THE LITURGY DOCUMENTS

SUPPLEMENTAL DOCUMENTS
FOR PARISH WORSHIP, DEVOTIONS,
FORMATION AND CATECHESIS

VOLUME FOUR

THE LITURGY DOCUMENTS

SUPPLEMENTAL DOCUMENTS
FOR PARISH WORSHIP, DEVOTIONS,
FORMATION AND CATECHESIS

Volume Four

LTP

LITURGY
TRAINING
PUBLICATIONS

Nihil Obstat
Very Reverend Daniel A. Smilanic, JCD
Vicar for Canonical Services
Archdiocese of Chicago
August 7, 2013

Imprimatur
Most Reverend Francis J. Kane, DD
Vicar General
Archdiocese of Chicago
August 7, 2013

The *Nihil Obstat* and *Imprimatur* are declarations that the material is free from doctrinal or moral error, and thus is granted permission to publish in accordance with c. 827. No legal responsibility is assumed by the grant of this permission. No implication is contained herein that those who have granted the *Nihil Obstat* and *Imprimatur* agree with the content, opinions, or statements expressed.

THE LITURGY DOCUMENTS, VOLUME FOUR: SUPPLEMENTAL DOCUMENTS FOR PARISH WORSHIP, DEVOTIONS, FORMATION AND CATECHESIS © 2013 Archdiocese of Chicago: Liturgy Training Publications, 3949 South Racine Avenue, Chicago IL 60609; 1-800-933-1800, fax 1-800-933- 7094, e-mail orders@ltp.org. All rights reserved. See our website at www.LTP.org.

Cover photo © John Zich

Printed in the United States of America.

Library of Congress Control Number: 2012940317

16   15   14   13   1   2   3   4   5

978-1-61671-126-9

LD4V1

. . . [T]he Eucharist is at the root of every form of holiness, and each of us is called to the fullness of life in the Holy Spirit.

This most holy mystery thus needs to be firmly believed, devoutly celebrated and intensely lived in the Church. Jesus' gift of himself in the sacrament which is the memorial of his passion tells us that the success of our lives is found in our participation in the trinitarian life offered to us truly and definitively in him. The celebration and worship of the Eucharist enable us to draw near to God's love and to persevere in that love until we are united with the Lord whom we love. The offering of our lives, our fellowship with the whole community of believers and our solidarity with all men and women are essential aspects of that . . . spiritual worship, holy and pleasing to God (cf.Rom 12:1), which transforms every aspect of our human existence, to the glory of God.

—*Sacramentum caritatis*, 94

CONTENTS

ABBREVIATIONS

Many texts listed here appear in *Documents on the Liturgy, 1963–1979: Conciliar, Papal and Curial Texts* (DOL) (Collegeville, MN: The Liturgical Press, 1982). This list is not all-inclusive of liturgical documents promulgated before and after the Second Vatican Council.

AAS	*Acta Apostolicae Sedis*
ADA	*Abhinc duos annos*
AG	*Ad gentes divinitus*
BB	Book of Blessings
BCDW	Bishops' Committee on Divine Worship
BCL	Bishops' Committee on the Liturgy
BG	Book of the Gospels
BLS	Built of Living Stones: Art, Architecture, and Worship
c.; cc.	canon; canons
CB	Ceremonial of Bishops
CCC	Catechism of the Catholic Church
CCCB	Canadian Conference of Catholic Bishops
CD	*Christus Dominus*
CDF	Congregation for the Doctrine of the Faith
CDWDS	Congregation for Divine Worship and the Discipline of the Sacraments
CHP	The Church at Prayer: A Holy Temple of the Lord
CI	Christian Initiation, General Introduction
CIC	1983 Code of Canon Law (*Codex Iuris Canonici*)
1917 CIC	1917 Code of Canon Law (*Codex Iuris Canonici*)
CMBVM(L)	Collection of Masses of the Blessed Virgin Mary: Lectionary
CMBVM(M)	Collection of Masses of the Blessed Virgin Mary: Missal
CP	*Comme le prévoit*
CSL	Constitution on the Sacred Liturgy
CSP	Chirograph of the Supreme Pontiff

CT	*Catechesi tradendae*
DA	*Divino afflatu*
DD	*Dies Domini*
DCS	*Divini cultus sanctitatem*
DE	Directory for the Application of Principles and Norms on Ecumenism
DedCh	Dedication of a Church and an Altar
DMC	Directory for Masses with Children
DOL	Documents on the Liturgy (ICEL)
DPPL	Directory on Popular Piety and the Liturgy: Principles and Guidelines
DSCAP	Directory on Sunday Celebrations in the Absence of a Priest
DSV	*De solemni vigilia paschali instauranda*
DV	*Dei Verbum*
EACW	Environment and Art in Catholic Worship
EE	*Ecclesia de Eucharistia*
EM	*Eucharisticum mysterium*
EN	*Evangelii nuntiandi*
EP	*Eucharistiae participationem*
EU	*Ecclesiae unitatem*
FYH	Fulfilled in Your Hearing: The Homily in the Sunday Assembly
GCD	General Catechetical Directory
GCE	Guidelines for the Concelebration of the Eucharist
GCSPD	Guidelines for the Celebration of the Sacraments with Persons with Disabilities
GDC	General Directory for Catechesis

GILOH	General Instruction of the Liturgy of the Hours
GIRM	The General Instruction of the Roman Missal
GMEF	God's Mercy Endures Forever: Guidelines on the Presentation of Jews and Judaism in Catholic Preaching
GrSim	*Graduale Simplex*
GS	*Gaudium et spes*
HCWEOM	Holy Communion and Worship of the Eucharist Outside Mass
IO	*Inter Oecumenici*
IST	In Spirit and Truth: Black Catholic Reflections on the Order of Mass
JD	*Jubilate Deo*
LA	*Liturgiam authenticam*
LetArt	Letter to Artists
LG	*Lumen gentium*
LI	*Liturgicae instaurationes*
LM	Lectionary for Mass
MarCul	*Marialis cultus*
MC	*Mirae caritatis*
MCC	*Mystici Corporis Christi*
MD	*Mediator Dei*
MS	*Musicam sacram*
MSD	*Musicae sacrae disciplina*
MSSL	*De Musica sacra et sacra Liturgia*
n.; nn.	number; numbers
NA	*Nostra aetate*
NCCB	National Conference of Catholic Bishops
NDRHC	Norms for the Distribution and Reception of Holy Communion Under Both Kinds in the Dioceses of the United States of America
NMI	*Novo millennio ineunte*
NSC	National Statutes on the Catechumenate
OCF	Order of Christian Funerals
OE	*Orientalium Ecclesiarum*
OEx	*Ordo Exsequiarum,* 1969
OT	*Optatam totius*
OU	*Oratio universalis*
PCS	Pastoral Care of the Sick: Rites of Anointing and Viaticum
PGR	Plenty Good Room: The Spirit and Truth of African American Catholic Worship
PO	*Presbyterorum Ordinis*
PS	*Paschale solemnitatis*
QAA	*Quattuor abhinc annos*
RBC	Rite of Baptism for Children
RC/ RConf	Rite of Confirmation
RCIA	Rite of Christian Initiation of Adults
RH	*Redemptor hominis*
RM/ RomM	The Roman Missal
RMarr	Rite of Marriage
RP	Roman Pontifical
RPen	Rite of Penance
RS	*Redemptionis sacramentum*
RVM	*Rosarium Virginis Mariae*
SacCar	*Sacramentum caritatis*
SacCom	*Sacram Communionem*
SC	*Sacrosanctum Concilium*
SCAP	Sunday Celebrations in the Absence of a Priest
SCC	To Speak as a Christian Community: Pastoral Message on Inclusive Language
SCh	*Sources chrétiennes*
SL	*Sacram Liturgiam*
SP	*Summorum Pontificum*
SS	*Spiritus et Sponsa*
STL	Sing to the Lord: Music in Divine Worship
TAA	*Tres abhinc annos*
TLS	*Tra le sollecitudini*
UE	*Universae ecclesiae*
UNLY	Universal Norms on the Liturgical Year and the General Roman Calendar
UR	*Unitatis redintegratio*
UP	*The Universal Prayer*
USCCB	United States Conference of Catholic Bishops
VD	*Verbum Domini*
VL	*Varietates legitimae*
VQA	*Vicesimus quintus annus*

GENERAL INTRODUCTION

Rev. Michael S. Driscoll

Volume Four of The Liturgy Documents series is a collection of supplemental documents for parish worship dealing with devotions, formation, and catechesis. In this volume there are two sorts of documents: those from the Holy See and those from the United States Conference of Catholic Bishops.

The first genre of Vatican documents is an instruction (*instructio*), which explains or amplifies a document that has legislative force—such as apostolic constitutions—and states how its precepts are to be applied. For example, the instruction *Liturgiam authenticam*, on liturgical translation, is an instruction on the correct implementation of the *Constitution on the Sacred Liturgy* that superseded an earlier instruction on translation entitled *Comme le Prévoit.* Thus, the manner of interpretation of conciliar documents can change and evolve over time. Two instructions have been included in this volume: *Varietates legitimae* (Fourth Instruction for the Right Application of the Conciliar Constitution on the Liturgy, March 29, 1994) and *Universae Ecclesiae* (originating from the Pontifical Commission *Ecclesia Dei* issued on April 8, 2011, dealing with the application of the apostolic letter *Summorum pontificum.*

Moving down the line of authoritative documents, we come to a genre dealing with the implementation of constitutions or decrees. A directory, while fully respecting the competence of authorities at different levels, is authorized by one of the Vatican dicasteries and gives orientations and norms of universal *application* to guide Catholic participation in ecumenical or pious activity. Two directories appear in this volume, one for ecumenical activity and the other for prayer activity in liturgical and non-liturgical forms: *Directory for the Application of Principles and Norms on Ecumenism* (Congregation for Christian Unity, March 25, 1993), and *Directory on Popular Piety and the Liturgy* (Congregation for Divine Worship and the Discipline of the Sacraments, December 2001). The last item, in what we might term as an implementational document, is *The Universal Prayer* (Consilium, April 17, 1966). In his *motu proprio Sacram Liturgiam* Pope Paul VI established the Consilium that authored this document. The Consilium promptly took up its two appointed tasks: to carry out the directives of the Constitution on the Sacred Liturgy (*Sacrosanctum Concilium*) and of *Sacram Liturgiam,* and to provide the means for interpreting these documents and putting them into practice. The document *Sacram Liturgiam* was the first document implementing the Second Vatican Council's liturgical reform. It was issued by Pope Paul VI the month following the release of the *Constitution on the Sacred Liturgy.* Pope Paul issued this apostolic letter *ex motu proprio* (literally "of one's own accord") on January 25, 1964. It provided the first authoritative guidelines on key matters (including vernacular translations) so that the Council's liturgical reform could proceed immediately. Also in January 1964, the special group of experts to implement the Council's liturgical reform was established. Known as the Consilium, the group had full authority over the reform of the liturgy from 1964 until it was disbanded in April 1970, following the establishment of the Sacred Congregation for Divine Worship on May 12, 1969.

In the years following the Second Vatican Council, and particularly during the pontificate of John Paul II, there have been special meetings of bishops to discuss defined topics. These gatherings are called Synods of Bishops. The Synod of Bishops was established by Pope Paul VI *ex motu proprio* in a document entitled *Apostolica sollicitudo* on September 15, 1965. Pope Paul VI gave the definition of the Synod of Bishops at the Sunday *Angelus* on September 22, 1974: "It is an ecclesiastic institution, which, on interrogating the signs of the times and as well as trying to provide a deeper interpretation of divine designs and the constitution of the Catholic Church, we set up after Vatican Council II in order to foster the unity and cooperation of bishops around the world with the Holy See. It does this by means of a common study concerning the conditions of the Church and a joint solution on matters concerning Her mission. It is neither a Council nor a Parliament but a special type of Synod." To date there have been thirteen such synods, two of which are of particular importance for the liturgy. In 2005 Benedict XVI presided over a synod convened by his predecessor John Paul II who died before it was convened. The topic was *The Eucharist: Source and Summit of the Life and Mission of the Church*. Two years later Benedict XVI wrote a post-synodal apostolic exhortation entitled *Sacramentum caritatis* (February 22, 2007), which summarized the main lines of discussion at the synod. Then in 2008 another general synod took place discussing the theme the *Word of God in the Life and Mission of the Church*. Two years hence, another post-synodal apostolic exhortation appeared from the pen of Benedict entitled *Verbum Domini* (September 30, 2010).

Another kind of papal document that ranks alongside encyclicals, apostolic letters, and apostolic exhortations is an apostolic letter *ex motu proprio*. This is a legislative document or decree issued by the pope on his own initiative, not in response to a request. These documents expound or explain existing law. Concerning the liturgy within this genre is *Summorum pontificum* (apostolic letter of Pope Benedict XVI, issued *ex motu proprio*, July 7, 2007). This document specified the rules for celebrating Mass according to the Missal promulgated by Pope John XXIII in 1962 in the Latin Rite of the Catholic Church. The form known as the Tridentine Mass is also used for administering most of the sacraments as they were done before the liturgical reforms following the Second Vatican Council. This document was accompanied by *Universae Ecclesiae*, an instruction on the application of *Summorum pontificum*. Pope Benedict XVI, in an audience granted to Cardinal William Levada, president of the Pontifical Commission *Ecclesia Dei* on April 8, 2011, approved this present Instruction and ordered its publication.

The next genre of Roman documents is called an apostolic letter, which is not necessarily issued *ex motu proprio*, but has authoritative weight nevertheless. In this volume there are four apostolic letters. The first is *Mane nobiscum Domine* ("Stay with us, Lord," October 7, 2004), addressed by John Paul II to the bishops, clergy, and faithful for the Year of the Eucharist (October 2004 to October 2005). In this letter, the pope speaks of the Eucharist with a profoundly personal tone in a heartfelt plea to rediscover the wealth of the Eucharist in the life of the Church and of the world. The second apostolic letter is entitled *Marialis cultus* and is a Mariological document issued by Pope Paul VI (February 2, 1974). The letter is subtitled *"For the Right Ordering and Development of Devotion to the Blessed Virgin Mary,"* focuses on Marian devotions, and it clarifies the way the Roman Catholic Church celebrates liturgies that commemorate Mary. The preparation of the document reportedly took four years. The third apostolic letter in this volume is entitled *Rosarium Virginis Mariae* ("Rosary of the Virgin Mary," October 16, 2002) issued by Pope John Paul II. This document deals with the Holy Rosary and views it as a compendium of the Gospel message. The letter reaffirms the Roman Catholic beliefs on the power of the Rosary and emphasizes total devotion to the Virgin Mary, as promoted by St. Louis de Montfort. This letter also introduces the "Mysteries of Light" into the Rosary's cycle of mysteries. They meditate on Christ's: (1) Baptism in the Jordan, (2) self-manifestation at the wedding of Cana, (3) proclamation of the Kingdom of God, (4) Transfiguration, and (5) institution of the Eucharist. The final apostolic letter is the *Letter to Artists* (issued Easter, 1999) authored by John Paul II, an artist in his own right both as a playwright and an actor. It is addressed "to all who are passionately dedicated to the search for new 'epiphanies' of beauty so that through their creative work as artists they may offer these as gifts to the world." In this letter the pope discusses the "special vocation" of the artist by beginning with the unique relationship between the artist and the creator. While God is the ultimate creator of all that is good and beautiful, the divine Artist (God) passes on to human artists a divine spark of his own surpassing wisdom, calling artists to share in God's creative power. Indeed, it was the pope's hope that all artists receive in abundance the gift of that creative inspiration, which is the starting point of every true work of art. Thus, it is the artist who is commissioned with this special vocation to bring beauty into the world and thereby promote the good. In doing so, the artist enriches the cultural heritage of each nation and of all humanity.

The final genre of documents belongs to the United States Conference of Catholic Bishops (USCCB). The episcopal conference of the Catholic Church in the United States was founded in 1966 as the joint *National Conference of Catholic Bishops* (NCCB) and the *United States Catholic Conference* (USCC). It is composed of all active and retired members of the Catholic hierarchy in the United States and the territory of the U.S. Virgin Islands. Episcopal conferences were first established as formal bodies by the Second Vatican Council[1] and implemented by Paul VI in his *motu proprio* entitled *Ecclesiae Sanctae* (1966). In order to fulfill the new requirements for national Conferences of Bishops, the American bishops established the National Conference of Catholic Bishops (NCCB) in 1966 and its secular arm, the United States Catholic Conference (USCC). As separate organizations with distinct responsibilities, the NCCB focused on internal ecclesiastical concerns while the USCC carried forward work in society at large. The NCCB enabled the bishops to deliberate and respond collectively on a broad range of issues, with work being carried out through various secretariats, standing committees, and ad hoc committees. On July 1,

---

1. See *Christus Dominus*, 38.

2001, the NCCB and the USCC combined to form the United States Conference of Catholic Bishops. The merger resulted in the continuation of all of the work formerly done by the NCCB and the USCC with the same staff.

Among the many kinds of documents produced by the United States Conference of Catholic Bishops and their standing committees, there are two kinds that appear in this volume: national directories and guidelines, and documents of special interest. Out of the various directories, two are presented in this volume: *Guidelines for Concelebration* and the *National Directory for Catechesis* (not in its entirety but only those parts that deal with the liturgy in chapters three and five). The *Constitution on the Sacred Liturgy, 57* makes provisions for concelebration on three specific occasions: (1) on the Thursday of the Lord's Supper, not only at the Mass of the Chrism, but also at the evening Mass, (2) at Masses during councils, Conferences of Bishops, and synods, and (3) at Masses for the blessing of an abbot. However, permission was given to the ordinary to decide whether concelebration is opportune on other occasions, such as at conventual Masses and at the principal Mass in churches, when the needs of the faithful do not require that all the priests available should celebrate individually, and at Masses celebrated at meetings of priests—whether the priests be secular or religious. The regulation of concelebration in the diocese pertains to the bishop. Additionally, Conferences of Bishops can issue guidelines to insure order and propriety in a country or region. This was the case for the document issued by the USCCB, November 12, 2003 and revised in 2013 to agree with the third edition of *The Roman Missal.*

The *National Directory for Catechesis* was approved by the bishops of the United States in June 2003. It received Vatican recognition on December 16, 2004. After years of collaboration, study, and writing, the *National Directory for Catechesis* represents a companion to the *General Directory for Catechesis* (GDC). It builds on some of the core themes of the GDC—like the relationship of catechesis to evangelization and worship—and provides practical tools for doing catechesis well.

Soon after the Second Vatican Council, an international commission was established to oversee the development of a universal catechetical directory. The commission's first step was to conduct a consultation directed to the bishops worldwide. On the basis of this first consultation, the commission developed a proposed outline that was reviewed at a special plenary session of the Congregation for the Clergy, the Holy See dicastery responsible for catechetical matters. As a result, a draft text was developed and then released to all the episcopal conferences for further consultation. Based on responses to this consultation and a review by both a special theological commission and the Congregation for the Doctrine of the Faith, the text of a *General Catechetical Directory* was developed and published in 1971. The purpose of this directory was to provide the basic principles of pastoral theology so that the ministry of the Word could be more fittingly directed and governed, but it encouraged bishops everywhere to develop national and/or regional directories in order to apply the principles and directives of the *General Catechetical Directory* to the concrete situations of their own people.

In the United States, the call to develop a national directory produced an almost immediate response. By April 1972, the National Conference of Catholic

Bishops formed a committee of seven bishops to oversee the development of a *National Catechetical Directory*. The following year a full-time project director and assistant director were named, and a twelve-member working committee of bishops, priests, religious, and laity was formed. The process of developing the first *National Catechetical Directory* involved several public consultations. A final draft was sent to the bishops in the summer of 1977. The text of the *National Catechetical Directory* was approved at the General Assembly of the Bishops in November of that year. Almost a year later, in October of 1978, the text received the required approval from the Holy See, and was released in March of 1979 with the title *Sharing the Light of Faith: The National Catechetical Directory*. Chapter 3 summarizes the criteria for authentic presentation of the Gospel message and contains sections that are pertinent to worship. It is, however, chapter 5 ("Catechesis in a Worshipping Community") that is of particular interest for this volume.

Over the decades since the Second Vatican Council, some documents issued from episcopal conferences have emerged that have special interest as they touch upon the liturgical and catechetical life of the Church in some capacity. There are two in this volume: The first is entitled *God's Mercy Endures Forever: Guidelines on the Presentation of Jews and Judaism in Catholic Preaching* (United States Conference of Catholic Bishops' Committee on the Liturgy, September 1988) and is particularly important for liturgical preaching; the second goes under the pithy title *Plenty Good Room* (United States Conference of Catholic Bishops, February 1991), and the subtitle *The Spirit and Truth of African American Catholic Worship* focuses attention on the purpose of this document calling for the installation of a distinctly African American flavor to the Catholic celebration. It lays the theological foundation for cultural adaptations and frames the discussion of the interplay between African American culture and liturgical celebration.

While the liturgy is the expression and the formation of the spirituality (self-understanding) of the Church, it is not alone in its impact on the formation of a believer's spiritual union with God and the Church. Devotions, novenas, Eucharistic adoration, and private prayers before and after Mass all play a supplementary role in developing our spiritual lives. While participation in the Eucharist is the source and the summit of the spiritual life of the faithful, other spiritual practices enable us to meet the challenges of the Christian life in our day and age. Only when our liturgical celebrations are supported by a rich exposure to the many treasures found in our Catholic prayer tradition can the liturgy truly be the high point toward which the activity of the Church is directed. It might seem to some people that the Church has an over-abundance of legislation on liturgical, devotional, and catechetical matters. On the other hand, the large corpus of liturgical legislation attests to the importance of the liturgy, devotions, and catechesis for the life of the Church and witnesses to the firm belief that Christ endowed his Church this means of prayer to draw all who pray closer to God. This collection of documents will serve our Catholic community well in developing a truly dynamic and liturgically appropriate experience of worship in the parishes and institutions of the Catholic Church.

SACRAMENTUM CARITATIS
ON THE EUCHARIST AS THE SOURCE AND SUMMIT OF THE CHURCH'S LIFE AND MISSION

POST-SYNODAL APOSTOLIC EXHORTATION
POPE BENEDICT XVI
FEBRUARY 22, 2007

AN OVERVIEW OF *SACRAMENTUM CARITATIS*
Rev. Mark E. Wedig, OP

During his papacy, Benedict XVI's ideas on the liturgy were often the subject of considerable discussion and disputation by the Church faithful. Those on the regularly vocal margins of the Church's left and right often viewed him as a proponent of reversing the reforms set in motion by the Second Vatican Council. Time and again such interpretations relied more on the writings and actions of Joseph Ratzinger, the theologian, than his thinking and pastoring as pontiff.[1] Contrary to those more extreme perspectives, it is the fundamental contention of this commentary on *Sacramentum caritatis* (SacCar) that such characterization wrongly interprets the pope's ecclesiological and liturgical intentions. This post-synodal apostolic exhortation on the Eucharist remains Benedict XVI's most comprehensive and authoritative writing on the liturgy as pontiff. Therefore *Sacramentum caritatis* stands as the foundational text of Pope Benedict on liturgy and represents his definitive viewpoint on the subject.[2] The post-synodal exhortation does not veer off course with a hermeneutics of the liturgy and the Eucharist set forth by the Liturgical Movement, the Second Vatican Council, and the subsequent work of the *Consilium* (theological and liturgical epxerts charged with the tasks of reforming the rites in light of the *Constitution on the Sacred Liturgy*), but in contrast remains fully in line with them.

This commentary is organized according to three basic movements of interpreting *Sacramentum caritatis*: its method, key theological insights of the exhortation, and liturgical correctives offered by the pope on misinterpretations of liturgical praxes in the post-Conciliar period. The overview of its method demonstrates the global organization that Benedict XVI takes in how to best understand liturgy and sacrament. Key insights highlight Benedict's liturgical and sacramental theology as viewed through the rites of the Eucharistic celebration. Liturgical correctives attempt to clarify what Benedict XVI sees as the misappropriation of the Eucharistic liturgy by celebrants and the assembly, especially in our contemporary period.

THE ORGANIZATION AND METHOD OF *SACRAMENTUM CARITATIS*

Sacramentum caritatis is arranged and systematically presented through the lens of three interrelated liturgical theological typologies: a mystery believed, celebrated, and lived. One can see from the arrangement that Benedict XVI is steeped in a contemporary liturgical theological method. For him, the twentieth-century Liturgical Movement and the reforms of the Second Vatican Council

---

1. Two examples of these interpretative extremes in relatively recent writings are as follows: Eamon Duff, "Benedict XVI and the Eucharist," *New Blackfriars* 88 (104): 195–212 and David G. Bonagura, Jr. "The Future of the Roman Rite: Reading Benedict in the Light of Ratzinger," *Antiphon* 13:3 (2009): 228–246.

2. See *Sacramentum caritatis* (SacCar), 5.

remain extraordinarily important phenomena for the life of the contemporary Church.[3] The organization reflects the revived and restored *lex orandi, lex credendi* relationship that is paramount to modern liturgical theology. For Benedict, believing, celebrating, and living the Eucharistic mystery are mutually interdependent realities. In other words, one cannot understand the Eucharistic celebration fully unless one views the mutually interdependent reality of its meaning, ritual performance, and relationship to everyday Christian life.[4] Moreover, the pope's organization and understanding of liturgy highlights the ancient axiom of *lex orandi, lex credendi,* and the more contemporary adage of *lex vivendi* or *lex agendi* that has been emphasized in twentieth-century liturgical theology.[5] The latter concept extends the relationship between belief and ritual to include the true interrelationship between doctrine and liturgy and the everyday living out the two.[6] *Sacrosanctum Concilium,* the Church's pastoral constitution on the liturgy from the Second Vatican Council, established this necessary and inclusive approach to liturgy as the foundation for understanding all the sacraments and liturgical rites. *Sacramentum caritatis* keeps in a balance how liturgy's doctrinal, ritual, and moral implications are derived from one central divine mystery.[7] (This is what *Sacramentum caritatis* means by full, conscious, and active participation in the life of the Church.[8]) Moreover the Eucharist, because of its centerpiece in the life of the ordinary Church, mediates the integral relationship between belief, symbolic action, and a spiritually authentic moral life.[9] Attempts to understand the sacraments solely as ideas or dogmas detached from their expression and ethical resonance shortchanges the way the Catholic tradition has distinguished one of its most precious and sacred of moments.[10]

Sacramentum caritatis identifies the unfortunate problem in the history of the Church of separating out sacramental belief from sacramental spirituality.[11] Such propositional fallacy has led to an ill-fated dualism in sacramental interpretation resulting in seeing sacraments as something only to be believed, not practiced. The twentieth-century Liturgical Movement and the Second Vatican Council set out to restore the ancient sacramental and especially Eucharistic practice of embodying the Risen Lord in the full life of the Church.[12] Consequently, the Church is most alive and authentically realized when she practices and believes her Eucharistic life. The overall schemata of *Sacramentum caritatis* underscores that a Christian spirituality that divorces liturgy from morality and vice versa is erroneously conceived.

---

3. See ibid., 3.

4. See ibid., 34.

5. See *Liturgy and the Moral Self: Humanity at Full Stretch Before God,* E. Byron Anderson and Bruce Morrill, editors. Collegeville, Minnesota: The Liturgical Press, 1998).

6. See SacCar, 71, 82, 89, 90, 91.

7. See ibid., 6.

8. See ibid., 15, 52, 53, 55.

9. See ibid., 16, 82.

10. See ibid., 88–92.

11. See ibid., 70.

12. See ibid., 5, 16.

Besides its contemporary liturgical method, *Sacramentum caritatis* also can be underscores fundamental theologies of the Eucharistic liturgy that are derived from a proper interpretation of Church tradition. Again Pope Benedict XVI shows himself to be a student of contemporary liturgical theology. His integration of key doctrines and the unique way they are embodied in the liturgy of the Church demonstrate how strongly he mirrors the *ressourcement* and *aggiorimento* of the twentieth-century theological movements. Here three key insights organize commentary on the exhortation: Eucharist as Trinitarian and ecclesial, Eucharist as Christological and symbolic, and Eucharist as mystagogical and ordinary.

Eucharist as Trinitarian and Ecclesial

In the post-Tridentine era one of the most hapless theological and pastoral phenomena in the Church's life was the much too frequent and purely juridical misappropriation of the Eucharist. Instead of viewing the Eucharist as the Church realizing her divine self, Eucharist was seen as something Catholics "had to do" in order to fend off purgatory and hell. The Eucharistic liturgy was less appropriated by Catholics as the marvelous way God was continuously offering himself to humankind and more as assurance of obtaining grace or heaven. As a result, such mishandling of the riches of the Church's tradition led more to seeing the sacramental life of the Church as an insurance policy for individual believers instead of as one of the seminal ways God self-communicates through the gathered Church. *Sacramentum caritatis* militates against such praxes and drives home that God and Church work as one divine reality.[13] When the two are extracted from the centerpiece of a human life then the very mystery of God as a self-communicating reality called Trinity and the unique way that comes to be in the gathered Church at Mass becomes terribly ill-conceived. Pope Benedict emphasizes that the way God fundamentally is (Trinitarian) leads to God being expressed, actualized, and realized through the Church assembled in her Eucharistic liturgy.[14]

Eucharist as Christological and Symbolic

Another central theological organizing principle of Benedict XVI's exhortation on the Eucharist is that the Christ is the celebrant par excellence of the liturgy and attempts to confuse that central symbolic truth have also led to mishap in interpreting the Church's tradition.[15] There is a fundamental difference between the historical Jesus and the Risen Lord manifest in the life of the Church. Jesus Christ dies and through the Holy Spirit leaves us the Church.[16] More literal Christologies led to confusion in this area, misappropriating the priest celebrant as an exact replica of Jesus Christ instead of the one who stands in for Christ.[17] Moreover, the Holy Spirit was de-emphasized as the source and manifestation

---

13. See ibid., 8, 12, 14, 15.
14. See ibid., 8.
15. See ibid., 36.
16. See ibid., 11, 12.
17. See ibid., 36, 37.

of the Christ as the *ecclesia* gathered around her altar.[18] Consequently, the sacrifice of the Mass was misperceived as something replicated instead of something shared. Contemporary theologies of the symbolic nature of the Christ uniquely manifested in the liturgy help us to realize the central Christological mystery. *Sacramentum caritatis* establishes that Christologies that are fundamentally pneumatological enable us to properly appropriate how the Eucharist makes the Church and the Church the Eucharist.[19] Without a nuanced theology of the symbol, Christian people always will attempt to interpret both the Eucharist and Christ himself in dichotomous ways, seeing them as either divine or human instead of both.[20]

Eucharist as Mystagogical and Ordinary

A final crucial and predominant theological insight of *Sacramentum caritatis* emphasizes how the Eucharist that is not preached, taught, and connected to everyday experience is bound for peril in the spiritual life of the faithful. Pope Benedict's liturgical theology is predicated on a modern liturgical revival of the ancient practice of mystagogy.[21] He advocates for this practice first developed in the early Church so that teaching and preaching the faith happened through the sacramental mysteries. Benedict underscores that Eucharistic reverence cannot be separated from everyday life and vice versa. Moreover when the meaning of the Eucharist is broken open and developed in the consciousness of the faithful, it allows them to connect central truths of Christianity (that is, Trinitarian, Christological, ecclesial) to their ordinary lives. The Eucharist that is explained in and connected to preaching, parish education, retreats, and social justice ministries takes hold in the imaginations of the Catholic faithful and transforms whole communities and dioceses.[22] In other words, the faithful hunger for the Eucharist because it has everything to do with what is meaningful, true, and relevant to a well-lived and ethical life. Like Dorothy Day, the faithful will not be able to minister to the poor and care for others without simultaneously hungering for the Eucharist.[23] There is no need to shame or disgrace the faithful into Eucharistic participation. Instead, through mystagogy, the faithful understand the intrinsic link between liturgy and life. And yet, Benedict stresses that there must be a converted clergy who preach this message at the ambo and demonstrate conviction to this with their lives.[24] Catechists must implement methods for religious education that integrate the weekly and daily celebrations of the Eucharist.[25]

---

18. See ibid., 13.
19. See ibid., 16.
20. See ibid., 40.
21. See ibid., 64.
22. See ibid., 84, 85.
23. See ibid., 88–90.
24. See ibid., 23, 24.
25. See ibid., 64.

As mentioned above, proponents of the liturgy from the margins of the Church too often misinterpreted the writings of Pope Benedict XVI as fundamentally opposed to the teachings and ecclesiological orientation of the Second Vatican Council. This commentary strongly takes issue with such interpretations, demonstrating how *Sacramentum caritatis* clearly and forthrightly advocates the conciliar teachings and does not intend a "reform of the reform." With that being said, this commentary contends that there are a few correctives to liturgical practices and interpretations that the pope wished to establish through the post-synodal exhortation, which can be organized into two fundamental issues: the presider's subjectification of the liturgy and a more mature understanding of full, conscious, and active participation in the liturgy.

The Presider's Subjectification of the Liturgy

Commentaries on the liturgy during recent decades have frequently addressed how one of the pitfalls unique to Eucharistic liturgical practice in the post-Conciliar period is revealed by what can be coined as the "subjectification" of the Mass by the presiding minister(s).[26] This is the tendency of liturgical ministers to overly interpret their role at the chair, altar, and ambo and therefore obscuring the intent of the prayers and rubrics by injecting personality into the prayer texts, gestures, and ritual phrases. *Sacramentum caritatis* clearly warns against such personality-driven extemporization.[27] The pope emphasizes that such ad-libbing and improvisation has been common in contemporary Eucharistic practice and resulted in unfortunate distraction from the intent of the reformed liturgy. Benedict also emphasizes that the priest celebrants must uniquely militate against such practices.[28]

Full, Conscious, and Active Participation in the Liturgy

Another liturgical corrective that Pope Benedict XVI takes up concerns what has been considered one of the central principles of *Sacrosanctum Concilium*. Without de-emphasizing the comprehensive need to inculturate the Mass through careful attention to symbol, language, and music, Benedict stresses that full, conscious, and active participation in the liturgy does not hinge on the personal and idiosyncratic tastes and invention of social trends.[29] Instead participation in the Mass requires catechesis and education in order to understand its richness. The Church's failure to create liturgical formation in the lives of the faithful has resulted in a comprehensive failure to appreciate these riches. The pope especially underlines how many of the improvements of the *Novus Ordo*—such as the variable Prefaces and multiple Eucharistic Prayers—are unfortunately unknown to the assembly. Without a revival of liturgical formation through

---

26. For a more elaborate explanation of "subjectification" of liturgical reality, see: M. Francis Mannion, "Liturgy and the Present Crisis of Culture," *Worship* (1989), reprinted in *Liturgy and Spirituality in Context*, ed. Eleanor Bernstein. Collegeville, Minnesota: The Liturgical Press, 1990, pp. 1–26.

27. See SacCar, 40.

28. See ibid., 23, 39, 80.

29. See ibid., 54.

mystagogy the spirit of the liturgy will not enrich the many people who hunger for its meaning.

CONCLUSION

It has been my hope in writing this essay to represent Pope Benedict XVI on his fundamental view of the liturgy and put to rest some of the contentiousness that typified interpretations of his viewpoint on liturgical matters. It is important to understand that in *Sacramentum caritatis* Benedict XVI undertook a different outlook on the Church's liturgy than he did as theologian and prefect for the Congregation for the Doctrine of the Faith. His 2007 document clearly demonstrates that the reforms inaugurated by the Liturgical Movement and the Second Vatican Council have been given another comprehensive sanctioning for providing the foundations of liturgical praxis for the contemporary Church.

OUTLINE

POST-SYNODAL
APOSTOLIC EXHORTATION
SACRAMENTUM CARITATIS

OF THE HOLY FATHER
BENEDICT XVI
TO THE BISHOPS, CLERGY,
CONSECRATED PERSONS
AND THE LAY FAITHFUL
ON THE EUCHARIST
AS THE SOURCE AND SUMMIT
OF THE CHURCH'S LIFE AND MISSION

INTRODUCTION

1.   The sacrament of charity,[1] the Holy Eucharist is the gift that Jesus Christ makes of himself, thus revealing to us God's infinite love for every man and woman. This wondrous sacrament makes manifest that "greater" love which led him to "lay down his life for his friends" (Jn 15:13). Jesus did indeed love them "to the end" (Jn 13:1). In those words the Evangelist introduces Christ's act of immense humility: before dying for us on the Cross, he tied a towel around himself and washed the feet of his disciples. In the same way, Jesus continues, in the sacrament of the Eucharist, to love us "to the end," even to offering us his body and his blood. What amazement must the Apostles have felt in witnessing what the Lord did and said during that Supper! What wonder must the eucharistic mystery also awaken in our own hearts!

The food of truth

2.   In the sacrament of the altar, the Lord meets us, men and women created in God's image and likeness (cf. Gen 1:27), and becomes our companion along the way. In this sacrament, the Lord truly becomes food for us, to satisfy our hunger for truth and freedom. Since only the truth can make us free (cf. Jn 8:32), Christ becomes for us the food of truth. With deep human insight, Saint Augustine clearly showed how we are moved spontaneously, and not by constraint, whenever we encounter something attractive and desirable. Asking himself what it is that can move us most deeply, the saintly Bishop went on to say: "What does our soul desire more passionately than truth?"[2] Each of us has an innate and

---

1. Cf. Saint Thomas Aquinas, *Summa Theologiae* III, q. 73, a. 3.
2. Saint Augustine, *In Iohannis Evangelium Tractatus*, 26, 5: PL 35, 1609.

irrepressible desire for ultimate and definitive truth. The Lord Jesus, "the way, and the truth, and the life" (Jn 14:6), speaks to our thirsting, pilgrim hearts, our hearts yearning for the source of life, our hearts longing for truth. Jesus Christ is the Truth in person, drawing the world to himself. "Jesus is the lodestar of human freedom: without him, freedom loses its focus, for without the knowledge of truth, freedom becomes debased, alienated and reduced to empty caprice. With him, freedom finds itself."[3] In the sacrament of the Eucharist, Jesus shows us in particular the *truth about the love* which is the very essence of God. It is this evangelical truth which challenges each of us and our whole being. For this reason, the Church, which finds in the Eucharist the very center of her life, is constantly concerned to proclaim to all, *opportune importune* (cf. 2 Tim 4:2), that God is love.[4] Precisely because Christ has become for us the food of truth, the Church turns to every man and woman, inviting them freely to accept God's gift.

The development of the eucharistic rite

3.   If we consider the bimillenary history of God's Church, guided by the wisdom of the Holy Spirit, we can gratefully admire the orderly development of the ritual forms in which we commemorate the event of our salvation. From the varied forms of the early centuries, still resplendent in the rites of the Ancient Churches of the East, up to the spread of the Roman rite; from the clear indications of the Council of Trent and the Missal of Saint Pius V to the liturgical renewal called for by the Second Vatican Council: in every age of the Church's history the eucharistic celebration, as the source and summit of her life and mission, shines forth in the liturgical rite in all its richness and variety. The Eleventh Ordinary General Assembly of the Synod of Bishops, held from October 2–23, 2005 in the Vatican, gratefully acknowledged the guidance of the Holy Spirit in this rich history. In a particular way, the Synod Fathers acknowledged and reaffirmed the beneficial influence on the Church's life of the liturgical renewal which began with the Second Vatican Ecumenical Council.[5] The Synod of Bishops was able to evaluate the reception of the renewal in the years following the Council. There were many expressions of appreciation. The difficulties and even the occasional abuses which were noted, it was affirmed, cannot overshadow the benefits and the validity of the liturgical renewal, whose riches are yet to be fully explored. Concretely, the changes which the Council called for need to be understood within the overall unity of the historical development of the rite itself, without the introduction of artificial discontinuities.[6]

The Synod of Bishops and the Year of the Eucharist

4.   We should also emphasize the relationship between the recent Synod of Bishops on the Eucharist and the events which have taken place in the Church's

---

3. Benedict XVI, Address to Participants in the Plenary Assembly of the Congregation for the Doctrine of the Faith (February 10, 2006): AAS 98 (2006), 255.

4. Benedict XVI, Address to the Members of the Ordinary Council of the General Secretariat of the Synod of Bishops (1 June 2006): *L'Osservatore Romano*, June 2, 2006, p. 5.

5. Cf. *Propositio* 2.

6. I am referring here to the need for a hermeneutic of continuity also with regard to the correct interpretation of the liturgical development which followed the Second Vatican Council: cf. Benedict Address to the Roman Curia (December 22, 2005): AAS 98 (2006), 44–45.

life in recent years. First of all, we should recall the Great Jubilee of the Year 2000, with which my beloved Predecessor, the Servant of God John Paul II, led the Church into the third Christian millennium. The Jubilee Year clearly had a significant eucharistic dimension. Nor can we forget that the Synod of Bishops was preceded, and in some sense prepared for, by the Year of the Eucharist which John Paul II had, with great foresight, wanted the whole Church to celebrate. That year, which began with the International Eucharistic Congress in Guadalajara in October 2004, ended on October 23, 2005, at the conclusion of the XI Synodal Assembly, with the canonization of five saints particularly distinguished for their eucharistic piety: Bishop Józef Bilczewski; Fathers Gaetano Catanoso, Zygmunt Gorazdowski, and Alberto Hurtado Cruchaga; and the Capuchin Fra Felice da Nicosia. Thanks to the teachings proposed by John Paul II in the Apostolic Letter *Mane Nobiscum Domine*[7] and to the helpful suggestions of the Congregation for Divine Worship and the Discipline of the Sacraments,[8] many initiatives were undertaken by Dioceses and various ecclesial groups in order to reawaken and increase eucharistic faith, to improve the quality of eucharistic celebration, to promote eucharistic adoration, and to encourage a practical solidarity which, starting from the Eucharist, would reach out to those in need. Finally, mention should be made of the significance of my venerable Predecessor's last Encyclical, *Ecclesia de Eucharistia*,[9] in which he left us a sure magisterial statement of the Church's teaching on the Eucharist and a final testimony of the central place that this divine sacrament had in his own life.

The purpose of this Exhortation

5.   This Post-Synodal Apostolic Exhortation seeks to take up the richness and variety of the reflections and proposals which emerged from the recent Ordinary General Assembly of the Synod of Bishops—from the *Lineamenta* to the *Propositiones*, along the way of the *Instrumentum Laboris*, the *Relationes ante* and *post disceptationem*, the interventions of the Synod Fathers, the *auditores*, and the fraternal delegates—and to offer some basic directions aimed at a renewed commitment to eucharistic enthusiasm and fervor in the Church. Conscious of the immense patrimony of doctrine and discipline accumulated over the centuries with regard to this sacrament,[10] I wish here to endorse the wishes expressed by the Synod Fathers[11] by encouraging the Christian people to deepen their understanding

---

7. Cf. AAS 97 (2005), 337–352.

8. *The Year of the Eucharist: Suggestions and Proposals* (October 15, 2004): *L'Osservatore Romano*, October 15, 2004, Supplement.

9. Cf. AAS 95 (2003), 433–475. Also, the Instruction of the Congregation for Divine Worship and the Discipline of the Sacraments *Redemptionis sacramentum* (March 25, 2004): AAS 96 (2004), 549–601, expressly desired by John Paul II.

10. To name only the more important documents: Ecumenical Council of Trent, *Doctrina et canones de ss. Missae sacrificio*, DS 1738–1759; Leo XIII, Encyclical Letter *Mirae caritatis* (May 28, 1902): ASS (1903), 115–136; Pius XII, Encyclical Letter *Mediator Dei* (November 20, 1947): AAS 39 (1947), 521–595; Paul VI, Encyclical Letter *Mysterium fidei* (September 3, 1965): AAS 57 (1965), 753–774; John Paul II, Encyclical Letter *Ecclesia de Eucharistia* (April 17, 2003): AAS 95 (2003), 433–475; Congregation for Divine Worship and the Discipline of the Sacraments, Instruction *Eucharisticum mysterium* (May 25, 1967): AAS 59 (1967), 539–573; Instruction *Liturgiam authenticam* (March 28, 2001): AAS 93 (2001), 685–726.

11. Cf. *Propositio* 1.

of the relationship between the *eucharistic mystery*, the *liturgical action*, and the *new spiritual worship* which derives from the Eucharist as the *sacrament of charity*. Consequently, I wish to set the present Exhortation alongside my first Encyclical Letter, *Deus Caritas Est*, in which I frequently mentioned the sacrament of the Eucharist and stressed its relationship to Christian love, both of God and of neighbor: "God incarnate draws us all to himself. We can thus understand how *agape* also became a term for the Eucharist: there God's own *agape* comes to us bodily, in order to continue his work in us and through us."[12]

PART ONE
THE EUCHARIST, A MYSTERY TO BE BELIEVED

"This is the work of God: that you believe in him whom he has sent." (Jn 6:29)

The Church's eucharistic faith

6.   *"The mystery of faith!"* With these words, spoken immediately after the words of consecration, the priest proclaims the mystery being celebrated and expresses his wonder before the substantial change of bread and wine into the body and blood of the Lord Jesus, a reality which surpasses all human understanding. The Eucharist is a "mystery of faith" par excellence: "the sum and summary of our faith."[13] The Church's faith is essentially a eucharistic faith, and it is especially nourished at the table of the Eucharist. Faith and the sacraments are two complementary aspects of ecclesial life. Awakened by the preaching of God's word, faith is nourished and grows in the grace-filled encounter with the Risen Lord which takes place in the sacraments: "faith is expressed in the rite, while the rite reinforces and strengthens faith."[14] For this reason, the Sacrament of the Altar is always at the heart of the Church's life: "thanks to the Eucharist, the Church is reborn ever anew!"[15] The more lively the eucharistic faith of the People of God, the deeper is its sharing in ecclesial life in steadfast commitment to the mission entrusted by Christ to his disciples. The Church's very history bears witness to this. Every great reform has in some way been linked to the rediscovery of belief in the Lord's eucharistic presence among his people.

THE BLESSED TRINITY AND THE EUCHARIST

The bread come down from heaven

7.   The first element of eucharistic faith is the mystery of God himself, trinitarian love. In Jesus' dialogue with Nicodemus, we find an illuminating expression in this regard: "God so loved the world that he gave his only Son, that whoever believes in him should not perish but have eternal life. For God sent the Son into the world, not to condemn the world, but that the world might be saved through him" (Jn 3:16–17). These words show the deepest source of God's

---

12. No. 14: AAS 98 (2006), 229.

13. *Catechism of the Catholic Church*, 1327.

14. *Propositio* 16.

15. Benedict XVI, Homily at the Mass of Installation in the Cathedral of Rome (May 7, 2005): AAS 97 (2005), 752.

gift. In the Eucharist Jesus does not give us a "thing," but himself; he offers his own body and pours out his own blood. He thus gives us the totality of his life and reveals the ultimate origin of this love. He is the eternal Son, given to us by the Father. In the Gospel we hear how Jesus, after feeding the crowds by multiplying the loaves and fishes, says to those who had followed him to the synagogue of Capernaum: "My Father gives you the true bread from heaven; for the bread of God is he who comes down from heaven, and gives life to the world" (Jn 6:32–33), and even identifies himself, his own flesh and blood, with that bread: "I am the living bread which came down from heaven; if anyone eats of this bread, he will live forever; and the bread which I shall give for the life of the world is my flesh" (Jn 6:51). Jesus thus shows that he is the bread of life which the eternal Father gives to mankind.

A free gift of the Blessed Trinity

8.   The Eucharist reveals the loving plan that guides all of salvation history (cf. Eph 1:10; 3:8–11). There the *Deus Trinitas*, who is essentially love (cf. 1 Jn 4:7–8), becomes fully a part of our human condition. In the bread and wine under whose appearances Christ gives himself to us in the paschal meal (cf. Lk 22:14–20; 1 Cor 11:23–26), God's whole life encounters us and is sacramentally shared with us. God is a perfect communion of love between Father, Son, and Holy Spirit. At creation itself, man was called to have some share in God's breath of life (cf. Gen 2:7). But it is in Christ, dead and risen, and in the outpouring of the Holy Spirit, given without measure (cf. Jn 3:34), that we have become sharers of God's inmost life.[16] Jesus Christ, who "through the eternal Spirit offered himself without blemish to God" (Heb 9:14), makes us, in the gift of the Eucharist, sharers in God's own life. This is an absolutely free gift, the superabundant fulfillment of God's promises. The Church receives, celebrates, and adores this gift in faithful obedience. The "mystery of faith" is thus a mystery of trinitarian love, a mystery in which we are called by grace to participate. We too should therefore exclaim with Saint Augustine: "If you see love, you see the Trinity."[17]

THE EUCHARIST: JESUS, THE TRUE SACRIFICIAL LAMB

The new and eternal covenant in the blood of the Lamb

9.   The mission for which Jesus came among us was accomplished in the Paschal Mystery. On the Cross from which he draws all people to himself (cf. Jn 12:32), just before "giving up the Spirit," he utters the words: "it is finished" (Jn 19:30). In the mystery of Christ's obedience unto death, even death on a Cross (cf. Phil 2:8), the new and eternal covenant was brought about. In his crucified flesh, God's freedom and our human freedom met definitively in an inviolable, eternally valid pact. Human sin was also redeemed once for all by God's Son (cf. Heb 7:27; 1 Jn 2:2; 4:10). As I have said elsewhere, "Christ's death on the Cross is the culmination of that turning of God against himself in which he gives himself in order to raise man up and save him. This is love in its most

---

16. Cf. *Propositio* 4.
17. *De Trinitate*, VIII, 8, 12: CCL 50, 287.

radical form."[18] In the Paschal Mystery, our deliverance from evil and death has taken place. In instituting the Eucharist, Jesus had spoken of the "new and eternal covenant" in the shedding of his blood (cf. Mt 26:28; Mk 14:24; Lk 22:20). This, the ultimate purpose of his mission, was clear from the very beginning of his public life. Indeed, when, on the banks of the Jordan, John the Baptist saw Jesus coming towards him, he cried out: "Behold, the Lamb of God, who takes away the sin of the world" (Jn 1:29). It is significant that these same words are repeated at every celebration of Holy Mass, when the priest invites us to approach the altar: "This is *the Lamb of God* who takes away the sins of the world. Happy are those who are called to his supper." Jesus is the *true* paschal lamb who freely gave himself in sacrifice for us, and thus brought about the new and eternal covenant. The Eucharist contains this radical newness, which is offered to us again at every celebration.[19]

The institution of the Eucharist

10.   This leads us to reflect on the institution of the Eucharist at the Last Supper. It took place within a ritual meal commemorating the foundational event of the people of Israel: their deliverance from slavery in Egypt. This ritual meal, which called for the sacrifice of lambs (cf. Ex 12:1–28, 43–51), was a remembrance of the past, but at the same time a prophetic remembrance, the proclamation of a deliverance yet to come. The people had come to realize that their earlier liberation was not definitive, for their history continued to be marked by slavery and sin. The remembrance of their ancient liberation thus expanded to the invocation and expectation of a yet more profound, radical, universal, and definitive salvation. This is the context in which Jesus introduces the newness of his gift. In the prayer of praise, the *Berakah*, he does not simply thank the Father for the great events of past history, but also for his own "exaltation." In instituting the sacrament of the Eucharist, Jesus anticipates and makes present the sacrifice of the Cross and the victory of the resurrection. At the same time, he reveals that he himself is the *true* sacrificial lamb, destined in the Father's plan from the foundation of the world, as we read in *The First Letter of Peter* (cf. 1:18–20). By placing his gift in this context, Jesus shows the salvific meaning of his death and resurrection, a mystery which renews history and the whole cosmos. The institution of the Eucharist demonstrates how Jesus' death, for all its violence and absurdity, became in him a supreme act of love and mankind's definitive deliverance from evil.

Figura transit in veritatem

11.   Jesus thus brings his own radical *novum* to the ancient Hebrew sacrificial meal. For us Christians, that meal no longer need be repeated. As the Church Fathers rightly say, *figura transit in veritatem*: the foreshadowing has given way to the truth itself. The ancient rite has been brought to fulfillment and definitively surpassed by the loving gift of the incarnate Son of God. The food of truth, Christ sacrificed for our sake, *dat figuris terminum*.[20] By his command to "do

---

18. Encyclical Letter *Deus caritas est* (December 25, 2005), 12: AAS 98 (2006), 228.
19. Cf. *Propositio* 3.
20. Roman Breviary, *Hymn for the Office of Readings of the Solemnity of Corpus Christi.*

this in remembrance of me" (Lk 22:19; 1 Cor 11:25), he asks us to respond to his gift and to make it sacramentally present. In these words the Lord expresses, as it were, his expectation that the Church, born of his sacrifice, will receive this gift, developing under the guidance of the Holy Spirit the liturgical form of the sacrament. The remembrance of his perfect gift consists not in the mere repetition of the Last Supper, but in the Eucharist itself, that is, in the radical newness of Christian worship. In this way, Jesus left us the task of entering into his "hour." "The Eucharist draws us into Jesus' act of self-oblation. More than just statically receiving the incarnate *Logos*, we enter into the very dynamic of his self-giving."[21] Jesus "draws us into himself."[22] The substantial conversion of bread and wine into his body and blood introduces within creation the principle of a radical change, a sort of "nuclear fission," to use an image familiar to us today, which penetrates to the heart of all being, a change meant to set off a process which transforms reality, a process leading ultimately to the transfiguration of the entire world, to the point where God will be all in all (cf. 1 Cor 15:28).

THE HOLY SPIRIT AND THE EUCHARIST

Jesus and the Holy Spirit

12.   With his word and with the elements of bread and wine, the Lord himself has given us the essentials of this new worship. The Church, his Bride, is called to celebrate the eucharistic banquet daily in his memory. She thus makes the redeeming sacrifice of her Bridegroom a part of human history and makes it sacramentally present in every culture. This great mystery is celebrated in the liturgical forms which the Church, guided by the Holy Spirit, develops in time and space.[23] We need a renewed awareness of the decisive role played by the Holy Spirit in the evolution of the liturgical form and the deepening understanding of the sacred mysteries. The Paraclete, Christ's first gift to those who believe,[24] already at work in Creation (cf. Gen 1:2), is fully present throughout the life of the incarnate Word: Jesus Christ is conceived by the Virgin Mary by the power of the Holy Spirit (cf. Mt 1:18; Lk 1:35); at the beginning of his public mission, on the banks of the Jordan, he sees the Spirit descend upon him in the form of a dove (cf. Mt 3:16 and parallels); he acts, speaks and rejoices in the Spirit (cf. Lk 10:21), and he can offer himself in the Spirit (cf. Heb 9:14). In the so-called "farewell discourse" reported by John, Jesus clearly relates the gift of his life in the paschal mystery to the gift of the Spirit to his own (cf. Jn 16:7). Once risen, bearing in his flesh the signs of the passion, he can pour out the Spirit upon them (cf. Jn 20:22), making them sharers in his own mission (cf. Jn 20:21). The Spirit would then teach the disciples all things and bring to their remembrance all that Christ had said (cf. Jn 14:26), since it falls to him, as the Spirit of truth (cf. Jn 15:26), to guide the disciples into all truth (cf. Jn 16:13). In the account in Acts, the Spirit descends on the Apostles gathered in prayer with Mary on the

---

21. Benedict XVI, Encyclical Letter *Deus caritas est* (December 25, 2005), 13: AAS 98 (2006), 228.
22. Benedict XVI, Homily at Marienfeld Esplanade (August 21, 2005): AAS 97 (2005), 891–892.
23. Cf. *Propositio* 3.
24. Cf. Roman Missal, *Eucharistic Prayer IV*.

day of Pentecost (cf. 2:1–4) and stirs them to undertake the mission of proclaiming the Good News to all peoples. Thus it is through the working of the Spirit that Christ himself continues to be present and active in his Church, starting with her vital center which is the Eucharist.

The Holy Spirit and the eucharistic celebration

13.   Against this backdrop we can understand the decisive role played by the Holy Spirit in the eucharistic celebration, particularly with regard to transubstantiation. An awareness of this is clearly evident in the Fathers of the Church. Saint Cyril of Jerusalem, in his *Catecheses*, states that we "call upon God in his mercy to send his Holy Spirit upon the offerings before us, to transform the bread into the body of Christ and the wine into the blood of Christ. Whatever the Holy Spirit touches is sanctified and completely transformed."[25] Saint John Chrysostom too notes that the priest invokes the Holy Spirit when he celebrates the sacrifice:[26] like Elijah, the minister calls down the Holy Spirit so that "as grace comes down upon the victim, the souls of all are thereby inflamed."[27] The spiritual life of the faithful can benefit greatly from a better appreciation of the richness of the anaphora: along with the words spoken by Christ at the Last Supper, it contains the epiclesis, the petition to the Father to send down the gift of the Spirit so that the bread and the wine will become the body and blood of Jesus Christ and that "the community as a whole will become ever more the body of Christ."[28] The Spirit invoked by the celebrant upon the gifts of bread and wine placed on the altar is the same Spirit who gathers the faithful "into one body" and makes of them a spiritual offering pleasing to the Father.[29]

THE EUCHARIST AND THE CHURCH

The eucharist, causal principle of the Church

14.   Through the sacrament of the Eucharist Jesus draws the faithful into his "hour;" he shows us the bond that he willed to establish between himself and us, between his own person and the Church. Indeed, in the sacrifice of the Cross, Christ gave birth to the Church as his Bride and his body. The Fathers of the Church often meditated on the relationship between Eve's coming forth from the side of Adam as he slept (cf. Gen 2:21–23) and the coming forth of the new Eve, the Church, from the open side of Christ sleeping in death: from Christ's pierced side, John recounts, there came forth blood and water (cf. Jn 19:34), the symbol of the sacraments.[30] A contemplative gaze "upon him whom they have pierced" (Jn 19:37) leads us to reflect on the causal connection between Christ's

---

25. *Cat.* XXIII, 7: PG 33, 1114ff.

26. Cf. *De Sacerdotio*, VI, 4: PG 48, 681.

27. Ibid., III, 4: PG 48, 642.

28. *Propositio* 22.

29. Cf. *Propositio* 42: "This eucharistic encounter takes place in the Holy Spirit, who transforms and sanctifies us. He reawakens in the disciple the firm desire to proclaim boldly to others all that he has heard and experienced, to bring them to the same encounter with Christ. Thus the disciple, sent forth by the Church, becomes open to a mission without frontiers."

30. Cf. Second Vatican Ecumenical Council, Dogmatic Constitution on the Church *Lumen gentium*, 3; for an example, see: Saint John Chrysostom, *Catechesis* 3, 13–19: SC 50, 174–177.

sacrifice, the Eucharist, and the Church. The Church "draws her life from the Eucharist."[31] Since the Eucharist makes present Christ's redeeming sacrifice, we must start by acknowledging that "there is a causal influence of the Eucharist at the Church's very origins."[32] The Eucharist is Christ who gives himself to us and continually builds us up as his body. Hence, in the striking interplay between the Eucharist which builds up the Church, and the Church herself which "makes" the Eucharist,[33] the primary causality is expressed in the first formula: the Church is able to celebrate and adore the mystery of Christ present in the Eucharist precisely because Christ first gave himself to her in the sacrifice of the Cross. The Church's ability to "make" the Eucharist is completely rooted in Christ's self-gift to her. Here we can see more clearly the meaning of Saint John's words: "he first loved us" (1 Jn 4:19). We too, at every celebration of the Eucharist, confess the primacy of Christ's gift. The causal influence of the Eucharist at the Church's origins definitively discloses both the chronological and ontological priority of the fact that it was Christ who loved us "first." For all eternity he remains the one who loves us first.

The Eucharist and ecclesial communion

15.   The Eucharist is thus constitutive of the Church's being and activity. This is why Christian antiquity used the same words, *Corpus Christi*, to designate Christ's body born of the Virgin Mary, his eucharistic body, and his ecclesial body.[34] This clear datum of the tradition helps us to appreciate the inseparability of Christ and the Church. The Lord Jesus, by offering himself in sacrifice for us, in his gift effectively pointed to the mystery of the Church. It is significant that the Second Eucharistic Prayer, invoking the Paraclete, formulates its prayer for the unity of the Church as follows: *"may all of us who share in the body and blood of Christ be brought together in unity by the Holy Spirit."* These words help us to see clearly how the *res* of the sacrament of the Eucharist is the unity of the faithful within ecclesial communion. The Eucharist is thus found at the root of the Church as a mystery of communion.[35]

The relationship between Eucharist and *communio* had already been pointed out by the Servant of God John Paul II in his Encyclical *Ecclesia de Eucharistia*. He spoke of the memorial of Christ as "the supreme sacramental manifestation of communion in the Church."[36] The unity of ecclesial communion is concretely manifested in the Christian communities and is renewed at the celebration of the Eucharist, which unites them and differentiates them in the particular Churches, *"in quibus et ex quibus una et unica Ecclesia catholica exsistit."*[37] The fact that the one Eucharist is celebrated in each Diocese around its own

---

31. John Paul II, Encyclical Letter *Ecclesia de Eucharistia* (April 17, 2003), 1: AAS 95 (2003), 433.

32. Ibid., 21: AAS 95 (2003), 447.

33. Cf. John Paul II, Encyclical Letter *Redemptor hominis* (March 4, 1979), 20: AAS 71 (1979), 309–316; Apostolic Letter *Dominicae Cenae* (February 24, 1980), 4: AAS 72 (1980), 119–121.

34. Cf. *Propositio* 5.

35. Cf. Saint Thomas Aquinas, *Summa Theologiae*, III, q. 80, a. 4.

36. No. 38: AAS 95 (2003), 458.

37. Second Vatican Ecumenical Council, Dogmatic Constitution on the Church *Lumen gentium*, 23.

Bishop helps us to see how those particular Churches subsist *in* and *ex Ecclesia*. Indeed, "the oneness and indivisibility of the eucharistic body of the Lord implies the oneness of his mystical body, which is the one and indivisible Church. From the eucharistic center arises the necessary openness of every celebrating community, of every particular Church. By allowing itself to be drawn into the open arms of the Lord, it achieves insertion into his one and undivided body."[38] Consequently, in the celebration of the Eucharist, the individual members of the faithful find themselves in *their* Church, that is, in the Church of Christ. From this eucharistic perspective, adequately understood, ecclesial communion is seen to be catholic by its very nature.[39] An emphasis on this eucharistic basis of ecclesial communion can also contribute greatly to the ecumenical dialogue with the Churches and Ecclesial Communities which are not in full communion with the See of Peter. The Eucharist objectively creates a powerful bond of unity between the Catholic Church and the Orthodox Churches, which have preserved the authentic and integral nature of the eucharistic mystery. At the same time, emphasis on the ecclesial character of the Eucharist can become an important element of the dialogue with the Communities of the Reformed tradition.[40]

THE EUCHARIST AND THE SACRAMENTS

The sacramentality of the Church

16.   The Second Vatican Council recalled that "all the sacraments, and indeed all ecclesiastical ministries and works of the apostolate, are bound up with the Eucharist and are directed towards it. For in the most blessed Eucharist is contained the entire spiritual wealth of the Church, namely Christ himself our Pasch and our living bread, who gives life to humanity through his flesh—that flesh which is given life and gives life by the Holy Spirit. Thus men and women are invited and led to offer themselves, their works, and all creation in union with Christ."[41] This close relationship of the Eucharist with the other sacraments and the Christian life can be most fully understood when we contemplate the mystery of the Church herself as a sacrament.[42] The Council in this regard stated that "the Church, in Christ, is a sacrament—a sign and instrument—of communion with God and of the unity of the entire human race."[43] To quote Saint Cyprian, as "a people made one by the unity of the Father, the Son, and the Holy Spirit,"[44] she is the sacrament of trinitarian communion.

---

38. Congregation for the Doctrine of the Faith, Letter on Some Aspects of the Church Understood as Communion *Communionis notio* (May 28, 1992), 11: AAS 85 (1993), 844–845.

39. *Propositio* 5: "The term 'catholic' expresses the universality deriving from the unity that the Eucharist, celebrated in each Church, fosters and builds up. The particular Churches in the universal Church thus have, in the Eucharist, the duty to make visible their own unity and diversity. This bond of fraternal love allows the trinitarian communion to become apparent. The Councils and Synods express in history this fraternal aspect of the Church."

40. Cf. ibid.

41. Decree on the Ministry and Life of Priests *Presbyterorum Ordinis*, 5.

42. Cf. *Propositio* 14.

43. Dogmatic Constitution on the Church *Lumen gentium*, 1.

44. *De Orat. Dom.*, 23: PL 4, 553.

The fact that the Church is the "universal sacrament of salvation"[45] shows how the sacramental economy ultimately determines the way that Christ, the one Savior, through the Spirit, reaches our lives in all their particularity. The Church *receives* and at the same time *expresses* what she herself is in the seven sacraments, thanks to which God's grace concretely influences the lives of the faithful, so that their whole existence, redeemed by Christ, can become an act of worship pleasing to God. From this perspective, I would like here to draw attention to some elements brought up by the Synod Fathers which may help us to grasp the relationship of each of the sacraments to the eucharistic mystery.

I. THE EUCHARIST AND CHRISTIAN INITIATION

The Eucharist, the fullness of Christian initiation

17.   If the Eucharist is truly the source and summit of the Church's life and mission, it follows that the process of Christian initiation must constantly be directed to the reception of this sacrament. As the Synod Fathers said, we need to ask ourselves whether in our Christian communities the close link between Baptism, Confirmation, and Eucharist is sufficiently recognized.[46] It must never be forgotten that our reception of Baptism and Confirmation is ordered to the Eucharist. Accordingly, our pastoral practice should reflect a more unitary understanding of the process of Christian initiation. The sacrament of Baptism, by which we were conformed to Christ,[47] incorporated in the Church and made children of God, is the portal to all the sacraments. It makes us part of the one Body of Christ (cf. 1 Cor 12:13), a priestly people. Still, it is our participation in the Eucharistic sacrifice which perfects within us the gifts given to us at Baptism. The gifts of the Spirit are given for the building up of Christ's Body (1 Cor 12) and for ever greater witness to the Gospel in the world.[48] The Holy Eucharist, then, brings Christian initiation to completion and represents the center and goal of all sacramental life.[49]

The order of the sacraments of initiation

18.   In this regard, attention needs to be paid to the order of the sacraments of initiation. Different traditions exist within the Church. There is a clear variation between, on the one hand, the ecclesial customs of the East[50] and the practice of the West regarding the initiation of adults,[51] and, on the other hand, the procedure adopted for children.[52] Yet these variations are not properly of the

---

45. Second Vatican Ecumenical Council, Dogmatic Constitution on the Church *Lumen gentium*, 48, cf. ibid., 9.

46. Cf. *Propositio* 13.

47. Cf. Second Vatican Ecumenical Council, Dogmatic Constitution on the Church *Lumen gentium*, 7.

48. Cf. ibid., 11; Second Vatican Ecumenical Council, Decree on the Church's Missionary Activity *Ad gentes*, 9, 13.

49. Cf. John Paul II, Apostolic Letter *Dominicae Cenae* (February 24, 1980), 7: AAS 72 (1980), 124–127; Second Vatican Ecumenical Council, Decree on the Ministry and Life of Priests *Presbyterorum Ordinis*, 5.

50. Cf. *Code of Canons of the Eastern Churches*, can. 710.

51. Cf. *Rite of the Christian Initiation of Adults*, General Introduction, 34–36.

52. Cf. *Rite of Baptism for Children*, Introduction, 18–19.

dogmatic order, but are pastoral in character. Concretely, it needs to be seen which practice better enables the faithful to put the sacrament of the Eucharist at the center, as the goal of the whole process of initiation. In close collaboration with the competent offices of the Roman Curia, Bishops' Conferences should examine the effectiveness of current approaches to Christian initiation, so that the faithful can be helped both to mature through the formation received in our communities and to give their lives an authentically eucharistic direction, so that they can offer a reason for the hope within them in a way suited to our times (cf. 1 Pet 3:15).

Initiation, the ecclesial community, and the family

19.   It should be kept in mind that the whole of Christian initiation is a process of conversion undertaken with God's help and with constant reference to the ecclesial community, both when an adult is seeking entry into the Church, as happens in places of first evangelization and in many secularized regions, and when parents request the sacraments for their children. In this regard, I would like to call particular attention to the relationship between Christian initiation and the family. In pastoral work it is always important to make Christian families part of the process of initiation. Receiving Baptism, Confirmation, and First Holy Communion are key moments not only for the individual receiving them but also for the entire family, which should be supported in its educational role by the various elements of the ecclesial community.[53] Here I would emphasize the importance of First Holy Communion. For many of the faithful, this day continues to be memorable as the moment when, even if in a rudimentary way, they first came to understand the importance of a personal encounter with Jesus. Parish pastoral programs should make the most of this highly significant moment.

II. THE EUCHARIST AND THE SACRAMENT OF RECONCILIATION

Their intrinsic relationship

20.   The Synod Fathers rightly stated that a love for the Eucharist leads to a growing appreciation of the sacrament of Reconciliation.[54] Given the connection between these sacraments, an authentic catechesis on the meaning of the Eucharist must include the call to pursue the path of penance (cf. 1 Cor 11:27–29). We know that the faithful are surrounded by a culture that tends to eliminate the sense of sin[55] and to promote a superficial approach that overlooks the need to be in a state of grace in order to approach sacramental communion worthily.[56] The loss of a consciousness of sin always entails a certain superficiality in the understanding of God's love. Bringing out the elements within the rite of Mass that express consciousness of personal sin and, at the same time, of God's mercy

---

53. Cf. *Propositio* 15.

54. Cf. *Propositio* 7; John Paul II, Encyclical Letter *Ecclesia de Eucharistia* (April 17, 2003), 36: AAS 95 (2003), 457–458.

55. Cf. John Paul II, Post-Synodal Apostolic Exhortation *Reconciliatio et Paenitentia* (December 2, 1984), 18: AAS 77 (1985), 224–228.

56. Cf. *Catechism of the Catholic Church*, 1385.

can prove most helpful to the faithful.[57] Furthermore, the relationship between the Eucharist and the sacrament of Reconciliation reminds us that sin is never a purely individual affair; it always damages the ecclesial communion that we have entered through Baptism. For this reason, Reconciliation, as the Fathers of the Church would say, is *laboriosus quidam baptismus*;[58] they thus emphasized that the outcome of the process of conversion is also the restoration of full ecclesial communion, expressed in a return to the Eucharist.[59]

Some pastoral concerns

21.   The Synod recalled that Bishops have the pastoral duty of promoting within their Dioceses a reinvigorated catechesis on the conversion born of the Eucharist and of encouraging frequent confession among the faithful. All priests should dedicate themselves with generosity, commitment, and competency to administering the sacrament of Reconciliation.[60] In this regard, it is important that the confessionals in our churches should be clearly visible expressions of the importance of this sacrament. I ask pastors to be vigilant with regard to the celebration of the sacrament of Reconciliation and to limit the practice of general absolution exclusively to the cases permitted,[61] since individual absolution is the only form intended for ordinary use.[62] Given the need to rediscover sacramental forgiveness, there ought to be a *Penitentiary* in every Diocese.[63] Finally, a balanced and sound practice of gaining *indulgences*, whether for oneself or for the dead, can be helpful for a renewed appreciation of the relationship between the Eucharist and Reconciliation. By this means the faithful obtain "remission before God of the temporal punishment due to sins whose guilt has already been forgiven."[64] The use of indulgences helps us to understand that by our efforts alone we would be incapable of making reparation for the wrong we have done, and that the sins of each individual harm the whole community. Furthermore, the practice of indulgences, which involves not only the doctrine of Christ's

---

57. For example, the *Confiteor*, or the words of the priest and people before receiving Communion: "*Lord, I am not worthy to receive you, but only say the word and I shall be healed.*" Not insignificantly does the liturgy also prescribe certain very beautiful prayers for the priest, handed down by tradition, which speak of the need for forgiveness, as, for example, the one recited quietly before inviting the faithful to sacramental communion: "*By the mystery of your body and blood, free me from all my sins and from every evil. Keep me always faithful to your teachings and never let me be parted from you.*"

58. Cf. Saint John Damascene, *Exposition of the Faith*, IV, 9: PG 94, 1124C; Saint Gregory Nazianzen, *Oratio* 39, 17: PG 36, 356A; Ecumenical Council of Trent, *Doctrina de sacramento paenitentiae*, Chapter 2: DS 1672.

59. Cf. Second Vatican Ecumenical Council, Dogmatic Constitution on the Church *Lumen gentium*, 11; John Paul II, Post-Synodal Apostolic Exhortation *Reconciliatio et Paenitentia* (December 2, 1984), 30: AAS 77 (1985), 256–257.

60. Cf. *Propositio* 7.

61. Cf. John Paul II, Motu Proprio *Misericordia Dei* (April 7, 2002): AAS 94 (2002), 452–459.

62. Together with the Synod Fathers I wish to note that the non-sacramental penitential services mentioned in the ritual of the sacrament of Reconciliation can be helpful for increasing the spirit of conversion and of communion in Christian communities, thereby preparing hearts for the celebration of the sacrament: cf. *Propositio* 7.

63. Cf. *Code of Canon Law*, can. 508.

64. Paul VI, Apostolic Constitution *Indulgentiarum doctrina* (January 1, 1967), *Norms*, No. 1: AAS 59 (1967), 21.

infinite merits, but also that of the communion of the saints, reminds us "how closely we are united to each other in Christ . . . and how the supernatural life of each can help others."[65] Since the conditions for gaining an indulgence include going to confession and receiving sacramental communion, this practice can effectively sustain the faithful on their journey of conversion and in rediscovering the centrality of the Eucharist in the Christian life.

III. THE EUCHARIST AND THE ANOINTING OF THE SICK

22.   Jesus did not only send his disciples forth to heal the sick (cf. Mt 10:8; Lk 9:2, 10:9); he also instituted a specific sacrament for them: the Anointing of the Sick.[66] The *Letter of James* attests to the presence of this sacramental sign in the early Christian community (cf. 5:14–16). If the Eucharist shows how Christ's sufferings and death have been transformed into love, the Anointing of the Sick, for its part, unites the sick with Christ's self-offering for the salvation of all, so that they too, within the mystery of the communion of saints, can participate in the redemption of the world. The relationship between these two sacraments becomes clear in situations of serious illness: "In addition to the Anointing of the Sick, the Church offers those who are about to leave this life the Eucharist as viaticum."[67] On their journey to the Father, communion in the Body and Blood of Christ appears as the seed of eternal life and the power of resurrection: "Anyone who eats my flesh and drinks my blood has eternal life and I will raise him up on the last day" (Jn 6:54). Since viaticum gives the sick a glimpse of the fullness of the Paschal Mystery, its administration should be readily provided for.[68] Attentive pastoral care shown to those who are ill brings great spiritual benefit to the entire community, since whatever we do to one of the least of our brothers and sisters, we do to Jesus himself (cf. Mt 25:40).

IV. THE EUCHARIST AND THE SACRAMENT OF HOLY ORDERS

In persona Christi capitis

23.   The intrinsic relationship between the Eucharist and the sacrament of Holy Orders clearly emerges from Jesus' own words in the Upper Room: "Do this in memory of me" (Lk 22:19). On the night before he died, Jesus instituted the Eucharist and at the same time established the *priesthood of the New Covenant*. He is priest, victim, and altar: the mediator between God the Father and his people (cf. Heb 5:5–10), the victim of atonement (cf. 1 Jn 2:2, 4:10) who offers himself on the altar of the Cross. No one can say "this is my body" and "this is the cup of my blood" except in the name and in the person of Christ, the one high priest of the new and eternal Covenant (cf. Heb 8–9). Earlier meetings of the Synod of Bishops had considered the question of the ordained priesthood,

---

65. Ibid., 9: AAS 59 (1967), 18–19.
66. Cf. *Catechism of the Catholic Church*, 1499–1532.
67. Ibid., 1524.
68. Cf. *Propositio* 44.

both with regard to the nature of the ministry[69] and the formation of candidates.[70] Here, in the light of the discussion that took place during the last Synod, I consider it important to recall several important points about the relationship between the sacrament of the Eucharist and Holy Orders. First of all, we need to stress once again that the connection between *Holy Orders and the Eucharist* is seen most clearly at Mass, when the Bishop or priest presides *in the person of Christ the Head.*

The Church teaches that priestly ordination is the indispensable condition for the valid celebration of the Eucharist.[71] Indeed, "in the ecclesial service of the ordained minister, it is Christ himself who is present to his Church as Head of his Body, Shepherd of his flock, High Priest of the redemptive sacrifice."[72] Certainly the ordained minister also acts "in the name of the whole Church, when presenting to God the prayer of the Church and above all when offering the eucharistic sacrifice."[73] As a result, priests should be conscious of the fact that in their ministry they must never put themselves or their personal opinions in first place, but Jesus Christ. Any attempt to make themselves the center of the liturgical action contradicts their very identity as priests. The priest is above all a servant of others, and he must continually work at being a sign pointing to Christ, a docile instrument in the Lord's hands. This is seen particularly in his humility in leading the liturgical assembly, in obedience to the rite, uniting himself to it in mind and heart, and avoiding anything that might give the impression of an inordinate emphasis on his own personality. I encourage the clergy always to see their eucharistic ministry as a humble service offered to Christ and his Church. The priesthood, as Saint Augustine said, is *amoris officium*,[74] it is the office of the good shepherd, who offers his life for his sheep (cf. Jn 10:14–15).

The Eucharist and priestly celibacy

24.   The Synod Fathers wished to emphasize that the ministerial priesthood, through ordination, calls for complete configuration to Christ. While respecting the different practice and tradition of the Eastern Churches, there is a need to reaffirm the profound meaning of priestly celibacy, which is rightly considered a priceless treasure and is also confirmed by the Eastern practice of choosing Bishops only from the ranks of the celibate. These Churches also greatly esteem the decision of many priests to embrace celibacy. This choice on the part of the priest expresses in a special way the dedication which conforms him to

---

69. Cf. Synod of Bishops, Second General Assembly, Document on the Ministerial Priesthood *Ultimis temporibus* (November 30, 1971): AAS 63 (1971), 898–942.

70. Cf. John Paul II, Post-Synodal Apostolic Exhortation *Pastores dabo vobis* (March 25, 1992), 42–69: AAS 84 (1992), 729–778.

71. Cf. Second Vatican Ecumenical Council, Dogmatic Constitution on the Church *Lumen gentium*, 10; Congregation for the Doctrine of the Faith, Letter on Certain Questions Concerning the Minister of the Eucharist *Sacerdotium ministeriale* (August 6, 1983): AAS 75 (1983), 1001–1009.

72. *Catechism of the Catholic Church*, 1548.

73. Ibid., 1552.

74. Cf. *In Iohannis Evangelium Tractatus*, 123, 5: PL 35, 1967.

Christ and his exclusive offering of himself for the Kingdom of God.[75] The fact that Christ himself, the eternal priest, lived his mission even to the sacrifice of the Cross in the state of virginity constitutes the sure point of reference for understanding the meaning of the tradition of the Latin Church. It is not sufficient to understand priestly celibacy in purely functional terms. Celibacy is really a special way of conforming oneself to Christ's own way of life. This choice has first and foremost a nuptial meaning; it is a profound identification with the heart of Christ the Bridegroom who gives his life for his Bride. In continuity with the great ecclesial tradition, with the Second Vatican Council,[76] and with my predecessors in the papacy,[77] I reaffirm the beauty and the importance of a priestly life lived in celibacy as a sign expressing total and exclusive devotion to Christ, to the Church, and to the Kingdom of God, and I therefore confirm that it remains obligatory in the Latin tradition. Priestly celibacy lived with maturity, joy, and dedication is an immense blessing for the Church and for society itself.

The clergy shortage and the pastoral care of vocations

25.   In the light of the connection between the sacrament of Holy Orders and the Eucharist, the Synod considered the difficult situation that has arisen in various Dioceses which face a shortage of priests. This happens not only in some areas of first evangelization, but also in many countries of long-standing Christian tradition. Certainly a more equitable distribution of clergy would help to solve the problem. Efforts need to be made to encourage a greater awareness of this situation at every level. Bishops should involve Institutes of Consecrated Life and the new ecclesial groups in their pastoral needs, while respecting their particular charisms, and they should invite the clergy to become more open to serving the Church wherever there is need, even if this calls for sacrifice.[78] The Synod also discussed pastoral initiatives aimed at promoting, especially among the young, an attitude of interior openness to a priestly calling. The situation cannot be resolved by purely practical decisions. On no account should Bishops react to real and understandable concerns about the shortage of priests by failing to carry out adequate vocational discernment, or by admitting to seminary formation and ordination candidates who lack the necessary qualities for priestly ministry.[79] An insufficiently formed clergy, admitted to ordination without the necessary discernment, will not easily be able to offer a witness capable of evoking

---

75. Cf. *Propositio* 11.

76. Cf. Decree on the Ministry and Life of Priests *Presbyterorum Ordinis*, 16.

77. Cf. John XXIII, Encyclical Letter *Sacerdotii nostri primordia* (August 1, 1959): AAS 51 (1959), 545–579; Paul VI, Encyclical Letter *Sacerdotalis coelibatus* (June 24, 1967): AAS 59 (1967), 657–697; John Paul II, Post-Synodal Apostolic Exhortation *Pastores dabo vobis* (March 25, 1992), 29: AAS 84 (1992), 703–705; Benedict XVI, Address to the Roman Curia (December 25, 2006): *L'Osservatore Romano*, December 23, 2006, p. 6.

78. Cf. *Propositio* 11.

79. Cf. Second Vatican Ecumenical Council, Decree on Priestly Formation *Optatam Totius*, 6; Code of Canon Law, can. 241, § 1 and can. 1029; Code of Canons of the Eastern Churches, can. 342 § 1 and can. 758; John Paul II, Post-Synodal Apostolic Exhortation *Pastores dabo vobis* (March 25, 1992), 11, 34, 50: AAS 84 (1992), 673–675; 712–714; 746–748; Congregation for the Clergy, Directory for the Ministry and Life of Priests *Dives Ecclesiae* (March 31, 1994), 58; Congregation for Catholic Education, Instruction Concerning the Criteria for the Discernment

in others the desire to respond generously to Christ's call. The pastoral care of vocations needs to involve the entire Christian community in every area of its life.[80] Obviously, this pastoral work on all levels also includes exploring the matter with families, which are often indifferent or even opposed to the idea of a priestly vocation. Families should generously embrace the gift of life and bring up their children to be open to doing God's will. In a word, they must have the courage to set before young people the radical decision to follow Christ, showing them how deeply rewarding it is.

Gratitude and hope

26.   Finally, we need to have ever greater faith and hope in God's providence. Even if there is a shortage of priests in some areas, we must never lose confidence that Christ continues to inspire men to leave everything behind and to dedicate themselves totally to celebrating the sacred mysteries, preaching the Gospel, and ministering to the flock. In this regard, I wish to express the gratitude of the whole Church for all those Bishops and priests who carry out their respective missions with fidelity, devotion and zeal. Naturally, the Church's gratitude also goes to deacons, who receive the laying on of hands "not for priesthood but for service."[81] As the Synod Assembly recommended, I offer a special word of thanks to those *Fidei Donum* priests who work faithfully and generously at building up the community by proclaiming the word of God and breaking the Bread of Life, devoting all their energy to serving the mission of the Church.[82] Let us thank God for all those priests who have suffered even to the sacrifice of their lives in order to serve Christ. The eloquence of their example shows what it means to be a priest to the end. Theirs is a moving witness that can inspire many young people to follow Christ and to expend their lives for others, and thus to discover true life.

V. THE EUCHARIST AND MATRIMONY

The Eucharist, a nuptial sacrament

27.   The Eucharist, as the sacrament of charity, has a particular relationship with the love of man and woman united in marriage. A deeper understanding of this relationship is needed at the present time.[83] Pope John Paul II frequently spoke of the nuptial character of the Eucharist and its special relationship with the sacrament of Matrimony: "The Eucharist is the sacrament of our redemption. It is the sacrament of the Bridegroom and of the Bride."[84] Moreover, "the entire Christian life bears the mark of the spousal love of Christ and the Church.

of Vocations with regard to Persons with Homosexual Tendencies in view of their Admission to the Seminary and to Holy Orders (November 4, 2005): AAS 97 (2005), 1007–1013.

80. Cf. *Propositio* 12; John Paul II, Post-Synodal Apostolic Exhortation *Pastores dabo vobis* (March 25, 1992), 41: AAS 84 (1992), 726–729.

81. Second Vatican Ecumenical Council, Dogmatic Constitution on the Church *Lumen gentium*, 29.

82. Cf. *Propositio* 38.

83. Cf. John Paul II, Post-Synodal Apostolic Exhortation *Familiaris consortio* (November 22, 1981), 57: AAS 74 (1982), 149–150.

84. Apostolic Letter *Mulieris dignitatem* (August 15, 1988), 26: AAS 80 (1988), 1715–1716.

Already Baptism, the entry into the People of God, is a nuptial mystery; it is so to speak the nuptial bath which precedes the wedding feast, the Eucharist."[85] The Eucharist inexhaustibly strengthens the indissoluble unity and love of every Christian marriage. By the power of the sacrament, the marriage bond is intrinsically linked to the eucharistic unity of Christ the Bridegroom and his Bride, the Church (cf. Eph 5:31–32). The mutual consent that husband and wife exchange in Christ, which establishes them as a community of life and love, also has a eucharistic dimension. Indeed, in the theology of Saint Paul, conjugal love is a sacramental sign of Christ's love for his Church, a love culminating in the Cross, the expression of his "marriage" with humanity and at the same time the origin and heart of the Eucharist. For this reason the Church manifests her particular spiritual closeness to all those who have built their family on the sacrament of Matrimony.[86] The family—the domestic Church[87]—is a primary sphere of the Church's life, especially because of its decisive role in the Christian education of children.[88] In this context, the Synod also called for an acknowledgment of the unique mission of women in the family and in society, a mission that needs to be defended, protected, and promoted.[89] Marriage and motherhood represent essential realities which must never be denigrated.

The Eucharist and the unicity of marriage

28.   In the light of this intrinsic relationship between marriage, the family, and the Eucharist, we can turn to several pastoral problems. The indissoluble, exclusive, and faithful bond uniting Christ and the Church, which finds sacramental expression in the Eucharist, corresponds to the basic anthropological fact that man is meant to be definitively united to one woman and vice versa (cf. Gen 2:24, Mt 19:5). With this in mind, the Synod of Bishops addressed the question of pastoral practice regarding people who come to the Gospel from cultures in which polygamy is practiced. Those living in this situation who open themselves to Christian faith need to be helped to integrate their life-plan into the radical newness of Christ. During the catechumenate, Christ encounters them in their specific circumstances and calls them to embrace the full truth of love, making whatever sacrifices are necessary in order to arrive at perfect ecclesial communion. The Church accompanies them with a pastoral care that is gentle yet firm,[90] above all by showing them the light shed by the Christian mysteries on nature and on human affections.

---

85. *Catechism of the Catholic Church*, 1617.

86. Cf. *Propositio* 8.

87. Cf. Second Vatican Ecumenical Council, Dogmatic Constitution on the Church *Lumen gentium*, 11.

88. Cf. *Propositio* 8.

89. Cf. John Paul II, Apostolic Letter *Mulieris dignitatem* (August 15, 1988): AAS 80 (1988), 1653–1729; Congregation for the Doctrine of the Faith, Letter to the Bishops of the Catholic Church on the Collaboration of Men and Women in the Church and in the World (May 31, 2004): AAS 96 (2004), 671–687.

90. Cf. *Propositio* 9.

The Eucharist and the indissolubility of marriage

29.   If the Eucharist expresses the irrevocable nature of God's love in Christ for his Church, we can then understand why it implies, with regard to the sacrament of Matrimony, that indissolubility to which all true love necessarily aspires.[91] There was good reason for the pastoral attention that the Synod gave to the painful situations experienced by some of the faithful who, having celebrated the sacrament of Matrimony, then divorced and remarried. This represents a complex and troubling pastoral problem, a real scourge for contemporary society, and one which increasingly affects the Catholic community as well. The Church's pastors, out of love for the truth, are obliged to discern different situations carefully in order to be able to offer appropriate spiritual guidance to the faithful involved.[92] The Synod of Bishops confirmed the Church's practice, based on Sacred Scripture (cf. Mk 10:2–12), of not admitting the divorced and remarried to the sacraments, since their state and their condition of life objectively contradict the loving union of Christ and the Church signified and made present in the Eucharist. Yet the divorced and remarried continue to belong to the Church, which accompanies them with special concern and encourages them to live as fully as possible the Christian life through regular participation at Mass, albeit without receiving communion, listening to the word of God, eucharistic adoration, prayer, participation in the life of the community, honest dialogue with a priest or spiritual director, dedication to the life of charity, works of penance, and commitment to the education of their children.

When legitimate doubts exist about the validity of the prior sacramental marriage, the necessary investigation must be carried out to establish if these are well-founded. Consequently there is a need to ensure, in full respect for canon law,[93] the presence of local ecclesiastical tribunals, their pastoral character, and their correct and prompt functioning.[94] Each Diocese should have a sufficient number of persons with the necessary preparation so that the ecclesiastical tribunals can operate in an expeditious manner. I repeat that "it is a grave obligation to bring the Church's institutional activity in her tribunals ever closer to the faithful."[95] At the same time, pastoral care must not be understood as if it were somehow in conflict with the law. Rather, one should begin by assuming that the fundamental point of encounter between the law and pastoral care is *love for the truth*: truth is never something purely abstract, but "a real part of the human and Christian journey of every member of the faithful."[96] Finally,

---

91. Cf. *Catechism of the Catholic Church*, 1640.

92. Cf. John Paul II, Post-Synodal Apostolic Exhortation *Familiaris Consortio* (November 22, 1981), 84: AAS 74 (1982), 184–186; Congregation for the Doctrine of the Faith, Letter to the Bishops of the Catholic Church concerning the Reception of Holy Communion by Divorced and Remarried Members of the Faithful *Annus Internationalis Familiae* (September 14, 1994): AAS 86 (1994), 974–979.

93. Cf. Pontifical Council for Legislative Texts, Instruction on the Norms to be Observed at Ecclesiastical Tribunals in Matrimonial Proceedings *Dignitas Connubii* (January 25, 2005), Vatican City, 2005.

94. Cf. *Propositio 40*.

95. Benedict XVI, Address to the Tribunal of the Roman Rota for the Inauguration of the Judicial Year (January 28, 2006): AAS 98 (2006), 138.

96. Cf. *Propositio 40*.

where the nullity of the marriage bond is not declared and objective circumstances make it impossible to cease cohabitation, the Church encourages these members of the faithful to commit themselves to living their relationship in fidelity to the demands of God's law, as friends, as brother and sister; in this way they will be able to return to the table of the Eucharist, taking care to observe the Church's established and approved practice in this regard. This path, if it is to be possible and fruitful, must be supported by pastors and by adequate ecclesial initiatives, nor can it ever involve the blessing of these relations, lest confusion arise among the faithful concerning the value of marriage.[97]

Given the complex cultural context which the Church today encounters in many countries, the Synod also recommended devoting maximum pastoral attention to training couples preparing for marriage and to ascertaining beforehand their convictions regarding the obligations required for the validity of the sacrament of Matrimony. Serious discernment in this matter will help to avoid situations where impulsive decisions or superficial reasons lead two young people to take on responsibilities that they are then incapable of honoring.[98] The good that the Church and society as a whole expect from marriage and from the family founded upon marriage is so great as to call for full pastoral commitment to this particular area. Marriage and the family are institutions that must be promoted and defended from every possible misrepresentation of their true nature, since whatever is injurious to them is injurious to society itself.

THE EUCHARIST AND ESCHATOLOGY

The Eucharist: a gift to men and women on their journey

30.   If it is true that the sacraments are part of the Church's pilgrimage through history[99] towards the full manifestation of the victory of the risen Christ, it is also true that, especially in the liturgy of the Eucharist, they give us a real foretaste of the eschatological fulfillment for which every human being and all creation are destined (cf. Rom 8:19ff.). Man is created for that true and eternal happiness which only God's love can give. But our wounded freedom would go astray were it not already able to experience something of that future fulfillment. Moreover, to move forward in the right direction, we all need to be guided towards our final goal. That goal is Christ himself, the Lord who conquered sin and death and who makes himself present to us in a special way in the eucharistic celebration. Even though we remain "aliens and exiles" in this world (1 Pet 2:11), through faith we already share in the fullness of risen life. The eucharistic banquet, by disclosing its powerful eschatological dimension, comes to the aid of our freedom as we continue our journey.

The eschatological banquet

31.   Reflecting on this mystery, we can say that Jesus' coming responded to an expectation present in the people of Israel, in the whole of humanity, and ultimately

---

97. Cf. ibid.
98. Cf. ibid.
99. Cf. Second Vatican Ecumenical Council, Dogmatic Constitution on the Church *Lumen gentium*, 48.

in creation itself. By his self-gift, he objectively inaugurated the eschatological age. Christ came to gather together the scattered People of God (cf. Jn 11:52) and clearly manifested his intention to gather together the community of the covenant, in order to bring to fulfillment the promises made by God to the fathers of old (cf. Jer 23:3; Lk 1:55, 70). In the calling of the Twelve, which is to be understood in relation to the twelve tribes of Israel, and in the command he gave them at the Last Supper, before his redemptive passion, to celebrate his memorial, Jesus showed that he wished to transfer to the entire community which he had founded the task of being, within history, the sign and instrument of the eschatological gathering that had its origin in him. Consequently, every eucharistic celebration sacramentally accomplishes the eschatological gathering of the People of God. For us, the eucharistic banquet is a real foretaste of the final banquet foretold by the prophets (cf. Is 25:6–9) and described in the New Testament as "the marriage-feast of the Lamb" (Rev 19:7–9) to be celebrated in the joy of the communion of saints.[100]

Prayer for the dead

32.   The eucharistic celebration, in which we proclaim that Christ has died and risen, and will come again, is a pledge of the future glory in which our bodies too will be glorified. Celebrating the memorial of our salvation strengthens our hope in the resurrection of the body and in the possibility of meeting once again, face to face, those who have gone before us marked with the sign of faith. In this context, I wish, together with the Synod Fathers, to remind all the faithful of the importance of prayers for the dead, especially the offering of Mass for them, so that, once purified, they can come to the beatific vision of God.[101] A rediscovery of the eschatological dimension inherent in the Eucharist, celebrated and adored, will help sustain us on our journey and comfort us in the hope of glory (cf. Rom 5:2; Tit 2:13).

THE EUCHARIST AND THE VIRGIN MARY

33.   From the relationship between the Eucharist and the individual sacraments, and from the eschatological significance of the sacred mysteries, the overall shape of the Christian life emerges, a life called at all times to be an act of spiritual worship, a self-offering pleasing to God. Although we are all still journeying towards the complete fulfillment of our hope, this does not mean that we cannot already gratefully acknowledge that God's gifts to us have found their perfect fulfillment in the Virgin Mary, Mother of God and our Mother. Mary's Assumption body and soul into heaven is for us a sign of sure hope, for it shows us, on our pilgrimage through time, the eschatological goal of which the sacrament of the Eucharist enables us even now to have a foretaste.

In Mary most holy, we also see perfectly fulfilled the "sacramental" way that God comes down to meet his creatures and involves them in his saving work.

---

100. Cf. *Propositio* 3.

101. Here I would recall the words filled with hope and consolation found in Eucharistic Prayer II: "*Remember our brothers and sisters who have gone to their rest in the hope of rising again. Bring them and all the departed into the light of your presence.*"

From the Annunciation to Pentecost, Mary of Nazareth appears as someone whose freedom is completely open to God's will. Her immaculate conception is revealed precisely in her unconditional docility to God's word. Obedient faith in response to God's work shapes her life at every moment. A virgin attentive to God's word, she lives in complete harmony with his will; she treasures in her heart the words that come to her from God and, piecing them together like a mosaic, she learns to understand them more deeply (cf. Lk 2:19, 51); Mary is the great Believer who places herself confidently in God's hands, abandoning herself to his will.[102] This mystery deepens as she becomes completely involved in the redemptive mission of Jesus. In the words of the Second Vatican Council, "the blessed Virgin advanced in her pilgrimage of faith, and faithfully persevered in her union with her Son until she stood at the Cross, in keeping with the divine plan (cf. Jn 19:25), suffering deeply with her only-begotten Son, associating herself with his sacrifice in her mother's heart, and lovingly consenting to the immolation of the victim who was born of her. Finally, she was given by the same Christ Jesus, dying on the Cross, as a mother to his disciple, with these words: 'Woman, behold your Son.'"[103] From the Annunciation to the Cross, Mary is the one who received the Word, made flesh within her and then silenced in death. It is she, lastly, who took into her arms the lifeless body of the one who truly loved his own "to the end" (Jn 13:1).

Consequently, every time we approach the Body and Blood of Christ in the eucharistic liturgy, we also turn to her who, by her complete fidelity, received Christ's sacrifice for the whole Church. The Synod Fathers rightly declared that "Mary inaugurates the Church's participation in the sacrifice of the Redeemer."[104] She is the Immaculata, who receives God's gift unconditionally and is thus associated with his work of salvation. Mary of Nazareth, icon of the nascent Church, is the model for each of us, called to receive the gift that Jesus makes of himself in the Eucharist.

PART TWO
THE EUCHARIST, A MYSTERY TO BE CELEBRATED

"Truly, truly, I say to you, it was not Moses who gave you the bread from heaven; my Father gives you the true bread from heaven." (Jn 6:32)

Lex orandi and lex credendi

34.   The Synod of Bishops reflected at length on the intrinsic relationship between eucharistic faith and eucharistic celebration, pointing out the connection between the *lex orandi* and the *lex credendi* and stressing the primacy of the *liturgical action*. The Eucharist should be experienced as a mystery of faith, celebrated authentically and with a clear awareness that "the *intellectus fidei* has a primordial relationship to the Church's liturgical action."[105] Theological reflection

---

102. Cf. Benedict XVI, Homily (December 8, 2005): AAS 98 (2006), 15–16.
103. Dogmatic Constitution on the Church *Lumen gentium*, 58.
104. *Propositio* 4.
105. *Relatio post disceptationem*, 4: *L'Osservatore Romano*, October 14, 2005, p. 5.

in this area can never prescind from the sacramental order instituted by Christ himself. On the other hand, the liturgical action can never be considered generically, prescinding from the mystery of faith. Our faith and the eucharistic liturgy both have their source in the same event: Christ's gift of himself in the Paschal Mystery.

Beauty and the liturgy

35.   This relationship between creed and worship is evidenced in a particular way by the rich theological and liturgical category of beauty. Like the rest of Christian Revelation, the liturgy is inherently linked to beauty: it is *veritatis splendor*. The liturgy is a radiant expression of the paschal mystery, in which Christ draws us to himself and calls us to communion. As Saint Bonaventure would say, in Jesus we contemplate beauty and splendor at their source.[106] This is no mere aestheticism, but the concrete way in which the truth of God's love in Christ encounters us, attracts us, and delights us, enabling us to emerge from ourselves and drawing us towards our true vocation, which is love.[107] God allows himself to be glimpsed first in creation, in the beauty and harmony of the cosmos (cf. Wis 13:5; Rom 1:19–20). In the Old Testament we see many signs of the grandeur of God's power as he manifests his glory in his wondrous deeds among the Chosen People (cf. Ex 14; 16:10; 24:12–18; Num 14:20–23). In the New Testament this epiphany of beauty reaches definitive fulfillment in God's revelation in Jesus Christ:[108] Christ is the full manifestation of the glory of God. In the glorification of the Son, the Father's glory shines forth and is communicated (cf. Jn 1:14; 8:54; 12:28; 17:1). Yet this beauty is not simply a harmony of proportion and form; "the fairest of the sons of men" (Ps 45[44]:3) is also, mysteriously, the one "who had no form or comeliness that we should look at him, and no beauty that we should desire him" (Is 53:2). Jesus Christ shows us how the truth of love can transform even the dark mystery of death into the radiant light of the resurrection. Here the splendor of God's glory surpasses all worldly beauty. The truest beauty is the love of God, who definitively revealed himself to us in the paschal mystery.

The beauty of the liturgy is part of this mystery; it is a sublime expression of God's glory and, in a certain sense, a glimpse of heaven on earth. The memorial of Jesus' redemptive sacrifice contains something of that beauty which Peter, James, and John beheld when the Master, making his way to Jerusalem, was transfigured before their eyes (cf. Mk 9:2). Beauty, then, is not mere decoration, but rather an essential element of the liturgical action, since it is an attribute of God himself and his revelation. These considerations should make us realize the care which is needed, if the liturgical action is to reflect its innate splendor.

---

106. Cf. *Serm.* 1, 7; 11, 10; 22, 7; 29, 76: *Sermones dominicales ad fidem codicum nunc denuo editi*, Grottaferrata, 1977, pp. 135, 209ff., 292ff.; 337; Benedict XVI, *Message to Ecclesial Movements and New Communities* (May 22, 2006): AAS 98 (2006), 463.

107. Cf. Second Vatican Ecumenical Council, Pastoral Constitution on the Church in the Modern World *Gaudium et spes*, 22.

108. Cf. Second Vatican Ecumenical Council, Dogmatic Constitution on Divine Revelation *Dei Verbum*, 2, 4.

THE EUCHARISTIC CELEBRATION, THE WORK OF "CHRISTUS TOTUS"

Christus totus in capite et in corpore

36. The "subject" of the liturgy's intrinsic beauty is Christ himself, risen and glorified in the Holy Spirit, who includes the Church in his work.[109] Here we can recall an evocative phrase of Saint Augustine which strikingly describes this dynamic of faith proper to the Eucharist. The great Bishop of Hippo, speaking specifically of the eucharistic mystery, stresses the fact that Christ assimilates us to himself: "The bread you see on the altar, sanctified by the word of God, is the body of Christ. The chalice, or rather, what the chalice contains, sanctified by the word of God, is the blood of Christ. In these signs, Christ the Lord willed to entrust to us his body and the blood which he shed for the forgiveness of our sins. If you have received them properly, you yourselves are what you have received."[110] Consequently, "not only have we become Christians, we have become Christ himself."[111] We can thus contemplate God's mysterious work, which brings about a profound unity between ourselves and the Lord Jesus: "one should not believe that Christ is in the head but not in the body; rather he is complete in the head and in the body."[112]

The Eucharist and the risen christ

37. Since the eucharistic liturgy is essentially an *actio Dei* which draws us into Christ through the Holy Spirit, its basic structure is not something within our power to change, nor can it be held hostage by the latest trends. Here too Saint Paul's irrefutable statement applies: "no one can lay any foundation other than the one that has been laid, which is Jesus Christ" (1 Cor 3:11). Again it is the Apostle of the Gentiles who assures us that, with regard to the Eucharist, he is presenting not his own teaching but what he himself has received (cf. 1 Cor 11:23). The celebration of the Eucharist implies and involves the living Tradition. The Church celebrates the eucharistic sacrifice in obedience to Christ's command, based on her experience of the Risen Lord and the outpouring of the Holy Spirit. For this reason, from the beginning, the Christian community has gathered for the *fractio panis* on the Lord's Day. Sunday, the day Christ rose from the dead, is also the first day of the week, the day which the Old Testament tradition saw as the beginning of God's work of creation. The day of creation has now become the day of the "new creation," the day of our liberation, when we commemorate Christ who died and rose again.[113]

ARS CELEBRANDI

38. In the course of the Synod, there was frequent insistence on the need to avoid any antithesis between the *ars celebrandi*, the art of proper celebration, and the full, active, and fruitful participation of all the faithful. The primary

---

109. *Propositio* 33.
110. *Sermo* 227, 1: PL 38, 1099.
111. *In Iohannis Evangelium Tractatus*, 21, 8: PL 35, 1568.
112. Ibid., 28, 1: PL 35, 1622.
113. Cf. *Propositio* 30. Weekday Masses, which the faithful are encouraged to attend, find their proper form on the day of the Lord, the day of Christ's resurrection; *Propositio* 43.

way to foster the participation of the People of God in the sacred rite is the proper celebration of the rite itself. The *ars celebrandi* is the best way to ensure their *actuosa participatio*.[114] The *ars celebrandi* is the fruit of faithful adherence to the liturgical norms in all their richness; indeed, for two thousand years this way of celebrating has sustained the faith life of all believers, called to take part in the celebration as the People of God, a royal priesthood, a holy nation (cf. 1 Pet 2:4–5, 9).[115]

The bishop, celebrant par excellence

39.   While it is true that the whole People of God participates in the eucharistic liturgy, a correct *ars celebrandi* necessarily entails a specific responsibility on the part of those who have received the sacrament of Holy Orders. Bishops, priests, and deacons, each according to his proper rank, must consider the celebration of the liturgy as their principal duty.[116] Above all, this is true of the Diocesan Bishop: as "the chief steward of the mysteries of God in the particular Church entrusted to his care, he is the moderator, promoter, and guardian of the whole of its liturgical life."[117] This is essential for the life of the particular Church, not only because communion with the Bishop is required for the lawfulness of every celebration within his territory, but also because he himself is the celebrant par excellence within his Diocese.[118] It is his responsibility to ensure unity and harmony in the celebrations taking place in his territory. Consequently the Bishop must be "determined that the priests, the deacons, and the lay Christian faithful grasp ever more deeply the genuine meaning of the rites and liturgical texts, and thereby be led to an active and fruitful celebration of the Eucharist."[119] I would ask that every effort be made to ensure that the liturgies which the Bishop celebrates in his Cathedral are carried out with complete respect for the *ars celebrandi*, so that they can be considered an example for the entire Diocese.[120]

Respect for the liturgical books and the richness of signs

40.   Emphasizing the importance of the *ars celebrandi* also leads to an appreciation of the value of the liturgical norms.[121] The *ars celebrandi* should foster a sense of the sacred and the use of outward signs which help to cultivate this sense, such as, for example, the harmony of the rite, the liturgical vestments,

---

114. Cf. *Propositio* 2.

115. Cf. *Propositio* 25.

116. Cf. *Propositio* 19. *Propositio* 25 states: "An authentic liturgical action expresses the sacredness of the eucharistic mystery. This should be evident from the words and actions of the priest who celebrates, as he intercedes to God the Father both with the faithful and on their behalf."

117. *General Instruction of the Roman Missal*, 22; Second Vatican Ecumenical Council, Constitution on the Sacred Liturgy *Sacrosanctum Concilium*, 41; cf. Congregation for Divine Worship and the Discipline of the Sacraments, Instruction *Redemptionis sacramentum* (March 25, 2004), 19–25: AAS 96 (2004), 555–557.

118. Cf. Second Vatican Ecumenical Council, Decree on the Pastoral Office of Bishops in the Church *Christus Dominus*, 14; Constitution on the Sacred Liturgy *Sacrosanctum Concilium*, 41.

119. *General Instruction of the Roman Missal*, 22.

120. Cf. ibid.

121. Cf. *Propositio* 25.

the furnishings, and the sacred space. The eucharistic celebration is enhanced when priests and liturgical leaders are committed to making known the current liturgical texts and norms, making available the great riches found in the *General Instruction of the Roman Missal* and the *Order of Readings for Mass*. Perhaps we take it for granted that our ecclesial communities already know and appreciate these resources, but this is not always the case. These texts contain riches which have preserved and expressed the faith and experience of the People of God over its two-thousand-year history. Equally important for a correct *ars celebrandi* is an attentiveness to the various kinds of language that the liturgy employs: words and music, gestures and silence, movement, the liturgical colors of the vestments. By its very nature the liturgy operates on different levels of communication which enable it to engage the whole human person. The simplicity of its gestures and the sobriety of its orderly sequence of signs communicate and inspire more than any contrived and inappropriate additions. Attentiveness and fidelity to the specific structure of the rite express both a recognition of the nature of Eucharist as a gift and, on the part of the minister, a docile openness to receiving this ineffable gift.

Art at the service of the liturgy

41.   The profound connection between beauty and the liturgy should make us attentive to every work of art placed at the service of the celebration.[122] Certainly an important element of sacred art is church architecture,[123] which should highlight the unity of the furnishings of the sanctuary, such as the altar, the crucifix, the tabernacle, the ambo and the celebrant's chair. Here it is important to remember that the purpose of sacred architecture is to offer the Church a fitting space for the celebration of the mysteries of faith, especially the Eucharist.[124] The very nature of a Christian church is defined by the liturgy, which is an assembly of the faithful (*ecclesia*) who are the living stones of the Church (cf. 1 Pet 2:5).

This same principle holds true for sacred art in general, especially painting and sculpture, where religious iconography should be directed to sacramental mystagogy. A solid knowledge of the history of sacred art can be advantageous for those responsible for commissioning artists and architects to create works of art for the liturgy. Consequently it is essential that the education of seminarians and priests include the study of art history, with special reference to sacred buildings and the corresponding liturgical norms. Everything related to the Eucharist should be marked by beauty. Special respect and care must also be given to the vestments, the furnishings, and the sacred vessels, so that by their harmonious and orderly arrangement they will foster awe for the mystery of God, manifest the unity of the faith and strengthen devotion.[125]

---

122. Cf. Second Vatican Ecumenical Council, Constitution on the Sacred Liturgy *Sacrosanctum Concilium*, 112–130.

123. Cf. *Propositio* 27.

124. Cf. ibid.

125. In these matters the provisions of the *General Instruction of the Roman Missal*, 319–351, are to be faithfully observed.

42. In the *ars celebrandi*, liturgical song has a pre-eminent place.[126] Saint Augustine rightly says in a famous sermon that "the new man sings a new song. Singing is an expression of joy and, if we consider the matter, an expression of love."[127] The People of God assembled for the liturgy sings the praises of God. In the course of her two-thousand-year history, the Church has created, and still creates, music and songs which represent a rich patrimony of faith and love. This heritage must not be lost. Certainly as far as the liturgy is concerned, we cannot say that one song is as good as another. Generic improvisation or the introduction of musical genres which fail to respect the meaning of the liturgy should be avoided. As an element of the liturgy, song should be well integrated into the overall celebration.[128] Consequently everything—texts, music, execution—ought to correspond to the meaning of the mystery being celebrated, the structure of the rite, and the liturgical seasons.[129] Finally, while respecting various styles and different and highly praiseworthy traditions, I desire, in accordance with the request advanced by the Synod Fathers, that Gregorian chant be suitably esteemed and employed[130] as the chant proper to the Roman liturgy.[131]

THE STRUCTURE OF THE EUCHARISTIC CELEBRATION

43. After mentioning the more significant elements of the *ars celebrandi* that emerged during the Synod, I would now like to turn to some specific aspects of the structure of the eucharistic celebration which require special attention at the present time, if we are to remain faithful to the underlying intention of the liturgical renewal called for by the Second Vatican Council, in continuity with the great ecclesial tradition.

The intrinsic unity of the liturgical action

44. First of all, there is a need to reflect on the inherent unity of the rite of Mass. Both in catechesis and in the actual manner of celebration, one must avoid giving the impression that the two parts of the rite are merely juxtaposed. The liturgy of the word and the Eucharistic liturgy, with the rites of introduction and conclusion, "are so closely interconnected that they form but one single act of worship."[132] There is an intrinsic bond between the word of God and the Eucharist. From listening to the word of God, faith is born or strengthened

---

126. Cf. *General Instruction of the Roman Missal*, 39–41; Second Vatican Ecumenical Council, Constitution on the Sacred Liturgy *Sacrosanctum Concilium*, 112–118.

127. *Sermo* 34, 1: PL 38, 210.

128. Cf. *Propositio* 25: "Like every artistic expression, singing must be closely adapted to the liturgy and contribute effectively to its aim; in other words, it must express faith, prayer, wonder, and love of Jesus present in the Eucharist."

129. Cf. *Propositio* 29.

130. Cf. *Propositio* 36.

131. Cf. Second Vatican Ecumenical Council, Constitution on the Sacred Liturgy *Sacrosanctum Concilium*, 116; *General Instruction of the Roman Missal*, 41.

132. *General Instruction of the Roman Missal*, 28; cf. Second Vatican Ecumenical Council, Constitution on the Sacred Liturgy *Sacrosanctum Concilium*, 56; Sacred Congregation of Rites, Instruction *Eucharisticum mysterium* (May 25, 1967), 3: AAS 59 (1967), 540–543.

(cf. Rom 10:17); in the Eucharist the Word made flesh gives himself to us as our spiritual food.[133] Thus, "from the two tables of the word of God and the Body of Christ, the Church receives and gives to the faithful the bread of life."[134] Consequently it must constantly be kept in mind that the word of God, read and proclaimed by the Church in the liturgy, leads to the Eucharist as to its own connatural end.

The liturgy of the word

45.   Together with the Synod, I ask that the liturgy of the word always be carefully prepared and celebrated. Consequently I urge that every effort be made to ensure that the liturgical proclamation of the word of God is entrusted to well-prepared readers. Let us never forget that "when the Sacred Scriptures are read in the Church, God himself speaks to his people, and Christ, present in his own word, proclaims the Gospel."[135] When circumstances so suggest, a few brief words of introduction could be offered in order to focus the attention of the faithful. If it is to be properly understood, the word of God must be listened to and accepted in a spirit of communion with the Church and with a clear awareness of its unity with the sacrament of the Eucharist. Indeed, the word which we proclaim and accept is the Word made flesh (cf. Jn 1:14); it is inseparably linked to Christ's person and the sacramental mode of his continued presence in our midst. Christ does not speak in the past, but in the present, even as he is present in the liturgical action. In this sacramental context of Christian revelation,[136] knowledge and study of the word of God enable us better to appreciate, celebrate and live the Eucharist. Here too, we can see how true it is that "ignorance of Scripture is ignorance of Christ."[137]

To this end, the faithful should be helped to appreciate the riches of Sacred Scripture found in the lectionary through pastoral initiatives, liturgies of the word, and reading in the context of prayer (*lectio divina*). Efforts should also be made to encourage those forms of prayer confirmed by tradition, such as the Liturgy of the Hours, especially Morning Prayer, Evening Prayer, and Night Prayer, and vigil celebrations. By praying the Psalms, the Scripture readings, and the readings drawn from the great tradition which are included in the Divine Office, we can come to a deeper experience of the Christ-event and the economy of salvation, which in turn can enrich our understanding and participation in the celebration of the Eucharist.[138]

---

133. Cf. *Propositio* 18.

134. Ibid.

135. *General Instruction of the Roman Missal*, 29.

136. Cf. John Paul II, Encyclical Letter *Fides et ratio* (September 14, 1998), 13: AAS 91 (1999), 15–16.

137. Saint Jerome, *Comm. in Is., Prol.*: PL 24, 17; cf. Second Vatican Ecumenical Council, Dogmatic Constitution on Divine Revelation *Dei Verbum*, 25.

138. Cf. *Propositio* 31.

The homily

46.   Given the importance of the word of God, the quality of homilies needs to be improved. The homily is "part of the liturgical action"[139] and is meant to foster a deeper understanding of the word of God, so that it can bear fruit in the lives of the faithful. Hence ordained ministers must "prepare the homily carefully, based on an adequate knowledge of Sacred Scripture."[140] Generic and abstract homilies should be avoided. In particular, I ask these ministers to preach in such a way that the homily closely relates the proclamation of the word of God to the sacramental celebration[141] and the life of the community, so that the word of God truly becomes the Church's vital nourishment and support.[142] The catechetical and paraenetic aim of the homily should not be forgotten. During the course of the liturgical year it is appropriate to offer the faithful, prudently and on the basis of the three-year lectionary, "thematic" homilies treating the great themes of the Christian faith, on the basis of what has been authoritatively proposed by the Magisterium in the four "pillars" of the *Catechism of the Catholic Church* and the recent *Compendium*, namely: the profession of faith, the celebration of the Christian mystery, life in Christ, and Christian prayer.[143]

The presentation of the gifts

47.   The Synod Fathers also drew attention to the presentation of the gifts. This is not to be viewed simply as a kind of "interval" between the liturgy of the word and the liturgy of the Eucharist. To do so would tend to weaken, at the least, the sense of a single rite made up of two interrelated parts. This humble and simple gesture is actually very significant: in the bread and wine that we bring to the altar, all creation is taken up by Christ the Redeemer to be transformed and presented to the Father.[144] In this way we also bring to the altar all the pain and suffering of the world, in the certainty that everything has value in God's eyes. The authentic meaning of this gesture can be clearly expressed without the need for undue emphasis or complexity. It enables us to appreciate how God invites man to participate in bringing to fulfillment his handiwork, and in so doing, gives human labor its authentic meaning, since, through the celebration of the Eucharist, it is united to the redemptive sacrifice of Christ.

The Eucharistic Prayer

48.   The Eucharistic Prayer is "the center and summit of the entire celebration."[145] Its importance deserves to be adequately emphasized. The different Eucharistic

---

139. *General Instruction of the Roman Missal*, 29; cf. Second Vatican Ecumenical Council, Constitution on the Sacred Liturgy *Sacrosanctum Concilium*, 7, 33, 52.

140. Cf. *Propositio* 19.

141. Second Vatican Ecumenical Council, Constitution on the Sacred Liturgy *Sacrosanctum Concilium*, 52.

142. Second Vatican Ecumenical Council, Dogmatic Constitution on Divine Revelation *Dei Verbum*, 21.

143. To this end the Synod has called for the preparation of pastoral aids based on the three-year lectionary to help connect the proclamation of the readings with the doctrine of the faith; cf. *Propositio* 19.

144. Cf. *Propositio* 20.

145. *General Instruction of the Roman Missal*, 78.

Prayers contained in the Missal have been handed down to us by the Church's living Tradition and are noteworthy for their inexhaustible theological and spiritual richness. The faithful need to be enabled to appreciate that richness. Here the *General Instruction of the Roman Missal* can help, with its list of the basic elements of every Eucharistic Prayer: thanksgiving, acclamation, epiclesis, institution narrative and consecration, anamnesis, offering, intercessions, and final doxology.[146] In a particular way, eucharistic spirituality and theological reflection are enriched if we contemplate in the anaphora the profound unity between the invocation of the Holy Spirit and the institution narrative[147] whereby "the sacrifice is carried out which Christ himself instituted at the Last Supper."[148] Indeed, "the Church implores the power of the Holy Spirit that the gifts offered by human hands be consecrated, that is, become Christ's Body and Blood, and that the spotless Victim to be received in communion be for the salvation of those who will partake of it."[149]

The sign of peace

49.   By its nature the Eucharist is the sacrament of peace. At Mass this dimension of the eucharistic mystery finds specific expression in the sign of peace. Certainly this sign has great value (cf. Jn 14:27). In our times, fraught with fear and conflict, this gesture has become particularly eloquent, as the Church has become increasingly conscious of her responsibility to pray insistently for the gift of peace and unity for herself and for the whole human family. Certainly there is an irrepressible desire for peace present in every heart. The Church gives voice to the hope for peace and reconciliation rising up from every man and woman of good will, directing it towards the one who "is our peace" (Eph 2:14) and who can bring peace to individuals and peoples when all human efforts fail. We can thus understand the emotion so often felt during the sign of peace at a liturgical celebration. Even so, during the Synod of Bishops there was discussion about the appropriateness of greater restraint in this gesture, which can be exaggerated and cause a certain distraction in the assembly just before the reception of Communion. It should be kept in mind that nothing is lost when the sign of peace is marked by a sobriety which preserves the proper spirit of the celebration, as, for example, when it is restricted to one's immediate neighbors.[150]

The distribution and reception of the Eucharist

50.   Another moment of the celebration needing to be mentioned is the distribution and reception of Holy Communion. I ask everyone, especially ordained ministers and those who, after adequate preparation and in cases of genuine need, are authorized to exercise the ministry of distributing the Eucharist, to

---

146. Cf. ibid., 78–79.

147. Cf. *Propositio* 22.

148. *General Instruction of the Roman Missal*, 79d.

149. Ibid., 79c.

150. Taking into account ancient and venerable customs and the wishes expressed by the Synod Fathers, I have asked the competent curial offices to study the possibility of moving the sign of peace to another place, such as before the presentation of the gifts at the altar. To do so would also serve as a significant reminder of the Lord's insistence that we be reconciled with others before offering our gifts to God (cf. Mt 5:23ff.); cf. *Propositio* 23.

make every effort to ensure that this simple act preserves its importance as a personal encounter with the Lord Jesus in the sacrament. For the rules governing correct practice in this regard, I would refer to those documents recently issued on the subject.[151] All Christian communities are to observe the current norms faithfully, seeing in them an expression of the faith and love with which we all must regard this sublime sacrament. Furthermore, the precious time of thanksgiving after communion should not be neglected: besides the singing of an appropriate hymn, it can also be most helpful to remain recollected in silence.[152]

In this regard, I would like to call attention to a pastoral problem frequently encountered nowadays. I am referring to the fact that on certain occasions—for example, wedding Masses, funerals, and the like—in addition to practicing Catholics there may be others present who have long since ceased to attend Mass or are living in a situation which does not permit them to receive the sacraments. At other times members of other Christian confessions and even other religions may be present. Similar situations can occur in churches that are frequently visited, especially in tourist areas. In these cases, there is a need to find a brief and clear way to remind those present of the meaning of sacramental communion and the conditions required for its reception. Wherever circumstances make it impossible to ensure that the meaning of the Eucharist is duly appreciated, the appropriateness of replacing the celebration of the Mass with a celebration of the word of God should be considered.[153]

The dismissal: "ite, missa est"

51.   Finally, I would like to comment briefly on the observations of the Synod Fathers regarding the dismissal at the end of the eucharistic celebration. After the blessing, the deacon or the priest dismisses the people with the words: *Ite, missa est*. These words help us to grasp the relationship between the Mass just celebrated and the mission of Christians in the world. In antiquity, *missa* simply meant "dismissal." However in Christian usage it gradually took on a deeper meaning. The word "dismissal" has come to imply a "mission." These few words succinctly express the missionary nature of the Church. The People of God might be helped to understand more clearly this essential dimension of the Church's life, taking the dismissal as a starting-point. In this context, it might also be helpful to provide new texts, duly approved, for the prayer over the people and the final blessing, in order to make this connection clear.[154]

---

151. Cf. Congregation for Divine Worship and the Discipline of the Sacraments, Instruction *Redemptionis sacramentum* (March 25, 2004), 80–96: AAS 96 (2004), 574–577.
152. Cf. *Propositio* 34.
153. Cf. *Propositio* 35.
154. Cf. *Propositio* 24.

ACTUOSA PARTICIPATIO

Authentic participation

52.   The Second Vatican Council rightly emphasized the active, full, and fruitful participation of the entire People of God in the eucharistic celebration.[155] Certainly, the renewal carried out in these past decades has made considerable progress towards fulfilling the wishes of the Council Fathers. Yet we must not overlook the fact that some misunderstanding has occasionally arisen concerning the precise meaning of this participation. It should be made clear that the word "participation" does not refer to mere external activity during the celebration. In fact, the active participation called for by the Council must be understood in more substantial terms, on the basis of a greater awareness of the mystery being celebrated and its relationship to daily life. The conciliar Constitution *Sacrosanctum Concilium* encouraged the faithful to take part in the eucharistic liturgy not "as strangers or silent spectators," but as participants "in the sacred action, conscious of what they are doing, actively and devoutly."[156] This exhortation has lost none of its force. The Council went on to say that the faithful "should be instructed by God's word, and nourished at the table of the Lord's Body. They should give thanks to God. Offering the immaculate Victim, not only through the hands of the priest but also together with him, they should learn to make an offering of themselves. Through Christ, the Mediator, they should be drawn day by day into ever more perfect union with God and each other."[157]

Participation and the priestly ministry

53.   The beauty and the harmony of the liturgy find eloquent expression in the order by which everyone is called to participate actively. This entails an acknowledgment of the distinct hierarchical roles involved in the celebration. It is helpful to recall that active participation is not per se equivalent to the exercise of a specific ministry. The active participation of the laity does not benefit from the confusion arising from an inability to distinguish, within the Church's communion, the different functions proper to each one.[158] There is a particular need for clarity with regard to the specific functions of the priest. He alone, and no other, as the tradition of the Church attests, presides over the entire eucharistic celebration, from the initial greeting to the final blessing. In virtue of his reception of Holy Orders, he represents Jesus Christ, the head of the Church, and, in a specific way, also the Church herself.[159] Every celebration of the Eucharist, in fact, is led by the Bishop, "either in person or through priests who are his

---

155. Cf. Second Vatican Ecumenical Council, Constitution on the Sacred Liturgy *Sacrosanctum Concilium*, 14–20; 30ff., 48ff.; Congregation for Divine Worship and the Discipline of the Sacraments, Instruction *Redemptionis sacramentum* (March 25, 2004), 36–42: AAS 96 (2004), 561–564.

156. No. 48.

157. Ibid.

158. Cf. Congregation for the Clergy, Instruction on Certain Questions Regarding the Collaboration of the Non-Ordained Faithful in the Ministry of Priests *Ecclesiae de mysterio* (August 15, 1997): AAS 89 (1997), 852–877.

159. Cf. *Propositio* 33.

helpers."[160] He is helped by a deacon, who has specific duties during the celebration: he prepares the altar, assists the priest, proclaims the Gospel, preaches the homily from time to time, reads the intentions of the Prayer of the Faithful, and distributes the Eucharist to the faithful.[161] Associated with these ministries linked to the sacrament of Holy Orders, there are also other ministries of liturgical service which can be carried out in a praiseworthy manner by religious and properly trained laity.[162]

The eucharistic celebration and inculturation

54.   On the basis of these fundamental statements of the Second Vatican Council, the Synod Fathers frequently stressed the importance of the active participation of the faithful in the eucharistic sacrifice. In order to foster this participation, provision may be made for a number of adaptations appropriate to different contexts and cultures.[163] The fact that certain abuses have occurred does not detract from this clear principle, which must be upheld in accordance with the real needs of the Church as she lives and celebrates the one mystery of Christ in a variety of cultural situations. In the mystery of the Incarnation, the Lord Jesus, born of woman and fully human (cf. Gal 4:4), entered directly into a relationship not only with the expectations present within the Old Testament, but also with those of all peoples. He thus showed that God wishes to encounter us in our own concrete situation. A more effective participation of the faithful in the holy mysteries will thus benefit from the continued inculturation of the eucharistic celebration, with due regard for the possibilities for adaptation provided in the *General Instruction of the Roman Missal*,[164] interpreted in the light of the criteria laid down by the Fourth Instruction of the Congregation for Divine Worship and the Discipline of the Sacraments *Varietates legitimae* of January 25, 1994[165] and the directives expressed by Pope John Paul II in the Post-Synodal Exhortations *Ecclesia in Africa, Ecclesia in America, Ecclesia in Asia, Ecclesia in Oceania* and *Ecclesia in Europa*.[166] To this end, I encourage Episcopal Conferences to

---

160. *General Instruction of the Roman Missal*, 92.

161. Cf. ibid., 94.

162. Cf. Second Vatican Ecumenical Council, Decree on the Apostolate of the Laity *Apostolicam actuositatem*, 24; *General Instruction of the Roman Missal*, 95–111; Congregation for Divine Worship and the Discipline of the Sacraments, Instruction *Redemptionis sacramentum* (March 25, 2004), 43–47: AAS 96 (2004), 564–566; *Propositio* 33: "These ministries must be introduced in accordance with a specific mandate and in accordance with the real needs of the celebrating community. Those entrusted with these liturgical services must be chosen with care, well prepared, and provided with ongoing formation. Their appointment must be for a limited term. They must be known to the community and be gratefully acknowledged by the community."

163. Cf. Second Vatican Ecumenical Council, Constitution on the Sacred Liturgy *Sacrosanctum Concilium*, 37–42.

164. Cf. *General Instruction of the Roman Missal*, 386–399.

165. Cf. Congregation for Divine Worship and the Discipline of the Sacraments, Instruction on the Roman Liturgy and Inculturation *Varietates legitimae* (January 25, 1994): AAS 87 (1995), 288–314.

166. Post-Synodal Apostolic Exhortation *Ecclesia in Africa* (September 14, 1995), 55–71: AAS 88 (1996), 34–47; Post-Synodal Apostolic Exhortation *Ecclesia in America* (January 22, 1999), 16, 40, 64, 70–72: AAS 91 (1999), 752–753, 775–776, 799, 805–809; Post-Synodal Apostolic Exhortation *Ecclesia in Asia* (November 6, 1999), 21ff.: AAS 92 (2000), 482–487; Post-Synodal

strive to maintain a proper balance between the criteria and directives already issued and new adaptations,[167] always in accord with the Apostolic See.

Personal conditions for an "active participation"

55.   In their consideration of the *actuosa participatio* of the faithful in the liturgy, the Synod Fathers also discussed the personal conditions required for fruitful participation on the part of individuals.[168] One of these is certainly the spirit of constant conversion which must mark the lives of all the faithful. Active participation in the eucharistic liturgy can hardly be expected if one approaches it superficially, without an examination of his or her life. This inner disposition can be fostered, for example, by recollection and silence for at least a few moments before the beginning of the liturgy, by fasting, and, when necessary, by sacramental confession. A heart reconciled to God makes genuine participation possible. The faithful need to be reminded that there can be no *actuosa participatio* in the sacred mysteries without an accompanying effort to participate actively in the life of the Church as a whole, including a missionary commitment to bring Christ's love into the life of society.

Clearly, full participation in the Eucharist takes place when the faithful approach the altar in person to receive communion.[169] Yet true as this is, care must be taken lest they conclude that the mere fact of their being present in church during the liturgy gives them a right or even an obligation to approach the table of the Eucharist. Even in cases where it is not possible to receive sacramental communion, participation at Mass remains necessary, important, meaningful, and fruitful. In such circumstances it is beneficial to cultivate a desire for full union with Christ through the practice of spiritual communion, praised by Pope John Paul II[170] and recommended by saints who were masters of the spiritual life.[171]

Participation by christians who are not catholic

56.   The subject of participation in the Eucharist inevitably raises the question of Christians belonging to Churches or Ecclesial Communities not in full communion with the Catholic Church. In this regard, it must be said that the intrinsic link between the Eucharist and the Church's unity inspires us to long for the day when we will be able to celebrate the Holy Eucharist together with all believers in Christ and in this way to express visibly the fullness of unity that Christ willed for his disciples (cf. Jn 17:21). On the other hand, the respect we owe to the sacrament of Christ's Body and Blood prevents us from making it a

---

Apostolic Exhortation *Ecclesia in Oceania* (November 22, 2001), 16: AAS 94 (2002), 382–384; Post-Synodal Apostolic Exhortation *Ecclesia in Europa* (June 28, 2003), 58–60: AAS 95 (2003), 685–686.

167. Cf. *Propositio* 26.

168. Cf. *Propositio* 35; Second Vatican Ecumenical Council, Constitution on the Sacred Liturgy *Sacrosanctum Concilium*, 11.

169. Cf. *Catechism of the Catholic Church*, 1388; Second Vatican Ecumenical Council, Constitution on the Sacred Liturgy *Sacrosanctum Concilium*, 55.

170. Cf. Encyclical Letter *Ecclesia de Eucharistia* (April 17, 2003), 34: AAS 95 (2003), 456.

171. See, for example, Saint Thomas Aquinas, *Summa Theologiae*, III, q. LXXX, a. 1, 2; Saint Teresa of Jesus, *The Way of Perfection*, Chapter 35. The doctrine was authoritatively confirmed by the Council of Trent, Session XIII, c. VIII.

mere "means" to be used indiscriminately in order to attain that unity.[172] The Eucharist in fact not only manifests our personal communion with Jesus Christ, but also implies full *communio* with the Church. This is the reason why, sadly albeit not without hope, we ask Christians who are not Catholic to understand and respect our conviction, which is grounded in the Bible and Tradition. We hold that eucharistic communion and ecclesial communion are so linked as to make it generally impossible for non-Catholic Christians to receive the former without enjoying the latter. There would be even less sense in actually concelebrating with ministers of Churches or ecclesial communities not in full communion with the Catholic Church. Yet it remains true that, for the sake of their eternal salvation, individual non-Catholic Christians can be admitted to the Eucharist, the sacrament of Reconciliation, and the Anointing of the Sick. But this is possible only in specific, exceptional situations and requires that certain precisely defined conditions be met.[173] These are clearly indicated in the *Catechism of the Catholic Church*[174] and in its *Compendium*.[175] Everyone is obliged to observe these norms faithfully.

Participation through the communications media

57.   Thanks to the remarkable development of the communications media, the word "participation" has taken on a broader meaning in recent decades. We all gladly acknowledge that the media have also opened up new possibilities for the celebration of the Eucharist.[176] This requires a specific preparation and a keen sense of responsibility on the part of pastoral workers in the sector. When Mass is broadcast on television, it inevitably tends to set an example. Particular care should therefore be taken to ensure that, in addition to taking place in suitable and well-appointed locations, the celebration respects the liturgical norms in force.

Finally, with regard to the value of taking part in Mass via the communications media, those who hear or view these broadcasts should be aware that, under normal circumstances, they do not fulfill the obligation of attending Mass. Visual images can represent reality, but they do not actually reproduce it.[177] While it is most praiseworthy that the elderly and the sick participate in Sunday Mass through radio and television, the same cannot be said of those who think that such broadcasts dispense them from going to church and sharing in the eucharistic assembly in the living Church.

---

172. Cf. John Paul II, Encyclical Letter *ut unum sint* (May 25, 1995), 8: AAS 87 (1995), 925–926.

173. Cf. *Propositio* 41; Second Vatican Ecumenical Council, Decree on Ecumenism *Unitatis redintegratio*, 8, 15; John Paul II, Encyclical Letter *ut unum sint* (May 25, 1995), 46: AAS 87 (1995), 948; Encyclical Letter *Ecclesia de Eucharistia* (April 17, 2003), 45–46: AAS 95 (2003), 463–464; *Code of Canon Law*, can. 844 §§ 3–4; *Code of Canons of the Eastern Churches*, can. 671 §§ 3–4; Pontifical Council for Promoting Christian Unity, *Directoire pour l'application des principes et des normes sur l'œcuménisme* (March 25, 1993), 125, 129–131: AAS 85 (1993), 1087, 1088–1089.

174. Cf. nos. 1398–1401.

175. Cf. no. 293.

176. Cf. Pontifical Council for Social Communications, Pastoral Instruction on Social Communications on the Twentieth Anniversary of "Communio et Progressio" *Aetatis novae* (February 22, 1992): AAS 84 (1992), 447–468.

177. Cf. *Propositio* 29.

Active participation by the sick

58. In thinking of those who cannot attend places of worship for reasons of health or advanced age, I wish to call the attention of the whole Church community to the pastoral importance of providing spiritual assistance to the sick, both those living at home and those in hospital. Their situation was often mentioned during the Synod of Bishops. These brothers and sisters of ours should have the opportunity to receive sacramental communion frequently. In this way they can strengthen their relationship with Christ, crucified and risen, and feel fully involved in the Church's life and mission by the offering of their sufferings in union with our Lord's sacrifice. Particular attention needs to be given to the disabled. When their condition so permits, the Christian community should make it possible for them to attend the place of worship. Buildings should be designed to provide ready access to the disabled. Finally, whenever possible, eucharistic communion should be made available to the mentally handicapped if they are baptized and confirmed: they receive the Eucharist in the faith also of the family or the community that accompanies them.[178]

Care for prisoners

59. The Church's spiritual tradition, basing itself on Christ's own words (cf. Mt 25:36), has designated the visiting of prisoners as one of the corporal works of mercy. Prisoners have a particular need to be visited personally by the Lord in the sacrament of the Eucharist. Experiencing the closeness of the ecclesial community, sharing in the Eucharist and receiving holy communion at this difficult and painful time can surely contribute to the quality of a prisoner's faith journey and to full social rehabilitation. Taking up the recommendation of the Synod, I ask Dioceses to do whatever is possible to ensure that sufficient pastoral resources are invested in the spiritual care of prisoners.[179]

Migrants and participation in the eucharist

60. Turning now to those people who for various reasons are forced to leave their native countries, the Synod expressed particular gratitude to all those engaged in the pastoral care of migrants. Specific attention needs to be paid to migrants belonging to the Eastern Catholic Churches; in addition to being far from home, they also encounter the difficulty of not being able to participate in the eucharistic liturgy in their own rite. For this reason, wherever possible, they should be served by priests of their rite. In all cases I would ask Bishops to welcome these brothers and sisters with the love of Christ. Contacts between the faithful of different rites can prove a source of mutual enrichment. In particular, I am thinking of the benefit that can come, especially for the clergy, from a knowledge of the different traditions.[180]

---

178. Cf. *Propositio* 44.
179. Cf. *Propositio* 48.
180. Candidates for the priesthood can be introduced to these traditions as part of their seminary training: cf. *Propositio* 45.

Large-scale concelebrations

61.   The Synod considered the quality of participation in the case of large-scale celebrations held on special occasions and involving not only a great number of the lay faithful, but also many concelebrating priests.[181] On the one hand, it is easy to appreciate the importance of these moments, especially when the Bishop himself celebrates, surrounded by his presbyterate and by the deacons. On the other hand, it is not always easy in such cases to give clear expression to the unity of the presbyterate, especially during the Eucharistic Prayer and the distribution of Holy Communion. Efforts need to be made lest these large-scale concelebrations lose their proper focus. This can be done by proper coordination and by arranging the place of worship so that priests and lay faithful are truly able to participate fully. It should be kept in mind, however, that here we are speaking of exceptional concelebrations, limited to extraordinary situations.

The latin language

62.   None of the above observations should cast doubt upon the importance of such large-scale liturgies. I am thinking here particularly of celebrations at international gatherings, which nowadays are held with greater frequency. The most should be made of these occasions. In order to express more clearly the unity and universality of the Church, I wish to endorse the proposal made by the Synod of Bishops, in harmony with the directives of the Second Vatican Council,[182] that, with the exception of the readings, the homily, and the prayer of the faithful, it is fitting that such liturgies be celebrated in Latin. Similarly, the better-known prayers[183] of the Church's tradition should be recited in Latin and, if possible, selections of Gregorian chant should be sung. Speaking more generally, I ask that future priests, from their time in the seminary, receive the preparation needed to understand and to celebrate Mass in Latin and also to use Latin texts and execute Gregorian chant; nor should we forget that the faithful can be taught to recite the more common prayers in Latin and also to sing parts of the liturgy to Gregorian chant.[184]

Eucharistic celebrations in small groups

63.   A very different situation arises when, in the interest of more conscious, active, and fruitful participation, pastoral circumstances favor small group celebrations. While acknowledging the formative value of this approach, it must be stated that such celebrations should always be consonant with the overall pastoral activity of the Diocese. These celebrations would actually lose their catechetical value if they were felt to be in competition with, or parallel to, the life of the particular Church. In this regard, the Synod set forth some necessary criteria: small groups must serve to unify the community, not to fragment it; the beneficial results ought to be clearly evident; these groups should encourage

---

181. Cf. *Propositio* 37.
182. Cf. Constitution on the Sacred Liturgy *Sacrosanctum Concilium*, 36, 54.
183. *Propositio* 36.
184. Cf. ibid.

the fruitful participation of the entire assembly and preserve as much as possible the unity of the liturgical life of individual families.[185]

INTERIOR PARTICIPATION IN THE CELEBRATION

Mystagogical catechesis

64.   The Church's great liturgical tradition teaches us that fruitful participation in the liturgy requires that one be personally conformed to the mystery being celebrated, offering one's life to God in unity with the sacrifice of Christ for the salvation of the whole world. For this reason, the Synod of Bishops asked that the faithful be helped to make their interior dispositions correspond to their gestures and words. Otherwise, however carefully planned and executed our liturgies may be, they would risk falling into a certain ritualism. Hence the need to provide an education in eucharistic faith capable of enabling the faithful to live personally what they celebrate. Given the vital importance of this personal and conscious *participatio*, what methods of formation are needed? The Synod Fathers unanimously indicated, in this regard, a mystagogical approach to catechesis, which would lead the faithful to understand more deeply the mysteries being celebrated.[186] In particular, given the close relationship between the *ars celebrandi* and an *actuosa participatio*, it must first be said that "the best catechesis on the Eucharist is the Eucharist itself, celebrated well.[187] By its nature, the liturgy can be pedagogically effective in helping the faithful to enter more deeply into the mystery being celebrated. That is why, in the Church's most ancient tradition, the process of Christian formation always had an experiential character. While not neglecting a systematic understanding of the content of the faith, it centered on a vital and convincing encounter with Christ, as proclaimed by authentic witnesses. It is first and foremost the witness who introduces others to the mysteries. Naturally, this initial encounter gains depth through catechesis and finds its source and summit in the celebration of the Eucharist. This basic structure of the Christian experience calls for a process of mystagogy which should always respect three elements:

> *a) It interprets the rites in the light of the events of our salvation*, in accordance with the Church's living tradition. The celebration of the Eucharist, in its infinite richness, makes constant reference to salvation history. In Christ crucified and risen, we truly celebrate the one who has united all things in himself (cf. Eph 1:10). From the beginning, the Christian community has interpreted the events of Jesus' life, and the Paschal Mystery in particular, in relation to the entire history of the Old Testament.

> *b)* A mystagogical catechesis must also be concerned with *presenting the meaning of the signs* contained in the rites. This is particularly important in a highly technological age like our own, which risks losing the ability to appreciate signs and symbols. More than simply conveying

---

185. Cf. *Propositio* 32.
186. Cf. *Propositio* 14.
187. *Propositio* 19.

information, a mystagogical catechesis should be capable of making the faithful more sensitive to the language of signs and gestures which, together with the word, make up the rite.

c) Finally, a mystagogical catechesis must be concerned with bringing out the *significance of the rites for the Christian life* in all its dimensions—work and responsibility, thoughts and emotions, activity and repose. Part of the mystagogical process is to demonstrate how the mysteries celebrated in the rite are linked to the missionary responsibility of the faithful. The mature fruit of mystagogy is an awareness that one's life is being progressively transformed by the holy mysteries being celebrated. The aim of all Christian education, moreover, is to train the believer in an adult faith that can make him a "new creation," capable of bearing witness in his surroundings to the Christian hope that inspires him.

If we are to succeed in carrying out this work of education in our ecclesial communities, those responsible for formation must be adequately prepared. Indeed, the whole people of God should feel involved in this formation. Each Christian community is called to be a place where people can be taught about the mysteries celebrated in faith. In this regard, the Synod Fathers called for greater involvement by communities of consecrated life, movements, and groups which, by their specific charisms, can give new impetus to Christian formation.[188] In our time, too, the Holy Spirit freely bestows his gifts to sustain the apostolic mission of the Church, which is charged with spreading the faith and bringing it to maturity.[189]

REVERENCE FOR THE EUCHARIST

65.   A convincing indication of the effectiveness of eucharistic catechesis is surely an increased sense of the mystery of God present among us. This can be expressed in concrete outward signs of reverence for the Eucharist which the process of mystagogy should inculcate in the faithful.[190] I am thinking in general of the importance of gestures and posture, such as kneeling during the central moments of the Eucharistic Prayer. Amid the legitimate diversity of signs used in the context of different cultures, everyone should be able to experience and express the awareness that at each celebration we stand before the infinite majesty of God, who comes to us in the lowliness of the sacramental signs.

ADORATION AND EUCHARISTIC DEVOTION

The intrinsic relationship between celebrbation and adoration

66.   One of the most moving moments of the Synod came when we gathered in Saint Peter's Basilica, together with a great number of the faithful, for eucharistic adoration. In this act of prayer, and not just in words, the assembly of Bishops wanted to point out the intrinsic relationship between eucharistic celebration and eucharistic adoration. A growing appreciation of this significant

---

188. Cf. *Propositio* 14.
189. Cf. Benedict XVI, Homily at First Vespers of Pentecost (June 3, 2006): AAS 98 (2006), 509.
190. Cf. *Propositio* 34.

aspect of the Church's faith has been an important part of our experience in the years following the liturgical renewal desired by the Second Vatican Council. During the early phases of the reform, the inherent relationship between Mass and adoration of the Blessed Sacrament was not always perceived with sufficient clarity. For example, an objection that was widespread at the time argued that the eucharistic bread was given to us not to be looked at, but to be eaten. In the light of the Church's experience of prayer, however, this was seen to be a false dichotomy. As Saint Augustine put it: "*nemo autem illam carnem manducat, nisi prius adoraverit; peccemus non adorando*—no one eats that flesh without first adoring it; we should sin were we not to adore it."[191] In the Eucharist, the Son of God comes to meet us and desires to become one with us; eucharistic adoration is simply the natural consequence of the eucharistic celebration, which is itself the Church's supreme act of adoration.[192] Receiving the Eucharist means adoring him whom we receive. Only in this way do we become one with him and are given, as it were, a foretaste of the beauty of the heavenly liturgy. The act of adoration outside Mass prolongs and intensifies all that takes place during the liturgical celebration itself. Indeed, "only in adoration can a profound and genuine reception mature. And it is precisely this personal encounter with the Lord that then strengthens the social mission contained in the Eucharist, which seeks to break down not only the walls that separate the Lord and ourselves, but also and especially the walls that separate us from one another."[193]

The practice of eucharistic adoration

67.   With the Synod Assembly, therefore, I heartily recommend to the Church's pastors and to the People of God the practice of eucharistic adoration, both individually and in community.[194] Great benefit would ensue from a suitable catechesis explaining the importance of this act of worship, which enables the faithful to experience the liturgical celebration more fully and more fruitfully. Wherever possible, it would be appropriate, especially in densely populated areas, to set aside specific churches or oratories for perpetual adoration. I also recommend that, in their catechetical training, and especially in their preparation for First Holy Communion, children be taught the meaning and the beauty of spending time with Jesus and helped to cultivate a sense of awe before his presence in the Eucharist.

Here I would like to express appreciation and support for all those Institutes of Consecrated Life whose members dedicate a significant amount of time to eucharistic adoration. In this way they give us an example of lives shaped by the Lord's real presence. I would also like to encourage those associations of the faithful and confraternities specifically devoted to eucharistic adoration; they serve as

---

191. *Enarrationes in Psalmos* 98:9, CCL XXXIX, 1385; cf. Benedict XVI, Address to the Roman Curia (December 22, 2005): AAS 98 (2006), 44–45.

192. Cf. *Propositio* 6.

193. Benedict XVI, Address to the Roman Curia (December 22, 2005): AAS 98 (2006), 45.

194. Cf. *Propositio* 6; Congregation for Divine Worship and the Discipline of the Sacraments, *Directory on Popular Piety and the Liturgy* (December 17, 2001), Nos. 164–165, Vatican City, 2002; Sacred Congregation of Rites, Instruction *Eucharisticum mysterium* (May 25, 1967): AAS 59 (1967), 539–573.

a leaven of contemplation for the whole Church and a summons to individuals and communities to place Christ at the center of their lives.

Forms of eucharistic devotion

68.   The personal relationship which the individual believer establishes with Jesus present in the Eucharist constantly points beyond itself to the whole communion of the Church and nourishes a fuller sense of membership in the Body of Christ. For this reason, besides encouraging individual believers to make time for personal prayer before the Sacrament of the Altar, I feel obliged to urge parishes and other church groups to set aside times for collective adoration. Naturally, already existing forms of eucharistic piety retain their full value. I am thinking, for example, of processions with the Blessed Sacrament, especially the traditional procession on the Solemnity of *Corpus Christi*; the Forty Hours devotion; local, national, and international Eucharistic Congresses; and other similar initiatives. If suitably updated and adapted to local circumstances, these forms of devotion are still worthy of being practiced today.[195]

The location of the tabernacle

69.   In considering the importance of eucharistic reservation and adoration, and reverence for the sacrament of Christ's sacrifice, the Synod of Bishops also discussed the question of the proper placement of the tabernacle in our churches.[196] The correct positioning of the tabernacle contributes to the recognition of Christ's real presence in the Blessed Sacrament. Therefore, the place where the eucharistic species are reserved, marked by a sanctuary lamp, should be readily visible to everyone entering the church. It is therefore necessary to take into account the building's architecture: in churches which do not have a Blessed Sacrament chapel, and where the high altar with its tabernacle is still in place, it is appropriate to continue to use this structure for the reservation and adoration of the Eucharist, taking care not to place the celebrant's chair in front of it. In new churches, it is good to position the Blessed Sacrament chapel close to the sanctuary; where this is not possible, it is preferable to locate the tabernacle in the sanctuary, in a sufficiently elevated place, at the center of the apse area, or in another place where it will be equally conspicuous. Attention to these considerations will lend dignity to the tabernacle, which must always be cared for, also from an artistic standpoint. Obviously it is necessary to follow the provisions of the Gen*eral Instruction of the Roman Missal* in this regard.[197] In any event, final judgment on these matters belongs to the Diocesan Bishop.

---

195. Cf. *Relatio post disceptationem*, 11: *L'Osservatore Romano*, October 14, 2005, p. 5.
196. Cf. *Propositio* 28.
197. Cf. no. 314.

PART THREE
THE EUCHARIST, A MYSTERY TO BE LIVED

*"As the living Father sent me, and I live because of the Father,
so he who eats me will live because of me." (Jn 6:57)*

THE EUCHARISTIC FORM OF THE CHRISTIAN LIFE

Spiritual worship—logiké latreía (Rom 12:1)

70.   The Lord Jesus, who became for us the food of truth and love, speaks of the gift of his life and assures us that "if any one eats of this bread, he will live for ever" (Jn 6:51). This "eternal life" begins in us even now, thanks to the transformation effected in us by the gift of the Eucharist: "He who eats me will live because of me" (Jn 6:57). These words of Jesus make us realize how the mystery "believed" and "celebrated" contains an innate power making it the principle of new life within us and the form of our Christian existence. By receiving the body and blood of Jesus Christ we become sharers in the divine life in an ever more adult and conscious way. Here too, we can apply Saint Augustine's words, in his *Confessions*, about the eternal *Logos* as the food of our souls. Stressing the mysterious nature of this food, Augustine imagines the Lord saying to him: "I am the food of grown men; grow, and you shall feed upon me; nor shall you change me, like the food of your flesh, into yourself, but you shall be changed into me."[198] It is not the eucharistic food that is changed into us, but rather we who are mysteriously transformed by it. Christ nourishes us by uniting us to himself; "he draws us into himself."[199]

Here the eucharistic celebration appears in all its power as the source and summit of the Church's life, since it expresses at once both the origin and the fulfillment of the new and definitive worship of God, the *logiké latreía*.[200] Saint Paul's exhortation to the Romans in this regard is a concise description of how the Eucharist makes our whole life a spiritual worship pleasing to God: "I appeal to you therefore, my brothers, by the mercies of God, to present your bodies as a living sacrifice, holy and acceptable to God, which is your spiritual worship" (Rom 12:1). In these words the new worship appears as a total self-offering made in communion with the whole Church. The Apostle's insistence on the offering of our bodies emphasizes the concrete human reality of a worship which is anything but disincarnate. The Bishop of Hippo goes on to say that "this is the sacrifice of Christians: that we, though many, are one body in Christ. The Church celebrates this mystery in the sacrament of the altar, as the faithful know, and there she shows them clearly that in what is offered, she herself is offered."[201] Catholic doctrine, in fact, affirms that the Eucharist, as the sacrifice of Christ,

---

198. VII, 10, 16: PL 32, 742.
199. Benedict XVI, Homily at Marienfeld Esplanade (August 21, 2005): AAS 97 (2005), 892; cf. Homily for the Vigil of Pentecost (June 3, 2006): AAS 98 (2006), 505.
200. Cf. *Relatio post disceptationem*, 6, 47: *L'Osservatore Romano*, October 14, 2005, pp. 5–6; *Propositio* 43.
201. *De civitate Dei*, X, 6: PL 41, 284.

is also the sacrifice of the Church, and thus of all the faithful.[202] This insistence on sacrifice—a "making sacred"—expresses all the existential depth implied in the transformation of our human reality as taken up by Christ (cf. Phil 3:12).

The all-encompassing effect of eucharistic worship

71.   Christianity's new worship includes and transfigures every aspect of life: "Whether you eat or drink, or whatever you do, do all to the glory of God" (1 Cor 10:31). Christians, in all their actions, are called to offer true worship to God. Here the intrinsically eucharistic nature of Christian life begins to take shape. The Eucharist, since it embraces the concrete, everyday existence of the believer, makes possible, day by day, the progressive transfiguration of all those called by grace to reflect the image of the Son of God (cf. Rom 8:29ff.). There is nothing authentically human—our thoughts and affections, our words and deeds—that does not find in the sacrament of the Eucharist the form it needs to be lived to the full. Here we can see the full human import of the radical newness brought by Christ in the Eucharist: the worship of God in our lives cannot be relegated to something private and individual, but tends by its nature to permeate every aspect of our existence. Worship pleasing to God thus becomes a new way of living our whole life, each particular moment of which is lifted up, since it is lived as part of a relationship with Christ and as an offering to God. The glory of God is the living man (cf. 1 Cor 10:31). And the life of man is the vision of God.[203]

Iuxta dominicam viventes—living in accordance with the Lord's Day

72.   From the beginning Christians were clearly conscious of this radical newness which the Eucharist brings to human life. The faithful immediately perceived the profound influence of the eucharistic celebration on their manner of life. Saint Ignatius of Antioch expressed this truth when he called Christians "those who have attained a new hope," and described them as "those living in accordance with the Lord's Day" (*iuxta dominicam viventes*).[204] This phrase of the great Antiochene martyr highlights the connection between the reality of the Eucharist and everyday Christian life. The Christians' customary practice of gathering on the first day after the Sabbath to celebrate the resurrection of Christ—according to the account of Saint Justin Martyr[205]—is also what defines the form of a life renewed by an encounter with Christ. Saint Ignatius' phrase—"living in accordance with the Lord's Day"—also emphasizes that this holy day becomes paradigmatic for every other day of the week. Indeed, it is defined by something more than the simple suspension of one's ordinary activities, a sort of parenthesis in one's usual daily rhythm. Christians have always experienced this day as the first day of the week, since it commemorates the radical newness brought by Christ. Sunday is thus the day when Christians rediscover the eucharistic form which their lives are meant to have. "Living in accordance with the Lord's Day" means living in the awareness of the libera-

---

202. Cf. *Catechism of the Catholic Church*, 1368.
203. Cf. Saint Irenaeus, *Adv. haer.*, IV, 20, 7: PG 7, 1037.
204. *Ad Magnes.*, 9, 1: PG 5, 670.
205. Cf. *I Apologia*, 67, 1–6; 66: PG 6, 430ff., 427, 430.

tion brought by Christ and making our lives a constant self-offering to God, so that his victory may be fully revealed to all humanity through a profoundly renewed existence.

Living the Sunday obligation

73. Conscious of this new vital principle which the Eucharist imparts to the Christian, the Synod Fathers reaffirmed the importance of the Sunday obligation for all the faithful, viewing it as a wellspring of authentic freedom enabling them to live each day in accordance with what they celebrated on "the Lord's Day." The life of faith is endangered when we lose the desire to share in the celebration of the Eucharist and its commemoration of the paschal victory. Participating in the Sunday liturgical assembly with all our brothers and sisters, with whom we form one body in Jesus Christ, is demanded by our Christian conscience and at the same time it forms that conscience. To lose a sense of Sunday as the Lord's Day, a day to be sanctified, is symptomatic of the loss of an authentic sense of Christian freedom, the freedom of the children of God.[206] Here some observations made by my venerable predecessor John Paul II in his Apostolic Letter *Dies Domini*[207] continue to have great value. Speaking of the various dimensions of the Christian celebration of Sunday, he said that it is *Dies Domini* with regard to the work of creation, *Dies Christi* as the day of the new creation and the Risen Lord's gift of the Holy Spirit, *Dies Ecclesiae* as the day on which the Christian community gathers for the celebration, and *Dies hominis* as the day of joy, rest, and fraternal charity.

Sunday thus appears as the primordial holy day, when all believers, wherever they are found, can become heralds and guardians of the true meaning of time. It gives rise to the Christian meaning of life and a new way of experiencing time, relationships, work, life, and death. On the Lord's Day, then, it is fitting that Church groups should organize, around Sunday Mass, the activities of the Christian community: social gatherings; programs for the faith formation of children, young people, and adults; pilgrimages; charitable works; and different moments of prayer. For the sake of these important values—while recognizing that Saturday evening, beginning with First Vespers, is already a part of Sunday and a time when the Sunday obligation can be fulfilled—we need to remember that it is Sunday itself that is meant to be kept holy, lest it end up as a day "empty of God."[208]

The meaning of rest and of work

74. Finally, it is particularly urgent nowadays to remember that the day of the Lord is also a day of rest from work. It is greatly to be hoped that this fact will also be recognized by civil society, so that individuals can be permitted to refrain from work without being penalized. Christians, not without reference to the meaning of the Sabbath in the Jewish tradition, have seen in the Lord's Day a day of rest from their daily exertions. This is highly significant, for *it relativizes work* and directs it to the person: work is for man and not man for work. It is

---

206. Cf. *Propositio* 30.
207. Cf. AAS 90 (1998), 713–766.
208. *Propositio* 30.

easy to see how this actually protects men and women, emancipating them from a possible form of enslavement. As I have had occasion to say, "work is of fundamental importance to the fulfillment of the human being and to the development of society. Thus, it must always be organized and carried out with full respect for human dignity and must always serve the common good. At the same time, it is indispensable that people not allow themselves to be enslaved by work or to idolize it, claiming to find in it the ultimate and definitive meaning of life."[209] It is on the day consecrated to God that men and women come to understand the meaning of their lives and also of their work.[210]

Sunday assemblies in the absence of a priest

75.   Rediscovering the significance of the Sunday celebration for the life of Christians naturally leads to a consideration of the problem of those Christian communities which lack priests and where, consequently, it is not possible to celebrate Mass on the Lord's Day. Here it should be stated that a wide variety of situations exists. The Synod recommended first that the faithful should go to one of the churches in their Diocese where the presence of a priest is assured, even when this demands a certain sacrifice.[211] Wherever great distances make it practically impossible to take part in the Sunday Eucharist, it is still important for Christian communities to gather together to praise the Lord and to commemorate the Day set apart for him. This needs, however, to be accompanied by an adequate instruction about the difference between Mass and Sunday assemblies in the absence of a priest. The Church's pastoral care must be expressed in the latter case by ensuring that the liturgy of the word—led by a deacon or a community leader to whom this ministry has been duly entrusted by competent authority—is carried out according to a specific ritual prepared and approved for this purpose by the Bishops' Conferences.[212] I reiterate that only Ordinaries may grant the faculty of distributing holy communion in such liturgies, taking account of the need for a certain selectiveness. Furthermore, care should be taken that these assemblies do not create confusion about the central role of the priest and the sacraments in the life of the Church. The importance of the role given to the laity, who should rightly be thanked for their generosity in the service of their communities, must never obscure the indispensable ministry of priests for the life of the Church.[213] Hence care must be taken to ensure that such assemblies in the absence of a priest do not encourage ecclesiological visions incompatible with the truth of the Gospel and the Church's tradition. Rather, they should be privileged moments of prayer for God to send holy priests after

209. Homily (March 19, 2006): AAS 98 (2006), 324.
210. The *Compendium of the Social Doctrine of the Church*, 258, rightly notes in this regard: "For man, bound as he is to the necessity of work, this rest opens to the prospect of a fuller freedom, that of the eternal Sabbath (cf. Heb 4:9–10). Rest gives men and women the possibility to remember and experience anew God's work, from Creation to Redemption, to recognize themselves as his work (cf. Eph 2:10), and to give thanks for their lives and for their subsistence to him who is their author."
211. Cf. *Propositio* 10.
212. Cf. ibid.
213. Cf. Benedict XVI, Address to the Bishops of Canada-Quebec during their Visit ad Limina (May 11, 2006): cf. *L'Osservatore Romano*, May 12, 2006, p. 5.

his own heart. It is touching, in this regard, to read the words of Pope John Paul II in his *Letter to Priests* for Holy Thursday 1979 about those places where the faithful, deprived of a priest by a dictatorial regime, would meet in a church or shrine, place on the altar a stole which they still kept, and recite the prayers of the eucharistic liturgy, halting in silence "at the moment that corresponds to the transubstantiation" as a sign of how "ardently they desire to hear the words that only the lips of a priest can efficaciously utter."[214] With this in mind, and considering the incomparable good which comes from the celebration of the Eucharist, I ask all priests to visit willingly and as often as possible the communities entrusted to their pastoral care, lest they remain too long without the sacrament of love.

A eucharistic form of Christian life, membership in the Church

76.   The importance of Sunday as the *Dies Ecclesiae* brings us back to the intrinsic relationship between Jesus' victory over evil and death and our membership in his ecclesial body. On the Lord's Day, each Christian rediscovers the communal dimension of his life as one who has been redeemed. Taking part in the liturgy and receiving the Body and Blood of Christ intensifies and deepens our belonging to the one who died for us (cf. 1 Cor 6:19ff.; 7:23). Truly, whoever eats of Christ lives for him. The eucharistic mystery helps us to understand the profound meaning of the *communio sanctorum*. Communion always and inseparably has both a vertical and a horizontal sense: it is communion with God and communion with our brothers and sisters. Both dimensions mysteriously converge in the gift of the Eucharist. "Wherever communion with God, which is communion with the Father, with the Son, and with the Holy Spirit, is destroyed, the root and source of our communion with one another is destroyed. And wherever we do not live communion among ourselves, communion with the Triune God is not alive and true either."[215] Called to be members of Christ and thus members of one another (cf. 1 Cor 12:27), we are a reality grounded ontologically in Baptism and nourished by the Eucharist, a reality that demands visible expression in the life of our communities.

The eucharistic form of Christian life is clearly an ecclesial and communitarian form. Through the Diocese and the parish, the fundamental structures of the Church in a particular territory, each individual believer can experience concretely what it means to be a member of Christ's Body. Associations, ecclesial movements and new communities—with their lively charisms bestowed by the Holy Spirit for the needs of our time—together with Institutes of Consecrated Life, have a particular responsibility for helping to make the faithful conscious that they *belong* to the Lord (cf. Rom 14:8). Secularization, with its inherent emphasis on individualism, has its most negative effects on individuals who are isolated and lack a sense of belonging. Christianity, from its very beginning, has meant fellowship, a network of relationships constantly strengthened by hearing God's word and sharing in the Eucharist and enlivened by the Holy Spirit.

214. No. 10: AAS 71 (1979), 414–415.
215. Benedict XVI, General Audience of March 29, 2006: *L'Osservatore Romano*, March 30, 2006, p. 4.

Spirituality and eucharistic culture

77.   Significantly, the Synod Fathers stated that "the Christian faithful need a fuller understanding of the relationship between the Eucharist and their daily lives. Eucharistic spirituality is not just participation in Mass and devotion to the Blessed Sacrament. It embraces the whole of life."[216] This observation is particularly insightful, given our situation today. It must be acknowledged that one of the most serious effects of the secularization just mentioned is that it has relegated the Christian faith to the margins of life as if it were irrelevant to everyday affairs. The futility of this way of living—"as if God did not exist"—is now evident to everyone. Today there is a need to rediscover that Jesus Christ is not just a private conviction or an abstract idea, but a real person, whose becoming part of human history is capable of renewing the life of every man and woman. Hence the Eucharist, as the source and summit of the Church's life and mission, must be translated into spirituality, into a life lived "according to the Spirit" (Rom 8:4ff.; cf. Gal 5:16, 25). It is significant that Saint Paul, in the passage of the *Letter to the Romans* where he invites his hearers to offer the new spiritual worship, also speaks of the need for a change in their way of living and thinking: "Do not be conformed to this world but be transformed by the renewal of your mind, that you may prove what is the will of God, what is good and acceptable and perfect" (12:2). In this way the Apostle of the Gentiles emphasizes the link between true spiritual worship and the need for a new way of understanding and living one's life. An integral part of the eucharistic form of the Christian life is a new way of thinking, "so that we may no longer be children tossed to and fro and carried about with every wind of doctrine" (Eph 4:14).

The Eucharist and the evangelization of cultures

78.   From what has been said thus far, it is clear that the eucharistic mystery puts us *in dialogue* with various cultures, but also in some way *challenges* them.[217] The intercultural character of this new worship, this *logiké latreía*, needs to be recognized. The presence of Jesus Christ and the outpouring of the Holy Spirit are events capable of engaging every cultural reality and bringing to it the leaven of the Gospel. It follows that we must be committed to promoting the evangelization of cultures, conscious that Christ himself is the truth for every man and woman and for all human history. The Eucharist becomes a criterion for our evaluation of everything that Christianity encounters in different cultures. In this important process of discernment, we can appreciate the full meaning of Saint Paul's exhortation, in his *First Letter to the Thessalonians*, to "test everything; and hold fast to what is good" (5:21).

The Eucharist and the lay faithful

79.   In Christ, Head of his Body, the Church, all Christians are "a chosen race, a royal priesthood, a holy nation, a people he claims for his own, to declare his wonderful deeds" (1 Pet 2:9). The Eucharist, as a mystery to be "lived," meets each of us as we are and makes our concrete existence the place where we experience daily the radical newness of the Christian life. The eucharistic sacrifice

---

216. *Propositio* 39.
217. Cf. *Relatio post disceptationem*, 30: *L'Osservatore Romano*, October 14, 2005, p. 6.

nourishes and increases within us all that we have already received at Baptism, with its call to holiness,[218] and this must be clearly evident from the way individual Christians live their lives. Day by day we become "a worship pleasing to God" by living our lives as a vocation. Beginning with the liturgical assembly, the sacrament of the Eucharist itself commits us, in our daily lives, to doing everything for God's glory.

And because the world is "the field" (Mt 13:38) in which God plants his children as good seed, the Christian laity, by virtue of their Baptism and Confirmation, and strengthened by the Eucharist, are called to live out the radical newness brought by Christ wherever they find themselves.[219] They should cultivate a desire that the Eucharist have an ever deeper effect on their daily lives, making them convincing witnesses in the workplace and in society at large.[220] I encourage families in particular to draw inspiration and strength from this sacrament. The love between man and woman, openness to life, and the raising of children are privileged spheres in which the Eucharist can reveal its power to transform life and give it its full meaning.[221] The Church's pastors should unfailingly support, guide, and encourage the lay faithful to live fully their vocation to holiness within this world which God so loved that he gave his Son to become its salvation (cf. Jn 3:16).

The Eucharist and priestly spirituality

80.   The eucharistic form of the Christian life is seen in a very special way in the priesthood. Priestly spirituality is intrinsically eucharistic. The seeds of this spirituality are already found in the words spoken by the Bishop during the ordination liturgy: "Receive the oblation of the holy people to be offered to God. Understand what you do, imitate what you celebrate, and conform your life to the mystery of the Lord's Cross."[222] In order to give an ever greater eucharistic form to his existence, the priest, beginning with his years in the seminary, should make his spiritual life his highest priority.[223] He is called to seek God tirelessly while remaining attuned to the concerns of his brothers and sisters. An intense spiritual life will enable him to enter more deeply into communion with the Lord and to let himself be possessed by God's love, bearing witness to that love at all times, even the darkest and most difficult. To this end I join the Synod Fathers in recommending "the daily celebration of Mass, even when the faithful are not present."[224] This recommendation is consistent with the objectively infinite value of every celebration of the Eucharist and is motivated by the Mass's unique spiritual fruitfulness. If celebrated in a faith-filled and

---

218. Cf. Second Vatican Ecumenical Council, Dogmatic Constitution on the Church *Lumen gentium*, 39–42.

219. Cf. John Paul II, Post-Synodal Apostolic Exhortation *Christifideles laici* (December 30, 1988), 14, 16: AAS 81 (1989), 409–413; 416–418.

220. Cf. *Propositio* 39.

221. Cf. ibid.

222. *The Roman Pontifical, Rites of Ordination of a Bishop, of Priests and of Deacons*, Ordination of a Priest, no. 135.

223. Cf. John Paul II, Post-Synodal Apostolic Exhortation *Pastores dabo vobis* (March 25, 1992), 19–33; 70–81: AAS 84 (1992), 686–712; 778–800.

224. *Propositio* 38.

attentive way, Mass is formative in the deepest sense of the word, since it fosters the priest's configuration to Christ and strengthens him in his vocation.

The Eucharist and the consecrated life

81.   The relationship of the Eucharist to the various ecclesial vocations is seen in a particularly vivid way in "the prophetic witness of consecrated men and women, who find in the celebration of the Eucharist and in eucharistic adoration the strength necessary for the radical following of Christ, obedient, poor, and chaste."[225] Though they provide many services in the area of human formation and care for the poor, education, and health care, consecrated men and women know that the principal purpose of their lives is "the contemplation of things divine and constant union with God in prayer."[226] The essential contribution that the Church expects from consecrated persons is much more in the order of being than of doing. Here I wish to reaffirm the importance of the witness of virginity, precisely in relation to the mystery of the Eucharist. In addition to its connection to priestly celibacy, the eucharistic mystery also has an intrinsic relationship to consecrated virginity, inasmuch as the latter is an expression of the Church's exclusive devotion to Christ, whom she accepts as her Bridegroom with a radical and fruitful fidelity.[227] In the Eucharist, consecrated virginity finds inspiration and nourishment for its complete dedication to Christ. From the Eucharist, moreover, it draws encouragement and strength to be a sign, in our own times too, of God's gracious and fruitful love for humanity. Finally, by its specific witness, consecrated life becomes an objective sign and foreshadowing of the "wedding-feast of the Lamb" (Rev 19:7–9) which is the goal of all salvation history. In this sense, it points to that eschatological horizon against which the choices and life decisions of every man and woman should be situated.

The Eucharist and moral transformation

82.   In discovering the beauty of the eucharistic form of the Christian life, we are also led to reflect on the moral energy it provides for sustaining the authentic freedom of the children of God. Here I wish to take up a discussion that took place during the Synod about the connection between the *eucharistic form of life* and *moral transformation*. Pope John Paul II stated that the moral life "has the value of a 'spiritual worship' (Rom 12:1; cf. Phil 3:3), flowing from and nourished by that inexhaustible source of holiness and glorification of God which is found in the sacraments, especially in the Eucharist: by sharing in the sacrifice of the Cross, the Christian partakes of Christ's self-giving love and is equipped and committed to live this same charity in all his thoughts and deeds."[228] In a word, "'worship' itself, eucharistic communion, includes the reality both of

225. *Propositio* 39. Cf. John Paul II, Post-Synodal Apostolic Exhortation *Vita consecrata* (March 25, 1996), 95: AAS 88 (1996), 470–471.
226. Code of Canon Law, can. 663 § 1.
227. Cf. John Paul II, Post-Synodal Apostolic Exhortation *Vita consecrata* (March 25, 1996), 34: AAS 88 (1996), 407–408.
228. Encyclical Letter *Veritatis splendor* (August 6, 1993), 107: AAS 85 (1993), 1216–1217.

being loved and of loving others in turn. A Eucharist which does not pass over into the concrete practice of love is intrinsically fragmented."[229]

This appeal to the moral value of spiritual worship should not be interpreted in a merely moralistic way. It is before all else the joy-filled discovery of love at work in the hearts of those who accept the Lord's gift, abandon themselves to him, and thus find true freedom. The moral transformation implicit in the new worship instituted by Christ is a heartfelt yearning to respond to the Lord's love with one's whole being, while remaining ever conscious of one's own weakness. This is clearly reflected in the Gospel story of Zacchaeus (cf. Lk 19:1–10). After welcoming Jesus to his home, the tax collector is completely changed: he decides to give half of his possessions to the poor and to repay fourfold those whom he had defrauded. The moral urgency born of welcoming Jesus into our lives is the fruit of gratitude for having experienced the Lord's unmerited closeness.

Eucharistic consistency

83.   Here it is important to consider what the Synod Fathers described as *eucharistic consistency*, a quality which our lives are objectively called to embody. Worship pleasing to God can never be a purely private matter, without consequences for our relationships with others: it demands a public witness to our faith. Evidently, this is true for all the baptized, yet it is especially incumbent upon those who, by virtue of their social or political position, must make decisions regarding fundamental values, such as respect for human life, its defense from conception to natural death, the family built upon marriage between a man and a woman, the freedom to educate one's children, and the promotion of the common good in all its forms.[230] These values are not negotiable. Consequently, Catholic politicians and legislators, conscious of their grave responsibility before society, must feel particularly bound, on the basis of a properly formed conscience, to introduce and support laws inspired by values grounded in human nature.[231] There is an objective connection here with the Eucharist (cf. 1 Cor 11:27–29). Bishops are bound to reaffirm constantly these values as part of their responsibility to the flock entrusted to them.[232]

THE EUCHARIST, A MYSTERY TO BE PROCLAIMED

The Eucharist and mission

84.   In my homily at the eucharistic celebration solemnly inaugurating my Petrine ministry, I said that "there is nothing more beautiful than to be surprised by the Gospel, by the encounter with Christ. There is nothing more beau-

---

229. Benedict XVI, Encyclical Letter *Deus caritas est* (December 25, 2005), 14: AAS 98 (2006), 229.
230. Cf. John Paul II, Encyclical Letter *Evangelium vitae* (March 25, 1995): AAS 87 (1995), 401–522; Benedict XVI, Address to the Pontifical Academy for Life (February 27, 2006): AAS 98 (2006), 264–265.
231. Cf. Congregation for the Doctrine of the Faith, Doctrinal Note on Some Questions Regarding the Participation of Catholics in Political Life (November 24, 2002): AAS 96 (2004), 359–370.
232. Cf. *Propositio* 46.

tiful than to know him and to speak to others of our friendship with him."[233] These words are all the more significant if we think of the mystery of the Eucharist. The love that we celebrate in the sacrament is not something we can keep to ourselves. By its very nature it demands to be shared with all. What the world needs is God's love; it needs to encounter Christ and to believe in him. The Eucharist is thus the source and summit not only of the Church's life, but also of her mission: "an authentically eucharistic Church is a missionary Church."[234] We too must be able to tell our brothers and sisters with conviction: "That which we have seen and heard we proclaim also to you, so that you may have fellowship with us" (1 Jn 1:3). Truly, nothing is more beautiful than to know Christ and to make him known to others. The institution of the Eucharist, for that matter, anticipates the very heart of Jesus' mission: he is the one sent by the Father for the redemption of the world (cf. Jn 3:16–17; Rom 8:32). At the Last Supper, Jesus entrusts to his disciples the sacrament which makes present his self-sacrifice for the salvation of us all, in obedience to the Father's will. We cannot approach the eucharistic table without being drawn into the mission which, beginning in the very heart of God, is meant to reach all people. Missionary outreach is thus an essential part of the eucharistic form of the Christian life.

The Eucharist and witness

85.   The first and fundamental mission that we receive from the sacred mysteries we celebrate is that of bearing witness by our lives. The wonder we experience at the gift God has made to us in Christ gives new impulse to our lives and commits us to becoming witnesses of his love. We become witnesses when, through our actions, words, and way of being, Another makes himself present. Witness could be described as the means by which the truth of God's love comes to men and women in history, inviting them to accept freely this radical newness. Through witness, God lays himself open, one might say, to the risk of human freedom. Jesus himself is the faithful and true witness (cf. Rev 1:5; 3:14), the one who came to testify to the truth (cf. Jn 18:37). Here I would like to reflect on a notion dear to the early Christians, which also speaks eloquently to us today: namely, witness even to the offering of one's own life, to the point of martyrdom. Throughout the history of the Church, this has always been seen as the culmination of the new spiritual worship: "Offer your bodies" (Rom 12:1). One thinks, for example, of the account of the martyrdom of Saint Polycarp of Smyrna, a disciple of Saint John: the entire drama is described as a liturgy, with the martyr himself becoming Eucharist.[235] We might also recall the eucharistic imagery with which Saint Ignatius of Antioch describes his own imminent martyrdom: he sees himself as "God's wheat" and desires to become in martyrdom "Christ's pure bread."[236] The Christian who offers his life in martyrdom enters into full communion with the Pasch of Jesus Christ and thus becomes Eucharist with him. Today too, the Church does not lack martyrs who offer the supreme witness to God's love. Even if the test of martyrdom is not asked of us,

---

233. AAS 97 (2005), 711.
234. *Propositio* 42.
235. Cf. *Mart. Polycarp.*, XV, 1: PG 5, 1039, 1042.
236. Saint Ignatius of Antioch, *Ad. Rom.*, IV, 1: PG 5, 690.

we know that worship pleasing to God demands that we should be inwardly prepared for it.[237] Such worship culminates in the joyful and convincing testimony of a consistent Christian life, wherever the Lord calls us to be his witnesses.

Christ Jesus, the one Savior

86.   Emphasis on the intrinsic relationship between the Eucharist and mission also leads to a rediscovery of the ultimate content of our proclamation. The more ardent the love for the Eucharist in the hearts of the Christian people, the more clearly will they recognize the goal of all mission: *to bring Christ to others*. Not just a theory or a way of life inspired by Christ, but the gift of his very person. Anyone who has not shared the truth of love with his brothers and sisters has not yet given enough. The Eucharist, as the sacrament of our salvation, inevitably reminds us of the unicity of Christ and the salvation that he won for us by his blood. The mystery of the Eucharist, believed in and celebrated, demands a constant catechesis on the need for all to engage in a missionary effort centered on the proclamation of Jesus as the one Savior.[238] This will help to avoid a reductive and purely sociological understanding of the vital work of human promotion present in every authentic process of evangelization.

Freedom of worship

87.   In this context, I wish to reiterate the concern expressed by the Synod Fathers about the grave difficulties affecting the mission of those Christian communities in areas where Christians are a minority or where they are denied religious freedom.[239] We should surely give thanks to the Lord for all those Bishops, priests, consecrated persons, and laity who devote themselves generously to the preaching of the Gospel and practice their faith at the risk of their lives. In not a few parts of the world, simply going to church represents a heroic witness that can result in marginalization and violence. Here too, I would like to reaffirm the solidarity of the whole Church with those who are denied freedom of worship. As we know, wherever religious freedom is lacking, people lack the most meaningful freedom of all, since it is through faith that men and women express their deepest decision about the ultimate meaning of their lives. Let us pray, therefore, for greater religious freedom in every nation, so that Christians, as well as the followers of other religions, can freely express their convictions, both as individuals and as communities.

THE EUCHARIST, A MYSTERY TO BE OFFERED TO THE WORLD

The Eucharist, bread broken for the life of the world

88.   "The bread I will give is my flesh, for the life of the world" (Jn 6:51). In these words the Lord reveals the true meaning of the gift of his life for all people. These words also reveal his deep compassion for every man and woman. The

---

237. Cf. Second Vatican Ecumenical Council, Dogmatic Constitution on the Church *Lumen gentium*, 42.
238. Cf. *Propositio* 42; Congregation for the Doctrine of the Faith, Declaration on the Unicity and Salvific Universality of Jesus Christ and the Church *Dominus Iesus* (August 6, 2000), 13–15: AAS 92 (2000), 754–755.
239. Cf. *Propositio* 42.

Gospels frequently speak of Jesus' feelings towards others, especially the suffering and sinners (cf. Mt 20:34; Mk 6:34; Lk 19:41). Through a profoundly human sensibility he expresses God's saving will for all people—that they may have true life. Each celebration of the Eucharist makes sacramentally present the gift that the crucified Lord made of his life, for us and for the whole world. In the Eucharist Jesus also makes us witnesses of God's compassion towards all our brothers and sisters. The eucharistic mystery thus gives rise to a service of charity towards neighbor, which "consists in the very fact that, in God and with God, I love even the person whom I do not like or even know. This can only take place on the basis of an intimate encounter with God, an encounter which has become a communion of will, affecting even my feelings. Then I learn to look on this other person not simply with my eyes and my feelings, but from the perspective of Jesus Christ."[240] In all those I meet, I recognize brothers or sisters for whom the Lord gave his life, loving them "to the end" (Jn 13:1). Our communities, when they celebrate the Eucharist, must become ever more conscious that the sacrifice of Christ is for all, and that the Eucharist thus compels all who believe in him to become "bread that is broken" for others, and to work for the building of a more just and fraternal world. Keeping in mind the multiplication of the loaves and fishes, we need to realize that Christ continues today to exhort his disciples to become personally engaged: "You yourselves, give them something to eat" (Mt 14:16). Each of us is truly called, together with Jesus, to be bread broken for the life of the world.

The social implications of the eucharistic mystery

89.   The union with Christ brought about by the Eucharist also brings a newness to our social relations: "this sacramental 'mysticism' is social in character." Indeed, "union with Christ is also union with all those to whom he gives himself. I cannot possess Christ just for myself; I can belong to him only in union with all those who have become, or who will become, his own."[241] The relationship between the eucharistic mystery and social commitment must be made explicit. The Eucharist is the sacrament of communion between brothers and sisters who allow themselves to be reconciled in Christ, who made of Jews and pagans one people, tearing down the wall of hostility which divided them (cf. Eph 2:14). Only this constant impulse towards reconciliation enables us to partake worthily of the Body and Blood of Christ (cf. Mt 5:23–24).[242] In the memorial of his sacrifice, the Lord strengthens our fraternal communion and, in a particular way, urges those in conflict to hasten their reconciliation by opening themselves to dialogue and a commitment to justice. Certainly, the restoration of justice, reconciliation, and forgiveness are the conditions for building true peace.[243] The recognition of this fact leads to a determination to transform unjust

---

240. Benedict XVI, Encyclical Letter *Deus caritas est* (December 25, 2005), 18: AAS 98 (2006), 232.
241. Ibid., 14.
242. During the Synod sessions we heard very moving and significant testimonies about the effectiveness of the Eucharist in peacemaking. In this regard, *Propositio* 49 states that: "Thanks to eucharistic celebrations, peoples engaged in conflict have been able to gather around the word of God, hear his prophetic message of reconciliation through gratuitous forgiveness, and receive the grace of conversion which allows them to share in the same bread and cup."
243. Cf. *Propositio* 48.

structures and to restore respect for the dignity of all men and women, created in God's image and likeness. Through the concrete fulfillment of this responsibility, the Eucharist becomes in life what it signifies in its celebration. As I have had occasion to say, it is not the proper task of the Church to engage in the political work of bringing about the most just society possible; nonetheless she cannot and must not remain on the sidelines in the struggle for justice. The Church "has to play her part through rational argument, and she has to reawaken the spiritual energy without which justice, which always demands sacrifice, cannot prevail and prosper."[244]

In discussing the social responsibility of all Christians, the Synod Fathers noted that the sacrifice of Christ is a mystery of liberation that constantly and insistently challenges us. I therefore urge all the faithful to be true promoters of peace and justice: "All who partake of the Eucharist must commit themselves to peacemaking in our world scarred by violence and war and, today in particular, by terrorism, economic corruption, and sexual exploitation."[245] All these problems give rise in turn to others no less troubling and disheartening. We know that there can be no superficial solutions to these issues. Precisely because of the mystery we celebrate, we must denounce situations contrary to human dignity, since Christ shed his blood for all, and at the same time affirm the inestimable value of each individual person.

The food of truth and human need

90.   We cannot remain passive before certain processes of globalization which not infrequently increase the gap between the rich and the poor worldwide. We must denounce those who squander the earth's riches, provoking inequalities that cry out to heaven (cf. Jas 5:4). For example, it is impossible to remain silent before the "distressing images of huge camps throughout the world of displaced persons and refugees, who are living in makeshift conditions in order to escape a worse fate, yet are still in dire need. Are these human beings not our brothers and sisters? Do their children not come into the world with the same legitimate expectations of happiness as other children?"[246] The Lord Jesus, the bread of eternal life, spurs us to be mindful of the situations of extreme poverty in which a great part of humanity still lives: these are situations for which human beings bear a clear and disquieting responsibility. Indeed, "on the basis of available statistical data, it can be said that less than half of the huge sums spent worldwide on armaments would be more than sufficient to liberate the immense masses of the poor from destitution. This challenges humanity's conscience. To peoples living below the poverty line, more as a result of situations to do with international political, commercial, and cultural relations than as a result of circumstances beyond anyone's control, our common commitment to truth can and must give new hope."[247]

---

244. Benedict XVI, Encyclical Letter *Deus caritas est* (December 25, 2005), 28: AAS 98 (2006), 239.
245. *Propositio* 48.
246. Benedict XVI, Address to the Diplomatic Corps Accredited to the Holy See (January 9, 2006): AAS 98 (2006), 127.
247. Ibid.

The food of truth demands that we denounce inhumane situations in which people starve to death because of injustice and exploitation, and it gives us renewed strength and courage to work tirelessly in the service of the civilization of love. From the beginning, Christians were concerned to share their goods (cf. Acts 4:32) and to help the poor (cf. Rom 15:26). The alms collected in our liturgical assemblies are an eloquent reminder of this, and they are also necessary for meeting today's needs. The Church's charitable institutions, especially *Caritas*, carry out at various levels the important work of assisting the needy, especially the poorest. Inspired by the Eucharist, the sacrament of charity, they become a concrete expression of that charity; they are to be praised and encouraged for their commitment to solidarity in our world.

The church's social teaching

91.   The mystery of the Eucharist inspires and impels us to work courageously within our world to bring about that renewal of relationships which has its inexhaustible source in God's gift. The prayer which we repeat at every Mass: "Give us this day our daily bread," obliges us to do everything possible, in cooperation with international, state, and private institutions, to end or at least reduce the scandal of hunger and malnutrition afflicting so many millions of people in our world, especially in developing countries. In a particular way, the Christian laity, formed at the school of the Eucharist, are called to assume their specific political and social responsibilities. To do so, they need to be adequately prepared through practical education in charity and justice. To this end, the Synod considered it necessary for Dioceses and Christian communities to teach and promote the Church's social doctrine.[248] In this precious legacy handed down from the earliest ecclesial tradition, we find elements of great wisdom that guide Christians in their involvement in today's burning social issues. This teaching, the fruit of the Church's whole history, is distinguished by realism and moderation; it can help to avoid misguided compromises or false utopias.

The sanctification of the world and the protection of creation

92.   Finally, to develop a profound eucharistic spirituality that is also capable of significantly affecting the fabric of society, the Christian people, in giving thanks to God through the Eucharist, should be conscious that they do so in the name of all creation, aspiring to the sanctification of the world and working intensely to that end.[249] The Eucharist itself powerfully illuminates human history and the whole cosmos. In this sacramental perspective we learn, day by day, that every ecclesial event is a kind of sign by which God makes himself known and challenges us. The eucharistic form of life can thus help foster a real change in the way we approach history and the world. The liturgy itself teaches us this, when, during the presentation of the gifts, the priest raises to God a prayer of blessing and petition over the bread and wine, "fruit of the earth," "fruit of the vine," and "work of human hands." With these words, the rite not only includes in our offering to God all human efforts and activity, but also leads

---

248. Cf. *Propositio* 48. In this regard, the *Compendium of the Social Doctrine of the Church* has proved most helpful.
249. Cf. *Propositio* 43.

us to see the world as God's creation, which brings forth everything we need for our sustenance. The world is not something indifferent, raw material to be utilized simply as we see fit. Rather, it is part of God's good plan, in which all of us are called to be sons and daughters in the one Son of God, Jesus Christ (cf. Eph 1:4–12). The justified concern about threats to the environment present in so many parts of the world is reinforced by Christian hope, which commits us to working responsibly for the protection of creation.[250] The relationship between the Eucharist and the cosmos helps us to see the unity of God's plan and to grasp the profound relationship between creation and the "new creation" inaugurated in the resurrection of Christ, the new Adam. Even now we take part in that new creation by virtue of our Baptism (cf. Col 2:12ff.). Our Christian life, nourished by the Eucharist, gives us a glimpse of that new world—new heavens and a new earth—where the new Jerusalem comes down from heaven, from God, "prepared as a bride adorned for her husband" (Rev 21:2).

The usefulness of a Eucharistic Compendium

93.   At the conclusion of these reflections, in which I have taken up a number of themes raised at the Synod, I also wish to accept the proposal which the Synod Fathers advanced as a means of helping the Christian people to believe, celebrate, and live ever more fully the mystery of the Eucharist. The competent offices of the Roman Curia will publish a *Compendium* which will assemble texts from the *Catechism of the Catholic Church*, prayers, explanations of the Eucharistic Prayers of the Roman Missal, and other useful aids for a correct understanding, celebration, and adoration of the Sacrament of the Altar.[251] It is my hope that this book will help make the memorial of the Passover of the Lord increasingly the source and summit of the Church's life and mission. This will encourage each member of the faithful to make his or her life a true act of spiritual worship.

CONCLUSION

94.   Dear brothers and sisters, the Eucharist is at the root of every form of holiness, and each of us is called to the fullness of life in the Holy Spirit. How many saints have advanced along the way of perfection thanks to their eucharistic devotion! From Saint Ignatius of Antioch to Saint Augustine, from Saint Anthony the Abbot to Saint Benedict, from Saint Francis of Assisi to Saint Thomas Aquinas, from Saint Clare of Assisi to Saint Catherine of Siena, from Saint Paschal Baylon to Saint Peter Julian Eymard, from Saint Alphonsus Liguori to Blessed Charles de Foucauld, from Saint John Mary Vianney to Saint Thérèse of Lisieux, from Saint Pius of Pietrelcina to Blessed Teresa of Calcutta, from Blessed Piergiorgio Frassati to Blessed Ivan Merz, to name only a few, holiness has always found its center in the sacrament of the Eucharist.

This most holy mystery thus needs to be firmly believed, devoutly celebrated, and intensely lived in the Church. Jesus' gift of himself in the sacrament which is the memorial of his passion tells us that the success of our lives is found in

---

250. Cf. *Propositio* 47.
251. Cf. *Propositio* 17.

our participation in the trinitarian life offered to us truly and definitively in him. The celebration and worship of the Eucharist enable us to draw near to God's love and to persevere in that love until we are united with the Lord whom we love. The offering of our lives, our fellowship with the whole community of believers and our solidarity with all men and women are essential aspects of that *logiké latreía*, spiritual worship, holy and pleasing to God (cf. Rom 12:1), which transforms every aspect of our human existence, to the glory of God. I therefore ask all pastors to spare no effort in promoting an authentically eucharistic Christian spirituality. Priests, deacons, and all those who carry out a eucharistic ministry should always be able to find in this service, exercised with care and constant preparation, the strength and inspiration needed for their personal and communal path of sanctification. I exhort the lay faithful, and families in particular, to find ever anew in the sacrament of Christ's love the energy needed to make their lives an authentic sign of the presence of the risen Lord. I ask all consecrated men and women to show by their eucharistic lives the splendor and the beauty of belonging totally to the Lord.

95.   At the beginning of the fourth century, Christian worship was still forbidden by the imperial authorities. Some Christians in North Africa, who felt bound to celebrate the Lord's Day, defied the prohibition. They were martyred after declaring that it was not possible for them to live without the Eucharist, the food of the Lord: *sine dominico non possumus.*[252] May these martyrs of Abitinae, in union with all those saints and beati who made the Eucharist the center of their lives, intercede for us and teach us to be faithful to our encounter with the risen Christ. We too cannot live without partaking of the sacrament of our salvation; we too desire to be *iuxta dominicam viventes*, to reflect in our lives what we celebrate on the Lord's Day. That day is the day of our definitive deliverance. Is it surprising, then, that we should wish to live every day in that newness of life which Christ has brought us in the mystery of the Eucharist?

96.   May Mary Most Holy, the Immaculate Virgin, ark of the new and eternal covenant, accompany us on our way to meet the Lord who comes. In her we find realized most perfectly the essence of the Church. The Church sees in Mary—"Woman of the Eucharist," as she was called by the Servant of God John Paul II[253]—her finest icon, and she contemplates Mary as a singular model of the eucharistic life. For this reason, as the priest prepares to receive on the altar the *verum Corpus natum de Maria Virgine*, speaking on behalf of the liturgical assembly, he says in the words of the canon: "We honor Mary, the ever-virgin mother of Jesus Christ our Lord and God."[254] Her holy name is also invoked and venerated in the canons of the Eastern Christian traditions. The faithful, for their part, "commend to Mary, Mother of the Church, their lives and the work of their hands. Striving to have the same sentiments as Mary, they help the whole community to become a living offering pleasing to the Father."[255] She is

---

252. *Martyrium Saturnini, Dativi et aliorum plurimorum*, 7, 9, 10: PL 8, 707, 709–710.
253. Cf. John Paul II, Encyclical Letter *Ecclesia de Eucharistia* (April 17, 2003), 53: AAS 95 (2003), 469.
254. *Eucharistic Prayer I (Roman Canon).*
255. *Propositio 50.*

the *tota pulchra*, the all-beautiful, for in her the radiance of God's glory shines forth. The beauty of the heavenly liturgy, which must be reflected in our own assemblies, is faithfully mirrored in her. From Mary we must learn to become men and women of the Eucharist and of the Church, and thus to present ourselves, in the words of Saint Paul, "holy and blameless" before the Lord, even as he wished us to be from the beginning (cf. Col 1:22; Eph 1:4).[256]

97.   Through the intercession of the Blessed Virgin Mary, may the Holy Spirit kindle within us the same ardor experienced by the disciples on the way to Emmaus (cf. Lk 24:13–35) and renew our "eucharistic wonder" through the splendor and beauty radiating from the liturgical rite, the efficacious sign of the infinite beauty of the holy mystery of God. Those disciples arose and returned in haste to Jerusalem in order to share their joy with their brothers and sisters in the faith. True joy is found in recognizing that the Lord is still with us, our faithful companion along the way. The Eucharist makes us discover that Christ, risen from the dead, is our contemporary in the mystery of the Church, his body. Of this mystery of love we have become witnesses. Let us encourage one another to walk joyfully, our hearts filled with wonder, towards our encounter with the Holy Eucharist, so that we may experience and proclaim to others the truth of the words with which Jesus took leave of his disciples: "Lo, I am with you always, until the end of the world" (Mt 28:20).

Given in Rome, at Saint Peter's, on February 22, the Feast of the Chair of Peter, in the year 2007, the second of my Pontificate.

BENEDICTUS PP. XVI

---

256. Cf. Benedict XVI, Homily (December 8, 2005): AAS 98 (2006), 15.

VERBUM DOMINI
ON THE WORD OF GOD IN THE LIFE
AND MISSION OF THE CHURCH

POST-SYNODAL APOSTOLIC EXHORTATION
POPE BENEDICT XVI
SEPTEMBER 30, 2010

AN OVERVIEW OF *VERBUM DOMINI*

S. Joyce Ann Zimmerman, CPPS

The *Constitution on the Sacred Liturgy* states that "Sacred Scripture is of the greatest importance in the celebration of the liturgy."[1] With Pope Benedict XVI's post-synodal apostolic exhortation *Verbum Domini*, he extends that deep appreciation for the sacredness of God's Word far beyond the liturgy so that it "will be ever more fully at the heart of every ecclesial activity."[2] This hope and prayer is stated in the first paragraph of the document. It undergirds all of the document's 124 articles. God's Word is at the heart of the whole life of the Church. Throughout the exhortation, Pope Benedict XVI plays between the Word as Sacred Scripture and the Word as the incarnated Son of God.

An apostolic exhortation is not doctrinal in intent; instead it is a communication to the Church urging her members to action. It carries the authority of the Holy Father himself. In *Verbum Domini* Pope Benedict XVI urges all of us to renew our encounter with God through the divinely inspired Word; our personal and communal encounter with the divine Son Jesus Christ, the Word made flesh; and to become heralds of the gift received in those encounters. In all of this Benedict desires that the gift of God's life might "spread ever more fully throughout the world."[3]

INTRODUCTION

In the brief, five-article introduction Pope Benedict XVI tries to convey to the whole Church the beauty and joy that he and the bishops felt in a renewed encounter with the Lord during the Twelfth Ordinary General Assembly of the Synod of Bishops on the Word of God.[4] The Synod drew from and built upon *Dei Verbum* (DV) and the previous Synod of Bishops on the Eucharist. This Synod of Bishops on the Word of God afforded an opportunity to "review the implementation of the Council's directives, and to confront the challenges which the present time sets before Christian believers."[5] The guide for the pope's remarks would be the Prologue to John's account of the Gospel, the text that proclaims that the Word was incarnate and dwells among us.[6] This focus on the Word incarnate is endemic to Benedict, who in so many ways in the years of his pontificate called us to make Christ the center of our lives. The pope hoped that the work of the Synod of Bishops on the Word of God would "have a real effect on the life of the Church."[7]

---

1. *Constitution on the Sacred Liturgy* (CSL), 24.
2. *Verbum Domini* (VD), 1.
3. VD, 2.
4. This synod was held at the Vatican, October 5 to 26, 2008, about two years before Pope Benedict XVI wrote this apostolic exhortation based on the synod's proceedings.
5. VD, 3.
6. See ibid., 5.
7. Ibid.

Anyone reading this introduction cannot help but be struck by its undercurrent of enthusiasm and joy. Several times Benedict uses the word "joy." Our engagement with Sacred Scripture ought not be a burden, but genuinely bring us to delight in God's gift of the Word to us.

The body of the exhortation is divided into three parts: the Word of God, the Word in the Church, and the Word to the world. This simple three-part structure witnesses beautifully to the progression of Benedict's thought on the divine Word: God is the source, the Church is the context, and spreading God's Word to the world is the mission.

PART I: VERBUM DEI

In this first and longest part of the document, Benedict begins by addressing the many ways that we speak about the "word of God"; he poetically refers to "a symphony of the word."[8] These many ways include, most importantly, the Word made flesh; creation in all its many forms, especially human beings made in the image of God; the Word that is salvation history; the Word of God spoken by the prophets; the apostolic word and preaching of the Apostles; the Church's living Tradition; and the divinely inspired Word of God in Sacred Scripture. Expounding upon these, Christ is given central place as the eternal Word of God who was with God from the very beginning. Benedict also brings out the important role of the Holy Spirit, not only in guiding us to hear God's Word, but also as the One who inspired the writers of the Sacred Scriptures.

The greater part of the pope's remarks on the Word of God are directed to interpretive and theological issues. Important points he makes include the relationship of inspiration and truth, the Word of God and faith, biblical studies and the Church's magisterium. He boldly addresses the thorny issues of the letter and spirit of God's Word, relationship of the Old and New Testaments, the difficult and "dark" passages of Scripture, fundamentalist interpretations, and biblical interpretation and ecumenism. For Benedict, faith is the key to overcoming dualisms and finding unity in these sometimes seemingly irreconcilable opposites. Here is where he also raises the pastoral dimensions of these issues.

PART II: VERBUM IN ECCLESIA

Throughout the document Pope Benedict XVI makes clear that interpreting the Word of God must take place within a community; specifically, the community of the Church. In this part of *Verbum Domini* Benedict explores how the Word comes alive in the community called Church.

The largest section of *Verbum in Ecclesia* concerns the preeminent "home" of God's Word, the Sacred Liturgy. Particularly during the Eucharistic celebration the Word of God proclaims Christ's saving events. Thus, Benedict XVI makes clear that at "the center of everything the paschal mystery shines forth" and that this mystery "unfolds each year in the liturgy."[9] He goes on to address Sacred Scripture in the sacraments, Lectionary, Homily, Liturgy of the Hours, Book of Blessings, celebrations of the Word, silence, ecumenical settings, and liturgical song.

---

8. Ibid., 7.
9. Ibid., 52.

Broadening his concerns, the pope addresses how the Bible is to inspire all the pastoral activity of the Church: in all "the ordinary activities of Christian communities,"[10] catechesis, and the fostering of vocations. He speaks to practical ways individuals within the Church community might come to a deeper appreciation of the Word in their lives, and includes two very helpful and practical paragraphs about the practice of *lectio divina*.[11] Informing all of his remarks on the Word in the Church is a focus on the presence and activity of Christ. Christ is the Head of his Body, the Church. At the very beginning of part II, the pope makes a clear and unequivocal statement, "Not to receive him [Christ] means not to listen to his voice, not to be conformed to the *Logos*."[12]

PART III: VERBUM MUNDO

We hear the Word of God, encounter the Word made flesh, then are called to spread God's Word throughout the world. This final section of *Verbum Domini* really is all about a topic near and dear to the heart of Benedict: evangelization.[13] "The Synod of Bishops forcefully reaffirmed the need within the Church for a revival of missionary consciousness."[14] As the community of the Church, we are all called through our Baptism to take up the mission of the Church,[15] which is nothing less than the mission of Christ himself.[16] We continue Jesus's mission of salvation and the Apostles's mission of preaching when we respond to the "Spirit of the Risen Lord [who] empowers us to proclaim the word everywhere by the witness of our lives."[17] Our "preaching" is the witness of fruitfully living in the Spirit.

Pope Benedict XVI encourages and underscores the importance of living lives of witness to the Gospel. He does so in very practical remarks extolling contemporary martyrs, urging us to spend our lives in commitment to bringing about justice in the world,[18] promoting peace and reconciliation,[19] and doing practical works of charity.[20] He reminds us of our obligation to help the younger generation hear and act on God's Word.[21] He speaks to the Word of God in relation to migrants,[22] those who are suffering,[23] and the poor.[24] He warns against

---

10. Ibid., 73.

11. See ibid., 86–87.

12. Ibid., 50.

13. Article 96 specifically addresses "Proclamation and the new evangelization," but this theme drives all Benedict's remarks in part III.

14. Ibid., 92.

15. See ibid., 95.

16. See ibid., 93.

17. Ibid., 91. articles 97 and 98 explain the relationship of the Word of God and Christian witness. It is the latter that makes the former credible.

18. See ibid., 99–100.

19. See ibid., 102.

20. See ibid., 103.

21. See ibid., 104.

22. See ibid., 105.

23. See ibid., 106.

24. See ibid., 107.

exploitation of creation, which was formed by God's Word.[25] He addresses the Word of God and culture from a number of perspectives, including the arts,[26] social communication,[27] inculturation,[28] and translations.[29] While greatly supporting and favoring the relationship of God's Word and culture, Benedict also makes clear that God's Word "overcomes the limits of individual cultures to create fellowship between different peoples."[30] The final four paragraphs of part III address interreligious dialogue[31] and religious freedom.[32]

CONCLUSION

In a brief conclusion of only four paragraphs, Pope Benedict XVI reiterates themes he has already developed: the definitive Word spoken by God is the Word made flesh. It is the Risen Christ whom we preach, his Good News of salvation, and it is this Word that brings us hope of one day enjoying eschatological fulfillment with him. Benedict once again emphasizes that a new and deeper appreciation of God's Word leads to a new evangelization. A new openness to God's Word will lead to a new Pentecost and brings us the "profound joy which has its origin in the very heart of the trinitarian life and which is communicated to us in the Son."[33]

THE WORD SHAPES LITURGY, OUR LIVES, US

Verbum Domini is a balanced mix of theological insights and pastoral recommendations, biblical spirituality, and liturgical mysticism. With ease Benedict weaves together a reflection on the revealed Word of Scripture and the Word made flesh. Throughout the document he upholds that Christ is clearly the center of our lives because he is the Word preeminently spoken by God. His apostolic exhortation urges us to study the Word in Scripture, appreciate the Word spoken through the Tradition, and live the Word spoken to us here and now in liturgy and in the works of justice and charity, reconciliation, and peace we undergo. With the Word informing our liturgy and lives, we cannot help but be conformed to Christ in the way that our Savior wishes.

A challenge for us as we reflect on God's Word is that we cannot limit ourselves to the written or spoken Word. In both part I and part II, Benedict XVI mentions the relationship of the Word and silence. Being silent in the face of God's Word reminds us that God is both distant and near. Silence, as the pope reminds us, is itself an expression of God's Word. We hear God's Word, and in a silent response we can enter into a mystical stance of awe, wonder, and joy.

---

25. See ibid., 108.
26. See ibid., 112.
27. See ibid., 113.
28. See ibid., 114.
29. See ibid., 115.
30. Ibid., 116.
31. Ibid., 117–119.
32. See ibid., 120.
33. Ibid., 123.

OUTLINE

POST-SYNODAL
APOSTOLIC EXHORTATION
VERBUM DOMINI

OF THE HOLY FATHER
BENEDICT XVI

TO THE BISHOPS, CLERGY, CONSECRATED PERSONS
AND THE LAY FAITHFUL ON THE WORD OF GOD
IN THE LIFE AND MISSION OF THE CHURCH

INTRODUCTION

1.   "The word of the Lord abides for ever. This word is the Gospel which was preached to you" (1 Pet 1:25; cf. Is 40:8). With this assertion from the First Letter of Saint Peter, which takes up the words of the Prophet Isaiah, we find ourselves before the mystery of God, who has made himself known through the gift of his word. This word, which abides for ever, entered into time. God spoke his eternal Word humanly; his Word "became flesh" (Jn 1:14). This is the good news. This is the proclamation which has come down the centuries to us today. The Twelfth Ordinary General Assembly of the Synod of Bishops, meeting in the Vatican from October 5–26, 2008, had as its theme: *The Word of God in the Life and Mission of the Church*. It was a profound experience of encounter with Christ, the Word of the Father, who is present where two or three are gathered in his name (cf. Mt 18:20). With this Post-Synodal Apostolic Exhortation, I readily respond to the request of the Synod Fathers to make known to the whole People of God the rich fruits which emerged from the synodal sessions and the recommendations which resulted from our common endeavor.[1] Consequently, I intend to revisit the work of the Synod in the light of its documents: the *Lineamenta*, the *Instrumentum laboris*, the *Relationes ante* and *post disceptationem*, the texts of the interventions, both those delivered on the Synod floor and those presented in written form, the reports of the smaller discussion groups, the Final Message to the People of God and, above all, a number of specific proposals (*Propositiones*) which the Fathers considered especially significant. In this way I wish to point out certain fundamental approaches to a rediscovery of God's word in the life of the Church as a wellspring of constant renewal. At the same time I express my hope that the word will be ever more fully at the heart of every ecclesial activity.

---

1. Cf. *Propositio* 1.

2.   Before all else, I would like to call to mind the beauty and pleasure of the renewed encounter with the Lord Jesus which we experienced during the synodal assembly. In union with the Synod Fathers, then, I address all the faithful in the words of Saint John in his first letter: "We proclaim to you the eternal life which was with the Father and which was made manifest to us—that which we have seen and heard we proclaim also to you, so that you may have fellowship with us; and our fellowship is with the Father and with his Son Jesus Christ" (1 Jn 1:2–3). The Apostle speaks to us of *hearing, seeing, touching and looking upon* (cf. 1 Jn 1:1) the word of life, since life itself was made manifest in Christ. Called to communion with God and among ourselves, we must proclaim this gift. From this kerygmatic standpoint, the synodal assembly was a testimony, before the Church and before the world, to the immense beauty of encountering the word of God in the communion of the Church. For this reason I encourage all the faithful to renew their personal and communal encounter with Christ, the word of life made visible, and to become his heralds, so that the gift of divine life—communion—can spread ever more fully throughout the world. Indeed, sharing in the life of God, a Trinity of love, is *complete joy* (cf. 1 Jn 1:4). And it is the Church's gift and inescapable duty to communicate that joy, born of an encounter with the person of Christ, the Word of God in our midst. In a world which often feels that God is superfluous or extraneous, we confess with Peter that he alone has "the words of eternal life" (Jn 6:68). There is no greater priority than this: to enable the people of our time once more to encounter God, the God who speaks to us and shares his love so that we might have life in abundance (cf. Jn 10:10).

FROM "DEI VERBUM" TO THE SYNOD ON THE WORD OF GOD

3.   With the Twelfth Ordinary General Assembly of the Synod of Bishops on the Word of God, we were conscious of dealing in a certain sense with the very *heart* of the Christian life, in continuity with the previous synodal assembly on *The Eucharist as the Source and Summit of the Church's Life and Mission.* Indeed, the Church is built upon the word of God; she is born from and lives by that word.[2] Throughout its history, the People of God has always found strength in the word of God, and today too the ecclesial community grows by hearing, celebrating, and studying that word. It must be acknowledged that in recent decades ecclesial life has grown more sensitive to this theme, particularly with reference to Christian revelation, the living Tradition and Sacred Scripture. Beginning with the pontificate of Pope Leo XIII, we can say that there has been a crescendo of interventions aimed at an increased awareness of the importance of the word of God and the study of the Bible in the life of the Church,[3] culminating in the Second Vatican Council and specifically in the promulgation of the Dogmatic Constitution on Divine Revelation *Dei Verbum.* The latter represented

---

2. Cf. Twelfth Ordinary General Assembly of the Synod of Bishops, *Instrumentum Laboris,* 27.

3. Cf. Leo XIII, Encyclical Letter *Providentissimus Deus* (November 18, 1893): ASS 26 (1893–94), 269–292; Benedict XV, Encyclical Letter *Spiritus Paraclitus* (September 15, 1920): AAS 12 (1920), 385–422; Pius XII, Encyclical Letter *Divino afflante Spiritu* (September 30, 1943): AAS 35 (1943), 297–325.

a milestone in the Church's history: "The Synod Fathers . . . acknowledge with gratitude the great benefits which this document brought to the life of the Church, on the exegetical, theological, spiritual, pastoral, and ecumenical plane."[4] The intervening years have also witnessed a growing awareness of the "trinitarian and salvation-historical horizon of revelation"[5] against which Jesus Christ is to be acknowledged as "mediator and fullness of all revelation."[6] To each generation the Church unceasingly proclaims that Christ "completed and perfected revelation. Everything to do with his presence and his self-manifestation was involved in achieving this: his words and works, signs and miracles, but above all his death and resurrection from the dead, and finally his sending of the Spirit of truth."[7]

Everyone is aware of the great impulse which the Dogmatic Constitution *Dei Verbum* gave to the revival of interest in the word of God in the life of the Church, to theological reflection on divine revelation, and to the study of Sacred Scripture. In the last forty years, the Church's magisterium has also issued numerous statements on these questions.[8] By celebrating this Synod, the Church, conscious of her continuing journey under the guidance of the Holy Spirit, felt called to further reflection on the theme of God's word, in order to review the implementation of the Council's directives, and to confront the new challenges which the present time sets before Christian believers.

THE SYNOD OF BISHOPS ON THE WORD OF GOD

4.   In the twelfth synodal assembly, Bishops from throughout the world gathered around the word of God and symbolically placed the text of the Bible at the center of the assembly, in order to stress anew something we risk taking for granted in everyday life: *the fact that God speaks and responds to our questions.*[9] Together we listened to and celebrated the word of the Lord. We recounted to one another all that the Lord is doing in the midst of the People of God, and we shared our hopes and concerns. All this made us realize that we can deepen

---

4. *Propositio* 2.

5. Ibid.

6. Second Vatican Ecumenical Council, Dogmatic Constitution on Divine Revelation *Dei Verbum*, 2.

7. Ibid., 4.

8. Noteworthy among various kinds of interventions are: Paul VI, Apostolic Letter *Summi Dei Verbum* (November 4, 1963): AAS 55 (1963), 979–995; Motu Proprio *Sedula cura* (June 27, 1971): AAS 63 (1971), 665–669; John Paul II, General Audience (May 1, 1985): *L'Osservatore Romano*, May 2–3, 1985, p. 6; Address on the Interpretation of the Bible in the Church (April 23, 1993): AAS 86 (1994), 232–243; Benedict XVI, Address to the International Congress held on the Fortieth Anniversary of *Dei Verbum* (September 16, 2005): AAS 97 (2005), 957; Angelus (November 6, 2005): *Insegnamenti* I (2005), 759–760. Also worthy of mention are the interventions of the Pontifical Biblical Commission, *De sacra Scriptura et christologia* (1984): *Enchiridion Vaticanum* 9, Nos. 1208–1339; *Unity and Diversity in the Church* (April 11, 1988): *Enchiridion Vaticanum* 11, Nos. 544–643; *The Interpretation of the Bible in the Church* (April 15, 1993): *Enchiridion Vaticanum* 13, Nos. 2846–3150; *The Jewish People and their Sacred Scriptures in the Christian Bible* (May 24, 2001): *Enchiridion Vaticanum* 20, Nos. 733–1150; *The Bible and Morality: Biblical Roots of Christian Conduct* (May 11, 2008): Vatican City, 2008.

9. Cf. Benedict XVI, Address to the Roman Curia (December 22, 2008): AAS 101 (2009), 49.

our relationship with the word of God only within the "we" of the Church, in mutual listening and acceptance. Hence our gratitude for the testimonies about the life of the Church in different parts of the world which emerged from the various interventions on the floor. It was also moving to hear the fraternal delegates, who accepted our invitation to take part in the synodal meeting. I think in particular of the meditation offered to us by His Holiness Bartholomaios I, Ecumenical Patriarch of Constantinople, for which the Fathers expressed deep appreciation.[10] Furthermore, for the first time ever, the Synod of Bishops also invited a rabbi to offer us a precious witness on the Hebrew Scriptures, which are also part of our own Sacred Scriptures.[11]

In this way we were able to acknowledge with joy and gratitude that "in the Church there is also a Pentecost today—in other words, the Church speaks in many tongues, and not only outwardly, in the sense that all the great languages of the world are represented in her, but, more profoundly, inasmuch as present within her are various ways of experiencing God and the world, a wealth of cultures, and only in this way do we come to see the vastness of the human experience and, as a result, the vastness of the word of God."[12] We were also able to see an ongoing Pentecost; various peoples are still waiting for the word of God to be proclaimed in their own language and in their own culture.

How can I fail to mention that throughout the Synod we were accompanied by the testimony of the Apostle Paul! It was providential that the Twelfth Ordinary General Assembly took place during the year dedicated to the great Apostle of the Nations on the two thousandth anniversary of his birth. Paul's life was completely marked by his zeal for the spread of God's word. How can we not be moved by his stirring words about his mission as a preacher of the word of God: "I do everything for the Gospel" (1 Cor 9:23); or, as he writes in the *Letter to the Romans*: "I am not ashamed of the Gospel; it is the power of God for salvation to every one who has faith" (1:16). Whenever we reflect on the word of God in the life and mission of the Church, we cannot but think of Saint Paul and his life spent in spreading the message of salvation in Christ to all peoples.

THE PROLOGUE OF JOHN'S GOSPEL AS A GUIDE

5.   With this Apostolic Exhortation I would like the work of the Synod to have a real effect on the life of the Church: on our personal relationship with the Sacred Scriptures, on their interpretation in the liturgy and catechesis, and in scientific research, so that the Bible may not be simply a word from the past, but a living and timely word. To accomplish this, I would like to present and develop the labors of the Synod by making constant reference to the *Prologue of John's Gospel* (Jn 1:1–18), which makes known to us the basis of our life: the Word, who from the beginning is with God, who became flesh, and who made his dwelling among us (cf. Jn 1:14). This is a magnificent text, one which offers a synthesis of the entire Christian faith. From his personal experience of having met and

---

10. Cf. *Propositio* 37.

11. Cf. Pontifical Biblical Commission, *The Jewish People and their Sacred Scriptures in the Christian Bible* (May 24, 2001): *Enchiridion Vaticanum* 20, Nos. 733–1150.

12. Benedict XVI, Address to the Roman Curia (December 22, 2008): AAS 101 (2009), 50.

followed Christ, John, whom tradition identifies as "the disciple whom Jesus loved" (Jn 13:23; 20:2; 21:7, 20), "came to a deep certainty: Jesus is the Wisdom of God incarnate, he is his eternal Word who became a mortal man."[13] May John, who "saw and believed" (cf. Jn 20:8) also help us to lean on the breast of Christ (cf. Jn 13:25), the source of the blood and water (cf. Jn 19:34) which are symbols of the Church's sacraments. Following the example of the Apostle John and the other inspired authors, may we allow ourselves to be led by the Holy Spirit to *an ever greater love of the word of God.*

PART ONE: *VERBUM DEI*

"In the beginning was the Word, and the Word was with God, and the Word was God . . . and the Word became flesh." (Jn 1:1, 14)

THE GOD WHO SPEAKS

GOD IN DIALOGUE

6. The novelty of biblical revelation consists in the fact that God becomes known through the dialogue which he desires to have with us.[14] The Dogmatic Constitution *Dei Verbum* had expressed this by acknowledging that the unseen God "from the fullness of his love, addresses men and women as his friends, and lives among them, in order to invite and receive them into his own company."[15] Yet we would not yet sufficiently grasp the message of the Prologue of Saint John if we stopped at the fact that God enters into loving communion with us. In reality, the Word of God, through whom "all things were made" (Jn 1:3) and who "became flesh" (Jn 1:14), is the same Word who is "in the beginning" (Jn 1:1). If we realize that this is an allusion to the beginning of the book of Genesis (cf. Gen 1:1), we find ourselves faced with *a beginning* which is absolute and which speaks to us of the inner life of God. The Johannine Prologue makes us realize that the *Logos* is truly *eternal*, and from eternity *is himself God.* God was never without his *Logos.* The Word exists before creation. Consequently at the heart of the divine life there is communion, there is absolute gift. "God is love" (1 Jn 4:16), as the same Apostle tells us elsewhere, thus pointing to "the Christian image of God and the resulting image of mankind and its destiny."[16] God makes himself known to us as a mystery of infinite love in which the Father eternally utters his Word in the Holy Spirit. Consequently the Word, who from the beginning is with God and is God, reveals God himself in the dialogue of love between the divine persons, and invites us to share in that love. Created in the image and likeness of the God who is love, we can thus understand ourselves only in accepting the Word and in docility to the work of the Holy Spirit. In the light of the revelation made by God's Word, the enigma of the human condition is definitively clarified.

---

13. Cf. Benedict XVI, Angelus (January 4, 2009): *Insegnamenti* V, 1 (2009), 13.

14. Cf. *Relatio ante disceptationem*, I.

15. Second Vatican Ecumenical Council, Dogmatic Constitution on Divine Revelation *Dei Verbum*, 2.

16. Benedict XVI, Encyclical Letter *Deus caritas est* (December 25, 2005), 1: AAS 98 (2006), 217–218.

7.   In the light of these considerations, born of meditation on the Christian mystery expressed in the Prologue of John, we now need to consider what the Synod Fathers affirmed about the different ways in which we speak of "the word of God." They rightly referred to a symphony of the word, to a single word expressed in multiple ways: "a polyphonic hymn."[17] The Synod Fathers pointed out that human language operates analogically in speaking of the word of God. In effect, this expression, while referring to God's self-communication, also takes on a number of different meanings which need to be carefully considered and related among themselves, from the standpoint both of theological reflection and pastoral practice. As the Prologue of John clearly shows us, the *Logos* refers in the first place to the eternal Word, the only Son, begotten of the Father before all ages and consubstantial with him: *the word was with God, and the word was God.* But this same Word, Saint John tells us, "became flesh" (Jn 1:14); hence Jesus Christ, born of the Virgin Mary, is truly the Word of God who has become consubstantial with us. Thus the expression "word of God" here refers to the person of Jesus Christ, the eternal Son of the Father, made man.

While the Christ event is at the heart of divine revelation, we also need to realize that creation itself, the *liber naturae*, is an essential part of this symphony of many voices in which the one word is spoken. We also profess our faith that God has spoken his word in salvation history; he has made his voice heard; by the power of his Spirit "he has spoken through the prophets."[18] God's word is thus spoken throughout the history of salvation, and most fully in the mystery of the incarnation, death, and resurrection of the Son of God. Then too, the word of God is that word preached by the Apostles in obedience to the command of the Risen Jesus: "Go into all the world and preach the Gospel to the whole creation" (Mk 16:15). The word of God is thus handed on in the Church's living Tradition. Finally, the word of God, attested and divinely inspired, is Sacred Scripture, the Old and New Testaments. All this helps us to see that, while in the Church we greatly venerate the Sacred Scriptures, the Christian faith is not a "religion of the book": Christianity is the "religion of the word of God," not of "a written and mute word, but of the incarnate and living Word."[19] Consequently the Scripture is to be proclaimed, heard, read, received, and experienced as the word of God, in the stream of the apostolic Tradition from which it is inseparable.[20]

As the Synod Fathers stated, the expression "word of God" is used analogically, and we should be aware of this. The faithful need to be better helped to grasp the different meanings of the expression, but also to understand its unitary sense. From the theological standpoint too, there is a need for further study of how the different meanings of this expression are interrelated, so that the unity

---

17. *Instrumentum laboris*, 9.

18. *Nicene-Constantinopolitan Creed*: DS 150.

19. Saint Bernard of Clairvaux, *Homilia super missus est*, IV, 11: PL 183, 86B.

20. Cf. Second Vatican Ecumenical Council, Dogmatic Constitution on Divine Revelation *Dei Verbum*, 10.

of God's plan and, within it, the centrality of the person of Christ, may shine forth more clearly.[21]

THE COSMIC DIMENSION OF THE WORD

8.   When we consider the basic meaning of the word of God as a reference to the eternal Word of God made flesh, the one Savior and mediator between God and humanity,[22] and we listen to this word, we are led by the biblical revelation to see that it is the foundation of all reality. The Prologue of Saint John says of the divine *Logos*, that "all things were made through him, and without him was not anything made that was made" (Jn 1:3); and in the *Letter to the Colossians* it is said of Christ, "the first-born of all creation" (1:15), that "all things were created through him and for him" (1:16). The author of the *Letter to the Hebrews* likewise states that "by faith we understand that the world was created by the word of God, so that what is seen was made out of things which do not appear" (11:3).

For us, this proclamation is a word of freedom. Scripture tells us that everything that exists does not exist by chance but is willed by God and part of his plan, at whose center is the invitation to partake, in Christ, in the divine life. Creation is born of the *Logos* and indelibly bears the mark of the *creative Reason which orders and directs it*; with joy-filled certainty the psalms sing: "By the word of the Lord the heavens were made, and all their host by the breath of his mouth" (Ps 33:6); and again, "he spoke, and it came to be; he commanded, and it stood forth" (Ps 33:9). All reality expresses this mystery: "The heavens are telling the glory of God; and the firmament proclaims his handiwork" (Ps 19:1). Thus Sacred Scripture itself invites us to acknowledge the Creator by contemplating his creation (cf. Wis 13:5; Rom 1:19–20). The tradition of Christian thought has developed this key element of the symphony of the word, as when, for example, Saint Bonaventure, who in the great tradition of the Greek Fathers sees all the possibilities of creation present in the *Logos*,[23] states that "every creature is a word of God, since it proclaims God."[24] The Dogmatic Constitution *Dei Verbum* synthesized this datum when it stated that "God, who creates and conserves all things by his word (cf. Jn 1:3), provides constant evidence of himself in created realities."[25]

---

21. Cf. *Propositio* 3.

22. Cf. Congregation for the doctrine of the faith, Declaration on the Unicity and Salvific Universality of Jesus Christ and of the Church *Dominus Iesus* (August 6, 2000), 13–15: AAS 92 (2000), 754–756.

23. Cf. *In Hexaemeron*, XX, 5: Opera Omnia V, Quaracchi 1891, pp. 425–426; *Breviloquium* I, 8: Opera Omnia V, Quaracchi 1891, pp. 216–217.

24. *Itinerarium mentis in Deum*, II, 12: Opera Omnia V, Quaracchi 1891, pp. 302–303; cf. *Commentarius in librum Ecclesiastes*, Cap. 1, vers. 11; *Quaestiones*, II, 3: Opera Omnia VI, Quaracchi 1891, p. 16.

25. Second Vatican Ecumenical Council, Dogmatic Constitution on Divine Revelation *Dei Verbum*, 3; cf. First Vatican Ecumenical Council, Dogmatic Constitution on the Catholic Faith *Dei Filius*, Chap. 2, De Revelatione: DS 3004.

9.   Reality, then is born of the word, as *creatura Verbi*, and everything is called to serve the word. Creation is the setting in which the entire history of the love between God and his creation develops; hence human salvation is the reason underlying everything. Contemplating the cosmos from the perspective of salvation history, we come to realize the unique and singular position occupied by man in creation: "God created man in his own image, in the image of God he created him: male and female he created them" (Gen 1:27). This enables us to acknowledge fully the precious gifts received from the Creator: the value of our body, the gift of reason, freedom, and conscience. Here too we discover what the philosophical tradition calls "the natural law."[26] In effect, "every human being who comes to consciousness and to responsibility has the experience of an inner call to do good"[27] and thus to avoid evil. As Saint Thomas Aquinas says, this principle is the basis of all the other precepts of the natural law.[28] Listening to the word of God leads us first and foremost to value the need to live in accordance with this law "written on human hearts" (cf. Rom 2:15; 7:23).[29] Jesus Christ then gives mankind the new law, the law of the Gospel, which takes up and eminently fulfills the natural law, setting us free from the law of sin, as a result of which, as Saint Paul says, "I can will what is right, but I cannot do it" (Rom 7:18). It likewise enables men and women, through grace, to share in the divine life and to overcome their selfishness.[30]

THE REALISM OF THE WORD

10.   Those who know God's word also know fully the significance of each creature. For if all things "hold together" in the one who is "before all things" (cf. Col 1:17), then those who build their lives on his word build in a truly sound and lasting way. The word of God makes us change our concept of realism: the realist is the one who recognizes in the word of God the foundation of all things.[31] This realism is particularly needed in our own time, when many things in which we trust for building our lives, things in which we are tempted to put our hopes, prove ephemeral. Possessions, pleasure, and power show themselves sooner or later to be incapable of fulfilling the deepest yearnings of the human heart. In building our lives we need solid foundations which will endure when human certainties fail. Truly, since "for ever, O Lord, your word is firmly fixed in the heavens" and the faithfulness of the Lord "endures to all generations" (Ps 119:89–90), whoever builds on this word builds the house of his life on rock (cf. Mt 7:24). May our heart be able to say to God each day: "You are my refuge

---

26. Cf. *Propositio* 13.

27. International Theological Commission, *In Search of a Universal Ethics: A New Look at the Natural Law*, Vatican City, 2009, No. 39.

28. Cf. *Summa Theologiae*, Ia-IIae, q. 94, a. 2.

29. Cf. Pontifical Biblical Commission, *The Bible and Morality: Biblical Roots of Christian Conduct* (May 11, 2008), Vatican City, 2008, Nos. 13, 32, 109.

30. Cf. International Theological Commission, *In Search of a Universal Ethics: A New Look at the Natural Law*, Vatican City, 2009, No. 102.

31. Cf. Benedict XVI, Homily during the Celebration of Terce at the Beginning of the First General Congregation of the Synod of Bishops (October 6, 2008): AAS 100 (2008), 758–761.

and my shield; I hope in your word" (Ps 119:114), and, like Saint Peter, may we entrust ourselves in our daily actions to the Lord Jesus: "At your word I will let down the nets" (Lk 5:5).

CHRISTOLOGY OF THE WORD

11.   From this glimpse at all reality as the handiwork of the Blessed Trinity through the divine Word, we can understand the statement made by the author of the *Letter to the Hebrews*: "in many and various ways God spoke of old to our fathers by the prophets; but in these last days he has spoken to us by a Son, whom he appointed the heir of all things, through whom also he created the world" (1:1–2). It is very beautiful to see how the entire Old Testament already appears to us as a history in which God communicates his word: indeed, "by his covenant with Abraham (cf. Gen 15:18) and, through Moses, with the race of Israel (cf. Ex 24:8), he gained a people for himself, and to them he revealed himself in words and deeds as the one, living, and true God. It was his plan that Israel might learn by experience God's ways with humanity and, by listening to the voice of God speaking to them through the prophets, might gradually understand his ways more fully and more clearly, and make them more widely known among the nations (cf. Ps 21:28–29; 95:1–3; Is 2:1–4; Jer 3:17)."[32]

This "condescension" of God is accomplished surpassingly in the incarnation of the Word. The eternal Word, expressed in creation and communicated in salvation history, in Christ became a man, "born of woman" (Gal 4:4). Here the word finds expression not primarily in discourse, concepts, or rules. Here we are set before the very person of Jesus. His unique and singular history is the definitive word which God speaks to humanity. We can see, then, why "being Christian is not the result of an ethical choice or a lofty idea, but the encounter with an event, a person, which gives life a new horizon and a definitive direction."[33] The constant renewal of this encounter and this awareness fills the hearts of believers with amazement at God's initiative, which human beings, with our own reason and imagination, could never have dreamt of. We are speaking of an unprecedented and humanly inconceivable novelty: "the word became flesh and dwelt among us" (Jn 1:14a). These words are no figure of speech; they point to a lived experience! Saint John, an eyewitness, tells us so: "We have beheld his glory, glory as of the only Son from the Father, full of grace and truth" (Jn 1:14b). The apostolic faith testifies that the eternal Word became one of us. The *divine Word* is truly expressed in *human words*.

12.   The patristic and medieval tradition, in contemplating this "Christology of the word," employed an evocative expression: *the word was "abbreviated."*[34] "The Fathers of the Church found in their Greek translation of the Old Testament a passage from the prophet Isaiah that Saint Paul also quotes in order to show how God's new ways had already been foretold in the Old Testament. There we

---

32. Second Vatican Ecumenical Council, Dogmatic Constitution on Divine Revelation *Dei Verbum*, 14.

33. Benedict XVI, Encyclical Letter *Deus caritas est* (December 25, 2005), 1: AAS 98 (2006), 217–218.

34. "Ho Logos pachynetai (or: brachynetai)." Cf. Origen, *Peri Archon*, I, 2,8: SC 252, 127–129.

read: 'The Lord made his word short, he abbreviated it' (Is 10:23; Rom 9:28). . . . The Son himself is the Word, the *Logos*: the eternal word became small—small enough to fit into a manger. He became a child, so that the word could be grasped by us."[35] Now the word is not simply audible; not only does it have a *voice*, now the word has a *face*, one which we can see: that of Jesus of Nazareth.[36]

Reading the Gospel accounts, we see how Jesus' own humanity appears in all its uniqueness precisely with regard to the word of God. In his perfect humanity he does the will of the Father at all times; Jesus hears his voice and obeys it with his entire being; he knows the Father and he keeps his word (cf. Jn 8:55); he speaks to us of what the Father has told him (cf. Jn 12:50); "I have given them the words which you gave me" (Jn 17:8). Jesus thus shows that he is the divine *Logos* which is given to us, but at the same time the new Adam, the true man, who unfailingly does not his own will but that of the Father. He "increased in wisdom and in stature, and in favor with God and man" (Lk 2:52). In a perfect way, he hears, embodies, and communicates to us the word of God (cf. Lk 5:1).

Jesus' mission is ultimately fulfilled in the paschal mystery: here we find ourselves before the "word of the cross" (1 Cor 1:18). The word is muted; it becomes mortal silence, for it has "spoken" exhaustively, holding back nothing of what it had to tell us. The Fathers of the Church, in pondering this mystery, attributed to the Mother of God this touching phrase: "Wordless is the Word of the Father, who made every creature which speaks, lifeless are the eyes of the one at whose word and whose nod all living things move."[37] Here that "greater" love, the love which gives its life for its friends (cf. Jn 15:13), is truly shared with us.

In this great mystery Jesus is revealed as *the word of the new and everlasting covenant*: divine freedom and human freedom have definitively met in his crucified flesh, in an indissoluble and eternally valid compact. Jesus himself, at the Last Supper, in instituting the Eucharist, had spoken of a "new and everlasting covenant" in the outpouring of his blood (cf. Mt 26:28; Mk 14:24; Lk 22:20), and shows himself to be the true sacrificial Lamb who brings about our definitive liberation from slavery.[38]

In the most luminous mystery of the resurrection, this silence of the word is shown in its authentic and definitive meaning. Christ, the incarnate, crucified, and risen Word of God, is Lord of all things; he is the victor, the *Pantocrator*, and so all things are gathered up forever in him (cf. Eph 1:10). Christ is thus "the light of the world" (Jn 8:12), the light which "shines in the darkness" (Jn 1:5) and which the darkness has not overcome (cf. Jn 1:5). Here we come to understand fully the meaning of the words of *Psalm 119*: "Your word is a lamp to my feet and a light to my path" (v. 105); the risen Word is this definitive light to our path.

---

35. Benedict XVI, *Homily on the Solemnity of the Birth of the Lord* (December 24, 2006): AAS 99 (2007), 12.

36. Cf. Final Message, II, 4–6.

37. Maximus the Confessor, *Life of Mary*, No. 89: *Testi mariani del primo millennio*, 2, Rome, 1989, p. 253.

38. Cf. Benedict XVI, Post-Synodal Apostolic Exhortation *Sacramentum caritatis* (February 22, 2007), 9–10: AAS 99 (2007), 111–112.

From the beginning, Christians realized that in Christ the word of God is present as a person. The word of God is the true light which men and women need. In the resurrection the Son of God truly emerged as the light of the world. Now, by living with him and in him, we can live in the light.

13.   Here, at the heart, as it were, of the "Christology of the word," it is important to stress the unity of the divine plan in the incarnate Word: the New Testament thus presents the paschal mystery as being in accordance with the Sacred Scriptures and as their deepest fulfillment. Saint Paul, in the *First Letter to the Corinthians*, states that Jesus Christ died for our sins "in accordance with the Scriptures" (15:3) and that he rose on the third day "in accordance with the Scriptures" (15:4). The Apostle thus relates the event of the Lord's death and resurrection to the history of the Old Covenant of God with his people. Indeed, he shows us that from that event history receives its inner logic and its true meaning. In the paschal mystery "the words of Scripture" are fulfilled; in other words, this death which took place "in accordance with the Scriptures" is an event containing a *logos*, an inner logic: the death of Christ testifies that the word of God became thoroughly human "flesh," human "history."[39] Similarly, the resurrection of Jesus takes place "on the third day in accordance with the Scriptures": since Jewish belief held that decay set in after the third day, the word of Scripture is fulfilled in Jesus who rises incorrupt. Thus Saint Paul, faithfully handing on the teaching of the Apostles (cf. 1 Cor 15:3), stresses that Christ's victory over death took place through the creative power of the word of God. This divine power brings hope and joy: this, in a word, is the liberating content of the paschal revelation. At Easter, God reveals himself and the power of the trinitarian love which shatters the baneful powers of evil and death.

Calling to mind these essential elements of our faith, we can contemplate the profound unity in Christ between creation, the new creation, and all salvation history. To use an example, we can compare the cosmos to a "book"—Galileo himself used this example—and consider it as "the work of an author who expresses himself through the 'symphony' of creation. In this symphony one finds, at a certain point, what would be called in musical terms a 'solo,' a theme entrusted to a single instrument or voice which is so important that the meaning of the entire work depends on it. This 'solo' is Jesus. . . . The Son of Man recapitulates in himself earth and heaven, creation and the Creator, flesh and Spirit. He is the center of the cosmos and of history, for in him converge without confusion the author and his work."[40]

THE ESCHATOLOGICAL DIMENSION OF THE WORD OF GOD

14.   In all of this, the Church gives voice to her awareness that with Jesus Christ she stands before the definitive word of God: he is "the first and the last" (Rev 1:17). He has given creation and history their definitive meaning; and hence we are called to live in time and in God's creation within this eschatological rhythm

---

39. Benedict XVI, General Audience (April 15, 2009): *L'Osservatore Romano*, April 16, 2009, p.1.

40. Id., Homily for the Solemnity of Epiphany (January 6, 2009): *L'Osservatore Romano*, January 7–8, 2009, p. 8.

of the word; "thus the Christian dispensation, since it is the new and definitive covenant, will never pass away; and no new public revelation is to be expected before the glorious manifestation of our Lord Jesus Christ (cf. 1 Tm 6:14 and Tit 2:13)."[41] Indeed, as the Fathers noted during the Synod, the "uniqueness of Christianity is manifested in the event which is Jesus Christ, the culmination of revelation, the fulfillment of God's promises and the mediator of the encounter between man and God. He who 'has made God known' (Jn 1:18) is the one, definitive word given to mankind."[42] Saint John of the Cross expresses this truth magnificently: "Since he has given us his Son, his only word (for he possesses no other), he spoke everything at once in this sole word—and he has no more to say . . . because what he spoke before to the prophets in parts, he has spoken all at once by giving us this All who is his Son. Any person questioning God or desiring some vision or revelation would be guilty not only of foolish behavior but also of offending him, by not fixing his eyes entirely on Christ and by living with the desire for some other novelty."[43]

Consequently the Synod pointed to the need to "help the faithful to distinguish the word of God from private revelations"[44] whose role "is not to 'complete' Christ's definitive revelation, but to help live more fully by it in a certain period of history."[45] The value of private revelations is essentially different from that of the one public revelation: the latter demands faith; in it God himself speaks to us through human words and the mediation of the living community of the Church. The criterion for judging the truth of a private revelation is its orientation to Christ himself. If it leads us away from him, then it certainly does not come from the Holy Spirit, who guides us more deeply into the Gospel, and not away from it. Private revelation is an aid to this faith, and it demonstrates its credibility precisely because it refers back to the one public revelation. Ecclesiastical approval of a private revelation essentially means that its message contains nothing contrary to faith and morals; it is licit to make it public and the faithful are authorized to give to it their prudent adhesion. A private revelation can introduce new emphases, give rise to new forms of piety, or deepen older ones. It can have a certain prophetic character (cf. 1 Thes 5:19–21) and can be a valuable aid for better understanding and living the Gospel at a certain time; consequently it should not be treated lightly. It is a help which is proffered, but its use is not obligatory. In any event, it must be a matter of nourishing faith, hope, and love, which are for everyone the permanent path of salvation.[46]

THE WORD OF GOD AND THE HOLY SPIRIT

15.   After reflecting on God's final and definitive word to the world, we need now to mention the mission of the Holy Spirit in relation to the divine word. In

41. Second Vatican Ecumenical Council, Dogmatic Constitution on Divine Revelation *Dei Verbum*, 4.

42. *Propositio* 4.

43. Saint John of the Cross, *Ascent of Mount Carmel*, II, 22.

44. *Propositio* 47.

45. *Catechism of the Catholic Church*, 67.

46. Cf. Congregation for the doctrine of the Faith, *The Message of Fatima* (June 26, 2000):*Enchiridion Vaticanum* 19, Nos. 974—1021.

fact there can be no authentic understanding of Christian revelation apart from the activity of the Paraclete. This is due to the fact that God's self-communication always involves the relationship of the Son and the Holy Spirit, whom Irenaeus of Lyons refers to as "the two hands of the Father."[47] Sacred Scripture itself speaks of the presence of the Holy Spirit in salvation history and particularly in the life of Jesus: he was conceived of the Virgin Mary by the power of the Holy Spirit (cf. Mt 1:18; Lk 1:35); at the beginning of his public mission, on the banks of the Jordan, he sees the Holy Spirit descend on him in the form of a dove (cf. Mt 3:16); in this same Spirit Jesus acts, speaks, and rejoices (cf. Lk 10:21); and in the Spirit he offers himself up (cf. Heb 9:14). As his mission draws to an end, according to the account of Saint John, Jesus himself clearly relates the giving of his life to the sending of the Spirit upon those who belong to him (cf. Jn 16:7). The Risen Jesus, bearing in his flesh the signs of the passion, then pours out the Spirit (cf. Jn 20:22), making his disciples sharers in his own mission (cf. Jn 20:21). The Holy Spirit was to teach the disciples all things and bring to their remembrance all that Christ had said (cf. Jn 14:26), since he, the Spirit of Truth (cf. Jn 15:26), will guide the disciples into all the truth (cf. Jn 16:13). Finally, in the *Acts of the Apostles*, we read that the Spirit descended on the Twelve gathered in prayer with Mary on the day of Pentecost (cf. 2:1–4), and impelled them to take up the mission of proclaiming to all peoples the Good News.[48]

The word of God is thus expressed in human words thanks to the working of the Holy Spirit. The missions of the Son and the Holy Spirit are inseparable and constitute a single economy of salvation. The same Spirit who acts in the incarnation of the Word in the womb of the Virgin Mary is the Spirit who guides Jesus throughout his mission and is promised to the disciples. The same Spirit who spoke through the prophets sustains and inspires the Church in her task of proclaiming the word of God and in the preaching of the Apostles; finally, it is this Spirit who inspires the authors of Sacred Scripture.

16.   Conscious of this pneumatological horizon, the Synod Fathers highlighted the importance of the Holy Spirit's work in the life of the Church and in the hearts of believers in relation to Sacred Scripture:[49] without the efficacious working of the "Spirit of Truth" (Jn 14:16), the words of the Lord cannot be understood. As Saint Irenaeus states: "Those who do not share in the Spirit do not draw from the bosom of their mother [the Church] the food of life; they receive nothing from the purest fountain that flows from the body of Christ."[50] Just as the word of God comes to us in the body of Christ, in his Eucharistic body and in the body of the Scriptures, through the working of the Holy Spirit, so too it can only be truly received and understood through that same Spirit.

The great writers of the Christian tradition speak unanimously of the place of the Holy Spirit in the relationship which believers are to have with the Scriptures.

---

47. *Adversus haereses*, IV, 7, 4: PG 7, 992–993; V, 1, 3: PG 7, 1123; V, 6, 1: PG 7, 1137; V, 28, 4: PG 7, 1200.

48. Cf. Benedict XVI, Post-Synodal Apostolic Exhortation *Sacramentum caritatis* (February 22, 2007), 12: AAS 99 (2007), 113–114.

49. Cf. *Propositio* 5.

50. *Adversus haereses*, III, 24, 1: PG 7, 966.

Saint John Chrysostom states that Scripture "needs the revelation of the Spirit, so that by discovering the true meaning of the things enclosed therein, we can reap abundant benefits."[51] Saint Jerome is likewise firmly convinced that "we cannot come to an understanding of Scripture without the assistance of the Holy Spirit who inspired it."[52] Saint Gregory the Great nicely emphasizes the work of the Spirit in the formation and interpretation of the Bible: "He himself created the words of the holy Testaments, he himself revealed their meaning."[53] Richard of Saint Victor points out that we need "the eyes of doves," enlightened and taught by the Spirit, in order to understand the sacred text.[54]

Here too I would like to emphasize the very significant witness to the relationship between the Holy Spirit and Scripture which we find in the texts of the liturgy, where the word of God is proclaimed, heard, and explained to the faithful. We find a witness to this in the ancient prayers which in the form of an epiclesis invoke the Spirit before the proclamation of the readings: "Send your Paraclete Spirit into our hearts and make us understand the Scriptures which he has inspired; and grant that I may interpret them worthily, so that the faithful assembled here may profit thereby." We also find prayers which, at the end of the homily, again ask God to send the gift of the Spirit upon the faithful: "God our Savior . . . we implore you for this people: send upon them the Holy Spirit; may the Lord Jesus come to visit them, speak to the minds of all, dispose their hearts to faith and lead our souls to you, God of mercies."[55] This makes it clear that we cannot come to understand the meaning of the word unless we are open to the working of the Paraclete in the Church and in the hearts of believers.

TRADITION AND SCRIPTURE

17.   In reaffirming the profound connection between the Holy Spirit and the word of God, we have also laid the basis for an understanding of the significance and the decisive value of the living Tradition and the Sacred Scriptures in the Church. Indeed, since God "so loved the world that he gave his only Son" (Jn 3:16), the divine word, spoken in time, is bestowed and "consigned" to the Church in a definitive way, so that the proclamation of salvation can be communicated effectively in every time and place. As the Dogmatic Constitution *Dei Verbum* reminds us, Jesus Christ himself "commanded the Apostles to preach the Gospel—promised beforehand by the prophets, fulfilled in his own person and promulgated by his own lips—to all as the source of all saving truth and moral law, communicating God's gifts to them. This was faithfully carried out; it was carried out by the Apostles who handed on, by oral preaching, by their example, by their ordinances, what they themselves had received—whether from the lips

---

51. *Homiliae in Genesim*, XXII, 1: PG 53, 175.

52. *Epistula* 120, 10: CSEL 55, 500–506.

53. *Homiliae in Ezechielem*, I, VII, 17: CC 142, p. 94.

54. "Oculi ergo devotae animae sunt columbarum quia sensus eius per Spiritum sanctum sunt illuminati et edocti, spiritualia sapientes. Nunc quidem aperitur animae talis sensus, ut intellegat Scripturas": Richard of Saint Victor, *Explicatio in Cantica Canticorum*, 15: PL 196, 450B and D.

55. *Sacramentarium Serapionis* II (XX): *Didascalia et Constitutiones Apostolorum*, ed F.X. Funk, II, Paderborn, 1906, p. 161.

of Christ, from his way of life and his works, or by coming to know it through the prompting of the Holy Spirit; it was carried out by those Apostles and others associated with them who, under the inspiration of the same Holy Spirit, committed the message of salvation to writing."[56]

The Second Vatican Council also states that this Tradition of apostolic origin is a living and dynamic reality: it "makes progress in the Church, with the help of the Holy Spirit;" yet not in the sense that it changes in its truth, which is perennial. Rather, "there is a growth in insight into the realities and the words that are being passed on," through contemplation and study, with the understanding granted by deeper spiritual experience and by the "preaching of those who, on succeeding to the office of bishop, have received the sure charism of truth."[57]

The living Tradition is essential for enabling the Church to grow through time in the understanding of the truth revealed in the Scriptures; indeed, "by means of the same tradition, the full canon of the sacred books is known to the Church and the holy Scriptures themselves are more thoroughly understood and constantly made effective in the Church."[58] Ultimately, it is the living Tradition of the Church which makes us adequately understand Sacred Scripture as the word of God. Although the word of God precedes and exceeds Sacred Scripture, nonetheless Scripture, as inspired by God, contains the divine word (cf. 2 Tim 3:16) "in an altogether singular way."[59]

18.   We see clearly, then, how important it is for the People of God to be properly taught and trained to approach the Sacred Scriptures in relation to the Church's living Tradition, and to recognize in them the very word of God. Fostering such an approach in the faithful is very important from the standpoint of the spiritual life. Here it might be helpful to recall the analogy drawn by the Fathers of the Church between the word of God which became "flesh" and the word which became a "book."[60] The Dogmatic Constitution *Dei Verbum* takes up this ancient tradition which holds, as Saint Ambrose says,[61] that "the body of the Son is the Scripture which we have received," and declares that "the words of God, expressed in human language, are in every way like human speech, just as the word of the eternal Father, when he took on himself the weak flesh of human beings, became like them."[62] When understood in this way, Sacred Scripture presents itself to us, in the variety of its many forms and content, as a single reality. Indeed, "through all the words of Sacred Scripture, God speaks only one single word, his one utterance, in whom he expresses himself completely (cf. Heb 1:1–3)."[63]

---

56. Second Vatican Ecumenical Council, Dogmatic Constitution on Divine Revelation *Dei Verbum*, 7.

57. Ibid., 8.

58. Ibid.

59. Cf. *Propositio 3*.

60. Cf. Final Message II, 5.

61. *Expositio Evangelii secundum Lucam*, 6, 33: PL 15, 1677.

62. Second Vatican Ecumenical Council, Dogmatic Constitution on Divine Revelation *Dei Verbum*, 13.

63. *Catechism of the Catholic Church*, 102; Cf. also Rupert of Deutz, *De operibus Spiritus Sancti*, I, 6: SC 131:72–74.

Saint Augustine had already made the point clearly: "Remember that one alone is the discourse of God which unfolds in all Sacred Scripture, and one alone is the word which resounds on the lips of all the holy writers."[64]

In short, by the work of the Holy Spirit and under the guidance of the magisterium, the Church hands on to every generation all that has been revealed in Christ. The Church lives in the certainty that her Lord, who spoke in the past, continues today to communicate his word in her living Tradition and in Sacred Scripture. Indeed, the word of God is given to us in Sacred Scripture as an inspired testimony to revelation; together with the Church's living Tradition, it constitutes the supreme rule of faith.[65]

SACRED SCRIPTURE, INSPIRATION, AND TRUTH

19.   A key concept for understanding the sacred text as the word of God in human words is certainly that of *inspiration*. Here too we can suggest an analogy: as the word of God became flesh by the power of the Holy Spirit in the womb of the Virgin Mary, so Sacred Scripture is born from the womb of the Church by the power of the same Spirit. Sacred Scripture is "the word of God set down in writing under the inspiration of the Holy Spirit."[66] In this way one recognizes the full importance of the human author who wrote the inspired texts and, at the same time, God himself as the true author.

As the Synod Fathers affirmed, the theme of inspiration is clearly decisive for an adequate approach to the Scriptures and their correct interpretation,[67] which for its part is to be done in the same Spirit in whom the sacred texts were written.[68] Whenever our awareness of its inspiration grows weak, we risk reading Scripture as an object of historical curiosity and not as the work of the Holy Spirit in which we can hear the Lord himself speak and recognize his presence in history.

The Synod Fathers also stressed the link between the theme of inspiration and that of the *truth of the Scriptures*.[69] A deeper study of the process of inspiration will doubtless lead to a greater understanding of the truth contained in the sacred books. As the Council's teaching states in this regard, the inspired books teach the truth: "since, therefore, all that the inspired authors, or sacred writers, affirm should be regarded as affirmed by the Holy Spirit, we must acknowledge that the books of Scripture firmly, faithfully, and without error, teach that truth which God, for the sake of our salvation, wished to see confided to the Sacred Scriptures. Thus, 'all scripture is inspired by God and is useful for teaching, for

---

64. *Enarrationes in Psalmos*, 103, IV, 1: PL 37, 1378. Similar statements in Origen, *In Iohannem* V, 5–6: SC 120, pp. 380–384.

65. Cf. Second Vatican Ecumenical Council, Dogmatic Constitution on Divine Revelation *Dei Verbum*, 21.

66. Ibid., 9.

67. Cf. *Propositiones* 5 and 12.

68. Cf. Second Vatican Ecumenical Council, Dogmatic Constitution on Divine Revelation *Dei Verbum*, 12.

69. Cf. *Propositio* 12.

reproof, for correction, and for training in righteousness, so that the man of God may be proficient, equipped for every good work' (2 Tm 3:16–17, Greek)."[70]

Certainly theological reflection has always considered inspiration and truth as two key concepts for an ecclesial hermeneutic of the Sacred Scriptures. Nonetheless, one must acknowledge the need today for a fuller and more adequate study of these realities, in order better to respond to the need to interpret the sacred texts in accordance with their nature. Here I would express my fervent hope that research in this field will progress and bear fruit both for biblical science and for the spiritual life of the faithful.

GOD THE FATHER, SOURCE AND ORIGIN OF THE WORD

20.   The economy of revelation has its beginning and origin in God the Father. By his word "the heavens were made, and all their host by the breath of his mouth" (Ps 33:6). It is he who has given us "the light of the knowledge of the glory of God in the face of Christ" (2 Cor 4:6; cf. Mt 16:17; Lk 9:29).

In the Son, "*Logos* made flesh" (cf. Jn 1:14), who came to accomplish the will of the one who sent him (cf. Jn 4:34), God, the source of revelation, reveals himself as Father and brings to completion the divine pedagogy which had previously been carried out through the words of the prophets and the wondrous deeds accomplished in creation and in the history of his people and all mankind. The revelation of God the Father culminates in the Son's gift of the Paraclete (cf. Jn 14:16), the Spirit of the Father and the Son, who guides us "into all the truth" (Jn 16:13).

All God's promises find their "yes" in Jesus Christ (cf. 2 Cor 1:20). Men and women are thus enabled to set out on the way that leads to the Father (cf. Jn 14:6), so that in the end "God may be everything to everyone" (1 Cor 15:28).

21.   As the cross of Christ demonstrates, God also speaks by his silence. The silence of God, the experience of the distance of the almighty Father, is a decisive stage in the earthly journey of the Son of God, the incarnate Word. Hanging from the wood of the cross, he lamented the suffering caused by that silence: "My God, my God, why have you forsaken me?" (Mk 15:34; Mt 27:46). Advancing in obedience to his very last breath, in the obscurity of death, Jesus called upon the Father. He commended himself to him at the moment of passage, through death, to eternal life: "Father, into your hands I commend my spirit" (Lk 23:46).

This experience of Jesus reflects the situation of all those who, having heard and acknowledged God's word, must also confront his silence. This has been the experience of countless saints and mystics, and even today is part of the journey of many believers. God's silence prolongs his earlier words. In these moments of darkness, he speaks through the mystery of his silence. Hence, in the dynamic of Christian revelation, silence appears as an important expression of the word of God.

---

70. Second Vatican Ecumenical Council, Dogmatic Constitution on Divine Revelation *Dei Verbum*, 11.

OUR RESPONSE TO THE GOD WHO SPEAKS

CALLED TO THE COVENANT WITH GOD

22.   By emphasizing the many forms of the word, we have been able to contemplate the number of ways in which God speaks to and encounters men and women, making himself known in dialogue. Certainly, as the Synod Fathers stated, "dialogue, when we are speaking of revelation, entails the *primacy* of the word of God addressed to man."[71] The mystery of the Covenant expresses this relationship between God who calls man with his word, and man who responds, albeit making clear that it is not a matter of a meeting of two peers; what we call the Old and New Covenant is not a contract between two equal parties, but a pure gift of God. By this gift of his love God bridges every distance and truly makes us his "partners," in order to bring about the nuptial mystery of the love between Christ and the Church. In this vision every man and woman appears as someone to whom the word speaks, challenges, and calls to enter this dialogue of love through a free response. Each of us is thus enabled by God to *hear and respond* to his word. We were created in the word and we live in the word; we cannot understand ourselves unless we are open to this dialogue. The word of God discloses the filial and relational nature of human existence. We are indeed called by grace to be conformed to Christ, the Son of the Father, and, in him, to be transformed.

GOD HEARS US AND RESPONDS TO OUR QUESTIONS

23.   In this dialogue with God we come to understand ourselves and we discover an answer to our heart's deepest questions. The word of God in fact is not inimical to us; it does not stifle our authentic desires, but rather illuminates them, purifies them, and brings them to fulfillment. How important it is for our time to discover that *God alone responds to the yearning present in the heart of every man and woman!* Sad to say, in our days, and in the West, there is a widespread notion that God is extraneous to people's lives and problems, and that his very presence can be a threat to human autonomy. Yet the entire economy of salvation demonstrates that God speaks and acts in history for our good and our integral salvation. Thus it is decisive, from the pastoral standpoint, to present the word of God in its capacity to enter into dialogue with the everyday problems which people face. Jesus himself says that he came that we might have life in abundance (cf. Jn 10:10). Consequently, we need to make every effort to share the word of God as an openness to our problems, a response to our questions, a broadening of our values and the fulfillment of our aspirations. The Church's pastoral activity needs to bring out clearly how God listens to our need and our plea for help. As Saint Bonaventure says in the *Breviloquium*: "The fruit of Sacred Scripture is not any fruit whatsoever, but the very fullness of eternal happiness. Sacred Scripture is the book containing the words of eternal life, so that we may not only believe in, but also possess eternal life, in which we will see and love, and all our desires will be fulfilled."[72]

---

71. *Propositio* 4.
72. *Prol*: Opera Omnia V, Quaracchi 1891, pp. 201–202.

24.   The word of God draws each of us into a conversation with the Lord: the God who speaks teaches us how to speak to him. Here we naturally think of the *Book of Psalms*, where God gives us words to speak to him, to place our lives before him, and thus to make life itself a path to God.[73] In the Psalms we find expressed every possible human feeling set masterfully in the sight of God; joy and pain, distress and hope, fear and trepidation: here all find expression. Along with the Psalms we think too of the many other passages of Sacred Scripture which express our turning to God in intercessory prayer (cf. Ex 33:12–16), in exultant songs of victory (cf. Ex 15) or in sorrow at the difficulties experienced in carrying out our mission (cf. Jer 20:7–18). In this way our word to God becomes God's word, thus confirming the dialogical nature of all Christian revelation,[74] and our whole existence becomes a dialogue with the God who speaks and listens, who calls us and gives direction to our lives. Here the word of God reveals that our entire life is under the divine call.[75]

THE WORD OF GOD AND FAITH

25.   "'The obedience of faith' (Rom 16:26; cf. Rom 1:5; 2 Cor 10:5–6) must be our response to God who reveals. By faith one freely commits oneself entirely to God, making 'the full submission of intellect and will to God who reveals' and willingly assenting to the revelation given by God."[76] In these words the Dogmatic Constitution *Dei Verbum* gave precise expression to the stance which we must have with regard to God. *The proper human response to the God who speaks is faith.* Here we see clearly that "in order to accept revelation, man must open his mind and heart to the working of the Holy Spirit who enables him to understand the word of God present in the Sacred Scriptures."[77] It is the preaching of the divine word, in fact, which gives rise to faith, whereby we give our heartfelt assent to the truth which has been revealed to us and we commit ourselves entirely to Christ: "faith comes from what is heard, and what is heard comes from the word of Christ" (Rom 10:17). The whole history of salvation progressively demonstrates this profound bond between the word of God and the faith which arises from an encounter with Christ. Faith thus takes shape as an encounter with a person to whom we entrust our whole life. Christ Jesus remains present today in history, in his body which is the Church; for this reason our act of faith is at once both personal and ecclesial.

SIN AS A REFUSAL TO HEAR THE WORD OF GOD

26.   The word of God also inevitably reveals the tragic possibility that human freedom can withdraw from this covenant dialogue with God for which we were

---

73. Cf. Benedict XVI, Address to Representatives of the World of Culture at the "Collège des Bernardins" *in Paris* (September 12, 2008): AAS 100 (2008), 721–730.

74. Cf. *Propositio* 4.

75. Cf. *Relatio post disceptationem*, 12.

76. Second Vatican Ecumenical Council, Dogmatic Constitution on Divine Revelation *Dei Verbum*, 5.

77. *Propositio* 4.

created. The divine word also discloses the sin that lurks in the human heart. Quite frequently in both the Old and in the New Testament, we find sin described as a *refusal to hear the word*, as a *breaking of the covenant* and thus as being closed to God who calls us to communion with himself.[78] Sacred Scripture shows how man's sin is essentially disobedience and refusal to hear. The radical obedience of Jesus even to his death on the cross (cf. Phil 2:8) completely unmasks this sin. His obedience brings about the New Covenant between God and man, and grants us the possibility of reconciliation. Jesus was sent by the Father as a sacrifice of atonement for our sins and for those of the whole world (cf. 1 Jn 2:2; 4:10; Heb 7:27). We are thus offered the merciful possibility of redemption and the start of a new life in Christ. For this reason it is important that the faithful be taught to acknowledge that the root of sin lies in the refusal to hear the word of the Lord, and to accept in Jesus, the Word of God, the forgiveness which opens us to salvation.

MARY, "MOTHER OF GOD'S WORD" AND "MOTHER OF FAITH"

27.   The Synod Fathers declared that the basic aim of the Twelfth Assembly was "to renew the Church's faith in the word of God." To do so, we need to look to the one in whom the interplay between the word of God and faith was brought to perfection, that is, to the Virgin Mary, "who by her 'yes' to the word of the covenant and her mission, perfectly fulfills the divine vocation of humanity."[79] The human reality created through the word finds its most perfect image in Mary's obedient faith. From the Annunciation to Pentecost she appears as a woman completely open to the will of God. She is the Immaculate Conception, the one whom God made "full of grace" (cf. Lk 1:28) and unconditionally docile to his word (cf. Lk 1:38). Her obedient faith shapes her life at every moment before God's plan. A Virgin ever attentive to God's word, she lives completely attuned to that word; she treasures in her heart the events of her Son, piecing them together as if in a single mosaic (cf. Lk 2:19, 51).[80]

In our day the faithful need to be helped to see more clearly the link between Mary of Nazareth and the faith-filled hearing of God's word. I would encourage scholars as well to study the relationship between *Mariology and the theology of the word*. This could prove most beneficial both for the spiritual life and for theological and biblical studies. Indeed, what the understanding of the faith has enabled us to know about Mary stands at the heart of Christian truth. The incarnation of the word cannot be conceived apart from the freedom of this young woman who by her assent decisively cooperated with the entrance of the eternal into time. Mary is the image of the Church in attentive hearing of the word of God, which took flesh in her. Mary also symbolizes openness to God and others; an active listening which interiorizes and assimilates, one in which the word becomes a way of life.

---

78. For example: Dt 28:1–2, 15, 45; 32:1; among the prophets, see: Jer 7:22–28; Ez 2:8; 3:10; 6:3; 13:2; up to the latest: cf. Zech 3:8. For Saint Paul, cf. Rom 10:14–18; 1 Th 2:13.

79. *Propositio* 55.

80. Cf. Benedict XVI, Post-Synodal Apostolic Exhortation *Sacramentum caritatis* (February 22, 2007), 33: AAS 99 (2007), 132–133.

28.   Here I would like to mention Mary's familiarity with the word of God. This is clearly evident in the *Magnificat*. There we see in some sense how she identifies with the word, enters into it; in this marvelous canticle of faith, the Virgin sings the praises of the Lord in his own words: "The *Magnificat*—a portrait, so to speak, of her soul—is entirely woven from threads of Holy Scripture, threads drawn from the word of God. Here we see how completely at home Mary is with the word of God, with ease she moves in and out of it. She speaks and thinks with the word of God; the word of God becomes her word, and her word issues from the word of God. Here we see how her thoughts are attuned to the thoughts of God, how her will is one with the will of God. Since Mary is completely imbued with the word of God, she is able to become the Mother of the Word Incarnate."[81]

Furthermore, in looking to the Mother of God, we see how God's activity in the world always engages our freedom, because through faith the divine word transforms us. Our apostolic and pastoral work can never be effective unless we learn from Mary how to be shaped by the working of God within us: "devout and loving attention to the figure of Mary as the model and archetype of the Church's faith is of capital importance for bringing about in our day a concrete paradigm shift in the Church's relation with the word, both in prayerful listening and in generous commitment to mission and proclamation."[82]

As we contemplate in the Mother of God a life totally shaped by the word, we realize that we too are called to enter into the mystery of faith, whereby Christ comes to dwell in our lives. Every Christian believer, Saint Ambrose reminds us, in some way interiorly conceives and gives birth to the word of God: even though there is only one Mother of Christ in the flesh, in the faith Christ is the progeny of us all.[83] Thus, what took place for Mary can daily take place in each of us, in the hearing of the word and in the celebration of the sacraments.

THE INTERPRETATION OF SACRED SCRIPTURE IN THE CHURCH

THE CHURCH AS THE PRIMARY SETTING FOR BIBLICAL HERMENEUTICS

29.   Another major theme that emerged during the Synod, to which I would now like to draw attention, is the *interpretation of Sacred Scripture in the Church*. The intrinsic link between the word and faith makes clear that authentic biblical hermeneutics can only be had within the faith of the Church, which has its paradigm in Mary's *fiat*. Saint Bonaventure states that without faith there is no key to throw open the sacred text: "This is the knowledge of Jesus Christ, from whom, as from a fountain, flow forth the certainty and the understanding of all Sacred Scripture. Therefore it is impossible for anyone to attain to knowledge of that truth unless he first have infused faith in Christ, which is the lamp, the gate, and the foundation of all Scripture."[84] And Saint Thomas Aquinas,

---

81. Id., Encyclical Letter *Deus caritas est* (December 25, 2005), 41: AAS 98 (2006), 251.
82. *Propositio* 55.
83. Cf. *Expositio Evangelii secundum Lucam*, 2, 19: PL 15, 1559–1560.
84. *Breviloquium*, *Prol.*: Opera Omnia, V, Quaracchi 1891, pp. 201–202.

citing Saint Augustine, insists that "the letter, even that of the Gospel, would kill, were there not the inward grace of healing faith."[85]

Here we can point to a fundamental criterion of biblical hermeneutics: *the primary setting for scriptural interpretation is the life of the Church*. This is not to uphold the ecclesial context as an extrinsic rule to which exegetes must submit, but rather is something demanded by the very nature of the Scriptures and the way they gradually came into being. "Faith traditions formed the living context for the literary activity of the authors of Sacred Scripture. Their insertion into this context also involved a sharing in both the liturgical and external life of the communities, in their intellectual world, in their culture, and in the ups and downs of their shared history. In like manner, the interpretation of Sacred Scripture requires full participation on the part of exegetes in the life and faith of the believing community of their own time."[86] Consequently, "since Sacred Scripture must be read and interpreted in the light of the same Spirit through whom it was written,"[87] exegetes, theologians, and the whole people of God must approach it as what it really is, the word of God conveyed to us through human words (cf. 1 Thes 2:13). This is a constant datum implicit in the Bible itself: "No prophecy of scripture is a matter of one's own interpretation, because no prophecy ever came by the impulse of man, but men moved by the Holy Spirit spoke from God" (2 Pt 1:20–21). Moreover, it is the faith of the Church that recognizes in the Bible the word of God; as Saint Augustine memorably put it: "I would not believe the Gospel, had not the authority of the Catholic Church led me to do so."[88] The Holy Spirit, who gives life to the Church, enables us to interpret the Scriptures authoritatively. The Bible is the Church's book, and its essential place in the Church's life gives rise to its genuine interpretation.

30.   Saint Jerome recalls that we can never read Scripture simply on our own. We come up against too many closed doors and we slip too easily into error. The Bible was written by the People of God for the People of God, under the inspiration of the Holy Spirit. Only in this communion with the People of God can we truly enter as a "we" into the heart of the truth that God himself wishes to convey to us.[89] Jerome, for whom "ignorance of the Scriptures is ignorance of Christ,"[90] states that the ecclesial dimension of biblical interpretation is not a requirement imposed from without: the Book is the very voice of the pilgrim People of God, and only within the faith of this People are we, so to speak, attuned to understand Sacred Scripture. An authentic interpretation of the Bible must always be in harmony with the faith of the Catholic Church. He thus wrote to a priest: "Remain firmly attached to the traditional doctrine that you have been taught,

---

85. *Summa Theologiae*, Ia-IIae, q. 106, art. 2.

86. Pontifical Biblical Commission, *The Interpretation of the Bible in the Church* (April 15, 1993), III, A, 3: *Enchiridion Vaticanum* 13, No. 3035.

87. Second Vatican Ecumenical Council, Dogmatic Constitution on Divine Revelation *Dei Verbum*, 12.

88. *Contra epistulam Manichaei quam vocant fundamenti*, V, 6: PL 42, 176.

89. Cf. Benedict XVI, General Audience (November 14, 2007): *Insegnamenti* III 2 (2007), 586–591.

90. *Commentariorum in Isaiam libri*, Prol.: PL 24, 17.

so that you may exhort according to sound doctrine and confound those who contradict it."[91]

Approaches to the sacred text that prescind from faith might suggest interesting elements on the level of textual structure and form, but would inevitably prove merely preliminary and structurally incomplete efforts. As the Pontifical Biblical Commission, echoing an accepted principle of modern hermeneutics, has stated: "access to a proper understanding of biblical texts is only granted to the person who has an affinity with what the text is saying on the basis of life experience."[92] All this brings out more clearly the relationship between the spiritual life and scriptural hermeneutics. "As the reader matures in the life of the Spirit, so there grows also his or her capacity to understand the realities of which the Bible speaks."[93] The intensity of an authentic ecclesial experience can only lead to the growth of genuine understanding in faith where the Scriptures are concerned; conversely, reading the Scriptures in faith leads to growth in ecclesial life itself. Here we can see once again the truth of the celebrated dictum of Saint Gregory the Great: "The divine words grow together with the one who reads them."[94] Listening to the word of God introduces and increases ecclesial communion with all those who walk by faith.

"THE SOUL OF SACRED THEOLOGY"

31.   "The study of the sacred page should be, as it were, the very soul of theology:"[95] this quotation from the Dogmatic Constitution *Dei Verbum* has become increasingly familiar over the years. Theological and exegetical scholarship, in the period after the Second Vatican Council, made frequent reference to this expression as symbolic of the renewed interest in Sacred Scripture. The Twelfth Assembly of the Synod of Bishops also frequently alluded to this well-known phrase in order to express the relationship between historical research and a hermeneutic of faith where the sacred text is concerned. The Fathers acknowledged with joy that study of the word of God in the Church has grown in recent decades, and they expressed *heartfelt gratitude to the many exegetes and theologians* who with dedication, commitment, and competence continue to make an essential contribution to the deeper understanding of the meaning of the Scriptures, as they address the complex issues facing biblical studies in our day.[96] *Sincere gratitude was also expressed to the members of the Pontifical Biblical Commission*, past and present, who in close collaboration with the Congregation for the Doctrine of the Faith continue to offer their expertise in the examination of particular questions raised by the study of Sacred Scripture.

---

91. *Epistula* 52:7: CSEL 54, p. 426.

92. Pontifical Biblical Commission, *The Interpretation of the Bible in the Church* (April 15, 1993), II, A, 2: *Enchiridion Vaticanum* 13, No. 2988.

93. Ibid., II, A, 2: *Enchiridion Vaticanum* 13, No. 2991.

94. *Homiliae in Ezechielem* I, VII, 8: PL 76, 843D.

95. Second Vatican Ecumenical Council, Dogmatic Constitution on Divine Revelation *Dei Verbum*, 24; cf. Leo XIII, Encyclical Letter *Providentissimus Deus* (November 18, 1893), Pars II, sub fine: ASS 26 (1893–94), 269–292; Benedict XV, Encyclical Letter *Spiritus Paraclitus* (September 15, 1920), Pars III: AAS 12 (1920), 385–422.

96. Cf. *Propositio* 26.

The Synod likewise felt a need to look into the present state of biblical studies and their standing within the field of theology. The pastoral effectiveness of the Church's activity and the spiritual life of the faithful depend to a great extent on the fruitfulness of the relationship between exegesis and theology. For this reason, I consider it important to take up some reflections that emerged in the discussion of this topic during the Synod sessions.

THE DEVELOPMENT OF BIBLICAL STUDIES AND THE CHURCH'S MAGISTERIUM

32.   Before all else, we need to acknowledge the benefits that historical-critical exegesis and other recently-developed methods of textual analysis have brought to the life of the Church.[97] For the Catholic understanding of Sacred Scripture, attention to such methods is indispensable, linked as it is to the realism of the Incarnation: "This necessity is a consequence of the Christian principle formulated in the Gospel of John 1:14: *Verbum caro factum est*. The historical fact is a constitutive dimension of the Christian faith. The history of salvation is not mythology, but a true history, and it should thus be studied with the methods of serious historical research."[98] The study of the Bible requires a knowledge of these methods of enquiry and their suitable application. While it is true that scholarship has come to a much greater appreciation of their importance in the modern period, albeit not everywhere to the same degree, nonetheless the sound ecclesial tradition has always demonstrated a love for the study of the "letter." Here we need but recall the monastic culture which is the ultimate foundation of European culture; at its root lies a concern for the word. The desire for God includes love for the word in all its dimensions: "because in the word of the Bible God comes to us and we to him, we must learn to penetrate the secret of language, to understand it in its structure and its mode of expression. Thus, because of the search for God, the secular sciences which lead to a greater understanding of language became important."[99]

33.   The Church's living magisterium, which is charged with "giving an authentic interpretation of the word of God, whether in its written form or in the form of tradition,"[100] intervened in a prudent and balanced way regarding the correct response to the introduction of new methods of historical analysis. I think in particular of the Encyclicals *Providentissimus Deus* of Pope Leo XIII and *Divino afflante Spiritu* of Pope Pius XII. My venerable predecessor John Paul II recalled the importance of these documents on the centenary and the fiftieth anniversary respectively of their promulgation.[101] Pope Leo XIII's intervention had the

---

97. Cf. Pontifical Biblical Commission, *The Interpretation of the Bible in the Church* (April 15, 1993), A-B: *Enchiridion Vaticanum* 13, nos. 2846–3150.

98. Benedict XVI, Intervention in the Fourteenth General Congregation of the Synod (October 14, 2008): *Insegnamenti* IV, 2 (2008), 492; cf. *Propositio* 25.

99. Id., Address to Representatives of the World of Culture at the "Collège des Bernardins" in Paris (September 12, 2008): AAS 100 (2008), 722–723.

100. Second Vatican Ecumenical Council, Dogmatic Constitution on Divine Revelation *Dei Verbum*, 10.

101. Cf. John Paul II, Address for the Celebration of the Centenary of the Encyclical *Providentissimus Deus* and the Fiftieth Anniversary of the Encyclical *Divino afflante Spiritu* (April 23, 1993): AAS 86 (1994), 232–243.

merit of protecting the Catholic interpretation of the Bible from the inroads of rationalism, without, however, seeking refuge in a spiritual meaning detached from history. Far from shunning scientific criticism, the Church was wary only of "preconceived opinions that claim to be based on science, but which in reality surreptitiously cause science to depart from its domain."[102] Pope Pius XII, on the other hand, was faced with attacks on the part of those who proposed a so-called mystical exegesis which rejected any form of scientific approach. The Encyclical *Divino afflante Spiritu* was careful to avoid any hint of a dichotomy between "scientific exegesis" for use in apologetics and "spiritual interpretation meant for internal use;" rather it affirmed both the "theological significance of the literal sense, methodically defined" and the fact that "determining the spiritual sense . . . belongs itself to the realm of exegetical science."[103] In this way, both documents rejected "a split between the human and the divine, between scientific research and respect for the faith, between the literal sense and the spiritual sense."[104] This balance was subsequently maintained by the 1993 document of the Pontifical Biblical Commission: "in their work of interpretation, Catholic exegetes must never forget that what they are interpreting is the *word of God*. Their common task is not finished when they have simply determined sources, defined forms, or explained literary procedures. They arrive at the true goal of their work only when they have explained the meaning of the biblical text as God's word for today."[105]

THE COUNCIL'S BIBLICAL HERMENEUTIC: A DIRECTIVE TO BE APPROPRIATED

34.   Against this background, one can better appreciate the great principles of interpretation proper to Catholic exegesis set forth by the Second Vatican Council, especially in the Dogmatic Constitution *Dei Verbum*: "Seeing that, in Sacred Scripture, God speaks through human beings in human fashion, it follows that the interpreters of Sacred Scripture, if they are to ascertain what God has wished to communicate to us, should carefully search out the meaning which the sacred writers really had in mind, that meaning which God had thought well to manifest through the medium of their words."[106] On the one hand, the Council emphasizes the study of literary genres and historical context as basic elements for understanding the meaning intended by the sacred author. On the other hand, since Scripture must be interpreted in the same Spirit in which it was written, the Dogmatic Constitution indicates three fundamental criteria for an appreciation of the divine dimension of the Bible: 1) the text must be interpreted with attention to *the unity of the whole of Scripture*; nowadays this is called canonical exegesis; 2) account is be taken of the *living Tradition of the whole Church*; and, finally, 3) respect must be shown for *the analogy of faith*. "Only where both methodological levels, the historical-critical and the theological,

---

102. Ibid., 4: AAS 86 (1994), 235.
103. Ibid., 5: AAS 86 (1994), 235.
104. Ibid., 5: AAS 86 (1994), 236.
105. Pontifical Biblical Commission, *The Interpretation of the Bible in the Church* (April 15, 1993), III, C, 1: *Enchiridion Vaticanum* 13, no. 3065.
106. No. 12.

are respected, can one speak of a theological exegesis, an exegesis worthy of this book."[107]

The Synod Fathers rightly stated that the positive fruit yielded by the use of modern historical-critical research is undeniable. While today's academic exegesis, including that of Catholic scholars, is highly competent in the field of historical-critical methodology and its latest developments, it must be said that comparable attention needs to be paid to the theological dimension of the biblical texts, so that they can be more deeply understood in accordance with the three elements indicated by the Dogmatic Constitution *Dei Verbum*.[108]

THE DANGER OF DUALISM AND A SECULARIZED HERMENEUTIC

35. In this regard we should mention the serious risk nowadays of a dualistic approach to Sacred Scripture. To distinguish two levels of approach to the Bible does not in any way mean to separate or oppose them, nor simply to juxtapose them. They exist only in reciprocity. Unfortunately, a sterile separation sometimes creates a barrier between exegesis and theology, and this "occurs even at the highest academic levels."[109] Here I would mention the most troubling consequences, which are to be avoided.

a) First and foremost, if the work of exegesis is restricted to the first level alone, Scripture ends up being *a text belonging only to the past*: "One can draw moral consequences from it, one can learn history, but the Book as such speaks only of the past, and exegesis is no longer truly theological, but becomes pure historiography, history of literature."[110] Clearly, such a reductive approach can never make it possible to comprehend the event of God's revelation through his word, which is handed down to us in the living Tradition and in Scripture.

b) The lack of a hermeneutic of faith with regard to Scripture entails more than a simple absence; in its place there inevitably enters another hermeneutic, a positivistic and *secularized hermeneutic* ultimately based on the conviction that the Divine does not intervene in human history. According to this hermeneutic, whenever a divine element seems present, it has to be explained in some other way, reducing everything to the human element. This leads to interpretations that deny the historicity of the divine elements.[111]

c) Such a position can only prove harmful to the life of the Church, casting doubt over fundamental mysteries of Christianity and their historicity—as, for example, the institution of the Eucharist and the resurrection of Christ. A philosophical hermeneutic is thus imposed, one which denies the possibility that the Divine can enter and be present within history. The adoption of this hermeneutic within theological studies inevitably introduces a sharp dichotomy between

107. Benedict XVI, Intervention at the Fourteenth General Congregation of the Synod (October 14, 2008): *Insegnamenti* IV, 2 (2008), 493; cf. *Propositio* 25.
108. Cf. *Propositio* 26.
109. *Propositio* 27.
110. Benedict XVI, Intervention at the Fourteenth General Congregation of the Synod (October 14, 2008): *Insegnamenti* IV, 2 (2008), 493; cf. *Propositio* 26.
111. Cf. ibid.

an exegesis limited solely to the first level and a theology tending towards a spiritualization of the meaning of the Scriptures, one which would fail to respect the historical character of revelation.

All this is also bound to have a negative impact on the spiritual life and on pastoral activity; "as a consequence of the absence of the second methodological level, a profound gulf is opened up between scientific exegesis and *lectio divina*. This can give rise to a lack of clarity in the preparation of homilies."[112] It must also be said that this dichotomy can create confusion and a lack of stability in the intellectual formation of candidates for ecclesial ministries.[113] In a word, "where exegesis is not theology, Scripture cannot be the soul of theology, and conversely, where theology is not essentially the interpretation of the Church's Scripture, such a theology no longer has a foundation."[114] Hence we need to take a more careful look at the indications provided by the Dogmatic Constitution *Dei Verbum* in this regard.

FAITH AND REASON IN THE APPROACH TO SCRIPTURE

36.   I believe that what Pope John Paul II wrote about this question in his Encyclical *Fides et ratio* can lead to a fuller understanding of exegesis and its relationship to the whole of theology. He stated that we should not underestimate "the danger inherent in seeking to derive the truth of Sacred Scripture from the use of one method alone, ignoring the need for a more comprehensive exegesis which enables the exegete, together with the whole Church, to arrive at the full sense of the texts. Those who devote themselves to the study of Sacred Scripture should always remember that the various hermeneutical approaches have their own philosophical underpinnings, which need to be carefully evaluated before they are applied to the sacred texts."[115]

This far-sighted reflection enables us to see how a hermeneutical approach to Sacred Scripture inevitably brings into play the proper relationship between faith and reason. Indeed, the secularized hermeneutic of Sacred Scripture is the product of reason's attempt structurally to exclude any possibility that God might enter into our lives and speak to us in human words. Here too, we need to urge a *broadening of the scope of reason*.[116] In applying methods of historical analysis, no criteria should be adopted which would rule out in advance God's self-disclosure in human history. The unity of the two levels at work in the interpretation of Sacred Scripture presupposes, in a word, *the harmony of faith and reason*. On the one hand, it calls for a faith which, by maintaining a proper relationship with right reason, never degenerates into fideism, which in the case of Scripture would end up in fundamentalism. On the other hand, it calls for a reason which, in its investigation of the historical elements present in the Bible,

---

112. Ibid.
113. Cf. *Propositio* 27.
114. Benedict XVI, Intervention at the Fourteenth General Congregation of the Synod (October 14, 2008): *Insegnamenti* IV, 2 (2008), 493–494.
115. John Paul II, Encyclical Letter *Fides et ratio* (September 14, 1998), 55: AAS 91 (1999), 49–50.
116. Cf. Benedict XVI, Address to the Fourth National Ecclesial Congress in Italy (October 19, 2006): AAS 98 (2006), 804–815.

is marked by openness and does not reject *a priori* anything beyond its own terms of reference. In any case, the religion of the incarnate *Logos* can hardly fail to appear profoundly reasonable to anyone who sincerely seeks the truth and the ultimate meaning of his or her own life and history.

LITERAL SENSE AND SPIRITUAL SENSE

37.　A significant contribution to the recovery of an adequate scriptural hermeneutic, as the synodal assembly stated, can also come from renewed attention to the Fathers of the Church and their exegetical approach.[117] The Church Fathers present a theology that still has great value today because at its heart is the study of Sacred Scripture as a whole. Indeed, the Fathers are primarily and essentially "commentators on Sacred Scripture."[118] Their example can "teach modern exegetes a truly religious approach to Sacred Scripture, and likewise an interpretation that is constantly attuned to the criterion of communion with the experience of the Church, which journeys through history under the guidance of the Holy Spirit."[119]

While obviously lacking the philological and historical resources at the disposal of modern exegesis, the patristic and medieval tradition could recognize the different senses of Scripture, beginning with the literal sense, namely, "the meaning conveyed by the words of Scripture and discovered by exegesis, following the rules of sound interpretation."[120] Saint Thomas of Aquinas, for example, states that "all the senses of Sacred Scripture are based on the literal sense."[121] It is necessary, however, to remember that in patristic and medieval times every form of exegesis, including the literal form, was carried out on the basis of faith, without there necessarily being any distinction between the *literal sense* and the *spiritual sense*. One may mention in this regard the medieval couplet which expresses the relationship between the different senses of Scripture:

> "*Littera gesta docet, quid credas allegoria,*
> *Moralis quid agas, quo tendas anagogia.*
>
> The letter speaks of deeds; allegory about the faith;
> The moral about our actions; anagogy about our destiny."[122]

Here we can note the unity and interrelation between the *literal sense* and the *spiritual sense*, which for its part is subdivided into three senses which deal with the contents of the faith, with the moral life, and with our eschatological aspiration.

In a word, while acknowledging the validity and necessity, as well as the limits, of the historical-critical method, we learn from the Fathers that exegesis "is

---

117. Cf. *Propositio* 6.
118. Cf. Saint Augustine, *De libero arbitrio*, III, XXI, 59: PL 32, 1300; *De Trinitate*, II, I, 2: PL 42, 845.
119. Congregation for Catholic Education, Instruction *Inspectis dierum* (November 10, 1989), 26: AAS 82 (1990), 618.
120. *Catechism of the Catholic Church*, 116.
121. *Summa Theologiae*, I, q. 1, art. 10, ad 1.
122. *Catechism of the Catholic Church*, 118.

truly faithful to the proper intention of biblical texts when it goes not only to the heart of their formulation to find the reality of faith there expressed, but also seeks to link this reality to the experience of faith in our present world."[123] Only against this horizon can we recognize that the word of God is living and addressed to each of us in the here and now of our lives. In this sense, the Pontifical Biblical Commission's definition of the spiritual sense, as understood by Christian faith, remains fully valid: it is "the meaning expressed by the biblical texts when read, under the influence of the Holy Spirit, in the context of the paschal mystery of Christ and of the new life which flows from it. This context truly exists. In it the New Testament recognizes the fulfillment of the Scriptures. It is therefore quite acceptable to re-read the Scriptures in the light of this new context, which is that of life in the Spirit."[124]

THE NEED TO TRANSCEND THE "LETTER"

38.   In rediscovering the interplay between the different senses of Scripture it thus becomes essential to grasp the *passage from letter to spirit*. This is not an automatic, spontaneous passage; rather, the letter needs to be transcended: "the word of God can never simply be equated with the letter of the text. To attain to it involves a progression and a process of understanding guided by the inner movement of the whole corpus, and hence it also has to become a vital process."[125] Here we see the reason why an authentic process of interpretation is never purely an intellectual process but also a lived one, demanding full engagement in the life of the Church, which is life "according to the Spirit" (Gal 5:16). The criteria set forth in number 12 of the Dogmatic Constitution *Dei Verbum* thus become clearer: this progression cannot take place with regard to an individual literary fragment unless it is seen in relation to the whole of Scripture. Indeed, the goal to which we are necessarily progressing is the one Word. There is an inner drama in this process, since the passage that takes place in the power of the Spirit inevitably engages each person's freedom. Saint Paul lived this passage to the full in his own life. In his words: *"the letter kills, but the Spirit gives life"* (2 Cor 3:6), he expressed in radical terms the significance of this process of transcending the letter and coming to understand it only in terms of the whole. Paul discovered that "the Spirit of freedom has a name, and hence that freedom has an inner criterion: 'The Lord is the Spirit and where the Spirit of the Lord is, there is freedom' (2 Cor 3:17). The Spirit of freedom is not simply the exegete's own idea, the exegete's own vision. The Spirit is Christ, and Christ is the Lord who shows us the way."[126] We know that for Saint Augustine too this passage was at once dramatic and liberating; he came to believe the Scriptures—which at first sight struck him as so disjointed in themselves and in places so coarse—through the very process of transcending the letter which he learned from Saint Ambrose in typological interpretation, wherein the entire Old Testament is a path to Jesus

---

123. Pontifical Biblical Commission, *The Interpretation of the Bible in the Church* (April 15, 1993), II, A, 2: *Enchiridion Vaticanum* 13, no. 2987.

124. Ibid., II, B, 2: *Enchiridion Vaticanum* 13, no. 3003.

125. Benedict XVI, Address to Representatives of the World of Culture at the "Collège des Bernardins" in Paris (September 12, 2008): AAS 100 (2008), 726.

126. Ibid.

Christ. For Saint Augustine, transcending the literal sense made the letter itself credible, and enabled him to find at last the answer to his deep inner restlessness and his thirst for truth.[127]

THE BIBLE'S INTRINSIC UNITY

39.   In the passage from letter to spirit, we also learn, within the Church's great tradition, to see the unity of all Scripture, grounded in the unity of God's word, which challenges our life and constantly calls us to conversion.[128] Here the words of Hugh of Saint Victor remain a sure guide: "All divine Scripture is one book, and this one book is Christ, speaks of Christ, and finds its fulfillment in Christ."[129] Viewed in purely historical or literary terms, of course, the Bible is not a single book, but a collection of literary texts composed over the course of a thousand years or more, and its individual books are not easily seen to possess an interior unity; instead, we see clear inconsistencies between them. This was already the case with the Bible of Israel, which we Christians call the Old Testament. It is all the more so when, as Christians, we relate the New Testament and its writings as a kind of hermeneutical key to Israel's Bible, thus interpreting the latter as a path to Christ. The New Testament generally does not employ the term "Scripture" (cf. Rom 4:3; 1 Pet 2:6), but rather "the Scriptures" (cf. Mt 21:43; Jn 5:39; Rom 1:2; 2 Pet 3:16), which nonetheless are seen in their entirety as the one word of God addressed to us.[130] This makes it clear that the person of Christ gives unity to all the "Scriptures" in relation to the one "Word." In this way we can understand the words of number 12 of the Dogmatic Constitution *Dei Verbum*, which point to the internal unity of the entire Bible as a decisive criterion for a correct hermeneutic of faith.

THE RELATIONSHIP BETWEEN THE OLD AND THE NEW TESTAMENTS

40.   Against this backdrop of the unity of the Scriptures in Christ, theologians and pastors alike need to be conscious of the relationship between Old and the New Testaments. First of all, it is evident that *the New Testament itself acknowledges the Old Testament as the word of God* and thus accepts the authority of the Sacred Scriptures of the Jewish people.[131] It implicitly acknowledges them by using the same language and by frequently referring to passages from these Scriptures. It explicitly acknowledges them by citing many parts of them as a basis for argument. In the New Testament, an argument based on texts from the Old Testament thus has a definitive quality, superior to that of mere human argumentation. In the Fourth Gospel, Jesus states that "Scripture cannot be rejected" (Jn 10:35) and Saint Paul specifically makes clear that the Old Testament revelation remains valid for us Christians (cf. Rom 15:4; 1 Cor 10:11).[132] We also

---

127. Cf. Id., General Audience (January 9, 2008): *Insegnamenti* IV, 1 (2008), 41–45.

128. Cf. *Propositio* 29.

129. *De arca Noe*, 2, 8: PL 176, 642C–D.

130. Cf. Benedict XVI, Address to Representatives of the World of Culture at the "Collège des Bernardins" in Paris (September 12, 2008): AAS 100 (2008), 725.

131. Cf. *Propositio* 10; Pontifical Biblical Commission, *The Jewish People and their Sacred Scriptures in the Christian Bible* (May 24, 2001): *Enchiridion Vaticanum* 20, nos. 748–755.

132. Cf. *Catechism of the Catholic Church*, 121–122.

affirm that "Jesus of Nazareth was a Jew and the Holy Land is the motherland of the Church:"[133] the roots of Christianity are found in the Old Testament, and Christianity continually draws nourishment from these roots. Consequently, sound Christian doctrine has always resisted all new forms of Marcionism, which tend, in different ways, to set the Old Testament in opposition to the New.[134]

Moreover, the New Testament itself claims to be consistent with the Old and proclaims that in the mystery of the life, death, and resurrection of Christ the Sacred Scriptures of the Jewish people have found their perfect fulfillment. It must be observed, however, that the concept of the fulfillment of the Scriptures is a complex one, since it has three dimensions: a basic aspect of *continuity* with the Old Testament revelation, an aspect of *discontinuity*, and an aspect of *fulfillment and transcendence*. The mystery of Christ stands in continuity of intent with the sacrificial cult of the Old Testament, but it came to pass in a very different way, corresponding to a number of prophetic statements and thus reaching a perfection never previously obtained. The Old Testament is itself replete with tensions between its institutional and its prophetic aspects. The paschal mystery of Christ is in complete conformity—albeit in a way that could not have been anticipated—with the prophecies and the foreshadowings of the Scriptures; yet it presents clear aspects of discontinuity with regard to the institutions of the Old Testament.

41.   These considerations show the unique importance of the Old Testament for Christians, while at the same time bringing out the *newness of Christological interpretation*. From apostolic times and in her living Tradition, the Church has stressed the unity of God's plan in the two Testaments through the use of typology; this procedure is in no way arbitrary, but is intrinsic to the events related in the sacred text and thus involves the whole of Scripture. Typology "discerns in God's works of the Old Covenant prefigurations of what he accomplished in the fullness of time in the person of his incarnate Son."[135] Christians, then, read the Old Testament in the light of Christ crucified and risen. While typological interpretation manifests the inexhaustible content of the Old Testament from the standpoint of the New, we must not forget that the Old Testament retains its own inherent value as revelation, as our Lord himself reaffirmed (cf. Mk 12:29–31). Consequently, "the New Testament has to be read in the light of the Old. Early Christian catechesis made constant use of the Old Testament (cf. 1 Cor 5:6–8; 1 Cor 10:1–11)."[136] For this reason the Synod Fathers stated that "the Jewish understanding of the Bible can prove helpful to Christians for their own understanding and study of the Scriptures."[137]

---

133. *Propositio* 52.
134. Cf. Pontifical Biblical Commission, *The Jewish People and their Sacred Scriptures in the Christian Bible* (May 24, 2001), 19: *Enchiridion Vaticanum* 20, nos. 799–801; Origen, *Homily on Numbers* 9, 4: SC 415, 238–242.
135. *Catechism of the Catholic Church*, 128.
136. Ibid., 129.
137. *Propositio* 52.

"The New Testament is hidden in the Old and the Old is made manifest in the New,"[138] as Saint Augustine perceptively noted. It is important, therefore, that in both pastoral and academic settings the close relationship between the two Testaments be clearly brought out, in keeping with the dictum of Saint Gregory the Great that "what the Old Testament promised, the New Testament made visible; what the former announces in a hidden way, the latter openly proclaims as present. Therefore the Old Testament is a prophecy of the New Testament; and the best commentary on the Old Testament is the New Testament."[139]

THE "DARK" PASSAGES OF THE BIBLE

42.   In discussing the relationship between the Old and the New Testaments, the Synod also considered those passages in the Bible which, due to the violence and immorality they occasionally contain, prove obscure and difficult. Here it must be remembered first and foremost that *biblical revelation is deeply rooted in history*. God's plan is manifested *progressively* and it is accomplished slowly, *in successive stages* and despite human resistance. God chose a people and patiently worked to guide and educate them. Revelation is suited to the cultural and moral level of distant times and thus describes facts and customs, such as cheating and trickery, and acts of violence and massacre, without explicitly denouncing the immorality of such things. This can be explained by the historical context, yet it can cause the modern reader to be taken aback, especially if he or she fails to take account of the many "dark" deeds carried out down the centuries, and also in our own day. In the Old Testament, the preaching of the prophets vigorously challenged every kind of injustice and violence, whether collective or individual, and thus became God's way of training his people in preparation for the Gospel. So it would be a mistake to neglect those passages of Scripture that strike us as problematic. Rather, we should be aware that the correct interpretation of these passages requires a degree of expertise, acquired through a training that interprets the texts in their historical-literary context and within the Christian perspective which has as its ultimate hermeneutical key "the Gospel and the new commandment of Jesus Christ brought about in the paschal mystery."[140] I encourage scholars and pastors to help all the faithful to approach these passages through an interpretation which enables their meaning to emerge in the light of the mystery of Christ.

CHRISTIANS, JEWS, AND THE SACRED SCRIPTURES

43.   Having considered the close relationship between the New Testament and the Old, we now naturally turn to the special bond which that relationship has engendered between Christians and Jews, a bond that must never be overlooked. Pope John Paul II, speaking to Jews, called them "our 'beloved brothers' in the faith of Abraham, our Patriarch."[141] To acknowledge this fact is in no way to

---

138. *Quaestiones in Heptateuchum*, 2, 73: PL 34, 623.

139. *Homiliae in Ezechielem* I, VI, 15: PL 76, 836B.

140. *Propositio* 29.

141. John Paul II, Message to the Chief Rabbi of Rome (May 22, 2004): *Insegnamenti* XXVII, 1 (2004), p. 655.

disregard the instances of discontinuity which the New Testament asserts with regard to the institutions of the Old Testament, much less the fulfillment of the Scriptures in the mystery of Jesus Christ, acknowledged as Messiah and Son of God. All the same, this profound and radical difference by no means implies mutual hostility. The example of Saint Paul (cf. Rom 9–11) shows on the contrary that "an attitude of respect, esteem, and love for the Jewish people is the only truly Christian attitude in the present situation, which is a mysterious part of God's wholly positive plan."[142] Indeed, Saint Paul says of the Jews that: "as regards election they are beloved for the sake of their forefathers, for the gifts and the call of God are irrevocable!" (Rom 11:28–29).

Saint Paul also uses the lovely image of the olive tree to describe the very close relationship between Christians and Jews: the Church of the Gentiles is like a wild olive shoot, grafted onto the good olive tree that is the people of the Covenant (cf. Rom 11:17–24). In other words, we draw our nourishment from the same spiritual roots. We encounter one another as brothers and sisters who at certain moments in their history have had a tense relationship, but are now firmly committed to building bridges of lasting friendship.[143] As Pope John Paul II said on another occasion: "We have much in common. Together we can do much for peace, justice, and for a more fraternal and more humane world."[144]

I wish to state once more how much the Church values her *dialogue with the Jews.* Wherever it seems appropriate, it would be good to create opportunities for encounter and exchange in public as well as in private, and thus to promote growth in reciprocal knowledge, in mutual esteem and cooperation, also in the study of the Sacred Scriptures.

THE FUNDAMENTALIST INTERPRETATION OF SACRED SCRIPTURE

44.   The attention we have been paying to different aspects of the theme of biblical hermeneutics now enables us to consider a subject which came up a number of times during the Synod: that of the fundamentalist interpretation of sacred Scripture.[145] The Pontifical Biblical Commission, in its document *The Interpretation of the Bible in the Church,* has laid down some important guidelines. Here I would like especially to deal with approaches which fail to respect the authenticity of the sacred text, but promote *subjective and arbitrary interpretations.* The "literalism" championed by the fundamentalist approach actually represents a betrayal of both the literal and the spiritual sense, and opens the way to various forms of manipulation, as, for example, by disseminating anti-ecclesial interpretations of the Scriptures. "The basic problem with fundamentalist interpretation is that, refusing to take into account the historical character of biblical revelation, it makes itself incapable of accepting the full

---

142. Cf. Pontifical Biblical Commission, *The Jewish People and their Sacred Scriptures in the Christian Bible* (May 24, 2001), 87: *Enchiridion Vaticanum* 20, no. 1150.

143. Cf. Benedict XVI, Farewell Discourse at Ben Gurion International Airport in Tel Aviv (May 15, 2009): *Insegnamenti,* V, 1 (2009), 847–849.

144. John Paul II, Address to the Chief Rabbis of Israel (March 23, 2000): *Insegnamenti* XXIII, 1 (2000), 434.

145. Cf. *Propositiones* 46 and 47.

truth of the incarnation itself. As regards relationships with God, fundamentalism seeks to escape any closeness of the divine and the human. . . . For this reason, it tends to treat the biblical text as if it had been dictated word for word by the Spirit. It fails to recognize that the word of God has been formulated in language and expression conditioned by various periods."[146] Christianity, on the other hand, perceives *in* the words *the* Word himself, the *Logos* who displays his mystery through this complexity and the reality of human history.[147] The true response to a fundamentalist approach is "the faith-filled interpretation of Sacred Scripture." This manner of interpretation, "practiced from antiquity within the Church's Tradition, seeks saving truth for the life of the individual Christian and for the Church. It recognizes the historical value of the biblical tradition. Precisely because of the tradition's value as a historical witness, this reading seeks to discover the living meaning of the Sacred Scriptures for the lives of believers today,"[148] while not ignoring the human mediation of the inspired text and its literary genres.

DIALOGUE BETWEEN PASTORS, THEOLOGIANS, AND EXEGETES

45. An authentic hermeneutic of faith has several important consequences for the Church's pastoral activity. The Synod Fathers themselves recommended, for example, a closer working relationship between pastors, exegetes, and theologians. Episcopal Conferences might foster such encounters with the "aim of promoting greater communion in the service of the word of God."[149] Cooperation of this sort will help all to carry out their work more effectively for the benefit of the whole Church. For scholars too, this pastoral orientation involves approaching the sacred text with the realization that it is a message which the Lord addresses to us for our salvation. In the words of the Dogmatic Constitution *Dei Verbum*, "Catholic exegetes and other workers in the field of sacred theology should work diligently with one another and under the watchful eye of the sacred magisterium. Using appropriate techniques, they should together set about examining and explaining the sacred texts in such a way that as many as possible of those who are ministers of God's word may be able to dispense fruitfully the nourishment of the Scriptures to the people of God. This nourishment enlightens the mind, strengthens the will, and fires the hearts of men and women with the love of God."[150]

THE BIBLE AND ECUMENISM

46. Conscious that the Church has her foundation in Christ, the incarnate Word of God, the Synod wished to emphasize the centrality of biblical studies within ecumenical dialogue aimed at the full expression of the unity of all

---

146. Pontifical Biblical Commission, *The Interpretation of the Bible in the Church* (April 15, 1993), I, F: *Enchiridion Vaticanum* 13, No. 2974.
147. Cf. Benedict XVI, Address to Representatives of the World of Culture at the "Collège des Bernardins" in Paris (September 12, 2008): AAS 100 (2008), 726.
148. *Propositio* 46.
149. *Propositio* 28.
150. Second Vatican Ecumenical Council, Dogmatic Constitution on Divine Revelation *Dei Verbum*, 23.

believers in Christ.[151] The Scriptures themselves contain Jesus' moving prayer to the Father that his disciples might be one, so that the world may believe (cf. Jn 17:21). All this can only strengthen our conviction that by listening and meditating together on the Scriptures, we experience a real, albeit not yet full communion;[152] "shared listening to the Scriptures thus spurs us on towards the dialogue of charity and enables growth in the dialogue of truth."[153] Listening together to the word of God, engaging in biblical *lectio divina*, letting ourselves be struck by the inexhaustible freshness of God's word which never grows old, overcoming our deafness to those words that do not fit our own opinions or prejudices, listening and studying within the communion of the believers of every age: all these things represent a way of coming to unity in faith as a response to hearing the word of God.[154] The words of the Second Vatican Council were clear in this regard: "in [ecumenical] dialogue itself, Sacred Scripture is a precious instrument in the mighty hand of God for attaining to that unity which the Savior holds out to all."[155] Consequently, there should be an increase in ecumenical study, discussion and celebrations of the word of God, with due respect for existing norms and the variety of traditions.[156] These celebrations advance the cause of ecumenism and, when suitably carried out, they represent intense moments of authentic prayer asking God to hasten the day when we will all be able at last to sit at the one table and drink from the one cup. Nonetheless, while it is praiseworthy and right to promote such services, care must be taken that they are not proposed to the faithful as alternatives to the celebration of Holy Mass on Sundays or holydays of obligation.

In this work of study and prayer, we serenely acknowledge those aspects which still need to be explored more deeply and those on which we still differ, such as the understanding of the authoritative subject of interpretation in the Church and the decisive role of the Magisterium.[157]

Finally, I wish to emphasize the statements of the Synod Fathers about the ecumenical importance of *translations of the Bible in the various languages*. We know that translating a text is no mere mechanical task, but belongs in some sense to the work of interpretation. In this regard, the Venerable John Paul II observed that "anyone who recalls how heavily debates about Scripture influenced divisions, especially in the West, can appreciate the significant step forward which these common translations represent."[158] Promoting common translations of the Bible is part of the ecumenical enterprise. I would like to

---

151. It should be recalled, however, that with regard to the so-called deuterocanonical books of the Old Testament and their inspiration, Catholics and Orthodox do not have exactly the same biblical canon as Anglicans and Protestants.

152. Cf. *Relatio post disceptationem*, 36.

153. *Propositio* 36.

154. Cf. Benedict XVI, Address to the Eleventh Ordinary Council of the General Secretariat of the Synod of Bishops (January 25, 2007): AAS 99 (2007), 85–86.

155. Second Vatican Ecumenical Council, Decree on Ecumenism *Unitatis Redintegratio*, 21.

156. Cf. *Propositio* 36.

157. Cf. Second Vatican Ecumenical Council, Dogmatic Constitution on Divine Revelation *Dei Verbum*, 10.

158. Encyclical Letter *Ut unum sint* (May 25, 1995), 44: AAS 87 (1995), 947.

thank all those engaged in this important work, and I encourage them to persevere in their efforts.

CONSEQUENCES FOR THE STUDY OF THEOLOGY

47.   A further consequence of an adequate hermeneutic of faith has to do with its necessary implications for exegetical and theological formation, particularly that of candidates for the priesthood. Care must be taken to ensure that the study of Sacred Scripture is truly the soul of theology inasmuch as it is acknowledged as the word of God addressed to today's world, to the Church and to each of us personally. It is important that the criteria indicated in number 12 of the Dogmatic Constitution *Dei Verbum* receive real attention and become the object of deeper study. A notion of scholarly research that would consider itself neutral with regard to Scripture should not be encouraged. As well as learning the original languages in which the Bible was written and suitable methods of interpretation, students need to have a deep spiritual life, in order to appreciate that the Scripture can only be understood if it is lived.

Along these lines, I urge that the study of the word of God, both handed down and written, be constantly carried out in a profoundly ecclesial spirit, and that academic formation take due account of the pertinent interventions of the Magisterium, which "is not superior to the word of God, but is rather its servant. It teaches only what has been handed on to it. At the divine command and with the help of the Holy Spirit, it listens to this devoutly, guards it reverently and expounds it faithfully."[159] Care must thus be taken that the instruction imparted acknowledge that "sacred Tradition, Sacred Scripture and the Magisterium of the Church are so connected and associated that one of them cannot stand without the others."[160] It is my hope that, in fidelity to the teaching of the Second Vatican Council, the study of Sacred Scripture, read within the communion of the universal Church, will truly be the soul of theological studies.[161]

THE SAINTS AND THE INTERPRETATION OF SCRIPTURE

48.   The interpretation of Sacred Scripture would remain incomplete were it not to include listening to *those who have truly lived the word of God: namely, the saints.*[162] Indeed, *"viva lectio est vita bonorum."*[163] The most profound interpretation of Scripture comes precisely from those who let themselves be shaped by the word of God through listening, reading, and assiduous meditation.

It is certainly not by chance that the great currents of spirituality in the Church's history originated with an explicit reference to Scripture. I am thinking for example of Saint Anthony the Abbot, who was moved by hearing Christ's words: "if you would be perfect, go, sell what you possess and give to the poor, and you

---

159. Second Vatican Ecumenical Council, Dogmatic Constitution on Divine Revelation *Dei Verbum*, 10.
160. Ibid.
161. Cf. ibid., 24.
162. Cf. *Propositio* 22.
163. Saint Gregory the Great, *Moralia in Job* XXIV, VIII, 16: PL 76, 295.

will have treasure in heaven; and come, follow me" (Mt 19:21).[164] No less striking is the question posed by Saint Basil the Great in the *Moralia*: "What is the distinctive mark of faith? Full and unhesitating certainty that the words inspired by God are true. . . . What is the distinctive mark of the faithful? Conforming their lives with the same complete certainty to the meaning of the words of Scripture, not daring to remove or add a single thing."[165] Saint Benedict, in his *Rule*, refers to Scripture as "a most perfect norm for human life."[166] Saint Francis of Assisi—we learn from Thomas of Celano—"upon hearing that the disciples of Christ must possess neither gold, nor silver, nor money, nor carry a bag, nor bread, nor a staff for the journey, nor sandals nor two tunics . . . exulting in the Holy Spirit, immediately cried out: 'This is what I want, this is what I ask for, this I long to do with all my heart!'"[167] Saint Clare of Assisi shared fully in the experience of Saint Francis: "The form of life of the Order of Poor Sisters—she writes—is this: to observe the holy Gospel of our Lord Jesus Christ."[168] So too, Saint Dominic "everywhere showed himself to be a man of the Gospel, in word as in deed,"[169] and wanted his friars likewise to be "men of the Gospel."[170] The Carmelite Saint Teresa of Avila, who in her writings constantly uses biblical images to explain her mystical experiences, says that Jesus himself revealed to her that "all the evil in the world is derived from not knowing clearly the truths of Sacred Scripture."[171] Saint Thérèse of the Child Jesus discovered that love was her personal vocation by poring over the Scriptures, especially Chapters 12 and 13 of the *First Letter to the Corinthians*;[172] the same saint describes the attraction of the Scriptures: "No sooner do I glance at the Gospel, but immediately I breathe in the fragrance of the life of Jesus and I know where to run."[173] Every saint is like a ray of light streaming forth from the word of God: we can think of Saint Ignatius of Loyola in his search for truth and in his discernment of spirits; Saint John Bosco in his passion for the education of the young; Saint John Mary Vianney in his awareness of the grandeur of the priesthood as gift and task; Saint Pius of Pietrelcina in his serving as an instrument of divine mercy; Saint Josemaría Escrivá in his preaching of the universal call to holiness; Blessed Teresa of Calcutta, the missionary of God's charity towards the poorest of the poor; and then the martyrs of Nazism and Communism, represented by Saint Teresa Benedicta of the Cross (Edith Stein), a Carmelite nun, and by Blessed Aloysius Stepinac, the Cardinal Archbishop of Zagreb.

49.   Holiness inspired by the word of God thus belongs in a way to the prophetic tradition, wherein the word of God sets the prophet's very life at its service. In

---

164. Cf. Saint Athanasius, *Vita Antonii*, II: PL 73:127.

165. *Moralia, Regula* LXXX, XXII: PG 31, 867.

166. *Rule*, 73, 3: SC 182, 672.

167. Thomas of Celano, *First Life of Saint Francis*, IX, 22: FF 356.

168. *Rule*, I, 1–2: FF 2750.

169. Blessed Jordan of Saxony, *Libellus de principiis Ordinis Praedicatorum*, 104; *Monumenta Fratrum Praedicatorum Historica*, Rome, 1935, 16, p. 75.

170. Order of Friars Preacher, *First Constitutions* or *Consuetudines*, II, XXXI.

171. *Vita*, 40, 1.

172. Cf. *Story of a Soul*, Ms B, 254.

173. Ibid., Ms C, 35v.

this sense, holiness in the Church constitutes an interpretation of Scripture which cannot be overlooked. The Holy Spirit who inspired the sacred authors is the same Spirit who impels the saints to offer their lives for the Gospel. In striving to learn from their example, we set out on the sure way towards a living and effective hermeneutic of the word of God.

We saw a direct witness to this link between holiness and the word of God during the Twelfth Assembly of the Synod when four new saints were canonized on October 12 in Saint Peter's Square: Gaetano Errico, priest and founder of the Congregation of Missionaries of the Sacred Hearts of Jesus and Mary; Mother Maria Bernarda Bütler, a native of Switzerland and a missionary in Ecuador and Colombia; Sister Alphonsa of the Immaculate Conception, the first canonized saint born in India; and the young Ecuadorian laywoman Narcisa de Jesús Martillo Morán. With their lives they testified before the world and the Church to the perennial fruitfulness of Christ's Gospel. Through the intercession of these saints canonized at the time of the synodal assembly on the word of God, let us ask the Lord that our own lives may be that "good soil" in which the divine sower plants the word, so that it may bear within us fruits of holiness, "thirtyfold, sixtyfold, a hundredfold" (Mk 4:20).

PART TWO: *VERBUM IN ECCLESIA*

"But to all who received him he gave power to become children of God." (Jn 1:12)

THE WORD OF GOD AND THE CHURCH

THE CHURCH RECEIVES THE WORD

50.   The Lord speaks his word so that it may be received by those who were created "through" that same word. "He came among his own" (Jn 1:11): his word is not something fundamentally alien to us, and creation was willed in a relationship of familiarity with God's own life. Yet the Prologue of the Fourth Gospel also places us before the rejection of God's word by "his own," who "received him not" (Jn 1:11). Not to receive him means not to listen to his voice, not to be conformed to the *Logos*. On the other hand, whenever men and women, albeit frail and sinful, are sincerely open to an encounter with Christ, a radical transformation begins to take place: "but to all who received him, he gave power to become children of God" (Jn 1:12). To receive the Word means to let oneself be shaped by him, and thus to be conformed by the power of the Holy Spirit to Christ, the "only Son from the Father" (Jn 1:14). It is the beginning of a new creation; a new creature is born, a new people comes to birth. Those who believe, that is to say, those who live the obedience of faith, are "born of God" (Jn 1:13) and made sharers in the divine life: *sons in the Son* (cf. Gal 4:5–6; Rom 8:14–17). As Saint Augustine puts it nicely in commenting on this passage from John's Gospel: "you were created through the word, but now through the word you must be recreated."[174] Here we can glimpse the face of the Church as a reality

---

174. *In Iohannis Evangelium Tractatus*, I, 12: PL 35, 1385.

defined by acceptance of the Word of God who, by taking flesh, came to pitch *his tent among us* (cf. Jn 1:14). This dwelling-place of God among men, this *shekinah* (cf. Ex 26:1), prefigured in the Old Testament, is now fulfilled in God's definitive presence among us in Christ.

CHRIST'S CONSTANT PRESENCE IN THE LIFE OF THE CHURCH

51.　The relationship between Christ, the Word of the Father, and the Church cannot be fully understood in terms of a mere past event; rather, it is a living relationship which each member of the faithful is personally called to enter into. We are speaking of the presence of God's word to us today: "Lo, I am with you always, to the close of the age" (Mt 28:20). As Pope John Paul II has said: "Christ's relevance for people of all times is shown forth in his body, which is the Church. For this reason the Lord promised his disciples the Holy Spirit, who would 'bring to their remembrance' and teach them to understand his commandments (cf. Jn 14:26), and who would be the principle and constant source of a new life in the world (cf. Jn 3:5–8; Rom 8:1–13)."[175] The Dogmatic Constitution *Dei Verbum* expresses this mystery by using the biblical metaphor of a nuptial dialogue: "God, who spoke in the past, continues to converse with the spouse of his beloved Son. And the Holy Spirit, through whom the living voice of the Gospel rings out in the Church—and through it in the world—leads believers to the full truth and makes the word of Christ dwell in them in all its richness (cf. Col 3:16)."[176]

The Bride of Christ—the great teacher of the art of listening—today too repeats in faith: "Speak, Lord, your Church is listening."[177] For this reason the Dogmatic Constitution *Dei Verbum* intentionally begins with the words: "Hearing the word of God reverently and proclaiming it confidently, this sacred Council. . . ."[178] Here we encounter a dynamic definition of the Church's life: "With these words the Council indicates a defining aspect of the Church: she is a community that hears and proclaims the word of God. The Church draws life not from herself but from the Gospel, and from the Gospel she discovers ever anew the direction for her journey. This is an approach that every Christian must understand and apply to himself or herself: only those who first place themselves in an attitude of listening to the word can go on to become its heralds."[179] In the word of God proclaimed and heard, and in the sacraments, Jesus says today, here and now, to each person: "I am yours, I give myself to you;" so that we can receive and respond, saying in return: "I am yours."[180] The Church thus emerges as the milieu in which, by grace, we can experience what John tells us in the Prologue of his Gospel: "to all who received him he gave power to become children of God" (Jn 1:12).

---

175. Encyclical Letter *Veritatis splendor* (August 6, 1993), 25: AAS 85 (1993), 1153.

176. Second Vatican Ecumenical Council, Dogmatic Constitution on Divine Revelation *Dei Verbum*, 8.

177. *Relatio post disceptationem*, 11.

178. No. 1.

179. Benedict XVI, Address to the International Congress "Sacred Scripture in the Life of the Church" (September 16, 2005): AAS 97 (2005), 956.

180. Cf. *Relatio post disceptationem*, 10.

THE LITURGY, PRIVILEGED SETTING FOR THE WORD OF GOD

52.   In considering the Church as *"the home of the word,"*[181] attention must first be given to the sacred liturgy, for the liturgy is the privileged setting in which God speaks to us in the midst of our lives; he speaks today to his people, who hear and respond. Every liturgical action is by its very nature steeped in Sacred Scripture. In the words of the Constitution *Sacrosanctum Concilium,* "Sacred Scripture is of the greatest importance in the celebration of the liturgy. From it are taken the readings, which are explained in the homily, and the psalms that are sung. From Scripture the petitions, prayers, and liturgical hymns receive their inspiration and substance. From Scripture the liturgical actions and signs draw their meaning."[182] Even more, it must be said that Christ himself "is present in his word, since it is he who speaks when Scripture is read in Church."[183] Indeed, "the liturgical celebration becomes the continuing, complete and effective presentation of God's word. The word of God, constantly proclaimed in the liturgy, is always a living and effective word through the power of the Holy Spirit. It expresses the Father's love that never fails in its effectiveness towards us."[184] The Church has always realized that in the liturgical action the word of God is accompanied by the interior working of the Holy Spirit who makes it effective in the hearts of the faithful. Thanks to the Paraclete, "the word of God becomes the foundation of the liturgical celebration, and the rule and support of all our life. The working of the same Holy Spirit . . . brings home to each person individually everything that in the proclamation of the word of God is spoken for the good of the whole gathering. In strengthening the unity of all, the Holy Spirit at the same time fosters a diversity of gifts and furthers their multiform operation."[185]

To understand the word of God, then, we need to appreciate and experience the essential meaning and value of the liturgical action. *A faith-filled understanding of Sacred Scripture must always refer back to the liturgy,* in which the word of God is celebrated as a timely and living word: "In the liturgy the Church faithfully adheres to the way Christ himself read and explained the Sacred Scriptures, beginning with his coming forth in the synagogue and urging all to search the Scriptures."[186]

Here one sees the sage pedagogy of the Church, which proclaims and listens to Sacred Scripture following the rhythm of the liturgical year. This expansion of God's word in time takes place above all in the Eucharistic celebration and in the Liturgy of the Hours. At the center of everything the paschal mystery shines forth, and around it radiate all the mysteries of Christ and the history of

---

181. Final Message, III, 6.
182. Second Vatican Ecumenical Council, Constitution on the Sacred Liturgy *Sacrosanctum Concilium,* 24.
183. Ibid., 7.
184. *Ordo Lectionum Missae,* 4.
185. Ibid, 9.
186. Ibid., 3; cf. *Lk* 4:16–21; 24:25–35, 44–49.

salvation which become sacramentally present: "By recalling in this way the mysteries of redemption, the Church opens up to the faithful the riches of the saving actions and the merits of her Lord, and makes them present to all times, allowing the faithful to enter into contact with them and to be filled with the grace of salvation."[187] For this reason I encourage the Church's Pastors and all engaged in pastoral work to see that all the faithful learn to savor the deep meaning of the word of God which unfolds each year in the liturgy, revealing the fundamental mysteries of our faith. This is in turn the basis for a correct approach to Sacred Scripture.

SACRED SCRIPTURE AND THE SACRAMENTS

53.   In discussing the importance of the liturgy for understanding the word of God, the Synod of Bishops highlighted the relationship between Sacred Scripture and the working of the sacraments. There is great need for a deeper investigation of the relationship between word and sacrament in the Church's pastoral activity and in theological reflection.[188] Certainly "the liturgy of the word is a decisive element in the celebration of each one of the sacraments of the Church;"[189] in pastoral practice, however, the faithful are not always conscious of this connection, nor do they appreciate the unity between gesture and word. It is "the task of priests and deacons, above all when they administer the sacraments, to explain the unity between word and sacrament in the ministry of the Church."[190] The relationship between word and sacramental gesture is the liturgical expression of God's activity in the history of salvation through the *performative character* of the word itself. In salvation history there is no separation between what God *says* and what he *does*. His word appears as alive and active (cf. Heb 4:12), as the Hebrew term *dabar* itself makes clear. In the liturgical action too, we encounter his word which accomplishes what it says. By educating the People of God to discover the performative character of God's word in the liturgy, we will help them to recognize his activity in salvation history and in their individual lives.

THE WORD OF GOD AND THE EUCHARIST

54.   What has been said in general about the relationship between the word and the sacraments takes on deeper meaning when we turn to the celebration of the Eucharist. The profound unity of word and Eucharist is grounded in the witness of Scripture (cf. Jn 6; Lk 24), attested to by the Fathers of the Church, and reaffirmed by the Second Vatican Council.[191] Here we think of Jesus' discourse on

---

187. Second Vatican Ecumenical Council, Constitution on Sacred Liturgy *Sacrosanctum Concilium*, 102.

188. Cf. Benedict XVI, Post-Synodal Apostolic Exhortation *Sacramentum caritatis* (February 22, 2007), 44–45: AAS 99 (2007) 139–141.

189. Pontifical Biblical Commission, *The Interpretation of the Bible in the Church* (April 15, 1993) IV, C, 1: *Enchiridion Vaticanum* 13, No. 3123.

190. Ibid., III, B, 3: *Enchiridion Vaticanum* 13, No. 3056.

191. Cf. Second Vatican Ecumenical Council, Constitution on the Sacred Liturgy *Sacrosanctum Concilium*, 48, 51, 56; Dogmatic Constitution on Divine Revelation *Dei Verbum*, 21, 26; Decree on the Missionary Activity of the Church *Ad gentes*, 6, 15; Decree on the Ministry and Life of

the bread of life in the synagogue of Capernaum (cf. Jn 6:22–69), with its under-lying comparison between Moses and Jesus, between the one who spoke face to face with God (cf. Ex 33:11) and the one who makes God known (cf. Jn 1:18). Jesus' discourse on the bread speaks of the gift of God, which Moses obtained for his people with the manna in the desert, which is really the *Torah*, the life-giving word of God (cf. Ps 119; Prv 9:5). In his own person Jesus brings to fulfillment the ancient image: "The bread of God is that which comes down from heaven and gives life to the world" . . . "I am the bread of life" (Jn 6:33–35). Here "the law has become a person. When we encounter Jesus, we feed on the living God himself, so to speak; we truly eat 'the bread from heaven.'"[192] In the discourse at Capernaum, John's Prologue is brought to a deeper level. There God's *Logos* became flesh, but here this flesh becomes *"bread"* given for the life of the world (cf. Jn 6:51), with an allusion to Jesus' self-gift in the mystery of the cross, con-firmed by the words about his blood being given as *drink* (cf. Jn 6:53). The mys-tery of the Eucharist reveals the true manna, the true bread of heaven: it is God's *Logos* made flesh, who gave himself up for us in the paschal mystery.

Luke's account of the disciples on the way to Emmaus enables us to reflect fur-ther on this link between the hearing of the word and the breaking of the bread (cf. Lk 24:13–35). Jesus approached the disciples on the day after the Sabbath, listened as they spoke of their dashed hopes, and, joining them on their journey, "interpreted to them in all the Scriptures the things concerning himself" (24:27). The two disciples began to look at the Scriptures in a new way in the company of this traveler who seemed so surprisingly familiar with their lives. What had taken place in those days no longer appeared to them as failure, but as fulfill-ment and a new beginning. And yet, apparently not even these words were enough for the two disciples. The *Gospel of Luke* relates that "their eyes were opened and they recognized him" (24:31) only when Jesus took the bread, said the blessing, broke it and gave it to them, whereas earlier "their eyes were kept from recognizing him" (24:16). The presence of Jesus, first with his words and then with the act of breaking bread, made it possible for the disciples to recog-nize him. Now they were able to appreciate in a new way all that they had pre-viously experienced with him: "Did not our hearts burn within us while he talked to us on the road, while he opened to us the Scriptures?" (24:32).

55.   From these accounts it is clear that Scripture itself points us towards an appreciation of its own unbreakable bond with the Eucharist. "It can never be forgotten that the divine word, read and proclaimed by the Church, has as its one purpose the sacrifice of the new covenant and the banquet of grace, that is,

---

Priests *Presbyterorum Ordinis*, 18; Decree on the Renewal of the Religious Life *Perfectae carita-tis*, 6. In the Church's great Tradition we find significant expressions such as *"Corpus Christi intelligitur etiam . . . Scriptura Dei"* ("God's Scripture is also understood as the Body of Christ"): Waltramus, *De unitate Ecclesiae conservanda*, 1, 14, ed. W. Schwenkenbecher, Hanoverae, 1883, p. 33; "The flesh of the Lord is true food and his blood true drink; this is the true good that is reserved for us in this present life, to nourish ourselves with his flesh and drink his blood, not only in the Eucharist but also in reading sacred Scripture. Indeed, true food and true drink is the word of God which we derive from the Scriptures": Saint Jerome, *Commentarius in Ecclesiasten*, III: PL 23, 1092A.
192. J. Ratzinger (Benedict XVI), *Jesus of Nazareth* (New York, 2007), 268.

the Eucharist."[193] Word and Eucharist are so deeply bound together that we cannot understand one without the other: the word of God sacramentally takes flesh in the event of the Eucharist. The Eucharist opens us to an understanding of Scripture, just as Scripture for its part illumines and explains the mystery of the Eucharist. Unless we acknowledge the Lord's real presence in the Eucharist, our understanding of Scripture remains imperfect. For this reason "the Church has honored the word of God and the Eucharistic mystery with the same reverence, although not with the same worship, and has always and everywhere insisted upon and sanctioned such honor. Moved by the example of her Founder, she has never ceased to celebrate his paschal mystery by coming together to read 'in all the Scriptures the things concerning him' (Lk 24:27) and to carry out the work of salvation through the celebration of the memorial of the Lord and through the sacraments."[194]

THE SACRAMENTALITY OF THE WORD

56. Reflection on the performative character of the word of God in the sacramental action and a growing appreciation of the relationship between word and Eucharist lead to yet another significant theme which emerged during the synodal assembly, that of the *sacramentality* of the word.[195] Here it may help to recall that Pope John Paul II had made reference to the "*sacramental* character of revelation" and in particular to "the sign of the Eucharist in which the indissoluble unity between the signifier and signified makes it possible to grasp the depths of the mystery."[196] We come to see that at the heart of the sacramentality of the word of God is the mystery of the Incarnation itself: "the Word became flesh" (Jn 1:14), the reality of the revealed mystery is offered to us in the "flesh" of the Son. The Word of God can be perceived by faith through the "sign" of human words and actions. Faith acknowledges God's Word by accepting the words and actions by which he makes himself known to us. The sacramental character of revelation points in turn to the history of salvation, to the way that word of God enters time and space, and speaks to men and women, who are called to accept his gift in faith.

The sacramentality of the word can thus be understood by analogy with the real presence of Christ under the appearances of the consecrated bread and wine.[197] By approaching the altar and partaking in the Eucharistic banquet we truly share in the body and blood of Christ. The proclamation of God's word at the celebration entails an acknowledgment that Christ himself is present, that he speaks to us,[198] and that he wishes to be heard. Saint Jerome speaks of the way we ought to approach both the Eucharist and the word of God: "We are reading the Sacred Scriptures. For me, the Gospel is the Body of Christ; for me, the holy Scriptures are his teaching. And when he says: *whoever does not eat my flesh and drink*

---

193. *Ordo Lectionum Missae*, 10.
194. Ibid.
195. Cf. *Propositio* 7.
196. Encyclical Letter *Fides et ratio* (September 14, 1998), 13: AAS 91 (1999), 16.
197. Cf. *Catechism of the Catholic Church*, 1373–1374.
198. Cf. Second Vatican Ecumenical Council, Constitution on Sacred Liturgy *Sacrosanctum Concilium*, 7.

my blood (Jn 6:53), even though these words can also be understood of the [Eucharistic] Mystery, Christ's body and blood are really the word of Scripture, God's teaching. When we approach the [Eucharistic] Mystery, if a crumb falls to the ground we are troubled. Yet when we are listening to the word of God, and God's Word and Christ's flesh and blood are being poured into our ears yet we pay no heed, what great peril should we not feel?"[199] Christ, truly present under the species of bread and wine, is analogously present in the word proclaimed in the liturgy. A deeper understanding of the sacramentality of God's word can thus lead us to a more unified understanding of the mystery of revelation, which takes place through "deeds and words intimately connected;"[200] an appreciation of this can only benefit the spiritual life of the faithful and the Church's pastoral activity.

SACRED SCRIPTURE AND THE LECTIONARY

57. In stressing the bond between word and Eucharist, the Synod also rightly wanted to call attention to certain aspects of the celebration which concern the service of the word. In the first place I wish to mention the importance of the Lectionary. The reform called for by the Second Vatican Council[201] has borne fruit in a richer access to Sacred Scripture, which is now offered in abundance, especially at Sunday Mass. The present structure of the Lectionary not only presents the more important texts of Scripture with some frequency, but also helps us to understand the unity of God's plan thanks to the interplay of the Old and New Testament readings, an interplay "in which Christ is the central figure, commemorated in his paschal mystery."[202] Any remaining difficulties in seeing the relationship between those readings should be approached in the light of canonical interpretation, that is to say, by referring to the inherent unity of the Bible as a whole. Wherever necessary, the competent offices and groups can make provision for publications aimed at bringing out the interconnection of the Lectionary readings, all of which are to be proclaimed to the liturgical assembly as called for by the liturgy of the day. Other problems or difficulties should be brought to the attention of the Congregation for Divine Worship and the Discipline of the Sacraments.

Nor should we overlook the fact that the current Lectionary of the Latin rite has ecumenical significance, since it is used and valued also by communities not yet in full communion with the Catholic Church. The issue of the Lectionary presents itself differently in the liturgies of the Eastern Catholic Churches; the Synod requested that this issue be "examined authoritatively,"[203] in accordance with the proper tradition and competences of the *sui iuris* Churches, likewise taking into account the ecumenical context.

---

199. *In Psalmum* 147: CCL 78, 337–338.
200. Second Vatican Ecumenical Council, Dogmatic Constitution on Divine Revelation *Dei Verbum*, 2.
201. Cf. Constitution on Sacred Liturgy *Sacrosanctum Concilium*, 107–108.
202. *Ordo Lectionum Missae*, 66.
203. *Propositio* 16.

58.   The Synod on the Eucharist had already called for greater care to be taken in the proclamation of the word of God.[204] As is known, while the Gospel is proclaimed by a priest or deacon, in the Latin tradition the first and second readings are proclaimed by an appointed reader, whether a man or a woman. I would like to echo the Synod Fathers who once more stressed the need for the adequate training[205] of those who exercise the *munus* of reader in liturgical celebrations,[206] and particularly those who exercise the ministry of Reader, which in the Latin rite is, as such, a lay ministry. All those entrusted with this office, even those not instituted in the ministry of Reader, should be truly suitable and carefully trained. This training should be biblical and liturgical, as well as technical: "The purpose of their biblical formation is to give readers the ability to understand the readings in context and to perceive by the light of faith central point of the revealed message. The liturgical formation ought to equip readers to have some grasp of the meaning and structure of the liturgy of the word and the significance of its connection with the liturgy of the Eucharist. The technical preparation should make the readers skilled in the art of reading publicly, either with the power of their own voice or with the help of sound equipment."[207]

THE IMPORTANCE OF THE HOMILY

59.   Each member of the People of God "has different duties and responsibilities with respect to the word of God. Accordingly, the faithful listen to God's word and meditate on it, but those who have the office of teaching by virtue of sacred ordination or have been entrusted with exercising that ministry," namely, bishops, priests and deacons, "expound the word of God."[208] Hence we can understand the attention paid to the homily throughout the Synod. In the Apostolic Exhortation *Sacramentum caritatis*, I pointed out that "given the importance of the word of God, the quality of homilies needs to be improved. The homily 'is part of the liturgical action' and is meant to foster a deeper understanding of the word of God, so that it can bear fruit in the lives of the faithful."[209] The homily is a means of bringing the scriptural message to life in a way that helps the faithful to realize that God's word is present and at work in their everyday lives. It should lead to an understanding of the mystery being celebrated, serve as a summons to mission, and prepare the assembly for the profession of faith, the universal prayer and the Eucharistic liturgy. Consequently, those who have been charged with preaching by virtue of a specific ministry ought to take this task to heart. Generic and abstract homilies which obscure the directness of God's word should be avoided, as well as useless digressions which risk drawing greater attention to the preacher than to the heart of the Gospel message. The faithful should be able to perceive clearly that the preacher has a compelling desire to

---

204. Benedict XVI, Post-Synodal Apostolic Exhortation *Sacramentum caritatis* (February 22, 2007), 45: AAS 99 (2007), 140–141.
205. Cf. *Propositio* 14.
206. Cf. *Code of Canon Law*, cc. 230 §2; 204 §1.
207. *Ordo Lectionum Missae*, 55.
208. Ibid., 8.
209. No. 46: AAS 99 (2007), 141.

present Christ, who must stand at the center of every homily. For this reason preachers need to be in close and constant contact with the sacred text;[210] they should prepare for the homily by meditation and prayer, so as to preach with conviction and passion. The synodal assembly asked that the following questions be kept in mind: "What are the Scriptures being proclaimed saying? What do they say to me personally? What should I say to the community in the light of its concrete situation?[211] The preacher "should be the first to hear the word of God which he proclaims,"[212] since, as Saint Augustine says: "He is undoubtedly barren who preaches outwardly the word of God without hearing it inwardly."[213] The homily for Sundays and solemnities should be prepared carefully, without neglecting, whenever possible, to offer at weekday Masses *cum populo* brief and timely reflections which can help the faithful to welcome the word which was proclaimed and to let it bear fruit in their lives.

THE FITTINGNESS OF A DIRECTORY ON HOMILETICS

60.   The art of good preaching based on the Lectionary is an art that needs to be cultivated. Therefore, in continuity with the desire expressed by the previous Synod,[214] I ask the competent authorities, along the lines of the Eucharistic Compendium,[215] also to prepare practical publications to assist ministers in carrying out their task as best they can: as for example a Directory on the homily, in which preachers can find useful assistance in preparing to exercise their ministry. As Saint Jerome reminds us, preaching needs to be accompanied by the witness of a good life: "Your actions should not contradict your words, lest when you preach in Church, someone may begin to think: 'So why don't you yourself act that way?' . . . In the priest of Christ, thought and word must be in agreement."[216]

THE WORD OF GOD, RECONCILIATION, AND THE ANOINTING OF THE SICK

61.   Though the Eucharist certainly remains central to the relationship between God's word and the sacraments, we must also stress the importance of Sacred Scripture in the other sacraments, especially the sacraments of healing, namely the sacrament of Reconciliation or Penance, and the sacrament of the Anointing of the Sick. The role of Sacred Scripture in these sacraments is often overlooked, yet it needs to be assured its proper place. We ought never to forget that "the word of God is a word of reconciliation, for in it God has reconciled all things to himself (cf. 2 Cor 5:18–20; Eph 1:10). The loving forgiveness of God, made

210. Cf. Second Vatican Ecumenical Council, Dogmatic Constitution on Divine Revelation *Dei Verbum*, 25.

211. *Propositio* 15.

212. Ibid.

213. *Sermo* 179, 1: PL 38, 966.

214. Cf. Benedict XVI, Post-Synodal Apostolic Exhortation *Sacramentum caritatis* (February 22, 2007), 93: AAS 99 (2007), 177.

215. Congregation for Divine Worship and the Discipline of the Sacraments, *Compendium Eucharisticum* (March 25, 2009), Vatican City, 2009.

216. *Epistula* 52, 7: CSEL 54, 426–427.

flesh in Jesus, raises up the sinner."[217] "Through the word of God the Christian receives light to recognize his sins and is called to conversion and to confidence in God's mercy."[218] To have a deeper experience of the reconciling power of God's word, the individual penitent should be encouraged to prepare for confession by meditating on a suitable text of Sacred Scripture and to begin confession by reading or listening to a biblical exhortation such as those provided in the rite. When expressing contrition it would be good if the penitent were to use "a prayer based on the words of Scripture,"[219] such as those indicated in the rite. When possible, it would be good that at particular times of the year, or whenever the opportunity presents itself, individual confession by a number of penitents should take place within penitential celebrations as provided for by the ritual, with due respect for the different liturgical traditions; here greater time can be devoted to the celebration of the word through the use of suitable readings.

In the case of the sacrament of the Anointing of the Sick too, it must not be forgotten that "the healing power of the word of God is a constant call to the listener's personal conversion."[220] Sacred Scripture contains countless pages which speak of the consolation, support, and healing which God brings. We can think particularly of Jesus' own closeness to those who suffer, and how he, God's incarnate Word, shouldered our pain and suffered out of love for us, thus giving meaning to sickness and death. It is good that in parishes and in hospitals, according to circumstances, community celebrations of the sacrament of the Anointing of the Sick should be held. On these occasions greater space should be given to the celebration of the word, and the sick helped to endure their sufferings in faith, in union with the redemptive sacrifice of Christ who delivers us from evil.

THE WORD OF GOD AND THE LITURGY OF THE HOURS

62.　Among the forms of prayer which emphasize Sacred Scripture, the Liturgy of the Hours has an undoubted place. The Synod Fathers called it "a privileged form of hearing the word of God, inasmuch as it brings the faithful into contact with Scripture and the living Tradition of the Church."[221] Above all, we should reflect on the profound theological and ecclesial dignity of this prayer. "In the Liturgy of the Hours, the Church, exercising the priestly office of her Head, offers 'incessantly' (1 Thes 5:17) to God the sacrifice of praise, that is, the fruit of lips that confess his name (cf. Heb 13:15). This prayer is 'the voice of a bride speaking to her bridegroom, it is the very prayer that Christ himself, together with his Body, addressed to the Father.'"[222] The Second Vatican Council stated in this regard that "all who take part in this prayer not only fulfill a duty of the Church, but also share in the high honor of the spouse of Christ; for by celebrating the praises of God, they stand before his throne in the name of the Church, their

---

217. *Propositio* 8.
218. *The Rite of Penance*, 17.
219. Ibid., 19.
220. *Propositio* 8.
221. *Propositio* 19.
222. *Principles and Norms for the Liturgy of the Hours*, III, 15.

Mother."[223] The Liturgy of the Hours, as the public prayer of the Church, sets forth the Christian ideal of the sanctification of the entire day, marked by the rhythm of hearing the word of God and praying the Psalms; in this way every activity can find its point of reference in the praise offered to God.

Those who by virtue of their state in life are obliged to pray the Liturgy of the Hours should carry out this duty faithfully for the benefit of the whole Church. Bishops, priests and deacons aspiring to the priesthood, all of whom have been charged by the Church to celebrate this liturgy, are obliged to pray all the Hours daily.[224] As for the obligation of celebrating this liturgy in the Eastern Catholic Churches *sui iuris*, the prescriptions of their proper law are to be followed.[225] I also encourage communities of consecrated life to be exemplary in the celebration of the Liturgy of the Hours, and thus to become a point of reference and an inspiration for the spiritual and pastoral life of the whole Church.

The Synod asked that this prayer become more widespread among the People of God, particularly the recitation of Morning Prayer and Evening Prayer. This could only lead to greater familiarity with the word of God on the part of the faithful. Emphasis should also be placed on the value of the Liturgy of the Hours for the First Vespers of Sundays and Solemnities, particularly in the Eastern Catholic Churches. To this end I recommend that, wherever possible, parishes and religious communities promote this prayer with the participation of the lay faithful.

THE WORD OF GOD AND THE BOOK OF BLESSINGS

63.   Likewise, in using the Book of Blessings attention should be paid to the space allotted to proclaiming, hearing, and briefly explaining the word of God. Indeed the act of blessing, in the cases provided for by the Church and requested by the faithful, should not be something isolated but related in its proper degree to the liturgical life of the People of God. In this sense a blessing, as a genuine sacred sign which "derives its meaning and effectiveness from God's word that is proclaimed."[226] So it is important also to use these situations as means of reawakening in the faithful a hunger and thirst for every word that comes from the mouth of God (cf. Mt 4:4).

SUGGESTIONS AND PRACTICAL PROPOSALS FOR PROMOTING FULLER PARTICIPATION IN THE LITURGY

64.   Having discussed some basic elements of the relationship between the liturgy and the word of God, I would now like to take up and develop several proposals and suggestions advanced by the Synod Fathers with a view to making the People of God ever more familiar with the word of God in the context of liturgical actions or, in any event, with reference to them.

---

223. Constitution on Sacred Liturgy *Sacrosanctum Concilium*, 85.
224. Cf. *Code of Canon Law*, cc. 276 § 3, 1174 § 1.
225. Cf. *Code of Canons of the Eastern Churches*, cc. 377; 473 § 1 and 2, 1°; 538 § 1; 881 § 1.
226. *Book of Blessings*, Introduction, 21.

a) Celebrations of the word of God

65.   The Synod Fathers encouraged all pastors to promote times devoted to the *celebration of the word* in the communities entrusted to their care.[227] These celebrations are privileged occasions for an encounter with the Lord. This practice will certainly benefit the faithful, and should be considered an important element of liturgical formation. Celebrations of this sort are particularly significant as a preparation for the Sunday Eucharist; they are also a way to help the faithful to delve deeply into the riches of the Lectionary, and to pray and meditate on Sacred Scripture, especially during the great liturgical seasons of Advent and Christmas, Lent and Easter. Celebrations of the word of God are to be highly recommended especially in those communities which, due to a shortage of clergy, are unable to celebrate the Eucharistic sacrifice on Sundays and holydays of obligation. Keeping in mind the indications already set forth in the Post-Synodal Apostolic Exhortation *Sacramentum caritatis* with regard to Sunday celebrations in the absence of a priest,[228] I recommend that competent authorities prepare ritual directories, drawing on the experience of the particular Churches. This will favor, in such circumstances, celebrations of the word capable of nourishing the faith of believers, while avoiding the danger of the latter being confused with celebrations of the Eucharist: "on the contrary, they should be privileged moments of prayer for God to send holy priests after his own heart."[229]

The Synod Fathers also recommended celebrations of the word of God on pilgrimages, special feasts, popular missions, spiritual retreats and special days of penance, reparation or pardon. The various expressions of popular piety, albeit not liturgical acts and not to be confused with liturgical celebrations, should nonetheless be inspired by the latter and, above all, give due space to the proclamation and hearing of God's word; "popular piety can find in the word of God an inexhaustible source of inspiration, insuperable models of prayer and fruitful points for reflection."[230]

b) The word and silence

66.   In their interventions, a good number of Synod Fathers insisted on the importance of silence in relation to the word of God and its reception in the lives of the faithful.[231] The word, in fact, can only be spoken and heard in silence, outward and inward. Ours is not an age which fosters recollection; at times one has the impression that people are afraid of detaching themselves, even for a moment, from the mass media. For this reason, it is necessary nowadays that the People of God be educated in the value of silence. Rediscovering the centrality of God's word in the life of the Church also means rediscovering a sense of

---

227. Cf. *Propositio* 18; Second Vatican Ecumenical Council, Constitution on Sacred the Liturgy *Sacrosanctum Concilium*, 35.

228. Cf. Benedict XVI, Post-Synodal Apostolic Exhortation *Sacramentum caritatis* (February 22, 2007), 745: AAS 99 (2007), 162–163.

229. Ibid.

230. Congregation for Divine Worship and the Discipline of the Sacraments, *Directory of Popular Piety and the Liturgy, Principles and Guidelines* (December 17, 2001), 87: *Enchiridion Vaticanum* 20, No. 2461.

231. Cf. *Propositio* 14.

recollection and inner repose. The great patristic tradition teaches us that the mysteries of Christ all involve silence.[232] Only in silence can the word of God find a home in us, as it did in Mary, woman of the word and, inseparably, woman of silence. Our liturgies must facilitate this attitude of authentic listening: *Verbo crescente, verba deficiunt*.[233]

The importance of all this is particularly evident in the Liturgy of the Word, "which should be celebrated in a way that favors meditation."[234] Silence, when called for, should be considered "a part of the celebration."[235] Hence I encourage Pastors to foster moments of recollection whereby, with the assistance of the Holy Spirit, the word of God can find a welcome in our hearts.

c) The solemn proclamation of the word of God

67.   Another suggestion which emerged from the Synod was that the proclamation of the word of God, and the Gospel in particular, should be made more solemn, especially on major liturgical feasts, through the use of the Gospel Book, carried in procession during the opening rites and then brought to the lectern by a deacon or priest for proclamation. This would help the people of God to realize that "the reading of the Gospel is the high point of the Liturgy of the Word."[236] Following the indications contained in the *Ordo Lectionum Missae*, it is good that the word of God, especially the Gospel, be enhanced by being proclaimed in song, particularly on certain solemnities. The greeting, the initial announcement: "A reading from the holy Gospel" and the concluding words: "The Gospel of the Lord," could well be sung as a way of emphasizing the importance of what was read.[237]

d) The word of God in Christian churches

68.   In order to facilitate hearing the word of God, consideration should be given to measures which can help focus the attention of the faithful. Concern should be shown for church acoustics, with due respect for liturgical and architectural norms. "Bishops, duly assisted, in the construction of churches should take care that they be adapted to the proclamation of the word, to meditation, and to the celebration of the Eucharist. Sacred spaces, even apart from the liturgical action, should be eloquent and should present the Christian mystery in relation to the word of God."[238]

Special attention should be given to the *ambo* as the liturgical space from which the word of God is proclaimed. It should be located in a clearly visible place to which the attention of the faithful will be naturally drawn during the liturgy of the word. It should be fixed, and decorated in aesthetic harmony with the

---

232. Cf. Saint Ignatius of Antioch, *Ad Ephesios*, XV, 2: *Patres Apostolici*, ed. F.X. Funk, Tubingae, 1901, I, 224.
233. Saint Augustine, *Sermo* 288, 5: PL 38, 1307; *Sermo* 120, 2: PL 38, 677.
234. *General Instruction of the Roman Missal*, 56.
235. Ibid., 45; cf.Second Vatican Ecumenical Council, Constitution on Sacred Liturgy *Sacrosanctum Concilium*, 30.
236. *Ordo Lectionum Missae*, 13.
237. Cf. ibid., 17.
238. *Propositio* 40.

altar, in order to present visibly the theological significance of *the double table of the word and of the Eucharist*. The readings, the responsorial psalm and the Exsultet are to be proclaimed from the ambo; it can also be used for the homily and the prayers of the faithful.[239]

The Synod Fathers also proposed that churches give a place of honor to the Sacred Scriptures, even *outside of liturgical celebrations*.[240] It is good that the book which contains the word of God should enjoy a visible place of honor inside the Christian temple, without prejudice to the central place proper to the tabernacle containing the Blessed Sacrament.[241]

e) The exclusive use of biblical texts in the liturgy

69.   The Synod also clearly reaffirmed a point already laid down by liturgical law,[242] namely that *the readings drawn from Sacred Scripture may never be replaced by other texts*, however significant the latter may be from a spiritual or pastoral standpoint: "No text of spirituality or literature can equal the value and riches contained in Sacred Scripture, which is the word of God."[243] This is an ancient rule of the Church which is to be maintained.[244] In the face of certain abuses, Pope John Paul II had already reiterated the importance of never using other readings in place of Sacred Scripture.[245] It should also be kept in mind that the *Responsorial Psalm* is also the word of God, and hence should not be replaced by other texts; indeed it is most appropriate that it be sung.

f) Biblically-inspired liturgical song

70.   As part of the enhancement of the word of God in the liturgy, attention should also be paid to the use of song at the times called for by the particular rite. Preference should be given to songs which are of clear biblical inspiration and which express, through the harmony of music and words, the beauty of God's word. We would do well to make the most of those songs handed down to us by the Church's tradition which respect this criterion. I think in particular of the importance of Gregorian chant.[246]

g) Particular concern for the visually and hearing impaired

71.   Here I wish also to recall the Synod's recommendation that special attention be given to those who encounter problems in participating actively in the liturgy; I think, for example, of the visually and hearing impaired. I encourage our Christian communities to offer every possible practical assistance to our

---

239. Cf. *General Instruction of the Roman Missal*, 309.

240. Cf. *Propositio* 14.

241. Benedict XVI, Post-Synodal Apostolic Exhortation *Sacramentum caritatis* (February 22, 2007), 69: AAS 99 (2007), 157.

242. Cf. *General Instruction of the Roman Missal*, 57.

243. *Propositio* 14.

244. Cf. Canon 36 of the *Synod of Hippo*, in the year 399: DS 186.

245. Cf. John Paul II, Apostolic Letter *Vicesimus quintus annus* (December 4, 1988), 13: AAS 81 (1989) 910; Congregation for Divine Worship and the Discipline of the Sacraments, Instruction *Redemptionis sacramentum* (March 25, 2004), 62: *Enchiridion Vaticanum* 22, No. 2248.

246. Cf. Second Vatican Ecumenical Council, Constitution on Sacred Liturgy *Sacrosanctum Concilium*, 116; *General Instruction of the Roman Missal*, 41.

brothers and sisters suffering from such impairments, so that they too can be able to experience a living contact with the word of the Lord.[247]

THE WORD OF GOD IN THE LIFE OF THE CHURCH

ENCOUNTERING THE WORD OF GOD IN SACRED SCRIPTURE

72.   If it is true that the liturgy is the privileged place for the proclamation, hearing, and celebration of the word of God, it is likewise the case that this encounter must be prepared in the hearts of the faithful and then deepened and assimilated, above all by them. The Christian life is essentially marked by an encounter with Jesus Christ, who calls us to follow him. For this reason, the Synod of Bishops frequently spoke of the importance of pastoral care in the Christian communities as the proper setting where a personal and communal journey based on the word of God can occur and truly serve as the basis for our spiritual life. With the Synod Fathers I express my heartfelt hope for the flowering of "a new season of greater love for Sacred Scripture on the part of every member of the People of God, so that their prayerful and faith-filled reading of the Bible will, with time, deepen their personal relationship with Jesus."[248]

Throughout the history of the Church, numerous saints have spoken of the need for knowledge of Scripture in order to grow in love for Christ. This is evident particularly in the Fathers of the Church. Saint Jerome, in his great love for the word of God, often wondered: "How could one live without the knowledge of Scripture, by which we come to know Christ himself, who is the life of believers?"[249] He knew well that the Bible is the means "by which God speaks daily to believers."[250] His advice to the Roman matron Leta about raising her daughter was this: "Be sure that she studies a passage of Scripture each day. . . . Prayer should follow reading, and reading follow prayer . . . so that in the place of jewelery and silk, she may love the divine books."[251] Jerome's counsel to the priest Nepotian can also be applied to us: "Read the divine Scriptures frequently; indeed, the sacred book should never be out of your hands. Learn there what you must teach."[252] Let us follow the example of this great saint who devoted his life to the study of the Bible and who gave the Church its Latin translation, the Vulgate, as well as the example of all those saints who made an encounter with Christ the center of their spiritual lives. Let us renew our efforts to understand deeply the word which God has given to his Church: thus we can aim for that "high standard of ordinary Christian living"[253] proposed by Pope John Paul II at the beginning of the third Christian millennium, which finds constant nourishment in attentively hearing the word of God.

---

247. Cf. *Propositio* 14.
248. *Propositio* 9.
249. *Epistula* 30, 7: CSEL 54, p. 246.
250. Id., *Epistula* 133, 13: CSEL 56, p. 260.
251. Id., *Epistula* 107, 9, 12: CSEL 55, pp. 300, 302.
252. Id., *Epistula* 52, 7: CSEL 54, p. 426.
253. John Paul II, Apostolic Letter *Novo millennio ineunte* (January 6, 2001), 31: AAS 93 (2001), 287–288.

73.   Along these lines the Synod called for a particular pastoral commitment to emphasizing the centrality of the word of God in the Church's life, and recommended a greater "biblical apostolate," not alongside other forms of pastoral work, but as *a means of letting the Bible inspire all pastoral work*.[254] This does not mean adding a meeting here or there in parishes or dioceses, but rather of examining the ordinary activities of Christian communities, in parishes, associations, and movements, to see if they are truly concerned with fostering a personal encounter with Christ, who gives himself to us in his word. Since "ignorance of the Scriptures is ignorance of Christ,"[255] making the Bible the inspiration of every ordinary and extraordinary pastoral outreach will lead to a greater awareness of the person of Christ, who reveals the Father and is the fullness of divine revelation.

For this reason I encourage pastors and the faithful to recognize the importance of this emphasis on the Bible: it will also be the best way to deal with certain pastoral problems which were discussed at the Synod and have to do, for example, with the *proliferation of sects* which spread a distorted and manipulative reading of Sacred Scripture. Where the faithful are not helped to know the Bible in accordance with the Church's faith and based on her living Tradition, this pastoral vacuum becomes fertile ground for realities like the sects to take root. Provision must also be made for the suitable preparation of priests and lay persons who can instruct the People of God in the genuine approach to Scripture.

Furthermore, as was brought out during the Synod sessions, it is good that pastoral activity also favor the growth of *small communities*, "formed by families or based in parishes or linked to the different ecclesial movements and new communities,"[256] which can help to promote formation, prayer, and knowledge of the Bible in accordance with the Church's faith.

THE BIBLICAL DIMENSION OF CATECHESIS

74.   An important aspect of the Church's pastoral work which, if used wisely, can help in rediscovering the centrality of God's word is catechesis, which in its various forms and levels must constantly accompany the journey of the People of God. Luke's description (cf. Lk 24:13–35) of the disciples who meet Jesus on the road to Emmaus represents, in some sense, the model of a catechesis centered on "the explanation of the Scriptures," an explanation which Christ alone can give (cf. Lk 24:27–28), as he shows that they are fulfilled in his person.[257] The hope which triumphs over every failure was thus reborn, and made those disciples convinced and credible witnesses of the Risen Lord.

---

254. *Propositio* 30; cf. Second Vatican Ecumenical Council, Dogmatic Constitution on Divine Revelation *Dei Verbum*, 24.
255. Saint Jerome, *Commentariorum in Isaiam libri, Prol.*: PL 24, 17B.
256. *Propositio* 21.
257. Cf. *Propositio* 23.

The *General Catechetical Directory* contains valuable guidelines for a biblically inspired catechesis and I readily encourage that these be consulted.[258] Here I wish first and foremost to stress that catechesis "must be permeated by the mindset, the spirit, and the outlook of the Bible and the Gospels through assiduous contact with the texts themselves; yet it also means remembering that catechesis will be all the richer and more effective for reading the texts with the mind and the heart of the Church,"[259] and for drawing inspiration from the two millennia of the Church's reflection and life. A knowledge of biblical personages, events, and well-known sayings should thus be encouraged; this can also be promoted by the judicious *memorization* of some passages which are particularly expressive of the Christian mysteries. Catechetical work always entails approaching Scripture in faith and in the Church's Tradition, so that its words can be perceived as living, just as Christ is alive today wherever two or three are gathered in his name (cf. Mt 18:20). Catechesis should communicate in a lively way the history of salvation and the content of the Church's faith, and so enable every member of the faithful to realize that this history is also a part of his or her own life.

Here it is important to stress the relationship between Sacred Scripture and the *Catechism of the Catholic Church*, as it is set forth in the *General Catechetical Directory*: "Sacred Scripture, in fact, as 'the word of God written under the inspiration of the Holy Spirit', and the Catechism of the Catholic Church, as a significant contemporary expression of the living Tradition of the Church and a sure norm for teaching the faith, are called, each in its own way and according to its specific authority, to nourish catechesis in the Church today."[260]

THE BIBLICAL FORMATION OF CHRISTIANS

75.   In order to achieve the goal set by the Synod, namely, an increased emphasis on the Bible in the Church's pastoral activity, all Christians, and catechists in particular, need to receive suitable training. Attention needs to be paid to the *biblical apostolate*, which is a very valuable means to that end, as the Church's experience has shown. The Synod Fathers also recommended that, possibly through the use of existing academic structures, centers of formation should be established where laity and missionaries can be trained to understand, live, and proclaim the word of God. Also, where needed, specialized institutes for biblical studies should be established to ensure that exegetes possess a solid understanding of theology and an appropriate appreciation for the contexts in which they carry out their mission.[261]

---

258. Cf. Congregation for the Clergy, *General Catechetical Directory* (August 15, 1997), 94–96; *Enchiridion Vaticanum*, 16, nos. 875–878; John Paul II, Apostolic Exhortation *Catechesi tradendae* (October 16, 1979), 27: AAS 71 (1979), 1298–1299.

259. Ibid., 127: *Enchiridion Vaticanum* 16, no. 935; cf. John Paul II, Apostolic Exhortation *Catechesi tradendae* (October 16, 1979), 27: AAS 71 (1979), 1299.

260. Ibid., 128: *Enchiridion Vaticanum* 16, no. 936.

261. Cf. *Propositio* 33.

76.   Among a variety of possible initiatives, the Synod suggested that in meetings, whether at the diocesan, national or international levels, greater emphasis be given to the importance of the word of God, its attentive hearing, and the faith-filled and prayerful reading of the Bible. In Eucharistic Congresses, whether national or international, at World Youth Days and other gatherings, it would be praiseworthy to make greater room for the celebration of the word and for biblically-inspired moments of formation.[262]

THE WORD OF GOD AND VOCATIONS

77.   In stressing faith's intrinsic summons to an ever deeper relationship with Christ, the word of God in our midst, the Synod also emphasized that this word calls each one of us personally, revealing that *life itself is a vocation* from God. In other words, the more we grow in our personal relationship with the Lord Jesus, the more we realize that he is calling us to holiness in and through the definitive choices by which we respond to his love in our lives, taking up tasks and ministries which help to build up the Church. This is why the Synod frequently encouraged all Christians to grow in their relationship with the word of God, not only because of their Baptism, but also in accordance with their call to various states in life. Here we touch upon one of the pivotal points in the teaching of the Second Vatican Council, which insisted that each member of the faithful is called to holiness according to his or her proper state in life.[263] Our call to holiness is revealed in Sacred Scripture: "Be holy, for I am holy" (Lev 11:44; 19:2; 20:7). Saint Paul then points out its Christological basis: in Christ, the Father "has chosen us before the foundation of the world, that we should be holy and blameless before him" (Eph 1:4). Paul's greeting to his brothers and sisters in the community of Rome can be taken as addressed to each of us: "To all God's beloved, who are called to be saints: grace to you and peace from God our Father and the Lord Jesus Christ!" (Rom 1:7).

a) Ordained ministers and the word of God

78.   I would like to speak first to the Church's ordained ministers, in order to remind them of the Synod's statement that "the word of God is indispensable in forming the heart of a good shepherd and minister of the word."[264] Bishops, priests, and deacons can hardly think that they are living out their vocation and mission apart from a decisive and renewed commitment to sanctification, one of whose pillars is contact with God's word.

79.   To those called to the *episcopate*, who are the first and most authoritative heralds of the word, I would repeat the words of Pope John Paul II in his Post-Synodal Apostolic Exhortation *Pastores gregis*. For the nourishment and progress of his spiritual life, the Bishop must always put "in first place, reading and meditation on the word of God. Every Bishop must commend himself and feel

---

262. Cf. *Propositio* 45.
263. Cf. Second Vatican Ecumenical Council, Dogmatic Constitution on the Church *Lumen gentium*, 39–42.
264. *Propositio* 31.

himself commended 'to the Lord and to the word of his grace, which is able to build up and to give the inheritance among all those who are sanctified' (Acts 20:32). Before becoming one who hands on the word, the Bishop, together with his priests and indeed like every member of the faithful, and like the Church herself, must be a hearer of the word. He should dwell 'within' the word and allow himself to be protected and nourished by it, as if by a mother's womb."[265] To all my brother Bishops I recommend frequent personal reading and study of Sacred Scripture, in imitation of Mary, *Virgo Audiens* and Queen of the Apostles.

80.   To *priests* too, I would recall the words of Pope John Paul II, who in the Post-Synodal Apostolic Exhortation *Pastores dabo vobis*, stated that "the priest is first of all a *minister of the word of God*, consecrated and sent to announce the Good News of the Kingdom to all, calling every person to the obedience of faith and leading believers to an ever increasing knowledge of and communion in the mystery of God, as revealed and communicated to us in Christ. For this reason the priest himself ought first of all to develop a great personal familiarity with the word of God. Knowledge of its linguistic and exegetical aspects, though certainly necessary, is not enough. He needs to approach the word with a docile and prayerful heart so that it may deeply penetrate his thoughts and feelings and bring about a new outlook in him—'the mind of Christ' (1 Cor 2:16)."[266] Consequently, his words, his choices and his behavior must increasingly become a reflection, proclamation, and witness of the Gospel; "only if he 'abides' in the word will the priest become a perfect disciple of the Lord. Only then then will he know the truth and be set truly free."[267]

In a word, the priestly vocation demands that one be *consecrated "in the truth."* Jesus states this clearly with regard to his disciples: "Sanctify them in the truth; your word is truth. As you have sent me into the world, so I have sent them into the world" (Jn 17:17–18). The disciples in a certain sense become "drawn into intimacy with God by being immersed in the word of God. God's word is, so to speak, the purifying bath, the creative power which changes them and makes them belong to God."[268] And since Christ himself is God's Word made flesh (Jn 1:14)—"the Truth" (Jn 14:6)—Jesus' prayer to the Father, "Sanctify them in the truth," means in the deepest sense: "Make them one with me, the Christ. Bind them to me. Draw them into me. For there is only one priest of the New Covenant, Jesus Christ himself."[269] Priests need to grow constantly in their awareness of this reality.

81.   I would also like to speak of the place of God's word in the life of those called to the *diaconate*, not only as the final step towards the order of priesthood, but as a permanent service. The *Directory for the Permanent Diaconate* states that "the deacon's theological identity clearly provides the features of his specific spirituality, which is presented essentially as a spirituality of service.

---

265. No. 15: AAS 96 (2004), 846–847.
266. No. 26: AAS 84 (1992), 698.
267. Ibid.
268. Benedict XVI, Homily at the Chrism Mass (April 9, 2009): AAS 101 (2009), 355.
269. Ibid., 356.

The model *par excellence* is Christ as servant, lived totally at the service of God, for the good of humanity."[270] From this perspective, one can see how, in the various dimensions of the diaconal ministry, a "characteristic element of diaconal spirituality is the word of God, of which the deacon is called to be an authoritative preacher, believing what he preaches, teaching what he believes, and living what he teaches."[271] Hence, I recommend that deacons nourish their lives by the faith-filled reading of Sacred Scripture, accompanied by study and prayer. They should be introduced to "Sacred Scripture and its correct interpretation; to the relationship between Scripture and Tradition; in particular to the use of Scripture in preaching, in catechesis, and in pastoral activity in general."[272]

b) The word of God and candidates for Holy Orders

82.   The Synod attributed particular importance to the decisive role that the word of God must play in the spiritual life of candidates for the ministerial priesthood: "Candidates for the priesthood must learn to love the word of God. Scripture should thus be the soul of their theological formation, and emphasis must be given to the indispensable interplay of exegesis, theology, spirituality, and mission."[273] Those aspiring to the ministerial priesthood are called to a profound personal relationship with God's word, particularly in *lectio divina*, so that this relationship will in turn nurture their vocation: it is in the light and strength of God's word that one's specific vocation can be discerned and appreciated, loved and followed, and one's proper mission carried out, by nourishing the heart with thoughts of God, so that faith, as our response to the word, may become a new criterion for judging and evaluating persons and things, events and issues.[274]

Such attention to the prayerful reading of Scripture must not in any way lead to a dichotomy with regard to the exegetical studies which are a part of formation. The Synod recommended that seminarians be concretely helped to see *the relationship between biblical studies and scriptural prayer*. The study of Scripture ought to lead to an increased awareness of the mystery of divine revelation and foster an attitude of prayerful response to the Lord who speaks. Conversely, an authentic life of prayer cannot fail to nurture in the candidate's heart a desire for greater knowledge of the God who has revealed himself in his word as infinite love. Hence, great care should be taken to ensure that seminarians always cultivate this *reciprocity between study and prayer* in their lives. This end will be served if candidates are introduced to the study of Scripture through methods which favor this integral approach.

---

270. Congregation for Catholic Education, *Fundamental Norms for the Formation of Permanent Deacons* (February 22, 1998), 11: *Enchiridion Vaticanum* 17, nos. 174–175.

271. Ibid., 74: *Enchiridion Vaticanum* 17, no. 263.

272. Ibid., 81: *Enchiridion Vaticanum* 17, no. 271.

273. *Propositio* 32.

274. Cf. John Paul II, Post-Synodal Apostolic Exhortation *Pastores dabo vobis* (March 25, 1992), 47: AAS 84 (1992), 740–742.

c) The word of God and the consecrated life

83.   With regard to the consecrated life, the Synod first recalled that it "is born from hearing the word of God and embracing the Gospel as its rule of life."[275] A life devoted to following Christ in his chastity, poverty, and obedience thus becomes "a living 'exegesis' of God's word."[276] The Holy Spirit, in whom the Bible was written, is the same Spirit who illumines "the word of God with new light for the founders and foundresses. Every charism and every rule springs from it and seeks to be an expression of it,"[277] thus opening up new pathways of Christian living marked by the radicalism of the Gospel.

Here I would mention that the great monastic tradition has always considered meditation on Sacred Scripture to be an essential part of its specific spirituality, particularly in the form of *lectio divina*. Today too, both old and new expressions of special consecration are called to be genuine schools of the spiritual life, where the Scriptures can be read according to the Holy Spirit in the Church, for the benefit of the entire People of God. The Synod therefore recommended that communities of consecrated life always make provision for solid instruction in the faith-filled reading of the Bible.[278]

Once again I would like to echo the consideration and gratitude that the Synod expressed with regard to those forms of *contemplative life* whose specific charism is to devote a great part of their day to imitating the Mother of God, who diligently pondered the words and deeds of her Son (cf. Lk 2:19, 51), and Mary of Bethany, who sat at the Lord's feet and listened attentively to his words (cf. Lk10:38). I think in particular of monks and cloistered nuns, who by virtue of their separation from the world are all the more closely united to Christ, the heart of the world. More than ever, the Church needs the witness of men and women resolved to "put nothing before the love of Christ."[279] The world today is often excessively caught up in outward activities and risks losing its bearings. Contemplative men and women, by their lives of prayer, attentive hearing and meditation on God's Word, remind us that man does not live by bread alone but by every word that comes from the mouth of God (cf. Mt 4:4). All the faithful, then, should be clearly conscious that this form of life "shows today's world what is most important, indeed, the one thing necessary: there is an ultimate reason which makes life worth living, and that is God and his inscrutable love."[280]

d) The word of God and the lay faithful

84.   The Synod frequently spoke of the laity and thanked them for their generous activity in spreading the Gospel in the various settings of daily life, at work

---

275. *Propositio* 24.

276. Benedict XVI, Homily for the World Day of Consecrated Life (February 2, 2008): AAS 100 (2008), 133; cf. John Paul II, Post-Synodal Apostolic Exhortation *Vita consecrata* (March 25, 1996), 82: AAS 88 (1996), 458–460.

277. Congregation for Institutes of Consecrated Life and for Societies of Apostolic Life, Instruction *Starting Afresh from Christ: A Renewed Commitment to Consecrated Life in the Third Millennium* (May 19, 2002), 24: *Enchiridion Vaticanum* 21, no. 447.

278. Cf. *Propositio* 24.

279. Saint Benedict, *Rule*, IV, 21: SC 181, 456–458.

280. Benedict XVI, Address at Heiligenkreuz Abbey (September 9, 2007): AAS 99 (2007), 856.

believing in and pleasing God. If during the *lectio* you encounter a closed door, knock and it will be opened to you by that guardian of whom Jesus said, 'The gatekeeper will open it for him'. By applying yourself in this way to *lectio divina*, search diligently and with unshakable trust in God for the meaning of the divine Scriptures, which is hidden in great fullness within. You ought not, however, to be satisfied merely with knocking and seeking: to understand the things of God, what is absolutely necessary is *oratio*. For this reason, the Savior told us not only: 'Seek and you will find,' and 'Knock and it shall be opened to you,' but also added, 'Ask and you shall receive.'"[293]

In this regard, however, one must *avoid the risk of an individualistic approach*, and remember that God's word is given to us precisely to build communion, to unite us in the Truth along our path to God. While it is a word addressed to each of us personally, it is also a word which builds community, which builds the Church. Consequently, *the sacred text must always be approached in the communion of the Church*. In effect, "a communal reading of Scripture is extremely important, because the living subject in the Sacred Scriptures is the People of God, it is the Church. . . . Scripture does not belong to the past, because its subject, the People of God inspired by God himself, is always the same, and therefore the word is always alive in the living subject. As such, it is important to read and experience Sacred Scripture in communion with the Church, that is, with all the great witnesses to this word, beginning with the earliest Fathers up to the saints of our own day, up to the present-day magisterium."[294]

For this reason, *the privileged place* for the prayerful reading of Sacred Scripture *is the liturgy*, and particularly *the Eucharist*, in which, as we celebrate the Body and Blood of Christ in the sacrament, the word itself is present and at work in our midst. In some sense the prayerful reading of the Bible, personal and communal, must always be related to the Eucharistic celebration. Just as the adoration of the Eucharist prepares for, accompanies and follows the liturgy of the Eucharist,[295] so too prayerful reading, personal and communal, prepares for, accompanies and deepens what the Church celebrates when she proclaims the word in a liturgical setting. By so closely relating *lectio* and liturgy, we can better grasp the criteria which should guide this practice in the area of pastoral care and in the spiritual life of the People of God.

87.   The documents produced before and during the Synod mentioned a number of methods for a faith-filled and fruitful approach to Sacred Scripture. Yet the greatest attention was paid to *lectio divina*, which is truly "capable of opening up to the faithful the treasures of God's word, but also of bringing about an encounter with Christ, the living word of God."[296] I would like here to review the basic steps of this procedure. It opens with the reading (*lectio*) of a text,

---

293. Origen, *Epistola ad Gregorium*, 3: PG 11, 92.

294. Benedict XVI, Address to the Students of the Roman Major Seminary (February 19, 2007): AAS 99 (2007), 253–254.

295. Cf. Id., Post-Synodal Apostolic Exhortation *Sacramentum caritatis* (February 22, 2007), 66; AAS 99 (2007), 155–156.

296. Final Message, III, 9.

which leads to a desire to understand its true content: w*hat does the biblical text say in itself?* Without this, there is always a risk that the text will become a pretext for never moving beyond our own ideas. Next comes meditation (*meditatio*), which asks: *what does the biblical text say to us?* Here, each person, individually but also as a member of the community, must let himself or herself be moved and challenged. Following this comes prayer (*oratio*), which asks the question: *what do we say to the Lord in response to his word?* Prayer, as petition, intercession, thanksgiving, and praise, is the primary way by which the word transforms us. Finally, *lectio divina* concludes with contemplation (*contemplatio*), during which we take up, as a gift from God, his own way of seeing and judging reality, and ask ourselves *what conversion of mind, heart, and life is the Lord asking of us?* In the *Letter to the Romans*, Saint Paul tells us: "Do not be conformed to this world, but be transformed by the renewal of your mind, that you may prove what is the will of God, what is good and acceptable and perfect" (12:2). Contemplation aims at creating within us a truly wise and discerning vision of reality, as God sees it, and at forming within us "the mind of Christ" (1 Cor 2:16). The word of God appears here as a criterion for discernment: it is "living and active, sharper than any two-edged sword, piercing to the division of soul and spirit, of joints and marrow, and discerning the thoughts and intentions of the heart" (Heb 4:12). We do well also to remember that the process of *lectio divina* is not concluded until it arrives at action (*actio*), which moves the believer to make his or her life a gift for others in charity.

We find the supreme synthesis and fulfillment of this process in the Mother of God. For every member of the faithful Mary is the model of docile acceptance of God's word, for she "kept all these things, pondering them in her heart" (Lk 2:19; cf. 2:51); she discovered the profound bond which unites, in God's great plan, apparently disparate events, actions and things.[297]

I would also like to echo what the Synod proposed about the importance of the personal reading of Scripture, also as a practice allowing for the possibility, in accordance with the Church's usual conditions, of gaining an indulgence either for oneself or for the faithful departed.[298] The practice of indulgences[299] implies the doctrine of the infinite merits of Christ—which the Church, as the minister of the redemption, dispenses and applies, but it also implies that of the communion of saints, and it teaches us that "to whatever degree we are united in Christ, we are united to one another, and the supernatural life of each one can be useful for the others."[300] From this standpoint, the reading of the word of God sustains us on our journey of penance and conversion, enables us to deepen our sense of belonging to the Church, and helps us to grow in familiarity with God. As Saint

---

297. Ibid.

298. "*Plenaria indulgentia* conceditur christifideli qui Sacram Scripturam, iuxta textum a competenti auctoritate adprobatum, cum veneratione divino eloquio debita et ad modum lectionis spiritalis, per dimidiam saltem horam legerit; si per minus tempus id egerit *indulgentia* erit partialis": apostolic penitentiary, *Enchiridion Indulgentiarum. Normae et concessiones* (July 16, 1999), 30, §1.

299. Cf. *Catechism of the Catholic Church*, 1471–1479.

300. Paul VI, Apostolic Constitution *Indulgentiarum doctrina* (January 1, 1967): AAS 59 (1967), 18–19.

Ambrose puts it, "When we take up the Sacred Scriptures in faith and read them with the Church, we walk once more with God in the Garden."[301]

THE WORD OF GOD AND MARIAN PRAYER

88. Mindful of the inseparable bond between the word of God and Mary of Nazareth, along with the Synod Fathers I urge that Marian prayer be encouraged among the faithful, above all in life of families, since it is an aid to meditating on the holy mysteries found in the Scriptures. A most helpful aid, for example, is the individual or communal recitation of the Holy Rosary,[302] which ponders the mysteries of Christ's life in union with Mary,[303] and which Pope John Paul II wished to enrich with the mysteries of light.[304] It is fitting that the announcement of each mystery be accompanied by a brief biblical text pertinent to that mystery, so as to encourage the memorization of brief biblical passages relevant to the mysteries of Christ's life.

The Synod also recommended that the faithful be encouraged to pray the *Angelus*. This prayer, simple yet profound, allows us "to commemorate daily the mystery of the Incarnate Word."[305] It is only right that the People of God, families, and communities of consecrated persons, be faithful to this Marian prayer traditionally recited at sunrise, midday, and sunset. In the *Angelus* we ask God to grant that, through Mary's intercession, we may imitate her in doing his will and in welcoming his word into our lives. This practice can help us to grow in an authentic love for the mystery of the incarnation.

The ancient prayers of the Christian East which contemplate the entire history of salvation in the light of the *Theotokos*, the Mother of God, are likewise worthy of being known, appreciated, and widely used. Here particular mention can be made of the *Akathist* and *Paraklesis* prayers. These hymns of praise, chanted in the form of a litany and steeped in the faith of the Church and in references to the Bible, help the faithful to meditate on the mysteries of Christ in union with Mary. In particular, the venerable *Akathist* hymn to the Mother of God—so-called because it is sung while standing—represents one of the highest expressions of the Marian piety of the Byzantine tradition.[306] Praying with these words opens wide the heart and disposes it to the peace that is from above, from God, to that peace which is Christ himself, born of Mary for our salvation.

---

301. Cf. *Epistula* 49, 3: PL 16, 1204A.

302. Cf. Congregation for Divine Worship and the Discipline of the Sacraments, *Directory on Popular Piety and the Liturgy. Principles and Orientations* (December 17, 2001), 197–202: *Enchiridion Vaticanum* 20, nos. 2638–2643.

303. Cf. *Propositio* 55.

304. Cf. John Paul II, Apostolic Letter *Rosarium Virginis Mariae* (October 16, 2002): AAS 95 (2003), 5–36.

305. *Propositio* 55.

306. Cf. Congregation for Divine Worship and the Discipline of the Sacraments, *Directory on Popular Piety and the Liturgy. Principles and Orientations* (December 17, 2001), 207:*Enchiridion Vaticanum* 20, nos. 2656–2657.

89.   As we call to mind the Word of God who became flesh in the womb of Mary of Nazareth, our heart now turns to the land where the mystery of our salvation was accomplished, and from which the word of God spread to the ends of the earth. By the power of the Holy Spirit, the Word became flesh in a specific time and place, in a strip of land on the edges of the Roman Empire. The more we appreciate the universality and the uniqueness of Christ's person, the more we look with gratitude to that land where Jesus was born, where he lived, and where he gave his life for us. The stones on which our Redeemer walked are still charged with his memory and continue to "cry out" the Good News. For this reason, the Synod Fathers recalled the felicitous phrase which speaks of the Holy Land as "the Fifth Gospel."[307] How important it is that in those places there be Christian communities, notwithstanding any number of hardships! The Synod of Bishops expressed profound closeness to all those Christians who dwell in the land of Jesus and bear witness to their faith in the Risen One. Christians there are called to serve not only as "a beacon of faith for the universal Church, but also as a leaven of harmony, wisdom, and equilibrium in the life of a society which traditionally has been, and continues to be, pluralistic, multi-ethnic, and multi-religious."[308]

The Holy Land today remains a goal of pilgrimage for the Christian people, a place of prayer and penance, as was testified to in antiquity by authors like Saint Jerome.[309] The more we turn our eyes and our hearts to the earthly Jerusalem, the more will our yearning be kindled for the heavenly Jerusalem, the true goal of every pilgrimage, along with our eager desire that the name of Jesus, the one name which brings salvation, may be acknowledged by all (cf. Acts 4:12).

PART THREE: *VERBUM MUNDO*

"No one has ever seen God. It is God the only Son, who is close to the Father's heart, who has made him known." (Jn 1:18)

THE CHURCH'S MISSION:
TO PROCLAIM THE WORD OF GOD TO THE WORLD

THE WORD FROM THE FATHER AND TO THE FATHER

90.   Saint John powerfully expresses the fundamental paradox of the Christian faith. On the one hand, he says that "no one has ever seen God" (Jn 1:18; cf. 1 Jn 4:12). In no way can our imaginations, our concepts or our words ever define or embrace the infinite reality of the Most High. He remains *Deus semper maior*. Yet Saint John also tells us that the Word truly "became flesh" (Jn 1:14). The only-begotten Son, who is ever with the Father, has made known the God whom

---

307. Cf. *Propositio* 51.
308. Benedict XVI, Homily at Mass in the Valley of Josaphat, Jerusalem (May 12, 2009): AAS 101 (2009), 473.
309. Cf. *Epistola* 108, 14: CSEL 55, pp. 324–325.

"no one has ever seen" (Jn 1:18). Jesus Christ comes to us, "full of grace and truth" (Jn 1:14), to give us these gifts (cf. Jn 1:17); and "from his fullness we have all received, grace upon grace" (Jn 1:16). In the Prologue of his Gospel, John thus contemplates the Word from his being with God to his becoming flesh and his return to the Father with our humanity, which he has assumed for ever. In this coming forth from God and returning to him (cf. Jn 13:3; 16:28; 17:8,10), Christ is presented as the one who "tells us" about God (cf. Jn 1:18). Indeed, as Saint Irenaeus of Lyons says, the Son "is the revealer of the Father."[310] Jesus of Nazareth is, so to speak, the "exegete" of the God whom "no one has ever seen." "He is the image of the invisible God" (Col 1:15). Here we see fulfilled the prophecy of Isaiah about the effectiveness of the Lord's word: as the rain and snow come down from heaven to water and to make the earth fruitful, so too the word of God "shall not return to me empty, but it shall accomplish that which I purpose, and prosper in the thing for which I sent it" (cf. Is 55:10–11.). Jesus Christ is this definitive and effective word which came forth from the Father and returned to him, perfectly accomplishing his will in the world.

PROCLAIMING TO THE WORLD THE "LOGOS" OF HOPE

91.   The word of God has bestowed upon us the divine life which transfigures the face of the earth, making all things new (cf. Rev 21:5). His word engages us not only as *hearers* of divine revelation, but also as its *heralds*. The one whom the Father has sent to do his will (cf. Jn 5:36–38; 6:38–40; 7:16–18) draws us to himself and makes us part of his life and mission. The Spirit of the Risen Lord empowers us to proclaim the word everywhere by the witness of our lives. This was experienced by the first Christian community, which saw the word spread through preaching and witness (cf. Acts 6:7). Here we can think in particular of the life of the Apostle Paul, a man completely caught up by the Lord (cf. Phil 3:12)—"it is no longer I who live, but Christ who lives in me" (Gal 2:20)—and by his mission: "woe to me if I do not proclaim the Gospel!" (1 Cor 9:16). Paul knew well that what was revealed in Christ is really salvation for all peoples, liberation from the slavery of sin in order to enjoy the freedom of the children of God.

What the Church proclaims to the world is the *Logos of Hope* (cf. 1 Pt 3:15); in order to be able to live fully each moment, men and women need "the great hope" which is "the God who possesses a human face and who 'has loved us to the end' (Jn 13:1)."[311] This is why the Church is missionary by her very nature. We cannot keep to ourselves the words of eternal life given to us in our encounter with Jesus Christ: they are meant for everyone, for every man and woman. Everyone today, whether he or she knows it or not, needs this message. May the Lord himself, as in the time of the prophet Amos, raise up in our midst a new hunger and thirst for the word of God (cf. Am 8:11). It is our responsibility to pass on what, by God's grace, we ourselves have received.

---

310. *Adversus haereses*, IV, 20, 7: PG 7, 1037.
311. Benedict XVI, Encyclical Letter *Spe salvi* (November 30, 2007), 31: AAS 99 (2007), 1010.

92. The Synod of Bishops forcefully reaffirmed the need within the Church for a revival of the missionary consciousness present in the People of God from the beginning. The first Christians saw their missionary preaching as a necessity rooted in the very nature of faith: the God in whom they believed was the God of all, the one true God who revealed himself in Israel's history and ultimately in his Son, who thus provided the response which, in their inmost being, all men and women awaited. The first Christian communities felt that their faith was not part of a particular cultural tradition, differing from one people to another, but belonged instead to the realm of truth, which concerns everyone equally.

Once more it is Saint Paul who, by his life, illustrates the meaning of the Christian mission and its fundamental universality. We can think here of the episode related in the *Acts of the Apostles* about the Athenian Areopagus (cf. 17:16–34). The Apostle of the Nations enters into dialogue with people of various cultures precisely because he is conscious that the mystery of God, Known yet Unknown, which every man and woman perceives, however confusedly, has really been revealed in history: "What therefore you worship as unknown, this I proclaim to you" (Acts 17:23). In fact, the newness of Christian proclamation is that we can tell all peoples: "God has shown himself. In person. And now the way to him is open. The novelty of the Christian message does not consist in an idea but in a fact: God has revealed himself."[312]

THE WORD AND THE KINGDOM OF GOD

93. Consequently, the Church's mission cannot be considered as an optional or supplementary element in her life. Rather it entails letting the Holy Spirit assimilate us to Christ himself, and thus to share in his own mission: "As the Father has sent me, so I send you" (Jn 20:21) to share the word with your entire life. It is the word itself which impels us towards our brothers and sisters: it is the word which illuminates, purifies, converts; we are only its servants.

We need, then, to discover ever anew the urgency and the beauty of the proclamation of the word for the coming of the Kingdom of God which Christ himself preached. Thus we grow in the realization, so clear to the Fathers of the Church, that the proclamation of the word has as its content the Kingdom of God (cf. Mk 1:14–15), which, in the memorable phrase of Origen,[313] *is the very person of Jesus* (*Autobasileia*). The Lord offers salvation to men and women in every age. All of us recognize how much the light of Christ needs to illumine every area of human life: the family, schools, culture, work, leisure, and the other aspects of social life.[314] It is not a matter of preaching a word of consolation, but rather a word which disrupts, which calls to conversion and which opens the way to an encounter with the one through whom a new humanity flowers.

---

312. Benedict XVI, Address to Representatives of the World of Culture at the "Collège des Bernardins" in Paris (September 12, 2008): AAS 100 (2008), 730.

313. Cf. *In Evangelium secundum Matthaeum* 17:7: PG 13, 1197B; Saint Jerome, *Translatio homiliarum Origenis in Lucam*, 36: PL 26, 324–325.

314. Cf. Benedict XVI, Homily for the Opening of the Twelfth Ordinary General Assembly of the Synod of Bishops (October 5, 2008): AAS 100 (2008), 757.

94.   Since the entire People of God is a people which has been "sent," the Synod reaffirmed that "the mission of proclaiming the word of God is the task of all of the disciples of Jesus Christ based on their Baptism."[315] No believer in Christ can feel dispensed from this responsibility which comes from the fact of our sacramentally belonging to the Body of Christ. A consciousness of this must be revived in every family, parish, community, association, and ecclesial movement. The Church, as a mystery of communion, is thus entirely missionary, and everyone, according to his or her proper state in life, is called to give an incisive contribution to the proclamation of Christ.

Bishops and *priests*, in accordance with their specific mission, are the first to be called to live a life completely at the service of the word, to proclaim the Gospel, to celebrate the sacraments and to form the faithful in the authentic knowledge of Scripture. *Deacons* too must feel themselves called to cooperate, in accordance with their specific mission, in this task of evangelization.

Throughout the Church's history *the consecrated life* has been outstanding for explicitly taking up the task of proclaiming and preaching the word of God in the *missio ad gentes* and in the most difficult situations, for being ever ready to adapt to new situations and for setting out courageously and boldly along fresh paths in meeting new challenges for the effective proclamation of God's word.[316]

The *laity* are called to exercise their own prophetic role, which derives directly from their Baptism, and to bear witness to the Gospel in daily life, wherever they find themselves. In this regard the Synod Fathers expressed "the greatest esteem, gratitude, and encouragement for the service to evangelization which so many of the lay faithful, and women in particular, provide with generosity and commitment in their communities throughout the world, following the example of Mary Magdalene, the first witness of the joy of Easter."[317] The Synod also recognized with gratitude that the ecclesial movements and the new communities are a great force for evangelization in our times and an incentive to the development of new ways of proclaiming the Gospel.[318]

THE NECESSITY OF THE *"MISSIO AD GENTES"*

95.   In calling upon all the faithful to proclaim God's word, the Synod Fathers restated the need in our day too for a decisive commitment to the *missio ad gentes*. In no way can the Church restrict her pastoral work to the "ordinary maintenance" of those who already know the Gospel of Christ. Missionary outreach is a clear sign of the maturity of an ecclesial community. The Fathers also insisted that the word of God is the saving truth which men and women in every age need to hear. For this reason, it must be explicitly proclaimed. The Church

---

315. *Propositio* 38.
316. Cf. Congregation for Institutes of consecrated life and for societies of apostolic life, Instruction *Starting Afresh from Christ: A Renewed Commitment to Consecrated Life in the Third Millennium* (May 19, 2002), 36: *Enchiridion Vaticanum* 21, nos. 488–491.
317. *Propositio* 30.
318. Cf. *Propositio* 38.

must go out to meet each person in the strength of the Spirit (cf. 1 Cor 2:5) and continue her prophetic defense of people's right and freedom to hear the word of God, while constantly seeking out the most effective ways of proclaiming that word, even at the risk of persecution.[319] The Church feels duty-bound to proclaim to every man and woman the word that saves (cf. Rom 1:14).

PROCLAMATION AND THE NEW EVANGELIZATION

96.   Pope John Paul II, taking up the prophetic words of Pope Paul VI in the Apostolic Exhortation *Evangelii nuntiandi*, had in a variety of ways reminded the faithful of the need for a new missionary season for the entire people of God.[320] At the dawn of the third millennium not only are there still many peoples who have not come to know the Good News, but also a great many Christians who need to have the word of God once more persuasively proclaimed to them, so that they can concretely experience the power of the Gospel. Many of our brothers and sisters are "baptized, but insufficiently evangelized."[321] In a number of cases, nations once rich in faith and in vocations are losing their identity under the influence of a secularized culture.[322] The need for a new evangelization, so deeply felt by my venerable Predecessor, must be valiantly reaffirmed, in the certainty that God's word is effective. The Church, sure of her Lord's fidelity, never tires of proclaiming the good news of the Gospel and invites all Christians to discover anew the attraction of following Christ.

THE WORD OF GOD AND CHRISTIAN WITNESS

97.   The immense horizons of the Church's mission and the complexity of today's situation call for new ways of effectively communicating the word of God. The Holy Spirit, the protagonist of all evangelization, will never fail to guide Christ's Church in this activity. Yet it is important that every form of proclamation keep in mind, first of all, the intrinsic relationship between *the communication of God*'s word and *Christian witness*. The very credibility of our proclamation depends on this. On the one hand, the word must communicate everything that the Lord himself has told us. On the other hand, it is indispensable, through witness, to make this word credible, lest it appear merely as a beautiful philosophy or utopia, rather than a reality that can be lived and itself give life. This reciprocity between word and witness reflects the way in which God himself communicated through the incarnation of his Word. The word of God reaches men and women "through an encounter with witnesses who make it present and alive."[323] In a particular way, young people need to be introduced to the word of God "through encounter and authentic witness by adults, through the positive influence of friends and the great company of the ecclesial community."[324]

---

319. Cf. *Propositio* 49.

320. Cf. John Paul II, Encyclical Letter *Redemptoris missio* (December 7, 1990): AAS 83 (1991), 294–340; Apostolic Letter *Novo millennio ineunte* (January 6, 2001), 40: AAS 93 (2001), 294–295.

321. *Propositio* 38.

322. Cf. Benedict XVI, Homily for the Opening of the Twelfth Ordinary General Assembly of the Synod of Bishops (October 5, 2008): AAS 100 (2008), 753–757.

323. *Propositio* 38.

324. Final Message, IV, 12.

There is a close relationship between the testimony of Scripture, as the self-attestation of God's word, and the witness given by the lives of believers. One implies and leads to the other. Christian witness communicates the word attested in the Scriptures. For their part, the Scriptures explain the witness which Christians are called to give by their lives. Those who encounter credible witnesses of the Gospel thus come to realize how effective God's word can be in those who receive it.

98.   In this interplay between witness and word we can understand what Pope Paul VI stated in the Apostolic Exhortation *Evangelii nuntiandi*. Our responsibility is not limited to suggesting shared values to the world; rather, we need to arrive at an explicit proclamation of the word of God. Only in this way will we be faithful to Christ's mandate: "The Good News proclaimed by the witness of life sooner or later has to be proclaimed by the word of life. There is no true evangelization unless the name, the teaching, the life, the promises, the Kingdom and the mystery of Jesus of Nazareth, the Son of God, are proclaimed."[325]

The fact that the proclamation of the word of God calls for the testimony of one's life is a datum clearly present in the Christian consciousness from the beginning. Christ himself is the faithful and true witness (cf. Acts 1:5; 3:14), it is he who testifies to the Truth (cf. Jn 18:37). Here I would like to echo the countless testimonials which we had the grace of hearing during the synodal assembly. We were profoundly moved to hear the stories of those who lived their faith and bore outstanding witness to the Gospel even under regimes hostile to Christianity or in situations of persecution.

None of this should cause us fear. Jesus himself said to his disciples: "A servant is not greater than his master. If they persecuted me, they will persecute you" (Jn 15:20). For this reason I would like, with the whole Church, to lift up to God a hymn of praise for the witness of our many faithful brothers and sisters who, even in our day, have given their lives to communicate the truth of God's love revealed to us in the crucified and risen Christ. I also express the whole Church's gratitude for those Christians who have not yielded in the face of obstacles and even persecutions for the sake of the Gospel. We likewise embrace with deep fraternal affection the faithful of all those Christian communities, particularly in Asia and in Africa, who presently risk their life or social segregation because of their faith. Here we encounter the true spirit of the Gospel, which proclaims blessed those who are persecuted on account of the Lord Jesus (cf. Mt 5:11). In so doing, we once more call upon the governments of nations to guarantee everyone freedom of conscience and religion, as well as the ability to express their faith publicly.[326]

---

325. Paul VI, Apostolic Exhortation *Evangelii nuntiandi* (December 8, 1975), 22: AAS 68 (1976), 20.
326. Cf. Second Vatican Ecumenical Council, Declaration on Religious Freedom *Dignitatis humanae*, 2 and 7.

THE WORD OF GOD AND COMMITMENT IN THE WORLD

99.   The word of God sheds light on human existence and stirs our conscience to take a deeper look at our lives, inasmuch as all human history stands under God's judgment: "When the Son of Man comes in his glory, and all the angels with him, then he will sit on his glorious throne. Before him will be gathered all the nations" (Mt 25:31–32). Nowadays we tend to halt in a superficial way before the importance of the passing moment, as if it had nothing to do with the future. The Gospel, on the other hand, reminds us that every moment of our life is important and must be lived intensely, in the knowledge that everyone will have to give an account of his or her life. In the twenty-fifth chapter of the *Gospel of Matthew*, the Son of Man considers whatever we do or do not do to "the least of his brethren" (cf. 25:40, 45) as done or not done to himself: "I was hungry and you gave me food, I was thirsty and you gave me drink, I was a stranger and you welcomed me, I was naked and you clothed me, I was sick and you visited me, I was in prison and you came to me" (25:35–36). The word of God itself emphasizes the need for our engagement in the world and our responsibility before Christ, the Lord of history. As we proclaim the Gospel, let us encourage one another to do good and to commit ourselves to justice, reconciliation, and peace.

THE WORD OF GOD AND COMMITMENT TO JUSTICE IN SOCIETY

100.   God's word inspires men and women to build relationships based on rectitude and justice, and testifies to the great value in God's eyes of every effort to create a more just and more livable world.[327] The word of God itself unambiguously denounces injustices and promotes solidarity and equality.[328] In the light of the Lord's words, let us discern the "signs of the times" present in history, and not flee from a commitment to those who suffer and the victims of forms of selfishness. The Synod recalled that a commitment to justice and to changing our world is an essential element of evangelization. In the words of Pope Paul VI, we must "reach and as it were overturn with the force of the Gospel the standards of judgment, the interests, the thought-patterns, the sources of inspiration, and lifestyles of humanity that are in contrast with the word of God and with his plan for salvation."[329]

For this reason, the Synod Fathers wished to say a special word to all those who take part in political and social life. Evangelization and the spread of God's word ought to inspire their activity in the world, as they work for the true common good in respecting and promoting the dignity of every person. Certainly it is not the direct task of the Church to create a more just society, although she does have the right and duty to intervene on ethical and moral issues related to the good of individuals and peoples. It is primarily the task of the lay faithful, formed

---

327. Cf. *Propositio* 39.

328. Cf. Benedict XVI, Message for the 2009 World Day of Peace (December 8, 2008): *Insegnamenti* IV, 2 (2008), 792–802.

329. Apostolic Exhortation *Evangelii nuntiandi* (December 8, 1975), 19: AAS 68 (1976), 18.

in the school of the Gospel, to be directly involved in political and social activity. For this reason, the Synod recommends that they receive a suitable formation in the principles of the Church's social teaching.[330]

101. I would like also to call the attention of everyone to the importance of defending and promoting the *human rights of every person*, based on the natural law written on the human heart, which, as such, are "universal, inviolable, and inalienable."[331] The Church expresses the hope that by the recognition of these rights human dignity will be more effectively acknowledged and universally promoted,[332] inasmuch as it is a distinctive mark imprinted by the Creator on his creatures, taken up and redeemed by Jesus Christ through his incarnation, death, and resurrection. The spread of the word of God cannot fail to strengthen the recognition of, and respect for, the human rights of every person.[333]

THE PROCLAMATION OF GOD'S WORD, RECONCILIATION AND PEACE BETWEEN PEOPLES

102. Among the many areas where commitment is needed, the Synod earnestly called for the promotion of reconciliation and peace. In the present context it is more necessary than ever to rediscover the word of God as a source of reconciliation and peace, since in that word God is reconciling to himself all things (cf. 2 Cor 5:18–20; Eph 1:10): Christ "is our peace" (Eph 2:14), the one who breaks down the walls of division. A number of interventions at the Synod documented the grave and violent conflicts and tensions present on our planet. At times these hostilities seem to take on the appearance of interreligious conflict. Here I wish to affirm once more that religion can never justify intolerance or war. We cannot kill in God's name![334] Each religion must encourage the right use of reason and promote ethical values that consolidate civil coexistence.

In fidelity to the work of reconciliation accomplished by God in Jesus Christ crucified and risen, Catholics and men and women of goodwill must commit themselves to being an example of reconciliation for the building of a just and peaceful society.[335] We should never forget that "where human words become powerless because the tragic clash of violence and arms prevails, the prophetic power of God's word does not waver, reminding us that peace is possible and that we ourselves must be instruments of reconciliation and peace."[336]

THE WORD OF GOD AND PRACTICAL CHARITY

103. Commitment to justice, reconciliation, and peace finds its ultimate foundation and fulfillment in the love revealed to us in Christ. By listening to the

---

330. Cf. *Propositio* 39.

331. John XXIII, Encyclical Letter *Pacem in terris* (April 11, 1963), 1: AAS 55 (1963), 259.

332. John Paul II, Encyclical letter *Centesimus annus* (May 1, 1991), 47: AAS 83 (1991), 851–852; Address to the General Assembly of the United Nations (October 2, 1979), 13: AAS 71 (1979), 1152–1153.

333. Cf. *Compendium of the Social Doctrine of the Church*, 152–159.

334. Cf. Benedict XVI, Message for the 2007 World Day of Peace (December 8, 2006), 10: *Insegnamenti* II, 2 (2006), 780.

335. Cf. *Propositio* 8.

336. Benedict XVI, Homily (January 25, 2009): *Insegnamenti* V, 1 (2009), 141.

testimonies offered during the Synod, we saw more clearly the bond between a love-filled hearing of God's word and selfless service of our brothers and sisters; all believers should see the need to "translate the word that we have heard into gestures of love, because this is the only way to make the Gospel proclamation credible, despite the human weakness that marks individuals."[337] Jesus passed through this world doing good (cf. Acts 10:38). Listening with docility to the word of God in the Church awakens "charity and justice towards all, especially towards the poor."[338] We should never forget that "love—*caritas*—will always prove necessary, even in the most just society . . . whoever wants to eliminate love is preparing to eliminate man as such."[339] I therefore encourage the faithful to meditate often on the Apostle Paul's hymn to charity and to draw inspiration from it: "Love is patient and kind; love is not jealous or boastful; it is not arrogant or rude. Love does not insist on its own way; it is not irritable or resentful; it does not rejoice at wrong but delights in the truth. Love bears all things, believes all things, hopes all things, endures all things. Love never ends" (1 Cor 13:4–8).

Love of neighbor, rooted in the love of God, ought to see us constantly committed as individuals and as an ecclesial community, both local and universal. As Saint Augustine says: "It is essential to realize that love is the fullness of the Law, as it is of all the divine Scriptures. . . . Whoever claims to have understood the Scriptures, or any part of them, without striving as a result to grow in this twofold love of God and neighbor, makes it clear that he has not yet understood them."[340]

THE PROCLAMATION OF THE WORD OF GOD AND YOUNG PEOPLE

104. The Synod paid particular attention to the proclamation of God's word to the younger generation. Young people are already active members of the Church and they represent its future. Often we encounter in them a spontaneous openness to hearing the word of God and a *sincere desire to know Jesus*. Youth is a time when genuine and irrepressible *questions* arise about the meaning of life and the direction our own lives should take. Only God can give the true answer to these questions. Concern for young people calls for courage and clarity in the message we proclaim; we need to help young people to gain confidence and familiarity with Sacred Scripture so it can become a compass pointing out the path to follow.[341] Young people need witnesses and teachers who can walk with them, teaching them to love the Gospel and to share it, especially with their peers, and thus to become authentic and credible messengers.[342]

---

337. Id., Homily at the Conclusion of the Twelfth Ordinary General Assembly of the Synod of Bishops (October 26, 2008): AAS 100 (2008), 779.

338. *Propositio* 11.

339. Benedict XVI, Encyclical letter *Deus caritas est* (December 25, 2005), 28: AAS 98 (2006), 240.

340. *De doctrina christiana*, I, 35, 39–36, 40: PL 34, 34.

341. Cf. Benedict XVI, Message for the Twenty-First World Youth Day (February 22, 2006): AAS 98 (2006), 282–286.

342. Cf. *Propositio* 34.

God's word needs to be presented in a way that brings out its implications for each person's vocation and assists young people in choosing the direction they will give to their lives, including that of total consecration to God.[343] Authentic vocations to the consecrated life and to the priesthood find fertile ground in a faith-filled contact with the word of God. I repeat once again the appeal I made at the beginning of my pontificate to open wide the doors to Christ: "If we let Christ into our lives, we lose nothing, nothing, absolutely nothing of what makes life free, beautiful, and great. No! Only in this friendship are the doors of life opened wide. Only in this friendship is the great potential of human existence truly revealed. . . . Dear young people: do not be afraid of Christ! He takes nothing away and he gives you everything. When we give ourselves to him, we receive a hundredfold in return. Yes, open, open wide the doors to Christ—and you will find true life."[344]

THE PROCLAMATION OF THE WORD OF GOD AND MIGRANTS

105. The word of God makes us attentive to history and to emerging realities. In considering the Church's mission of evangelization, the Synod thus decided to address as well the complex phenomenon of movements of migration, which in recent years have taken on unprecedented proportions. This issue is fraught with extremely delicate questions about the *security* of nations and the *welcome* to be given to those seeking refuge or improved conditions of living, health, and work. Large numbers of people who know nothing of Christ, or who have an inadequate understanding of him, are settling in countries of Christian tradition. At the same time, persons from nations deeply marked by Christian faith are emigrating to countries where Christ needs to be proclaimed and a new evangelization is demanded. These situations offer new possibilities for the spread of God's word. In this regard the Synod Fathers stated that migrants are entitled to hear the *kerygma*, which is to be proposed, not imposed. If they are Christians, they require forms of pastoral care which can enable them to grow in the faith and to become in turn messengers of the Gospel. Taking into account the complexity of the phenomenon, a mobilization of all dioceses involved is essential, so that movements of migration will also be seen as an opportunity to discover new forms of presence and proclamation. It is also necessary that they ensure, to the extent possible, that these our brothers and sisters receive adequate welcome and attention, so that, touched by the Good News, they will be able to be heralds of God's word and witnesses to the Risen Jesus, the hope of the world.[345]

THE PROCLAMATION OF THE WORD OF GOD AND THE SUFFERING

106. During the work of the Synod, the Fathers also considered the need to proclaim God's word to all those who are suffering, whether physically, psychologically, or spiritually. It is in times of pain that *the ultimate questions about the meaning of one's life* make themselves acutely felt. If human words seem

---

343. Cf. ibid.

344. Homily (April 24, 2005): AAS 97 (2005), 712.

345. Cf. *Propositio* 38.

to fall silent before the mystery of evil and suffering, and if our society appears to value life only when it corresponds to certain standards of efficiency and well-being, the word of God makes us see that even these moments are mysteriously "embraced" by God's love. Faith born of an encounter with God's word helps us to realize that *human life deserves to be lived fully, even when weakened by illness and pain.* God created us for happiness and for life, whereas sickness and death came into the world as a result of sin (cf. Wis 2:23–24). Yet the Father of life is mankind's physician *par excellence,* and he does not cease to bend lovingly over suffering humanity. We contemplate the culmination of God's closeness to our sufferings in Jesus himself, "the Word incarnate. He suffered and died for us. By his passion and death he took our weakness upon himself and totally transformed it."[346]

Jesus' closeness to those who suffer is constant: it is prolonged in time thanks to the working of the Holy Spirit in the mission of the Church, in the word and in the sacraments, in men and women of good will, and in charitable initiatives undertaken with fraternal love by communities, thus making known God's true face and his love. The Synod thanked God for the luminous witness, often hidden, of all the many Christians—priests, religious, and lay faithful—who have lent and continue to lend their hands, eyes, and hearts to Christ, the true physician of body and soul. It exhorts all to continue to care for the infirm and to bring them the life-giving presence of the Lord Jesus in the word and in the Eucharist. Those who suffer should be helped to read the Scriptures and to realize that their condition itself enables them to share in a special way in Christ's redemptive suffering for the salvation of the world (cf. 2 Cor 4:8–11, 14).[347]

THE PROCLAMATION OF THE WORD OF GOD AND THE POOR

107. Sacred Scripture manifests God's special love for the poor and the needy (cf. Mt 25:31–46). The Synod Fathers frequently spoke of the importance of enabling these, our brothers and sisters, to hear the Gospel message and to experience the closeness of their pastors and communities. Indeed, "the poor are the first ones entitled to hear the proclamation of the Gospel; they need not only bread, but also words of life."[348] The diaconia of charity, which must never be lacking in our churches, should always be bound to the proclamation of the word and the celebration of the sacred mysteries.[349] Yet we also need to recognize and appreciate the fact that the poor are themselves agents of evangelization. In the Bible, the true poor are those who entrust themselves totally to God; in the Gospel Jesus calls them *blessed*, "for theirs is the Kingdom of Heaven" (Mt 5:3; cf. Lk 6:20). The Lord exalts the simplicity of heart of those who find in God true riches, placing their hope in him, and not in the things of this world. The Church cannot let the poor down: "Pastors are called to listen to them, to learn

---

346. Benedict XVI, Homily for the Seventeenth World Day of the Sick (February 11, 2009): *Insegnamenti* V, 1 (2009), 232.

347. Cf. *Propositio* 35.

348. *Propositio* 11.

349. Cf. Benedict XVI, Encyclical Letter *Deus caritas est* (December 25, 2005), 25: AAS 98 (2006), 236–237.

from them, to guide them in their faith and to encourage them to take respon-sibility for lives."[350]

The Church also knows that poverty can exist as a *virtue*, to be cultivated and chosen freely, as so many saints have done. Poverty can likewise exist as *indigence*, often due to injustice or selfishness, marked by hunger and need, and as a source of conflict. In her proclamation of God's word, the Church knows that a "virtuous circle" must be promoted between the poverty which is *to be chosen* and the poverty which is *to be combated*; we need to rediscover "moderation and solidarity, these values of the Gospel that are also universal. . . . This entails decisions marked by justice and moderation."[351]

THE PROCLAMATION OF THE WORD OF GOD AND THE PROTECTION OF CREATION

108. Engagement with the world, as demanded by God's word, makes us look with new eyes at the entire created cosmos, which contains traces of that word through whom all things were made (cf. Jn 1:2). As men and women who believe in and proclaim the Gospel, we have a responsibility towards creation. Revelation makes known God's plan for the cosmos, yet it also leads us to denounce that mistaken attitude which refuses to view all created realities as a reflection of their Creator, but instead as mere raw material, to be exploited without scruple. Man thus lacks that essential humility which would enable him to see creation as a gift from God, to be received and used in accordance with his plan. Instead, the arrogance of human beings who live "as if God did not exist" leads them to exploit and disfigure nature, failing to see it as the handiwork of the creative word. In this theological context, I would like to echo the statements of the Synod Fathers who reminded us that "accepting the word of God, attested to by Scripture and by the Church's living Tradition, gives rise to a new way of seeing things, promotes an authentic ecology which has its deepest roots in the obedience of faith . . . [and] develops a renewed theological sensitivity to the goodness of all things, which are created in Christ."[352] We need to be reeducated in wonder and in the ability to recognize the beauty made manifest in created realities.[353]

THE WORD OF GOD AND CULTURE

THE VALUE OF CULTURE FOR THE LIFE OF HUMANITY

109. Saint John's proclamation that the Word became flesh reveals the insepa-rable bond between *God's word* and the *human words* by which he communi-cates with us. In this context the Synod Fathers considered the relationship between the word of God and culture. God does not reveal himself in the abstract, but by using languages, imagery, and expressions that are bound to different cultures. This relationship has proved fruitful, as the history of the Church abundantly testifies. Today it is entering a new phase due to the spread of the

---

350. *Propositio* 11.

351. Benedict XVI, Homily (January 1, 2009): *Insegnamenti* V, 1 (2009), 236–237.

352. *Propositio* 54.

353. Cf. Benedict XVI, Post-Synodal Apostolic Exhortation *Sacramentum caritatis* (February 22, 2007), 92: AAS 99 (2007), 176–177.

Gospel and its taking root within different cultures, as well as more recent developments in the culture of the West. It calls in the first place for a recognition of the importance of culture as such for the life of every man and woman. The phenomenon of culture is, in its various aspects, an essential datum of human experience. "Man lives always according to a culture which is properly his, and which in turn creates among persons a bond which is properly theirs, one which determines the inter-human and social character of human existence."[354]

Down the centuries the word of God has inspired different cultures, giving rise to fundamental moral values, outstanding expressions of art and exemplary lifestyles.[355] Hence, in looking to a renewed encounter between the Bible and culture, I wish to reassure all those who are part of the world of culture that they have nothing to fear from openness to God's word, which never destroys true culture, but rather is a constant stimulus to seek ever more appropriate, meaningful, and humane forms of expression. Every authentic culture, if it is truly to be at the service of humanity, has to be open to transcendence and, in the end, to God.

THE BIBLE, A GREAT CODE FOR CULTURES

110. The Synod Fathers greatly stressed the importance of promoting a suitable knowledge of the Bible among those engaged in the area of culture, also in secularized contexts and among non-believers.[356] Sacred Scripture contains anthropological and philosophical values that have had a positive influence on humanity as a whole.[357] A sense of the Bible as a great code for cultures needs to be fully recovered.

KNOWLEDGE OF THE BIBLE IN SCHOOLS AND UNIVERSITIES

111. One particular setting for an encounter between the word of God and culture is that of schools and universities. Pastors should be especially attentive to this milieu, promoting a deeper knowledge of the Bible and a grasp of its fruitful cultural implications also for the present day. Study centers supported by Catholic groups offer a distinct contribution to the promotion of culture and education—and this ought to be recognized. Nor must *religious education* be neglected, and religion teachers should be given careful training. Religious education is often the sole opportunity available for students to encounter the message of faith. In the teaching of religion, emphasis should be laid on knowledge of Sacred Scripture, as a means of overcoming prejudices old and new, and enabling its truth to be better known.[358]

---

354. John Paul II, Address to UNESCO (June 2, 1980), 6: AAS 72 (1980), 738.

355. Cf. *Propositio* 41.

356. Cf. ibid.

357. John Paul II, Encyclical Letter *Fides et ratio* (September 14, 1998), 80: AAS 91 (1999), 67–68.

358. Cf. *Lineamenta* 23.

112. The relationship between the word of God and culture has found expression in many areas, especially in *the arts*. For this reason the great tradition of East and West has always esteemed works of art inspired by Sacred Scripture, as for example the figurative arts and architecture, literature, and music. I think too of the ancient language expressed by *icons*, which from the Eastern tradition is gradually spreading throughout the world. With the Synod Fathers, the whole Church expresses her appreciation, esteem, and admiration of those artists "enamored of beauty" who have drawn inspiration from the sacred texts. They have contributed to the decoration of our churches, to the celebration of our faith, to the enrichment of our liturgy, and many of them have helped to make somehow perceptible, in time and space, realities that are unseen and eternal.[359] I encourage the competent offices and groups to promote in the Church a solid formation of artists with regard to Sacred Scripture in the light of the Church's living Tradition and her magisterium.

THE WORD OF GOD AND THE MEANS OF SOCIAL COMMUNICATION

113. Linked to the relationship between the word of God and culture is the need for a careful and intelligent use of the communications media, both old and new. The Synod Fathers called for a proper knowledge of these media; they noted their rapid development and different levels of interaction, and asked for greater efforts to be made in gaining expertise in the various sectors involved, particularly in the *new media*, such as the *internet*. The Church already has a significant presence in the world of mass communications, and her magisterium has frequently intervened on the subject, beginning with the Second Vatican Council.[360] Discovering new methods of transmitting the Gospel message is part of the continuing evangelizing outreach of those who believe. Communications today take place through a worldwide network, and thus give new meaning to Christ's words: "What I tell you in the dark, utter in the light; and what you hear whispered, proclaim upon the housetops" (Mt 10:27). God's word should resound not only in the print media, but in other forms of communication as well.[361] For this reason, together with the Synod Fathers, I express gratitude to those Catholics who are making serious efforts to promote a significant presence in the world of the media, and I ask for an ever wider and more qualified commitment in this regard.[362]

---

359. Cf. *Propositio* 40.

360. Cf. Second Vatican Ecumenical Council, Decree on the Instruments of Social Communication *Inter mirifica*; Pontifical Council for Social Communications, Pastoral Instruction *Communio et progressio* (May 23, 1971): AAS 63 (1971), 596–656; John Paul II, Apostolic Letter *The Rapid Development* (January 24, 2005): AAS 97 (2005) 265–274; Pontifical Council for Social Communications, Pastoral Instruction *Aetatis novae* (February 22, 1992): AAS 84 (1992), 447–468; *The Church and Internet* (February 22, 2002): *Enchiridion Vaticanum* 21, nos. 66–95; *Ethics in Internet* (February 22, 2002): *Enchiridion Vaticanum* 21, nos. 96–127.

361. Cf. Final Message, IV, 11; Benedict XVI, Message for the 2009 World Day of Social Communications (January 24, 2009): *Insegnamenti* V, 1 (2009), 123–127.

362. Cf. *Propositio* 44.

Among the new forms of mass communication, nowadays we need to recognize the increased role of the *internet*, which represents a new forum for making the Gospel heard. Yet we also need to be aware that the virtual world will never be able to replace the real world, and that evangelization will be able to make use of the *virtual world* offered by the new media in order to create meaningful relationships only if it is able to offer the *personal contact* which remains indispensable. In the world of the internet, which enables billions of images to appear on millions of screens throughout the world, *the face of Christ* needs to be seen and his voice heard, for "if there is no room for Christ, there is no room for man."[363]

THE BIBLE AND INCULTURATION

114. The mystery of the incarnation tells us that while God always communicates in a concrete history, taking up the cultural codes embedded therein, the same word can and must also be passed on in different cultures, transforming them from within through what Pope Paul VI called *the evangelization of cultures*.[364] The word of God, like the Christian faith itself, has a profoundly *intercultural* character; it is capable of encountering different cultures and in turn enabling them to encounter one another.[365]

Here too we come to appreciate the importance of the *inculturation* of the Gospel.[366] The Church is firmly convinced that the word of God is inherently capable of speaking to all human persons in the context of their own culture: "this conviction springs from the Bible itself, which, right from the Book of Genesis, adopts a universalist stance (cf. Gen 1:27–28), maintains it subsequently in the blessing promised to all peoples through Abraham and his offspring (cf. Gen 12:3; 18:18), and confirms it definitively in extending to 'all nations' the proclamation of the Gospel."[367] For this reason, inculturation is not to be confused with processes of superficial adaptation, much less with a confused syncretism which would dilute the uniqueness of the Gospel in an attempt to make it more easily accepted.[368] The authentic paradigm of inculturation is the incarnation itself of the Word: "'Acculturation' or 'inculturation' will truly be a reflection of the incarnation of the Word when a culture, transformed and regenerated by the Gospel, brings forth from its own living tradition original expressions of Christian life, celebration, and thought,"[369] serving as a leaven within the local

363. John Paul II, Message for the XXXVI World Communications Day (January 24, 2002): *Insegnamenti* XXV, 1 (2002), 94–95.

364. Cf. Apostolic Exhortation *Evangelii nuntiandi* (December 8, 1975), 20: AAS 68 (1976), 18–19.

365. Cf. Benedict XVI, Post-Synodal Apostolic Exhortation *Sacramentum caritatis* (February 22, 2007), 78: AAS 99 (2007), 165.

366. Cf. *Propositio* 48.

367. Pontifical Biblical Commission, *The Interpretation of the Bible in the Church* (April 15, 1993), IV, B: *Enchiridion Vaticanum*, 13, no. 3112.

368. Cf. Second Vatican Ecumenical Council, Decree on the Church's Missionary Activity *Ad gentes*, 22; Pontifical Biblical Commission, *The Interpretation of the Bible in the Church* (April 15, 1993), IV, B: *Enchiridion Vaticanum*, 13, nos. 3111–3117.

369. John Paul II, Address to the Bishops of Kenya (May 7, 1980), 6: AAS 72 (1980), 497.

culture, enhancing the *semina Verbi* and all those positive elements present within that culture, thus opening it to the values of the Gospel.[370]

TRANSLATING THE BIBLE AND MAKING IT MORE WIDELY AVAILABLE

115. The inculturation of God's word is an integral part of the Church's mission in the world, and a decisive moment in this process is the diffusion of the Bible through the precious work of translation into different languages. Here it should always be remembered that the work of translation of the Scriptures had been undertaken "already in the Old Testament period, when the Hebrew text of the Bible was translated orally into Aramaic (Neh 8:8, 12) and later in written form into Greek. A translation, of course, is always more than a simple transcription of the original texts. The passage from one language to another necessarily involves a change of cultural context: concepts are not identical and symbols have a different meaning, for they come up against other traditions of thought and other ways of life."[371]

During the Synod, it was clear that a number of local Churches still lack a complete translation of the Bible in their own languages. How many people today hunger and thirst for the word of God, yet remain deprived of the "widely available access to Sacred Scripture"[372] desired by the Second Vatican Council! For this reason the Synod considered it important, above all, to train specialists committed to translating the Bible into the various languages.[373] I would encourage the investment of resources in this area. In particular I wish to recommend supporting the work of the Catholic Biblical Federation, with the aim of further increasing the number of translations of Sacred Scripture and their wide diffusion.[374] Given the very nature of such an enterprise, it should be carried out as much as possible in cooperation with the different Bible Societies.

GOD'S WORD TRANSCENDS CULTURAL LIMITS

116. The synodal assembly, in its discussion of the relationship between God's word and cultures, felt the need to reaffirm something that the earliest Christians had experienced beginning on the day of Pentecost (Acts 2:1–2). The word of God is capable of entering into and finding expression in various cultures and languages, yet that same word overcomes the limits of individual cultures to create fellowship between different peoples. The Lord's word summons us to advance towards an ever more vast communion. "We escape the limitations of our experience and we enter into the reality that is truly universal. Entering into communion with the word of God, we enter into the communion of the Church which lives the word of God. . . . It means going beyond the limits of

---

370. Cf. *Instrumentum laboris*, 56.

371. Pontifical Biblical Commission, *The Interpretation of the Bible in the Church* (April 15, 1993), IV, B: *Enchiridion Vaticanum* 13, no. 3113.

372. Second Vatican Ecumenical Council, Dogmatic Constitution on Divine Revelation *Dei Verbum*, 22.

373. Cf. *Propositio* 42.

374. Cf. *Propositio* 43.

the individual cultures into the universality that connects all, unites all, makes us all brothers and sisters."[375] The proclamation of God's work thus always demands, of us in the first place, a new exodus, as we leave behind our own limited standards and imaginations in order to make room for the presence of Christ.

THE WORD OF GOD AND INTERRELIGIOUS DIALOGUE

THE VALUE OF INTERRELIGIOUS DIALOGUE

117. The Church considers an essential part of the proclamation of the word to consist in encounter, dialogue, and cooperation with all people of good will, particularly with the followers of the different religious traditions of humanity. This is to take place without forms of syncretism and relativism, but along the lines indicated by the Second Vatican Council's Declaration *Nostra aetate* and subsequently developed by the magisterium of the Popes.[376] Nowadays the quickened pace of globalization makes it possible for people of different cultures and religions to be in closer contact. This represents a providential opportunity for demonstrating how authentic religiosity can foster relationships of universal fraternity. Today, in our frequently secularized societies, it is very important that the religions be capable of fostering a mentality that sees Almighty God as the foundation of all good, the inexhaustible source of the moral life, and the bulwark of a profound sense of universal brotherhood.

In the Judeo-Christian tradition, for example, one finds a moving witness to God's love for all peoples: in the covenant with Noah he joins them in one great embrace symbolized by the "bow in the clouds" (Gen 9:13, 14, 16) and, according to the words of the prophets, he desires to gather them into a single universal family (cf. Is 2:2ff.; 42:6; 66:18–21; Jer 4:2; Ps 47). Evidence of a close connection between a relationship with God and the ethics of love for everyone is found in many great religious traditions.

DIALOGUE BETWEEN CHRISTIANS AND MUSLIMS

118. Among the various religions the Church also looks with respect to Muslims, who adore the one God.[377] They look to Abraham and worship God above all through prayer, almsgiving, and fasting. We acknowledge that the Islamic tradition includes countless biblical figures, symbols, and themes. Taking up the efforts begun by the Venerable John Paul II, I express my hope that the trust-filled relationships established between Christians and Muslims over the years

---

375. Benedict XVI, Homily during the Celebration of Terce at the beginning of the First General Congregation of the Synod of Bishops (October 6, 2008): AAS 100 (2008), 760.

376. Among numerous interventions of various genres, see: John Paul II, Encyclical Letter *Dominum et vivificantem* (May 18, 1986): AAS 78 (1986), 809–900; Encyclical Letter *Redemptoris missio* (December 7, 1990): AAS 83 (1991), 249–340; Addresses and Homilies in Assisi for the October 27, 1986 Day of Prayer for Peace: *Insegnamenti* IX, 2 (1986), 1249–1273; Day of Prayer for World Peace (January 24, 2002): *Insegnamenti* XXV, 1 (2002), 97–108; Congregation for the Doctrine of the Faith, Declaration *Dominus Iesus* on the Unicity and Salvific Universality of Jesus Christ and of the Church (August 6, 2000): AAS 92 (2000), 742–765.

377. Cf. Second Vatican Ecumenical Council, Declaration on the Relation of the Church to Non-Christian Religions *Nostra aetate*, 3.

will continue to develop in a spirit of sincere and respectful dialogue.[378] In this dialogue the Synod asked for a deeper reflection on respect for life as a fundamental value, the inalienable rights of men and women, and their equal dignity. Taking into account the important distinction to be made between the socio-political order and the religious order, the various religions must make their specific contribution to the common good. The Synod asked Conferences of Bishops, wherever it is appropriate and helpful, to encourage meetings aimed at helping Christians and Muslims to come to better knowledge of one another, in order to promote the values which society needs for a peaceful and positive coexistence.[379]

DIALOGUE WITH OTHER RELIGIONS

119. Here too I wish to voice the Church's respect for the ancient religions and spiritual traditions of the various continents. These contain values which can greatly advance understanding between individuals and peoples.[380] Frequently we note a consonance with values expressed also in their religious books, such as, in Buddhism, respect for life, contemplation, silence, simplicity; in Hinduism, the sense of the sacred, sacrifice, and fasting; and again, in Confucianism, family and social values. We are also gratified to find in other religious experiences a genuine concern for the transcendence of God, acknowledged as Creator, as well as respect for life, marriage and the family, and a strong sense of solidarity.

DIALOGUE AND RELIGIOUS FREEDOM

120. All the same, dialogue would not prove fruitful unless it included authentic respect for each person and the ability of all freely to practice their religion. Hence the Synod, while encouraging cooperation between the followers of the different religions, also pointed out "the need for the freedom to profess one's religion, privately and publicly, and freedom of conscience to be effectively guaranteed to all believers":[381] indeed, "respect and dialogue require reciprocity in all spheres, especially in that which concerns basic freedoms, more particularly religious freedom. Such respect and dialogue foster peace and understanding between peoples."[382]

CONCLUSION

GOD'S DEFINITIVE WORD

121. At the conclusion of these reflections with which I have sought to gather up and examine more fully the rich fruits of the Twelfth Ordinary General Assembly of the Synod of Bishops on the word of God in the life and mission of

---

378. Cf. Benedict XVI, Address to Ambassadors of Predominantly Muslim Countries Accredited to the Holy See (September 25, 2006): AAS 98 (2006), 704–706.
379. Cf. *Propositio* 53.
380. Cf. *Propositio* 50.
381. Ibid.
382. John Paul II, Address at the Meeting with Young Muslims in Casablanca, Morocco (August 19, 1985), 5: AAS 78 (1986), 99.

the Church, I wish once more to encourage all the People of God, pastors, consecrated persons, and the laity, to become increasingly familiar with the sacred Scriptures. We must never forget that all authentic and living Christian spirituality is based on *the word of God proclaimed, accepted, celebrated, and meditated upon in the Church*. This deepening relationship with the divine word will take place with even greater enthusiasm if we are conscious that, in Scripture and the Church's living Tradition, we stand before God's definitive word on the cosmos and on history.

The Prologue of John's Gospel leads us to ponder the fact that everything that exists is under the sign of the Word. The Word goes forth from the Father, comes to dwell in our midst and then returns to the Father in order to bring with him the whole of creation which was made in him and for him. The Church now carries out her mission in eager expectation of the eschatological manifestation of the Bridegroom: "the Spirit and the bride say: 'Come!'" (Rev 22:17). This expectation is never passive; rather it is a missionary drive to proclaim the word of God which heals and redeems every man. Today too the Risen Jesus says to us: "Go into all the world and proclaim the Gospel to the whole creation" (Mk 16:15).

NEW EVANGELIZATION AND A NEW HEARING

122. Our own time, then, must be increasingly marked by a new hearing of God's word and a new evangelization. Recovering the centrality of the divine word in the Christian life leads us to appreciate anew the deepest meaning of the forceful appeal of Pope John Paul II: to pursue the *missio ad gentes* and vigorously to embark upon the new evangelization, especially in those nations where the Gospel has been forgotten or meets with indifference as a result of widespread secularism. May the Holy Spirit awaken a hunger and thirst for the word of God, and raise up zealous heralds and witnesses of the Gospel.

Following the example of the great Apostle of the Nations, who changed the course of his life after hearing the voice of the Lord (cf. Acts 9:1–30), let us too hear God's word as it speaks to us, ever personally, here and now. The Holy Spirit, we are told in the *Acts of the Apostles*, set Paul and Barnabas apart to proclaim and spread the Good News (cf. 13:2). In our day too, the Holy Spirit constantly calls convinced and persuasive hearers and preachers of the word of the Lord.

THE WORD AND JOY

123. The greater our openness to God's word, the more will we be able to recognize that today too the mystery of Pentecost is taking place in God's Church. The Spirit of the Lord continues to pour out his gifts upon the Church to guide us into all truth, to show us the meaning of the Scriptures and to make us credible heralds of the word of salvation before the world. Thus we return to the *First Letter of Saint John*. In God's word, we too have heard, we too have seen and touched the Word of life. We have welcomed by grace the proclamation that eternal life has been revealed, and thus we have come to acknowledge our

fellowship with one another, with those who have gone before us marked with the sign of faith, and with all those who throughout the world hear the word, celebrate the Eucharist and by their lives bear witness to charity. This proclamation has been shared with us—the Apostle John reminds us—so that "our joy may be complete" (1 Jn 1:4).

The synodal assembly enabled us to experience all that Saint John speaks of: the proclamation of the word creates *communion* and brings about *joy*. This is a profound joy which has its origin in the very heart of the trinitarian life and which is communicated to us in the Son. This joy is an ineffable gift which the world cannot give. Celebrations can be organized, but not joy. According to the Scripture, joy is the fruit of the Holy Spirit (cf. Gal 5:22) who enables us to enter into the word and enables the divine word to enter into us and to bear fruit for eternal life. By proclaiming God's word in the power of the Holy Spirit, we also wish to share the source of true joy, not a superficial and fleeting joy, but the joy born of the awareness that the Lord Jesus alone has words of everlasting life (cf. Jn 6:68).

"MATER VERBI ET MATER LAETITIAE"

124. This close relationship between God's word and joy is evident in the Mother of God. Let us recall the words of Saint Elizabeth: "Blessed is she who believed that there would be a fulfillment of what was spoken to her by the Lord" (Lk 1:45). Mary is blessed because she has faith, because she believed, and in this faith she received the Word of God into her womb in order to give him to the world. The joy born of the Word can now expand to all those who, by faith, let themselves be changed by God's word. The *Gospel of Luke* presents this mystery of hearing and joy in two texts. Jesus says: "My mother and my brothers are those who hear the word of God and do it" (8:21). And in reply to a woman from the crowd who blesses the womb that bore him and the breasts that nursed him, Jesus reveals the secret of true joy: "Blessed rather are those who hear the word of God and obey it!" (11:28). Jesus points out Mary's true grandeur, making it possible for each of us to attain that blessedness which is born of the word received and put into practice. I remind all Christians that our personal and communal relationship with God depends on our growing familiarity with the word of God. Finally, I turn to every man and woman, including those who have fallen away from the Church, who have left the faith, or who have never heard the proclamation of salvation. To everyone the Lord says: "Behold, I stand at the door and knock; if anyone hears my voice and opens the door, I will come in to him and eat with him, and he with me" (Rev 3:20).

May every day of our lives thus be shaped by a renewed encounter with Christ, the Word of the Father made flesh: he stands at the beginning and the end, and "in him all things hold together" (Col 1:17). Let us be silent in order to hear the Lord's word and to meditate upon it, so that by the working of the Holy Spirit it may remain in our hearts and speak to us all the days of our lives. In this way the Church will always be renewed and rejuvenated, thanks to the word of the

Lord which remains for ever (cf. 1 Pt 1:25; Is 40:8). Thus we too will enter into the great nuptial dialogue which concludes Sacred Scripture: "The Spirit and the bride say: 'Come.' And let everyone who hears say: 'Come!'" The one who testifies to these things, says: 'Surely I am coming soon!' Amen. Come, Lord Jesus!" (Rev 22:17, 20).

Given in Rome, at Saint Peter's, on September 30, the Memorial of Saint Jerome, in the year 2010, the sixth of my Pontificate.

BENEDICT XVI

MANE NOBISCUM DOMINE
STAY WITH US, LORD

APOSTOLIC LETTER
POPE JOHN PAUL II
OCTOBER 7, 2004

AN OVERVIEW OF *MANE NOBISCUM DOMINE*

Corinna Laughlin

Mane nobiscum Domine, an apostolic letter of Pope John Paul II, was issued on October 7, 2004 to mark the beginning of the Year of the Eucharist, which continued until October of 2005. The letter would prove to be one of the last significant teachings of Pope John Paul II. It is not a legislative document, but rather an exhortation to greater intentionality in the celebration and adoration of the Eucharist. The title is drawn from the Gospel account of the Emmaus encounter with the risen Christ[1]: "Stay with us, Lord, for it is almost evening."[2] The first chapter places the letter and the Year of the Eucharist in the context of earlier documents and observances, and then highlights three key dimensions of the Eucharist: light, Communion, and mission.

CONTEXT

Part I of the letter situates *Mane nobiscum Domine* "In the Wake of the Council and the Great Jubilee." The observance of the Great Jubilee was more than "a simple chronological event."[3] It was an expression of the "enthusiasm" of the Council, which proclaimed Christ "the goal of human history, the focal point of the desires of history and civilization."[4] The Eucharist was at the heart of the Great Jubilee, and of the teaching of Pope John Paul II, from his first encyclical, *Redemptor hominis* (1979), through the various documents that prepared the way for the Jubilee, including *Dies Domini* (1998).

That Eucharistic trajectory, John Paul II observes, has continued in the years following the Jubilee. He points to the apostolic letter *Novo millennio ineunte* (2001), which called the Church to "contemplation of the face of Christ . . . through the art of prayer."[5] That call bore fruit in the Year of the Rosary, the purpose of which was "contemplating the face of Christ, *now from a Marian perspective*,"[6] and it now culminates in the Year of the Eucharist, which is likewise an invitation to contemplate the face of Christ through this central mystery of faith.

Pope John Paul II carefully traces the context of the letter in order to present the Year of the Eucharist as both a "synthesis" of what had come before, and *"the high point of a journey in progress."*[7] Coming after so many other documents, so many other celebrations, *Mane nobiscum Domine* is not intended to

---

1. See Luke 24:13–35.
2. *Mane nobiscum Domine* (MND), 1; quoting Luke 24:29.
3. MND, 6.
4. Ibid., 6; quoting *Gaudium et spes* (GS), 45.
5. Ibid., 8.
6. Ibid., 9.
7. Ibid., 10.

offer new teachings or to lay out strategies for an elaborate observance. Rather, it simply offers "some reflections"[8] and a number of pastoral suggestions.

LIGHT

The second and longest part of the letter evokes the Year of the Rosary, which expanded the Rosary by adding the Mysteries of Light, in calling the Eucharist "a mystery of light." The Eucharist is light because the celebration of the sacrament is always paired with the Word of God "in the unity of the two 'tables,' the table of the Word and the table of the Bread."[9] So close is the unity of the two tables that Pope John Paul II invites communities to use the Year of the Eucharist "to evaluate their progress"[10] in the areas of the proclamation and preaching of the Word. Only if we are able to feast at the first table, the table of the Word, can we truly know who is coming to us at the table of the Eucharist.

The Eucharist is light; it is also mystery. In a wonderful line, John Paul II writes, "We are constantly tempted to reduce the Eucharist to our own dimensions, while in reality *it is we who must open ourselves up to the dimensions of the Mystery.*"[11] The Eucharist is a meal, but it is a meal with "a profoundly and primarily *sacrificial* meaning."[12] The Eucharist is a "mystery of presence," for it is an encounter with the Risen Christ, who still bears the wounds of his Passion, and it proclaims Christ's coming at the end of time.[13] It is our faith in the Real Presence of Christ in the Eucharist that takes all these dimensions of the Eucharist "far beyond mere symbolism."[14] This mystery of presence is the keynote of the entire letter: "remain with us, Lord."

Pope John Paul II echoes some of the concerns of previous documents, especially *Ecclesia de Eucharistia* and *Redemptionis sacramentum*, as he highlights the need for dignified Eucharistic celebrations, carried out in accordance with the norms, with "suitably 'sacred'" music, and the full participation of the faithful.[15] He also encourages "'mystagogical' catechesis" like that of the Church Fathers so that the faithful can more fully appreciate and understand the mystery in which they share. He urges that Eucharistic adoration outside of Mass, focused on prayer of reparation and adoration, become a commitment for individuals and communities. The Year of the Eucharist should also see a greater intentionality in our celebration of the Solemnity of the Most Holy Body and Blood of Christ (*Corpus Christi*) and the procession with the Blessed Sacrament. Thus, through the liturgy, the Eucharist as a mystery of light—of understanding and awareness of the presence of Christ—will shine more brightly in our communities.

---

8. Ibid., 11.

9. Ibid., 12; echoing *Constitution on the Sacred Liturgy* (CSL), 9.

10. Ibid., 13.

11. Ibid., 14.

12. Ibid., 15.

13. Ibid.

14. Ibid., 16.

15. Ibid., 17.

The third part of the letter speaks of the Eucharist as the "source and the manifestation of communion."[16] To receive Communion is to enter "into a profound communion with Jesus . . . *a certain foretaste of heaven on earth.*"[17] But reception of Holy Communion cannot be separated from "ecclesial communion."[18] The Eucharist not only brings us the abiding presence of Christ; it brings us into communion with one another, forming us into the one Body of Christ. And that makes demands of us. In a memorable phrase, Pope John Paul II says "The Eucharist is an *epiphany of communion*"[19]: it manifests our union in the Body of Christ. Thus, "the conditions for full participation in the celebration of the Eucharist" are well founded.[20] In order that the *"hierarchical* communion"[21] of the Church might be more clearly seen, John Paul II urges that the stational Masses of the bishop at the cathedral church be celebrated in their fullness, and that priests *"be even more attentive to Sunday Mass,"*[22] the expression of the community's unity in diversity.

MISSION

In the final section of the letter, the Eucharist is seen as both the principle and the plan of the Church's mission (an echo of the emphasis on the apostolicity of the Eucharist in *Ecclesia de Eucharistia*). When we truly find the Risen Lord in the Eucharist, we cannot keep it to ourselves: we want everyone to come to this table. The Eucharist is thus the impetus for and the goal of evangelization: to share in this meal is to become a missionary.[23] And there is more: the Eucharist is the very plan for mission. "The Eucharist is a mode of being, which passes from Jesus into each Christian"; the Eucharist must form our "values . . . attitudes . . . resolutions"[24] as individuals and as a Church.

What exactly is this Eucharistic "mode of being"?[25] It is an attitude of thanksgiving to God, the source of everything we have and are.[26] A Eucharistic attitude has a "transcendent point of reference," a constant awareness of the presence and action of God, from whom and through whom all things exist.[27] Pope John Paul II speaks of a "culture of the Eucharist," a culture of dialogue, in which Christians acknowledge the presence and action of God, even in public life.[28] There is no room for intolerance here: "One who learns to say 'thank

---

16. The title for chapter III.
17. Ibid., 19.
18. MND, 20.
19. Ibid., 21.
20. Ibid.
21. Ibid.
22. Ibid., 23.
23. Ibid., 24.
24. Ibid., 25.
25. Ibid.
26. Ibid., 26.
27. Ibid.
28. See ibid.

you' in the manner of the crucified Christ might end up as a martyr, but never as a persecutor."[29]

The Eucharist not only shapes our attitudes, but sets our agenda. And that agenda is solidarity, not only with God, but with other people: The Eucharist points us to the poor. So inevitable is the connection between Eucharist and charity that Pope John Paul II can say: "We cannot delude ourselves: by our mutual love, and, in particular, by our concern for those in need we will be recognized as true followers of Christ (cf. Jn 13:35; Mt 25:31–46). This will be the criterion by which the authenticity of our Eucharistic celebrations is judged."[30] In other words, a Eucharist that does not lead to charity is not truly a Eucharist. (Pope Benedict XVI would echo this in his first encyclical: "A Eucharist which does not pass over into the concrete practice of love is intrinsically fragmented."[31]) Pope John Paul II encourages local communities to use the Year of the Eucharist to respond to the problems of hunger and disease, especially in the developing world, and to the plight of the elderly, the unemployed, and immigrants. This agenda, he says, is inherent in the Eucharist itself.

CONCLUSION

In *Mane nobiscum Domine*, Pope John Paul II urges the entire Church to a renewed awareness of the gift of the Eucharist. He is realistic in his expectations, but perennially hopeful that the letter and the Year of the Eucharist will bear fruit in the Church: "I do not ask . . . for anything extraordinary, but rather that every initiative be marked by a profound interiority," he writes, but adds: "it is good to aim high, and not to be content with mediocrity."[32] The letter, that began with the "enthusiasm"[33] of the Second Vatican Council, also concludes with enthusiasm and an echo of the Council: "may the Church discover new enthusiasm for her mission and come to acknowledge ever more fully that the Eucharist is the source and summit of her entire life."[34]

Ten years later, *Mane nobiscum Domine* continues to be valuable both as a kind of coda to the teachings of *Ecclesia de Eucharistia* and the instruction *Redemptionis sacramentum*, and in its own right, especially for its juxtaposition of the mystery and mission of the Eucharist.

---

29. Ibid.
30. Ibid., 28.
31. *Deus caritas est* (DCE), 14.
32. MND, 29.
33. Ibid., 6.
34. Ibid., 31; echoing CSL, 10.

OUTLINE

APOSTOLIC LETTER
MANE NOBISCUM DOMINE

OF THE HOLY FATHER
JOHN PAUL II TO THE BISHOPS, CLERGY
AND FAITHFUL
FOR THE YEAR OF THE EUCHARIST

OCTOBER 2004–OCTOBER 2005

INTRODUCTION

1.   "Stay with us, Lord, for it is almost evening" (cf. Lk 24:29). This was the insistent invitation that the two disciples journeying to Emmaus on the evening of the day of the resurrection addressed to the Wayfarer who had accompanied them on their journey. Weighed down with sadness, they never imagined that this stranger was none other than their Master, risen from the dead. Yet they felt their hearts burning within them (cf. v. 32) as he spoke to them and "explained" the Scriptures. The light of the Word unlocked the hardness of their hearts and "opened their eyes" (cf. v. 31). Amid the shadows of the passing day and the darkness that clouded their spirit, the Wayfarer brought a ray of light which rekindled their hope and led their hearts to yearn for the fullness of light. "Stay with us," they pleaded. And he agreed. Soon afterwards, Jesus' face would disappear, yet the Master would "stay" with them, hidden in the "breaking of the bread" which had opened their eyes to recognize him.

2.   The *image of the disciples on the way to Emmaus* can serve as a fitting guide for a year when the Church will be particularly engaged in living out the mystery of the Holy Eucharist. Amid our questions and difficulties, and even our bitter disappointments, the divine Wayfarer continues to walk at our side, opening to us the Scriptures and leading us to a deeper understanding of the mysteries of God. When we meet him fully, we will pass from the light of the Word to the light streaming from the "Bread of life," the supreme fulfillment of his promise to "be with us always, to the end of the age" (cf. Mt 28:20).

3.   The "breaking of bread"—as the Eucharist was called in earliest times—has always been at the center of the Church's life. Through it Christ makes present within time the mystery of his death and resurrection. In it he is received in person as the "living bread come down from heaven" (Jn 6:51), and with him we receive the pledge of eternal life and a foretaste of the eternal banquet of the heavenly Jerusalem. Following the teaching of the Fathers, the Ecumenical

Councils and my own Predecessors, I have frequently urged the Church to reflect upon the Eucharist, most recently in the Encyclical *Ecclesia de Eucharistia*. Here I do not intend to repeat this teaching, which I trust will be more deeply studied and understood. At the same time I thought it helpful for this purpose *to dedicate an entire Year to this wonderful sacrament*.

4.   As is known, the *year of the Eucharist* will be celebrated from October 2004 to October 2005. The idea for this celebration came from two events which will serve to mark its beginning and end: the *International Eucharistic Congress*, which will take place from October 10–17, 2004 in Guadalajara, Mexico, and the *Ordinary Assembly of the Synod of Bishops*, which will be held in the Vatican from October 2–29, 2005 on the theme: "The Eucharist: Source and Summit of the Life and Mission of the Church." I was also guided by another consideration: this year's *World Youth Day* will take place in Cologne from August 16–21, 2005. I would like the young people to gather around the Eucharist as the vital source which nourishes their faith and enthusiasm. A Eucharistic initiative of this kind had been on my mind for some time: it is a natural development of the pastoral impulse which I wanted to give to the Church, particularly during the years of preparation for the Jubilee and in the years that followed it.

5.   In the present Apostolic Letter, I wish to reaffirm this pastoral continuity and to help everyone to grasp its spiritual significance. As for the particular form which the *Year of the Eucharist* will take, I am counting on the personal involvement of the Pastors of the particular Churches, whose devotion to this great Mystery will not fail to suggest suitable approaches. My Brother Bishops will certainly understand that this initiative, coming as it does so soon after the celebration of the *Year of the Rosary*, is meant to take place on a deeply spiritual level, so that it will in no way interfere with the pastoral programs of the individual Churches. Rather, it can shed light upon those programs, anchoring them, so to speak, in the very Mystery which nourishes the spiritual life of the faithful and the initiatives of each local Church. I am not asking the individual Churches to alter their pastoral programs, but to emphasize the Eucharistic dimension which is part of the whole Christian life. For my part, I would like in this Letter to offer *some basic guidelines*; and I am confident that the People of God, at every level, will welcome my proposal with enthusiasm and fervent love.

I

IN THE WAKE OF THE COUNCIL AND THE GREAT JUBILEE

LOOKING TOWARDS CHRIST

6.   Ten years ago, in *Tertio millennio adveniente* (November 10, 1994), I had the joy of proposing to the Church a program of preparation for the *Great Jubilee of the Year 2000*. It seemed to me that this historic moment presented itself as a great grace. I realized, of course, that a simple chronological event, however evocative, could not by itself bring about great changes. Unfortunately the Millennium began with events which were in tragic continuity with the past, and often with its worst aspects. A scenario emerged which, despite certain positive elements, is marred by acts of violence and bloodshed which cause

continued concern. Even so, in inviting the Church to celebrate the Jubilee of the two-thousandth anniversary of the Incarnation, I was convinced—and I still am, more than ever!—that this celebration would be of benefit to humanity in the "long term."

Jesus Christ stands at the center not just of the history of the Church, but also the history of humanity. In him, all things are drawn together (cf. Eph 1:10; Col 1:15–20). How could we forget the enthusiasm with which the Second Vatican Council, quoting Pope Paul VI, proclaimed that Christ is "the goal of human history, the focal point of the desires of history and civilization, the center of mankind, the joy of all hearts, and the fulfillment of all aspirations"?[1] The Council's teaching gave added depth to our understanding of the nature of the Church, and gave believers a clearer insight not only into the mysteries of faith but also into earthly realities, seen in the light of Christ. In the Incarnate Word, both the mystery of God and the mystery of man are revealed.[2] In him, humanity finds redemption and fulfillment.

7.   In the Encyclical *Redemptor hominis*, at the beginning of my Pontificate, I developed this idea, and I have frequently returned to it on other occasions. The Jubilee was a fitting time to invite believers once again to consider this fundamental truth. The preparation for the great event was fully Trinitarian and Christocentric. Within this plan, there clearly had to be a place for the Eucharist. At the start of this Year of the Eucharist, I repeat the words which I wrote in *Tertio millennio adveniente*: "The Year 2000 will be intensely Eucharistic; in the *Sacrament of the Eucharist* the Savior, who took flesh in Mary's womb twenty centuries ago, continues to offer himself to humanity as the source of divine life."[3] The International Eucharistic Congress, held that year in Rome, also helped to focus attention on this aspect of the Great Jubilee. It is also worth recalling that my Apostolic Letter *Dies Domini*, written in preparation for the Jubilee, invited believers to meditate on Sunday as the day of the Risen Lord and the special day of the Church. At that time I urged everyone to rediscover the celebration of the Eucharist as the heart of Sunday.[4]

CONTEMPLATING WITH MARY THE FACE OF CHRIST

8.   The fruits of the Great Jubilee were collected in the Apostolic Letter *Novo millennio ineunte*. In this programmatic document, I suggested an ever greater pastoral engagement based on the contemplation of the face of Christ, as part of an ecclesial pedagogy aimed at "the high standard" of holiness and carried out especially through the art of prayer.[5] How could such a program be complete without a commitment to the liturgy and in particular to the *cultivation of Eucharistic life*? As I said at the time: "In the twentieth century, especially since the Council, there has been a great development in the way the Christian community celebrates the Sacraments, especially the Eucharist. It is necessary to

---

1. Pastoral Constitution on the Church in the Modern World *Gaudium et spes*, 45.
2. Cf. ibid., 22.
3. No. 55: AAS 87 (1995), 38.
4. Cf. nos. 32–34: AAS 90 (1998), 732–734.
5. Cf. nos. 30–32: AAS 93 (2001), 287–289.

continue in this direction, and to stress particularly *the Sunday Eucharist* and *Sunday* itself, experienced as a special day of faith, the day of the Risen Lord and of the gift of the Spirit, the true weekly Easter."[6] In this context of a training in prayer, I recommended the celebration of the *Liturgy of the Hours*, by which the Church sanctifies the different hours of the day and the passage of time through the liturgical year.

9.   Subsequently, with the proclamation of the Year of the Rosary and the publication of the Apostolic Letter *Rosarium Virginis Mariae*, I returned to the theme of contemplating the face of Christ, now *from a Marian perspective*, by encouraging once more the recitation of the Rosary. This traditional prayer, so highly recommended by the Magisterium and so dear to the People of God, has a markedly biblical and evangelical character, focused on the name and the face of Jesus as contemplated in the mysteries and by the repetition of the "Hail Mary." In its flow of repetitions, it represents *a kind of pedagogy of love*, aimed at evoking within our hearts the same love that Mary bore for her Son. For this reason, developing a centuries-old tradition by the addition of the mysteries of light, I sought to make this privileged form of contemplation an even more complete "compendium of the Gospel."[7] And how could the mysteries of light not culminate in the Holy Eucharist?

FROM THE YEAR OF THE ROSARY TO THE YEAR OF THE EUCHARIST

10.   In the midst of the *Year of the Rosary*, I issued the Encyclical Letter *Ecclesia de Eucharistia*, with the intention of shedding light on the mystery of the Eucharist in its inseparable and vital relation to the Church. I urged all the faithful to celebrate the Eucharistic sacrifice with due reverence, offering to Jesus present in the Eucharist, both within and outside Mass, the worship demanded by so great a Mystery. Above all, I suggested once again the need for a Eucharistic spirituality and pointed to Mary, "woman of the Eucharist,"[8] as its model.

The *Year of the Eucharist* takes place against *a background which has been enriched by the passage of the years*, while remaining ever rooted in the theme of Christ and the contemplation of his face. In a certain sense, it is meant to be a year of synthesis, *the high point of a journey in progress*. Much could be said about how to celebrate this year. I would simply offer some reflections intended to help us all to experience it in a deeper and more fruitful way.

---

6. Ibid., 35: loc. cit., 290–291.

7. Cf. Apostolic Letter *Rosarium Virginis Mariae* (October 16, 2002), 19–21: AAS 95 (2003), 18–20.

8. Encyclical Letter *Ecclesia de Eucharistia* (April 17, 2003), 53: AAS 95 (2003), 469.

II
THE EUCHARIST, A MYSTERY OF LIGHT

"he interpreted to them in all the scriptures the things concerning himself" (lk 24:27)

11.   The account of the Risen Jesus appearing to the two disciples on the road to Emmaus helps us to focus on a primary aspect of the Eucharistic mystery, one which should always be present in the devotion of the People of God: *The Eucharist is a mystery of light!* What does this mean, and what are its implications for Christian life and spirituality?

Jesus described himself as the "light of the world" (Jn 8:12), and this quality clearly appears at those moments in his life, like the Transfiguration and the Resurrection, in which his divine glory shines forth brightly. Yet in the Eucharist the glory of Christ remains veiled. The Eucharist is preeminently a *mysterium fidei*. Through the mystery of his complete hiddenness, Christ becomes a mystery of light, thanks to which believers are led into the depths of the divine life. By a happy intuition, Rublëv's celebrated icon of the Trinity clearly places the Eucharist at the center of the life of the Trinity.

12.   The Eucharist is light above all because at every Mass the liturgy of the Word of God precedes the liturgy of the Eucharist in the unity of the two "tables," the table of the Word and the table of the Bread. This continuity is expressed in the Eucharistic discourse of Saint John's Gospel, where Jesus begins his teaching by speaking of the mystery of his person and then goes on to draw out its Eucharistic dimension: "My flesh is food indeed, and my blood is drink indeed" (Jn 6:55). We know that this was troubling for most of his listeners, which led Peter to express the faith of the other Apostles and of the Church throughout history: "Lord, to whom can we go? You have the words of eternal life" (Jn 6:68). In the account of the disciples on the road to Emmaus, Christ himself intervenes to show, "beginning with Moses and all the prophets," how "all the Scriptures" point to the mystery of his person (cf. Lk 24:27). His words make the hearts of the disciples "burn" within them, drawing them out of the darkness of sorrow and despair, and awakening in them a desire to remain with him: "Stay with us, Lord" (cf. v. 29).

13.   The Fathers of the Second Vatican Council, in the Constitution *Sacrosanctum Concilium*, sought to make "the table of the word" offer the treasures of Scripture more fully to the faithful.[9] Consequently they allowed the biblical readings of the liturgy to be proclaimed in a language understood by all. It is Christ himself who speaks when the Holy Scriptures are read in the Church.[10] The Council Fathers also urged the celebrant to treat the homily as part of the liturgy, aimed at explaining the word of God and drawing out its meaning for the Christian life.[11] Forty years after the Council, the *Year of the Eucharist* can serve as an important opportunity for Christian communities *to evaluate their progress in*

---

9. Cf. no. 51.

10. Ibid., 7.

11. Cf ibid., 52.

this area. It is not enough that the biblical passages are read in the vernacular, if they are not also proclaimed with the care, preparation, devout attention and meditative silence that enable the word of God to touch people's minds and hearts.

14.   It is significant that the two disciples on the road to Emmaus, duly prepared by our Lord's words, recognized him at table through the simple gesture of the "breaking of bread." When minds are enlightened and hearts are enkindled, signs begin to "speak." The Eucharist unfolds in a dynamic context of signs containing a rich and luminous message. Through these signs the mystery in some way opens up before the eyes of the believer.

As I emphasized in my Encyclical *Ecclesia de Eucharistia*, it is important that no dimension of this sacrament should be neglected. We are constantly tempted to reduce the Eucharist to our own dimensions, while in reality *it is we who must open ourselves up to the dimensions of the Mystery*. "The Eucharist is too great a gift to tolerate ambiguity and depreciation."[12]

15.   There is no doubt that the most evident dimension of the Eucharist is that it is a *meal*. The Eucharist was born, on the evening of Holy Thursday, in the setting of the Passover meal. *Being a meal* is part of its very structure. "Take, eat. . . . Then he took a cup and . . . gave it to them, saying: Drink from it, all of you" (Mt 26:26, 27). As such, it expresses the fellowship which God wishes to establish with us and which we ourselves must build with one another.

Yet it must not be forgotten that the Eucharistic meal also has a profoundly and primarily *sacrificial* meaning.[13] In the Eucharist, Christ makes present to us anew *the sacrifice offered once for all on Golgotha*. Present in the Eucharist as the Risen Lord, he nonetheless bears the marks of his passion, of which every Mass is a "memorial," as the Liturgy reminds us in the acclamation following the consecration: "We announce your death, Lord, we proclaim your resurrection . . ." At the same time, while the Eucharist makes present what occurred in the past, it also *impels us towards the future, when Christ will come again* at the end of history. This "eschatological" aspect makes the Sacrament of the Eucharist an event which draws us into itself and fills our Christian journey with hope.

16.   All these dimensions of the Eucharist come together in one aspect which more than any other makes a demand on our faith: *the mystery of the "real" presence*. With the entire tradition of the Church, we believe that Jesus is truly present under the Eucharistic species. This presence—as Pope Paul VI rightly

---

12. Encyclical Letter *Ecclesia de Eucharistia* (April 17, 2003), 10: AAS 95 (2003), 439.

13. Cf. John Paul II, Encyclical Letter *Ecclesia de Eucharistia* (April 17, 2003), 10: AAS 95 (2003), 439. Congregation for Divine Worship and the Discipline of the Sacraments, Instruction *Redemptionis sacramentum* on certain matters to be observed or to be avoided regarding the Most Holy Eucharist (March 25, 2004), 38: *L'Osservatore Romano*, Weekly Edition in English, April 28, 2004, Special Insert, p.3.

explained—is called "real" not in an exclusive way, as if to suggest that other forms of Christ's presence are not real, but *par excellence*, because Christ thereby becomes substantially present, whole and entire, in the reality of his body and blood.[14] Faith demands that we approach the Eucharist fully aware that we are approaching Christ himself. It is precisely his presence which gives the other aspects of the Eucharist—as meal, as memorial of the Paschal Mystery, as eschatological anticipation—a significance which goes far beyond mere symbolism. The Eucharist is a mystery of presence, the perfect fulfillment of Jesus' promise to remain with us until the end of the world.

CELEBRATING, WORSHIPING, CONTEMPLATING

17.   The Eucharist is a great mystery! And it is one which above all must be *well celebrated*. Holy Mass needs to be set at the center of the Christian life and celebrated in a dignified manner by every community, in accordance with established norms, with the participation of the assembly, with the presence of ministers who carry out their assigned tasks, and with a serious concern that singing and *liturgical music* be suitably "sacred." One specific project of this *Year of the Eucharist* might be for each parish community to study the General Instruction of the Roman Missal. The best way to enter into the mystery of salvation made present in the sacred "signs" remains that of following faithfully the unfolding of the liturgical year. Pastors should be committed to that *"mystagogical" catechesis* so dear to the Fathers of the Church, by which the faithful are helped to understand the meaning of the liturgy's words and actions, to pass from its signs to the mystery which they contain, and to enter into that mystery in every aspect of their lives.

18.   There is a particular need to cultivate *a lively awareness of Christ's real presence*, both in the celebration of Mass and in the worship of the Eucharist outside Mass. Care should be taken to show that awareness through tone of voice, gestures, posture and bearing. In this regard, liturgical law recalls—and I myself have recently reaffirmed[15]—the importance of moments of silence both in the celebration of Mass and in Eucharistic adoration. The way that the ministers and the faithful treat the Eucharist should be marked by profound respect.[16] The presence of Jesus in the tabernacle must be a kind of *magnetic pole* attracting an ever greater number of souls enamored of him, ready to wait patiently to hear his voice and, as it were, to sense the beating of his heart. "O taste and see that the Lord is good!" (Ps 34:8).

---

14. Cf. Encyclical Letter *Mysterium fidei* (September 3, 1965), 39: *AAS* 57 (1965), 764; Sacred Congregation of Rites, Instruction *Eucharisticum mysterium* on the Worship of the Eucharistic Mystery (May 25, 1967), 9: AAS 59 (1967), 547.

15. Cf. Message *spiritus et sponsa*, for the fortieth anniversary of the Constitution on the Sacred Liturgy *Sacrosanctum Concilium* (December 4, 2003), 13: AAS 96 (2004), 425.

16. Cf. Congregation for Divine Worship and the Discipline of the Sacraments, Instruction *Redemptionis sacramentum* on certain matters to be observed or to be avoided regarding the Most Holy Eucharist (March 25, 2004): *L'Osservatore Romano*, Weekly Edition in English, April 28, 2004, Special Insert.

During this year *Eucharistic adoration outside Mass* should become a particular commitment for individual parish and religious communities. Let us take the time to kneel before Jesus present in the Eucharist, in order to make reparation by our faith and love for the acts of carelessness and neglect, and even the insults which our Savior must endure in many parts of the world. Let us deepen through adoration our personal and communal contemplation, drawing upon aids to prayer inspired by the word of God and the experience of so many mystics, old and new. The Rosary itself, when it is profoundly understood in the biblical and christocentric form which I recommended in the Apostolic Letter *Rosarium Virginis Mariae*, will prove a particularly fitting introduction to Eucharistic contemplation, a contemplation carried out with Mary as our companion and guide.[17]

This year let us also celebrate with particular devotion the Solemnity of *Corpus Christi*, with its traditional procession. Our faith in the God who took flesh in order to become our companion along the way needs to be everywhere proclaimed, especially in our streets and homes, as an expression of our grateful love and as an inexhaustible source of blessings.

III

THE EUCHARIST, SOURCE AND MANIFESTATION OF COMMUNION

"ABIDE IN ME, AND I IN YOU" (JN 15:4)

19.   When the disciples on the way to Emmaus asked Jesus to stay "with" them, he responded by giving them a much greater gift: through the Sacrament of the Eucharist he found a way to stay "in" them. Receiving the Eucharist means entering into a profound communion with Jesus. "Abide in me, and I in you" (Jn 15:4). This relationship of profound and mutual "abiding" *enables us to have a certain foretaste of heaven on earth.* Is this not the greatest of human yearnings? Is this not what God had in mind when he brought about in history his plan of salvation? God has placed in human hearts a "hunger" for his word (cf. Am 8:11), a hunger which will be satisfied only by full union with him. Eucharistic communion was given so that we might be "sated" with God here on earth, in expectation of our complete fulfillment in heaven.

ONE BREAD, ONE BODY

20.   This special closeness which comes about in Eucharistic "communion" cannot be adequately understood or fully experienced apart from ecclesial communion. I emphasized this repeatedly in my Encyclical *Ecclesia de Eucharistia*. The Church is the Body of Christ: we walk "with Christ" to the extent that we are in relationship "with his body." Christ provided for the creation and growth of this unity by the outpouring of his Holy Spirit. And he himself constantly builds it up by his Eucharistic presence. It is the one Eucharistic bread which makes us one body. As the Apostle Paul states: "Because there is one bread, we who are many are one body, for we all partake of the one bread" (1 Cor 10:17). In

---

17. Cf. ibid., 137, loc. cit., p. 11.

the mystery of the Eucharist Jesus builds up the Church as a communion, in accordance with the supreme model evoked in his *priestly prayer:* "Even as you, Father, are in me, and I in you, that they may also be in us, so that the world may believe that you have sent me" (Jn 17:21).

21. The Eucharist is both the *source* of ecclesial unity and its greatest *manifestation*. The Eucharist is an *epiphany of communion*. For this reason the Church sets conditions for full participation in the celebration of the Eucharist.[18] These various limitations ought to make us ever more conscious of *the demands made by the communion which Jesus asks of us*. It is a *hierarchical* communion, based on the awareness of a variety of roles and ministries, as is seen by the reference to the Pope and the Diocesan Bishop in the Eucharistic Prayer. It is a *fraternal* communion, cultivated by a "spirituality of communion" which fosters reciprocal openness, affection, understanding and forgiveness.[19]

"... OF ONE HEART AND SOUL" (ACTS 4:32)

22. At each Holy Mass we are called to measure ourselves against the ideal of communion which the *Acts of the Apostles* paints as a model for the Church in every age. It is the Church gathered around the Apostles, called by the word of God, capable of sharing in spiritual goods but in material goods as well (cf. Acts 2:42–47; 4:32–35). In this *Year of the Eucharist* the Lord invites us to draw as closely as possible to this ideal. Every effort should be made to experience fully those occasions mentioned in the liturgy for the Bishop's "Stational Mass," which he celebrates in the cathedral together with his presbyters and deacons, with the participation of the whole People of God. Here we see the principal "manifestation" of the Church.[20] It would be praiseworthy to specify *other significant occasions*, also on the parochial level, which would increase a sense of communion and find in the Eucharistic celebration a source of renewed fervor.

THE LORD'S DAY

23. In a particular way I ask that every effort be made this year to experience Sunday as the day of the Lord and the day of the Church. I would be happy if everyone would reflect once more on my words in the Apostolic Letter *Dies Domini*. "At Sunday Mass, Christians relive with particular intensity the experience of the Apostles on the evening of Easter, when the Risen Lord appeared to them as they were gathered together (cf. Jn 20:19). In a sense, the People of God of all times were present in that small nucleus of disciples, the first-fruits

---

18. Cf. John Paul II, Encyclical Letter *Ecclesia de Eucharistia* (April 17, 2003), 44: AAS 95 (2003), 462; *Code of Canon Law*, canon 908; *Code of Canons of the Eastern Churches*, canon 702; Pontifical Council for Promoting Christian Unity, *Directorium oecumenicum* (March 25, 1993), 122–125, 129–131: AAS 85 (1993), 1086–1089; Congregation for the Doctrine of the Faith, Letter *Ad exsequendam* (May 18, 2001): AAS 93 (2001), 786.

19. Cf. John Paul II, Apostolic Letter *Novo millennio ineunte* (January 6, 2001), 43: AAS 93 (2001), 297.

20. Cf. Second Vatican Ecumenical Council, Constitution on the Sacred Liturgy *Sacrosanctum Concilium*, 41.

of the Church."[21] During this year of grace, priests in their pastoral ministry should *be even more attentive to Sunday Mass* as the celebration which brings together the entire parish community, with the participation of different groups, movements and associations.

IV
THE EUCHARIST, PRINCIPLE AND PLAN OF "MISSION"

"THEY SET OUT IMMEDIATELY" (CF. LK 24:33)

24.   The two disciples of Emmaus, upon recognizing the Lord, "set out imme-diately" (cf. Lk 24:33), in order to report what they had seen and heard. Once we have truly met the Risen One by partaking of his body and blood, we cannot keep to ourselves the joy we have experienced. The encounter with Christ, con-stantly intensified and deepened in the Eucharist, issues in the Church and in every Christian *an urgent summons to testimony and evangelization*. I wished to emphasize this in my homily announcing the *Year of the Eucharist*, based on the words of Saint Paul: "As often as you eat this bread and drink the cup, you proclaim the Lord's death until he comes" (1 Cor 11:26). The Apostle closely relates meal and proclamation: entering into communion with Christ in the memorial of his Pasch also means sensing the duty to be a missionary of the event made present in that rite.[22] The dismissal at the end of each Mass is *a charge* given to Christians, inviting them to work for the spread of the Gospel and the imbuing of society with Christian values.

25.   The Eucharist not only provides the interior strength needed for this mis-sion, but is also—in some sense—*its plan*. For the Eucharist is a mode of being, which passes from Jesus into each Christian, through whose testimony it is meant to spread throughout society and culture. For this to happen, each mem-ber of the faithful must assimilate, through personal and communal meditation, the values which the Eucharist expresses, the attitudes it inspires, the resolu-tions to which it gives rise. Can we not see here *a special charge* which could emerge from this *Year of the Eucharist?*

GIVING THANKS

26.   One fundamental element of this *plan* is found in the very meaning of the word "Eucharist": thanksgiving. In Jesus, in his sacrifice, in his unconditional "yes" to the will of the Father, is contained the "yes," the "thank you" and the "amen" of all humanity. The Church is called to remind men and women of this great truth. This is especially urgent in the context of our secularized cul-ture, characterized as it is by a forgetfulness of God and a vain pursuit of human self-sufficiency. Incarnating the Eucharistic "plan" in daily life, wherever peo-ple live and work—in families, schools, the workplace, in all of life's settings—means bearing witness that *human reality cannot be justified without reference*

---

21. No. 33: AAS 90 (1998), 733.

22. Cf. Homily for the Solemnity of the Body and Blood of Christ (June 10, 2004): *L'Osservatore Romano*, June 11–12, 2004, p.6.

to the Creator: "Without the Creator the creature would disappear."[23] This transcendent point of reference, which commits us constantly to give thanks for all that we have and are—in other words, to a "Eucharistic" attitude—in no way detracts from the legitimate autonomy of earthly realities,[24] but grounds that autonomy more firmly by setting it within its proper limits.

In this *Year of the Eucharist* Christians ought to be committed to bearing more forceful witness to God's presence in the world. We should not be afraid to speak about God and to bear proud witness to our faith. The "culture of the Eucharist" promotes a culture of dialogue, which here finds strength and nourishment. It is a mistake to think that any public reference to faith will somehow undermine the rightful autonomy of the State and civil institutions, or that it can even encourage attitudes of intolerance. If history demonstrates that mistakes have also been made in this area by believers, as I acknowledged on the occasion of the Jubilee, this must be attributed not to "Christian roots," but to the failure of Christians to be faithful to those roots. One who learns to say "thank you" in the manner of the crucified Christ might end up as a martyr, but never as a persecutor.

THE WAY OF SOLIDARITY

27.   The Eucharist is not merely an expression of communion in the Church's life; it is also a *project of solidarity* for all of humanity. In the celebration of the Eucharist the Church constantly renews her awareness of being a "sign and instrument" not only of intimate union with God but also of the unity of the whole human race.[25] Each Mass, even when celebrated in obscurity or in isolation, always has a universal character. The Christian who takes part in the Eucharist learns to become a *promoter of communion, peace and solidarity* in every situation. More than ever, our troubled world, which began the new Millennium with the specter of terrorism and the tragedy of war, demands that Christians learn to experience the Eucharist as *a great school of peace*, forming men and women who, at various levels of responsibility in social, cultural and political life, can become promoters of dialogue and communion.

AT THE SERVICE OF THE LEAST

28.   There is one other point which I would like to emphasize, since it significantly affects the authenticity of our communal sharing in the Eucharist. It is the impulse which the Eucharist gives to the community for *a practical commitment to building a more just and fraternal society*. In the Eucharist our God has shown love in the extreme, overturning all those criteria of power which too often govern human relations and radically affirming the criterion of service: "If anyone would be first, he must be last of all and servant of all" (Mc 9:35). It is not by chance that the Gospel of John contains no account of the institution

---

23. Second Vatican Ecumenical Council, Pastoral Constitution on the Church in the Modern World *Gaudium et spes*, 36.

24. Ibid.

25. Cf. Second Vatican Ecumenical Council, Pastoral Constitution on the Church *Lumen gentium*, 1.

of the Eucharist, but instead relates the "washing of feet" (cf. Jn 13:1–20): by bending down to wash the feet of his disciples, Jesus explains the meaning of the Eucharist unequivocally. Saint Paul vigorously reaffirms the impropriety of a Eucharistic celebration lacking charity expressed by practical sharing with the poor (cf. 1 Cor 11:17–22, 27–34).

Can we not make this *Year of the Eucharist* an occasion for diocesan and parish communities to commit themselves in a particular way to responding with fraternal solicitude to one of the many forms of poverty present in our world? I think for example of the tragedy of hunger which plagues hundreds of millions of human beings, the diseases which afflict developing countries, the loneliness of the elderly, the hardships faced by the unemployed, the struggles of immigrants. These are evils which are present—albeit to a different degree—even in areas of immense wealth. We cannot delude ourselves: by our mutual love and, in particular, by our concern for those in need we will be recognized as true followers of Christ (cf. Jn 13:35; Mt 25:31–46). This will be the criterion by which the authenticity of our Eucharistic celebrations is judged.

CONCLUSION

29.   *O Sacrum Convivium, in quo Christus sumitur!* The *Year of the Eucharist* has its source in the amazement with which the Church contemplates this great Mystery. It is an amazement which I myself constantly experience. It prompted my Encyclical *Ecclesia de Eucharistia*. As I look forward to the twenty-seventh year of my Petrine ministry, I consider it a great grace to be able to call the whole Church to contemplate, praise, and adore in a special way this ineffable Sacrament. May the *Year of the Eucharist* be for everyone a precious opportunity to grow in awareness of the incomparable treasure which Christ has entrusted to his Church. May it encourage a more lively and fervent celebration of the Eucharist, leading to a Christian life transformed by love.

There is room here for any number of initiatives, according to the judgment of the Pastors of the particular Churches. The *Congregation for Divine Worship and the Discipline of the Sacraments* will not fail to provide some helpful suggestions and proposals. I do not ask, however, for anything extraordinary, but rather that every initiative be marked by a profound interiority. If the only result of this Year were the revival in all Christian communities of the celebration of Sunday Mass and an increase in Eucharistic worship outside Mass, this Year of grace would be abundantly successful. At the same time, it is good to aim high, and not to be content with mediocrity, since we know we can always count on God's help.

30.   To you, dear *Brother Bishops*, I commend this Year, confident that you will welcome my invitation with full apostolic zeal.

Dear *priests*, who repeat the words of consecration each day, and are witnesses and heralds of the great miracle of love which takes place at your hands: be challenged by the grace of this special Year; celebrate Holy Mass each day with the same joy and fervor with which you celebrated your first Mass, and willingly spend time in prayer before the tabernacle.

May this be a Year of grace also for you, *deacons*, who are so closely engaged in the ministry of the word and the service of the altar. I ask you, *lectors, acolytes and extraordinary ministers of holy communion*, to become ever more aware of the gift you have received in the service entrusted to you for a more worthy celebration of the Eucharist.

In particular I appeal to you, *the priests of the future*. During your time in the seminary make every effort to experience the beauty not only of taking part daily in Holy Mass, but also of spending a certain amount of time in dialogue with the Eucharistic Lord.

Consecrated men and women, called by that very consecration to more prolonged contemplation: never forget that Jesus in the tabernacle wants you to be at his side, so that he can fill your hearts with the experience of his friendship, which alone gives meaning and fulfillment to your lives.

May all of you, *the Christian faithful*, rediscover the gift of the Eucharist as light and strength for your daily lives in the world, in the exercise of your respective professions amid so many different situations. Rediscover this above all in order to experience fully the beauty and the mission of the *family*.

I have great expectations of you, *young people*, as I look forward to our meeting at the next *World Youth Day* in Cologne. The theme of our meeting—*"We have come to worship him"*—suggests how you can best experience this Eucharistic year. Bring to your encounter with Jesus, hidden in the Eucharist, all the enthusiasm of your age, all your hopes, all your desire to love.

31.   We have before us the example of the Saints, who in the Eucharist found nourishment on their journey towards perfection. How many times did they shed tears of profound emotion in the presence of this great mystery, or experience hours of inexpressible "spousal" joy before the sacrament of the altar! May we be helped above all by the Blessed Virgin Mary, whose whole life incarnated the meaning of the Eucharist. "The Church, which looks to Mary as a model, is also called to imitate her in her relationship with this most holy mystery."[26] The Eucharistic Bread which we receive is the spotless flesh of her Son: *Ave verum corpus natum de Maria Virgine*. In this Year of grace, sustained by Mary, may the Church discover new enthusiasm for her mission and come to acknowledge ever more fully that the Eucharist is the source and summit of her entire life.

To all of you I impart my Blessing as a pledge of grace and joy.

From the Vatican, on October 7, the Memorial of Our Lady of the Rosary, in the year 2004, the twenty-sixth of my Pontificate.

IOANNES PAULUS PP.II

---

26. John Paul II, Encyclical Letter *Ecclesia de Eucharistia* (April 17, 2003), 53: AAS 95 (2003), 469.

ORATIO UNIVERSALIS
THE UNIVERSAL PRAYER OR
PRAYER OF THE FAITHFUL

CONSILIUM
SACRED CONGREGATION OF RITES
JANUARY 17, 1965;
REVISED APRIL 17, 1966 (SECOND EDITION)

AN OVERVIEW OF *ORATIO UNIVERSALIS*
Paul F. Ford

Yesterday's revolution can become today's commonplace; monumental changes can be taken for granted; and great reforms can be weakened or even reversed through inattention, misunderstanding, and misuse. Such forgetfulness and indifference can afflict Catholics with respect to the great modernizing and updating the Church has been through since 1963. In liturgy, who still recognizes the restoration of the General Intercessions as one of the great changes of the Second Vatican Council? And yet it is. In the Universal Prayer[1] the priestly people of God rediscover in the Order of Mass their proper and irreplaceable role of interceding for the needs of the Church and the world.

It is only a slight exaggeration to call, *Oratio universalis* (OU), or in English, *The Universal Prayer* or *Prayer of the Faithful* (UP) the firstfruit of the liturgical reform of the Second Vatican Council.[2] Originally released on January 13, 1965 as a provisional thirty-two-page text and used at the Masses of the Council's fourth session,[3] the second edition, a 182–page booklet,[4] was published on April 17, 1966, fewer than five months after the end of the Council. UP contains:

- A twenty-article *praenotanda* (introduction);

- One hundred and forty-one pages containing fifty-four samples of the Universal Prayer in Latin and French;[5]

- A seventeen-article history of the Universal Prayer;

- Three pages of eight musical formularies (that are later included in the *Graduale Simplex*);

- Three indexes (systematic, alphabetic, and general).

Alas, little of UP was available in English until its *praenotanda* and its introduction to the samples appeared as number 239 in *Documents on the Liturgy: 1963–1979*, a joint publication of The Liturgical Press and the International Commission on English in the Liturgy (ICEL). As such, it is one of the most neglected foundational documents of the liturgical reform.

---

1. Also known as Prayer of the Faithful (GIRM, 69), Bidding Prayers (Order of Mass, 20), or General Intercessions.

2. Only the *Kyriale Simplex* is older, by a month (December 14, 1964), a reworking of familiar materials, eventually included in the 1968 *Graduale Simplex*.

3. *De oratione communi seu fidelium. Eius natura, momentum ac structura. Criteria atque specimina ad experimentum Coetibus territorialibus Episcoporum proposita.* Libreria Editrice Vaticana, 1965.

4. *Oratio Universalis: De oratione communi seu fidelium / Natura, momentum ac structura / Criteria atque specimina / Coetibus territorialibus Episcoporum proposita.* Libreria Editrice Vaticana, 1966.

5. Eleven of which are in the third edition of *The Roman Missal* (RM), *Appendix V: Examples of Formularies for the Universal Prayer.*

The Universal Prayer was restored by article 53 of the *Constitution on the Sacred Liturgy*:

> Especially on Sundays and feasts of obligation there is to be restored, after the Gospel and the homily, "the common prayer" or "the prayer of the faithful." By this prayer, in which the people are to take part, intercession will be made for holy Church, for the civil authorities, for those oppressed by various needs, for all mankind, and for the salvation of the entire world.

Permission to commence praying the Universal Prayer was given by article 56 of *Inter oecumenici*, the instruction on implementing liturgical norms, promulgated September 26, 1964.

THE THEOLOGY OF THE UNIVERSAL PRAYER

Pope John Paul II said: "When our people realize . . . that they are called to be 'a royal priesthood . . .' and . . . that all their prayers of petition are united to an infinite act of the praying Christ, then there is fresh hope and new encouragement for the Christian people."[6]

In fact UP makes two bold analogies: (1) Just as Holy Communion is the climax of the liturgy of the Eucharist, so the Prayer of the Faithful is the climax of the entire Liturgy of the Word; and (2) this prayer is the hinge between the two parts of the Mass.[7] As the theologian Robert Cabié summarizes,

> The General Intercessions can be seen to mark the end of the entire Liturgy of the Word and at the same time to be, as it were, the threshold of the Eucharist proper. Coming as they do after the dismissal of the catechumens, they are the privilege of the faithful, and they underscore the latter's priestly character. To present to God the appeals and hopes of the entire human race is to share in the care and concern of the Priest of the New Covenant who gave his life for the salvation of the world; it is to share in his mission. We may say that the intercessions represent the other side of evangelization, since speaking of human beings to God is inseparable from speaking of God to human beings.[8]

Cabié reflects the Church's vision for this prayer:

> The place proper to the prayer of the faithful is at the end of every celebration of the word of God; as a rule it takes place even if the eucharistic sacrifice is not to follow.
>
> The reason is that this prayer is the fruit, as it were, of the working of the word of God in the hearts of the faithful: instructed, stirred and renewed by the word, all stand together to offer prayer for the needs of the whole Church and the whole world.[9]

---

6. *Newsletter*, XIX (August/September 1983).
7. See *Oratio universalis* (OU) §4.
8. Cabié, 75.
9. OU, 4.

But is this the experience of average Catholics? Or do they hear "canned" intentions, or laundry lists of persons who are sick or deceased, or petitions for every conceivable need, to which they respond with a rattled off "Lord, hear our prayer"? Do ordinary people look forward to this prayer with the same longing as they have for receiving Holy Communion? Do they experience the same sort of satisfaction after this prayer as they do after Holy Communion?

Seven years after it issued UP, Rome had to remind Conferences of Bishops throughout the world, "*Much* is to be made of the general intercessions which . . . is the community's response to the word of God proclaimed and received."[10] But do we make *much* of this prayer? Do people feel that the Church is *only* "X, our Pope, X, our bishop, and all the clergy" or that they are the "gathered Church . . . , the great entreater and advocate appointed for all humanity?"[11]

American Catholics come by their misunderstanding and/or misuse of the Universal Prayer honestly. One of the most effective and life-giving substitutes for liturgical spirituality before the Second Vatican Council was the weekly novena devotion. People avidly filled out slips of paper with their intentions, including the all-covering and ever-intriguing "Special Intention." But there is perhaps nothing more contrary to the *universal* and liturgical character of the Prayer of the Faithful than voicing at it the very *particular* and devotional novena petition, "for a special intention." Special intentions do have their place in liturgy: during the silence for prayer at the time of the Collect.

So, in order for people to experience their "liturgical dignity" the Universal Prayer needs to become what it was designed to be:

> In the light of God's word and in a sense in response to it, the congregation of the faithful prays in the universal prayer as a rule for the needs of the universal Church and the local community, for the salvation of the world and those oppressed by any burden, and for special categories of people.

> The celebrant introduces the prayer; a deacon, another minister, or some of the faithful may propose intentions that are short and phrased with a measure of freedom. In these petitions "the people, exercising its priestly function, makes intercession for all men and women," (GIRM, 45) with the result that, as the liturgy of the word has its full effects in the faithful, they are better prepared to proceed to the liturgy of the Eucharist.[12]

Thus, the readings for Mass contain many matters from which intercessions might be made. But how do we make this ideal real in our parishes and communities?

THE UNIVERSAL PRAYER IN PRACTICE

The task of composing the Prayer of the Faithful belongs to the deacon, cantor, or "intentionist" working together with those who prepare the liturgy. There is

---

10. *Eucharistiæ participationem*, 16; April 27, 1973 (DOL 248: 1990), emphasis added.
11. OU, 3.
12. "Introduction" to the *Lectionary for Mass*, 30.

a series of questions they can address to the readings themselves (and to the Holy Spirit who wrote them and who wants to inspire our prayer). The answers to these questions form the raw material out of which the Universal Prayer can be made. (In the following list, anything in *italics* is from UP, 9, a passage that expands upon the four categories of the *General Instruction of the Roman Missal* ([GIRM] 69–70.) Mark the Lectionary readings with the letters **(c)**, **(w)**, **(n)**, and **(l)** for the many possible intentions.)

First the preliminary questions: Where do these readings and where does this liturgy fit in the liturgical year? In the world/national/regional/local secular calendar? Then,

- Do the readings remind one of **[c** = Church] *the needs of the Church universal, for example, for the pope, the bishops and pastors of the Church, missions, Christian unity, vocations to the priesthood and religious life*? Does any reading suggest any particular profession, vocation, or job which the lay faithful occupy and for the doing of which they need God's help? About any kinds of ministry in the Church today? Is there anything about any reading particularly applicable to women in the Church? To the young in our Church (children, adolescents, and young adults) and ministry to them?

- Do the readings remind one of [**w** = world] *national or world affairs, for example peace, leaders of government, good weather, the safety of crops, elections, economic crises, and so on*? Is there anything about any reading particularly applicable to the needs of women around the world? To the needs of the youth of the world (children, adolescents, and young adults)?

- Do the readings remind one of [**n** = those is special need] *those beset by poverty or tribulation, for example, for those absent, the persecuted, the unemployed, the sick and infirm, the dying, prisoners, exiles, and so on*? Is there anything about any reading particularly applicable to women in crisis? To the young in special need?

- Do the readings remind one of [**l** = local] *the congregation and members of the local community, for example, those in the parish preparing for Baptism, Confirmation, Holy Orders, Marriage, for pastors, for a coming parish mission, for first communicants, and so on*? Is there anything about any reading particularly applicable to women in this local community of faith? To the young of this community?

To see how the Universal Prayer is structured, it is instructive to look at the eleven sample formulas in *The Roman Missal*, Appendix V. Every Universal Prayer begins with the priest celebrant's invitation to pray and concludes with a short prayer. UP instructs the priest celebrant, that, in his invitation (which is not addressed to God but to the people), his responsibility is to motivate (the Latin says *excitare*) them to pray; his concluding prayer is "limited to asking God to hear the petitions poured forth."[13]

---

13. OU, 7 is about the invitation and OU, 14 is about the conclusion.

UP, 12 directs that the intentions are composed in one of three forms:

1. The full form ("Let us pray for . . . that"), which states those to be prayed for and what is to be prayed for.[14] There is a pause for the silent prayer of the people after "for . . ." and before "that . . . "

2. A first partial form ("Let us pray that . . ."), which immediately mentions the favor to be requested.[15]

3. A second partial form ("Let us pray for . . ."), which states only those being prayed for.[16]

Notice too that only examples 3 and 9 pray for the pope and for the bishop. This means that prayers for the needs of the Church are not exhausted by prayers for them.

The prayer of the people may be either: (1) a short acclamation, (2) silent prayer, (3) a long formula that the people recite (this is how the Universal Prayer is done at morning and evening prayer in the Liturgy of the Hours), and (4) a combination of the first two: silent prayer followed by a short acclamation in answer to the deacon's invitation.

We are most familiar with the short acclamation but this familiarity has bred confusion. Many think that the intention is the prayer and the acclamation is a mere response, like a mere *Amen*. In order to reeducate ourselves, we need to use silence alone or silence followed by an acclamation. Silence set aside for the faithful's prayer is the key to recovery of the Prayer of the Faithful.

CONCLUSION

Now restored to our worship, the Universal Prayer should be composed with care and earnestly prayed. For the Church's power of prayer is great. The whole Church, the baptized praying with united voices and hearts, interceding for the needs, not only of its own, but especially for all humanity, is moving the world ever nearer to the kingdom of God's reign over the earth.

These reflections underscore the final reason why we should pray well the Universal Prayer. As Jews believe that with every Passover and every Sabbath well celebrated the coming of the Messiah is hastened, so ancient Christians believed that every Eucharist shortens the time until the Second Coming. The Bride has only to join her voice to the Spirit's to be able to say, "Maranatha! Come, Lord Jesus!"

---

14. OU, 12; examples 1, 4, 5, 8, and 10.
15. Ibid.; examples 3, 6, 7, and 11.
16. Ibid.; examples 2 and 9.

THE UNIVERSAL PRAYER OR PRAYER
OF THE FAITHFUL

DIRECTORY

CONSILIUM FOR THE IMPLEMENTATION
OF THE CONSTITUTION ON THE SACRED LITURGY

13, JANUARY 1965 (FIRST EDITION)
17 APRIL 1966 (SECOND EDITION)

INTRODUCTION

The Constitution on the Liturgy has taught and decreed (art. 53) the following on the universal prayer or prayer of the faithful: "Especially on Sundays and holydays of obligation there is to be restored, after the gospel and the homily, 'the universal prayer' or 'the prayer of the faithful.' By this prayer, in which the people are to take part, intercession will be made for holy Church, for the civil authorities, for those oppressed by various needs, for all people, and for the salvation of the entire world."*

On the same point the Congregation of Rites' instruction on the orderly carrying out of the Constitution on the Liturgy, 26 September 1964, has this to say (no. 56): "In places where the universal prayer or prayer of the faithful is already the custom, it shall take place before the offertory, after the *Oremus*, and, for the time being, with formularies in use in individual regions. The celebrant is to lead the prayer at either his chair, the altar, the lectern, or the edge of the sanctuary. A deacon, cantor, or other suitable minister may sing the intentions or intercessions. The celebrant takes the introduction and concluding prayer, this being ordinarily the *Deus refugium nostrum et virtus* (Missale Romanum, Orationes diversae no. 20) or another prayer more suited to particular needs. In places where the universal prayer or prayer of the faithful is not the custom, the competent territorial authority may decree its use in the manner already indicated and with formularies approved provisorily by that authority."

This present booklet, composed under the care and effort of the Consilium, has as its purpose to give illustrative samples of such texts in order to provide the competent ecclesiastical authority with models for the correct preparation, in its own region, of formularies or with criteria for its approval of such formularies. The series of texts presented here are therefore not to be taken as obligatory.

*This text is from the second edition.

A French translation is printed alongside the Latin text in order to facilitate the work of the territorial authority in the preparation of vernacular texts. This arrangement shows to what extent intelligent adaptations may be made in keeping with the idiom and rules of each language.

The samples of sets of intentions here generally correspond to the sets of chants for Mass in the *Graduale simplex* (Vatican Polyglot Press, Vatican City, 17 April 1966).

CHAPTER I

PRACTICAL DIRECTORY

§ I. Nature and Pastoral Value of the Prayer of the Faithful

1.   "Universal prayer" is a term for a prayer or intercession directed to God, made at the invitation of the proper minister and by the faithful as a group. This prayer makes intercession for the various needs of the Church, especially the universal Church, and of the whole world.

2.   Thus this prayer has three noteworthy characteristics:

   a. *It is a petition addressed to God.* Therefore it is not the expression of adoration or thanksgiving alone; nor is it in praise of some saint or a summary to give instruction on truths about religious obligations or the nature of the Mass.

   b. *It is a petition to God chiefly for blessings of a universal kind*: on behalf of the whole Church, the world, all those "beset by various needs"; nevertheless it is proper also to pray for the faithful actually making up the assembly.

   c. *It belongs to the whole congregation* ("with the people taking part"), because the assembly responds to the minister's invitations and does not through a single *Amen* simply conclude petitions made by the minister alone.

3.   There is a place for this prayer not simply during Mass, but also in popular devotions and in the other rites of the liturgy, in keeping with what the Constitution on the Liturgy has described. Firm in its faith in the communion of saints and in its own all-embracing vocation, the gathered Church in offering this prayer stands as the great entreater and advocate appointed for all humanity. The holy people of God exercise their royal priesthood to the fullest above all by sharing in the sacraments, but also by joining in this prayer. Of its nature this supplication still belongs only to the faithful, not to catechumens.

4.   The place proper to the prayer of the faithful is at the end of every celebration of the word of God; as a rule it takes place even if the eucharistic sacrifice is not to follow (see the instruction of 26 September 1964, nos. 37 and 73 c).

The reason is that this prayer is the fruit, as it were, of the working of the word of God in the hearts of the faithful: instructed, stirred and renewed by the word, all stand together to offer prayer for the needs of the whole Church and the whole world.

Thus there is an analogy: sacramental communion is the conclusion and, in regard to the people's participation, the climax of the liturgy of the eucharist; the prayer of the faithful, according to the witness of antiquity, appears as the conclusion and, in regard to the people's participation, the climax of the entire liturgy of the word. This is why the Constitution (art. 54) and the Instruction cited (no. 57), when dealing with use of the vernacular in the liturgy, both first of all make mention of the readings and of this prayer.

But the prayer can also be seen in another way as a hinge between the two parts of the Mass: it terminates the liturgy of the word in which God's wonderful works and the Christian calling are brought to mind; it ushers in the liturgy of the eucharist by stating some of those general and particular intentions for which the sacrifice is to be offered.

5.   The prayer of the faithful is to be put into use as often as possible, so that it may "be restored especially on Sundays and holydays of obligation" (SC art. 53) and also on weekdays at all Masses celebrated with a large number of people present.

§ II. Parts and Ministers

6.   The prayer of the faithful consists of several parts: the announcement or statement of the intentions; the responses of the assembly; the concluding formularies. Another part that may be included is an introductory commentary.

7.   It is the celebrant's responsibility to motivate the people in regard to this prayer by introductory comments on its liturgical and pastoral significance. Such an introduction, normally brief and addressed not to God but to the people, may touch on the liturgical season or on the theme of the feast or of the saint being celebrated, and it should connect these with the ensuing prayer. But an introduction may be omitted for a good reason, especially when the prayer of the faithful immediately follows the homily.

8.   In the style of the ancient Roman usage, the priest himself may propose the intentions to the people. But, in accord with *Inter Oecumenici* (no. 56), this function usually belongs to the deacon.

In Masses with no deacon present the function should be assigned to some other suitable person assisting (e.g., a commentator) or to the celebrant or one of the concelebrants.

If the intentions are set to music, which is desirable, the minister or the person assisting must be able to sing properly.

When the celebrant himself does not announce the intentions, he responds along with the congregation and does not continue Mass until the universal prayer is over, thus following the rule given by *Inter Oecumenici* in the case of confirmation or marriage celebrated within Mass (nos. 66 and 72).

9.   After the priest's introductory comments (designated in the formulas of this booklet as "Section A"), there are usually four sets of intentions in any prayer of the faithful (excepting the cases in no. 10), namely, for:

> B. the needs of the Church universal, e.g., for the pope, the bishops and pastors of the Church, missions, Christian unity, vocations to the priesthood and religious life (Section B);

> C. national or world affairs, e.g., peace, leaders of government, good weather, the safety of crops, elections, economic crises, etc. (Section C);

> D. those beset by poverty or tribulation, e.g., for those absent, the persecuted, the unemployed, the sick and infirm, the dying, prisoners, exiles, etc. (Section D);

> E. the congregation and members of the local community, e.g., those in the parish preparing for baptism, confirmation, orders, marriage, for pastors, for a coming parish mission, for first communicants, etc. (Section E).

At least one intention from each set is to be announced.

10.   In such votive celebrations as weddings or funerals more scope is allowed for the appropriate votive intention, but never by completely omitting the general intentions.

11.   *As to structure*, the intentions *usually are expressed in one of three forms* (as is indicated in the historical summary in this booklet):

> a. the full form ("Let us pray *for . . . that*"), which states those to be prayed for and what is to be prayed for. An example is the invitations to prayer or first part of each of the solemn prayers on Good Friday;

> b. a first partial form ("Let us pray *that . . .*"), which immediately mentions the favor to be requested, referring in only one word to the persons prayed for. An example is the petitions of the final section of the Litany of the Saints;

> c. a second partial form ("Let us pray *for . . .*"), which states only those being prayed for. Examples are some of the litanic "deprecations" in both the East and the West.

12.   Of utmost importance is the part of the prayer of the faithful involving the congregation's participation. For this to be real and active it is better that it be repeated with each invitation to pray. There are four ways of doing so:

> a. a short acclamation, always the same in the same celebration; this is the easiest form of participation and established by the long usage known by the name "litany";

b. participation through silent prayer during a suitable pause; though seemingly passive this silent participation, tested by its Roman usage in the solemn prayers, can contribute a great deal to prayer;

c. the communal recitation of a rather long intercessory formulary; to avoid boredom, however, it is necessary that there be variety in the texts and that the faithful have written copies of them;

d. finally, a combination of the first and second: after a brief silence, the deacon in a second, very short invitation calls for the congregation's acclamation. This way can be used on certain more solemn occasions.

Without doubt the first way has the most to recommend it, even though it is right that there be complete freedom to use any of the others.

13.   Because the Constitution on the Liturgy calls for participation by the people and this is really the principal element in the prayer of the faithful, it is completely out of place in Masses with a congregation for only the choir or ministers to respond to the one announcing the intentions.

14.   The conclusion of the prayer belongs to the one presiding (see *Inter Oecumenici* no. 56). As a rule, the conclusion takes place only once at the end of the whole prayer and usually in the form of a concluding prayer, limited to asking God to hear the petitions poured forth. This concluding prayer should in no way be a repetition of the opening prayer of the day. But in votive celebrations, where most of the petitions relate to the votive intention (see no. 10), the priest's concluding prayer may also express this special intention.

§ *III. Respecting Freedom in the Use of the Prayer of the Faithful*

15.   In order that the prayer of the faithful may be an expression of the authentic prayer of the Church as universal yet at home in every place and period, there must be a strong preference for the freedom to vary formularies and match them to the character of regions or peoples.

16.   Greater conformity can be required for the concluding part and a degree of uniformity in the people's responses for individual nations or neighboring regions sharing the same language. More freedom is left in regard to the choice of petitions and the ways of participation. But such freedom must respect the essential properties of the prayer of the faithful already stated.

17.   For the Roman Rite as a whole, the Consilium sets out the *principles* and *rules* governing the right arrangement of the prayer of the faithful.

18.   But it is for the territorial bodies of bishops and, where applicable, for local Ordinaries to approve formularies (see *Inter Oecumenici* no. 56) and to provide pastors with an ample collection of intentions to choose from.

19.   It is proper to leave it to the pastor of a church:

    a. to choose from among the many approved formularies for intentions those to be announced for each set;

    b. to add a few other intentions of his own composition, provided he respects the rule on keeping the four classes of intention indicated in no. 9 and writes out the text ahead of time.

20.   To ensure that the prayer of the faithful will not become an aggravation to the people because of its length, the competent authority may stipulate the maximum number of intentions for any Mass, if this seems warranted. But it will be permissible to exceed this number on a given occasion, e.g., at a celebration of the word, at a pilgrimage, or at some extraordinary gathering.

CHAPTER II

SAMPLES FOR COMPOSING A PLAN FOR THE UNIVERSAL PRAYER

There is no need to translate the samples given into the various languages. It is better that the texts be made to suit the character or language of each people.

The term *oratio communis* or *oratio fidelium* itself can be quite readily expressed by synonyms, for example, *prex* or *deprecatio universalis*. The expressions *oratio communis* or *oratio fidelium* are retained in documents because they are the accepted terms in antiquity and because of their *technical* meaning. Even so, a literal translation of them does not seem to be the best translation: the whole Mass is a universal prayer of participation and the Lord's Prayer is distinctively the prayer of the faithful.

These various samples do not rule out other styles of composing the prayer of the faithful, especially in regions where this prayer is already the practice.[1] The formularies assigned for the various seasons or feasts are offered merely as examples and others may be substituted at the discretion of the conferences of bishops. In individual formularies the sequence of intentions (B, C, D, E), although generally preferable, is not entirely obligatory (see formulary 52 for weddings): e.g., in votive celebrations it will sometimes be better to begin the prayer of the faithful with the votive intentions, which are more on the minds of congregation, so as to go from these particular intentions to the more general. [. . .]*

*Samples of formularies in Latin with French translation follow here in the booklet, 16–159.

APPENDIX I

HISTORY OF THE UNIVERSAL PRAYER OR PRAYER OF THE FAITHFUL

1.   The prayer of the faithful, which still exists in almost all rites and seems at one time to have existed in all, very probably had an apostolic or even a Jewish

---

    1. For example, certain regions have the custom of proposing intentions in the manner used in the final part of the Litany of the Saints.

origin. That is true even if the text of 1 Timothy cited by the Constitution on the Liturgy[2] is not a specific reference to this particular form of liturgical petition but a generic reference to the Christian's obligation to pray.

2.   We find a more explicit link with the liturgical prayer of the faithful in its technical sense at the end of the Letter of Pope St. Clement written before the end of the first century. After a homiletic exhortation to the Corinthians, the successor of St. Peter invites them: "Let us entreat the Creator of all things with urgent petition and supplication that through his beloved Son Jesus Christ he preserve intact those counted among his elect throughout the world."

After this brief appeal to the Corinthians, Clement immediately begins a great petition addressed to God—for the people of God, those afflicted by various needs, for pardon for sin, for peace, for rulers—then concludes with a magnificent doxology.

3.   But, as is well known, we find the first explicit mention of the prayer of the faithful in 150 AD as a part of the liturgy following the homily or the rite of baptism, before the kiss of peace and the eucharistic sacrifice. In his *Apologia I* St. Justin Martyr writes that [on Sunday after the reading of Scripture and the homily of the one presiding] "we all stand together and offer prayers" (67). On the occasion of baptism, "we bring [the one newly baptized] into the assembly and offer communal prayers for ourselves, for the one baptized, and for all others wherever they may be. We pray that we may become worthy adherents to the truth, spend our lives in good works, and keep the commandments so that we may reach eternal salvation" (65). Justin makes a distinction between these "universal prayers" of the whole assembly and the "eucharist and prayer" that "after the kiss of peace the one presiding utters over the bread and wine" and at whose conclusion the people respond: *Amen.*

4.   In the early years of the third century, with similar words Hippolytus of Rome in his *Traditio apostolica* directs that after receiving baptism the neophytes "then pray together with all the people, for they do not do so before they have received all these things [the rites of baptism]." Hippolytus indicates that the kiss of peace and the offering of the bread and wine then follow.[3]

5.   *Many of the Fathers make frequent allusions* to the universal prayer (in the West: Cyprian, Tertullian, Ambrose, Arnobius, Augustine, Siricius; in the East: Clement of Alexandria, Dionysius of Alexandria, Origen, Athanasius, Chrysostom, and others). Even though in some texts it is not clear whether the subject is this part of the liturgy of the Mass, in many others it is.

But as far as the specific form of the prayer and its intentions is concerned, the statements of Fathers of the second and fourth century, are ambiguous. Tertullian

---

2. "I exhort therefore that first of all there be supplications, prayers, intercessions, and thanksgiving for all people; for rulers and for all that are in authority; that we may lead a quiet and peaceable life in all godliness and uprightness. For this is good and acceptable in the sight of God our Savior, whose will is that all should be saved and come to know the truth" (1 Tm 2:1–4).

3. B. Botte, ed. (Münster, 1963) 54; (Paris, 1946) 53.

in passing reminds Christians "to pray also for rulers, their ministers and officers, the state of the world, the peace of its affairs, and the delay of its end" (*Apologeticum* 39, 2). And Ambrose: "prayer is requested for the people, for rulers, for others" (*De sacramentis* 4, 14).

6.   The solemn prayers concluding the liturgy of Good Friday are the oldest surviving text and the oldest form of the prayer of the faithful in the Roman Rite. Baumstark and Jungmann assign the text to the third century; St. Prosper of Aquitaine in the fifth century clearly refers to it. Later use of this prayer was limited to Holy Week, but at the beginning of the eighth century Roman Ordinal 24 is evidence of its continuance in use not only on Good Friday but also on the Wednesday of Holy Week.

As we know, in these solemn prayers there is a sequence of nine intentions: for the Church, the pope, all ranks of the people of God, the emperor, catechumens, those with various needs, heretics and schismatics, Jews, and pagans. Their form is as follows:

   a. Nine times the priest himself invites the congregation to prayer, announcing the intention in the fuller form: "Let us pray . . . for . . . *that.*"

   b. After each invitation, at the direction of the deacon, the people kneel and pray in silence.

   c. Then, again at the deacon's direction, all rise and the priest, exercising his proper function, recites aloud the concluding collect addressed to God.

   d. Finally, the people acclaim their assent to the concluding collect with their *Amen.*

7.   The *litany* is another form of the universal prayer that was current in the East earlier and that the Roman liturgy adopted at the end of the fifth century. It is a formulary of "deprecation" in which:

   a. The deacon announces the intentions in a way shorter than in the solemn Roman prayers, either in the longer form, "Let us pray . . . for . . . *that,*" or in the short form, "Let us pray *that* . . . ," or in the shorter form, "Let us pray *for* . . . ," without mention of what is to be prayed for, but only of the beneficiaries of the prayer. As the formularies of petition become shortened their number greatly increases and new ones appear: for the fruits of the earth, benefactors, the dead, etc.; for the assembly there are individual intentions for pardon for sin, protection by the angels, a Christian way of life, a happy death, etc.

   b. The people respond to each invitation of the deacon with a very short acclamation of petition; as the number of intentions increases this is repeated as many as fifteen or twenty times (the *Testamentum Domini* in a fifth-century Syrian text) or even thirty-five times (the same litany of the *Testamentum Domini* in a text of the Ethiopian liturgy).

c. The priest, conflating a number of intentions into a series, makes three, two, or even one collect of the people's prayers at the end of the whole litany.[4]

8.   It is hard to say whether this kind of litany is the primitive form of the universal prayer in the Eastern, especially the Syrian, liturgies. Its composition in some Eastern texts seems to date from the third century. Whatever its origins, this form was in full use throughout the East at the end of the fourth century.

In the following centuries this form also spread remarkably throughout the West, often being substituted for the original local form of the prayer of the faithful. A literal translation of Greek formularies appeared in the Celtic-Germanic litany called the *Deprecatio Sancti Martini* and the Ambrosian litany *Divinae pacis*,[5] still used in Milan during Lent. In Rome the *Deprecatio Gelasii Papae*, much superior in style, was introduced at the end of the fifth century and from the outset, or soon thereafter, was placed at the *Introit* of the papal Mass. Except during Holy Week, it supplanted the ancient Roman form of the prayer of the faithful, until it itself was reduced, before the end of the seventh century, to the simple acclamation, *Kyrie, eleison*.

9.   It is clear that the prayer of the faithful was not only part of the Mass but was a *conclusion of every major noneucharistic celebration.*[6] Its oldest Roman form remains at the end of the liturgy of the word on Good Friday. Use of the litany at the end of the morning and evening offices continues in the Byzantine, Armenian, and other rites; this also was at one time the Roman usage, the traces of which are the weekday and Sunday *preces* of the divine office.

10.   In the fourth century, first in the East and later in Rome, the practice began of the *priest's intercession* at the end of the anaphora or in the midst of the canon. It is a recapitulation of the intentions and in many cases of the very words of the prayer of the faithful. The practice is abundantly documented and continues in all rites, except the Mozarabic.[7]

11.   *In the Visigothic liturgy of Spain* (and in the Gallican liturgies), a distinctive form of the prayer seems to have existed. It comprised an exhortation prefacing

---

4. See M. Righetti, *Storia liturgica* v. 3 (2nd ed., Milan, 1956) 264. The first legislation on this matter is in canon 19 of the Council of Laodicea in the middle of the fourth century (before AD 381): "After the addresses of the bishops the first thing must be the prayer over the catechumens; after the catechumens have left, come the prayers over penitents. Once these have left . . . the prayers of the faithful are to be completed, one, namely the first, in silence, the second and third with the customary acclamations. Then the sign of peace is given . . . and the sacrifice offered" (Hefele-Leclerq, *Histoire des Conciles* 1, 1010).

5. The last part of the Litany of the Saints seems to have had the same origin (see H. Bishop, *Liturgica historia* 142). These litanies, of obscure origin, were used in the Carolingian period as a common petition of the faithful, but in processions, not at Mass.

6. "All the major nonliturgical *synaxes*, that is, assemblies for readings and prayers without celebration of the eucharist, for example, morning prayer and evening prayer, were ended with a prayer of the faithful" (P. Borella, *Il rito ambrosiano*, Brescia, 1964) 164.

7. But the Mozarabic rite makes mention of those making the offering at the time when the gifts are offered at the altar, that is, at what we call the offertory.

the particular announcements of intentions or a general invitation to prayer addressed to the congregation (the Gauls referred to it as the "preface of the Mass").

12.   In regions where the Roman Rite displaced the Gallican rites, the Sunday use of the prayer of the faithful, often at the end of the liturgy of the word before the eucharist, apparently never ceased.

There is evidence of this use in France from the Council of Lyons in AD 517, which refers to "the prayer of the people said after the gospel"; also from a commentary on the Mass by the Pseudo-Germain of Paris in the seventh century, which discusses a diaconal litany combined with a priest's prayer.

Very probably formularies from these Gallican usages passed into the Roman Mass; the texts exist in documents of the ninth to the eleventh century, Germanic and Lotharingian (the Missal of Leofric of Exeter), Celtic and Anglo-Saxon (the Drummond Missal, the York Gospel Book).

13.   From the beginning of the 10th century in Germanic and Gallican collections of canon law a canon is repeated that is said to be taken from a council at Orleans: "On Sundays and feast days after the sermon in the Mass the priest must exhort the people to offer together to the Lord prayers for various needs, in keeping with the teaching of the apostles: for their king, bishop, and the pastors of their churches, for peace, against the plague, for those of the parish sick in bed, for the recently deceased. During each petition the people are to say the Lord's Prayer in silence, while the priest is to say solemnly the prayer expressing the need pertinent to each intention. After this the sacrifice is celebrated."[8]

14.   Different twelfth-century formularies of the prayer of the faithful survive from Germany and Bohemia; among them a special place belongs to one that Honorius of Autun wrote in his homiliary entitled *Speculum Ecclesiae*. The formulary begins in this way: "Brothers, you must not stand here idle, but pray for yourselves and for the entire holy Church of God, that he . . . will deign to give it peace, etc." The fourteen, long intention announcements concern: the Church and the clergy (4), the king and judges (2), those beset by needs (5), the whole Christian people (1), the celebrant (1), and the assembly (1). The conclusion is: "Come now and raise your prayers aloud to heaven and sing God's praises: *Kyrie, eleison.*"

15.   This or similar texts seems to be the source of several, late-medieval formularies for announcing intentions (called in France *Formules du Prône* or *Prières du Prône*). There is evidence of these or even the actual texts from the thirteenth to the sixteenth century from nearly all regions of the Roman Rite: Spain, France, England, Germany, Iceland, Poland, Bohemia, and also from the city of Siena in Italy. The Sienese evidence is as follows: "Weekly . . . on Sunday . . . he asks the people to pray for peace, for those entering or in God's service, that God may allow them . . . and us so to live in this world that with them we may share in the kingdom of heaven. For those also who are sick in

---

8. Mansi 8, 361. PL 132, 224; 140, 658; 161, 193.

soul or in body, that. . . . Then he urges the people to pray for the souls of the dead. . . . And he tells them to sing the Lord's Prayer and the clergy to recite a psalm. . . ."

In the late-medieval centuries the priest recited twelve or even fifteen intention announcements in the vernacular, using the fuller form: "Pray (or let us pray) *for . . . that . . .*"; then one or two psalms and prayers were often said by the clergy alone, while the people silently recited the Lord's Prayer.

There is no evidence up to now of such a practice in Rome.

16. From the time of the sixteenth-century Reformers and especially after the Council of Trent, in many regions this medieval form of the universal prayer underwent major changes.

Suddenly or gradually these prayers disappeared in Italy, Spain, and Poland, as the new books of the Roman liturgy and different forms of popular devotion were introduced.

In Germany St. Peter Canisius in 1556 composed a beautiful formulary addressed to God by the whole assembly, which replaced the medieval prayers until the present century. Then it was revised in the form of a litany, with the people taking a very active part and often, in the style of the Canisian formulary, after the announcement of the intentions by the presiding priest or commentator.

In France in the 17th century the *Preces pronai* (as they were then called) were given an inappropriate place before the homily and were encumbered with purely didactic elements. In the next centuries they were reduced little by little to a mere vestige of what they had been and this remained the case until the present.

17. Bossuet, however, was still speaking of the great importance of the prayer of the faithful when in 1687 he wrote in the second part of his catechism for the instruction of the people of his diocese: "Why is it better to hear the parish Mass rather than another? Because at this Mass there is an assembly of the faithful. For any other reason? Because at the parish Mass the *prières du prône* take place. What are they? They consist of two main parts. What are they? The first is the prayer of the faithful that God prescribes for the whole Church, for pastors, for rulers, for the sick, for the afflicted, and for all the needs of the people of God, both general and special. Is such a prayer heard by God? By all means, especially when it is the communal prayer of the pastor and all the faithful gathered together in the assembly."[9]

---

9. *Catéchisme du Diocèse de Meaux* (Paris, 1687) Part 2, 4–5.

GUIDELINES FOR CONCELEBRATION OF THE EUCHARIST

UNITED STATES CONFERENCE OF CATHOLIC BISHOPS
NOVEMBER 12, 2003

AN OVERVIEW OF
GUIDELINES FOR CONCELEBRATION OF THE EUCHARIST
Rev. Msgr. Joseph DeGrocco

The brief document *Guidelines for Concelebration of the Eucharist* (a mere fifty-three articles long) was issued November 12, 2003 by the United States Conference of Catholic Bishops. The document is meant to summarize the Church's practice of Eucharistic concelebration. As such, the document does not present any new liturgical laws, but it does have the authority of law where it cites other documents with the force of law. The scope of the document is limited, however, in that it deals only with the specific issue of Eucharistic concelebration; It should not be seen as or used as a comprehensive treatment of Eucharistic theology or of other questions of liturgical theology regarding the celebration of the Eucharist. Diocesan bishops may adapt the guidelines within the limits accorded them in liturgical law,[1] and a diocesan bishop, since he is the one to regulate the norms concerning concelebration, may establish diocesan policies concerning it.[2]

A new rite for concelebration was called for in article 58 of the *Constitution on the Sacred Liturgy* (CSL). Subsequent to CSL, the document *Ecclesiae semper*, dated March 7, 1965 was issued, promulgating the *Rite of Concelebration*. *Ecclesiae semper* noted three "marks and properties" that are "intrinsically and necessarily" present in every Mass: the unity of the sacrifice of the Cross; the unity of the priesthood; and that Mass is "an activity that belongs to the entire people of God."[3] These three "marks and properties" can be found as underlying themes that permeate the current *Guidelines for Concelebration of the Eucharist*, and, indeed, much of the content of this document remains substantially unchanged from *Ecclesiae semper*. While these themes run throughout the entire document at least implicitly, they are clearly exhibited in the first twenty articles, which are of a more general nature and deal with broader issues.

Taken together, these themes underscore that the meaning of a priest's concelebration of the Eucharist (as is also true of his presiding at the celebration as the main celebrant) is not to be centered on his own personal devotion or piety but rather in the activity of the Church. While of course a priest should

---

1. See *Guidelines for Concelebration of the Eucharist* (GCE), 4.

2. See ibid., 5.

3. Sacred Congregation of Rites (Consilium), Decree *Ecclesiae semper*, promulgating the *editio typica* of the rites of concelebration and of communion under both kinds, March 7, 1965: AAS 57 (1965), 410–412 as found in *Documents on the Liturgy 1963–1979: Conciliar, Papal, and Curial Texts*. Collegeville, MN: The Liturgical Press, 1982.

bring devotion and reverence to his role, any hint of personal "ownership" of the Mass as an exclusively clerical endeavor or as an action of a priest without reference to the larger assembly is to be avoided. The priest, whether as main celebrant or concelebrant, is not acting on his own, but rather acts always as a minister of the Church, and the liturgical action is always one of the entire Body of Christ. First and foremost, then, the meaning of concelebration is to be found under the larger theme of the celebration of the Eucharist as a manifestation of the reality and true nature of the Church.

Thus, the *Guidelines for Concelebration of the Eucharist* highlight from the very beginning how concelebration is "an expression of 'the unity of the priesthood'" as priests come together to act "with one voice and one will" and "offer a single sacrifice by a single sacrament."[4] This is shown through various practical considerations, for example, that the vestments of the concelebrants should not differ in size, shape, or ornamentation.[5] The principle being elucidated is that a priest participates not as an individual priest but rather as a member of the presbyterate, precisely in the liturgical role of concelebrant. Therefore, a priest's right to celebrate the Eucharist is not without conditions—while a priest is permitted to celebrate the Eucharist individually, he is not permitted to do so at the same time a concelebrated Mass is being celebrated in the same church or oratory.[6] Other conditions may be applied, for example, a limit on the number of concelebrants when a large number might compromise the dignity of the rite (such as, inadequate size of the church and the altar, or when the faithful's view of the rite would be impaired[7]). The guidelines make it a point to note, however, that such limitation on the number of concelebrants has nothing to do with exclusion, but rather is a pastoral response to the limitations of space.[8] Once again, then, we see that it is the demands of the liturgical celebration of the Church, and not individual piety, that take precedence.

The notion of the unity of the priesthood is further underscored by the document's directive that concelebrants should be seated together in a distinct area, or, if this is not possible, then at least seating those who do not fit in the presbyterium in another area that "physically and visually unites them with the other concelebrants;"[9] they are not to be intermingled among the members of the assembly.

Another point to be made under the theme of the unity of the priesthood is that concelebration in no way diminishes their identity as priests: "Concelebration should be understood as an appropriate way for priests to participate in the celebration of the Eucharist, expressive of their unique relationship with Christ the High Priest and of the unity of the priesthood."[10] In fact, concelebration is "always encouraged"[11] and, one might argue, even to be preferred over private celebration, in light of CSL 27. which stressed that "whenever

---

4. GCE, 1; quoting CSL, 1.2a.
5. See ibid., 20.
6. See ibid., 5.
7. See ibid., 11.
8. See ibid., 12.
9. Ibid., 14.
10. Ibid., 3.
11. Ibid., 7.

rites, according to their specific nature, make provision for communal celebration involving the presence and participation of the faithful . . . this way of celebrating them is to be preferred, as far as possible, to a celebration that is individual and, so to speak, private. This applies with especial force to the celebration of Mass and the administration of the sacraments."

This principle of unity is further manifested as the document explains that concelebration is important on more than just a practical level (for example, to save the inconvenience of having many priests celebrate individual Masses); rather, "concelebration at Mass is expressive of the one sacrifice of the cross."[12] That one sacrifice is celebrated by the entire People of God; the Eucharist is an action of "the entire People of God, 'ordered and acting hierarchically.'"[13] The full, conscious, and active participation of everyone in the assembly is affirmed, and the presence of concelebrating priests is not to in any way diminish or impede this participation by all. This vision of the Church as the hierarchically-ordered body where all members participate equally-yet-distinctly, each according to one's role and identity in the assembly, is demonstrated in various practical considerations, for example, that concelebrants are not to obscure the bishop or the presiding priest or other ministers,[14] showing that concelebration is not to be interpreted as a clerical "takeover" of the liturgy.

Yet, even though participation as a concelebrant occurs within an action of the entire People of God, such participation in no way diminishes a priest's unique identity. In fact, care is to be taken to maintain that unique identity of priests: When participating in the Eucharist, priests should always fulfill their office "according to their proper order, that is by celebrating Mass rather than merely receiving communion as lay persons."[15] Participating according to their proper order is emphasized by the fact that not only must concelebrants wear an alb with a stole, but the chasuble is to be worn as well, unless a lack of vestments makes wearing the chasuble impossible.[16] However, the alb and stole are always to be worn: secular attire, clerical garb without the liturgical vesture, and wearing a stole over a cassock or religious order habit are all prohibited.[17]

There are certain rituals where the rite itself stipulates that the Mass is to be concelebrated, namely, the Ordination of a bishop and priests, the blessing of an abbot, and the Chrism Mass. Furthermore, concelebration is recommended on other occasions when it is advantageous to express the unity of the priesthood, for example, at the evening Mass of the Lord's Supper on Holy Thursday, at meetings of bishops, or at meetings of priests.[18] Additionally, when the bishop presides, priests should concelebrate with him, so as to manifest through the

---

12. Ibid., 3.

13. Ibid.; quoting *Ecclesiae semper*, 7.

14. See ibid., 15.

15. Ibid., 6. One might lament the use of the infelicitous phrase "merely receiving communion as lay persons." However, it is best to not read this as a denigration of the laity's participation in the celebration of the Eucharist and instead to read the intent behind the phrasing, that is, that the legitimate unique identity and role of the ordained priest in the life of the Church and in the liturgical assembly should never be compromised or obscured.

16. See GCE, 17.

17. See ibid., 19.

18. See ibid., 8.

Eucharistic celebration both the "mystery of the unity of the Church" and that priests are "the presbyterate of the Bishop."[19]

After these broader themes are dealt with in the first twenty articles, articles 21–54 describe the rite of concelebration itself. It is instructive to take note of some particular points that at times are perhaps overlooked or misunderstood.

If a deacon is not present, a concelebrant is to read the Gospel, not the presiding priest, thus underscoring the proclamation of the Gospel as a ministerial, not a presidential, function. A concelebrant receives the blessing before the Gospel from a bishop, but not from another priest.[20]

A concelebrant may be permitted to preach, but this is at the invitation of the principal celebrant, thus underscoring that the presider is the usual (ordinary) homilist.[21]

Concelebrants approach the altar to participate in the Eucharistic Prayer before the prayer begins, which means they are in place before the introductory dialogue of the prayer begins; a common mistake is for the concelebrants to move during or after the Holy, Holy, Holy. They are to begin to move immediately as the principal celebrant concludes the Prayer over the Offerings, and the principal celebrant should wait until the concelebrants are in place before beginning the introductory dialogue.[22]

The parts the concelebrants recite are delineated: the epiclesis, the words of consecration, the anamnesis, and the post-consecratory epiclesis are the parts to be recited, and only those parts; concelebrants should not be saying any other parts of the prayer, even if they are merely whispering them. The parts they do say are to be said "in a very low voice, so that the congregation is able to hear the text without difficulty."[23] Thus, the role of the presiding priest is not to be eclipsed; there is only one presider. This is especially emphasized in the case of the doxology of the Eucharistic Prayer; actually, their joining in the doxology is optional so there is no requirement for concelebrants to do so. However, it seems to be an almost universal custom that priests join in singing this. When they do, though, they cannot overshadow the principal celebrant: The guidelines forcefully state, *"The collective voice of the concelebrants should not, however, overwhelm the voice of the principal celebrant."*[24] The concelebrants listen in silence to all other parts of the prayer.

Various other procedures are outlined, such as how concelebrants may assist in the fractioning of the bread. It is explicitly stated that each concelebrant need not receive one-half of a so-called large host (which in most cases is not really very large at all[25]). Various means by which concelebrants may self-communicate, either by approaching the altar to take the consecrated elements themselves or by having the consecrated bread and the chalice passed to them, are described in articles 44 and 47–50. When elements are passed to them, the formulae "The Body of Christ" and "The Blood of Christ" are not said, and the concelebrants

---

19. Ibid., 9.
20. See ibid., 22.
21. See ibid., 23.
22. See ibid., 25.
23. Ibid., 27.
24. Ibid., 37.
25. See ibid., 42.

genuflect before taking the them if they are taking elements from the altar, but do not genuflect if the elements are being handed to them by a deacon, another priest, or if they are being passed among the concelebrants. Also, intinction is mentioned as a possibility for their self-communication.

Gestures for concelebrants are also explained: they are to stretch out both their hands toward the elements during the epiclesis (the same gesture as the principal celebrant[26]); they are to extend their right hand toward the bread and the chalice during the consecration[27]; they are to bow profoundly when the principal celebrant genuflects after the consecration of the bread and after the consecration of the wine[28]; and their hands are extended in the *orans* gesture for the anamnesis and the post-consecratory epiclesis, but not during any other part of the Prayer.[29]Additional gestures are indicated for the Roman Canon.[30] The *orans* gesture is also used for the Lord's Prayer, but not for the embolism that follows it.[31]

Lastly, it must be emphasized that yet again there is a call for the faithful to receive Holy Communion from bread that has been consecrated at that same Mass, rather than going to the tabernacle for hosts—this practice is "strongly recommended."[32] However, it is clearly states that concelebrants "must never be given Holy Communion consecrated at another Mass and reserved in the tabernacle, and they are to receive under both species."[33]

Although the document is largely concerned with procedure and points of practice, these procedures nonetheless reiterate the vision of the reformed liturgy promulgated by the Second Vatican Council. The guidelines do not deal in depth with theological questions *per se*, but they do reinforce and reaffirm the celebration of the Eucharist as an action of the whole Church, a Church that is hierarchically ordered. It also affirms the identity and role of concelebrants within the Eucharistic celebration: Concelebration manifests the unity of the priesthood, a unity manifested in its proper place within the entire liturgical assembly.

---

26. See ibid., 29.
27. See ibid., 30.
28. See ibid., 31.
29. See ibid., 32.
30. See ibid., 33.
31. See ibid., 38.
32. Ibid., 43.
33. Ibid.

OUTLINE

GUIDELINES FOR CONCELEBRATION OF THE EUCHARIST

INTRODUCTION

1.   Concelebration is the practice by which "several priests, in virtue of Christ's own Priesthood and in the person of the High Priest, act together with one voice and one will; so also do they confect and offer a single sacrifice by a single sacramental act and likewise partake of the same."[1]

2.   The Fathers of the Second Vatican Council recommended concelebration as an expression of "the unity of the priesthood"[2] and chose to extend permission for the practice to a number of particular instances, granting the Bishop of each diocese the authority to decide when concelebration was opportune at other times. The Council further directed that "a new rite for concelebration . . . be drawn up and inserted into the *Pontifical* and into the *Roman Missal*."[3]

3.   On March 7, 1965, the Council's directives were fulfilled in the publication of the Decree *Ecclesiae semper* and the accompanying *Rite of Concelebration*. From the earliest days of the Church, concelebration, while taking a variety of forms, has been celebrated for "much more than merely practical considerations."[4] For such concelebration at Mass is expressive of the one sacrifice of the cross, the priesthood, and the action of the entire People of God, "ordered and acting hierarchically."[5] Concelebration should be understood as an appropriate way for priests to participate in the celebration of the Eucharist, expressive of their unique relationship with Christ the High Priest and of the unity of the priesthood.

---

1. Sacred Congregation of Rites, *Ecclesiae Semper* (ES), 7 March 1965.

2. See Second Vatican Council, *Sacrosanctum Concilium* (SC), December 4, 1963, no. 57 §1, 2a: "at conventual Mass, and at the principal Mass in churches when the needs of the faithful do not require that all priests available should celebrate individually and at Masses celebrated at any kind of priests' meetings, whether the priests be secular clergy or religious," and SC, 57 §1, 1: (a) on the Thursday of the Lord's Supper, not only at the Mass of the Chrism, but also at the evening Mass; (b) at Masses during councils, Bishops' conferences, and synods; (c) at the Mass for the blessing of an abbot.

3. SC, no. 58.

4. ES.

5. ES.

GENERAL PRINCIPLES

REGULATION OF CONCELEBRATION

4.   The purpose of these guidelines is to provide a summary of the Church's practice in regard to Eucharistic concelebration. They do not constitute new liturgical law, but enjoy the authority of the law cited. These guidelines may be adapted by diocesan Bishops within the parameters of liturgical law. This document is limited to questions directly pertaining to Eucharistic concelebration.

5.   The regulation of concelebration belongs to the diocesan Bishop, who may establish diocesan guidelines regarding concelebration.[6] "An individual priest is, however, permitted to celebrate the Eucharist individually, though not at the same time as a concelebration is taking place in the same church or oratory. On Holy Thursday, however, and for Mass of the Easter Vigil, it is not permitted to celebrate individually."[7]

PARTICIPATION IN CONCELEBRATION

6.   "[Priests] 'as ministers of holy things, above all in the Sacrifice of the Mass, act especially in the person of Christ' (*Presbyterorum Ordinis*, no. 13, see also *Lumen Gentium*, no. 28). Hence it is fitting that, because of the sign value (*ratione signi*), priests should participate in the Eucharist, fulfilling their office according to their proper order, that is by celebrating Mass rather than merely receiving communion as lay persons."[8]

7.   Therefore, concelebration is always encouraged, "unless the welfare of the Christian faithful requires or urges otherwise."[9] "Visiting priests should be gladly welcomed to Eucharistic concelebration, as long as their priestly standing is ascertained,"[10] and "a superior may not prohibit a priest from concelebrating,"[11] except in the instances described in no. 10, below.

8.   Concelebration is "prescribed by the rite itself for the Ordination of a Bishop and of priests, at the blessing of an abbot, and at the Chrism Mass"[12] because it

---

6. See *General Instruction of the Roman Missal, third typical edition* (GIRM), April 20, 2000, no. 202.

7. GIRM, no. 199; see SC, 57 §2.

8. Sacred Congregation of Rites, *Eucharisticum Mysterium* (EM), May 25, 1967, no. 43.

9. *Code of Canon Law*, Canon 902: "Priests may concelebrate the Eucharist unless the welfare of the Christian faithful requires or urges otherwise but with due regard for the freedom of each priest to celebrate the Eucharist individually, though not during the time when there is a concelebration in the same church or oratory."

10. GIRM, no. 200.

11. In a *responsum ad dubium*, dated July 3, 1999 (prot. 1411/99), the Congregation for Divine Worship and the Discipline of the Sacraments has reinforced the freedom of all priests to concelebrate. No superior may prohibit a priest from concelebrating. The response also notes that "it is laudable that [priests enjoying the faculty of celebrating Mass in the rite in force before the liturgical renewal of Vatican Council II] concelebrate freely especially for the Mass of the Thursday of Holy Week, with the diocesan Bishop presiding. . . . The sign of communion inherent in concelebration is so particular that it ought not to be omitted in the Chrism Mass except for grave reasons."

12. GIRM, no. 199.

"appropriately expresses the unity of the priesthood, of the Sacrifice, and also of the whole People of God."[13] Concelebration is also recommended at the evening Mass on Holy Thursday, the Mass for councils, meetings of Bishops, synods, the conventual Mass, the principal Mass in churches and oratories, and the Mass for any kind of meeting of priests, either secular or religious.[14]

9.   "In a Eucharistic celebration at which the Bishop presides, priests should concelebrate with him, so that the mystery of the unity of the Church is manifested through the Eucharist and that priests appear before the community as the presbyterate of the Bishop."[15]

10.   "No one is ever to enter into a concelebration or to be admitted as a concelebrant once the Mass has already begun."[16]

NUMBER OF CONCELEBRANTS

11.   Each Ordinary or the Major Superior of clerical non-exempt religious and of societies of clerics living in common[17] may limit the number of concelebrants if, in consideration of the size of the church and the altar and whether the faithful's view of the rite is impaired, he decides "that the dignity of the rite requires this."[18]

12.   In those instances where it is advisable to limit the number of concelebrants, the priests chosen to concelebrate should be truly representative of the larger group. Such a limitation on the number of concelebrants should be understood as a pastoral response to the problems of space which may occur because of the great number of priests who may be present rather than as an attempt at exclusion.

13.   In those cases when the number of concelebrants is limited for legitimate reasons, those in charge of planning should provide opportunities for the non-concelebrating priests to celebrate the Eucharist at another time.

PHYSICAL ARRANGEMENTS

14.   Concelebrants should be seated together in a distinct area (*presbyterium*). They should not be intermingled with the assembly nor should anyone be seated between the concelebrants and the altar. If the space in the *presbyterium* is not large enough to accommodate all the concelebrants appropriately, some are seated in another area which physically and visually unites them with the other concelebrants.

---

13. GIRM, no. 199.

14. See GIRM, no. 199.

15. *Caeremoniale Episcoporum* (CE), September 14, 1984, no. 21. Translation by the USCCB Secretariat for the Liturgy.

16. GIRM, no. 206.

17. "It is for the Bishop, in accordance with the norm of law, to regulate the discipline for concelebration in all churches and oratories of his diocese": GIRM, no. 202.

18. Sacred Congregation of Rites, *Rite of Concelebration* (RC), March 7, 1965, nos. 3 and 4.

15.   The position of the concelebrants should not obscure the fact that only one Bishop or one priest presides over the whole celebration. Furthermore, the position of the concelebrants should not usurp the positions or limit the functioning of other liturgical ministers. Unless it is unavoidable, concelebrants should not impede the full view of the assembly, since members of the congregation are called upon to kneel at various times during Mass.[19]

VESTURE

16.   "In the Church, which is the Body of Christ, not all members have the same office. This variety of offices in the celebration of the Eucharist is shown outwardly by the diversity of sacred vestments, which should therefore be a sign of the office proper to each minister. At the same time, however, the sacred vestments should also contribute to the beauty of the sacred action itself."[20]

17.   Concelebrating priests wear an alb with a stole and chasuble. However, if "a good reason arise[s] (e.g., a large number of concelebrants or a lack of vestments), concelebrants other than the principal celebrant may omit the chasuble and simply wear the stole over the alb."[21]

18.   The principal celebrant is to wear the alb with a stole and chasuble.[22]

19.   Priests may not concelebrate in secular attire, in ordinary clerical garb, or by wearing the stole over the cassock. Nor may priests of religious institutes concelebrate merely by placing a stole over the monastic cowl or habit.[23]

20.   If chasubles are worn by all the concelebrants, they should be simpler in their decoration than that of the principal celebrant. Vestments that differ in size, shape, and ornamentation can obscure unity, emphasize individualism, and detract from the presidential role of the principal celebrant. The vestments of the concelebrants should be of the color proper to the Mass being celebrated. "However, the proper color being kept by the principal celebrant, the concelebrants may in case of necessity use white. . . ."[24]

RITE OF CONCELEBRATION

REVERENCE TO THE ALTAR

21.   Concelebrants should participate in the entrance or recessional chant or maintain a reverential silence. The principal celebrant and deacon(s), together with concelebrants and other ministers in the procession, bow to the altar on arrival as a sign of reverence. "If, however, the tabernacle with the Most Blessed

---

19. See GIRM, no. 43.

20. GIRM, no. 335.

21. GIRM, no. 209.

22. See GIRM, no. 209.

23. See Sacred Congregation for Divine Worship, *Liturgicae Instaurationes*, September 5, 1970, no. 8c.

24. See CE, no. 12.

Sacrament is present in the sanctuary, the priest, the deacon, and the other ministers [including concelebrants] genuflect when they approach the altar and when they depart from it, but not during the celebration of Mass itself."[25] The principal celebrant, the deacon(s), and any concelebrants then venerate the altar with a kiss.[26]

THE GOSPEL

22.   When there is no deacon present, a concelebrant proclaims the Gospel.[27] If the principal celebrant is a Bishop, the concelebrant asks for and receives a blessing from the Bishop, and proclaims the gospel reading in the usual way.[28] If the principal celebrant is not a Bishop, the concelebrant bows before the altar and prays inaudibly, *Almighty God, cleanse my heart*, and proclaims the gospel reading in the usual way.[29] After the proclamation of the Gospel, if the *Book of the Gospels* is brought to the Bishop, the concelebrants remain standing.

THE HOMILY

23.   The homily is usually given by the principal celebrant or, at his invitation, by one of the concelebrants,[30] or even, in some cases, by a deacon.[31]

PREPARATION OF THE ALTAR AND THE GIFTS

24.   "The Preparation of the Gifts (cf. nos. 139–146) is carried out by the principal celebrant, while the other concelebrants remain at their places."[32] When there are to be great numbers of communicants and all the ciboria cannot conveniently be placed on the altar, some of the concelebrants may hold the ciboria in their hands during the Eucharistic Prayer.

AT THE ALTAR

25.   The concelebrants approach the altar for the Eucharistic Prayer after the principal celebrant has concluded the prayer over the offerings. If there is a great number of concelebrants, only some of them should be invited to stand with the principal celebrant at the altar. The deacons remain "behind the concelebrants, but in such a way that one of them may assist at the cup and the book as needed."[33] The Eucharistic Prayer should be chosen prior to the celebration. The principal celebrant begins the Eucharistic Prayer only after the concelebrants have taken their places.

---

25. See GIRM, no. 274.

26. See GIRM, no. 211.

27. See GIRM, no. 212; see *Books of the Gospels for Use in the Dioceses of the United States of America* (BOG), no. 14.

28. See BOG, no. 15.

29. *Lectionary for Mass for Use in the Dioceses of the United States of America* (LFM), November 29, 1998, no. 17.

30. See GIRM, no. 213.

31. See GIRM, no. 66.

32. GIRM, no. 214.

33. GIRM, no. 215; see CE, no. 153.

26.   It is very appropriate that the principal celebrant sing those parts of the Eucharistic Prayer for which musical notation in the *Missal* is provided and that concelebrants sing together the parts assigned to them.[34] However, the Eucharistic Prayer should not be sung unless the principal celebrant and the concelebrants know the music and are able to sing it well.

PROCLAMATION OF THE EUCHARISTIC PRAYER

27.   When it is not sung, the Eucharistic Prayer should be proclaimed by the principal celebrant in a loud and clear voice. Concelebrating priests recite the epiclesis, words of consecration, anamnesis, and post-consecratory epiclesis in a very low voice, so that the congregation is able to hear the text without difficulty.[35] The concelebrants listen in silence during the post-sanctus and the intercessions.

DEACONS AND OTHER MINISTERS

28.   When neither a deacon nor other ministers assist in a concelebrated Mass, their functions are to be carried out by one or more of the concelebrants.[36] However, every effort should be made to provide a deacon and other ministers.

EPICLESIS

29.   In accord with ancient tradition, concelebrating priests stretch out both their hands toward the elements during the epiclesis.[37] The full impact of this gesture can be achieved if the concelebrants adopt the same gesture as the principal celebrant.

CONSECRATION

30.   During the consecration, each concelebrant extends the right hand toward the bread and the chalice.[38]

31.   All bow profoundly when the principal celebrant genuflects after the consecration of the bread and after the consecration of the wine.

ANAMNESIS AND EPICLESIS

32.   The concelebrants hold their hands outstretched in an *orans* gesture during the anamnesis and the post-consecratory epiclesis, but not during the other parts of the Eucharistic Prayer.

---

34. See GIRM, nos. 147, 218.
35. See GIRM, no. 218.
36. See GIRM, no. 208.
37. See GIRM, nos. 222a, 227a, 230a, 233a.
38. See GIRM, nos. 222c, 227c, 230c, 233c.

ADDITIONAL GESTURES IN THE ROMAN CANON

33.   When praying the First Eucharistic Prayer (Roman Canon), concelebrants make two additional gestures. From *Almighty God, we pray* to *the sacred body and blood of your Son* inclusive, they bow with hands joined; then they stand upright and cross themselves at the words *let us be filled.*[39] At the words *Though we are sinners,* each concelebrant strikes his breast.[40]

THE INTERCESSIONS

34.   If they are to be prayed by designated concelebrants, the intercessions within the Eucharistic Prayer should be assigned prior to the beginning of the celebration. Cards or booklets containing the Eucharistic Prayer should be provided to those concelebrants who will read one or more of the intercessions. In this way, the passing of the *Sacramentary* on the altar from one concelebrant to another will be avoided.

35.   Each individual concelebrant chosen to pray the intercessions does so with his hands extended. Careful attention should be given to the manner in which the intercessions are divided.[41] The principal celebrant may also say the intercessions by himself.

DOXOLOGY OF THE EUCHARISTIC PRAYER

36.   During the final doxology of the Eucharistic Prayer only the principal celebrant elevates the paten with the consecrated bread, while the deacon raises the chalice. The concelebrants do not elevate other chalices, ciboria, or other sacred vessels. If no deacon is present, one of the concelebrants may elevate the chalice.

37.   All the concelebrants may join in the singing or recitation of the doxology if this is desirable or it may be sung or recited by the principal celebrant alone.[42] *The collective voice of the concelebrants should not, however, overwhelm the voice of the principal celebrant.* The procedure to be followed should be decided by the principal celebrant before the celebration begins.

THE LORD'S PRAYER

38.   "The principal celebrant, with hands extended, says the introduction to the Lord's Prayer. Then, together with the concelebrants, who also extend their hands, he says the Lord's Prayer with the people."[43] Only the principal celebrant maintains the *orans* posture for the *Deliver us, Lord, from every evil. . . .*

---

39. See GIRM, no. 222e.
40. See GIRM, no. 224.
41. See GIRM, nos. 216–236.
42. See GIRM, no. 236.
43. GIRM, no. 237 (translation by Bishops' Committee on the Liturgy); see CE, no. 159.

39.   The celebrant's parts of the Communion Rite are said by the principal cele-brant alone. They may not be distributed for recitation by the concelebrants. Nor may they be recited by the concelebrants together with the principal celebrant.[44]

SIGN OF PEACE

40.   The sign of peace should not be overextended, thus delaying the rite of the breaking of the consecrated bread.[45]

BREAKING OF THE BREAD

41.   The Lamb of God begins only after the sign of peace is completed. During this litany the deacon (or, in his absence, one or more of the concelebrants) assists the principal celebrant in the breaking of the consecrated bread.[46]

42.   It is not necessary that each concelebrant receive one-half of a large host. But at least some of the Eucharistic bread should be broken for the concelebrants and the people.

43.   It is strongly recommended that the faithful receive the Lord's Body from the bread consecrated at the same Mass.[47] Concelebrants must never be given Holy Communion consecrated at another Mass and reserved in the tabernacle, and they are to receive under both species.[48]

44.   The concelebrants can receive hosts in two ways. When the principal cel-ebrant's private prayer before Communion is finished, the principal celebrant genuflects and steps back a little. One after another, the concelebrants come to the middle of the altar, genuflect, and reverently take the Body of Christ from the altar. Then, holding the Eucharistic bread in one hand, with the other hand under it, they return to their places. Alternately, the concelebrants may remain in their places and take the Body of Christ from the paten presented to them by the principal celebrant, or by one or more of the concelebrants or deacons, or also from the paten as it is passed from one to another.[49] The formula *The Body of Christ* is not said.

45.   When sufficient concelebrants are present, they assist the principal cele-brant in the distribution of Holy Communion. When the number of ordinary ministers of Holy Communion is insufficient, extraordinary ministers of Holy Communion may assist in the distribution of the Eucharist. Such extraordinary ministers do not receive Holy Communion in the manner of concelebrants.

---

44. See GIRM, nos. 238, 241.

45. See GIRM, no. 154.

46. See GIRM, no. 240.

47. See SC, no. 55; GIRM, no. 85; EM, no. 31.

48. For an exception, see the circular letter of the Congregation for Doctrine of the Faith dated July 24, 2003 (Prot. 89/78–17498), no. B3.

49. See GIRM, no. 242.

Rather, they receive the Body and Blood of the Lord after the principal celebrant and the deacon.

INVITATION TO HOLY COMMUNION

46.   Only the principal celebrant shows the consecrated host to the people when he proclaims, *This is the Lamb of God.*[50] Concelebrants do not elevate their hosts; rather, they reverently hold the consecrated bread in the right hand with the left hand under it.

RECEIVING THE BODY OF THE LORD

47.   After the invitation to Communion, the principal celebrant alone says in a lower voice, *May the Body of Christ bring me to everlasting life.* He then consumes the Body of Christ. If the concelebrants are holding the consecrated bread in their hands, they consume it at this time.[51]

RECEIVING THE PRECIOUS BLOOD

48.   The Precious Blood is received[52] in one of the following ways: The concelebrants approach the altar one after another or, if two chalices are used, two by two. They genuflect, partake of the Blood of Christ, wipe the rim of the chalice, and return to their seats, or the concelebrants may receive the Precious Blood while remaining in their places. They drink from the chalice presented to them by the deacon or one of the concelebrants, or else passed from one to the other. The chalice is wiped either by the one who drinks from it or by the one who presents it. The chalice is offered to each concelebrant without saying the formula *The Blood of Christ.*[53]

ALTERNATE FORM OF RECEIVING HOLY COMMUNION

49.   A second form of distributing Holy Communion to concelebrants is described by the *General Instruction.* "After the principal celebrant's Communion, the chalice is placed on another corporal at the side of the altar. The concelebrants approach the middle of the altar one after another, genuflect, and receive the Body of the Lord; then they go to the side of the altar and consume the Blood of

---

50. See GIRM, no. 243.

51. See GIRM, nos. 244.

52. The following is excerpted from a circular letter to the Presidents of Episcopal Conferences from Cardinal Joseph Ratzinger, Prefect of the Congregation for the Doctrine of the Faith (prot. 89/78): "Concerning permission to use *mustum*: (A) The preferred solution continues to be Communion *per intinctionem*, or in concelebration under the species of bread alone. . . .) In general, those who have received permission to use *mustum* are prohibited from presiding at concelebrated Masses. There may be some exceptions however: in the case of a Bishop or Superior General; or, with prior approval of the Ordinary, at the celebration of the anniversary of priestly ordination or other similar occasions. In these cases, the one who presides is to communicate under both the species of bread and that of *mustum*, while for the other concelebrants a chalice shall be provided in which normal wine is to be consecrated."

53. See GIRM, no. 246.

the Lord, following the rite chosen for Communion from the chalice, as has just been said."[54]

50.   "If the concelebrants' Communion is by intinction, the principal celebrant receives the Body and Blood of the Lord in the usual way, but making sure that enough of the Precious Blood remains in the chalice for the Communion of the concelebrants. Then the deacon, or one of the concelebrants, arranges the chalice as appropriate in the center of the altar or at the side on another corporal together with the paten containing particles of the host. The concelebrants approach the altar one after another, genuflect, and take a particle, dip it partly into the chalice, and, holding a purificator under their chin, consume the intincted particle. They then return to their places as at the beginning of Mass."[55]

DISTRIBUTION OF HOLY COMMUNION TO THE FAITHFUL

51.   If there are many concelebrating priests, the Communion of the liturgical assembly should not be delayed. There is no need for all the concelebrants to finish receiving Holy Communion before distribution to the assembly can commence.

PURIFICATION OF SACRED VESSELS

52.   After Communion, the Precious Blood is to be consumed immediately.[56] The sacred vessels are purified or are covered on a side table to be purified after Mass.[57]

REVERENCE TO THE ALTAR

53.   Before leaving it, the concelebrants make a profound bow to the altar when the principal celebrant with the deacon venerates the altar with a kiss.[58] If the tabernacle is present in the sanctuary, they genuflect to it.

---

54. GIRM, no. 248.
55. GIRM, no. 249.
56. See GIRM, no. 182.
57. See GIRM, no. 183.
58. See GIRM, no. 251.

VARIETATES LEGITIMAE
INCULTURATION AND
THE ROMAN LITURGY

FOURTH INSTRUCTION FOR THE RIGHT APPLICATION OF THE
CONCILIAR CONSTITUTION ON THE LITURGY (NOS. 37–40)

CONGREGATION FOR DIVINE WORSHIP AND
THE DISCIPLINE OF THE SACRAMENTS
MARCH 29, 1994

AN OVERVIEW OF *VARIETATIS LEGITIMAE*

Rev. Ricky Manalo, CSP

INTRODUCTION AND SIGNIFICANCE

Varietatis legitimae (VL) is a significant and pivotal document in the worship life of the Roman Catholic Church. It is significant since it articulates the relationship between liturgy and culture from an official position. It is pivotal in that it continues the dialogue between liturgy and culture that began with the Second Vatican Council and it includes the insights of John Paul II, under whose pontificate this statement was issued. In addition to the *Constitution on the Sacred Liturgy* (CSL), VL is another document that subsequent documents refer to regarding questions surrounding the inculturation of the liturgy. The purpose of this introduction is to provide a historical background of VL, summarize its content and principles, and offer various suggestions with regard to its pastoral application.[1]

HISTORICAL BACKGROUND

VL was issued on January 25, 1994, by the Congregation of Divine Worship and the Discipline of the Sacraments (CDWDS). Its full English title is *Inculturation and the Roman Liturgy: Fourth Instruction for the Right Application of the Conciliar Constitution on the Liturgy (Nos. 37–40)*. A shorter English title, *The Roman Liturgy and Inculturation*, is more popularly used, as is the Latin title, *Varietates legitimae* ("Legitimate differences"), which is taken from the first two words of the Latin text. Finding its foundation in *Sacrosanctum Concilium*, VL is the fourth instruction of its kind that follows three previous instructions on the correct implementation of CSL: *Inter oecumenici* (IO, 1964), *Tres abhinc annos* (TAA, 1967), and *Liturgicae instaurationes* (LI, 1970). A fifth instruction, *Liturgiam authenticam* (LA), was issued on March 28, 2001, seven years after VL.[2] That instruction, which focuses on the translation of liturgical texts and the use of vernacular language in the publication of the official books, is to be read in conjunction with VL.[3]

---

1. It is important to note that *Varietates legitimae* (VL) is addressed to the Conferences of Bishops in their attempt to apply articles 37–40 of the *Constitution on the Sacred Liturgy*. This entry is an introduction for all ecclesial, liturgical, and pastoral leaders who may look to this document for inspiration and guidance.

2. These instructions are included in *The Liturgy Documents, Volume Three: Foundational Documents on the Origins and Implementation of* Sacrosanctum Concilium. Chicago, Illinois: Liturgy Training Publications, 2013.

3. *Liturgicam authenticam* (LA), 8 states: "The norms set forth in this Instruction are to be substituted for all norms previously published on the matter, with the exception of the Instruction *Varietates legitimae*, published by the Congregation for Divine Worship and the Discipline of the Sacraments on 25 January 1994, in conjunction with which the norms in this present Instruction are to be understood."

Between the promulgation of Liturgiacae instaurationes in 1970 and Varietatis legitimae in 1994, a wellspring of academic, pastoral, and official resources emerged that focused on the terminology, methods, and processes surrounding the dialogue among the Church, her worship life, and culture. One of the crowning achievements that emerged from this period was the development of the term "inculturation," a theological term that expresses the twofold dialogue between the Church and culture. At the official level, the revisions of the sacraments and other rites that occurred during this period included guidelines for cultural adaptations. Paul VI and John Paul II expressed their own reflections through a series of apostolic letters, exhortations, and encyclicals. Inspired by his own travels throughout the world and his experiences of the many varied forms of worship, John Paul II would eventually request that the Congregation of Divine Worship and the Discipline of the Sacraments write a fourth instruction that would address the interpretation of articles 37–40 of CSL, the section that focuses on the cultural adaptation of the liturgy.

OUTLINE AND SUMMARY

VL is divided into an introduction, followed by four major sections, and a conclusion. The introductory paragraphs provide the historical background that led to the writing of VL since the Second Vatican Council. Three goals are named: 1) to assist bishops and episcopal conferences in the cultural adaptation of the liturgy in their local contexts; 2) to provide a framework from which these conferences could re-evaluate the work of liturgical inculturation that had taken place since the Second Vatican Council; and 3) present further clarification on matters that call for "more profound" and "more difficult"[4] adaptations. Utilizing the event of the Incarnation as a theological paradigm, inculturation is defined as "the incarnation of the Gospel in autonomous cultures and at the same time the introduction of these cultures into the life of the church."[5] This "double movement" consists in the proclamation of the Gospel message in particular cultural contexts, and, at the same time, the assimilation of those cultural values that are compatible with the Gospel into the life of the Church. Included here is the distinction between the term adaptation, which "could lead one to think of modifications of a somewhat transitory and external nature,"[6] and the term *inculturation*, which "is a better expression to designate a double movement."[7] Yet, despite this distinction and preference for the term *inculturation*, VL as a whole continues to use the term *adaptation*.

Part I provides a historical survey of salvation history through the prism of inculturation. It takes into account the different historical strands that had developed throughout time, and the complexity and variety of cultural contexts within which and from which Christianity took root. It begins with its Judaic roots, moves through the Old Testament prophets, and considers the particular sociocultural milieu during Jesus's own lifetime. It continues with Jesus's sending forth of the disciples to all nations and notes how the Church reinterpreted

---

4. VL, 3.

5. Ibid., 4; quoting *Slavorum apostoli*, 21.

6. VL, 4.

7. Ibid.

its Judaic roots in light of what constituted Christian membership and practices. Cultural adaptations had always been one of the hallmarks of the Church's worship and sacramental life. Through the process of discernment under the guidance of the Holy Spirit, such adaptations led to a variety of liturgical forms and expressions.

Part II notes preliminary conditions that ought to be taken into account. It begins with an ecclesial exposition of the nature of the liturgy. Local or particular Churches are united to the universal Church in liturgical celebrations, through which the Church glorifies the Triune God and through which humankind is sanctified. Since the liturgy is a community act, legislative frameworks for the organization of liturgical worship are required. Evangelization as the proclamation of the Word of God provides the preliminary condition for the inculturation of the liturgy. But the levels of reception vary from location to location due to the different histories of Christianity that have taken (or not taken) root. For this reason, episcopal conferences should call upon those who are not only familiar with the liturgical tradition of the Roman Rite, but also those who are indigenous to the local culture and who remain appreciative of the values and traditions of that culture.

Three general principles and practical norms for liturgical inculturation are presented in part III. Citing article 21 of CSL, the first goal is to ensure that the "texts and rites . . . be so drawn up that they express more clearly the holy things they signify"[8] and "that the Christian people, as far as possible, may be able to understand them with ease and to take part in the rites fully, actively and as befits a community."[9] The second goal calls for the maintenance of the substantial unity of the Roman Rite throughout the process of inculturation as it is expressed in the typical editions. And third, liturgical adaptations are to depend on Church authority. When aligning these three principles in proper balance, adaptations of liturgical actions and artistic expressions—including the use of language, music, gesture, posture, environment, and art—should reference the historical value of the liturgical elements, particularly their biblical and patristic origins, as well as their function and role within the liturgy. Finally, liturgical innovations require a prudent approach, one that grows organically from already existing forms.

Part IV examines more closely two types of adaptations: adaptations in the liturgical books and adaptations envisaged by article 40 of CSL. Concerning the first type of adaptation, the Holy See is to provide the directives for the completion of translations. Throughout the process, there is to be a respect of literary genres and preservation of the theological content found in the Latin typical editions. The rest of this section moves through specific sacramental celebrations, pointing to the norms for cultural adaptations and regulations of such adaptations by the episcopal conferences. The second section is devoted to the interpretation of article 40 of CSL that considers even more radical adaptation of the liturgy. Episcopal conferences may pursue these adaptations only after they have exhausted all other possible adaptations, so long as they "do not envisage

---

8. Ibid., 35.
9. Ibid.

a transformation of the Roman rite, but are made within the context of the Roman rite." After each of these sections, specific procedures are presented.

Finally, the short conclusion calls for the development of a pastoral plan, one that balances the diverse cultural expressions with the substantial unity of the Roman Rite.

PASTORAL SUGGESTIONS FOR THE APPLICATION OF *VARIETATES LEGITIMAE* TO LOCAL WORSHIP CONTEXTS

If liturgical inculturation is to be viewed as a twofold movement between the Church and culture—particularly, how this movement manifests itself and is experienced within worship contexts—then much of what is written in VL arguably stresses one side of this movement, that of the official Church. It is, after all, an *official* statement and is addressed to the bishops and episcopal conferences. For example, while VL suggests that Church authorities seek the advice and feedback from local cultural representatives and specialists, not much is written about *how* one goes about this process in light of more recent intercultural communication theories and post-colonial approaches. At the same time, while it is addressed to episcopal conferences, other leaders, including worship leaders and liturgical theologians, could gain much insight from this document and view VL as a starting point in the process of preparing meaningful worship services. The following section offers some suggestions that are meant to guide pastoral leaders in the application of VL to their own local worship contexts. My thoughts in this section are meant to offer complementary insights to VL from a pastoral perspective. Throughout this section, the use of the term "cultural" is not limited to ethnic racial groups, but extends to all sociocultural groups that more or less share similar traits in everyday practices, worldviews, and artistic expressions.

PASTORAL TIME AND ENERGY

Our Roman Catholic Tradition has a rich repertoire of resources from magisterial, theological, and pastoral perspectives. Studying these resources should be a priority. However, much time should equally be spent (if not more) in simply getting to know the various cultural groups and peoples in our local communities. Book or musical knowledge alone does not suffice! Getting to know the various cultural groups entails a more *affective use of time* (as distinct from an approach that merely seeks to attain "an effect" or strategic plan or goal), from visiting people in their own locations outside of official liturgical spaces, to learning how they view and interpret the available resources *from their own eyes and worldviews*. Centuries of experience have shown that unless this is fostered, the rich content from available resources stands the chance of falling on deaf ears.

AWARENESS AND FOSTERING OF INTERCULTURAL DYNAMICS THROUGHOUT THE ENTIRE PREPARATION PROCESS

Different cultural groups have different codes and patterns for communication. Learning how to communicate the content of VL to the various cultural groups throughout the process of liturgical inculturation entails developing better inter-cultural communication skills. We are not born with these skills! For example, how one goes about inviting cultural representatives around the table of liturgi-cal preparation varies from culture to culture. Some cultural groups allow indi-vidual members to speak for themselves; others expect a more collective response and agreed-upon representation. It is equally important that those who are invited to speak on behalf of their respective cultural groups *be given permission* to differ and share their own opinions and/or interpretations. Creating an environ-ment of trust and openness will allow the Holy Spirit to move more effectively throughout the intercultural exchange. Lastly, intercultural dynamics does not end with the invitation and conversation stages, but continues throughout the entire process, from rehearsal to celebration to evaluation.

DEFINING THE QUALIFICATIONS WITHIN THE DOCUMENT

When reading some of the qualifications that appear within VL, realize that interpretations of these qualifications are culturally and historically conditioned. For example, article 39 addresses the use of liturgical language and states that it must always express "the grandeur and holiness of the mysteries which are being celebrated."[10] Interpretations of "grandeur and holiness" vary, whether one is celebrating within an African American Gospel Mass or a Vesper service within a Trappist monastery. At the same time, VL offers much insight as to other factors that need to be taken into account, including the suitability and functionality of particular cultural symbols. Tradition is also a factor, but, as the section on history proved, the Roman Catholic liturgical tradition has always varied from place to place and from period to period. The key to interpreting these qualifications is to place all of the above factors in conversation with one another, while learning how to elicit and coordinate the various interpretations that emerge from the representative cultural groups.

MOVING BEYOND THE BOUNDARIES OF LITURGICAL CELEBRATIONS

Applying intercultural skills toward liturgical celebrations entails being aware of the plethora of cultural worship and spirituality practices that move to, from, and around these celebrations. This applies to our use of pastoral time and energy when it comes to becoming acquainted with the various cultural groups *outside* of our liturgies. But this also includes being aware of other worship forms that occur in everyday life, including popular devotions, domestic prayer rituals, and the use of media, such as the Internet, cell phones, and so on. All of these socio-cultural practices (and more) come to influence (for better or for worse) our expe-riences of liturgy. There are some sociocultural practices that are compatible with the message of the Gospel, and others that are not. In short, developing one's cultural sensibility entails remaining open to the transboundaring char-acteristics of cultural practices in order to discern the level of appropriateness of these practices within our liturgies.

---

10. Ibid., 39.

I place this suggestion at the end in order to conclude and highlight the pastoral reality that all cultural processes take time. The incarnational paradigm that the term inculturation is based upon (a paradigm that points to the humanity and divinity of Christ) is helpful in expressing the unity and diversity that exists within local communities and the relationship between these local communities and the larger universal Church. But other theological terms, such as eschatology, may also be employed in order to illustrate the unfolding revelation of how God works through the multitude of cultural expressions. In order to fully appropriate the theological and official content of VL (a more vertical paradigm), worshipping communities should equally develop and continually foster a pastoral methodology (a more horizontal paradigm) that moves organically from the ground up. Keeping both of these paradigms in proper balance is the key to preparing and celebrating culturally rich liturgies.

OUTLINE

VARIETATES LEGITIMAE
INCULTURATION AND THE ROMAN LITURGY

FOURTH INSTRUCTION FOR THE RIGHT APPLICATION OF THE CONCILIAR CONSTITUTION ON THE LITURGY (NOS. 37–40)

CONGREGATION FOR DIVINE WORSHIP AND THE
DISCIPLINE OF THE SACRAMENTS
MARCH 29, 1994

INTRODUCTION

1.   Legitimate differences in the Roman rite were allowed in the past and were foreseen by the Second Vatican Council in the Constitution on the Sacred Liturgy *Sacrosanctum Concilium*, especially in the missions.[1] "Even in the liturgy the church has no wish to impose a rigid uniformity in matters that do not affect the faith or the good of the whole community."[2] It has known and still knows many different forms and liturgical families, and considers that this diversity, far from harming her unity, underlines its value.[3]

2.   In his apostolic letter *Vicesimus quintus annus*, the Holy Father Pope John Paul II described the attempt to make the liturgy take root in different cultures as an important task for liturgical renewal.[4] This work was foreseen in earlier instructions and in liturgical books, and it must be followed up in the light of experience, welcoming where necessary cultural values "which are compatible with the true and authentic spirit of the liturgy, always respecting the substantial unity of the Roman rite as expressed in the liturgical books."[5]

A) NATURE OF THIS INSTRUCTION

3.   By order of the supreme pontiff, the Congregation for Divine Worship and the Discipline of the Sacraments has prepared this instruction: The norms for the adaptation of the liturgy to the temperament and conditions of different peoples, which were given in Articles 37–40 of the constitution *Sacrosanctum Concilium*, are here defined; certain principles expressed in general terms in

---

1. Cf. SC, 38; cf. also no. 40.
2. SC, 37.
3. Cf. OE, 2; SC, 3 and 4; CCC, 1200–1206, especially 1204–1206.
4. Cf. VQA, 16: AAS 81 (1989), 912.
5. Ibid.

those articles are explained more precisely, the directives are set out in a more appropriate way and the order to be followed is clearly set out, so that in the future this will be considered the only correct procedure. Since the theological principles relating to questions of faith and inculturation have still to be examined in depth, this congregation wishes to help bishops and episcopal conferences to consider or put into effect, according to the law, such adaptations as are already foreseen in the liturgical books; to re-examine critically arrangements that have already been made; and if in certain cultures pastoral need requires that form of adaptation of the liturgy which the constitution calls "more profound" and at the same time considers "more difficult," to make arrangements for putting it into effect in accordance with the law.

B) PRELIMINARY OBSERVATIONS

4. The constitution *Sacrosanctum Concilium* spoke of the different forms of liturgical adaptation.[6] Subsequently the magisterium of the church has used the term *inculturation* to define more precisely "the incarnation of the Gospel in autonomous cultures and at the same time the introduction of these cultures into the life of the church."[7] Inculturation signifies "an intimate transformation of the authentic cultural values by their integration into Christianity and the implantation of Christianity into different human cultures."[8]

The change of vocabulary is understandable, even in the liturgical sphere. The expression *adaptation*, taken from missionary terminology, could lead one to think of modifications of a somewhat transitory and external nature.[9] The term *inculturation* is a better expression to designate a double movement: "By inculturation, the church makes the Gospel incarnate in different cultures and at the same times introduces peoples, together with their cultures, into her own community."[10] On the one hand the penetration of the Gospel into a given sociocultural milieu "gives inner fruitfulness to the spiritual qualities and gifts proper to each people . . . , strengthens these qualities, perfects them and restores them in Christ."[11]

On the other hand, the church assimilates these values, when they are compatible with the Gospel, "to deepen understanding of Christ's message and give it more effective expression in the liturgy and in the many different aspects of the life of the community of believers."[12] This double movement in the work of inculturation thus expresses one the component elements of the mystery of the incarnation.[13]

---

6. SC, 37–40.

7. John Paul II, Encyclical *Slavorum Apostoli*, June 2,1985, no. 21: AAS 77 (1985), 802–803; discourse to the Pontifical Council for Culture, plenary assembly, January 17, 1987, no. 5: AAS 79 (1987), 1204–1205.

8. RM, 52: AAS 83 (1991), 300.

9. Cf. ibid., and Synod of Bishops, Final Report *Exeunte coetu secundo*, December 7, 1985, D 4.

10. RM, 52.

11. GS, 58.

12. GS, 58.

13. Cf. CT, 53: AAS 71 (1979), 1319.

5.   Inculturation thus understood has its place in worship as in other areas of the life of the church.[14] It constitutes one of the aspects of the inculturation of the Gospel, which calls for true integration[15] in the life of faith of each people of the permanent values of a culture rather than their transient expressions. It must, then, be in full solidarity with a much greater action, a unified pastoral strategy which takes account of the human situation.[16] As in all forms of the work of evangelization, this patient and complex undertaking calls for methodical research and ongoing discernment.[17] The inculturation of the Christian life and of liturgical celebrations must be the fruit of a progressive maturity in the faith of the people.[18]

6.   The present instruction has different situations in view. There are in the first place those countries which do not have a Christian tradition or where the Gospel has been proclaimed in modern times by missionaries who brought the Roman rite with them. It is now more evident that "coming into contact with different cultures, the church must welcome all that can be reconciled with the Gospel in the tradition of a people to bring to it the riches of Christ and to be enriched in turn by the many different forms of wisdom of the nations of the earth."[19]

7.   The situation is different in the countries with a long-standing Western Christian tradition, where the culture has already been penetrated for a long time by the faith and the liturgy expressed in the Roman rite. That has helped the welcome given to liturgical reform in these countries, and the measures of adaptation envisaged in the liturgical books were considered, on the whole, sufficient to allow for legitimate local diversity (cf. below nos. 53–61). In some countries, however, where several cultures coexist, especially as a result of

---

14. Cf. CCEC, c. 584.2: *"Evangelizatio gentium ita fiat, ut servata integritate fidei et morum Evangelium se in cultura singulorum populorum exprimere possit, in catechesi scilicet, in ritibus propriis liturgicis, in arte sacra in iure particulari ac demum in tota vita ecclesiali."*

15. Cf. CT, 53: "concerning evangelization in general, we can say that it is a call to bring the strength of the Gospel to the heart of culture and cultures. . . . It is in this way that it can propose to cultures the knowledge of the mystery hidden and help them to make of their own living tradition original expressions of life, celebration and Christian thought."

16. Cf. RM, 52: "Inculturation is a slow process covering the whole of missionary life and involves all who are active in the mission *ad gentes* and Christian communities in the measure that they are developing." Discourse to Pontifical Council for Culture plenary assembly: "I strongly reaffirm the need to mobilize the whole church into a creative effort toward a renewed evangelization of both people and cultures. It is only by a joint effort that the church will be able to bring the hope of Christ into the heart of cultures and present-day ways of thinking."

17. Cf. Pontifical Biblical Commission, *Foi et culture à la lumière de la Bible*, 1981; and International Theological Commission, "Faith and Inculturation," 1988.

18. Cf. John Paul II, discourse to the bishops of Zaire, April 12, 1983, no. 5: AAS 75 (1983), 620: "How is it that a faith which has truly matured, is deep and firm, does not succeed in expressing itself in a language, in a catechesis, in theological reflection, in prayer, in the liturgy, in art, in the institutions which are truly related to the African soul of your compatriots? There is the key to the important and complex question of the liturgy, to mention just one area. Satisfactory progress in this domain can only be the fruit of a progressive growth in faith, linked with spiritual discernment, theological clarity, a sense of the universal church."

19. Discourse to Pontifical Council for Culture, 5: "In coming into contact with the cultures, the church must welcome all that in the traditions of peoples is compatible with the Gospel, to give all the riches of Christ to them and to enrich itself of the varied wisdom of the nations of the earth."

immigration, it is necessary to take account of the particular problems which this poses (cf. below no. 49).

8.   It is necessary to be equally attentive to the progressive growth both in countries with a Christian tradition and in others of a culture marked by indifference or disinterest in religion.[20] In the face of this situation, it is not so much a matter of inculturation, which assumes that there are pre-existent religious values and evangelizes them, but rather a matter of insisting on liturgical formation[21] and finding the most suitable means to reach spirits and hearts.

I. PROCESS OF INCULTURATION THROUGHOUT THE HISTORY OF SALVATION

9.   Light is shed upon the problems being posed about the inculturation of the Roman rite in the history of salvation. The process of inculturation was a process which developed in many ways.

The people of Israel throughout its history preserved the certain knowledge that it was the chosen people of God, the witness of his action and love in the midst of the nations. It took from neighboring peoples certain forms of worship, but its faith in the God of Abraham, Isaac and Jacob subjected these borrowings to profound modifications, principally changes of significance but also often changes in the form, as it incorporated these elements into its religious practice in order to celebrate the memory of God's wonderful deeds in its history.

The encounter between the Jewish world and Greek wisdom gave rise to a new form of inculturation: the translation of the Bible into Greek introduced the word of God into a world that had been closed to it and caused, under divine inspiration, an enrichment of the Scriptures.

10.   "The law of Moses, the prophets and the psalms" (cf. Luke 24:27 and 44) was a preparation for the coming of the Son of God upon earth. The Old Testament, comprising the life and culture of the people of Israel, is also the history of salvation.

On coming to the earth the Son of God, "born of a woman, born under the law" (Galatians 4:4), associated himself with social and cultural conditions of the people of the alliance, with whom he lived and prayed.[22] In becoming a man he became a member of a people, a country and an epoch "and in a certain way, he thereby united himself to the whole human race."[23] For "we are all one in Christ, and the common nature of our humanity takes life in him. It is for this that he was called the 'new Adam.'"[24]

---

20. Cf. discourse to the Pontifical Council for Culture, 5; cf. also VQA, 17.
21. Cf. SC, 19 and 35.
22. Cf. AG, 10.
23. GS, 22.
24. St. Cyril of Alexandria, *In Ioannem*, I 14: PG, 73, 162C.

11.   Christ, who wanted to share our human condition (cf. Hebrews 2:14), died for all in order to gather into unity the scattered children of God (cf. John 11:52). By his death he wanted to break down the wall of separation between mankind, to make Israel and the nations one people. By the power of his resurrection he drew all people to himself and created out of them a single new man (cf. Ephesians 2:14–16; John 12:32). In him a new world has been born (cf. 2 Corinthians 5:16–17), and everyone can become a new creature. In him, darkness has given place to light, promise became reality and all the religious aspirations of humanity found their fulfillment. By the offering that he made of his body, once for all (cf. Hebrews 10:10), Christ Jesus brought about the fullness of worship in spirit and in truth in the renewal which he wished for his disciples (cf. John 4:23–24).

12.   "In Christ . . . the fullness of divine worship has come to us."[25] In him we have the high priest, taken from among men (cf. Hebrews 5:15; 10:19–21), put to death in the flesh but brought to life in the spirit (cf. 1 Peter 3:18). As Christ and Lord, he has made out of the new people "a kingdom of priests for God his Father" (cf. Revelation 1:6; 5:9 –10).[26] But before inaugurating by the shedding of his blood the paschal mystery,[27] which constitutes the essential element of Christian worship,[28] Christ wanted to institute the eucharist, the memorial of his death and resurrection, until he comes again. Here is to be found the fundamental principle of Christian liturgy and the kernel of its ritual expression.

13.   At the moment of his going to his Father, the risen Christ assures his disciples of his presence and sends them to proclaim the Gospel to the whole of creation, to make disciples of all nations and baptize them (cf. Matthew 28:15; Mark 16:15; Acts 1:8). On the day of Pentecost, the coming of the Holy Spirit created a new community with the human race, uniting all in spite of the differences of language, which were a sign of division (cf. Acts 2:1–11). Henceforth the wonders of God will be made known to people of every language and culture (cf. Acts 10:44–48). Those redeemed by the blood of the Lamb and united in fraternal communion (cf. Acts 2:42) are called from "every tribe, language, people and nation" (cf. Revelation 5:9).

14.   Faith in Christ offers to all nations the possibility of being beneficiaries of the promise and of sharing in the heritage of the people of the covenant (cf. Ephesians 3:6), without renouncing their culture. Under the inspiration of the Holy Spirit, following the example of St. Peter (cf. Acts 10), St. Paul opened the doors of the church, not keeping the Gospel within the restrictions of the Mosaic law but keeping what he himself had received of the tradition which came from the Lord (cf. 1 Corinthians 11:23). Thus, from the beginning, the church did not demand of converts who were uncircumcised "anything beyond what was necessary" according to the decision of the apostolic assembly of Jerusalem (cf. Acts 15:28).

---

25. SC, 5.

26. Cf. LG, 10.

27. Cf. RomM, Fifth Weekday of the Passion of the Lord, 5: Prayer One: ". . . per suum cruorem instituit paschale mysterium."

28. Cf. Paul VI, apostolic letter Mysterii paschalis, February 14, 1969: AAS 61 (1969), 222–226.

15.   In gathering together to break the bread on the first day of the week, which became the day of the Lord (cf. Acts 20:7; Revelation 1:10), the first Christian communities followed the command of Jesus who, in the context of the memorial of the Jewish pasch, instituted the memorial of his passion. In continuity with the unique history of salvation, they spontaneously took the forms and texts of Jewish worship and adapted them to express the radical newness of Christian worship.[29] Under the guidance of the Holy Spirit, discernment was exercised between what could be kept and what was to be discarded of the Jewish heritage of worship.

16.   The spread of the Gospel in the world gave rise to other types of ritual in the churches coming from the gentiles, under the influence of different cultural traditions. Under the constant guidance of the Holy Spirit, discernment was exercised to distinguish those elements coming from "pagan" cultures which were incompatible with Christianity from those which could be accepted in harmony with apostolic tradition and in fidelity to the gospel of salvation.

17.   The creation and the development of the forms of Christian celebration developed gradually according to local conditions in the great cultural areas where the good news was proclaimed. Thus were born distinct liturgical families of the churches of the West and of the East. Their rich patrimony preserves faithfully the Christian tradition in its fullness.[30] The church of the West has sometimes drawn elements of its liturgy from the patrimony of the liturgical families of the East.[31] The church of Rome adopted in its liturgy the living language of the people, first Greek and then Latin, and, like other Latin churches, accepted into its worship important events of social life and gave them a Christian significance. During the course of the centuries, the Roman rite has known how to integrate texts, chants, gestures and rites from various sources[32] and to adapt itself in local cultures in mission territories,[33] even if at certain periods a desire for liturgical uniformity obscured this fact.

18.   In our own time, the Second Vatican Council recalled that the church "fosters and assumes the ability, resources and customs of each people. In assuming them, the church purifies, strengthens and ennobles them. . . . Whatever good lies latent in the religious practices and cultures of diverse peoples, it is not only saved from destruction but it is also cleansed, raised up and made perfect unto

---

29. Cf. CCC, 1096.

30. Cf. CCC, 1200–1203.

31. Cf. UR, 14–15.

32. Texts: cf. the sources of the prayers, the prefaces and the eucharistic prayers of the RomM; chants: for example the antiphons for Jan. 1, baptism of the Lord; Sept. 8, the *Improperia* of Good Friday, the hymns of the Liturgy of the Hours; gestures: for example the sprinkling of holy water, use of incense, genuflection, hands joined; rites: for example Palm Sunday procession, the adoration of the cross on Good Friday, the rogations.

33. Cf. in the past St. Gregory the Great, Letter to Mellitus: Reg. XI, 59: CIC 140A, 961–962; John VIII, Bull *Industriae tuae*, June 26, 880: PL, 126, 904; Congregation for the Propagation of the Faith, Instruction to the Apostolic Vicars of China and Indochina (1654): *Collectanea S.C. de Propaganda Fide*, I 1 Rome, 1907, no. 135; instruction *Plane compertum*, December 8, 1939: AAS 32 (1940), 2426.

the glory of God, the confounding of the devil, and the happiness of mankind."[34] So the liturgy of the church must not be foreign to any country, people or individual, and at the same time it should transcend the particularity of race and nation. It must be capable of expressing itself in every human culture, all the while maintaining its identity through fidelity to the tradition which comes to it from the Lord.[35]

19. The liturgy, like the Gospel, must respect cultures, but at the same time invite them to purify and sanctify themselves.

In adhering to Christ by faith, the Jews remained faithful to the Old Testament, which led to Jesus, the Messiah of Israel; they knew that he had fulfilled the Mosaic alliance, as the mediator of the new and eternal covenant, sealed in his blood on the cross. They knew that, by his one perfect sacrifice, he is the authentic high priest and the definitive temple (cf. Hebrews 6–10), and the prescriptions of circumcision (cf. Galatians 5:1–6), the Sabbath (cf. Matthew 12:8 and similar),[36] and the sacrifices of the temple (cf. Hebrews 10) became of only relative significance.

In a more radical way Christians coming from paganism had to renounce idols, myths, superstitions (cf. Acts 19:18–19; 1 Corinthians 10:14–22; 2:20–22; 1 John 5:21) when they adhered to Christ.

But whatever their ethnic or cultural origin, Christians have to recognize the promise, the prophecy and the history of their salvation in the history of Israel. They must accept as the word of God the books of the Old Testament as well as those of the New.[37] They welcome the sacramental signs, which can only be understood fully in the context of Holy Scripture and the life of the church.[38]

20. The challenge which faced the first Christians, whether they came from the chosen people or from a pagan background, was to reconcile the renunciations demanded by faith in Christ with fidelity to the culture and traditions of the people to which they belonged.

And so it will be for Christians of all times, as the words of St. Paul affirm: "We proclaim Christ crucified, scandal for the Jews, foolishness for the pagans" (1 Corinthians 1:23).

The discernment exercised during the course of the church's history remains necessary, so that through the liturgy the work of salvation accomplished by

---

34. LG, 17 also 13.

35. Cf. CT, 52–53; RM, 53–54; CCC 1204–1206.

36. Cf., also St. Ignatius of Antioch, Letter to the Magnesians, 9: Funk 1, 199: "We have seen how former adherents of the ancient customs have since attained to a new hope; so that they have given up keeping the sabbath, and now order their lives by the Lord's day instead."

37. Cf. DV, 14–16; Ordo Lectionum Missae ed. typica altera Praenotanda, 5: "It is the same mystery of Christ that the church announces when she proclaims the Old and New Testament in the celebration of the liturgy. The New Testament is, indeed, hidden in the Old and, in the New the Old is revealed. Because Christ is the center and fullness of all Scripture, as also of the whole liturgical celebration"; CCC, 120–123, 128–130, 1093–1095.

38. Cf. CCC, 1093–1096.

Christ may continue faithfully in the church by the power of the Spirit in different countries and times and in different human cultures.

II. REQUIREMENTS AND PRELIMINARY CONDITIONS FOR LITURGICAL INCULTURATION

A) REQUIREMENTS EMERGING FROM THE NATURE OF THE LITURGY

21.   Before any research on inculturation begins, it is necessary to keep in mind the nature of the liturgy. It "is, in fact the privileged place where Christians meet God and the one whom he has sent, Jesus Christ" (cf. John 17:3).[39] It is at once the action of Christ the priest and the action of the church which is his body, because in order to accomplish his work of glorifying God and sanctifying mankind, achieved through visible signs, he always associates with himself the church, which, through him and in the Holy Spirit, gives the Father the worship which is pleasing to him.[40]

22.   The nature of liturgy is intimately linked up with the nature of the church; indeed, it is above all in the liturgy that the nature of the church is manifested.[41] Now the church has specific characteristics which distinguish it from every other assembly and community.

It is not gathered together by a human decision, but is called by God in the Holy Spirit and responds in faith to his gratuitous call (*ekklesia* derives from *klesis*, "call"). This singular characteristic of the church is revealed by its coming together as a priestly people, especially on the Lord's day, by the word which God addresses to his people and by the ministry of the priest, who through the sacrament of orders acts in the person of Christ the head.[42]

Because it is catholic, the church overcomes the barriers which divide humanity: By baptism all become children of God and form in Christ Jesus one people where "there is neither Jew nor Greek, neither slave nor free, neither male nor female" (Galatians 3:28). Thus church is called to gather all peoples, to speak the languages, to penetrate all cultures.

Finally, the church is a pilgrim on the earth far from the Lord (cf. 2 Corinthians 5:6): It bears the marks of the present time in the sacraments and in its institutions, but is waiting in joyful hope for the coming of Jesus Christ (cf. Titus 2:13).[43] This is expressed in the prayers of petition: It shows that we are citizens of heaven (cf. Philippians 3:20), at the same time attentive to the needs of mankind and of society (cf. 1 Timothy 2:1–4).

23.   The church is nourished on the word of God written in the Old and New Testaments. When the church proclaims the word in the liturgy, it welcomes it as a way in which Christ is present: "It is he who speaks when the sacred

---

39. VQA, 7.
40. Cf. SC, 5–7.
41. Cf. SC, 2; VQA, 9.
42. Cf. PO, 2.
43. Cf. LG, 48; SC, 2 and 8.

Scriptures are read in church."[44] For this reason the word of God is so important in the celebration of the liturgy[45] that the holy Scripture must not be replaced by any other text, no matter how venerable it may be.[46] Likewise the Bible is the indispensable source of the liturgy's language, of its signs and of its prayer, especially in the psalms.[47]

24. Since the church is the fruit of Christ's sacrifice, the liturgy is always the celebration of the paschal mystery of Christ, the glorification of God the Father and the sanctification of mankind by the power of the Holy Spirit.[48] Christian worship thus finds its most fundamental expression when every Sunday throughout the whole world Christians gather around the altar under the leadership of the priest, celebrate the eucharist, listen to the word of God, and recall the death and resurrection of Christ, while awaiting his coming in glory.[49] Around this focal point, the paschal mystery is made present in different ways in the celebration of each of the sacraments.

25. The whole life of the liturgy gravitates in the first place around the eucharistic sacrifice and the other sacraments given by Christ to his church.[50] The church has the duty to transmit them carefully and faithfully to every generation. In virtue of its pastoral authority, the church can make dispositions to provide for the good of the faithful, according to circumstances, times and places.[51] But it has no power over the things which are directly related to the will of Christ and which constitute the unchangeable part of the liturgy.[52] To break the link that the sacraments have with Christ, who instituted them, and with the very beginnings of the church,[53] would no longer be to inculturate them, but to empty them of their substance.

26. The church of Christ is made present and signified in a given place and in a given time by the local or particular churches, which through the liturgy reveal the church in its true nature.[54] That is why every particular church must be united with the universal church not only in belief and sacramentals, but also in those practices received through the church as part of the uninterrupted

---

44. SC, 7.

45. Cf. SC, 24.

46. Cf. Ordo Lectionem Missae Praenotanda, 12: "It is not allowed to suppress or reduce either the biblical readings in the celebration of Mass or the chants that are drawn from sacred Scripture. It is absolutely forbidden to replace these readings by other nonbiblical readings. It is through the word of God in the Scriptures that 'God continues to speak to his people' (SC, 33), and it is through familiarity with the Holy Scripture that the people of God, made docile by the Holy Spirit in the light of faith, can by their life and way of living witness to Christ before the whole world."

47. Cf. CCC, 2585–2589.

48. Cf. SC, 7.

49. Cf. SC, 6, 47, 56, 102, 106; cf. GIRM, 1, 7, 8.

50. Cf. SC, 6.

51. Cf. Council of Trent, Session 21, Chap. 2: Denz-Schonm. 1728; SC, 48ff, 62ff.

52. Cf. SC, 21.

53. Cf. CDF, Inter insigniores, October 15, 1976: AAS 69 (1977), 107–108.

54. Cf. LG, 28; also no. 26.

apostolic tradition.[55] This includes, for example, daily prayer,[56] sanctification of Sunday and the rhythm of the week, the celebration of Easter and the unfolding of the mystery of Christ throughout the liturgical year,[57] the practice of penance and fasting,[58] the sacraments of Christian initiation, the celebration of the memorial of the Lord and the relationship between the Liturgy of the Word and the eucharistic liturgy, the forgiveness of sins, the ordained ministry, marriage and the anointing of the sick.

27.   In the liturgy the faith of the church is expressed in a symbolic and communitarian form: This explains the need for a legislative framework for the organization of worship, the preparation of texts and the celebration of rites.[59] The reason for the preceptive character of this legislation throughout the centuries and still today is to ensure the orthodoxy of worship; that is to say, not only to avoid errors, but also to pass on the faith in the integrity so that the "rule of prayer" (*lex orandi*) of the church may correspond to the "rule of faith" (*lex credendi*).[60]

However deep inculturation may go, the liturgy cannot do without legislation and vigilance on the part of those who have received this responsibility in the church: the Apostolic See and, according to the prescriptions of the law, the episcopal conference for its territory and the bishop for his diocese.[61]

B) PRELIMINARY CONDITIONS FOR INCULTURATION OF THE LITURGY

28.   The missionary tradition of the church has always sought to evangelize people in their own language. Often indeed, it was the first apostles of a country who wrote down languages which up till then had only been oral. And this is right, as it is by the mother language, which conveys the mentality and the culture of a people, that one can reach the soul, mold it in the Christian spirit and allow to share more deeply in the prayer of the church.[62]

After the first evangelization, the proclamation of the word of God in the language of a country remains very useful for the people in their liturgical celebrations. The translation of the Bible, or at least of the biblical texts used in the liturgy, is the first necessary step in the process of the inculturation of the liturgy.[63]

---

55. Cf. St. Irenaeus, *Against the Heresies*, III, 2, 1–3; 3, 1–2: SCh, 211, 24–31; cf. St. Augustine, *Letter to Januarius* 54, 1: PL 33, 200: "But regarding those other observances which we keep and all the world keeps, and which do not derive from Scripture but from tradition, we are given to understand that they have been ordained or recommended to be kept by the apostles themselves or by the plenary councils, whose authority is well founded in the church"; cf. RM, 53– 4; cf. CDF, *Letter to Bishops of the Catholic Church on Certain Aspects of the Church Understood as Communion*, May 28, 1992, nos. 7–10.

56. Cf. SC, 83.

57. Cf. SC, 102, 106 and App.

58. Cf. Paul VI, apostolic constitution *Paenitemini*, February 17, 1966: AAS 58 (1966), 177–198.

59. Cf. SC, 22; 26; 28; 40, 43 and 128; CIC, c. 2 and *passim*.

60. Cf. GIRM, 2; Paul VI, *Discourse to the Consilium for the Application of the Constitution on the Liturgy*, October 13, 1966: AAS 58 (1966), 1146; October 14, 1968: AAS 60 (1968), 734.

61. Cf. SC, 22; 36; 40; 44–46; CIC, cc. 47ff and 838.

62. Cf. RM, 53.

63. Cf. SC, 35 and 36; CIC, c. 825.1.

So that the word of God may be received in a right and fruitful way, "it is necessary to foster a taste for holy Scripture, as is witnessed by the ancient traditions of the rites of both East and West."[64] Thus inculturation of the liturgy presupposes the reception of the sacred Scripture into a given culture.[65]

29. The different situations in which the church finds itself are an important factor in judging the degree of liturgical inculturation that is necessary. The situation of countries that were evangelized centuries ago and where the Christian faith continues to influence the culture is different from countries which were evangelized more recently or where the Gospel has not penetrated deeply into cultural values.[66] Different again is the situation of a church where Christians are a minority of the population. A more complex situation is found when the population has different languages and cultures. A precise evaluation of the situation is necessary in order to achieve satisfactory solutions.

30. To prepare an inculturation of the liturgy, episcopal conferences should call upon people who are competent both in the liturgical tradition of the Roman rite and in the appreciation of local cultural values. Preliminary studies of a historical, anthropological, exegetical and theological character are necessary. But these need to be examined in the light of the pastoral experience of the local clergy, especially those born in the country.[67] The advice of "wise people" of the country, whose human wisdom is enriched by the light of the Gospel, would also be valuable. Liturgical inculturation should try to satisfy the needs of traditional culture[68] and at the same time take account of the needs of those affected by an urban and industrial culture.

c) THE RESPONSIBILITY OF THE EPISCOPAL CONFERENCE

31. Since it is a question of local culture, it is understandable that the constitution *Sacrosanctum Concilium* assigned special responsibility in this matter to the "various kinds of competent territorial bodies of bishops legitimately established."[69] In regard to this, episcopal conferences must consider "carefully and prudently what elements taken from the traditions and cultures of individual peoples may properly be admitted into divine worship."[70] They can sometimes introduce "into the liturgy such elements as are not bound up with superstition and error . . . provided they are in keeping with the true and authentic spirit of the liturgy."[71]

32. Conferences may determine, according to the procedure given below (cf. nos. 62 and 65–69), whether the introduction into the liturgy of elements borrowed from the social and religious rites of a people, and which form a living

---

64. SC, 24.

65. Cf. SC; CT, 55.

66. In SC, attention is drawn to nos. 38 and 40: "above all in the missions."

67. Cf. AG, 16 and 17.

68. Cf. AG, 19.

69. SC, 22; cf. AG, 39 and 40; CIC, cc. 447–448ff.

70. SC, 40.

71. SC, 37.

part of their culture, will enrich their understanding of liturgical actions without producing negative effects on their faith and piety. They will always be careful to avoid the danger of introducing elements that might appear to the faithful as the return to a period before evangelization (cf. below, no. 47).

In any case, if changes in rites or texts are judged to be necessary, they must be harmonized with the rest of the liturgical life and, before being put into practice, still more before being made mandatory, they should first be presented to the clergy and then to the faithful in such a way as to avoid the danger of troubling them without good reason (cf. below, nos. 46 and 69).

III. PRINCIPLES AND PRACTICAL NORMS FOR INCULTURATION OF THE ROMAN RITE

33.   As particular churches, especially the young churches, deepen their understanding of the liturgical heritage they have received from the Roman church which gave them birth, they will be able in turn to find in their own cultural heritage appropriate forms which can be integrated into the Roman rite where this is judged useful and necessary.

The liturgical formation of the faithful and the clergy, which is called for by the constitution *Sacrosanctum Concilium*,[72] ought to help them to understand the meaning of the texts and the rites given in the present liturgical books. Often this will mean that elements which come from the tradition of the Roman rite do not have to be changed or suppressed.

A) GENERAL PRINCIPLES

34.   In the planning and execution of the inculturation of the Roman rite, the following points should be kept in mind: 1) the goal of inculturation; 2) the substantial unity of the Roman rite; 3) the competent authority.

35.   The goal which should guide the inculturation of the Roman rite is that laid down by the Second Vatican Council as the basis of the general restoration of the liturgy: "Both texts and rites should be so drawn up that they express more clearly the holy things they signify and so that the Christian people, as far as possible, may be able to understand them with ease and to take part in the rites fully, actively and as befits a community."[73]

Rites also need "to be adapted to the capacity of the faithful and that there should not be a need for numerous explanations for them to be understood."[74] However, the nature of the liturgy always has to be borne in mind, as does the biblical and traditional character of its structure and the particular way in which it is expressed (cf. above, nos. 21–27).

---

72. Cf. SC, 14–19.
73. SC, 21.
74. Cf. SC, 34.

36. The process of inculturation should maintain the substantial unity of the Roman rite.[75] This unity is currently expressed in the typical editions of liturgical books, published by authority of the supreme pontiff and in the liturgical books approved by the episcopal conferences for their areas and confirmed by the Apostolic See.[76] The work of inculturation does not foresee the creation of new families of rites; inculturation responds to the needs of a particular culture and leads to adaptations which still remain part of the Roman rite.[77]

37. Adaptations of the Roman rite, even in the field of inculturation, depend completely on the authority of the church. This authority belongs to the Apostolic See, which exercises it through the Congregation for Divine Worship and the Discipline of the Sacraments;[78] it also belongs, within the limits fixed by law, to episcopal conferences[79] and to the diocesan bishop.[80] "No other person, not even if he is a priest, may on his own initiative add, remove or change anything in the liturgy."[81] Inculturation is not left to the personal initiative of celebrants or to the collective initiative of an assembly.[82]

Likewise concessions granted to one region cannot be extended to other regions without the necessary authorization, even if an episcopal conference considers that there are sufficient reasons for adopting such measures in its own area.

B) ADAPTATIONS WHICH CAN BE MADE

38. In an analysis of a liturgical action with a view to its inculturation, it is necessary to consider the traditional value of the elements of the action and in particular their biblical or patristic origin (cf. above, nos. 21–26), because it is not sufficient to distinguish between what can be changed and what is unchangeable.

---

75. Cf. SC, 37–40.

76. Cf. VQA, 16.

77. Cf. John Paul II, discourse to the plenary assembly of the Congregation for Divine Worship and the Discipline of the Sacraments, January 26, 1991, no. 3: AAS 83 (1991), 940: "This is not to suggest to the particular churches that they have a new task to undertake following the application of liturgical reform, that is to say, adaptation or inculturation. Nor is it intended to mean inculturation as the creation of alternative rites. . . . It is a of collaborating so that the Roman rite, maintaining its own identity, may incorporate suitable adaptations."

78. Cf. SC, 22; CIC, cc. 838.1 and 838.2; John Paul II, apostolic constitution Pastor Bonus, 62, 64.3: AAS 80 (1988), 876 – 877; VQA, 19.

79. Cf. SC, 22 and cc. 447ff and 838.1 and 838.3; VQA, 20.

80. Cf. SC, 22, and CIC, cc. 838.1 and 838.4; VQA, 21.

81. Cf. SC, 22.

82. The situation is different when, in the liturgical books published after the constitution, the introductions and the rubrics envisaged adaptations and the possibility of leaving a choice to the pastoral sensitivity of the one presiding, for example, when it says "if it is opportune," "in these or similar terms," "also," "according to circumstances," "either . . . or," "if convenient," "normally," "the most suitable form can be chosen." In making a choice, the celebrant should seek the good of the assembly, taking into account the spiritual preparation and mentality of the participants rather than his own or the easiest solution. In celebrations for particular groups, other possibilities are available. Nonetheless, prudence and discretion are always called for in order to avoid the breaking up of the local church into little "churches" or "chapels" closed in upon themselves.

39. Language, which is a means of communication between people; in liturgical celebrations its purpose is to announce to the faithful the good news of salvation[83] and to express the church's prayer to the Lord. For this reason it must always express, along with the truths of the faith, the grandeur and holiness of the mysteries which are being celebrated.

Careful consideration therefore needs to be given to determine which elements in the language of the people can properly be introduced into liturgical celebrations, and in particular whether it is suitable or not to use expressions from non-Christian religions. It is just as important to take account of the different literary genres used in the liturgy: biblical texts, presidential prayers, psalmody, acclamations, refrains, responsories, hymns and litanies.

40. Music and singing, which express the soul of people, have pride of place in the liturgy. And so singing must be promoted, in the first place singing the liturgical text, so that the voices of the faithful may be heard in the liturgical actions themselves.[84] "In some parts of the world, especially mission lands, there are people who have their own musical traditions, and these play a great part in their religious and social life. Due importance is to be attached to their music and a suitable place given to it, not only in forming their attitude toward religion, but also in adapting worship to their native genius."[85]

It is important to note that a text which is sung is more deeply engraved in the memory than when it is read, which means that it is necessary to be demanding about the biblical and liturgical inspiration and the literary quality of texts which are meant to be sung.

Musical forms, melodies and musical instruments could be used in divine worship as long as they "are suitable, or can be made suitable, for sacred use, and provided they are in accord with the dignity of the place of worship and truly contribute to the uplifting of the faithful."[86]

41. The liturgy is an action, and so gesture and posture are especially important. Those which belong to the essential rites of the sacraments and which are required for their validity must be preserved just as they have been approved or determined by the supreme authority of the church.[87]

The gestures and postures of the celebrating priest must express his special function: He presides over the assembly in the person of Christ.[88]

---

83. Cf. CIC, cc. 762–772, esp. c. 769.

84. Cf. SC, 118; also no. 54: While allowing that "a suitable place be allotted to the language of the country" in the chants, "steps should be taken so that the faithful may also be able to say or sign together in Latin those parts of the ordinary of the Mass which pertain to them," especially the Our Father, cf. GIRM, 19.

85. SC, 119.

86. SC, 120.

87. Cf. CIC, c. 841.

88. Cf. SC, 33; CIC, c. 899.2.

The gestures and postures of the assembly are signs of its unity and express its active participation and foster the spiritual attitude of the participants.[89] Each culture will choose those gestures and bodily postures which express the attitude of humanity before God, giving them a Christian significance, having some relationship if possible, with the gestures and postures of the Bible.

42. Among some peoples, singing is instinctively accompanied by hand clapping, rhythmic swaying and dance movements on the part of the participants. Such forms of external expression can have a place in the liturgical actions of these peoples on condition that they are always the expression of true communal prayer of adoration, praise, offering and supplication, and not simply a performance.

43. The liturgical celebration is enriched by the presence of art, which helps the faithful to celebrate, meet God and pray. Art in the church, which is made up of all peoples and nations, should enjoy the freedom of expression as long as it enhances the beauty of the buildings and liturgical rites, investing them with the respect and honor which is their due.[90] The arts should also be truly significant in the life and tradition of the people.

The same applies to the shape, location and decoration of the altar,[91] the place for the proclamation of the word of God[92] and for baptism,[93] all the liturgical furnishings, vessels, vestments and colors.[94] Preference should be given to materials, forms and colors which are in use in the country.

44. The constitution *Sacrosanctum Concilium* has firmly maintained the constant practice of the church of encouraging the veneration by the faithful of images of Christ, the Virgin Mary and the saints,[95] because the honor "given to the image is given to its subject."[96] In different cultures believers can be helped in their prayer and in their spiritual life by seeing works of art which attempt, according to the genius of the people, to express the divine mysteries.

45. Alongside liturgical celebrations and related to them, in some particular churches there are various manifestations of popular devotion. These were sometimes introduced by missionaries at the time of the initial evangelization, and they often develop according to local custom.

The introduction of devotional practices into liturgical celebrations under the pretext of inculturation cannot be allowed "because by its nature, (the liturgy) is superior to them."[97]

---

89. Cf. SC, 30.

90. Cf. SC, 123–124; CIC, c. 1216.

91. Cf. GIRM, 259–270; CIC, cc. 1235–1239, esp. c. 1236.

92. Cf. GIRM, 272.

93. Cf. *De Benedictionibus, Ordo benedictionis Baptisterii seu novi Fontis batismalis*, 832–837.

94. Cf. GIRM, 287–310.

95. Cf. SC, 125; LG, 67; CIC, c. 1188.

96. Council of Nicea II: Denz.-Schonm. 601; cf. St. Basil, "On the Holy Spirit," XVIII, 45; SCh 17, 194.

97. SC, 13.

It belongs to the local ordinary[98] to organize such devotions, to encourage them as supports for the life and faith of Christians, and to purify them when necessary, because they need to be constantly permeated by the Gospel.[99] He will take care to ensure that they do not replace liturgical celebrations or become mixed up with them.[100]

c) NECESSARY PRUDENCE

46. "Innovations should only be made when the good of the church genuinely and certainly requires them; care must be taken that any new forms adopted should in some way grow organically from forms already existing."[101] This norm was given in the constitution *Sacrosanctum Concilium* in relation to the restoration of the liturgy, and it also applies, in due measure, to the inculturation of the Roman rite. In this field changes need to be gradual and adequate explanation given in order to avoid the danger of rejection or simply an artificial grafting onto previous forms.

47. The liturgy is the expression of faith and Christian life, and so it is necessary to ensure that liturgical inculturation is not marked, even in appearance, by religious syncretism. This would be the case if the places of worship, the liturgical objects and vestments, gestures and postures let it appear as if rites had the same significance in Christian celebrations as they did before evangelization. The syncretism will be still worse if biblical readings and chants (cf. above, no. 26) or the prayers were replaced by texts from other religions, even if these contain an undeniable religious and moral value.[102]

48. The constitution *Sacrosanctum Concilium* envisaged the admission of rites or gestures according to local custom into rituals of Christian initiation, marriage and funerals.[103] This is a stage of inculturation, but there is also the danger that the truth of the Christian rite and the expression of the Christian faith could be easily diminished in the eyes of the faithful. Fidelity to traditional usages must be accompanied by purification and, if necessary, a break with the past. The same applies, for example, to the possibility of Christianizing pagan festivals or holy places, or to the priest using the signs of authority reserved to the heads of civil society or for the veneration of ancestors. In every case it is necessary to avoid any ambiguity. Obviously the Christian liturgy cannot accept magic rites, superstition, spiritism, vengeance or rites with a sexual connotation.

49. In a number of countries there are several cultures which coexist and sometimes influence each other in such a way as to lead gradually to the formation

---

98. Cf. CIC, c. 839.2.
99. VQA, 18.
100. Cf. ibid.
101. SC, 23.
102. These texts can be used profitably in the homily because it is one of the tasks of the homily "to show the points of convergence between revealed divine wisdom and noble human thought, seeking the truth by various paths" (John Paul II, apostolic letter *Dominicae Cenae*, February 24, 1980, no. 10: AAS 72 [1980], 137).
103. SC, 65, 77, 81. Cf. 30–31, 79–81, 88–89; *Ordo celebrandi Matrimonium, editio typica altera, Praenotanda*, 41–44; *Ordo exsequiarum, Praenotanda*, 21–22.

of a new culture, while at times they seek to affirm their proper identity or even oppose each other in order to stress their own existence. It can happen that customs may have little more than folkloric interest. The episcopal conference will examine each case individually with care: They should respect the riches of each culture and those who defend them, but they should not ignore or neglect a minority culture with which they are not familiar. They should weigh the risk of a Christian community becoming inward looking and also the use of inculturation for political ends. In those countries with a customary culture, account must also be taken of the extent to which modernization has affected the people.

50.   Sometimes there are many languages in use in the one country, even though each one may be spoken only by a small group of persons or a single tribe. In such cases a balance must be found which respects the individual rights of these groups or tribes but without carrying to extremes the localization of the liturgical celebrations. It is also sometimes possible that a country may be moving toward the use of a principal language.

51.   To promote liturgical inculturation in a cultural area bigger than one country, the episcopal conferences concerned must work together and decide the measures which have to be taken so that "as far as possible, there are not notable ritual differences in regions bordering on one another."[104]

IV. AREAS OF ADAPTATION IN THE ROMAN RITE

52.   The constitution *Sacrosanctum Concilium* had in mind an inculturation of the Roman rite when it gave norms for the adaptation of the liturgy to the mentality and needs of different peoples, when it provided for a degree of adaptation in the liturgical books (cf. below, nos. 53– 61), and also when it envisaged the possibility of more profound adaptations in some circumstances, especially in mission countries (cf. below, nos. 63–64).

A) ADAPTATIONS IN THE LITURGICAL BOOKS

53.   The first significant measure of inculturation is the translation of liturgical books into the language of the people.[105] The completion of translations and their revision, where necessary, should be effected according to the directives given by the Holy See on this subject.[106] Different literary genres are to be respected, and the content of the texts of the Latin typical edition is to be preserved; at the same time the translations must be understandable to participants (cf. above, no. 39), suitable for proclamation and singing, with appropriate responses and acclamations by the assembly.

All peoples, even the most primitive, have a religious language which is suitable for expressing prayer, but liturgical language has its own special characteristics: It is deeply impregnated by the Bible; certain words in current Latin use *(memoria, sacramentum)* took on a new meaning in the Christian faith.

---

104. SC, 23.
105. Cf. SC, 36, 54, 63.
106. Cf. VQA, 20.

Certain Christian expressions can be transmitted from one language to another, as has happened in the past, for example in the case of *ecclesia, evangelium, baptisma, eucharistia.*

Moreover, translators must be attentive to the relationship between the text and the liturgical action, aware of the needs of oral communication and sensitive to the literary qualities of the living language of the people. The qualities needed for liturgical translations are also required in the case of new compositions, when they are envisaged.

54. For the celebration of the eucharist, the Roman Missal, "while allowing . . . for legitimate differences and adaptations according to the prescriptions of the Second Vatican Council," must remain "a sign and instrument of unity"[107] of the Roman rite in different languages. The General Instruction on the Roman Missal foresees that "in accordance with the constitution on the liturgy, each conference of bishops has the power to lay down norms for its own territory that are suited to the traditions and character of peoples, regions and different communities."[108] The same also applies to the gestures and postures of the faithful,[109] the way in which the altar and the book of the gospels are venerated,[110] the texts of the opening chants,[111] the song at the preparation of the gifts[112] and the communion song,[113] the rite of peace,[114] conditions regulating communion with the chalice,[115] the materials for the construction of the altar and liturgical furniture,[116] the material and form of sacred vessels,[117] liturgical vestments.[118] Episcopal conferences can also determine the manner of distributing communion.[119]

55. For the other sacraments and for sacramentals, the Latin typical edition of each ritual indicates the adaptations which pertain to the episcopal conferences[120]

---

107. Cf. Paul VI, apostolic constitution *Missale Romanum*, April 3, 1969: AAS 61 (1969), 221.
108. GIRM, 6; cf. also *Ordo Lectionum Missae, editio typica altera, Praenotanda,* 111–118.
109. GIRM, 22.
110. Cf. GIRM, 232.
111. Cf. GIRM, 26.
112. Cf. GIRM, 50.
113. Cf. GIRM, 56 i.
114. Cf. GIRM, 56 b.
115. Cf. GIRM, 242.
116. Cf. GIRM, 263 and 288.
117. Cf. GIRM, 290.
118. Cf. GIRM, 304, 305, 308.
119. Cf. *De sacra communione et de cultu Mysterii eucharistici extra Missam, Praenotanda,* 21.
120. Cf. *Ordo initiationis christianae adultorum, Praenotanda Generalia,* 30–33; *Praenotanda,* 12, 20, 47, 64–65; *Ordo,* 312; Appendix, 12; *Ordo Baptismi parvulorum, Praenotanda,* 8, 23–25; *Ordo Confirmationis, Praenotanda,* 11–12, 16–17; *De sacra communione et de cultu Mysterii eucharistici extra Missam, Praenotanda,* 12; *Ordo Paenitentiae, Praenotanda,* 35b, 38; *Ordo Unctionis infirmorum eorumque pastoralis curae, Praenotanda,* 38–39; *Ordo celebrandi Matrimonium, editio typica altera, Praenotanda,* 39–44; *De Ordinatione Episcopi, Presbyterorum et Diaconorum, editio typica altera, Praenotanda,* 11; *De Benedictionibus, Praenotanda generalia,* 39.

or to individual bishops in particular circumstances.[121] These adaptations concern texts, gestures and sometimes the ordering of the rite. When the typical edition gives alternative formulas, conferences of bishops can add other formulas of the same kind.

56. For the rites of Christian initiation, episcopal conferences are "to examine with care and prudence what can properly be admitted from the traditions and character of each people"[122] and "in mission countries to judge whether initiation ceremonies practiced among the people can be adapted into the rite of Christian initiation and to decide whether they should be used."[123] It is necessary to remember, however, that the term *initiation* does not have the same meaning or designate the same reality when it is used of social rites of initiation among certain people or when it is contrary to the process of Christian initiation, which leads through the rites of the catechumenate to incorporation into Christ in the church by means of the sacraments of baptism, confirmation and eucharist.

57. In many places it is the marriage rite that calls for the greatest degree of adaptation so as not to be foreign to social customs. To adapt it to the customs of different regions and peoples, each episcopal conference has the "faculty to prepare its own proper marriage rite, which must always conform to the law which requires that the ordained minister or the assisting layperson,[124] according to the case, must ask for and obtain the consent of the contracting parties and give them the nuptial blessing."[125] This proper rite must obviously bring out clearly the Christian meaning of marriage, emphasize the grace of the sacrament and underline the duties of the spouses.[126]

58. Among all peoples, funerals are always surrounded with special rites, often of great expressive value. To answer to the needs of different countries, the Roman Ritual offers several forms of funerals.[127] Episcopal conferences must choose those which correspond best to local customs.[128] They will wish to preserve all that is good in family traditions and local customs, and ensure that funeral rites manifest the Christian faith in the resurrection and bear witness to the true values of the Gospel.[129] It is in this perspective that funeral rituals can incorporate the customs of different cultures and respond as best they can to the needs and traditions of each region.[130]

59. The blessing of persons, places or things touches the everyday life of the faithful and answers their immediate needs. They offer many possibilities for

---

121. Cf. *Ordo initiationis christianae adultorum, Praenotanda,* 66; *Ordo Baptismi parvulorum, Praenotanda,* 26; *Ordo Paenitentiae, Praenotanda,* 39; *Ordo celebrandi Matrimonium, editio typica altera, Praenotanda,* 36.
122. *Ordo initiationis christianae adultorum, Praenotanda Generalia,* 30.2.
123. Ibid., 31; cf. SC, 65.
124. Cf. CIC, cc. 1108 and 1112.
125. SC, 77; *Ordo celebrandi Matrimonium, editio typica altera, Praenotanda,* 42.
126. Cf. SC, 77.
127. Cf. *Ordo exsequiarum, Praenotanda,* 4.
128. Cf. ibid., 9 and 21.1–21.3.
129. Cf. ibid., 2.
130. Cf. SC, 81.

adaptation, for maintaining local customs and admitting popular usages.[131] Episcopal conferences will be able to employ the foreseen dispositions and be attentive to the needs of the country.

60.   As regards the liturgical year, each particular church and religious family adds its own celebrations to those of the universal church, after approval by the Apostolic See.[132] Episcopal conferences can also, with the prior approval of the Apostolic See, suppress the obligation of certain feasts or transfer them to a Sunday.[133] They also decide the time and manner of celebrating rogationtide and ember days.[134]

61.   The Liturgy of the Hours has as its goal the praise of God and the sanctification by prayer of the day and all human activity. Episcopal conferences can make adaptations in the second reading of the office of readings, hymns and intercessions and in the final Marian antiphons.[135]

procedure

62.   When an episcopal conference prepares its own edition of liturgical books, it decides about the translations and also the adaptations which are envisaged by the law.[136] The acts of the conference, together with the final vote, are signed by the president and secretary of the conference and sent to the Congregation for Divine Worship and the Discipline of the Sacraments, along with two copies of the approved text.

Moreover along with the complete dossier should be sent:

a) A succinct and precise explanation of the reasons for the adaptations that have been introduced.

b) Indications as to which sections have been taken from other already approved liturgical books and which are newly composed.

After the recognition by the Apostolic See has been received according to the law,[137] the episcopal conference promulgates the decree and determines the date when the new text comes into force.

B) ADAPTATIONS ENVISAGED BY NO. 40 OF THE CONCILIAR CONSTITUTION ON THE LITURGY

63.   Apart from the adaptations provided for in the liturgical books, it may be that "in some places and circumstances an even more radical adaptation of the liturgy is needed, and this entails greater difficulties."[138] This is more than the

---

131. Cf. SC, 79; *De Benedictionibus, Praenotanda generalia*, 39; *Ordo Professionis religiosae, Praenotanda*, 12–15.
132. Cf. GNLY, 49, 55; CDW, Instruction *Calendaria particularia*, June 24, 1970: AAS, 62 (1970), 349–370.
133. Cf. CIC, c. 1246.2.
134. Cf. GNLY, 46.
135. GILOH, 92, 162, 178, 184.
136. Cf. CIC, cc. 455.2 and 838.3; that is also the case for a new edition, cf. VQA, 20.
137. CIC, c. 838.3
138. SC, 40.

sort of adaptations envisaged by the general instructions and the *praenotanda* of the liturgical books.

It presupposes that an episcopal conference has exhausted all the possibilities of adaptation offered by the liturgical books; that it has made an evaluation of the adaptations already introduced and maybe revised them before proceeding to more far-reaching adaptations.

The desirability or need for an adaptation of this sort can emerge in one of the areas mentioned above (cf. nos. 53–61) without the others being affected. Moreover, adaptations of this kind do not envisage a transformation of the Roman rite, but are made within the context of the Roman rite.

64.   In some places when there are still problems about the participation of the faithful, a bishop or several bishops can set out their difficulties to their colleagues in the episcopal conferences and examine with them the desirability of introducing more profound adaptations, if the good of souls truly requires it.[139]

It is the function of episcopal conferences to propose to the Apostolic See the modifications it wishes to adopt following the procedure set out below.[140]

The Congregation for Divine Worship and the Discipline of the Sacraments is ready to receive the proposals of episcopal conferences and examine them, keeping in mind the good of the local churches concerned and the common good of the universal church, and to assist the process of inculturation where it is desirable or necessary. It will do this in accordance with the principles laid down in this instruction (cf. above, nos. 33–51), and in a spirit of confident collaboration and shared responsibility.

procedure

65.   The episcopal conference will examine what has to be modified in liturgical celebrations because of the traditions and mentality of peoples. It will ask the national or regional liturgical commission to study the matter and examine the different aspects of the elements of local culture and their eventual inclusion in the liturgical celebrations. The commission is to ensure that it receives the appropriate expert advice. It may be sometimes opportune to ask the advice of members of non-Christian religions about the religious or civil value of this or that element (cf. above, nos. 30–32).

If the situation requires it, this preliminary examination will be made in collaboration with the episcopal conferences of neighboring countries or those with the same culture (cf. above, nos. 33–51).

66.   The episcopal conference will present the proposal to the congregation before any experimentation takes place. The presentation should include a description of the innovations proposed, the reasons for their adoption, the criteria used, the times and places chosen for a preliminary experiment and an indication

---

139. Cf. Congregation for Bishops, *Directory on the Pastoral Ministry of Bishops*, February 22, 1973, no. 84.
140. Cf. SC, 40.

which groups will make it, and finally the acts of the discussion and the vote of the conference.

After an examination of the proposal carried out together by the episcopal conference and the congregation, the latter will grant the episcopal conference a faculty to make an experiment for a definite period of time, where this is appropriate.[141]

67.   The episcopal conference will supervise the process of experimentation,[142] normally with the help of the national or regional liturgical commission. The conference will also take care to ensure that the experimentation does not exceed the limits of time and place that were fixed. It will also ensure pastors and the faithful know about the limited and provisional nature of the experiment, and it will not give it publicity of a sort which could have an effect on the liturgical practice of the country. At the end of the period of experimentation, the episcopal conference will decide whether it matches up to the goal that was proposed or whether it needs revision, and it will communicate its conclusions to the congregation along with full information about the experiment.

68.   After examining the dossier, the congregation will issue a decree giving its consent, possibly with some qualifications, so that the changes can be introduced into the territory covered by the episcopal conference.

69.   The faithful, both lay people and clergy, should be well informed about the changes and prepared for their introduction into the liturgical celebrations. The changes are to be put into effect as circumstances require, with a transition period if this is appropriate (cf. above, no. 61).

CONCLUSION

70.   The Congregation for Divine Worship and the Discipline of the Sacraments presents these rules to the episcopal conferences to govern the work of liturgical inculturation envisaged by the Second Vatican Council as a response to the pastoral needs of peoples of different cultures. Liturgical inculturation should be carefully integrated into a pastoral plan for the inculturation of the Gospel into the many different human situations that are to be found. The Congregation for Divine Worship and the Discipline of the Sacraments hopes that each particular church, especially the young churches, will discover that the diversity of certain elements of liturgical celebrations can be a source of enrichment, while respecting the substantial unity of the Roman rite, the unity of the whole church and the integrity of the faith transmitted to the saints for all time (cf. Jude 3).

The present instruction was prepared by the Congregation for Divine Worship and the Discipline of the Sacraments, by order of His Holiness Pope John Paul II, who approved it and ordered that it be published.

From the Congregation for Divine Worship and the Discipline of the Sacraments, January 25, 1994.

---

141. Cf. SC, 40.
142. Cf. SC, 40.

GOD'S MERCY
ENDURES FOREVER
GUIDELINES ON THE PRESENTATION
OF JEWS AND JUDAISM
IN CATHOLIC PREACHING

STATEMENT AND GUIDELINES
BISHOPS' COMMITTEE ON THE LITURGY

NATIONAL CONFERENCE OF CATHOLIC BISHOPS
SEPTEMBER, 1988

AN OVERVIEW OF *GOD'S MERCY ENDURES FOREVER: GUIDELINES ON THE PRESENTATION OF JEWS AND JUDAISM IN CATHOLIC PREACHING*

Rev. John T. Pawlikowski, OSM

The 1970s and the 1980s were both decades of considerable significance in terms of Catholic-Jewish relations. Both here in the United States and globally, the Church turned her attention to the concrete implementation of the renewed vision of the Church's relationship with the Jewish people that began with the passage of the declaration *Nostra aetate* at the Second Vatican Council. Chapter IV of *Nostra aetate,* which had the strong support of the American hierarchy, recast the Church's understanding of her relationship with Judaism in a whole new light. The Council repudiated previous claims by many in the Church that Judaism ended as a serious religious tradition with the coming of Christ and that Jews lost their covenantal status in light of their rejection of him.

Nostra aetate's chapter IV made three great assertions: (1) Jews were not collectively responsible for the Death of Jesus; (2) Hence the basis for Jewish exclusion from a covenantal relationship with God after the coming of Christ was invalidated. Jews were still covenantal partners with God alongside of Christians; and (3) Jesus drew richly upon parts of the Jewish tradition of his day for many of the key themes of his public ministry.

These three themes provided the new bedrock for a Catholic approach to Judaism. But the feeling remained that, though these three assertions stood at the heart of the new understanding of the continuing Jewish religious tradition on the part of Catholicism, there was need to amplify them and integrate them more fully into the ongoing life of the Church. Three documents tried to respond to this felt need in the Church. Two of them were issued at the global level; the third was released under the auspices of the National Conference of Catholic Bishops in the United States. The first, which appeared on December 1, 1974, titled *Guidelines and Suggestions for Implementing the Conciliar Declaration "Nostra Aetate," No. 4* urged due diligence on the part of homilists in ensuring that the Word of God be presented in a way that casts a positive light on the sacred texts of Judaism, including the Old Testament. Homilists must be especially vigilant in dealing with certain texts in the New Testament that appear at first glance to present Judaism in an unfavorable way but in fact represent certain tensions within the Jewish community of Jesus's time rather a wholesale condemnation of the Jewish religious tradition.

In the American context, the National Conference of Catholic Bishops (now the United States Conference of Catholic Bishops) promulgated a statement that follows up on chapter IV of *Nostra aetate* as well as the Holy See's 1974 *Guidelines.* This document was dated November 20, 1975. It gave a mandate to catechists and homilists to coordinate efforts in helping the community better appreciate the rich spiritual heritage of the Jewish tradition and how that tradition impacted the development of early Christian teaching, including Jesus's own perspectives. The document referred to the "spiritual giants" of the Old Testament—such as Abraham, Moses, the biblical prophets, and the psalmists—as potentially rich sources for Christian spiritual reflection. Pope Benedict XVI reinforced this mandate and added to it by recommending post-biblical Jewish texts as an additional resource for Christians in his address to the synagogue in Rome in January 2010.

Returning to the global scene, June 1985 saw the publication of a document commemorating the twentieth anniversary of *Nostra aetate*. Following up on the thrust of the preceding 1974 statement, this document, called *Notes on the Correct Way to Present Jews and Judaism in Preaching and Catechesis in the Roman Catholic Church* (simply referred to as *Notes*), reemphasized the obligation incumbent upon homilists to present Jews and Judaism in the correct light. It specifically addressed one issue that has been a perennial source of denigration of Judaism in Catholic catechism and preaching: the image of the Pharisees. The textbook study on the texts most widely used in Catholic schools by the late S. Rose Thering, OP, listed the negative image of the Pharisees as one of the three major distortions of Judaism present in these texts. And who of us has not heard a homilist denounce the Pharisees as people totally opposed to Jesus's teachings? Yet, based on recent biblical scholarship, the 1985 *Notes* argue that Jesus was closer to Pharisaism in a positive sense than any other Jewish movement of the time.

The 1985 *Notes* also strongly affirm the positive influence of Judaism on Jesus and his basic rootedness in the Jewish community of his day. These are the actual words of the *Notes* in this regard: "Jesus was and always remained a Jew . . . Jesus is fully a man of his time, and his environment—the Jewish Palestinian one of the first century, the anxieties and hopes of which he shared."[1] The *Notes* were able to make such a claim relative to Jesus's relationship with Judaism because of the scholarship of people such as Cardinal Carlo Martini, SJ, the retired Archbishop of Milan and a former professor at the Biblicum in Rome who penned the words that parallel those of the *Notes*: "Without a sincere feeling for the Jewish world and a direct experience of it, one cannot fully understand Christianity. Jesus is fully Jewish, the apostles are Jewish, and one cannot doubt their attachment to the traditions of their forefathers."[2]

Though these three Catholic documents without question advanced the original vision of *Nostra aetate* they basically remained on a general level without discussing concrete situations found in the Church's Missal, the aforementioned statement on Jesus and Pharisaism being one of the few exceptions in this regard. As a result, a number of Catholic scholars who had been active in the dialogue with Jewish counterparts generated by *Nostra aetate*, some of whom served on the United States Conference of Catholic Bishops' Advisory Committee

---

1. *Notes*, 1.
2. Carlo Maria Martini, SJ, "Christianity and Judaism: A Historical and Theological Overview," in *Jews and Christians Exploring the Past, Present and Future*, ed. James H. Charlesworth. New York: Crossroad Publishing Company, 1990, p. 19.

on Catholic-Jewish Relations, felt the need for a more detailed statement focusing on specific seasons of the liturgical year if the vision of chapter IV of *Nostra aetate* were to acquire deep roots in the postconciliar consciousness of the Catholic community. It was decided to approach the United States Conference of Catholic Bishops' Committee on the Liturgy to propose a collaborative document that would raise awareness among Catholic homilists of the mandate presented by the three previous documents and do so for each major liturgical season. The leadership of the Committee on the Liturgy agreed to this proposition to work with the United States Conference of Catholic Bishops' Committee on Ecumenical and Interreligious Affairs in drafting a text and also understood that such a document would have greater influence if released under the aegis of the Committee on the Liturgy.

This is how *God's Mercy Endures Forever: Guidelines on the Presentation of Jews and Judaism in Catholic Preaching* (GMEF) came to be born in September 1988. Its authoritative dimensions rest primarily on its release as a document from the Committee on the Liturgy (now the Committee on Divine), which is charged with overseeing Catholic worship in the United States. But its overall strength also comes from the input of Catholic scholars who have been deeply involved in the name of the Church in the ongoing encounter with the Jewish community.

During his long papacy Pope John Paul II became a major force in the implementation of the Second Vatican Council's new vision of the Catholic-Jewish relationship. In numerous speeches he portrayed Judaism as deeply embedded in the Christian soul. For him, authentic Christian expression must show the Church's deep-seated connection with Judaism. He was fond of emphasizing that when we look into the heart of Christianity there we will find Judaism. Hence reincorporating the Jewish context of Christianity will have significant implications for how the Church presents its self-understanding in a liturgical context and how homilists might present this new sense of Jewish-Catholic integration in a clear and sustained fashion to a worshipping assembly. This is the challenge that *God's Mercy Endures Forever* takes up in a comprehensive way. In its introductory articles the document pulls no punches. Increased sharpening of sensitivities rooted in the Church's growing understanding of biblical and post-biblical Judaism will be required if its stated goal is to be realized.

God's Mercy Endures Forever begins with a brief overview of how the principal celebrations of the Church's liturgical year owe their origins to the Jewish tradition. While these celebrations have been given new interpretations within Catholicism, an appreciation of their origins is critical for the full manifestation of their spiritual potential. It becomes the responsibility of the homilist as the "mediator of meaning" to make these connections visible for the community as it follows the yearly liturgical cycle. Basic liturgical concepts such as "Church," "ordo," and "anamnesis" were inherited from the Jewish tradition. Catholicism's most central ritual celebration, the Eucharist, has its base in a certain part of the Jewish spirituality that existed in Jesus's day. Jesus, throughout his public ministry, involved himself in public worship. As a result no understanding of the origins of worship in the name of Jesus is complete without the awareness of this reality. The depth and meaning of the Eucharistic tradition remain incomplete minus such awareness. And what has become a central prayer of the Church over the centuries, both within Catholicism's formal liturgy and in its non-liturgical settings, the Our Father, is Jewish to the core. When public Jewish worship was allowed once more in Spain in the latter part of the twentieth century the rededication of the principal synagogue in Madrid was celebrated with a joint Catholic-Jewish service during which the Our Father was prayed together by both communities.

God's Mercy Endures Forever confronts the unfortunate history of Catholic liturgical practice in terms of Jews and Judaism. The continuing connections between the Christian expression and the Jewish tradition that existed in the Church for several centuries was regrettably pushed aside when the Church became overwhelmingly Gentile and certain Christian writers such as Marcion cast a negative light on the entirety of the Jewish tradition, including disparaging the Old Testament as an ongoing source of spiritual insight for Christians. This anti-Jewish thrust in Catholic liturgy needs to be rectified and *God's Mercy Endures Forever* envisions homilists as having a central role in overcoming this anti-Jewish legacy in Catholicism's public worship. Catholic liturgy, following the directions promoted by Pope John Paul II, needs to affirm the continuity of the Jewish covenant after the coming of Christ and homilists must begin to preach on the liturgical texts from the Old Testament in a way that sees these texts as ongoing, positive sources for Christian spirituality.

Making Old Testament texts focal points of homilies will require considerable preparation and commitment. Examining how such texts are read and interpreted by Jewish preachers would be an important first step. Turning to other sources would prove very beneficial in this regard, including texts such as the *Jewish Annotated New Testament: New Revised Standard Version* edited by Amy-Jill Levine and Marc Z. Brettler[3] and *The Jewish People and Their Sacred Scriptures in the Christian Bible* from the Pontifical Biblical Commission in Rome.[4] Until now, I suspect few Catholic homilies have preached on the liturgical readings from the Old Testament.

Against a background of these more general observations *God's Mercy Endures Forever* moves to a consideration of issues in each of the major periods of the liturgical year. This is done chronologically beginning with Advent. A key issue in this liturgical season is the interpretation of the prophetic texts that appear with great frequency. The document reminds homilists that these prophetic texts are not to be regarded merely as temporal Messianic readings but as visions of an ultimate eschatological era. Church tradition has always presented Jesus's Messiahship as not yet complete. Hence Jews were not blind in rejecting such fulfillment in a particular temporal moment. In addition, these prophetic texts were not only instructing us about the future, they were also evaluating the quality of covenantal faithfulness within the believing community. So they ought to be presented by the homilist as yearly evaluations of the quality of faithfulness to our covenantal obligations today just as they served this purpose in ancient days.

---

3. *Jewish Annotated New Testament: New Revised Standard Version*, eds. Amy-Jill Levine and Marc Z. Brettler. Oxford, United Kingdom: Oxford University Press, 2011.
4. *The Jewish People and Their Sacred Scriptures in the Christian Bible*. Vatican City: Pontifical Biblical Commission, 2001.

Following the liturgical year, *God's Mercy Endures Forever* moves on to consider issues related to Lent and Holy Week. The use of prophetic texts is once more a challenge though not as compelling as during Advent. Greater concern arises over some of the texts used in this season that seem on the surface to present Judaism in a very unfavorable light. The culmination of this process occurs in Holy Week, which can prove a painful experience for Jews and historically was often the time when certain Christians launched physical attacks against Jewish communities in parts of Europe. The document tries to help the homilist transform the Passion into a moment of reconciliation between Jews and Christians rather than a source of hostility. It does so in part by quoting from Pope John Paul II's speech to the Jewish leaders gathered in Miami in September 1987: "Considering this mystery of the suffering of Israel's children, their witness of hope, of faith, and of humanity under dehumanizing outrages, the Church experiences ever more deeply her common bond with the Jewish people and with their treasure of spiritual riches in the past and in the present."[5]

God's Mercy Endures Forever closes with a reference to Easter Time. Although not traditionally thought of as a central problem in Catholic-Jewish relations, closer examination of the readings of this season from the Epistle of Peter and other biblical books can easily convey the impression that early Christians were charging the Jewish community with deicide for which there is little or no historical evidence. So this liturgical season needs far more attention than it has generally received.

The basic thrust of *God's Mercy Endures Forever* is toward a recognition by homilists that the Catholic-Jewish relationship must be of concern throughout the liturgical year and not merely during specially selected periods such as Holy Week. The new vision of Catholic-Jewish reconciliation proclaimed in *Nostra aetate* must permeate the Church's fundamental identity whenever it is presented by homilists.

---

5. As quoted in GMEF, 25.

OUTLINE

GOD'S MERCY ENDURES FOREVER

On June 24, 1985, the solemnity of the Birth of John the Baptist, the Holy See's Commission for Religious Relations with the Jews issued its *Notes on the Correct Way to Present the Jews and Judaism in Preaching and Catechesis of the Roman Catholic Church* (hereafter, *1985 Notes*). The *1985 Notes* rested on a foundation of previous Church statements, addressing the tasks given Catholic homilists by the Second Vatican Council's *Declaration on the Relationship of the Church to Non-Christian Religions (Nostra Aetate)*, no. 4.

On December 1, 1974, for example, the Holy See had issued *Guidelines and Suggestions for Implementing the Conciliar Declaration "Nostra Aetate," no. 4* (hereafter, 1974 *Guidelines*). The second and third sections of this document placed central emphasis on the important and indispensable role of the homilist in ensuring that God's Word be received without prejudice toward the Jewish people or their religious traditions, asking "with respect to liturgical readings," that "care be taken to see that homilies based on them will not distort their meaning, especially when it is a question of passages which seem to show the Jewish people as such in unfavorable light" (1974 *Guidelines*, no. 2).

In this country, the National Conference of Catholic Bishops, in 1975, similarly urged catechists and homilists to work together to develop among Catholics increasing "appreciation of the Jewishness of that heritage and rich spirituality which we derive from Abraham, Moses, the prophets, the psalmists, and other spiritual giants of the Hebrew Scriptures" (*Statement on Catholic-Jewish Relations*, November 20, 1975, no. 12).

Much progress has been made since then. As it continues, sensitivities will need even further sharpening, founded on the Church's growing understanding of biblical and rabbinic Judaism.

It is the purpose of these present *Guidelines* to assist the homilist in these continuing efforts by indicating some of the major areas where challenges and opportunities occur and by offering perspectives and suggestions for dealing with them.

JEWISH ROOTS OF THE LITURGY

1. "Our common spiritual heritage [with Judaism] is considerable. To assess it carefully in itself and with due awareness of the faith and religious life of the Jewish people as they are professed and practiced still today, can greatly help us to understand better certain aspects of the life of the Church. Such is the case

with the liturgy, whose Jewish roots remain still to be examined more deeply, and in any case should be better known and appreciated by the faithful" (Pope John Paul II, March 6, 1982).

2.   Nowhere is the deep spiritual bond between Judaism and Christianity more apparent than in the liturgy. The very concepts of a liturgical cycle of feasts and the *lectio continua* principle of the lectionary that so mark Catholic tradition are adopted from Jewish liturgical practice. Easter and Pentecost have historical roots in the Jewish feasts of Passover and Shavuot. Though their Christian meaning is quite distinct, an awareness of their original context in the story of Israel is vital to their understanding, as the lectionary readings themselves suggest. Where appropriate, such relationships should be pointed out. The homilist, as a "mediator of meaning" (NCCB Committee on Priestly Life and Ministry, *Fulfilled in Your Hearing*, 1982) interprets for the liturgical assembly not only the Scriptures but their liturgical context as well.

3.   The central action of Christian worship, the eucharistic celebration, is likewise linked historically with Jewish ritual. The term for Church, *ecclesia*, like the original sense of the word *synagogue*, is an equivalent for the Hebrew *keneset* or *kenessiyah* (assembly). The Christian understanding of *ecclesia* is based on the biblical understanding of *qahal* as the formal "gathering" of the people of God. The Christian *ordo* (order of worship) is an exact rendering of the earliest rabbinic idea of prayer, called a *seder*, that is, an "order" of service. Moreover, the Christian *ordo* takes its form and structure from the Jewish *seder*: the Liturgy of the Word, with its alternating biblical readings, doxologies, and blessings; and the liturgical form of the Eucharist, rooted in Jewish meal liturgy, with its blessings over bread and wine. Theologically, the Christian concept of *anamnesis* coincides with the Jewish understanding of *zikkaron* (memorial reenactment). Applied to the Passover celebration, *zikkaron* refers to the fact that God's saving deed is not only recalled but actually relived through the ritual meal. The synoptic gospels present Jesus as instituting the Eucharist during a Passover *seder* celebrated with his followers, giving to it a new and distinctly Christian "memory."

4.   In addition to the liturgical seasons and the Eucharist, numerous details of prayer forms and ritual exemplify the Church's continuing relationship with the Jewish people through the ages. The liturgy of the hours and the formulas of many of the Church's most memorable prayers, such as the "Our Father," continue to resonate with rabbinic Judaism and contemporary synagogue prayers.

HISTORICAL PERSPECTIVES AND CONTEMPORARY PROCLAMATION

5.   The strongly Jewish character of Jesus' teaching and that of the primitive Church was culturally adapted by the growing Gentile majority and later blurred by controversies alienating Christianity from emerging rabbinic Judaism at the end of the first century. "By the third century, however, a de-Judaizing process had set in which tended to undervalue the Jewish origins of the Church, a tendency that has surfaced from time to time in devious ways throughout Christian history" (*Statement on Catholic-Jewish Relations*, no. 12).

6. This process has manifested itself in various ways in Christian history. In the second century, Marcion carried it to its absurd extreme, teaching a complete opposition between the Hebrew and Christian Scriptures and declaring that different Gods had inspired the two Testaments. Despite the Church's condemnation of Marcion's teachings, some Christians over the centuries continued to dichotomize the Bible into two mutually contradictory parts. They argued, for example, that the New Covenant "abrogated" or "superseded" the Old, and that the Sinai Covenant was discarded by God and replaced with another. The Second Vatican Council, in *Dei Verbum* and *Nostra Aetate*, rejected these theories of the relationship between the Scriptures. In a major address in 1980, Pope John Paul II linked the renewed understanding of Scripture with the Church's understanding of its relationship with the Jewish people, stating that the dialogue, as "the meeting between the people of God of the Old Covenant, never revoked by God, is at the same time a dialogue within our Church, that is to say, a dialogue between the first and second part of its Bible" (Pope John Paul II, Mainz, November 17, 1980).

7. Another misunderstanding rejected by the Second Vatican Council was the notion of collective guilt, which charged the Jewish people *as a whole* with responsibility for Jesus' death (cf. nos. 21–25 below, on Holy Week). From the theory of collective guilt, it followed for some that Jewish suffering over the ages reflected divine retribution on the Jews for an alleged "deicide." While both rabbinic Judaism and early Christianity saw in the destruction of the Jerusalem Temple in AD 70 a sense of divine punishment (see Luke 19:42–44), the theory of collective guilt went well beyond Jesus' poignant expression of his love as a Jew for Jerusalem and the destruction it would face at the hands of Imperial Rome. Collective guilt implied that because "the Jews" had rejected Jesus, God had rejected them. With direct reference to Luke 19:44, the Second Vatican Council reminded Catholics that "nevertheless, now as before, God holds the Jews most dear for the sake of their fathers; he does not repent of the gifts he makes or of the calls he issues," and established as an overriding hermeneutical principle for homilists dealing with such passages that "the Jews should not be represented as rejected by God or accursed, as if this followed from Holy Scripture" (*Nostra Aetate*, no. 4; cf. 1985 *Notes*, VI:33).

8. Reasons for increased sensitivity to the ways in which Jews and Judaism are presented in homilies are multiple. First, understanding of the biblical readings and of the structure of Catholic liturgy will be enhanced by an appreciation of their ancient sources and their continuing spiritual links with Judaism. The Christian proclamation of the saving deeds of the One God through Jesus was formed in the context of Second Temple Judaism and cannot be understood thoroughly without that context. It is a proclamation that, at its heart, stands in solidarity with the continuing Jewish witness in affirming the One God as Lord of history. Further, false or demeaning portraits of a repudiated Israel may undermine Christianity as well. How can one confidently affirm the truth of God's covenant with all humanity and creation in Christ (see Romans 8:21) without at the same time affirming God's faithfulness to the Covenant with Israel that also lies at the heart of the biblical testimony?

9.   As Catholic homilists know, the liturgical year presents both opportunities and challenges. One can show the parallels between the Jewish and Catholic liturgical cycles. And one can, with clarity, confront misinterpretations of the meaning of the lectionary readings, which have been too familiar in the past. Specifically, homilists can guide people away from a triumphalism that would equate the pilgrim Church with the Reign of God, which is the Church's mission to herald and proclaim. Likewise, homilists can confront the unconscious transmission of anti-Judaism through cliches that derive from an unhistorical overgeneralization of the self-critical aspects of the story of Israel as told in the Scriptures (e.g., "hardheartedness" of the Jews, "blindness," "legalism," "materialism," "rejection of Jesus," etc.). From Advent through Passover/Easter, to Yom Kippur and Rosh Hashana, the Catholic and Jewish liturgical cycles spiral around one another in a stately progression of challenges to God's people to repent, to remain faithful to God's call, and to prepare the world for the coming of God's Reign. While each is distinct and unique, they are related to one another. Christianity is engrafted on and continues to draw sustenance from the common root, biblical Israel (Romans 11:13–24).

10.   In this respect, the 1985 *Notes,* stressing "the unity of the divine plan" (no. 11), caution against a simplistic framing of the relationship of Christianity and Judaism as "two parallel ways of salvation" (no. 7). The Church proclaims the universal salvific significance of the Christ-event and looks forward to the day when "there shall be one flock and one shepherd" (John 10:16; cf. Isaiah 66:2; Zephaniah 3:9; Jeremiah 23:3; Ezra 11:17; see also no. 31e below). So intimate is this relationship that the Church "encounters the mystery of Israel" when "pondering her own mystery" (*1974 Guidelines,* no.5).

ADVENT: THE RELATIONSHIP BETWEEN THE SCRIPTURES

11.   The lectionary readings from the prophets are selected to bring out the ancient Christian theme that Jesus is the "fulfillment" of the biblical message of hope and promise, the inauguration of the "days to come" described, for example, by the daily Advent Masses, and on Sundays by Isaiah in cycle A and Jeremiah in cycle C for the First Sunday of Advent. This truth needs to be framed very carefully. Christians believe that Jesus is the promised Messiah who has come (see Luke 4:22), but also know that his messianic kingdom is not yet fully realized. The ancient messianic prophecies are not merely temporal predictions but profound expressions of eschatological hope. Since this dimension can be misunderstood or even missed altogether, the homilist needs to raise clearly the hope found in the prophets and heightened in the proclamation of Christ. This hope includes trust in what is promised but not yet seen. While the biblical prophecies of an age of universal *shalom* are "fulfilled" (i.e., irreversibly inaugurated) in Christ's coming, the fulfillment is not yet completely worked out in each person's life or perfected in the world at large (*1974 Guidelines,* no. 2). It is the mission of the Church, as also that of the Jewish people, to proclaim and to work to prepare the world for the full flowering of God's Reign, which is, but is "not yet" (cf. *1974 Guidelines,* II). Both the Christian "Our Father" and the Jewish *Kaddish* exemplify this message. Thus, both Christianity and Judaism seal their worship with a common hope: "Thy kingdom come!"

12.   Christians proclaim that the Messiah has indeed come and that God's Reign is "at hand." With the Jewish people, we await the complete realization of the messianic age.

> In underlining the eschatological dimension of Christianity, we shall reach a greater awareness that the people of God of the Old and the New Testament are tending toward a like end in the future: the coming or return of the Messiah—even if they start from two different points of view (1985 Notes, nos. 18–19).

13.   Other difficulties may be less theologically momentous but can still be troublesome. For example, the reading from Baruch in cycle C or from Isaiah in cycle A for the Second Sunday of Advent can leave the impression that pre-Jesus Israel was wholly guilt-ridden and in mourning, and Judaism virtually moribund. In fact, in their original historical settings, such passages reveal Judaism's remarkable capacity for self-criticism. While Israel had periods of deep mourning (see Lamentations) and was justly accused of sinfulness (e.g., see Jeremiah), it also experienced periods of joy, return from Exile, and continuing *teshuvah*, turning back to God in faithful repentance. Judaism was and is incredibly complex and vital, with a wide variety of creative spiritual movements vying for the people's adherence.

14.   The reform of the liturgy initiated by the Second Vatican Council reintroduced regular readings from the Old Testament into the lectionary. For Catholics, the Old Testament is that collection that contains the Hebrew Scriptures and the seven deuterocanonical books. Using postbiblical Jewish sources, with respect for the essential differences between Christian and Jewish traditions of biblical interpretation, can enliven the approach to the biblical text (cf. nos. 31a and 31i below). The opportunity also presents a challenge for the homilist. Principles of selection of passages vary. Sometimes the readings are cyclic, providing a continuity of narrative over a period of time. At other times, especially during Advent and Lent, a reading from the prophets or one of the historical books of the Old Testament and a gospel pericope are "paired," based on such liturgical traditions as the *sensus plenior* (fuller meaning) or, as is especially the case in Ordinary Time, according to the principle of *typology*, in which biblical figures and events are seen as "types" prefiguring Jesus (see no. 31e below).

15.   Many of these pairings represent natural associations of similar events and teachings. Others rely on New Testament precedent and interpretation of the messianic psalms and prophetic passages. Matthew 1:23, for example, quotes the Septuagint, which translates the Hebrew *almah* (young woman) as the Greek for *virgin* in its rendering of Isaiah 7:14. The same biblical text, therefore, can have more than one valid hermeneutical interpretation, ranging from its original historical context and intent to traditional Christological applications. The *1985 Notes* describe this phenomenon as flowing from the "unfathomable riches" and "inexhaustible content" of the Hebrew Bible. For Christians, the unity of the Bible depends on understanding all Scripture in the light of Christ. Typology is one form, rooted in the New Testament itself, of expressing this unity of Scripture and of the divine plan (see no. 31e below). As such, it "should not lead

us to forget that it [the Hebrew Bible] retains its own value as Revelation that the New Testament often does no more than resume" (*1985 Notes*, no. 15; cf. *Dei Verbum*, 14–18).

LENT: CONTROVERSIES AND CONFLICTS

16.   The Lenten lectionary presents just as many challenges. Prophetic texts such as Joel (Ash Wednesday), Jeremiah's "new covenant" (cycle B, Fifth Sunday), and Isaiah (cycle C, Fifth Sunday) call the assembly to proclaim Jesus as the Christ while avoiding negativism toward Judaism.

17.   In addition, many of the New Testament texts, such as Matthew's references to "hypocrites in the synagogue" (Ash Wednesday), John's depiction of Jesus in the Temple (cycle B, Third Sunday), and Jesus' conflicts with the Pharisees (e.g., Luke, cycle C, Fourth Sunday) can give the impression that the Judaism of Jesus' day was devoid of spiritual depth and essentially at odds with Jesus' teaching. References to earlier divine punishments of the Jews (e.g., 1 Corinthians, cycle C, Third Sunday) can further intensify a false image of Jews and Judaism as a people rejected by God.

18.   In fact, however, as the *1985 Notes* are at pains to clarify (sec. III and IV), Jesus was observant of the Torah (e.g, in the details of his circumcision and purification given in Luke 2:21–24), he extolled respect for it (see Matthew 5:17–20), and he invited obedience to it (see Matthew 8:4). Jesus taught in the synagogues (see Matthew 4:23 and 9:35; Luke 4:15–18; John 18:20) and in the Temple, which he frequented, as did the disciples even after the Resurrection (see Acts 2:46; 3:1ff). While Jesus showed uniqueness and authority in his interpretation of God's word in the Torah—in a manner that scandalized some Jews and impressed others—he did not oppose it, nor did he wish to abrogate it.

19.   Jesus was perhaps closer to the Pharisees in his religious vision than to any other group of his time. The *1985 Notes* suggest that this affinity with Pharisaism may be a reason for many of his apparent controversies with them (see no. 27). Jesus shared with the Pharisees a number of distinctive doctrines: the resurrection of the body; forms of piety such as almsgiving, daily prayer, and fasting; the liturgical practice of addressing God as Father; and the priority of the love commandment (see no. 25). Many scholars are of the view that Jesus was not so much arguing against "the Pharisees" as a group, as he was condemning excesses of some Pharisees, excesses of a sort that can be found among some Christians as well. In some cases, Jesus appears to have been participating in internal Pharisaic debates on various points of interpretation of God's law. In the case of divorce (see Mark 10:2–12), an issue that was debated hotly between the Pharisaic schools of Hillel and Shammai, Jesus goes beyond even the more stringent position of the House of Shammai. In other cases, such as the rejection of a literal interpretation of the *lex talionis* ("An eye for an eye . . . . "), Jesus' interpretation of biblical law is similar to that found in some of the prophets and ultimately adopted by rabbinic tradition as can be seen in the *Talmud*.

20. After the church had distanced itself from Judaism (cf. no. 5 above), it tended to telescope the long historical process whereby the gospels were set down some generations after Jesus' death. Thus, certain controversies that may actually have taken place between church leaders and rabbis toward the end of the first century were "read back" into the life of Jesus:

> Some [New Testament] references hostile or less than favorable to Jews have their historical context in conflicts between the nascent Church and the Jewish community. Certain controversies reflect Christian-Jewish relations long after the time of Jesus. To establish this is of capital importance if we wish to bring out the meaning of certain gospel texts for the Christians of today. All this should be taken into account when preparing catechesis and homilies for the weeks of Lent and Holy Week (*1985 Notes*, no. 29; see no. 26 below).

HOLY WEEK: THE PASSION NARRATIVES

21. Because of the tragic history of the "Christ-killer" charge as providing a rallying cry for anti-Semites over the centuries, a strong and careful homiletic stance is necessary to combat its lingering effects today. Homilists and catechists should seek to provide a proper context for the proclamation of the passion narratives. A particularly useful and detailed discussion of the theological and historical principles involved in presentations of the passions can be found in *Criteria for the Evaluation of Dramatizations of the Passion* issued by the Bishops' Committee for Ecumenical and Interreligious Affairs (March 1988).

22. The message of the liturgy in proclaiming the passion narratives in full is to enable the assembly to see vividly the love of Christ for each person, despite their sins, a love that even death could not vanquish. "Christ in his boundless love freely underwent his passion and death because of the sins of all so that all might attain salvation" (*Nostra Aetate*, no. 4). To the extent that Christians over the centuries made Jews the scapegoat for Christ's death, they drew themselves away from the paschal mystery. For it is only by dying to one's sins that we can hope to rise with Christ to new life. This is a central truth of the Catholic faith stated by the Catechism of the Council of Trent in the sixteenth century and reaffirmed by the *1985 Notes* (no. 30).

23. It is necessary to remember that the passion narratives do not offer eyewitness accounts or a modern transcript of historical events. Rather, the events have had their meaning focused, as it were, through the four theological "lenses" of the gospels. By comparing what is shared and what distinguishes the various gospel accounts from each other, the homilist can discern the core from the particular optics of each. One can then better see the significant theological differences between the passion narratives. The differences also are part of the inspired Word of God.

24. Certain historical essentials are shared by all four accounts: a growing hostility against Jesus on the part of some Jewish religious leaders (note that the Synoptic gospels do not mention the Pharisees as being involved in the events

leading to Jesus' death, but only the "chief priests, scribes, and elders"); the Last Supper with the disciples; betrayal by Judas; arrest outside the city (an action conducted covertly by the Roman and Temple authorities because of Jesus' popularity among his fellow Jews); interrogation before a high priest (not necessarily a Sanhedrin trial); formal condemnation by Pontius Pilate (cf. The Apostles' and Nicene Creeds, which mention *only* Pilate, even though some Jews were involved); crucifixion by Roman soldiers; affixing the title "King of the Jews" on the cross; death; burial; and resurrection. Many other elements, such as the crowds shouting "His blood be on us and on our children" in Matthew, or the generic use of the term "the Jews" in John, are unique to a given author and must be understood within the context of the author's overall theological scheme. Often, these unique elements reflect the perceived needs and emphases of the author's particular community at the end of the first century, *after* the split between Jews and Christians was well underway. The bitterness toward synagogue Judaism seen in John's gospel (e.g., John 9:22;16:2) most likely reflects the bitterness felt by John's own community after its "parting of the ways" with the Jewish community, and the martyrdom of St. Stephen illustrates that verbal disputes could, at times, lead to violence by Jews against fellow Jews who believed in Jesus.

25.   Christian reflection on the passion should lead to a deep sense of the need for reconciliation with the Jewish community today. Pope John Paul II has said:

> Considering history in the light of the principles of faith in God, we must also reflect on the catastrophic event of the *Shoah* . . . .
>
> Considering this mystery of the suffering of Israel's children, their witness of hope, of faith, and of humanity under dehumanizing outrages, the Church experiences ever more deeply her common bond with the Jewish people and with their treasure of spiritual riches in the past and in the present (*Address to Jewish Leadership*, Miami, September 11, 1987).

THE EASTER SEASON

26.   The readings of the Easter season, especially those from the book of Acts, which is used extensively throughout this liturgical period, require particular attention from the homilist in light of the enduring bond between Jews and Christians. Some of these readings from Acts (e.g., cycles A and B for the Third and Fourth Sundays of Easter) can leave an impression of collective Jewish responsibility for the crucifixion ("You put to death the author of life . . . . " Acts 3:15). In such cases, the homilist should put before the assembly the teachings of *Nostra Aetate* in this regard (see no. 22 above), as well as the fact noted in Acts 3:17 that what was done by some individual Jews was done "out of ignorance" so that no unwarranted conclusion about collective guilt is drawn by the hearers. The Acts may be dealing with a reflection of the Jewish-Christian relationship as it existed toward the end of the first century (when Acts was composed) rather than with the actual attitudes of the post-Easter Jerusalem Church. Homilists should desire to convey the spirit and enthusiasm of the early Church that marks these Easter season readings. But in doing so, statements about Jewish

responsibility have to be kept in context. This is part of the reconciliation between Jews and Christians to which we are all called.

PASTORAL ACTIVITY DURING HOLY WEEK AND THE EASTER SEASON

27.   Pope John Paul II's visit to the Chief Rabbi of Rome on Good Friday, 1987, gives a lead for pastoral activities during Holy Week in local churches. Some dioceses and parishes, for example, have begun traditions such as holding a "Service of Reconciliation" with Jews on Palm Sunday, or inviting Holocaust survivors to address their congregations during Lent.

28.   It is becoming familiar in many parishes and Catholic homes to participate in a Passover Seder during Holy Week. This practice can have educational and spiritual value. It is wrong, however, to "baptize" the Seder by ending it with New Testament readings about the Last Supper or, worse, turn it into a prologue to the Eucharist. Such mergings distort both traditions. The following advice should prove useful:

> When Christians celebrate this sacred feast among themselves, the rites of the *haggadah* for the seder should be respected in all their integrity. The seder . . . should be celebrated in a dignified manner and with sensitivity to those to whom the seder truly belongs. The primary reason why Christians may celebrate the festival of Passover should be to acknowledge common roots in the history of salvation. Any sense of restaging the Last Supper of the Lord Jesus should be avoided. . . . The rites of the Triduum are the [Church's] annual memorial of the events of Jesus' dying and rising (Bishops' Committee on the Liturgy *Newsletter*, March 1980, p. 12).

Seders arranged at or in cooperation with local synagogues are encouraged.

29.   Also encouraged are joint memorial services commemorating the victims of the *Shoah* (Holocaust). These should be prepared for with catechetical and adult education programming to ensure a proper spirit of shared reverence. Addressing the Jewish community of Warsaw, Pope John Paul II stressed the uniqueness and significance of Jewish memory of the *Shoah:* "More than anyone else, it is precisely you who have become this saving warning. I think that in this sense you continue your particular vocation, showing yourselves to be still the heirs of that election to which God is faithful. This is your mission in the contemporary world before . . . all of humanity" (Warsaw, June 14, 1987). On the Sunday closest to *Yom ha Shoah*, Catholics should pray for the victims of the Holocaust and their survivors. The following serve as examples of petitions for the general intercessions at Mass:

- For the victims of the Holocaust, their families, and all our Jewish brothers and sisters, that the violence and hatred they experienced may never again be repeated, we pray to the Lord.

- For the Church, that the Holocaust may be a reminder to us that we can never be indifferent to the sufferings of others, we pray to the Lord.

- For our Jewish brothers and sisters, that their confidence in the face of long-suffering may spur us on to a greater faith and trust in God, we pray to the Lord.

PREACHING THROUGHOUT THE YEAR

30.   The challenges that peak in the seasons of Advent, Lent, and Easter are present throughout the year in the juxtaposition of the lectionary readings. There are many occasions when it is difficult to avoid a reference either to Jews or Judaism in a homily based upon a text from the Scriptures. For all Scripture, including the New Testament, deals with Jews and Jewish themes.

31.   Throughout the year, the following general principles will be helpful:

a) Consistently affirm the value of the whole Bible. While "among all the Scriptures, even those of the New Testament, the Gospels have a special pre-eminence" (*Dei Verbum*, 18), the Hebrew Scriptures are the word of God and have validity and dignity in and of themselves (ibid., 15). Keep in view the intentions of the biblical authors (ibid., 19).

b) Place the typology inherent in the lectionary in a proper context, neither overemphasizing nor avoiding it. Show that the meaning of the Hebrew Scriptures for their original audience is not limited to nor diminished by New Testament applications (*1985 Notes*, II).

c) Communicate a reverence for the Hebrew Scriptures and avoid approaches that reduce them to a propaedeutic or background for the New Testament. It is God who speaks, communicating himself through divine revelation (*Dei Verbum*, 6).

d) Show the connectedness between the Scriptures. The Hebrew Bible and the Jewish tradition founded on it must not be set against the New Testament in such a way that the former seems to constitute a religion of only retributive justice, fear, and legalism, with no appeal to love of God and neighbor (cf. Deuteronomy 6:5; Leviticus 19:18,32; Hosea 11:1-9; Matthew 22:34-40).

e) Enliven the eschatological hope, the "not yet" aspect of the *kerygma*. The biblical promises are realized in Christ. But the Church awaits their perfect fulfillment in Christ's glorious return when all creation is made free (*1974 Guidelines*, II).

f) Emphasize the Jewishness of Jesus and his teachings and highlight the similarities of the teachings and highlight the similarities of the teachings of the Pharisees with those of Christ (*1985 Notes*, III and IV).

g) Respect the continuing validity of God's covenant with the Jewish people and their responsive faithfulness, despite centuries of suffering, to the divine call that is theirs (*1985 Notes*, VI).

h) Frame homilies to show that Christians and Jews together are "trustees and witnesses of an ethic marked by the Ten Commandments, in the observance of which humanity finds its truth and freedom" (John Paul II, Rome Synagogue, April 13, 1986).

i) Be free to draw on Jewish sources (rabbinic, medieval, and modern) in expounding the meaning of the Hebrew Scriptures and the apostolic writings. The *1974 Guidelines* observe that "the history of Judaism did not end with the destruction of Jerusalem, but went on to develop a religious tradition . . . rich in religious values." The *1985 Notes* (no. 14) thus speak of Christians "profiting discerningly from the traditions of Jewish readings" of the sacred texts.

32.   The *1985 Notes* describe what is central to the role of the homilist: "Attentive to the same God who has spoken, hanging on the same word, we have to witness to one same memory and one common hope in him who is master of history. We must also accept our responsibility to prepare the world for the coming of the Messiah by working together for social justice, respect for the rights of persons and nations, and for social and international reconciliation. To this we are driven, Jews and Christians, by the command to love our neighbor, by a common hope for the kingdom of God, and by the great heritage of the prophets" (*1985 Notes*, no. 19; see also Leviticus 19:18, 32).

PLENTY GOOD ROOM
THE SPIRIT AND TRUTH OF AFRICAN AMERICAN CATHOLIC WORSHIP

PASTORAL LETTER
SECRETARIAT FOR THE LITURGY
AND SECRETARIAT FOR BLACK CATHOLICS
NATIONAL CONFERENCE OF CATHOLIC BISHOPS
AUGUST 28, 1990

AN OVERVIEW OF *PLENTY GOOD ROOM:* *THE SPIRIT AND TRUTH OF AFRICAN AMERICAN CATHOLIC WORSHIP*

Most Reverend Wilton D. Gregory

Many African American spirituals unsurprisingly go unattributed to any specific author or composer. Most of the spirituals were created at a moment in time when copyright laws may not have been as precise as they are currently or as universally observed. Even more important, the spirituals originated at a time when the artists who composed them would not have been considered very noteworthy or artistically significant. Yet African American spirituals remain among the truly indigenous and culturally grounded music of our nation. They often reveal both scriptural as well as social wisdom that continues to serve and inspire those who listen to them. "Plenty Good Room" is the title of the spiritual that was borrowed to name the document prepared by the Bishops' Secretariat for the Liturgy in collaboration with the Bishops' Secretariat for black Catholics published in 1991 to serve as a compendium and exposé of some of the elements to be found in traditional African American religious motifs and how these might successfully and appropriately be used in the liturgical inculturation of the Roman Rite.[1]

As the title indicates, it was written to suggest that there is ample room in the Roman Rite for some of these elements to be employed in Catholic liturgy, as this liturgical structure has accommodated elements from many other cultures and traditions multiple times throughout its history. The question is always how this process must follow the principles outlined in the *Constitution on the Sacred Liturgy*:

> Even in the liturgy the Church has no wish to impose a rigid uniformity in matters that do not affect the faith or the good of the whole community; rather, the Church respects and fosters the genius and talents of the various races and peoples. The Church considers with sympathy and, if possible, preserves intact the elements in these peoples' way of life that are not indissolubly bound up with superstition and error. Sometimes in fact the Church admits such elements into the liturgy itself, provided they are in keeping with the true and authentic spirit of the liturgy.[2]

Plenty Good Room was conceived as a project of these aforementioned secretariats to study how many elements of time-honored African American religious traditions might be appropriately used in Roman Catholic liturgy. In other words, it was an exercise to undertake that invitation found in the *Constitution on the Sacred Liturgy* to allow the religious heritage of African

---

1. For reference, the text of this spiritual is reprinted in this collection on page 268.
2. *Constitution on the Sacred Liturgy* (CSL), 37.

American peoples to be used in Catholic worship. *Plenty Good Room* includes a panoramic descriptive overview of how the Church has welcomed the cultural contributions of many other people in her long heritage of liturgical development. In many respects it offers an opportunity for all Catholics to revisit the Church's liturgical development throughout the centuries and to consider the spiritual culture and traditions of African Americans with a pastoral eye to incorporating some of those gifts within Catholic liturgy. It was intended to serve as a sequel document to the earlier resource, *In Spirit and Truth: Black Catholic Reflections on the Order of Mass*, published in 1988 as a focused examination of the opportunities within the then existing Order of Mass where inculturation of African American spiritual traditions might be used. This earlier work was limited to the task of considering the adaptation possibilities within the Order of Mass while *Plenty Good Room* was designed to explore the broader issue of the principles and the history that are to be found within the Church as she has adopted cultural and ethnic traditions throughout her history and used them in the liturgy.

Plenty Good Room is an *apologia* for reaching out and capturing some of the cultural and spiritual gifts that are to be found within the expansive African American spiritual community and considering how they might be used in Catholic worship. It is a pastoral work and not a legislative manuscript and it never claimed to be an all-inclusive listing of every cultural element to be found within the black spiritual heritage. Nor did it profess to be the final word on the topic of liturgical inculturation. It is rather a careful pastoral reflection on a number of the important questions that involve cultural liturgical adaptation and therefore its principles are applicable beyond merely the African American religious context.

Plenty Good Room explores how one can bring his or her cultural heritage to the life of the Church and how the Church herself has been enriched by these additions employed prudently within her liturgy. No one gave greater expression of the possibility of such an interchange than did Pope John Paul II in his many and varied travels throughout the world. In his very person, the successor of Peter encountered multiple cultures and ethnic traditions that were found the world over. He effectively used these travels to recognize and to affirm the heritages of the peoples of the Church and he did so apparently with obvious delight. Whether in Africa, Asia, Central or Latin America, the Pacific Rim, or Europe itself, he allowed traditional garb, music, tempo, and traditions to be involved with the liturgical celebrations over which he presided as the Church's Universal Pastor and Supreme Pontiff. His pastoral sensitivity in the area of liturgical inculturation had been previously affirmed by Pope Paul VI in his exhortation to the Churches in Africa at the closing of the Symposium for African Bishops in 1969 at Kampala.[3]

Plenty Good Room was also a summons to the African American community ourselves to continue our own efforts to deepen our appreciation of and our pride in our own treasured heritage and to bring that same heritage to the Catholic Church that we love as an offering and as a valued gift. This invitation

---

3. Documentation of Pope Paul's 1969 visit to Uganda can be found on the Vatican website: www.vatican.va/holy_father/paul_vi/travels/sub-index/index_uganda.htm.

occasionally provided a challenge for some African Americans to view our heritage as a true blessing in spite of the residual experience of hesitancy on the part of some that the gift would indeed be welcomed or of any real value. Every culture has gifts and treasures that both distinguish it from other cultures but also hold the possibility of inspiring respect, admiration, and delight on the part of others. Cultures are not so much in competition with one another for supremacy as they should be in a complementary relationship. The Church throughout the ages has selected certain elements from the vast array to be found in the many cultures of humanity to enrich her liturgy and to allow the message and the truth of the Gospel to penetrate, engage, and transform the people of every nation and land.

The document also acknowledges the rich diversity that exists within the African American community itself as is the case with all cultural or racial categories of people. It explores some of the variety of backgrounds that distinguish the African American community as well as those common experiences that bind us together in spite of those differences. It is a document that ponders carefully the spiritual and religious elements that the black community in the United States preserves from our African origins—oftentimes wrapped in regional variations but always subtly reflecting residual ties to older African cultural traditions. Among the residual essentials to be found in African American spiritual practices is the deeply African value of viewing religion as a pervasive reality for all of creation. In today's cultural environment, which seemingly moves more aggressively toward a secularist point of view, African religious traditions seem countercultural. The African spiritual heritage considers all of reality to be a part of a sacred or mystical drama. This can be seen frequently in the close affinity that African Americans presume between pulpit and government, between minister and political figure, between Church and polling place. Perhaps this is best understood by a community whose first public elected officials were often the ministers of the people. At a time when the best educated and most articulate members were the pastors of the community, this close affinity has endured—even in an environment that seeks to draw wider and clearer distinctions between religious institutions and civic public entities.

African American religious practices invariably exalt in the Word of God. Scripture is paramount in the spiritual traditions that distinguish black Church customs. Traditional black preaching is an art form, a source of moral guidance, and a living spiritual drama. The proclamation of the Word of God and its compelling exposition in the sermon have long been recognized as highpoints of the black Church. And while the Catholic Church's liturgy is the intimate and inextricable union of the celebration of Word and Sacrament, the spirit and vitality of traditional black preaching offers a model and an incentive to inspire our own preaching without disintegrating into banal artificiality or insulting charade. *Plenty Good Room* does not call for the style of black preachers to become the archetype in Catholic worship, but the energy, the passion, and the inspiration that any vibrant and eloquent preaching offers to the assembly should become a touchstone for improving every preacher's skill.

African American spiritual songs are closely related to the Word of God. Many of them employ paraphrases of scriptural texts or make liberal use of the biblical images that flow from Sacred Scripture. They often reflect an intimate union between the Word of God and the human condition in which people of color have found themselves. Nonetheless, Catholic ritual traditions call for the use of music that corresponds to the ritual action of the liturgy. Catholic service music is integral to the celebration of the liturgy and thus not every song fits well into Catholic ritual—even songs that are scripturally inspired. Mass texts are established as specific to the celebration of the liturgy and cannot be substituted even with songs that are clearly biblical in origin. Nonetheless, there are opportunities within the celebration of the Church's rituals that allow for music that underscores the union and complementarity of the Word of God and the sacramental action being celebrated. The treasury of African American religious music provides many examples that can be and have been effectively included within Catholic liturgy. The recently published second edition of the hymnal *Lead Me, Guide Me*[4] provides a very helpful anthology of musical selections and also serves as a resource for adapting African American spiritual music to Catholic ritual in conformity to the newly issued English language Roman Missal.

Plenty Good Room addresses two communities—first, the African American community that even today continues to discover the many rich components within our heritage that for too long went unexplored and undervalued. These cultural treasures were frequently dismissed by many people—both black and white—because of the negative impact of slavery and racism and too often were not even considered worthy of study and examination. Thus, the document invites African American Catholics to unearth many of the elements of our African heritage and to take pride in that discovery. The other audience is the larger Catholic community itself that also seeks to encounter the spiritual gifts of the sons and daughters of African ancestry and to welcome those treasures as the Church has welcomed the cultural gifts of others throughout the entire history of Catholicism. Both audiences will find ample material upon which to reflect in this fine, pioneering resource.

The closing section of *Plenty Good Room* includes some suggestions and recommendations about where elements of the African American spiritual heritage might be used as part of the celebration of the Sunday Eucharist. These observations are now twenty years old and need to be viewed in light of the recently published English language Roman Missal as well as from the vantage point of the events and changes that have taken place during the intervening years. Some of these recommendations have been in place in many different parishes for almost a generation and others have extended to parishes that may or may not have a predominately African American community. Some of them are practical and others may not appear to be exclusively the tradition of any particular community. Almost every Catholic parish now has a welcoming opening comment before the Mass begins that asks people to acknowledge their neighbors (some more expressively than others), turn off all cell phones and electronic devices, and place themselves in the mood and spiritual state to praise God together. When *Plenty Good Room* made such a suggestion more than twenty years ago, it might have seemed novel, but now it is routine for most parishes. The intent of such welcoming comments was to highlight the need

---

4. *Lead Me, Guide Me*, Second Edition, ed., Robert J. Batastini. Chicago, Illinois: GIA Publications, Inc., 2012.

for a spirit of hospitality that has long held an important place in African American Church traditions. Now such expressions of welcome and cordiality are widely present in most parish communities well beyond Catholicism and even the black Church. In keeping with the tradition of hospitality so important to black Church practices, *Plenty Good Room* suggests that parishes might welcome those who are present as guests or first time visitors—perhaps at the time of the parish announcements. Here again, many Catholic communities publicly acknowledge the presence of visitors and extend to them a warm invitation to make the parish their church home or to come back again. These gestures of hospitality have enriched not only black Catholic parishes, but parishes in general who have found such gestures not only effective in strengthening the spirit of community but even as a means of responding to the Church's call to promote a new evangelization of the society in general.

Sunday Mass is the ordinary moment when most Catholics experience the Church's liturgy. It is the touchstone of most of our parishes where the majority of the assembly gathers for worship and pastoral life. African American parishes, like all other Catholic parishes, have experienced a diminution in the numbers of people who attend Sunday Mass regularly. Pastors serving in predominately black parishes like all others must explore ways to welcome and then to retain parishioners at this vitally important ecclesial moment. Sunday Mass should be the very heart of the Church week and all Catholics must be invited to a renewal of the value of this shared time together in prayer. Even after more than two decades, *Plenty Good Room* offers helpful insights into achieving that end.

PLENTY GOOD ROOM
Refrain
There's plenty good room,
plenty good room,
plenty good room in ma Father's kingdom,
Plenty good room,
plenty good room,
just choose your seat and sit down.

Verse 1
I would not be a sinner,
I'll tell you the reason why;
I'm afraid my Lord might call on me,
and I wouldn't be ready to die.

Verse 2
I would not be a liar,
I'll tell you the reason why;
I'm afraid my Lord might call on me,
and I wouldn't be ready to die.

Verse 3
I would not be a cheater,
I'll tell you the reason why;
I'm afraid my Lord might call on me,
And I wouldn't be ready to die.

OUTLINE

PLENTY GOOD ROOM: THE SPIRIT AND TRUTH OF AFRICAN AMERICAN CATHOLIC WORSHIP

I. LITURGY AND SYMBOLIC REALITY

You awake us to delight in your praise, for you have made us for yourself, and our heart is restless until it rests in you.[1]

A. AN EXAMINATION OF RITUAL

1.   Public worship, rooted in humanity's response to God's self-revelation, is a rich and complex reality. Although every people attempts to convey its awareness of absolute mystery, dread, awe, wonder, and love in its experience of the holy, ultimately, there are no adequate words for this ineffable mystery. The experience nonetheless is real, and it leads to a profound sense of total dependence, of utter creaturehood in the presence of the Creator. This experience of the absolute majesty of God, the One who dwells in unapproachable light, who is the source of life and goodness, is tempered by the equally powerful sense of the fascinating nearness and familiarity of God, who created all things and fills them with every blessing.[2]

> For without God all of our efforts turn to ashes and our sunrises into darkest nights. Without God, life is a meaningless drama with the decisive scenes missing. But with God we are able to rise from the fatigue of despair to the buoyancy of hope. With God we are able to rise from the midnight of desperation to the daybreak of joy. Saint Augustine was right—we were made for God and we will be restless until we find rest in God.[3]

This is uniquely true in the Christian tradition, because in Jesus Christ the mystery of the divine and of the human are both made manifest.[4] For by his dying and rising, "Jesus revealed the human face of God and transformed the face of humanity."[5] He is, as Saint Paul says, an unshakable "Yes" both to God and to us (see 2 Corinthians 1:18–22).

2.   Liturgy celebrates and evokes that divine reality that is at once remote and intimate, transcendent and immanent, beyond our reach and ever present. As a

---

1. Saint Augustine, *Confessions* 1, i, 1.

2. Cf. Eucharistic Prayer IV; Psalms 145:16 and 136:25.

3. Coretta Scott King, ed., *The Words of Martin Luther King, Jr.* (New York: Newmarket Press, 1987), p. 64.

4. Cf. Joseph Gelineau, SJ, *Liturgy: Today and Tomorrow* (New York: Paulist Press, 1978).

5. Gilbert Ostdiek, OFM, *Catechesis for Liturgy* (Washington, DC: The Pastoral Press, 1986), p. 50.

result, liturgy has an undeniable density and complexity even when worshipers and religious leaders themselves do not advert to it.[6] Liturgy evokes a world that is at once shared with others and is at the same time beyond ordinary life. To borrow the words of Howard Thurman, liturgy "bathes one's whole being with something more wonderful than words can ever tell."[7]

B. SYMBOLS

3.   Precisely because liturgy is concerned with realities of faith that go beyond immediate experience, it celebrates mystery by means of symbols and signs.[8] Liturgical activity, therefore, is not principally concerned about directly producing effects in the world as it is, except insofar as they relate to the coming of God's reign. Thus, in ritual activity, the faithful do not eat and drink only to feed their bodies. They do not sing only to make music. They do not speak only to teach and to learn. They do not pray only to restore psychic equilibrium. By using space, time, action, and speech in a new way, worship turns the attention of the assembly toward realities that would otherwise go unattended.[9] Worship lifts people up and moves them into the soul-stirring, the awe-inspiring, the transcendent, and the inciting[10] so that, ultimately, they may worship in spirit and truth (cf. John 4:24), so that they may not honor Christ in worship clothed in silk vestments, only to pass him by unclothed and frozen outside.[11]

4.   Since liturgy is possible only by reason of humanity's intrinsic symbol-making genius, and because of the depth and complexity of both humanity and its symbols, it is possible for our symbols to be misused and misunderstood in the Sunday liturgy.

5.   First, one cannot arbitrarily make or establish symbols. Symbols are not merely things. Certain realities become symbolic in particular circumstances and only in relation to a human community. In and of themselves bread, wine, water, oil, fire, incense, a cross, a fish, a white robe, an organ melody, a purple cloth, a paragraph from Scripture may not be symbolic. They become symbolic because of their resonating with the members of a given historical, cultural, ethnic, and racial community. They can assume levels of meaning that make sense of birth, life, and death—by means of tradition, community, and grace.[12]

6.   Second, symbols are not to be confused with signs. Signs have conventional meanings established by the community. The purpose of a sign is clear and

---

6. Cf. Mercea Eliade, *The Sacred and the Profane* (New York: Harper Torchbook, 1959).

7. Howard Thurman, *The Growing Edge* (Richmond, Indiana: Friends United Press, 1956), p. 117.

8. For an extensive explanation of symbol, see Edward K. Braxton, "Reflections from a Theological Perspective," *This Far by Faith: American Black Catholic Worship and Its African Roots* (Washington, DC: The Liturgical Conference, 1977).

9. Cf. *Catechesis for Liturgy.*

10. Cf. Sean Swayne, *Gather Around the Lord: A Vision for Renewal of the Sunday Eucharist* (Dublin: The Columba Press, 1987), pp. 32–36.

11. Cf. Saint John Chrysostom, *Homilies on the Gospel of Matthew,* Matthew 14:23–24, no. 50, para. 3–4.

12. Cf. Paul Ricoeur, *The Symbolism of Evil* (Boston: Beacon Press, 1967).

unambiguous (e.g., a red light means stop, and only stop; a green light means go, and only go). They are signs. There is no ambiguity. This is not the case with symbols. Symbols are necessarily ambiguous, that is, they evoke multiple meanings and associations. Water, for example, is a primal symbol. For different people, in different circumstances, a body of water may evoke very diverse symbolic associations: coolness, calm, life, storm, danger, drowning, flood, death. For this reason, symbols cannot be strictly controlled in an effort to manage and predict exactly what associations and feelings people will have in their presence.[13]

7.   This is why people can participate in the same celebration of the Eucharist on Sunday and find different meanings in the Scriptures proclaimed, the hymns sung, the preparation of the gifts, the eucharistic prayer, the sign of peace, the sharing in the Body and Blood of the Lord. This is also why people of different ethnic and cultural backgrounds may have different subjective responses to the same objective symbolic activity.

8.   Third, it is inadequate to think of symbols primarily as bearers of knowledge or information. While there is a catechetical and instructional dimension to the liturgy, the Eucharist is not the same as a religion class. It is a serious mistake to judge the impact of symbols by what people explicitly understand by them, and even worse by what they can put into words. Moved by symbols, the faithful often know and understand far more than they can say.

9.   The Second Vatican Council and the postconciliar liturgical instructions of the Church enriched the symbols of the liturgy by restoring to the rites much of their original simplicity and beauty. This restoration emphasized the importance of the participation of the assembly, revised all existing rites, expanded the use of Scripture, and encouraged a greater degree of cultural diversity. As a result, the liturgy should be more understandable to the assembly and should invite the participation of all. Moreover, these enriched symbols have an authentic driving force even when they seem beyond comprehension. A person may be particularly moved by the singing of a certain hymn, by an element in one of the rites of Christian initiation, by the ritualized actions of vested ministers, or by the rich ceremonies of Holy Week without fully understanding them in the cognitive sense. Were they asked, "What do these symbols mean?" they might respond, "I don't know. I didn't even know they were symbols!" This would not imply that they have not experienced meaning in their symbolic activity. They have, for symbols are truly multi-dimensional phenomena.

10.   Again, if people are asked why they are deeply moved by the recitation of a poem by Langston Hughes, a sermon preached by Martin Luther King, Jr., jazz played by Mary Lou Williams, music scored by Lionel Hampton, the blues sung by Ray Charles, an aria performed by Marian Anderson, or a ballet choreographed by Alvin Ailey, they might be able to discourse on aesthetic theory, but they might not be able to say why the work moves them so. The interplay between symbol and person is far more than that of cause and effect. Symbols draw upon the accumulated wisdom and heritage of a people. They combine concepts and

---

13. Cf. *Liturgy: Today and Tomorrow.*

values, while appealing to memory and imagination. They derive much of their power through association with the collective experience and history of a people. Perhaps one of the reasons why some Catholic assemblies do not experience the full depth of their liturgical prayer is that the seeming ordinariness of their lives and daily work in some way separates them from poetic, artistic, and symbolic language. Such a difficulty might suggest a greater catechesis *through* and *for* the liturgy by "attending to what we and others actually experience in liturgy; reflecting on what our experience and that of others means; applying what we have learned to future liturgies."[14]

II. LITURGY AND THE CHRIST EVENT

A. WHO AND WHAT LITURGY CELEBRATES

11.   Liturgy celebrates the landscapes of human experience: happiness, sadness, renewal, and grief. Liturgy provides rites of passage in human life: birth, maturity, vocation, commitment, old age, death. Liturgy also celebrates the universal human need for communion, healing, and reconciliation. Christian liturgy embraces all these and far more by celebrating the new meaning that the life, death, and resurrection of Jesus Christ give to the lives of all people. In the liturgy, the Church proclaims the paschal mystery, the paradigmatic event that transforms the past, the present, and the future. In faith, and in fact, the liturgy is the memorial that joins the worshipers to the past experience of the mystery of Christ that radically changed the lives of his followers and altered the history of the world. It is this memorial that directs worshipers into the future, the "not-yet" of Christ's coming in glory.[15]

12.   In the liturgy, Christ speaks to each person and each community in their lived conditions. Saint Augustine reminds us: "He [Christ] has ascended without leaving us. While in heaven he is also with us, and while on earth we are also with him."[16] In this manner, people are able to unite the drama of their own sufferings with the paschal mystery of the Lord. The liturgy encourages the people of God, nourished by Christ's Body and Blood and filled with his Holy Spirit,[17] to approach the future with hope and trust. Even though this future is unknown, faith guarantees that Christ will be there. This confident hope embraces everyone's personal history as well as the future of the world. Believers realize that their faith in Christ makes them conscious that they must do everything they can to overcome personal problems and world discord, to be a living sacrifice of praise.[18] The liturgy also reminds them that when they have done all they can, they should not despair, because Christ is still with them. Events and experiences that seem random and confusing to them may be a part of a larger, providential design beyond their complete understanding. It is this Christ event that all Catholics celebrate in the liturgy. It is this Christ event without

---

14. *Catechesis for Liturgy*, pp. 13–20.

15. Cf. Braxton, *This Far by Faith*, p. 74.

16. Saint Augustine, *Sermon on the Words of the Gospel*, Luke 7:2, para. 1.

17. Cf. Eucharistic Prayer III; Acts 2:33.

18. Cf. Eucharistic Prayer IV; Romans 12:1, Ephesians 1:14.

which we cannot go on living.[19] It is this Christ event that is the hinge event of history, whose meaning surpasses the limits of time and locality.

B. THE ENCOUNTER WITH CHRIST

13.   In whatever locality he preached, Jesus preached that the reign of God was at hand (see Mark 1:15). Wherever he traveled, Jesus turned people's hearts to God (see Luke 18:42–43). Whenever he proclaimed the Good News, Jesus showed the way to God's prodigal love and mercy (see Luke 15:11–32). Whoever followed him experienced in Jesus the very mystery of God. In him, their longings for a coming High Priest, Prophet, King, Suffering Servant, Savior, and Messiah were all fulfilled. He was the Christ, the Son of the living God (see Matthew 16:13–23). The encounter with Christ changed their lives completely (see Luke 8:1–3). They could never forget the sacred meal that he left them (see 1 Corinthians 11:23–26), the meal that kept the memory of the Passover of the Lord but which they would now eat in memory of the Lord's dying and rising "until he comes" (see 1 Corinthians 11:26).[20] They experienced the devastation of his death (see Matthew 27:45–66) and the joyous reality of his resurrection (see John 20:1–21, 25). These experiences drew them deeper into the mystery of God. They preserved and passed onto others the meaning and truth of their encounter with Christ by means of oral and written accounts, by creeds, and most important, by liturgical symbols and rites (see Acts 2:42). These symbols and rites have been continually adapted, depending upon the varying cultures encountered. The goal of the adaptations has always been to intensify the experience of the mystery of Christ and God's saving power for all peoples—even to the very ends of the earth (see Matthew 28:16–20).

III. LITURGY AND CULTURE

A. THE ENCOUNTER WITH CHRIST CONTINUED: CULTURAL ADAPTATION OF THE LITURGY THROUGHOUT HISTORY

14.   From the beginning, in order to recall and relive the experience of Christ in their midst, the Church, at Jesus' command and under the guidance of the Holy Spirit, engaged and transformed many Jewish rituals, symbols, gestures, and customs beloved by Jesus and his original disciples.

15.   In this early and fertile Jewish period (c. 33 to c. 100), the Church harvested not only many followers but also words and phrases such as: *alleluia; amen;* "holy, holy, holy"; "it is right and just to give thanks and praise"; and "let us pray." It likewise gave a Christian meaning to the essential structure of the Eucharistic Prayer, intercessory prayer, and the liturgy of the word; baptismal

---

19. Cf. *Gather Around the Lord*, pp. 12–20.

20. Anscar J. Chupungco, OSB, *Cultural Adaptation of the Liturgy* (New York: Paulist Press, 1982), p. 7.

rites, devotion to the saints, and laying on of hands; and designation of Sunday as the weekly day of worship.[21]

16.   As the Church grew, it continued its mission to the very ends of the earth. It encountered and labored among both the Hellenistic and Roman worlds. From this period (c. 100 and c. 321), the Church acquired the wisdom of Justin Martyr, Clement of Alexandria, Tertullian, Hippolytus and other learned doctors; words and phrases such as: *acclamation; advent; agape; anamnesis; canon; epiclesis; epiphany; eucharist; eulogy; Lord, have mercy; mystery;* and *preface;* the concepts of formulary prayer, sacrament, and silence; the rites of anointing, exorcism; the Church calendar;[22] and the *domus ecclesiae* (house of the Church), which was complete with an atrium where the assembly gathered, a large tank of water where the initiates could be baptized, and a table where the leader presided—all of which became the model space for the assembly's worship.[23]

17.   With the peace established between Constantine and the Church in 313 with the Edict of Milan, the Church gained not only official recognition but also the new and free ideas of those such as Cyril of Jerusalem, Ambrose of Milan, John Chrysostom, and Augustine of Hippo; the concepts of mystagogy and of facing the East during prayer—prayer that was prayed through Christ, with Christ, and in Christ;[24] the continuing development of the Roman and Oriental Rites, baptismal candles, the washing of feet at baptism, and white baptismal garments; imperial court ceremonials; high esteem for the bishop and his office; liturgical vesture and ornaments, especially the pallium and ring; kissing the altar; and the establishment of the solemnity of Christmas—a prime example of cultural adaptation.[25]

18.   As the Church continued to develop, it heralded the Good News of the Christ-event to countless others. In the process of this proclamation, the Church became incarnate in new and varying cultures. From the Franco-Germanic period

---

21. Theodor Klauser, *A Short History of the Western Liturgy* (Oxford: Oxford University Press, 1979), pp. 4–7.

22. Cf. ibid., p. 7.

23. Cf. *Cultural Adaptation of the Liturgy*, p. 11.

24. Cf. *A Short History of the Western Liturgy*, pp. 30–32. This custom of praying through, with, and in Christ is one that is practiced and reaffirmed even to this day:

Christ Jesus, High Priest of the new and eternal covenant, taking human nature, introduced into this earthly exile the hymn that is sung throughout all ages in the halls of heaven. He joins the entire human community to himself, associating it with his own singing of this canticle of divine praise (SC, 83).

Or in short:

Jesus sings the only song that is heard in heaven, those whose voices would be heard must sing along with Christ (Austin Fleming, *Preparing for Liturgy* [Washington, DC: The Pastoral Press, 1985], p. 17).

25. Cf. *Cultural Adaptation of the Liturgy*, pp. 20–22. Father Chupungco provides early definitions of *acculturation* and *inculturation*. Acculturation is "the process whereby cultural elements that are compatible with Roman Liturgy are incorporated into it either as substitutes for or illustrations of ritual elements of the Roman Rite." Inculturation is "the process whereby a pre-Christian rite is permanently given a Christian meaning" (ibid., pp. 81–86). In a later work *Liturgies of the Future: The Process and Methods of Inculturation* (Mahwah, NJ: Paulist Press, 1989), Father Chupungco further develops these definitions.

(c. 590 to c. 1073), the Church renewed its liturgical life and added to it by the families of sacramentaries attributed to Leo the Great, Gelasius, and Gregory the Great; the lyrics of the "Veni Creator" and "Victimae Paschali"; devotion to the saints, liturgical drama, and verbal flourishes in prayer; the procession with palms on Palm Sunday, footwashing on Holy Thursday, the veneration of the cross on Good Friday; the blessing of the new fire, the greeting of the Light of Christ, the "Exultet," the blessing of the baptismal water at the Easter Vigil; Romanesque churches and their rites of dedication.[26] Simultaneously, from the East the Church reaped the bounty of the greatness of Cyril and Methodius in their adapting the Byzantine liturgy to the culture and language of the Slavic peoples.[27] All this activity served as powerful testimony to Saint Peter's early admonition: "In truth, I see that God shows no partiality. Rather, in every nation whoever fears him and acts uprightly is acceptable to him" (Acts 10:34–35).[28]

19.   With the passage of time, the Church continued to grow even further and farther and reached the very limits of the known world. Having converged with the world's manifold cultures and having adapted worthily to them, the Church regrettably, as Anscar Chupungco has stated, entered upon a period of "luxuriant growth in which the liturgy was both reinterpreted and misinterpreted."[29] The first chill in the midwinter of the Church's liturgical adaptation was felt in the political policies of Saint Pope Gregory VII (c. 1021–1085); the unification of the Western liturgies through the agency of mendicant preachers; elaborate liturgical plays, with actors supplanting the solemn liturgical actions of the assembly; the multiplication of Masses, with the attendant diminution of the liturgical ministries coupled with an exaggerated piety toward the Eucharist apart from the eucharistic action and the reception of Holy Communion; and all this to the increased accompaniment of sacring-bells and the song of paid chantry clerks.[30] Of this age, Walter Howard Frere writes:

> Equally unfortunate was the effect on persons. The Mass-priest became dominant. Now, so long as he had a serving boy, he could dispense with deacon and other ministers; he could supersede the congregation also. With the disappearance of the sense of sacrifice there disappeared also not only the layman's communion but also the sense of his lay-priesthood. The ideal

---

26. Cf. ibid., pp. 27–29.

27. Cf. Joseph P. Fitzpatrick, SJ, *One Culture Many Cultures: Challenge of Diversity* (Kansas City, MO: Sheed and Ward, 1987), pp. 54–61.

28. Pope Gregory the Great addressed a similar theme in his letter to Augustine of Canterbury: "You, brother, know the usage of the Roman Church in which you were brought up: hold it very much in affection. But as far as I am concerned, if you have found something more pleasing to Almighty God, either in the Frankish or in any other Church, make a careful choice and institute in the Church of the English—which as yet is new to the faith—the best usages which you have gathered together from many Churches. For we should love things not because of the places where they are found, but places because of the good things they contain. Therefore choose from each particular Church what is godly, religious and sound, and gathering all together as it were into a dish, place it on the table of the English for their customary diet" (*Cultural Adaptation of the Liturgy*, p. 26).

29. *A Short History of the Western Liturgy*, p. 2.

30. Cf. David A. Novak, "A Brief History of the Eucharist," Address to Eucharistic Ministers in the Diocese of Cleveland (November 12, 1989).

layman was the boy who would serve the priest's Mass. Drill superseded worship and the Mass was commercialized. The hour of Low Mass arrived; and the hour of revulsion drew on.[31]

20.   Because of the aforementioned factors, and out of the rapid expansion and sometimes unregulated practices of the Middle Ages, there arose a call for strict uniformity. A heightened rubrical approach followed the Council of Trent, whose principal aim was to curb abuses and institute reforms, not to introduce new adaptations. With the reform of the Roman Misal by Saint Pius V in 1570 and the establishment of the Sacred Congregation of Rites by Sixtus V in 1588, the centralizing effort of Trent was realized, free development of the liturgy in local churches was greatly curtailed, and the cultural accommodation of liturgy came to a virtual standstill.[32] One need only examine the Chinese Rites controversy to see how creative and daring adaptations of the faith and its practices to the Chinese Confucian culture of the sixteenth and seventeenth centuries came into direct conflict with the Church's desire for unification.[33] Liturgical creativity took avenues other than the Mass: devotion to the Blessed Sacrament, which gave rise to the use of tabernacles, sanctuary lights, elevations, exposition, and benediction.[34]

21.   In reaction to this period of strict uniformity and its consequent alienation of the assembly came the Age of the Baroque with its "flair for festivity, external manifestations of grandeur and triumphalism, especially through pilgrimages and processions, and sensuousness in artistic expression and pious devotions."[35]

22.   In time, some protested the inflexibility of the state of the liturgical life of the post-Tridentine Church as well as the externalism of the Baroque. With this protest developed the advent of Romanticism and its subsequent stress on history. The Church began to reexamine the origins and meaning of liturgical gestures, vestments, vessels, rites, and feasts.

23.   From the nineteenth century onward came renowned liturgists such as Prosper Gueranger, Virgil Michel, Odo Casel, Pius Parsch, Lambert Beauduin, and Romano Guardini; and the great liturgical centers at Solesmes, Beuron, Maredsous, Maria Laach, and Malines.[36] These scholars and outstanding centers of renewed liturgical life provided the foundation of the Liturgical Movement of the early 1900s, which culminated in Pius XII's encyclical on the sacred liturgy, *Mediator Dei*, in 1947; the reformation of the Holy Week Rites in 1955; and finally, the magna carta of contemporary liturgical renewal, the *Constitution on the Sacred Liturgy* of the Second Vatican Council, which was promulgated by Paul VI on December 4, 1963.[37]

---

31. Walter Howard Frere, *The Anaphora or Great Eucharistic Prayer* (London: SPCK Press, 1938), p. 138.
32. Cf. *A Short History of the Western Liturgy*, pp. 117–123.
33. Cf. *One Culture Many Cultures*, pp. 61–91.
34. Cf. *A Short History of the Western Liturgy*, pp. 135–140.
35. *Cultural Adaptation of the Liturgy*, p. 34.
36. Cf. *A Short History of the Western Liturgy*, p. 122.
37. Cf. *Cultural Adaptation of the Liturgy*, pp. 37–38.

B. CULTURAL ADAPTATION AND THE SECOND VATICAN COUNCIL

24. Throughout much of its history, the Church was firmly committed to cultural adaptation in public worship for the good of the people of God. The same is true of the Church today. The *Constitution on the Liturgy*, the principal guide for the pastoral adaptation of the liturgy, reminds us of the communal and unifying nature of the liturgy:

> Liturgical services are not private functions, but are celebrations belonging to the Church, which is the "sacrament of unity," namely, the holy people united and ordered under their bishops.[38]

Yet, recognizing the diversity of Christian communities, the missionary nature of the Church, and the exigencies of evangelization, the Church teaches that liturgical rites may be adapted to the temperaments and traditions of different ethnic, language, cultural, and racial groups. With due respect for the common good and unity of faith, the Church does not wish to impart a rigid uniformity upon liturgical expression. Rather, when local customs are free of superstition and error, they may be admitted into the liturgy "provided they are in keeping with the true and authentic spirit of the liturgy."[39]

25. While clearly calling for the safeguarding of the substantial unity of the Roman Rite, the Church insists that there be legitimate variations and adaptations to different groups, regions, and peoples in drawing up rites, determining rubrics, and revising liturgical books. This is particularly important in areas where the Church is still very young or very small.[40] Therefore, within the limits specified by the liturgical books themselves, specific adaptations may be made in the style of celebrating the sacraments, sacramentals, processions, liturgical language, music, and art by competent territorial ecclesiastical authority.[41]

26. Because the bishops of the Second Vatican Council, assembled from all over the world, were quite aware of the racial, cultural, and spiritual differences of the people of their local churches and the millions of people yet to hear or respond to the gospel of Christ, they provided for "even more radical adaptations." Such adaptations are always to be guided by the following considerations:

> a) The competent, territorial ecclesiastical authority mentioned in art. 22, par. 2, must, in this matter, carefully, and prudently weigh what elements from the traditions and culture of individual peoples may be appropriately admitted into divine worship. They are to propose to the Apostolic See adaptations considered useful or necessary that will be introduced with its consent.

> b) To ensure that adaptations are made with all the circumspection they demand, the Apostolic See will grant power to this same territorial ecclesiastical authority to permit and to direct, as the case requires, the

---

38. SC, 26.
39. SC, 37.
40. Cf. SC, 38.
41. Cf. SC, 39.

necessary preliminary experiments within certain groups suited for the purpose and for a fixed time.

c) Because liturgical laws often involve special difficulties with respect to adaptation, particularly in mission lands,[42] experts in these matters must be employed to formulate them.[43]

27.   The Church further recognized that there is a necessary connection between liturgical adaptations and ongoing catechesis. The *Constitution on the Liturgy* expressed well the Church's desire to ensure that no one in the Church feel estranged or alienated, but that those who are invited to the feast may be able to participate fully:

> The Church, therefore, earnestly desires that Christ's faithful, when present at this mystery of faith, should not be there as strangers or silent spectators; on the contrary, through a good understanding of the rites and prayers they should take part in the sacred service conscious of what they are doing, with devotion and full involvement. They should be instructed by God's word and be nourished at the table of the Lord's body; they should give thanks to God; by offering the immaculate Victim, not only through the hands of the priest, but also with him, they should learn to offer themselves as well; through Christ the Mediator, they should be formed day by day into an ever more perfect unity with God and with each other, so that finally God may be all in all.[44]

28.   In its continuing implementation of the reforms initiated by the Second Vatican Council, the Church has spoken still further on the direct connection between liturgical adaptation and evangelization:

> In the work of evangelization the liturgy clearly holds a place of primary importance: it stands as a high point at which the preached mystery of salvation becomes actual; pastorally it offers to evangelization privileged occasions and a sound and effective formation. . . . The intimate union between evangelization and liturgy also gives rise to the duty of renewing the liturgical celebration; this will unfailingly have a strong impact on the life of the Church.[45]

---

42. ". . . 'Missions' is the name generally given to those special endeavors by which heralds of the Gospel sent by the Church and going out into the whole world fulfill the office of preaching the Gospel and of implanting the Church among peoples or groups not yet believing in Christ" (AG, 6). According to this definition, would not "unchurched" African Americans be considered a valid mission?

43. SC, 40.

44. SC, 48.

45. Secretariat of State, "Letter of Cardinal Jean Villot to Bishop R. Alberti, President of the Department of Liturgy of CELAM," On the Occasion of the Second Latin American Meeting on the Liturgy (Caracas, July 12–14, 1977), *Notitiae* 13 (1977): 459–467.

IV. LITURGICAL ADAPTATION IN THE AFRICAN AMERICAN COMMUNITY

A. THE CALL

29.   The aforementioned summary statements about liturgical uniformity, diversity, catechesis, and evangelization should make it clear that the Church is sincerely and fundamentally committed to translating its liturgical rites to the many voices of various people, creating, it is hoped, one song of praise.

30.   Nowhere is this commitment more profoundly expressed than in Paul VI's speech to the young churches in Africa:

> The expression, that is, the language and mode of manifesting this one faith, may be manifold; hence, it may be original, suited to the tongue, the style, the character, the genius and the culture of one who professes this one faith. From this point of view, a certain pluralism is not only legitimate, but desirable. An adaptation of the Christian life in the fields of pastoral, ritual, didactic and spiritual activities is not only possible, it is even favored by the Church. The liturgical renewal is a living example of this. And in this sense you may, and you must, have an African Christianity. Indeed you possess human values and characteristic forms of culture which rise up to perfection such as to find in Christianity and for Christianity a true superior fullness and prove to be capable of a richness of expression all its own, and genuinely African. . . . You will be capable of bringing to the Catholic Church the precious and original contribution of "Blackness" which she particularly needs in this historic hour.[46]

31.   What Paul VI asked of Africans for the universal Church, the Church in the United States asks of its African American daughters and sons—the gift of "Blackness," a gift so intensely expressive and so alive that it comes from the very depths of the Black soul, a gift not just to improve the work of evangelization but to further the very Catholic nature that is the Church's.[47]

32.   The Catholic Church indeed welcomes the genius and talents of African Americans. Witness but a few of the many recent signs of growth and vitality of the Church in that community:

- *Discrimination and Christian Conscience* (1958); *On Racial Harmony* (1963); *A Statement on the National Race Crisis* (1968); *Brothers and Sisters to Us* (1979)[48]—challenging statements and pastoral letters of the

---

46. Paul VI, "Address at the Closing of the Symposium of African Bishops Given at Kampala," Excerpt on the Liturgy and Different Cultures, (July 31, 1969), AAS 61 (1969): 573–578.

47. Cf. Clarence Joseph Rivers on the definition of "soul" in *Soulfull Worship* (Washington, DC: National Office for Black Catholics, 1974), p. 14.

48. These statements and pastoral letters are contained in the four-volume *Pastoral Letters of the United States Bishops, 1792–1983* (Washington DC: USCC Office for Publishing and Promotion Services, 1984).

National Conference of Catholic Bishops condemning the sin of racism and calling for a commitment to eradicate it;

- the ordination of our African American brothers to the episcopacy and the issuing of *What We Have Seen and Heard*,[49] their illustrative pastoral letter on the nature of evangelization in the African American community;

- the clear inclusion of African American leaders at all levels of church government;

- the establishment of diocesan offices of ministry to the African American community;

- the creation of a Secretariat for Black Catholics at the National Conference of Catholic Bishops;

- the Sixth National Black Catholic Congress, its subsequent compelling Pastoral Plan, and its continuing conferences and workshops to assist those who minister in the African American community;

- the introduction and publication of *Lead Me, Guide Me* (GIA Publications, Inc., 1987), the first African American Catholic hymnal, and *In Spirit and Truth: Black Catholic Reflections on the Order of Mass* (USCC, 1987);

- the secure foundation of quality liturgical programs throughout the United States for African Americans;

- a host of diocesan-wide revivals and festive celebrations commemorating Dr. Martin Luther King, Jr. and Black History Month;

- the ever-increasing creation of African American choirs to employ the wide range of the African American musical heritage; and

- John Paul II's spirited meeting with representatives of the African American Catholic community in New Orleans during his 1987 pastoral visit, where he stated:

While remaining faithful to her doctrine and discipline, the Church esteems and honors all cultures; she respects them in all her evangelizing efforts among the various peoples. At the first Pentecost, those present heard the apostles speaking in their own languages (cf. Acts 2:4ff.). With the guidance of the Holy Spirit, we try in every age to bring the gospel convincingly and understandably to people of all races, languages, and cultures. It is important to realize that there is no black Church, no white Church, no American Church; but there is and must be, in the one Church of Jesus Christ, a home for blacks, whites, Americans, every culture and race. What I said on another occasion, I willingly repeat: "The Church is catholic . . . because she is able to present in every

---

49. Jospeh L. Howze, et al., *What We Have Seen and Heard: A Pastoral Letter on Evangelization from the Black Bishops of the United States* [= WWHSH] (Cincinnati: St. Anthony Messenger Press, 1984).

human context the revealed truth, preserved by her intact in its divine content, in such a way as to bring it into contact with the lofty thoughts and just expectations of every individual and every people." (*Slavorum Apostoli*, 18).

Dear brothers and sisters, your black cultural heritage enriches the Church and makes her witness of universality more complete. In a real way the Church needs you, just as much as you need the Church, for you are part of the Church and the Church is part of you. . . .[50]

33.   The Church's commitment to and call for liturgical adaptation are clear. The Church's commitment to and call for liturgical adaptation in the African American community are clear and unequivocal. Yet, the continuation of the task at hand is involved and complex.

B. THE EARLY YEARS OF THE CHURCH IN THE UNITED STATES: A DOMINANCE OF WESTERN CULTURE THROUGH MISSIONARY ACTIVITY

34.   Sadly, many Americans, even a number of African American Catholics, perceive and experience the Catholic Church in the United States as an exclusively white European reality. This is due in part to the centuries-old Catholic tradition associated with countries like Italy, France, Spain, Germany, Poland, and Ireland and with the great missionaries of the Church who were noted for having brought the faith from these Christian countries to peoples of distant lands.

35.   In the United States, Catholicism was introduced primarily through the colonizing vigor of the Spanish, French, and English.[51]

36.   Inspired by the drive to announce the reign of God to Native Americans and European settlers, Franciscans, Dominicans, Jesuits, and Sulpicians evangelized Florida, the Southwest, Texas, California, Canada, the Great Lakes region, Maryland, Pennsylvania, and New York.

37.   During this Spanish, French, and English missionary activity, Catholicism was so intimately wed to the culture of the missionaries that, doubtless, many of them could not easily distinguish the Gospel that they preached from their own particular cultural expression of it. As a result, because of its links to Europe and its history, the Church in America, like most American institutions, tended to assume that European cultures were the only cultures and found it extremely difficult to imagine, much less value, cultures other than their own.

38.   Happily, for the better part of this century, there has been a gradual change in the understanding of human experience and human perception, particularly

---

50. "Meeting with Black Catholic Leadership," *Unity in the Work of Service*, p. 55.
51. Cf. John Tracy Ellis, *American Catholicism* (Chicago: The University of Chicago Press, 1956), pp. 1–39; Dennis R. Clark, *Our Catholic Roots* (New York: Sadlier-Oxford, 1988), pp. 2–27.

by those who are expert observers and evaluators of culture. There is a greater awareness that European cultures are not normative.

39. As long as Europe was recognized as the "center of gravity," many people perceived European cultures as the norm, as the only "real" cultures. In scholarly circles and in common parlance, these cultures came to be called "classical." They were viewed as a distillation of the great achievements of ancient Greek philosophy, Roman political systems, and Western European philosophy, art, music, architecture, and social values. And they were viewed as universal, providing the normative understanding of the human condition, the nature of religion, and the social order. For generations, these "classical" cultures held sway, and in some quarters they continue to hold sway even today as the only authentic expressions of culture. Consequently, the mores, customs, traditions, folkways, rituals, and symbols of people who are not European were rarely, if ever, considered expressions of culture, especially as these people were viewed as "primitive," "barbaric," and "uncivilized." Recent evidence for this can be found, for example, in the way Native, African, and Asian American peoples were portrayed in American film and television from the 1930s until the late 1960s and in the fact that the art and artifacts of Africa have only recently been deemed truly worthy of a place in American and European art museums.

C. CONTEMPORARY UNDERSTANDING OF CULTURE

40. Fortunately, contemporary understanding of culture is quite different. In the contemporary view, no one culture is normative, and all races and ethnic groups are to be taken seriously. Indeed, all peoples have customs, mores, artistic expressions, and traditions that constitute genuine culture. Furthermore, this contemporary view of culture has a historical perspective. It accepts and embraces diversity and pluralism in a manner that the "classical" cultures never could. European "classical" culture is accepted as one among many expressions of culture.

41. For centuries, the Church shaped and influenced European cultures in an intimate way, and, most assuredly, European cultures had an equal impact on the Church. The necessary process of ridding what is obsolete in this "classical" view of culture and assimilating what is of value in the contemporary view of culture is painstakingly difficult. Nevertheless, it is just such a process that is essential in promoting liturgical adaptation in the African American community.

42. The fact that the Church is renewing its recognition of and warmly embracing a plurality of cultures does not mean that it must abandon the rich liturgical and aesthetic traditions developed in Europe.[52] What must happen, and indeed what is already happening, is that the Church welcomes and strongly encourages the equally rich and diverse traditions of all peoples in every time and in every place.

---

52. For a discussion of the relationship between religion and culture see Bernard J. F. Lonergan, SJ, *Method in Theology* (New York: Herder and Herder, 1972).

V. THE AFRICAN AMERICAN RELIGIOUS EXPERIENCE IN THE UNITED STATES

A. A VARIED PEOPLE

43.   Before all else, and in order better to understand Roman Catholic worship in the African American community, it must first be stated that the African American community is not monolithic. Even the term "African American" is not universally used. Many people prefer other descriptions, such as "Negro," "African," "Afro-American," "Black," or simply "people of color." Still others think of themselves only as human beings. Race, for them, is a secondary reality that merits neither discrimination nor special treatment.

44.   African Americans live, work, study, and recreate in a wide variety of social settings. There is indeed a great diversity in nations of origin, socioeconomic status, religious and political persuasions, historical backgrounds, and life-styles. Strictly speaking, African American enslavement was not the universal experience of all "African" people in the United States. Yet, while slavery was not an experience common to all African Americans, racism, which has been part of the social fabric of America since its European colonization and which persists still today in many blatant and covert ways, was.

45.   Some African Americans do not wish to be thought of as "African American Catholics." Rather, they simply regard themselves as Catholics. They may cherish the Gregorian *Missa Orbis Factor* or may relish singing traditional hymns and contemporary songs as much as their white counterparts. These traditional Black Catholics should not be treated as "odd, misinformed, or pitiable souls," but they must be respected, for all Catholics are indeed our brothers and sisters in the faith. They, along with many other Catholics, may also need to be reminded that, some twenty-five years after the Second Vatican Council, reform and renewal of the liturgy are at the very heart of the Church's life and mission today. Others, unfortunately, may have to be persuaded to overcome in themselves any subtle forms of self-hatred that is an unsightly fragment of years of sustained racism.

46.   Despite this diversity, the vast majority of African American Catholics, both convert and "cradle Catholic," upper middle-class and poor, would attest with their African American brothers in the episcopacy that

> There is a richness in our Black experience that we must share with the entire people of God. These are gifts that are part of an African past. For we have heard with Black ears and have seen with Black eyes and we have understood with an African heart. We thank God for the gifts of our Catholic faith and we give thanks for the gifts of our Blackness. In all humility we turn to the whole Church that it might share our gifts so that "our joy may be complete."

> To be Catholic is to be universal. To be universal is not to be uniform. It does mean, however, that the gifts of individuals and of particular groups become the common heritage shared by all. Just as we lay claim to the gifts

of Blackness, so we share these gifts within the Black community at large and within the Church. This will be our part in the building up of the whole Church. This will also be our way of enriching ourselves. "For it is in giving that we receive." Finally, it is our way to witness to our brothers and sisters within the Black community that the Catholic Church is both one and also home to us all.[53]

B. THE BROADER CONTEXT

47.   African American religious experience is shaped by African factors as well as by those on these shores. To begin with, several key concepts should be noted:

- that religion is an all-pervasive reality for African peoples;[54]
- that a sense of the holy encompasses the whole mystery of life, beginning before birth and continuing after death;[55]
- that for most Africans, to live is to participate in a religious drama;[56] and
- that African people see themselves as totally immersed in a sacred cosmos.[57]

This was the religious cultural matrix of many African Americans who accepted Christianity in this country.

48.   Although current evidence seems to suggest that those Africans who were enslaved here were not brought from African territories where Christianity may have existed, we must nevertheless remember that Christianity was indeed no stranger to African cultures. Actually, Christianity had been well established in much of North Africa, parts of the Sudan, Egypt, and Ethiopia. This was a dynamic Christianity, one that produced great scholars and theologians like Clement of Alexandria, Tertullian, Origen, Cyprian of Carthage, Augustine of Hippo, and Pope Gelasius. Ethiopia was evangelized in the fourth century by Saint Frumentius, whom Saint Athanasius selected to be bishop. In the sixth century, the Emperor Justinian and the Empress Theodora, respectively, sent two groups of missionaries to evangelize Nubia (modern-day Sudan). Until Islamic armies conquered the area in the seventh century, many North Africans made significant contributions to the Church. The Moslem conquest reduced the Church in North Africa to a mere remnant, and by the year 1000 much of North Africa's Church was extinct.

49.   Once in the United States, enslaved Africans had some contact with the Catholic Church in those areas where Catholics were numerous. In other areas where the slave holders were Protestant, they had little, if any, initial contact with the Catholic Church. These enslaved people responded most favorably, however, to the evangelizing efforts of Methodist and Baptist preachers. The fact that these preachers were willing to allow the enslaved to express freely

---

53. WWHSH, p. 4.
54. Cf. John S. Mbiti, *African Religions and Philosophy* (New York: Praeger, 1970).
55. Cf. for example, ibid., pp. 100–162.
56. Cf. ibid., p. 108.
57. Cf. J. S. Mbiti, *Concepts of God in Africa* (New York: Praeger, 1970), pp. 1–154.

the religious feelings of their hearts contributed greatly to the growth of the Protestant churches among Africans in the United States. Protestant revivals,[58] camp meetings, and the growth of the "secret church," that is, the church under the trees, the church in chains, the church in the fields—the church not doctrinally, institutionally, nor juridically denominational; that church of the slave quarters and family gatherings, where the spirituals were born, sung, danced, prayed, shouted, sermonized; where the sin-sick soul was healed—all gave the enslaved Africans hope of at least a spiritual escape from their oppression.

C. THE U.S. RELIGIOUS EXPERIENCE IN DETAIL

50. The experience of the African American religious origins here in the United States bears a deeper scrutiny. The enslaved African women and men brought with them to this continent a concept of the Supreme Being, who was deeply and continually involved in the practical affairs of their daily lives, but in a different way than the Christian God.[59]

> For Africans believed in a God who was not only omnipresent, omniscient, omnipotent, and eternal, they believed in a God, who as Supreme Being, had a radical moral relationship with humanity. This Being was approachable through many intermediaries, especially nature—all symbolic representatives of the living, pulsating environment in which humans subsist and through which we are related to the spirits of natural things and the ancestors, but preeminently with the Supreme Being, the God who is above all gods and who is known as Creator, Judge, and Redeemer.[60]

This God and their belief in this God helped them to survive.

SCRIPTURE

51. When the enslaved began to learn Bible stories, beginning with Adam and Eve and continuing through to the ministry of Jesus; Jesus' suffering, death, and resurrection; and the Day of Judgment,[61] they developed a unique theological vision that spoke directly to their plight. They concluded that the God of the Bible was the same universal guide and ruler of the religion of their forebears:

> God is a God.
> God don't never change!
> God is a God.
> An' He always will be God.
> (Spiritual: "God Is A God")[62]

---

58. Cf. Diana L. Hayes, "Black Catholic Revivalism: The Emergence of a New Form of Worship," *The Journal of the Interdenominational Theological Center* XIV:1–2 (Fall 1986/Spring 1987): 87–107.

59. Cf. Gayraud S. Wilmore, *Black Religion and Black Radicalism*, Second Edition (New York: Orbis Books, 1983), p. 15.

60. Ibid., p. 16.

61. Cf. Charles B. Copher, "Biblical Characters, Events, Places, and Images Remembered and Celebrated in Black Church Worship," *The Journal of the Interdenominational Theological Center* XIV:1–2 (Fall 1986/Spring 1987): 75–86.

62. See *Songs of Zion* [= SOZ] (Nashville: Abingdon Press, 1981), no. 140.

This God cared for and rewarded all people who were good and punished all who were wicked. This God was not partial to the enslaved or the free; men or women; black or white; brown, yellow or red; for there would be "plenty good room in my Father's Kingdom" (Spiritual: "Plenty Good Room").[63]

52.　Though uprooted and far from home, the enslaved now found a basic orientation and harmony in the scriptural world. These enslaved people from Africa, now baptized, knew that the God of the Bible was a God of liberation, a God who set captives free, who sent Moses "to tell ole Pharaoh to let my people go" (Spiritual: "Go Down, Moses").[64] They understood that this God did not accept slavery any more than sin. And they decided that, if the God of Hebrew children would work to free them and give them a homeland, and if the God of Jesus Christ so loved the world that the only-begotten Son was given to the world to be its Savior, then this same God must love them too. This God would not leave them in bondage under the taskmaster's whip forever. They would indeed be "free at last. Thank God Almighty we're free at last!" (Spiritual: "Free At Last").[65]

53.　Those few enslaved who were able to read were particularly ignited by the Scriptures and often went from camp to camp sharing the encouraging word of what God had done and what God could indeed still do.

54.　In continuing to tell the Bible's story to each other again and again, the slaves came to recognize more powerfully their own story in the Bible. They were a scattered people of many tribal origins, all of whom involuntarily had been enslaved for the service of another nation. They had cried out to the God of their ancestors for deliverance, and they had been answered by a God they did not at first know. They soon learned that this God was the God of their ancestors, and entering their lives, this God constituted them a beloved people, a light to the nations (see Isaiah 42:6).

55.　These enslaved Africans discovered their own story in the story of Jesus as well, for he identified with those who were poor, blind, and suffering. Like so many of them, Jesus had been born into an oppressed class, suffered real pain, carried a real cross, died a real human death. But he had overcome it all for their sake. And in his resurrection, Jesus showed himself their Lord and Savior, guaranteeing deliverance to his friends, promising to come again when "the Lord shall bear my spirit home."[66]

56.　Enslaved African people in America accepted Christianity because it explained their unique situation: God saw a suffering people; Jesus took up their burden, and he had changed the world, changed the history of the African American slave, lifting it and pointing it toward divine expectations: the freedom of the children of God (see Romans 8:21).

---

63. See *Lead Me, Guide Me: The African American Catholic Hymnal* [= LMGM] (Chicago: GIA Publications, Inc., 1987), no. 318.

64. See LMGM, no. 292.

65. See LMGM, no. 293.

66. James H. Cone, *The Spirituals and the Blues: An Interpretation* (New York: Seabury Press, 1972), p. 54.

57.   This unique Christian vision of enslaved African Americans resulted in a religion that strengthened them in times of great adversity.[67] This same vision gave birth to the "Black church"—the "invisible institution"[68]—when, out of fear of the African American uprisings, religious services by the enslaved were forbidden unless overseen by whites. This church "became the religion of double blackness, carried on in the shadows and under cover of the night, always in danger of interruption and punishment so severe that it might even mean death."[69] Like any other highly developed religion, the "invisible institution," whose vestiges are visible even today, had its sacred space, sacred time, and sacred action.[70]

58.   Its sacred space was the woods in the evening, groupings around camp fires, secret gatherings in a cabin, stealing away under trees, standing in an open field. These places were called "hush-harbors," places where softly spoken words and sacred chants were secretly, yet boldly uttered.

59.   Its sacred time was a gentle combination of God's time and their own life cycle. It was a time in which one, wearing a white robe, could be fully immersed in the saving waters of baptism and enfolded in the community's love. It was a time where two, who could be sold separately, were made one in the midst of a joyous community. It was a time when one could die, but not be forgotten, ever living in the hearts and minds of a remembering community.

60.   Its sacred action was prayer, preaching, and conversion supported by gesture and sacred song. The Scripture was proclaimed and broken open by one who was "acquainted with the source of sacred knowledge."[71] The preacher's ability to dramatize and apply the sacred texts to the assembly's lives in burning oratory, and sometimes solemnly chanted sermons, had to be unparalleled. It had to lead people to "conversion," a radical change of heart ending in a sense of cleanliness, certainty, and reintegration—the three things every enslaved person was denied in life.[72] The minister's ability to lift up the assembly by eloquent, poetic prayer, large gestures, and spirited song encouraged the assembly to do the same.

---

67. This strength in times of adversity is true even today:
Recognizing the necessity for suffering I have tried to make it a virtue. If only to save myself from bitterness. . . . I have lived these last few years with the conviction that unearned suffering is redemptive. . . . So like the Apostle Paul, I can now humbly yet proudly say, "I bear in my body the marks of the Lord Jesus." The suffering and agonizing moments through which I have passed over the last few years have also drawn me closer to God. More than ever before, I am convinced of the reality of a personal God (Martin Luther King, Jr., in an interview with the *Christian Century* [April 27, 1960], as quoted in James M. Washington, *A Testament of Hope: The Essential Writings of Martin Luther King, Jr.* [San Francisco: Harper and Row, 1986], p. 41.)

68. E. Franklin Frazier, *The Negro in America* (New York: Schocken Books, 1974), p. 23.

69. Catherine L. Albanese, *America: Religions and Religion* (Belmont, Calif.: Wadsworth Publishing Company, 1981), p. 120.

70. Cf. ibid., pp. 119–123.

71. *The Negro in America*, p. 24.

72. Cf. Clifton H. Johnson, ed., *God Struck Me Dead: Religious Conversion Experiences and Autobiographies of Ex-Slaves* (Philadelphia: Pilgrim Press, 1969).

61.   Recalling the melodies of Mother Africa; using the hymnody of a new land; recalling the stories from the Bible; and using clapping, moaning, shouting, waving hands, and dance, this community sang songs of life and death, suffering and sorrow, love and judgment, grace and hope, justice and mercy. They sang ardently and lovingly, often hoping against hope. And in singing these "spirituals" they expressed all manner of things:[73]

- their anguish in slavery ("I've Been Buked And I've Been Scorned");[74]

- their trust in God's mighty arm ("Didn't My Lord Deliver Daniel?");[75]

- their belief in God's care ("Nobody Knows The Trouble I See");[76]

- their identification with Jesus' suffering, a suffering like their own ("Were You There When They Crucified My Lord?");[77]

- their belief in the resurrection ("Soon-a Will Be Done");[78]

- their desire for freedom ("O Freedom");[79]

- their assurance of certain freedom now sung in "double coded" songs ("Steal Away");[80] and

- their need for constant conversion and prayer ("Wade In The Water"; "Standin' In The Need Of Prayer").[81]

62.   What must be noted here is that the Scriptures cited in these "spirituals" were not from the Douai-Rheims translation of the Bible, but from the King James translation. This is yet another one of the many clear reminders to us Roman Catholics that when the "Black church" was developed, most of the enslaved knew almost nothing about the Catholic Church.

EFFORTS AT EVANGELIZATION

63.   Though it is true that in the British colonies, during the seventeenth and eighteenth centuries, Roman Catholics were numerically and culturally an insignificant minority—most being found only in Maryland, in parts of Pennsylvania, and, by the beginning of the nineteenth century, in Kentucky and Louisiana—the Catholic Church, except in some isolated instances, was not at all aggressive in the evangelization of the Africans in America or in supporting the Abolitionist Movement to end slavery. As a result, the Church failed to seize the initiative in the evangelizing and converting of the African American population. This failure was due in great part to the acceptance of slavery as an institution by

---

73. Cf. James H. Cone, *The Spiritual and the Blues.*
74. See LMGM, no. 53.
75. See SOZ, no. 106.
76. See SOZ, no. 170.
77. See LMGM, no. 43.
78. See SOZ, no. 158.
79. See SOZ, no. 102.
80. See LMGM, no. 319.
81. See LMGM, no. 107, 216.

many of the Christian faithful and clergy. Tragically, there seems to have been no Saint Peter Claver or Bishop Bartolomé de Las Casas to cry out in the wilderness of the United States.

64.   Furthermore, there is one sad fact we can neither excuse nor ignore: the clergy and people of the Church in America did very little to evangelize African Americans; to expose them to the rich graces and strengths of Catholic life, tradition, and worship; or to lighten the weight of their suffering.

65.   What efforts were made to evangelize African Americans began in earnest with the advent of Mary Elizabeth Lange and the Oblate Sisters of Providence in 1828, in Baltimore; Henriette Delille and the Sisters of the Holy Family in 1842, in New Orleans; the arrival of the Mill Hill Fathers (Josephites) from England in 1871, in Baltimore; and the founding of the Sisters of the Blessed Sacrament by Blessed Katharine Drexel two decades later in Philadelphia.[82]

66.   In the 1920s and 1930s, African Americans migrated to the North in large numbers, hoping to escape the blatant racism in the South and searching for employment. The Jim Crow laws and the no less blatant segregation practiced in all northern cities resulted in "Negro parishes," similar to those already established in the South. Because there was no contact with "white parishes," there was little or limited shared experience of a common church life.

67.   Whenever a parish changed from serving white Americans to serving African Americans, the ordinary policy of most dioceses was to turn parish administration over to religious orders that were willing to take up the special ministry to African Americans. One dubious result of this segregated ministry was that certain religious orders attracted at least a few African American vocations, while most diocesan seminaries and communities of religious women attracted almost none.

68.   Unfortunately, because of this attitude toward African Americans, many in this century believe that the Church saw its work as little more than a burdensome endeavor to educate African Americans out of their "uncivilized and barbaric" traditions and into the European-American culture with which the Church seemed so fundamentally identified. That is why the Church's present efforts at evangelization and liturgical adaptation are all the more necessary and urgent, and yet all the more difficult to accomplish.

VI. THE AFRICAN AMERICAN CHURCH

A. AFRICAN VESTIGES

69.   The religious history of Africans and their descendants in this country is certainly a long and complex one. But, in spite of this troubled history, continuity with a rich African ritual has survived in the "Black church," if only in

---

82. Cf. Cyprian Davis, osb, "Black Catholics in Nineteenth-century America," *U.S. Catholic Historian* 5:1 (1986): 4–17.

fragmentary ways, even to this very day. W. E. B. Du Bois, Albert J. Raboteau, and George Ofori-atta-Thomas inform us that ancient West African worship was marked by dramatic prayer, storytelling, teaching, song, poetic intensity, and by postures of praise, beauty of symbol, kinship, and healing. *Griots* (African storytellers) and others—persons who assisted the community in its encounter with the sacred—presided over these rituals, told the ancient story, and reminded the assembled who they were and whose they were.[83]

70.   Robert C. Williams, Robert Farris Thompson, and Ulysses D. Jenkins tell us that the enslaved Africans, combining these ancient elements with a new understanding of the God of Jesus, created a ritual process that was dramatic in character, influenced by the shout, and was the means by which conversion and God were experienced. They were thus enabled to follow a more or less orderly means of ritually seeking solutions to their problems—to "sing a song of the Lord in a foreign land" (Psalm 137:4).[84]

B. THE "BLACK CHURCH" TODAY

71.   The vestiges of this transformed ritual process are present even now in many African American Protestant traditions. Today, we can still hear dramatic prayer:

> Dear God,
>   Enable us, we pray, to see your acts and to hear your voice amidst the rumbling and confusion of these earthquaking days. Equip us to seize the time that we may be vigilant in our freedom, committed in our callings, and just in our relations with all. *Amen.*[85]

72.   We can still hear the sermon "preached," employing Scripture, drama, sustained tones, intonation, rhythm, call-and-response, congregational identification, and a call to conversion:[86]

> As they went up to the temple to pray, a certain man—don't know the man's name, but the next few words tell us somewhat of his condition—a certain man that was lame from his mother's womb. When he said "a lame man," that made me feel sorry for him because it is a pitiful thing when a person has been useful and now has lost that usefulness.

---

83. See George Ofori-atta-Thomas, "African Inheritance in the Black Church Worship," *The Journal of the Interdenominational Theological Center* XIV:1–2 (Fall 1986/Spring 1987): 43–74. See also W.E.B. Du Bois, *The Gift of Black Folk* (Greenwich, Conn.: Fawcett, 1903); and Albert J. Raboteau, *Slave Religion* (Oxford: Oxford University Press, 1978).

84. See Robert C. Williams, "Worship and Anti-structure in Thurman's Vision of the Sacred," *The Journal of the Interdenominational Theological Center* XIV: 1–2 (Fall 1986/Spring 1987): 173. See also Robert Farris Thompson, *Flash of the Spirit* (New York: Vintage Books, 1983); and Ulysses D. Jenkins, *Ancient African Religion and the African-American Church* (Jacksonville, N.C.: Flame International, 1978).

85. See O. Richard Bowyer, Betty L. Hart, Charlotte A. Meade, eds., *Prayer in the Black Tradition* (Nashville: The Upper Room, 1986).

86. Cf. Henry H. Mitchell, *Black Preaching* (San Francisco: Harper and Row, 1979).

But when I got to thinking about this man who was lame, and I remember the writer said that he was lame from his mother's womb, that made it all the more pitiful to me. For not only was he a lame man, but he had been lame all his life. And I can think of nothing more pitiful than a lame baby—one who was born into the world and whose parents have ever hoped some day he will be strong and healthy. I can see those parents watching him day in and day out, but he never had any use of his limbs. He grew old in age, but still lame.

I think it was last fall, or some time recently, a teenager was told that one of his legs would have to be amputated. He just hated the idea. "Here I am a teenager, where all of the other children my age are active in getting around, doing this and that; and conditions are such that I will have to lose one of my legs and be a cripple the rest of my life."

Well, it is a pitiful thing to see a teenager lame. But, here, this man had never been able to use his limbs, and had been lame from his mother's womb. This man had to be carried. You know we can understand this man's condition because he couldn't help himself. I know a lot of people in the church that are healthy and strong but still want to be carried. . . . They had to carry this man and they brought him daily and laid him at a gate called Beautiful. Now they carried him daily, it means that he must have been receiving something that kept him coming back. . . . Look at that man that was made by the hands of God. That man is lame and twisted, and had to be carried.

Well, when he saw Peter and John going into the temple, he got glad because, you know, he had begged so long until he could just look at a person as he approached and he could tell what kind of gift he was going to get. I can understand, somehow, how he felt. At one time I used to hop bells at a hotel. And, you know, after a few years I could look at a guest when he pulled up in front of the door and I could pretty well tell what kind of tip I was going to get. Oh, I could look at his bags, yes, I could . . . I could look at the way he was dressed and I could tell the type, the size of tip I was going to get.

Well, this man had been in this business so long until he could look and size up the kind of gift he was going to get. But this time he underestimated. Yes, he did! He knew he was looking for alms. He was looking for something that he could exchange at the supermarket. Oh, but Peter and John said, "Look on us." And every one of us who is representative of the Lord ought to be able to tell the world to "look on us . . ."[87]

73.   We can still hear syncopated, heart-throbbing, feeling-thumping song, as varied as: "Do, Lord, Remember Me"[88] or Andre Crouch's "Soon And Very Soon"[89] or Leon Robert's "Holy, Holy, Holy."[90]

74.   We can still hear kinship in warm, heartfelt fellowship:

87. Ibid., 196–271.
88. See SOZ, no. 119.
89. See LMGM, no. 4.
90. See LMGM, no. 426.

On Sundays when services are to be held, the congregation gathers long before it is time to begin. As they drop in one or two at a time, there is much merriment. Each new arrival means a round of handshaking and earnest inquiry as to health.[91]

75.   We can still hear partnership expressed:

Preacher: "Let the church say Amen!"

Church: "Amen. Praise the Lord. Hallelujah!"

      or

"I hear you! Say so. Look out now. Go head!"

76.   We can still feel the healing when persons "get the spirit" or "fall out" or are "slain in the Spirit." We see this healing acclaimed in witness, testimony, and spontaneous song as well.

VII. TOWARD AN AUTHENTIC AFRICAN AMERICAN CATHOLIC WORSHIP

A. WORD AND SACRAMENT

77.   First, when African American Catholics began to thirst for African American cultural expressions in Roman Catholic worship, they turned to those vestigial African traditions still found in the Protestant churches. Initially, some Catholics may have attempted to bring whole structures of African American Protestant worship into Catholic liturgy exactly as they experienced them. However, ecclesiological and credal differences, as well as, theological and sociological analyses suggest that most Baptist, Methodist, and Pentecostal practices simply cannot be, nor should they be, translated into Catholic liturgy. Specifically:

> Though our liturgy is Catholic in that it is open to welcome the spiritual contributions of all peoples which are consistent with our biblical faith and our historical continuity, it is also Catholic in that everything that is done in our worship clearly serves (and does not interrupt) this ritual action of Word and sacrament which has its own rhythm and movement, all built on the directions, rites, and forms of the Roman Catholic liturgy as they are approved and promulgated.[92]

African American Catholics "understand the clear distinction between the Roman Catholic Church as a sacramental-eucharistic community and Christian churches of the Protestant tradition as evangelical."[93]

---

91. *God Struck Me Dead*, p. 2.

92. See J-Glenn Murray, sj, "The Liturgy of the Roman Rite and African American Worship," in LMGM.

93. Donald M. Clark, as cited in Bishop James P. Lyke, ofm, "Liturgical Expression in the Black Community," *Worship* 57:1 (January 1983): 20.

B. SPIRITUALITY

78. Second, African American Catholics turned to "Black theology" for inspiration. This theology, which is concerned with the desire of the African American community to know itself and to know God in the context of African American experience, history, and culture, is as old as the first sermon preached by enslaved Africans to their brothers and sisters huddled together in some plantation swamp, and as new as the reflections of James Cone, Major Jones, J. Deotis Roberts, Cecil Cone, and others beginning in the 1960s.[94] It is a theology of, about, and by African Americans. And while the formal proponents of this theology were a group of creative Protestant scholars, African American Catholic thinkers have used it as a point of departure to elaborate theological reflection that is both African American and Catholic.[95] The contributions made to this theology are decidedly significant, but what they added to the discussion on the nature of authentic African American Catholic liturgy is invaluable.

79. These theologians state that spirituality must be the starting point of a distinctively African American Catholic liturgy. It is a spirituality that is born of moments of the African American sense of "conversion." This conversion is neither "confected" nor produced in liturgy as much as it is nourished and sustained.[96]

80. The African American bishops, in their pastoral letter, *What We Have Seen And Heard*, spoke eloquently of some of the qualities of an African American spirituality. They called particular attention to its contemplative, holistic, joyful, and communitarian nature.

CONTEMPLATIVE

81. African American spirituality "senses the awe of God's transcendence and the vital intimacy of His closeness."[97] Lifted up into God's presence, African Americans respond by surrendering and basking completely in marvelous mystery, whether in church on bended knee or at home in labor or at rest. This contemplative prayer is central and pervasive in the African American tradition.

HOLISTIC

82. African American spirituality involves the whole person: intellect and emotion, spirit and body, action and contemplation, individual and community, secular and sacred.

> In keeping with our African heritage, we are not ashamed of our emotions. For us, the religious experience is an experience of the whole human being, both the feeling and the intellect, the heart as well as the head. It is a spirituality grounded in the doctrine of the Incarnation—our belief that Jesus is both divine and human.[98]

---

94. Cf. Eric Lincoln, *The Black Church Since Frazier* (New York: Schocken, 1974).

95. Cf. Gayraud S. Wilmore and James H. Cone, eds., *Black Theology: A Documented History* (Maryknoll, NY: Orbis Books, 1979).

96. Cf. *Preparing for Liturgy*, p. 82.

97. WWHSH, p. 8.

98. Ibid.

It is a spirituality needed in a society that produces "progressive dehumanization brought about by a technocratic society."[99]

JOYFUL

83. African American spirituality explodes in the joy of movement, song, rhythm, feeling, color, and sensation. "This joy is a result of our conviction that 'in the time of trouble, He will lead me.' . . . This joy comes from the teaching and wisdom of our mothers and fathers in the Faith."[100]

COMMUNITARIAN

84. African American spirituality means community. Worship is always a celebration of community. Because in this spirituality, "I" takes its meaning from "we"; "community means social concern for human suffering and other people's concerns."[101]

C. EMOTION: A WAY OF LEARNING

85. Third, the qualities of an African American spirituality suggest that this spirituality, which is deeply rooted in faith, has a strongly intuitive and emotive base. Nathan Jones, Jawanza Kunjufu, Alvin Pouissant, Na'im Akbar, and many others tell us that there are many ways of knowing and relating to the world.[102] The intellect is not the only way to experience reality. Reality may be experienced by emotion. Leopold Sedar Senghor expresses it best:

> The elan vital of Black Africans, their self-abandonment to the Other (emotion) is, therefore, animated by reason—reason, note, that is not the reason of "seeing" of European whites, which is more a reason of set categories into which the outside world is forced. African reason is more *logos* (word) than *ratio* (intellect). For *ratio* is compasses, square and sextant, scale and yardstick, whereas *logos* is the living Word, the most specifically human expression of the neuro-sensorial impression. . . . The Black African logos in its ascent to the *Verbum* (transcendent) removes the rust from reality to bring out its primordial color, grain, texture, sound, and color.[103]

---

99. Ibid., p. 9.

100. Ibid.

101. Ibid., p. 10.

102. Cf. Nathan Jones, *Sharing the Old, Old Story: Educational Ministry in the Black Community* (Winona, MN: Saint Mary's Press, 1982); Jawanza Kunjufu, *Developing Positive Self-Images and Discipline in Black Children* (Chicago: African-American Images, 1984); Alvin F. Pouissant, *Why Blacks Kill Blacks* (New York: Emerson Hall Publishers, 1972); Na'im Akbar, *Chains and Images of Psychological Slavery* (Jersey City: New Mind Productions, 1984); Reginald Lanier Jones, *Black Psychology* (New York: Harper and Row, 1972); and Alfred B. Pasteur and Ivory L. Toldson, *Roots of Soul: The Psychology of Black Expressiveness* (New York: Anchor Press, 1982).

103. Leopold Sedar Senghor, "The Psychology of the African Negro," *Freeing the Spirit*, as cited in Clarence Joseph Rivers, "The Oral African Tradition versus the Ocular Western Tradition," *This Far by Faith*, p. 41.

This emotive way of knowing is not based primarily on the sense of sight as in the ocular, print-oriented culture of Europe, but on the African oral tradition, which tends to be poetic rather than literal.

86.   Whereas the European way might be summarized in Descartes' "I think, therefore, I am," the African model might be "I am, I dance the Other, I am." For,

> Africans do not make a distinction between themselves and the Object, whether it be tree or stone, human or beast. . . . They become receptive to the impression it emanates, and, like the blind, take hold of it, full of life, with no attempt to hold it in store, without killing it. . . . Black Africans are children of the third day of creation, pure sensory fields.[104]

87.   Father Clarence Joseph Rivers, noted African American liturgist, informs us that in this way of knowing "there is a natural tendency for interpenetration and interplay, creating a concert or orchestration in which the ear sees, the eye hears, and where one both smells and tastes color; wherein all the senses, unmuted, engage in every experience."[105] This way of knowing does not exclude a discursive dimension. It simply states that emotion is the primary way of knowing among African peoples and their descendants. It attests that objective detachment and analytical explanations are useful, but are not the sole means of communicating faith.[106] And lastly, it asserts that peoples everywhere are not poetic or discursive, but both poetic and discursive.

D. SOME RITUAL EMPHASES

88.   Fourth and finally, this articulated African American spirituality comes to full expression in ritual activity, that activity where the Creator and creation meet; where the assembled look upon the face of God and do not die but are sustained;[107] where special attention is paid to space, time, action, language, preaching, and song.

SPACE

89.   The hush-harbors, places of conversion and wholeness, of prayer and preaching, of solace and forgiveness, of shout and dance, were the places where the enslaved went to worship. It was in these small-group spaces that they responded to the God of their forebears in praise, adoration, and reverence. It was in these places that God brought healing, meaning, sustenance, and wholeness to them as individuals and as a group.[108] Today, the holy ground on which the African American assembly gathers, hears God's life-giving Word, gives thanks in a sacrificial meal, and is sent back into the world must be a hush-harbor. As in former

---

104. Ibid.

105. "The Oral African Tradition," p. 45.

106. See ibid., p. 49.

107. Cf. *Preparing for Liturgy*, p. 19.

108. Cf. Edward P. Wimberly, "The Dynamics of Black Worship: A Psychological Exploration of the Impulses That Lie at the Roots of Black Worship," *The Journal of the Interdenominational Theological Center*, Volume XIV:1–2 (Fall 1986/Spring 1987):198.

times, these hush-harbors may be anywhere, but they must reflect the assembly whose roots are both African and American, not simply African or American. For as surely as the hush-harbors of old formed the assembly, our new African American liturgical environments will shape those worshiping today. And as the worshipers are shaped, so the world too is in which they live.

90.   The current hush-harbors must be "houses of the Church." They must be spaces that have "the power to anchor and map our human world and our Christian journey through it."[109] They must be places that give full sway to the rich array of the auditory, tactile, visual, and olfactory senses.[110] They must communicate relations with an African heritage and with the struggle of people today. They must be places that speak clearly to the reality that here in this sacred space is an African American, Roman Catholic people gathered for the celebration of word and sacrament. Consequently, this space must be attentive to and mindful of not only all that the African American community has to say, but all that the Church has to say about environment as well, especially in chapters 5 and 6 of the *General Instruction of the Roman Missal* and the statement of the Bishops' Committee on the Liturgy, *Environment and Art in Catholic Worship.*

TIME

91.   The expressions, "We're going to have a good time" and "We're going to have church," sum up the African American's experience of sacred time. Although it is our duty and salvation always and everywhere to give thanks to God, gathering for liturgy is not simply an obligation. Gathering for liturgy is a time of glory and praise. Gathering for liturgy is "passing time" with the Lord. It is a time to heal the "sin-sick" soul. It is a time to give the Spirit breathing room. It is a time to tell the ancient story, at dawn and at dusk, on Sunday, and in every season. It is preeminently a time for the liturgical re-presentation of the paschal mystery: the dying and rising of Christ, that event of "the life of Jesus of Nazareth who was born, lived, taught, ministered, suffered, was put to death, transcended death paradoxically and was proclaimed and exalted as the Christ. . . . [This event] is celebrated in liturgy in such a way that its interpretation of the past event has a plenitude of meaning for the present. That past event becomes sacred time."[111]

ACTION

92.   Holy hands lifted in prayer, bowed heads, bended knee, jumping, dancing, and shouting were all accepted movements in ancient African American worship, because they were creative (i.e., created by the Spirit, who moves us to do so) (see Romans 8:15). In an African American liturgy today, this movement must still play a vital part, not merely because it is a vestige of an African heritage but because gesture is a long-standing tradition of Roman Catholic worship

---

109. *Catechesis for Liturgy,* p. 70.
110. Cf. Bishops' Committee on hte Liturgy, National Conference of Catholic Bishops, *Environment and Art in Catholic Worhsip* [= EACW](Washington, D.C.: USCC Office for Publishing and Promotion Serivces, 1978), 12..
111. "Reflections from a Theological Perspective," p. 74.

as well.[112] Gestures reveal our inner feelings, hopes, fears, dreams, and longings for freedom. Furthermore:

> If we attend to our experience of bodily interaction with others, we discover that we become the persons we are through that interaction. We learn from the caring touch of a parent that we are valued and loved, and that incites in us the ability to value and love others in return. The attentive, engrossed look on the face of a conversation partner encourages us to share and develop the feelings and ideas within us. The forgiving hug of a friend loosens in us an unsuspected power to forgive. A hand stretched out to us in a moment of need teaches us how to rise above self-concern in dealing with others. In other words, we are called forth to become the persons we are by the deeds of others.[113]

93. In both the Church and the African American community, there is great evidence of the power of posture in prayer.

> Prayer said standing with head and hands upraised becomes prayer of praise and self-commitment. Bended knees and bowed head plead and repent. Raised hands speak of hearts lifted to God. A handshake or an embrace offers a peace which the world cannot give. Hands folded as mirror images of each other bring an inner quiet and peace of soul. Sitting hollows out in us a lap-like receptivity to receive a word in faith.[114]

94. Crying out soars to heaven and joins in the great seraphic hymn. Waving hands proclaim a deep-down praise and thanks when mere words fail. And being slain in the spirit brings an abiding and quickening rest to a world-weary soul. One caveat:

> The liturgy of the Church has been rich in a tradition of ritual movement and gestures. These actions, subtly, yet really, contribute to an environment which can foster prayer or which can distract from prayer. When the gestures are done in common, they contribute to the unity of the worshiping assembly. Gestures which are broad and full in both a visual and tactile sense, support the entire symbolic ritual. When gestures are done by the presiding minister, they can either engage the entire assembly and bring them into even greater unity, or if done poorly, they can isolate.[115]

LANGUAGE: PRAYER

95. African American liturgy is marked by a rich narrative quality. Words are important. And how words are used in prayer is critical.

> Prayer in the Black Tradition is the very center of the Christian life of Black people and continues to be the basis of hope. In those days when they dwelt

---

112. Cf. EACW 56.
113. *Catechesis for Liturgy*, p. 126.
114. Ibid., p. 128.
115. EACW 56.

in the dark valley of bondage hope was yet unborn. It was through prayer in which they found solace and temporary escape from their sordid condition. . . . The prayers were so fervent, they seemed to ring up heaven. A significant and cogent feature of the prayers was the theological and sociological aspects. Their God was the same God of Abraham, Isaac, and Jacob; a captain who never lost a battle; a God of unrelenting love and forgiveness. Yet their prayers were always mindful of their brothers and sisters who shared some hope for freedom some day. . . . Today in an unsupportive society, prayer for Black people is still the "soul's sincere desire."[116]

96.   The language of African American liturgy can be proclamatory in "witnessing" and attentive in listening; very personal without being exclusive; immanent while genuinely transcendent; exuberant and profoundly silent. It is a language that promotes the assembly's full active participation.[117]

LANGUAGE: PREACHING

97.   Words are also important in the art of preaching. James Weldon Johnson has described the role of preaching in African American worship this way

> The old-time Negro preacher was above all an orator, and in good measure, an actor. He knew the secret of oratory, that at bottom it is a progression of rhythmic words more than anything else. I have witnessed congregations moved to ecstasy by the rhythmic intonations. He was a master of all the modes of eloquence. He often possessed a voice that was a marvelous instrument, a voice he could modulate from a sepulchral whisper to a crashing thunderclap. His discourse was generally kept at a high pitch of fervency, but occasionally he dropped into colloquialisms and, less often, into humor. He preached a personal and anthropomorphic God, a sure-enough heaven and red-hot hell. His imagination was bold and unfettered. He had the power to sweep his hearers before him; and so he himself was often swept away. At such times his language was not prose but poetry.[118]

98.   Preaching frequently becomes a dialogue involving the preacher and the assembly. When the preacher delivers a sermon or makes an important point, the congregation may respond from their hearts: "Amen!"; "Yes, Lord!"; "Thank you, Jesus!" They may hum. And sometimes worshipers may simply raise their hands on high in silent gestures of praise, gratitude, and affirmation. These responses are an acclamation of faith that neither demand nor expect any rubrics.

99.   Because of the African American aesthetic appreciation of the vivid narrative form, the celebration of the Word of God in African American worship must be viewed as an experience of communal storytelling through which salvation history is related to the day-to-day lives of the faithful. The presiding

---

116. *Prayer in the Black Tradition*, pp. 13–14.

117. Cf. SC 30.

118. James Weldon Johnson, *God's Trombones: Seven Negro Sermons in Verse* (New York: The Viking Press, 1969), p. 5.

minister is the leader of this storytelling experience. The presiding minister is a person of the "Book" (the Scriptures), whose role is to articulate the tale of the Christ event so that people can relate the salvation experience to their lives.[119]

100. Both preaching and praying are always in need of improvement. Those who are called to minister in the African American community must see it as their sacred trust to develop effective, spirit-filled, sound preaching and prayer. Both are a folk art. Thus, white and African American preacher-presiding ministers alike can benefit by learning more about the techniques of this African American liturgical art and regularly evaluating their ministry.

SACRED SONG

101. The "soul" in African American liturgy calls forth a great deal of musical improvisation and creativity. It also calls forth a greater sense of spontaneity. The African American assembly is not a passive, silent, nonparticipating assembly. It participates by responding with its own interjections and acclamations, with expressions of approval and encouragement.

102. This congregational response becomes a part of the ritualized order of the celebration. The assembly has a sense of when and how to respond in ways that would no more disrupt the liturgy than applause would interrupt a politician's speech or laughter a comedian's monologue. The deadly silence of an unresponsive assembly gives the impression that the Spirit is absent from the community's act of praise.[120]

103. African Americans are heirs to the West African music aesthetic of the call-and-response structure, extensive melodic ornamentation (e.g., slides, slurs, bends, moans, shouts, wails, and so forth), complex rhythmic structures, and the integration of song and dance.[121] As a result, African American sacred song, as Thea Bowman noted, is:

> *holistic:* challenging the full engagement of mind, imagination, memory, feeling, emotion, voice, and body;
>
> *participatory:* inviting the worshiping community to join in contemplation, in celebration, and in prayer;
>
> *real:* celebrating the immediate concrete reality of the worshiping community—grief or separation, struggle or oppression, determination or joy—bringing that reality to prayer within the community of believers;

---

119. Cf. Giles Conwill, "Black Preaching and Catholicism," *Ministry among Black Americans* (Indianapolis: Lilly Endowment, Inc., 1980), pp. 31–43.

120. "To promote active participation, the people should be encouraged to take part by means of acclamations, responses, psalmody, antiphons, and songs, as well as by actions, gestures, and bearing. And at the proper times all should observe a reverent silence" (SC 30).

121. Cf. Portia K. Maultsby, "The Use and Performance of Hymnody, Spirituals and Gospels in the Black Church," *The Journal of the Interdenominational Theological Center* XIV:1–2 (Fall 1986/Spring 1987): 141–160.

spirit-filled: energetic, engrossing, intense; and

life-giving: refreshing, encouraging, consoling, invigorating, sustaining.[122]

African American sacred song is also the song of the people, a people "who share and claim a common history, a common experience, a common oppression, common values, hopes, dreams, and visions."[123]

104. African American Catholic worship may be greatly enhanced by spirituals and gospel music, both of which are representations of this aesthetic. But classical music; anthems; African Christian hymns; jazz; South American, African-Caribbean, and Haitian music may all be used where appropriate. It is not just the style of music that makes it African American, but the African American assembly that sings it and the people whose spirits are uplifted by it.

VIII. AN AFRICAN AMERICAN CATHOLIC WORSHIP MODEL: *IN SPIRIT AND TRUTH*

A. THE IMPORTANCE OF SUNDAY WORSHIP

105. The one Church of Jesus Christ is indeed a home to us all, a place where all cultures meet and contribute to the one Body of Christ. The liturgy is the summit toward which the activity of this family (the Church) is directed; at the same time it is the fount from which all its power flows.[124] Of preeminence is the Church's Sunday Eucharist:

> For on this day Christ's faithful must gather together, so that, by hearing the word of God and taking part in the eucharist, they may call to mind the passion, resurrection, and glorification of the Lord Jesus and may thank God, who "has begotten them again unto a living hope through the resurrection of Jesus Christ from the dead" (1 Peter 1:3).[125]

106. This Sunday celebration of the dying and rising of Christ has several principal requisites:

> a. the gathering of the faithful to manifest the Church, not simply on their own initiative but as called together by God, that is, as the people of God in their organic structure, presided over by a priest, who acts in the person of Christ;
>
> b. their instruction in the paschal mystery through the Scriptures that are proclaimed and that are explained by a priest or deacon;

---

122. See Thea Bowman, FSPA, "The Gift of African American Sacred Song," in LMGM, p. 3.
123. Ibid., p. 5.
124. Cf. SC 10.
125. SC 106.

c. the celebration of the eucharistic sacrifice, by which the paschal mystery is expressed, and which is carried out by the priest in the person of Christ and offered in the name of the entire Christian people.[126]

107. African American Catholics and those ministering with them are most sincerely thankful for and respectful of this Sunday liturgy. While realizing that the Church's eucharistic and sacramental tradition is not the same as that of the Protestant evangelical tradition, many African Americans recognize that a more caring celebration of the Roman Rite encourages a wedding of the Gospel of Jesus Christ and the rich heritage of the African American culture—a process in which the liturgy is not adapted to the culture as much as the liturgical assembly absorbing the best and most fitting cultural elements into itself in a rich diversity of ways and over long periods of time.[127]

108. Currently, there may be no worshiping community to which the Church in the United States can turn as an ideal example of authentic indigenous African American Catholic worship. One parish may have the appropriate balance of choir and congregational participation.[128] Another may have a powerful preaching tradition that does not eclipse an equally important liturgy of the Eucharist. Still another may have found ways to relate heroes from the larger African American experience with more traditional Catholic saints. Yet another may have found ways to respect the diversity of the African American worshiping community itself, taking care not to impose something on older people or younger people or Catholics from different parts of the country.

B. PRINCIPLES OF CULTURAL ADAPTATION

109. Although no model worshiping community presently exists, there are principles, based on the very nature of the liturgy itself, that should guide those African Americans who are in the ardent search of such a model:[129]

- " . . . the liturgy is above all things the worship of the divine majesty" (SC 33). It is humanity's personal encounter with God in faith, hope, and love through Christ in the community of the Church;

- Christ and his paschal mystery are at the very center of every liturgical act, whether the liturgy celebrates Baptism, or Eucharist, or the Liturgy of the Hours. The Church continually proclaims Christ and his salvific act of dying and rising;

- the Church prays through Christ, with Christ, and in Christ to God, the Father, in the union of the Holy Spirit;

---

126. Congregation for Divine Worship, *Directory for Sunday Celebrations in the Absence of a Priest* (June 2, 1988) ICEL trans. (Washington, DC: USCC Office for Publishing and Promotion Services, 1988), p. 12.

127. Cf. Aidan Kavanagh, OSB, *Elements of Rite: A Handbook of Liturgical Style* (New York: Pueblo Publishing Company, 1982), pp. 55–57.

128. Cf. J. Wendell Mapson, Jr., *The Ministry of Music in the Black Church* (Valley Forge: Judson Press, 1984), pp. 43–54.

129. *Cultural Adaptation of the Liturgy*, pp. 63–74.

- "the liturgy is made up of unchangeable elements divinely instituted (e.g., water for baptism, food and drink for eucharist), and elements subject to change" (signs dependent upon the culture and tradition of the people, e.g., the method used for the exchange of peace during the sign of peace);

- "Sacred Scripture is of the greatest importance in the celebration of the liturgy" (SC 24), that is, the Word of God is a sacramental that effects what it says. Therefore, non-biblical literature should not be used in the place of God's Word or in such a way as to draw the assembly's attention away from this Word;

- the assembly's full, conscious, and active participation in liturgical celebrations is called for by the very nature of the liturgy (SC 14), while respecting the simplicity of the rites and the varying roles of the liturgical ministers within these rites;

- there is an educative and catechetical value present in every liturgy, since each liturgy "contains rich instruction for the faithful. For in the liturgy God is speaking to his people and Christ is still proclaiming his Gospel"(SC 33);

- the use of a language that reflects the thought of the people, native symbols, and motifs can help make signs and symbols clear.

C. *IN SPIRIT AND TRUTH:* A MODEL

110. Though no model African American Catholic community exists, there is a signpost—based on a love of the Church's liturgy, an equal love of the powerful, religious traditions of the African American community, and the guidelines articulated above—that may assist in pointing the way to such a worshiping community. That signpost is *In Spirit and Truth: Black Catholic Reflections on the Order of Mass.*

111. The Black Liturgy Subcommittee of the Bishops' Committee on the Liturgy prepared those reflections to assist and enhance the liturgical life of parish communities and to present the many opportunities already present for the accommodation of the liturgy to the "genius and talents" of the many ethnic, cultural, and racial groups that make up the Church in the United States, particularly the African American community.[130]

PRELIMINARY GATHERING

112. Noting the long-standing traditions of "fellowship" and "witnessing" in the Black Church, *In Spirit and Truth* suggests a preliminary gathering:

---

130. Cf. Bishops' Committee on hte Liutrgy, National Conference of Catholic Bishops, *In Spirit and Truth: Black Catholic Reflections on the Order of Mass,* [= IST](Washington, D.C.: USCC Office for Publishing and Promotion Services, 1987), Preface, p. 1.

The purpose of this preliminary gathering is most commonly to help the congregation experience Christ's presence and to build up fellowship within the assembly. . . .[131]

Later, while discussing the sign of peace in the Communion Rite, *In Spirit and Truth* offers this reflection:

The warmth and affection of Black Catholic communities may prompt the extension or enlargement of this ritual [the sign of peace] to the point that it overshadows the sharing of the Bread of life, the richest sign of Christians' oneness in Christ. Extended greetings and signs of communicating affection are more properly given during the *Preliminary Gathering of the Assembly* and not at this time.[132]

113. A preliminary gathering, presided over by a deacon or lay minister, might resemble the following:[133]

• An organ or choral prelude as the assembly gathers.

• A well-known congregational hymn that engenders a sense of fellowship or reflects the theme of that day's Scripture readings.

• A scriptural greeting and testimony.

This is a time when many or a few members of the church stand and utter their praises to God for what God has done. This time need "not be eternal to be immortal (see Matthew 6:7–8). It lifts people from the habit of rote prayers, and it causes them to say in one or two lines exactly the thought they would utter to God."[134]

As an example, the presiding minister might say:

They that hope in the Lord
Will renew their strength,
They will soar as with eagles' wings;
They will run and not grow weary,
Walk and not grow faint (Isaiah 40:31).

What a mighty God we serve! Amen? Amen!
Is there anyone who wishes to witness to the Lord's goodness this morning?

One who gives testimony might say:

Saints of God, I have been coming up the rough side of the mountain all week. Along the way I thought I wouldn't make it. But I kept on praying,

---

131. IST 9.
132. IST 51.
133. Cf. J-Glenn Murray, SJ, "Enfleshing *In Spirit and Truth*," Address Given to the African American Catholic Liturgical Ministers (Los Angeles, February 18, 1988).
134. Harold A. Carter, *The Prayer Tradition of Black People* (Valley Forge: Judson Press, 1976), p. 123.

and the Lord has brought me through. He has made a way out of no way, and I am here to tell the story! Amen!

or:

> This week has been a particularly rough one for me, my friends. But I have survived because the Lord is truly like a mother who forgets not her child. And I'm so glad that God has not forgotten me.

- A prayer.

    After the leader has discerned when these testimonies should come to an end,[135] he or she may collect all these praises into one prayer, summarizing the concerns of those who have spoken.

- Fellowship.

    This is a time when those who form the assembly may greet one another enthusiastically.[136]

    For example, the leader might say:

    > The Lord's kindness never fails. Let us ready ourselves to receive that kindness in abundance. Let us stand and greet one another in fellowship, for this is the day the Lord has made. Let us rejoice and be glad!

    This preliminary gathering may also take the form of hymn singing, catechesis, instruction for the liturgy, and fellowship.

PRAYER

114. Recalling the African American community's rich tradition of prayer, *In Spirit and Truth* states:

> The invitation *Let us pray* is always addressed to the assembly and never to God. This invitation may be extended and adapted to the needs of the assembly, in the style of alternative opening prayers found in the *Sacramentary*. Any variation in this invitation should focus upon the opening prayer prescribed for the day, which must always be said. . . .[137]

Compare:

> Let us pray
> [to the Father whose kindness never fails]
> (Eighteenth Sunday in Ordinary Time)

---

135. Cf. ibid., p. 123.

136. "I advanced towards the people. The church was full. Cries of joy echoed through it: 'Glory to God! God be praised!' Nobody was silent. Shouts were coming from everywhere. I greeted the people, and again they began to cry out in their enthusiasm. Finally, when silence was restored, the readings from the Sacred Scripture were proclaimed." (Saint Augustine, *The City of God*, Book vii, 22 as cited in R. Cabie, *The Church at Prayer*, volume 2 (London: Geoffrey Chapman, 1986], p.50).

137. IST 22.

with:

> Let us pray
> to the Father whose kindness never fails.
> Let us pray
> to the God of our salvation.
> Let us pray
> for peace and life and guidance
> on our pilgrim way.

or:

> Our God is good, yes? Yes! Amen!
> Our God is gracious, yes? Yes! Amen!
> Our God has helped us, yes? Yes! Amen!
> Helped us travel this lonesome valley, yes? Yes! Amen!
> Then let us open our hearts and bow our heads
> And pray to our God whose kindness never fails.[138]

115. The penitential rite and the general intercessions are additional opportunities for using the beauty and poetry of African American prayer to great effect:[139]

A Possible Penitential Rite for the Eighteenth Sunday
in Ordinary Time, Sunday Cycle A[140]

Priest or Deacon:

> Mindful of our many sins
> and hungering for forgiveness,
> let us remember God's mercy
> made manifest in Christ Jesus our Lord.
> (pause)

> Lord Jesus Christ, you are our Bread of heaven, Lamb of God and Word of life. Lord, have mercy.

> Lord Jesus Christ, you are our Rock in a weary land, and our Shelter in the storm. Christ, have mercy.

> Lord Jesus Christ, you are our soon-coming King.
> Lord, have mercy.

---

138. "Enfleshing *In Spirit and Truth*."
139. Cf. IST 17, 18, 39–40.
140. "Enfleshing *In Spirit and Truth*."

A Possible Litany for the General Intercessions for the Eighteenth Sunday in Ordinary Time, Sunday, Cycle A[141]

Priest:

> O brothers and sisters,
> drawn together by Jesus, the Bread of Life,
> and mindful of God's manifold blessings,
> we cry out that the many hungers of the world
> may indeed be satisfied.

Minister:

> For the Church scattered throughout the world and longing to spread the Good News of God's most merciful reign, we pray to the Lord. Lord, have mercy.
>
> For our elected leaders who labor for an abiding justice and a peace unending, we pray to the Lord. Lord, have mercy.
>
> For the homeless who ache for shelter, the poor who hunt for bread, the young who starve for love, we pray to the Lord. Lord, have mercy.
>
> For the broken in mind and body who set their hearts on wholeness, especially those for whom we now pray (pause to allow the congregation to voice names of the sick), we pray to the Lord. Lord, have mercy.
>
> For the dead who yearn for eternal rest, especially those for whom we now pray (pause to allow the congregation to voice names of the dead), we pray to the Lord. Lord, have mercy.

Priest:

> Heavenly Father,
> hear us in what we ask
> and perfect us in what we do
> and, at last, gather us into your kingdom
> where our deepest needs will be satisfied
> through Christ our Lord.

SCRIPTURE

116. Keeping in mind the African American community's unbroken love of Scripture, *In Spirit and Truth* observes:

> "In the dark days of slavery, reading was forbidden, but for our ancestors the Bible was never a closed book. The stories were told and retold in sermons, spirituals and shouts, proverbs and turns of phrases borrowed freely from the Bible. . . . Thus, when the word of Scripture is proclaimed in the Black community, it is not a new message but a new challenge" (*What We Have Seen And Heard*, pp. 4–5). . . .

---

141. Ibid.

. . . [Consequently] a reader may, according to his or her talent, lend a spirit of enthusiasm to the proclamation of the Scripture texts. Many Black Americans have long grown accustomed to such a spirited proclamation of God's word. So long as the word of God is announced with faith, clarity, and sincerity such styles may be appropriate in the Eucharist.[142]

HOMILY

117. Acknowledging the fertile past of the African American preaching, *In Spirit and Truth* reminds us:

[T]he homily is an application of the Scripture readings and the meaning of the solemnity or feast to everyday Christian living and continued conversion.

The style and manner of preaching should be influenced by "the composition and expectations of the congregation to which it is addressed and not exclusively by the preference of the preacher" (see Bishops' Committee on Priestly Life and Ministry, *Fulfilled in Your Hearing: The Homily in the Sunday Assembly*, p. 25:1). . . .

. . . Traditionally, good "Black preaching" is rich in content and expression, relies heavily on the biblical text, and draws generously from story, song, poetry, humor, anecdote, and descriptive language. Good Black preaching balances emotion and content and never descends to crass affectation. . . .[143]

LITURGY OF THE EUCHARIST

118. Remembering the African American community's longing for continual conversion, its desire to stand at the foot of the cross, and the zeal of souls who sing "How great Thou art!" beckons the community to gather around the table of the Lord.[144] *In Spirit and Truth* remarks:[145]

"At the last supper Christ instituted the sacrifice and paschal meal that make the sacrifice of the cross to be continuously present in the Church, when the priest, representing Christ the Lord, carries out what the Lord did and handed over to his disciples to do in his memory" (*General Instruction of the Roman Missal*, 48). . . .

The eucharistic prayer, also called the anaphora, "a prayer of thanksgiving and sanctification, is the center of the entire celebration" (Bishops' Committee on the Liturgy, *Music in Catholic Worship*, 47).

---

142. IST 23, 26.
143. IST 33–35.
144. See Stuart K. Hine, "How Great Thou Art," in LMGM, no. 181.
145. IST 41, 44.

119. Observing the African American community's characteristic for dialogue and acclamation, and its passion for singing the Lord's song, *In Spirit and Truth* urges the examination of the use of music:[146]

- in the Entrance Song;
- at the Gloria;
- as the assembly prepares to hear God's word;
- in the Responsorial Psalm;
- at the Gospel procession;
- after the proclamation of the Gospel;
- in the General Intercessions;
- at the Preparation of the Altar and the Gifts;
- for the acclamations in the Eucharistic Prayer;
- for the Lord's Prayer;[147]
- at the Breaking of the Bread;
- for the Communion procession;
- for the Psalm or Hymn of Praise after Communion; and
- at the Recessional.

GESTURE

120. Understanding the African American community's affection for gesture, *In Spirit and Truth* points out those places where gesture and other movements are appropriate:[148]

- the Entrance Procession;
- the Gospel Procession;
- the Preparation of the Altar and the Gifts;
- the Communion Rite;[149] and
- the Recessional.

---

146. See IST 11, 20, 24, 28, 30, 32, 40, 42, 45, 49, 55, 57, 58, 59, 65.

147. Musical settings of the Lord's Prayer should always include the embolism (Deliver us, Lord . . .") a development of the last petition of the Lord's Prayer that begs, on behalf of the entire community of the faithful, deliverance from the power of evil (GIRM, 56a). Given the times of great anxiety in which we live, this embolism surely needs to be prayed.

148. See IST 12–13, 31, 43, 66.

149. It might be suggested that the assembly stand in *orans* for the Lord's Prayer (see Tertullian, *De oratione*, 14), embrace at the Sign of Peace (GIRM, 56b), and make a proper reverence before the reception of Communion (GIRM, 244c).

121. Appreciating the African American community's sense of profound silence, *In Spirit and Truth* calls to mind the liturgy's call to silence:[150]

- during the Opening Prayer and Prayer after Communion; and

- after Communion.

The liturgical celebration will be served by this additional reminder:

> Silence should be observed at the designated times as part of the celebration. Its function depends on the time it occurs in each part of the celebration. Thus at the penitential rite and again after the invitation to pray, all recollect themselves; at the conclusion of a reading or the homily, all meditate briefly on what has been heard; after communion, all praise God in silent prayer (*General Instruction of the Roman Missal*, 23).

WELCOMING OF GUESTS

122. Finally, as was noted earlier, fellowship and hospitality are a fundamental element of the Black Church experience. One manifestation of that hospitality is the warm attention paid to visitors and guests. In many Black churches where this tradition survives, the welcoming of guests is an important part of the pastor's announcements.[151] In keeping with that tradition and noting the placement of announcements at the beginning of the Concluding Rites of the Sunday liturgy,[152] we might suggest the following as one of those brief announcements:

> Mindful of the Lord's words:
> "Anyone who welcomes you, welcomes me," (Matthew 10:40)
> we welcome all our guests.
> To those of you who are Catholic
> and have no church home,
> please feel free to see me or one of our ushers
> about becoming an active member of our church family.
> To those of you who may possibly be seeking membership
> in the Catholic Church, please see me
> about initiating so wondrous a step.
> Again, know that you are all welcome.

D. CONCLUSION

123. *In Spirit and Truth* provides an excellent model and serves as a worthy signpost. But it must be remembered that African American Catholics are in the process of developing and continuing a tradition, a laudatory and difficult

---

150. See IST 21, 60.
151. Cf. Rawn Harbor, "Music and the Black Church Experience," Talk Given at the Black Catholic Worship Conference (Archdiocese of Detroit, February 3, 1989).
152. Cf. GIRM 123.

task.[153] This task is one in which we welcome from the African American culture all that is "compatible with aspects of the true and authentic spirit of the liturgy, in respect for the substantial unity of the Roman Rite."[154] This task, as John Paul II reminds us, ". . . demands a serious formation in theology, history, and culture as well as a sound judgment in discerning what is necessary or useful and what is not useful or even dangerous to faith. . . ."[155] It will take time for people who are authentically African American and truly Catholic and who know the nature of the liturgy and worship to nurture this tradition. In the meantime, African American Catholics must establish, with the authority of the Congregation for Divine Worship and the Discipline of the Sacraments, the Bishops' Committee on the Liturgy, and their local bishops, various liturgical centers of pastoral sensitivity and academic excellence where liturgists, scholars, artists, musicians, and pastors may continue to dedicate their skills in God's service.[156] Furthermore, these prayerful men and women might do well to look beyond these shores to Africa. As Bishop Wilton D. Gregory has exhorted:

> It might well be, and in many cases I suspect that it will be true that there is much that the Church in service to African Americans can learn from and use from the Catholic Church in Africa. Our people need to continue to explore the genuine and authentic African heritage that is ours, but has been denied or denigrated for far too long. What we do not need are facile, inaccurate, incomplete, uninformed exposure to certain African traditions which ignore the complexity of their origin used in a Catholic ritual context without proper explanation and reverence for either the ritual or African custom.[157]

124. And finally, African Americans all must pray:

> Be in the fleeting word, our Father, the stumbling effort.
> Touch mind and heart and life,
> that as we move from this place
> into the way that we must take,
> we shall not be alone,
> but feel Thy Presence beside us, all the way.[158]

African Americans must pray so as to continue exploring and searching the established traditions of the Church and the powerful gifts of the African American culture, in order to determine what is the best result for the Church—all to the greater honor and glory of God, in whose house there is plenty good room!

---

153. Cf. Bishop Wilton D. Gregory, "Black Catholic Liturgy: What Do You Say It Is?" *U.S. Catholic Historian* 7:2–3 (Spring/Summer 1988): 316–319.

154. John Paul II, Apostolic Letter *On the Twenty-fifth Anniversary of the "Constitution on the Sacred Liturgy"* (December 4, 1988) (Washington DC: USCC Office for Publishing and Promotion Services, 1989), 16.

155. Ibid.

156. Cf. WWHSH, pp. 30–33.

157. Bishop Wilton D. Gregory, "Children of the Same Mother," Talk Given at the Workshop for Pastors Serving in the African American Catholic Community (Atlanta, May 12, 1990), pp. 11–12.

158. *The Growing Edge*, p. 154.

DIRECTORY FOR THE
APPLICATION OF PRINCIPLES
AND
NORMS ON ECUMENISM

LITURGICAL EXCERPTS

DIRECTORY
PONTIFICAL COUNCIL
FOR PROMOTING CHRISTIAN UNITY
1993

OVERVIEW OF THE *DIRECTORY FOR THE APPLICATION OF PRINCIPLES AND NORMS ON ECUMENISM*

Rev. Paul Turner

May a non-Catholic serve as a godparent for a Catholic Baptism? May a Catholic be the best man at a non-Catholic wedding? May someone from an Eastern Orthodox Church receive Holy Communion at a Roman Catholic Mass? May a Catholic receive Holy Communion at a non-Catholic Church? These and other questions that Catholics often face due to their family, business, and other social relationships are answered in the *Directory for the Application of Principles and Norms on Ecumenism* (DE).

The directory, published by the Pontifical Council for Promoting Christian Unity in 1993, updated and expanded the information previously offered in two post-Conciliar documents: *A Directory for the Application of the Second Vatican Council's Decisions on Ecumenism* (1967), and its second part, subtitled *Ecumenism in Higher Education* (1970).

Through the Second Vatican Council (1962–1965) the Catholic Church entered a time of self-reflection, probing her identity more deeply and refreshing her dialogue with the world. The fruits of the Council's labor became immediately evident in the Church's worship, but its complete goals were broader still.

Among the major areas the Council pursued was ecumenism. Other Churches and ecclesial communities had already entered the arena. By the beginning of the Second Vatican Council, the World Council of Churches had already formed, and some churches were already merging. Formerly, the ecumenical strategy of the Catholic Church seemed to have two goals: the conversion of Protestants and an end to the Orthodox schism. The Council Fathers took a broader look at the ecumenical picture, striking a balance between their convictions already noted in *Lumen gentium (Dogmatic Constitution on the Church)*: first, that the church of Christ "subsists in the Catholic Church"; and second, that "many elements of sanctification and of truth are found outside its visible confines."[1] In doing so, they called for a deep respect for the personal faith of all. The resulting *Decree on Ecumenism, Unitatis redintegratio*, catapulted the Catholic Church into the ecumenical movement. Its opening words called the restoration of unity one of the principal concerns of the Council, and it criticized division among churches as contrary to the will of Christ and a scandal to the world.

Unitatis redintegratio still captures the heady enthusiasm of the Second Vatican Council. It launched a sweeping agenda for the Church by calling for not only the promotion of but the practice of ecumenism. It also recognized the distinct concerns issuing from relationships between the Catholic Church and

---

1. *Lumen gentium* (LG), 8.

other Eastern and Western Churches. By its nature, the document towered with vision while abstaining from specifics.

The specifics of the *Decree on Ecumenism* fell to post-Conciliar work. The Secretariat for Promoting Christian Unity accepted the responsibility and set about developing its *Directory for the Application of the Second Vatican Council's Decisions on Ecumenism*, published in two parts—in 1967 and 1970.

The first part of the directory (1967) dealt with several practical concerns. These included the creation of diocesan and regional ecumenical commissions necessary for working out the ideals of the Council. It also affirmed the validity of Baptism administered by ministers of other Churches and ecclesial communities, and promoted sharing among Churches where possible.

The second part (1970) laid more groundwork. It presented the general principles that undergird ecumenism and then worked out particular norms for ecumenical formation and collaboration, especially regarding schools and institutions.

The *Directory for the Application of the Second Vatican Council's Decisions on Ecumenism* served the Church well. However, other concurrent developments began to influence ecumenical progress. Most significantly, the *Code of Canon Law* for the Roman Catholic Church was revised in 1983, and the *Code of Canons of the Eastern Churches* was published in 1990. It also became evident that the directory had not adequately treated topics like Marriage between Catholics and other Christians. A more coherent integration of all this material, it seemed, would better serve the cause of ecumenism and the Church's commitment to it.

Consequently, in 1985, speaking on the twenty-fifth anniversary of the founding of the Secretariat for Promoting Christian Unity, Pope John Paul II called for the revision of the ecumenical directory. The Secretariat once again assumed the task, and thus began a long process of development and consultation for the generation of the revised document. Before its completion in 1993, DE passed through several committees, received reactions from national conferences of bishops around the world, underwent further refinements with the Congregation for the Doctrine of the Faith, and finally won the approval of Pope John Paul II. On March 25, 1993, DE was promulgated under the auspices of the renamed Pontifical Council for Promoting Christian Unity.

The finished document contains five sections. It opens with a chapter on the search for Christian unity—new theological material rooted in the Second Vatican Council's *Unitatis redintegratio* and *Lumen gentium*. It then treats the organization of the Catholic Church in its service to Christian unity, calling for internal commissions and international cooperation. The third section discusses the formation of Catholics in ecumenism, an attempt to widen participation in the ecumenical movement. The fourth gathers the practical matters of communion of life and spiritual activity among the baptized. The final section calls for collaboration, dialogue, and common witness to ecumenism.

The excerpt included in this volume of *The Liturgy Documents, Volume Four* draws from the fourth and fifth sections of DE, articles 92–160 and 183–187. These articles concern specific matters that pertain to liturgical prayer among the Christian Churches and ecclesial communities. The first and lengthier part of the excerpt considers prayer and the sacraments. The document gives special consideration to Baptism and Marriage. However, in a middle section entitled "Sharing Spiritual Activities and Resources," one finds other substantial concerns: principles for prayer in common; sharing in non-sacramental liturgical worship; and sharing in the sacramental life of the Church, especially in the Eucharist, but also in Reconciliation and Anointing of the Sick. The shorter, second part of the excerpt concerns the development of common scriptural and liturgical texts.

The Sacrament of Baptism prompts several concerns, including conditions for its validity and the role of godparents. Regarding validity, DE assumes the validity of Baptisms in which the minister uses the proper matter and form, and has the same intention as the Church. This affirmation represents a change in policy. Formerly, the validity of Baptisms performed by other Christians was generally considered doubtful; if other Christians desired acceptance into the Catholic Church, the priest usually administered a conditional Baptism. In fact, this practice was so common that the formula for conditional Baptism appeared in the Roman Ritual together with the standard one for hundreds of years. Today, the Baptisms of other Christians in the mainline Churches and ecclesial communities are presumed to be valid. If any of those Christians desire the full communion of the Catholic Church, they celebrate the Rite of Reception; the priest who receives them also confirms them. If a conditional Baptism must be performed, it is to happen in private.[2]

The question of whether Christians of one denomination may serve as godparents in another has vexed many Catholics. DE explains that Baptism is celebrated within a given Church or ecclesial community. Only a person within that Church or ecclesial community may function as a godparent, but other baptized Christians may serve as witnesses together with the godparent. The prescription advises Catholic parents to seek a Catholic godparent, even if they wish to include a witness of another Christian tradition; it also permits Catholics to serve as witnesses for Baptisms in other Church communities when the host church provides a godparent.[3]

In sharing spiritual activities and resources, DE encourages Catholics to make full use of what they share in common with others. Many non-sacramental occasions may draw churches together for prayer; the funeral of a member of a non-Catholic Church may even be celebrated in a Catholic church.[4] Catholics may share buildings and religious objects with members of non-Catholic Churches, as long as each community's faith is respected.[5] Students from other Churches or ecclesial communities in Catholic schools may have access to their own ministers,[6] as may patients of other communities in Catholic hospitals.[7]

The question of sharing other sacraments requires much more nuance, and the possibilities depend first on whether or not an Eastern Church is involved. The Catholic Church recognizes the sacraments of all Eastern Churches. It

---

2. See *Directory for the Application of Principles and Norms on Ecumenism* (DE), 93–95, 99–100.

3. See ibid., 98.

4. See ibid., 120–121.

5. See ibid., 137–140.

6. See ibid., 141.

7. See ibid., 142.

extends its willingness to share the sacraments with them, but not all Eastern Churches are able to extend the same invitation back.[8]

The sharing of Eucharist, Penance, and Anointing of the Sick with Christians of Western Churches and ecclesial communities is more difficult. For Catholics, the Eucharist is a sign of ecclesial communion; being outside that communion excludes members of other Christian communities from ordinary participation. However, there are occasions when the sharing of these sacraments "may be permitted or even commended."[9] DE offers four conditions: "that the person be unable to have recourse for the sacrament desired to a minister of his or her own church or ecclesial community, ask for the sacrament of his or her own initiative, manifest Catholic faith in this sacrament and be properly disposed."[10] Catholics under similar circumstances may only receive from those churches whose sacraments are considered valid.[11] Hence, Catholics cannot accept a reciprocal invitation to communion in a non-Catholic Church, even in these extraordinary circumstances.

The sense of "communion" at sacramental worship extends also to certain ministries: The reader and homilist at a Catholic Eucharistic liturgy should be Catholic. Outside of Eucharistic celebrations they need not be.[12] Those who witness marriages as best man, maid of honor, or as another member of the wedding party need not be from the same Church as the bride or groom, whether the wedding takes place in a Catholic church or elsewhere.[13]

Marriages between Catholics and members of other Churches or ecclesial communities pose special pastoral concerns. Even before Marriage, couples should discuss the exercise of their faith as part of their preparation for the celebration of the sacrament. One should be firm in one's own faith and learn about the faith of the partner; still, respecting the partner's faith should not invite indifference about one's own. The pastors of each partner should collaborate before the wedding. The couple is exhorted to pray together.[14]

Of primary concern in Marriage is the faith of the children. The Catholic party is asked to promise to do all in his or her power to raise the children in the Catholic faith, beginning with Baptism. The non-Catholic party is to be informed of this promise, but is not asked to assent or sign anything. The Catholic parent is to act always with respect for the religious freedom and conscience of the other parent when sharing the Catholic faith with the children.[15]

The wedding ceremony should affirm the significance of the sacrament. Marriages between Catholics and Eastern Christians should stress what the faiths share in common. A Catholic who wishes to marry a member of another Church or ecclesial community is still bound by the canonical form of marriage but may obtain a dispensation for various reasons, including "the maintaining of family harmony, obtaining parental consent to the marriage, the recognition

8. See ibid., 122–128.

9. DE, 129.

10. DE, 131.

11. See ibid., 132.

12. See ibid., 133–135.

13. See ibid., 136.

14. See ibid., 143–149.

15. See ibid., 150–151.

of the particular religious commitment of the non-Catholic partner or his/her blood relationship with a minister of another Church or ecclesial community."[16] Still, a single public ceremony is required; a couple may not give consent twice.[17] The Catholic minister may join or be joined by the minister of another community at the wedding; the visiting minister may recite a prayer, proclaim a reading, offer an exhortation, or give a blessing.[18] DE states that the wedding between a Catholic and a person from another Church or ecclesial community will ordinarily not take place within the context of a celebration of the Eucharist. If the non-Catholic partner desires Holy Communion at the wedding, the norms found in article 131 still apply.[19] The bishops of South Africa notably clarified these permissions after DE was published.

The last excerpt included here[20] comes from the closing section of DE and deals with common Bible work and common liturgical texts. Since DE calls on Christians to seek occasions for common prayer, it also encourages the recognition of Bible and liturgy texts that many ecclesial communities might hold in common.

When Catholics in all parts of the world are drawn on a regular basis into conversation and commerce with those of other beliefs, they find the experience both rich and challenging. The *Directory for the Application of Principles and Norms on Ecumenism* aims to help Catholics enter that experience strong in their faith yet committed to the cause of ecumenism.

---

16. Ibid., 154.
17. See ibid., 156.
18. See ibid., 157–158.
19. See ibid., 159–160.
20. See ibid., 183–187.

OUTLINE

The outline that follows pertains to the liturgical excerpts of the Directory for the Application of Principles and Norms on Ecumenism.

DIRECTORY FOR THE APPLICATION OF PRINCIPLES AND NORMS ON ECUMENISM—EXCERPTS

IV. COMMUNION IN LIFE AND SPIRITUAL ACTIVITY AMONG THE BAPTIZED

A. SACRAMENT OF BAPTISM

92.   By the sacrament of baptism a person is truly incorporated into Christ and into his church and is reborn to a sharing of the divine life.[1] Baptism, therefore, constitutes the sacramental bond of unity existing among all who through it are reborn. Baptism, of itself, is the beginning, for it is directed toward the acquiring of fullness of life in Christ. It is thus ordered to the profession of faith, to the full integration into the economy of salvation and to eucharistic communion.[2] Instituted by the Lord himself, baptism, by which one participates in the mystery of his death and resurrection, involves conversion, faith, the remission of sin and the gift of grace.

93.   Baptism is conferred with water and with a formula that clearly indicates that baptism is done in the name of the Father, Son and Holy Spirit. It is therefore of the utmost importance for all the disciples of Christ that baptism be administered in this manner by all and that the various churches and ecclesial communities arrive as closely as possible at an agreement about its significance and valid celebration.

94.   It is strongly recommended that the dialogue concerning both the significance and the valid celebration of baptism take place between Catholic authorities and those of other churches and ecclesial communities at the diocesan or episcopal conference levels. Thus it should be possible to arrive at common statements through which they express mutual recognition of baptisms as well as procedures for considering cases in which a doubt may arise as to the validity of a particular baptism.

95.   In arriving at these expressions of common agreement, the following points should be kept in mind:

a) Baptism by immersion or by pouring, together with the Trinitarian formula, is of itself valid. Therefore, if the rituals, liturgical books or established customs of a church or ecclesial community prescribe either of these ways of baptism, the sacrament is to be considered valid unless there are serious reasons

---

1. Cf. UR, 22.
2. Cf. UR, 22.

for doubting that the minister has observed the regulations of his/her own community or church.

b) The minister's insufficient faith concerning baptism never of itself makes baptism invalid. Sufficient intention in a minister who baptizes is to be presumed, unless there is serious ground for doubting that the minister intended to do what the church does.

c) Wherever doubts arise about whether or how water was used,[3] respect for the sacrament and deference toward these ecclesial communities require that serious investigation of the practice of the community concerned be made before any judgment is passed on the validity of its baptism.

96.   According to the local situation and as occasion may arise, Catholics may, in common celebration with other Christians, commemorate the baptism which unites them by renewing the engagement to undertake a full Christian life which they have assumed in the promises of their baptism and by pledging to cooperate with the grace of the Holy Spirit in striving to heal the divisions which exist among Christians.

97.   While by baptism a person is incorporated into Christ and his church, this is only done in practice in a given church or ecclesial community. Baptism, therefore, may not be conferred jointly by two ministers belonging to different churches or ecclesial communities. Moreover, according to Catholic liturgical and theological tradition, baptism is celebrated by just one celebrant. For pastoral reasons, in particular circumstances the local ordinary may sometimes permit, however, that a minister of another church or ecclesial community take part in the celebration by reading a lesson, offering a prayer, etc. Reciprocity is possible only if a baptism celebrated in another community does not conflict with Catholic principles or discipline.[4]

98.   It is the Catholic understanding that godparents, in a liturgical and canonical sense, should themselves be members of the church or ecclesial community in which the baptism is being celebrated. They do not merely undertake a responsibility for the Christian education of the person being baptized (or confirmed) as a relative or friend; they are also there as representatives of a community of faith, standing as guarantees of the candidate's faith and desire for ecclesial communion.

a) However, based on the common baptism and because of ties of blood or friendship, a baptized person who belongs to another ecclesial community may be admitted as a witness to the baptism, but only together with a Catholic godparent.[5] A Catholic may do the same for a person being baptized in another ecclesial community.

---

3. With regard to all Christians, consideration should be given to the danger of invalidity when baptism is administered by sprinkling, especially of several people at once.

4. Cf. Ecumenical Directory (1967).

5. Cf. CIC, c. 874.2. According to the explanation given by the *Acta Commissionis* (Communicationes 5, 1983, p. 182) the wording *communitas ecclesialis* does not include the Eastern Orthodox churches not in full communion with the Catholic church *(Notatur insuper ecclesias Orientales Orthodoxas in schemate sub nomine communitatis ecclesialis non venire)*.

b) Because of the close communion between the Catholic church and the Eastern Orthodox churches, it is permissible for a just cause for an Eastern faithful to act as godparent together with a Catholic godparent at the baptism of a Catholic infant or adult, so long as there is provision for the Catholic education of the person being baptized and it is clear that the godparent is a suitable one.

A Catholic is not forbidden to stand as godparent in an Eastern Orthodox church if he/she is so invited. In this case, the duty of providing for the Christian education binds in the first place the godparent who belongs to the church in which the child is baptized.[6]

99. Every Christian has the right for conscientious religious reasons freely to decide to come into full Catholic communion.[7] The work of preparing the reception of an individual who wishes to be received into full communion with the Catholic church is of its nature distinct from ecumenical activity.[8] The Rite of Christian Initiation of Adults provides a formula for receiving such persons into full Catholic communion. However, in such cases, as well as in cases of mixed marriages, the Catholic authority may consider it necessary to inquire as to whether the baptism already received was validly celebrated. The following recommendations should be observed in carrying out this inquiry.

a) There is no doubt about the validity of baptism as conferred in the various Eastern churches. It is enough to establish the fact of the baptism. In these churches the sacrament of confirmation (chrismation) is properly administered by the priest at the same time as baptism. There it often happens that no mention is made of confirmation in the canonical testimony of baptism. This does not give grounds for doubting that this sacrament was also conferred.

b) With regard to Christians from other churches and ecclesial communities, before considering the validity of baptism of an individual Christian, one should determine whether an agreement on baptism (as mentioned above, No. 94) has been made by the churches and ecclesial communities of the regions or localities involved and whether baptism has in fact been administered according to this agreement. It should be noted, however, that the absence of a formal agreement about baptism should not automatically lead to doubt about the validity of baptism.

c) With regard to these Christians, where an official ecclesiastical attestation has been given there is no reason for doubting the validity of the baptism conferred in their churches and ecclesial communities unless, in a particular case, an examination clearly shows that a serious reason exists for having a doubt about one of the following: the matter and form and words used in the conferral of baptism, the intention of an adult baptized or the minister of the baptism.[9]

d) If, even after careful investigation, a serious doubt persists about the proper administration of the baptism and it is judged necessary to baptize conditionally, the Catholic minister should show proper regard for the doctrine

---

6. Cf. Ecumenical Directory, 48; CCEC, c. 685.3.
7. Cf. UR, 4; CCEC, c. 896–901.
8. Cf. UR, 4.
9. CIC, c. 869.2.

that baptism may be conferred only once by explaining to the person involved both why in this case he is baptizing conditionally and what is the significance of the rite of conditional baptism. Furthermore, the rite of conditional baptism is to be carried out in private and not in public.[10]

e) It is desirable that synods of Eastern Catholic churches and episcopal conferences issue guidelines for the reception into full communion of Christians baptized into other churches and ecclesial communities. Account is to be taken of the fact that they are not catechumens and of the degree of knowledge and practice of the Christian faith which they may have.

100. According to the rite of Christian Initiation of Adults, those adhering to Christ for the first time are normally baptized during the Paschal Vigil. Where the celebration of this rite includes the reception into full communion of those already baptized, a clear distinction must be made between them and those who are not yet baptized.

101. In the present state of our relations with the ecclesial communities of the Reformation of the 16th century, we have not yet reached agreement about the significance or sacramental nature or even of the administration of the sacrament of confirmation. Therefore, under present circumstances, persons entering into full communion with the Catholic church from one of these communities are to receive the sacrament of confirmation according to the doctrine and rite of the Catholic church before being admitted to eucharistic communion.

B. SHARING SPIRITUAL ACTIVITIES AND RESOURCES

GENERAL PRINCIPLES

102. Christians may be encouraged to share in spiritual activities and resources, i.e. to share that spiritual heritage they have in common in a manner and to a degree appropriate to their present divided state.[11]

103. The term "sharing in spiritual activities and resources" covers such things as prayer offered in common, sharing in liturgical worship in the strict sense as described below in No. 116, as well as common use of sacred places and of all necessary objects.

104. The principles which should direct this spiritual sharing are the following:

a) In spite of the serious difficulties which prevent full ecclesial communion, it is clear that all those who by baptism are incorporated into Christ share many elements of the Christian life. There thus exists a real even if imperfect communion among Christians which can be expressed in many ways, including sharing in prayer and liturgical worship,[12] as will be indicated in the paragraph which follows.

---

10. Cf. CIC, c. 869.1 and .3.
11. UR, 8.
12. Cf. UR, 3 and 8; see also n. 116 below.

b) According to Catholic faith, the Catholic Church has been endowed with the whole of revealed truth and all the means of salvation as a gift which cannot be lost.[13] Nevertheless, among the elements and gifts which belong to the Catholic Church (e.g., the written word of God, the life of grace, faith, hope and charity etc.) many can exist outside its visible limits. The churches and ecclesial communities not in full communion with the Catholic Church have by no means been deprived of significance and value in the mystery of salvation, for the Spirit of Christ has not refrained from using them as means of salvation.[14] In ways that vary according to the condition of each church or ecclesial community, their celebrations are able to nourish the life of grace in their members who participate in them and provide access to the communion of salvation.[15]

c) The sharing of spiritual activities and resources, therefore, must reflect this double fact:

1) The real communion in the life of the Spirit which already exists among Christians and is expressed in their prayer and liturgical worship.

2) The incomplete character of this communion because of differences of faith and understanding which are incompatible with an unrestricted mutual sharing of spiritual endowments.

d) Fidelity to this complex reality makes it necessary to establish norms for spiritual sharing which take into account the diverse ecclesial situations of the churches and ecclesial communities involved, so that as Christians esteem and rejoice in the spiritual riches they have in common they are also made more aware of the necessity of overcoming the separations which still exist.

e) Since eucharistic concelebration is a visible manifestation of full communion in faith, worship and community life of the Catholic Church, expressed by ministers of that church, it is not permitted to concelebrate the eucharist with ministers of other churches or ecclesial communities.[16]

105. There should be a certain "reciprocity" since sharing in spiritual activities and resources, even with defined limits, is a contribution, in a spirit of mutual good will and charity, to the growth of harmony among Christians.

106. It is recommended that consultations on this sharing take place between appropriate Catholic authorities and those of other communions to seek out the possibilities for lawful reciprocity according to the doctrine and traditions of different communities.

107. Catholics ought to show a sincere respect for the liturgical and sacramental discipline of other churches and ecclesial communities, and these in their turn are asked to show the same respect for Catholic discipline. One of the objectives of the consultation mentioned above should be a greater mutual understanding of each other's discipline and even an agreement on how to manage a situation

---

13. Cf. LG, 8; UR, 4.
14. Cf. UR, 3.
15. Cf. UR, 3, 15, 22.
16. Cf. CIC, c. 908; CCEC, c. 702.

in which the discipline of one church calls into question or conflicts with the discipline of another.

108. Where appropriate, Catholics should be encouraged, in accordance with the church's norms, to join in prayer with Christians of other churches and ecclesial communities. Such prayers in common are certainly a very effective means of petitioning for the grace of unity, and they are a genuine expression of the ties which still bind Catholics to these other Christians.[17] Shared prayer is in itself a way to spiritual reconciliation.

109. Prayer in common is recommended for Catholics and other Christians so that together they may put before God the needs and problems they share—e.g., peace, social concerns, mutual charity among people, the dignity of the family, the effects of poverty, hunger and violence, etc. The same may be said of occasions when, according to circumstances, a nation, region or community wishes to make a common act of thanksgiving or petition to God, as on a national holiday, at a time of public disaster or mourning, on a day set aside for remembrance of those who have died for their country, etc. This kind of prayer is also recommended when Christians hold meetings for study or common action.

110. Shared prayer should, however, be particularly concerned with the restoration of Christian unity. It can center, e.g., on the mystery of the church and its unity, on baptism as a sacramental bond of unity or on the renewal of personal and community life as a necessary means to achieving unity. Prayer of this type is particularly recommended during the Week of Prayer for Christian Unity or in the period between Ascension and Pentecost.

111. Representatives of the churches, ecclesial communities or other groups concerned should cooperate and prepare together such prayer. They should decide among themselves the way in which each is to take part, choose the themes and select the scripture readings, hymns and prayers.

a) In such a service there is room for any reading, prayer and hymn which manifests the faith or spiritual life shared by all Christian people. There is a place for an exhortation, address or biblical meditation drawing on the common Christian inheritance and able to promote mutual good will and unity.

b) Care should be taken that the versions of holy scripture used be acceptable to all and be faithful translations of the original text.

c) It is desirable that the structure of these celebrations should take account of the different patterns of community prayer in harmony with the liturgical renewal in many churches and ecclesial communities, with particular regard being given to common heritage of hymns, of texts taken from lectionaries and of liturgical prayers.

d) When services are arranged between Catholics and those of an Eastern church, particular mention should be given to the liturgical discipline of each church, in accordance with No. 115 below.

---

17. Cf. UR, 8.

112. Although a church building is a place in which a community is normally accustomed to celebrating its own liturgy, the common services mentioned above may be celebrated in the church of one or other of the communities concerned if that is acceptable to all the participants. Whatever place is used should be agreeable to all, be capable of being properly prepared and be conducive to devotion.

113. Where there is a common agreement among the participants, those who have a function in a ceremony may use the dress proper to their ecclesiastical rank and to the nature of the celebration.

114. Under the direction of those who have proper formation and experience, it may be helpful in certain cases to arrange for spiritual sharing in the form of days of recollection, spiritual exercises, groups for the study and sharing of traditions of spirituality, and more stable associations for a deeper exploration of a common spiritual life. Serious attention must always be given to what has been said concerning the recognition of the real differences of doctrine which exist as well as to the teaching and discipline of the Catholic Church concerning sacramental sharing.

115. Since the celebration of the eucharist on the Lord's Day is the foundation and center of the whole liturgical year,[18] Catholics—but those of Eastern churches according to their own law[19]—are obliged to attend Mass on that day and on days of precept.[20] It is not advisable therefore to organize ecumenical services on Sundays, and it must be remembered that even when Catholics participate in ecumenical services or in services of other churches and ecclesial communities, the obligation of participating at Mass on these days remains.

SHARING IN NONSACRAMENTAL LITURGICAL WORSHIP

116. By liturgical worship is meant worship carried out according to books, prescriptions and customs of a church or ecclesial community presided over by a minister or delegate of that church or community. This liturgical worship may be of a nonsacramental kind or may be the celebration of one or more of the Christian sacraments. The concern here is nonsacramental worship.

117. In some situations, the official prayer of a church may be preferred to ecumenical services specially prepared for the occasion. Participation in such celebrations as morning or evening prayer, special vigils, etc., will enable people of different liturgical traditions—Catholic, Eastern, Anglican and Protestant—to understand each other's community prayer better and to share more deeply in traditions which often have developed from common roots.

118. In liturgical celebrations taking place in other churches and ecclesial communities, Catholics are encouraged to take part in the psalms, responses, hymns and common actions of the church in which they are guests. If invited by their hosts, they may read a lesson or preach.

---

18. Cf. SC, 106.
19. Cf. CCEC, c. 881.1; CIC, c. 1247.
20. Cf. CIC, c. 1247; CCEC, c. 881.1.

119. Regarding assistance at liturgical worship of this type, there should be a meticulous regard for the sensibilities of the clergy and people of all the Christian communities concerned, as well as for local customs that may vary according to time, place, persons and circumstances. In a Catholic liturgical celebration, ministers of other churches and ecclesial communities may have the place and liturgical honors proper to their rank and their role, if this is judged desirable. Catholic clergy invited to be present at a celebration of another church or ecclesial community may wear the appropriate dress or insignia of their ecclesiastical office if it is agreeable to their hosts.

120. In the prudent judgment of the local ordinary, the funeral rites of the Catholic Church may be granted to members of a non-Catholic Church or ecclesial community unless it is evidently contrary to their will and provided that their own minister is unavailable[21] and that the general provisions of canon law do not forbid it.[22]

121. Blessings ordinarily given for the benefit of Catholics may also be given to other Christians who request them, according to the nature and object of the blessing. Public prayer for other Christians, living or dead, and for the needs and intentions of other churches and ecclesial communities and their spiritual heads may be offered during the litanies and other invocations of a liturgical service, but not during the eucharistic anaphora. Ancient Christian liturgical and ecclesiological tradition permits the specific mention in the eucharistic anaphora only of the names of persons who are in full communion with the church celebrating the eucharist.

SHARING IN SACRAMENTAL LIFE, ESPECIALLY THE EUCHARIST

a) With Members of Various Eastern Churches

122. Between the Catholic Church and the Eastern churches not in full communion with it, there is still a very close communion in matters of faith.[23] Moreover, "through the celebration of the eucharist of the Lord in each of these churches, the church of God is built up and grows in stature" and "although separated from us, these churches still possess true sacraments, above all—by apostolic succession—the priesthood and the eucharist."[24] This offers ecclesiological and sacramental grounds, according to the understanding of the Catholic church, for allowing and even encouraging some sharing in liturgical worship, even of the eucharist, with these churches, "given suitable circumstances and the approval of church authorities."[25] It is recognized, however, that Eastern Churches, on the basis of their own ecclesiological understanding, may have more restrictive disciplines in this matter, which others should respect. Pastors should carefully instruct the faithful so that they will be clearly aware of the

---

21. Cf. CIC, c. 1183.3; CCEC, c. 876.2.
22. Cf. CIC, c. 1184; CCEC, c. 887.
23. Cf. UR, 14.
24. UR, 22.
25. UR, 22.

proper reasons for this kind of sharing in liturgical worship and of the variety of discipline which may exist in this connection.

123. Whenever necessity requires or a genuine spiritual advantage suggests, and provided that the danger of error or indifferentism is avoided, it is lawful for any Catholic for whom it is physically or morally impossible to approach a Catholic minister, to receive the sacraments of penance, eucharist and anointing of the sick from a minister of an Eastern church.[26]

124. Since practice differs between Catholics and Eastern Christians in the matter of frequent communion, confession before communion and the eucharistic fast, care must be taken to avoid scandal and suspicion among Eastern Christians through Catholics not following the Eastern usage. A Catholic who legitimately wishes to communicate with Eastern Christians must respect the Eastern discipline as much as possible and refrain from communicating if that church restricts sacramental communion to its own members to the exclusion of others.

125. Catholic ministers may lawfully administer the sacraments of penance, eucharist and the anointing of the sick to members of the Eastern churches who ask for these sacraments of their own free will and are properly disposed. In these particular cases also, due consideration should be given to the discipline of the Eastern churches for their own faithful, and any suggestion of proselytism should be avoided.[27]

126. Catholics may read lessons at a sacramental liturgical celebration in the Eastern churches if they are invited to do so. An Eastern Christian may be invited to read the lessons at similar services in Catholic churches.

127. A Catholic minister may be present and take part in the celebration of a marriage being properly celebrated between Eastern Christians or between a Catholic and an Eastern Christian in the Eastern church if invited to do so by the Eastern church authority and if it is in accord with the norms given below concerning mixed marriages, where they apply.

128. A member of an Eastern church may act as bridesmaid or best man at a wedding in a Catholic Church; a Catholic also may be bridesmaid or best man at a marriage properly celebrated in Eastern church. In all cases this practice must conform to the general discipline of both churches regarding the requirements for participating in such marriages.

b) With Christians of Other Churches and Ecclesial Communities.

129. A sacrament is an act of Christ and of the church through the Spirit.[28] Its celebration in a concrete community is the sign of the reality of its unity in faith, worship and community life. As well as being signs, sacraments—most specially

---

26. Cf. CIC, c. 844.2 and CCEC, c. 671.2.
27. Cf. CIC, c. 844.3 and cf. n. 106 above.
28. Cf. CIC, c. 840 and CCEC, c. 667.

the eucharist—are sources of the unity of the Christian community and of spiritual life, and are means for building them up. Thus eucharistic communion is inseparably linked to full ecclesial communion and its visible expression.

At the same time, the Catholic Church teaches that by baptism members of other churches and ecclesial communities are brought into a real, even if imperfect, communion with the Catholic Church[29] and that "baptism, which constitutes the sacramental bond of unity existing among all who through it are reborn . . . is wholly directed toward the acquiring of fullness of life in Christ."[30] The eucharist is, for the baptized, a spiritual food which enables them to overcome sin and to live the very life of Christ, to be incorporated more profoundly in him and share more intensely in the whole economy of the mystery of Christ.

It is in the light of these two basic principles, which must always be taken into account together, that in general the Catholic Church permits access to its eucharistic communion and to the sacraments of penance and anointing of the sick only to those who share its oneness in faith, worship and ecclesial life.[31] For the same reasons it also recognizes that in certain circumstances, by way of exception and under certain conditions, access to these sacraments may be permitted or even commended for Christians of other churches and ecclesial communities.[32]

130. In case of danger of death, Catholic ministers may administer these sacraments when the conditions given below (No. 131) are present. In other cases, it is strongly recommended that the diocesan bishop, taking into account any norms which may have been established for this matter by the episcopal conference or by the synods of Eastern Catholic churches, establish general norms for judging situations of grave and pressing need and for verifying the conditions mentioned below (No. 131).[33] In accord with canon law,[34] these general norms are to be established only after consultation with at least the local competent authority of the other interested church or ecclesial community. Catholic ministers will judge individual cases and administer these sacraments only in accord with these established norms, where they exist. Otherwise they will judge according to the norms of this directory.

131. The conditions under which a Catholic minister may administer the sacraments of the eucharist, of penance and of the anointing of the sick to a baptized person who may be found in the circumstances given above (No. 130) are that the person be unable to have recourse for the sacrament desired to a minister of his or her own church or ecclesial community, ask for the sacrament of his or her own initiative, manifest Catholic faith in this sacrament and be properly disposed.[35]

---

29. Cf. UR, 3.
30. UR, 22.
31. Cf. UR, 8; CIC, c. 844.1 and CCEC, c. 671.1.
32. Cf. CIC, c. 844.4 and CCEC, c. 671.4.
33. For the establishing of these norms we refer to the following documents: "On Admitting Other Christians to Eucharistic Communion in the Catholic Church" (1972) and "Note Interpreting the Instruction on Admitting Other Christians to Eucharistic Communion Under Certain Circumstances" (1973).
34. Cf. CIC, c. 844.5 and CCEC, c. 671.5.
35. Cf. CIC, c. 844.4 and CCEC, c. 671.4.

132. On the basis of the Catholic doctrine concerning the sacraments and their validity, a Catholic who finds himself or herself in the circumstances mentioned above (Nos. 130 and 131) may ask for these sacraments only from a minister in whose church these sacraments are valid or from one who is known to be validly ordained according to the Catholic teaching on ordination.

133. The reading of Scripture during a eucharistic celebration in the Catholic Church is to be done by members of that church. On exceptional occasions and for a just cause, the bishop of the diocese may permit a member of another church or ecclesial community to take on the task of reader.

134. In the Catholic eucharistic liturgy the homily which forms part of the liturgy itself is reserved to the priest or deacon, since it is the presentation of the mysteries of faith and the norms of Christian living in accordance with Catholic teaching and tradition.[36]

135. For the reading of Scripture and preaching during other than eucharistic celebrations, the norms given above (No. 118) are to be applied.

136. Members of other churches or ecclesial communities may be witnesses at the celebration of marriage in a Catholic Church. Catholics may also be witnesses at marriages which are celebrated in other churches or ecclesial communities.

SHARING OTHER RESOURCES FOR SPIRITUAL LIFE AND ACTIVITY

137. Catholic churches are consecrated or blessed buildings which have an important theological and liturgical significance for the Catholic community. They are therefore generally reserved for Catholic worship. However, if priests, ministers or communities not in full communion with the Catholic Church do not have a place or the liturgical objects necessary for celebrating worthily their religious ceremonies, the diocesan bishop may allow them the use of a church or a Catholic building and also lend them what may be necessary for their services. Under similar circumstances, permission may be given to them for interment or for the celebration of services at Catholic cemeteries.

138. Because of developments in society, the rapid growth of population and urbanization, and for financial motives, where there is a good ecumenical relationship and understanding between the communities the shared ownership or use of church premises over an extended period of time may become a matter of practical interest.

139. When authorization for such ownership or use is given by the diocesan bishop according to any norms which may be established by the episcopal conference or the Holy See, judicious consideration should be given to the reservation of the blessed sacrament so that this question is resolved on the basis of a sound sacramental theology with the respect that is due, while also taking account of the sensitivities of those who will use the building, e.g. by construction a separate room or chapel.

---

36. Cf. CIC, c. 767 and CCEC, c. 614.4.

140. Before making plans for a shared building, the authorities of the communities concerned should first reach agreement as to how their various disciplines will be observed, particularly in regard to the sacraments. Furthermore, a written agreement should be made which will clearly and adequately take care of all questions which may arise concerning financial matters and the obligations arising from church and civil law.

141. In Catholic schools and institutions every effort should be made to respect the faith and conscience of students or teachers who belong to other churches or ecclesial communities. In accordance with their own approved statutes, the authorities of these schools and institutions should take care that clergy of other communities have every facility for giving spiritual and sacramental ministration to their own faithful who attend such schools or institutions. As far as circumstances allow, with the permission of the diocesan bishop these facilities can be offered on the Catholic premises, including the church or chapel.

142. In hospitals, homes for the aged and similar institutions conducted by Catholics, the authorities should promptly advise priests and ministers of other communities of the presence of their faithful, and afford them every facility to visit these persons and give them spiritual and sacramental ministrations under dignified and reverent conditions, including the use of the chapel.

C. MIXED MARRIAGES

143. This section of the Ecumenical Directory does not attempt to give an extended treatment of all the pastoral and canonical questions connected with either the actual celebration of the sacrament of Christian marriage or the pastoral care to be given to Christian families, since such questions form part of the general pastoral care of every bishop or regional conference of bishops. What follows below focuses on specific issues related to mixed marriages and should be understood in the context. The term mixed marriage refers to any marriage between a Catholic and a baptized Christian who is not in full communion with the Catholic church.[37]

144. In all marriages, the primary concern of the church is to uphold the strength and stability of the indissoluble marital union and the family life that flows from it. The perfect union of persons and full sharing of life which constitutes the married state are more easily assured when both partners belong to the same faith community. In addition, practical experience and the observations obtained in various dialogues between representatives of churches and ecclesial communities indicate that mixed marriages frequently present difficulties for the couples themselves and for the children born to them in maintaining their Christian faith and commitment, and for the harmony of family life. For all these reasons, marriage between persons of the same ecclesial community remains the objective to be recommended and encouraged.

---

37. Cf. CIC, c. 1124 and CCEC, c. 813.

145. In view, however, of the growing number of mixed marriages in many parts of the world, the church includes within its urgent pastoral solicitude couples preparing to enter, or already having entered, such marriages. These marriages, even if they have their own particular difficulties, "contain numerous elements that could well be made good use of and developed both for their intrinsic value and for the contribution they can make to the ecumenical movement. This is particularly true when both parties are faithful to their religious duties. Their common baptism and the dynamism of grace provide the spouses in these marriages with the basis and motivation for expressing unity in the sphere of moral and spiritual values."[38]

146. It is the abiding responsibility of all, especially priests and deacons and those who assist them in pastoral ministry, to provide special instruction and support for the Catholic party in living his or her faith as well as for the couples in mixed marriages both in the preparation for the marriage, in its sacramental celebration and for the life together that follows the marriage ceremony. This pastoral care should take into account the concrete spiritual condition of each partner, their formation in their faith and their practice of it. At the same time respect should be shown for the particular circumstances of each couple's situation, the conscience of each partner and the holiness of the state of sacramental marriage itself. Where judged useful, diocesan bishops, synods of Eastern Catholic churches or episcopal conferences could draw up more specific guidelines for this pastoral care.

147. In fulfilling this responsibility, where the situation warrants it positive steps should be taken, if possible, to establish contacts with the minister of the other church or ecclesial community, even if this may not always prove easy. In general, mutual consultation between Christian pastors for supporting such marriages and upholding their values can be a fruitful field of ecumenical collaboration.

148. In preparing the necessary marriage preparation programs, the priest or deacon and those who assist him should stress the positive aspects of what the couple share together as Christians in the life of grace, in faith, hope and love, along with the other interior gifts of the Holy Spirit.[39] Each party, while continuing to be faithful to his or her Christian commitment and to the practice of it, should seek to foster all that can lead to unity and harmony, without minimizing real differences and while avoiding an attitude of religious indifference.

149. In the interest of greater understanding and unity, both parties should learn more about their partner's religious convictions and the teaching and religious practices of the church or ecclesial community to which he or she belongs. To help them live the Christian inheritance they have in common, they should be reminded that prayer together is essential for their spiritual harmony and that reading and study of the sacred Scriptures are especially important. In the period of preparation, the couple's effort to understand their individual religious and

---

38. Cf. John Paul II, apostolic exhortation *Familiaris consortio* (on the family), Nov. 22, 1981: 78.
39. Cf. UR, 3.

ecclesial traditions, and serious consideration of the differences that exist can lead to greater honesty, charity and understanding of these realities and also of the marriage itself.

150. When, for a just and reasonable cause, permission for a mixed marriage is requested, both parties are to be instructed on the essential ends and properties of marriage which are not to be excluded by either party. Furthermore, the Catholic party will be asked to affirm, in the form established by the particular law of the Eastern Catholic churches or by the episcopal conference, that he or she is prepared to avoid the dangers of abandoning the faith and to promise sincerely to do all in his/her power to see that the children of the marriage be baptized and educated in the Catholic Church. The other partner is to be informed of these promises and responsibilities.[40] At the same time it should be recognized that the non-Catholic partner may feel a like obligation because of his/her own Christian commitment. It is to be noted that no formal written or oral promise is required of this partner in canon law.

Those who wish to enter into a mixed marriage should, in the course of the contacts that are made in this connection, be invited and encouraged to discuss the Catholic baptism and education of the children they will have and where possible come to a decision on this question before the marriage.

In order to judge the existence or otherwise of a "just and reasonable cause" with regard to granting permission for this mixed marriage, the local ordinary will take account, among other things, of an explicit refusal on the part of the non-Catholic party.

151. In carrying out this duty of transmitting the Catholic faith to the children the Catholic parent will do so with respect for the religious freedom and conscience of the other parent and with due regard for the unity and permanence of the marriage and for the maintenance of the communion of the family. If, notwithstanding the Catholic's best efforts, the children are not baptized and brought up in the Catholic Church, the Catholic parent does not fall subject to the censure of canon law.[41] At the same time, his/her obligation to share the Catholic faith with the children does not cease. It continues to make its demands, which could be met, for example, by playing an active part in contributing to the Christian atmosphere of the home; doing all that is possible by word and example to enable the other members of the family to appreciate the specific values of the Catholic tradition; taking whatever steps are necessary to be well informed about his/her own faith so as to be able to explain and discuss it with them; praying with the family for the grace of Christian unity as the Lord wills it.

152. While keeping clearly in mind that doctrinal differences impede full sacramental and canonical communion between the Catholic Church and the various Eastern churches, in the pastoral care of marriages between Catholics and Eastern Christians particular attention should be given to the sound and consistent teaching of the faith which is shared by both and to the fact that in the

---

40. Cf. CIC, cc. 1125, 1126 and CCEC, cc. 814, 815.
41. Cf. CIC, c. 1366 and CCEC, c. 1439.

Eastern churches are to be found "true sacraments, and above all, by apostolic succession, the priesthood and the eucharist, whereby they are still joined to us in closest intimacy."[42] If proper pastoral care is given to persons involved in these marriages, the faithful of both communions can be helped to understand how children born of such marriages will be initiated into and spiritually nourished by the sacramental mysteries of Christ. Their formation in authentic Christian doctrine and ways of Christian living would, for the most part, be similar in each church. Diversity in liturgical life and private devotion can be made to encourage rather than hinder family prayer.

153. A marriage between a Catholic and a member of an Eastern church is valid if it has taken place with the celebration of a religious rite by an ordained minister, as long as any other requirements of law for validity have been observed. For lawfulness in these cases, the canonical form of celebration is to be observed.[43] Canonical form is required for the validity of marriages between Catholics and Christians of churches and ecclesial communities.[44]

154. The local ordinary of the Catholic partner, after having consulted the local ordinary of the place where the marriage will be celebrated, may for grave reasons and without prejudice to the law of the Eastern churches[45] dispense the Catholic partner from the observance of the canonical form of marriage.[46] Among these reasons for dispensation may be considered the maintaining of family harmony, obtaining parental consent to the marriage, the recognition of the particular religious commitment of the non-Catholic partner or his/her blood relationship with a minister of another church or ecclesial community. Episcopal conferences are to issue norms by which such a dispensation may be granted in accordance with a common practice.

155. The obligation imposed by some churches or ecclesial communities for the observance of their own form of marriage is not a motive for automatic dispensation from the Catholic canonical form. Such particular situations should form the subject of dialogue between the churches, at least at the local level.

156. One must keep in mind that if the wedding is celebrated with a dispensation from canonical form some public form of celebration is still required for validity.[47] To emphasize the unity of marriage, it is not permitted to have two separate religious services in which the exchange of consent would be expressed twice, or even one service which would celebrate two such exchanges of consent jointly or successively.[48]

---

42. Cf. UR, 15.
43. Cf. CIC, c. 1127.1 and CCEC, c. 834.2.
44. Cf. CIC, c. 1127.1 and CCEC, c. 834.1.
45. Cf. CCEC, c. 835.
46. Cf. CIC, c. 1127.2.
47. Cf. ibid.
48. Cf. CIC, c. 1127.3 and CCEC, c. 839.

157. With the previous authorization of the local ordinary, and if invited to do so, a Catholic priest or deacon may attend or participate in some way in the celebration of mixed marriages in situations where the dispensation from canonical form has been granted. In these cases there may be only one ceremony in which the presiding person receives the marriage vows. At the invitation of this celebrant, the Catholic priest or deacon may offer other appropriate prayers, read from the Scriptures, give a brief exhortation and bless the couple.

158. Upon request of the couple, the local ordinary may permit the Catholic priest to invite the minister of the party of the other church or ecclesial community to participate in the celebration of the marriage, to read from the Scriptures, give a brief exhortation and bless the couple.

159. Because of problems concerning eucharistic sharing which may arise from the presence of non-Catholic witnesses and guests, a mixed marriage celebrated according to the Catholic form ordinarily takes place outside the eucharistic liturgy. For a just cause, however, the diocesan bishop may permit the celebration of the eucharist.[49] In the latter case, the decision as to whether the non-Catholic party of the marriage may be admitted to eucharistic communion is to be made in keeping with the general norms existing in the matter both for Eastern Christians[50] and for other Christians,[51] taking into account the particular situation of the reception of the sacrament of Christian marriage by two baptized Christians.

160. Although the spouses in a mixed marriage share the sacraments of baptism and marriage, eucharistic sharing can only be exceptional and in each case the norms stated above concerning the admission of a non-Catholic Christian to eucharistic communion,[52] as well as those concerning the participation of a Catholic in eucharistic communion in an other church,[53] must be observed.

V. ECUMENICAL COOPERATION, DIALOGUE AND COMMON WITNESS

COMMON BIBLE WORK

183. The word of God that is written in the Scriptures nourishes the life of the church in manifold ways[54] and is "a precious instrument in the mighty hand of God for attaining to that unity which the Savior holds out to all men."[55] Veneration of the Scriptures is a fundamental bond of unity between Christians, one that holds firm even when the churches and communities to which they belong are not in full communion with each other. Everything that can be done to make

---

49. RMarr, 8.
50. Cf. above, n. 125.
51. Cf. above, nn. 129–131.
52. Cf. above, nn. 125, 130 and 131.
53. Cf. above, n. 132.
54. Cf. DV, Ch. 6.
55. UR, 21.

members of the churches and ecclesial communities read the word of God, and to do that together when possible (e.g., Bible Weeks), reinforces this bond of unity that already unites them, helps them to be open to the unifying action of God and strengthens the common witness to the saving word of God which they give to the world. The provision and diffusion of suitable editions of the Bible is a prerequisite to the hearing of the word. While the Catholic Church continues to produce editions of the Bible that meet her own specific standards and requirements, it also cooperates willingly with other churches and ecclesial communities in the making of translations and in the publication of common editions in accordance with what was foreseen by the Second Vatican Council and is provided for in the Code of Canon Law.[56] It sees ecumenical cooperation in this field as a valuable form of common service and common witness in the church and to the world.

184. The Catholic Church is involved in this cooperation in many ways and at different levels. The Pontifical Council for Promoting Christian Unity was involved in the setting up, in 1969, of the World Catholic Federation for the Biblical Apostolate (now Catholic Biblical Federation), as an international Catholic organization of a public character to further the pastoral implementation of Dei Verbum, Ch. VI. In accordance with this objective, whenever local circumstances allow, collaboration at the level of local churches as well as at the regional level, between the ecumenical officer and the local sections of the federation should be strongly encouraged.

185. Through the general secretariat of the Catholic Biblical Federation, the Pontifical Council for Promoting Christian Unity maintains and develops relations with the United Bible Societies, an international Christian organization which has published jointly with the secretariat "Guidelines for Interconfessional Cooperation in Translating the Bible."[57] This document sets out the principles, methods and concrete orientations of this special type of collaboration in the biblical field. This collaboration has already yielded good results. Similar contacts and cooperation between institutions devoted to the publication and use of the Bible are encouraged on all levels of the life of the church. They can help cooperation between the churches and ecclesial communities in missionary work, catechetics and religious education, as well as in common prayer and study. They can often result in the joint production of a Bible that may be used by several churches and ecclesial communities in a given cultural area, or for specific purposes such as study or liturgical life.[58] Cooperation of this kind can be an antidote to the use of the Bible in a fundamentalist way or for sectarian purposes.

---

56. Cf. CIC, c. 825.2 and CCEC, c. 655.1.

57. New revised edition 1987 of the first 1968 version. Published in Information Service of the SPCU, 65 (1987): 140–145.

58. In accordance with the norms laid down in CIC, cc. 825–827, 838 and in CCEC, cc. 655–659 and the decree of the Congregation for the Doctrine of the Faith *Ecclesiae pastorum de Ecclesiae pastorum vigilantia circa libros* (March 19, 1975) in AAS 1975, 281–184.

186. Catholics can share the study of the Scriptures with members of other churches and ecclesial communities in many different ways and on many different levels. This sharing goes from the kind of work that can be done in neighborhood or parochial groups to that of scholarly research among professional exegetes. In order to have ecumenical value, at whatever level it is done, this work needs to be grounded on faith and to nourish faith. It will often bring home to the participants how the doctrinal positions of different churches and ecclesial communities, and differences in their approaches to the use and exegesis of the Bible, lead to different interpretations of particular passages. It is helpful for Catholics when the editions of the Scriptures that they use actually draw attention to passages in which the doctrine of the church is at issue. They will want to face up to any difficulties and disagreements that come from the ecumenical use of the Scriptures with an understanding of and a loyalty to the teaching of the church. But this need not prevent them from recognizing how much they are at one with other Christians in the interpretation of the Scriptures. They will come to appreciate the light that the experience and traditions of the different churches can throw on parts of the Scriptures that are especially significant for them. They will become more open to the possibility of finding new starting points in the Scriptures themselves for discussion about controversial issues. They will be challenged to discover the meaning of God's word in relation to contemporary human situations that they share with their fellow Christians. Moreover, they will experiences with joy the unifying power of God's word.

COMMON LITURGICAL TEXTS

187. Churches and ecclesial communities whose members live within a culturally homogeneous area should draw up together, where possible, a text of the most important Christian prayers (the Lord's Prayer, Apostles' Creed, Nicene-Constantinopolitan Creed, a Trinitarian doxology, the Glory to God in the Highest). These would be for regular use by all the churches and ecclesial communities or at least for use when they pray together on ecumenical occasions. Agreement on a version of the psalter for liturgical use, or at least of some of the more frequently used psalms would also be desirable; a similar agreement for common scriptural readings for liturgical use should also be explored. The use of liturgical and other prayers that come from the period of the undivided church can help to foster an ecumenical sense. Common hymn books, or at least common collections of hymns to be included in the books of the different churches and ecclesial communities, as well as cooperation in developing liturgical music, are also to be recommended. When Christians pray together with one voice, their common witness reaches to heaven as well as being heard on earth.

DIRECTORY ON POPULAR PIETY
AND THE LITURGY
PRINCIPLES AND GUIDELINES

CONGREGATION FOR DIVINE WORSHIP
AND THE DISCIPLINE OF THE SACRAMENTS
DECEMBER 14, 2001

AN OVERVIEW OF THE *DIRECTORY ON POPULAR PIETY AND THE LITURGY: PRINCIPLES AND GUIDELINES*

Rev. Mark R. Francis, CSV

The *Directory on Popular Piety and the Liturgy* (DPPL) was published by the Congregation for Divine Worship and the Discipline of the Sacraments (CDWDS) on December 17, 2001 with the approval of Pope John Paul II. The introduction to the document, while reaffirming the Congregation's desire to promote the liturgy as the source and summit of the life of the Church, seeks to "draw attention to the need to ensure that the other forms of piety among the Christian people are not overlooked, nor their useful contribution to living in unity with Christ, in the Church, be forgotten."[1] DPPL seeks to offer guidelines on popular religious practices and their relationship to the liturgy of the Church and prevent "abuses or deviations"[2] through a systematic restating of the teaching of the magisterium on the place of popular piety in the life of Christians.

After presenting extracts from an address on the importance of popular piety by Pope John Paul II to the CDWDS, the decree authorizing the publication of the *Directory*, and an introduction that sets the context for the document,[3] the *Directory* itself is divided into two parts. The first part, "Emerging Trends," offers background information to allow a more profound understanding of popular piety. It is composed of three chapters: "Liturgy and Popular Piety in a Historical Perspective"; "Liturgy and Popular Piety in the Church's Magisterium"; and "Theological Principles for an Evaluation and Renewal of Popular Piety." The second part of the *Directory*, entitled "Guidelines for the Harmonization of Popular Piety with the Liturgy," is of a more practical, pastoral nature and contains five chapters entitled: "The Liturgical Year"; "Veneration of the Mother of God"; "Cult of the Saints and Beati"; "Suffrage for the Dead"; and "Shrines and Pilgrimages." The document ends with a conclusion that briefly restates the purpose of the *Directory*.

AUTHORITY OF THE DOCUMENT

The document was published in the form of a "directory." This relatively new form of communication by dicasteries of the Roman Curia was developed after the Second Vatican Council in order to deal with practical issues that arise in the life of the Church. Similar to "instructions," examples of documents issued as directories are: the *General Catechetical Directory* issued by the Congregation

---

1. *Directory on Popular Piety and the Liturgy* (DPPL), 1.

2. Ibid., 4.

3. The papal address and decree are not included in this collection. To view these documents, please visit the Vatican website: www.vatican.va/roman_curia/congregations/ccdds/documents/rc_con_ccdds_doc_20020513_vers-direttorio_en.html.

for the Clergy in 1971; *On the Ministry and Life of Priests* published by the same Congregation in 1994; *For the Application of Principles and Norms on Ecumenism* by the Council for Promoting Christian Unity in 1967 and 1970. Other well-known directories issued by the CDWDS are the *Directory for Masses with Children* in 1973 and the *Directory on Sunday Celebration in the Absence of a Priest* in 1998. The purpose of this kind of document is well explained by a noted canonist:

> The intent of a directory is to provide norms for pastoral practice. The text usually combines theory and disciplinary norms; the theological foundations of the norms are quite clearly elaborated. Directories usually provide broad guidelines for various kinds of ministry in the Church. It is difficult to specify the weight that should be attached to them. Some are clearly legislative documents and contain statements to that effect; others are not legislative in character. The advantage of issuing statements in the form of directories is that the legislation can be adequately situated in its proper theological context.[4]

As DPPL states in its introduction, the document does not contain new teachings or principles, but does establish practical guidelines for applying the already established principles and teachings already articulated by the magisterium. Its authority derives from conciliar, papal, and curial teaching on this topic that is systematically presented in DPPL with a "view to assisting the Bishops in promoting and honoring the prayers and pious practices of the Christian people, that fully reflect the norms of the Church."[5]

SOURCES FOR THE *DIRECTORY*

DPPL cites previous magisterial pronouncements that speak of the relationship of popular piety and liturgy. The most fundamental reference is the treatment of this relationship in *Sacrosanctum Concilium* (SC):

> Popular devotions of the Christian people are to be highly commended, provided they accord with the laws and norms of the Church, above all when they are ordered by the Apostolic See.

> Devotions proper to individual Churches also have a special dignity if they are undertaken by mandate of the bishops according to customs or books lawfully approved.

> But these devotions should be so drawn up that they harmonize with the liturgical seasons, accord with the sacred liturgy, are in some fashion derived from it, and lead the people to it, since, in fact, the liturgy by its very nature far surpasses any of them.[6]

It could be argued that the entire DPPL is simply a commentary on this one article of SC. The relationship between liturgy and popular piety, though,

---

4. Seasoltz, R. Kevin. *New Liturgy, New Laws.* (Collegeville MN: The Liturgical Press, 1980), 179.
5. DPPL, 3.
6. *Sacrosanctum Concilium* (SC), 13.

continued to be the object of official commentary in the years following the Second Vatican Council. Pope Paul VI, in his groundbreaking 1975 apostolic exhortation *Evangelii nuntiandi* (EN) spoke of the need to take seriously the potential contributions of popular religiosity to the Church's efforts at evangelization, asserting that despite some of its limits, "when it is well oriented, this popular religiosity can be more and more for multitudes of our people a true encounter with God in Jesus Christ."[7] The second article of DPPL extensively quotes Pope John Paul II's apostolic letter *Vicesimus quintus annus* (1988). Following the lead of this letter, the document announces two major orientations: (1) popular piety represents a legitimate religious attitude that must be respected but needs to be constantly evangelized; (2) pious exercises of the Christian people can be recommended provided that they do not replace the liturgy or become integrated into liturgical celebrations. The authentic pastoral approach to the liturgy is to use the riches of popular devotions to build the liturgy, purifying them and directing them to the liturgy "as an offering of the people."[8]

Two other magisterial documents also deal with the topic of liturgy and popular piety. The 1994 *Catechism of the Catholic Church* (CCC) devotes several articles to the topic[9] encouraging catechesis to take into account the "various forms of piety surrounding the Church's sacramental life."[10] While the document of the CDWDS, *Varietates legitimae* (VL) warns against introducing practices of "popular devotion"[11] into the liturgy under the pretext of inculturation this document does allow for the introduction of local practices in the liturgical celebrations of Marriage and funerals provided that they are purified of any appearance of syncretism or superstition.[12]

PROPOSED CLARIFICATION OF TERMINOLOGY

In the magisterial documents and the scholarly studies that preceded DPPL, various terms were used to describe the phenomenon of "popular religiosity" or "popular piety." Although acknowledging that there is no universally accepted definition for either of these terms, in order to offer some precision, DPPL proposes its own definitions for four expressions that appear in discussing this topic: pious exercises, devotions, popular piety, and popular religiosity.

Pious exercises are those non-liturgical public or private expressions of Christian piety that "are considered to be in harmony with the spirit, norms, and rhythms of the Liturgy."[13] These expressions are inspired by the liturgy and are also part of the cultic patrimony of a particular culture or religious family. They are practiced in conformity with the laws and customs of the Church and refer to public divine revelation.

---

7. *Evangelii nuntiandi* (EN), 48.
8. DPPL, 2.
9. See *Catechism of the Catholic Church* (CCC), 1674–1676, 1679.
10. CCC, 1674.
11. *Varietates legitimae* (VL), 45.
12. Ibid., 48.
13. DPPL, 7.

Devotions are described as external practices such as prayers, hymns, and observances attached to particular times or places, insignias, medals, and habits that manifest a particular relationship with the Divine Persons, with the Blessed Virgin Mary, or with the saints. Unlike pious exercises, devotions are not necessarily inspired by the liturgy.[14] These practices are largely private or individual.

Popular piety refers to diverse expressions of worship, public or private, which are inspired predominantly by local cultures and not by the liturgy. DPPL sees popular piety as "a treasure of the people of God"[15] because it is an expression of the thirst for God among the poor and humble who see God as a loving presence and provident Father.[16] It also generates interior attitudes of "patience, awareness of the Cross in everyday life, detachment, openness to others and devotion."[17]

Popular religiosity refers to an awareness of and a response to the transcendent that is present in all peoples. It gives form to ritual expressions that articulate a given culture's concepts of nature, society, and history.[18] Popular religiosity, though, does not necessarily refer to Christian revelation.[19]

THE THREE PRINCIPLES THAT SHAPE THE *DIRECTORY*

There are three guiding principles that influence DPPL's treatment of popular piety. The first, which we have seen, comes from *Sacrosanctum Concilium* which categorically states that the liturgy is preeminent and always surpasses all forms of popular piety.[20]

Acknowledging the primacy of the liturgy over other forms of worship, however laudable, is crucial, since the liturgy is a sacred action, carried out by the Christ, the priest, and Christ's Body, the Church, and takes precedence over all other forms of worship. As DPPL points out: "While sacramental actions are *necessary* to life in Christ, the various forms of popular piety are *optional.*"[21]

The second principle, though, is to encourage the various forms of popular piety—especially pious exercises. These forms, though, are to be judged in the light of the Gospel in order to avoid magical and superstitious interpretations. In evaluating and renewing popular piety, any given practice needs to be imbued with four spirits or characteristics: a biblical spirit, a liturgical spirit, an ecumenical spirit, and an anthropological spirit.[22] The importance of the direct or indirect relationship of popular piety to the Sacred Scriptures is obvious. The connection with the liturgy is also crucial in promoting a relationship with the mysteries celebrated and in disposing the faithful to celebrate them. Popular religious practice needs to be aware of the sensibilities and traditions of other Christians. Finally, DPPL's use of the term "anthropological" refers to a respect that is due to the symbols and expressions of the cultural context of the local

---

14. See ibid., 8.
15. Ibid., 9.
16. Ibid.
17. Ibid.
18. See ibid., 10.
19. Ibid.
20. See SC, 13.
21. DPPL, 11.
22. See ibid., 12.

church without, however, idealizing or proposing popular religious practices that are no longer followed (senseless archaisms).

The third principle is that popular piety ought to be in harmony with, but distinct from, the liturgy. DPPL calls upon the bishops of the Church to assure that the faithful are aware of the distinction between the liturgy and pious customs, avoiding superimposing pious practices that have their own "language, rhythm, course and theological emphasis"[23] different from those of the liturgy.

SIGNIFICANCE OF THE *DIRECTORY* IN THE LIFE OF THE CHURCH

DPPL represents a step forward in providing authoritative pastoral orientations on the important relationship between liturgy and popular religious practices. It is the product of a mature reflection on the whole of the liturgical reform initiated by the Second Vatican Council that in practice tended to emphasize the liturgy in such a way that other sources of Christian life were marginalized. This document maintains that popular religious practices should not be seen in opposition to the liturgy. Rather, they form part of the rich spiritual patrimony of Catholics that are capable of deepening our life of faith.

Though liturgy and popular piety are not "equal" in importance, attention to popular religious practices can be an important source for both evangelization and for the inculturation of the Gospel message in the many cultures where the Church is present. As DPPL points out, "popular piety, because of its symbolic and expressive qualities, can often provide the Liturgy with important insights for inculturation and stimulate an effective dynamic creativity."[24] The *Directory on Popular Piety and the Liturgy* is a rich resource for all pastors and liturgical ministers in their efforts at continuing the renewal of the liturgy begun by the Second Vatican Council.

---

23. DPPL, 13.
24. Ibid., 58.

OUTLINE

CONGREGATION FOR DIVINE WORSHIP
AND THE DISCIPLINE OF THE SACRAMENTS

DIRECTORY
ON POPULAR PIETY AND THE LITURGY
PRINCIPLES AND GUIDELINES

VATICAN CITY
DECEMBER 2001

INTRODUCTION

1.   In accordance with the teaching of the Second Vatican Council, this Congregation, in furthering and promoting the Liturgy, "the summit toward which the activity of the Church is directed . . . and the fount from which all her power flows,"[1] wishes to draw attention to the need to ensure that other forms of piety among the Christian people are not overlooked, nor their useful contribution to living in unity with Christ, in the Church, be forgotten.[2]

Following on the conciliar renewal, the situation with regard to Christian popular piety varies according to country and local traditions. Contradictory attitudes to popular piety can be noted: manifest and hasty abandonment of inherited forms of popular piety resulting in a void not easily filled; attachments to imperfect or erroneous types of devotion which are estranged from genuine Biblical revelation and compete with the economy of the sacraments; unjustified criticism of the piety of the common people in the name of a presumed "purity" of faith; a need to preserve the riches of popular piety, which is an expression of the profound and mature religious feeling of the people at a given moment in space and time; a need to purify popular piety of equivocation and of the dangers deriving from syncretism; the renewed vitality of popular religiosity in resisting, or in reaction to, a pragmatic technological culture and economic utilitarianism; decline of interest in popular piety ensuing on the rise of secularized ideologies and the aggressive activities of "sects" hostile to it.

The question constantly occupies the attention of Bishops, priests, deacons, pastoral assistants, and scholars, who are concerned both to promote the liturgical life among the faithful and to utilize popular piety.

---

1. SC 10.
2. Cf. SC 12 and 13.

2.   In its constitution on the Liturgy, the Second Vatican Council explicitly touched upon the relationship between the Liturgy and pious exercises.[3] The question of popular piety has been more amply considered on various occasions by the Apostolic See[4] and by the Conferences of Bishops.[5] In his Apostolic Letter *Vicesimus Quintus Annus*, John Paul II raised the question again in relation to the liturgical renewal and indicated that it remained among those to be addressed at a future date: "popular piety can neither be ignored nor treated with indifference or disrespect because of its richness and because in itself it represents an religious attitude in relation to God. However, it has to be continually evangelized, so that the faith which it expresses may become more mature and authentic. The pious exercises of the Christian people and other forms of devotion can be accepted and recommended provided that they do not become substitutes for the Liturgy or integrated into the Liturgical celebrations. An authentic pastoral promotion of the liturgy, will know how to build on the riches of popular piety, purify them and direct them towards the Liturgy as an offering of the people."[6]

3.   With a view, therefore, to assisting the Bishops in "promoting and honoring the prayers and pious practices of the Christian people, that fully reflect the norms of the Church,"[7] in addition to the Liturgy, the preparation of this present *Directory* appears opportune to this Dicastery. In a general way, it considers the various connections between the Liturgy and popular piety. This *Directory* also reaffirms some principles and establishes guidelines for their practical application.

NATURE AND STRUCTURE

4.   This Directory contains two parts. The first, entitled *Emerging trends*, provides the elements necessary for the harmonization of Liturgy and popular piety. It draws on the experience which has matured during the long history and emergence of the contemporary problematic (Chapter 1). The teachings of the Magisterium are systematically restated since they are indispensable for ecclesial communion and fruitful action (Chapter 2). Finally, the theological principles, according to which difficulties concerning the relationship between Liturgy and popular piety are approached and resolved, are stated (Chapter 3). The possibility of realizing a true and fruitful harmonization of Liturgy and

---

3. Cf. SC 13.

4. Cf. Sacred Congregation of Rites, Instruction *Eucharisticum mysterium* April 25, 1967), 58–67; Paul VI, Apostolic Exhortation *Marialis cultus* (February 2, 1974), 24–58; Apostolic Exhortation *Evangelii nuntiandi* (December 8, 1975), 48; John Paul II, Apostolic Exhortation *Catechesi tradendae* (October 16, 1979), 54; Apostolic Exhortation *Familiaris consorti* (November 22, 1981) 59–62; Congregation for the Clergy, *General Directory on Catechesis* (August 15, 1997), Libreria Editrice Vaticana, Città del Vaticano 1997, nn. 195–196.

5. See, for example, III Conferencia General del Episcopado Latino-Americano, *Documento de Puebla*, 444–469, 910–915, 935–937, 959–963; Conferencia Episcopal de España, Documento pastoral de la Comision episcopal de Liturgia, *Evangelización y renovación de la piedad popular*, Madrid 1987; *Liturgia y piedad popular*, Directorio Liturgico-Pastoral, Secretariado Nacional de Liturgia, Madrid 1989; Conferencia General del Episcopado Latino-Americano, *Documento de Santo Domingo*, 36, 39, 53.

6. John Paul II, Apostolic Letter *Vicemus Quintus Annus* (December 4, 1988), 18.

7. John Paul II, Apostolic Constitution *Pastor Bonus* (June 28, 1988), 70.

popular piety can only be achieved by a wise and committed respect for these presuppositions. Conversely, overlooking them leads to nothing but reciprocal and futile ignorance, damaging confusion and contradictory polemics.

The second part, entitled *Guidelines*, offers a series of practical proposals. It does not claim to be able to include every usage or practice of popular piety to be found in particular locations throughout the world. Mention of particular practices or expressions of popular piety is not to be regarded as an invitation to adopt them where they are not already practiced. This section is elaborated in reference to the Liturgical Year (Chapter 4); to the special veneration given by the Church to the Mother of our Savior (Chapter 5); to devotion to the Holy Angels, the Saints and the Beatified (Chapter 6); to suffrage for the dead (Chapter 7) and to pilgrimage and examples of popular piety connected with shrines (Chapter 8).

The object of this *Directory* is to offer guidelines and, where necessary, to prevent abuses or deviations. Its tone is positive and constructive. In the same context, it provides short historical notes on several popular devotions in its *Guidelines*. It records the various pious exercises attached to these devotions while signaling their theological underpinning, and making practical suggestions in relation to time, place, language and other factors, so as to harmonize them with the Liturgy.

THOSE TO WHOM THE DIRECTORY IS ADDRESSED

5.   The operative proposals of this Directory, which are intended solely for the Latin Church and primarily for the Roman Rite, are addressed firstly to the Bishops, whose office entails presiding over the worshipping community of the dioceses, promoting the liturgical life and coordinating other forms of worship[8] with it. They are also intended for the Bishops' closest collaborators—their episcopal Vicars, priests, deacons and especially the Rectors of sanctuaries. These proposals are also intended for the major Superiors of the institutes of consecrated life—both male and female, since many forms of popular piety arose within, and were developed by, such institutes, and because the religious and the members of the secular institutes can contribute much to the proper harmonization of the various forms of popular piety with the Liturgy.

6.   The history of the Western Church is marked by the flowering among the Christian people of multiple and varied expressions of simple and fervent faith in God, of love for Christ the Redeemer, of invocations of the Holy Spirit, of devotion to the Blessed Virgin Mary, of the veneration of the Saints, of commitment to conversion and of fraternal charity. These expressions have grown up alongside the Liturgy. Treatment of this vast and complex material which is

---

8. Cf. LG 21; SC 41; Decree *Christus Dominus*, 15; Sacred Congregation for Bishops, *Directorium de pastorali ministerio Episcoporum*, Typis Polyglotis Vaticanis 1973, 75–76, 82, 90–91; CIC, can. 835, §1 and can. 839, §2; John Paul II, Apostolic Letter *Vicesimus quintus annus*, 21.

sometimes referred to as "popular religiosity" or "popular piety"[9] lacks a uniform terminology. Hence it will be necessary to adopt a certain precision of language. Without pretending to resolve all difficulties in this area, it will be useful to outline the commonly understood meaning of certain terms employed in this document.

Pious Exercises

7.   The expression "pious exercise" in this Directory refers to those public or private expressions of Christian piety which, although not part of the Liturgy, are considered to be in harmony with the spirit, norms, and rhythms of the Liturgy. Moreover, such pious exercises are inspired to some degree by the Liturgy and lead the Christian people to the Liturgy.[10] Some pious exercises have been established by mandate of the Apostolic See or by mandate of the Bishops.[11] Many of these exercises are part of the cultic patrimony of particular Churches or religious families. Pious exercises always refer to public divine revelation and to an ecclesial background. They often refer to the grace revealed by God in Jesus Christ and, in conformity with the laws of the Church, they are practiced "in accordance with approved customs or books."[12]

Devotions

8.   In the present context, this term is used to describe various external practices (e.g. prayers, hymns, observances attached to particular times or places, insignia, medals, habits or customs). Animated by an attitude of faith, such external practices manifest the particular relationship of the faithful with the Divine Persons, or the Blessed Virgin Mary in her privileges of grace and those of her titles which express them, or with the Saints in their configuration with Christ or in their role in the Church's life.[13]

Popular Piety

9.   The term "popular piety" designates those diverse cultic expressions of a private or community nature which, in the context of the Christian faith, are

---

9. Treating of the same material, the Apostolic Exhortation, *Evangelii nuntiandi*, 48, for example, having recalled its richness, states: "because of this we gladly call it *popular piety*, that is, religion of the people, rather than religiosity of the people;" the Apostolic Exhortation *Catechesi tradendae*, 54, uses the expression "popular piety;" the *Code of Canon Law*, can. 1234, §1, adopts the term "popular piety;" John Paul II uses the term "popular piety" in the Apostolic Letter *Vicesimus quintus annus*; the *Catechism of the Catholic Church*, 1674–1676, uses the expression "popular religiosity" but is also aware of the term "popular piety" (1679); the fourth Instruction for the correct implementation of the conciliar Constitution on the Sacred Liturgy (37–40) *Varietates legitimae*, published by the Congregation for Divine Worship and the Discipline of the Sacraments (January 25, 1994) employs the expression "popular piety" in article 45.

10. Cf. SC 13.

11. Cf. SC 13.

12. SC 13.

13. Cf. Council of Trent, *Decretum de invocatione, veneratione, et reliquiis Sanctorum, et sacris imaginibus* (December 3, 1563), in DS 1821–1825; Pius XII, Encyclical Letter *Mediator Dei*, in AAS 39 (1947), 581–582; SC 104; LG 50.

inspired predominantly not by the Sacred Liturgy but by forms deriving from a particular nation or people or from their culture.

Popular piety has rightly been regarded as "a treasure of the people of God"[14] and "manifests a thirst for God known only to the poor and to the humble, rendering them capable of a generosity and of sacrifice to the point of heroism in testifying to the faith while displaying an acute sense of the profound attributes of God: paternity, providence, His constant and loving presence. It also generates interior attitudes otherwise rarely seen to the same degree: patience, an awareness of the Cross in everyday life, detachment, openness to others and devotion."[15]

Popular Religiosity

10.   "Popular religiosity" refers to a universal experience: there is always a religious dimension in the hearts of people, nations, and their collective expressions. All peoples tend to give expression to their totalizing view of the transcendent, their concept of nature, society, and history through cultic means. Such characteristic syntheses are of major spiritual and human importance.

Popular religiosity does not always necessarily refer to Christian revelation.

SOME PRINCIPLES

An overview of the present Directory can be obtained from the following principles which are more fully developed and explained in the subsequent text.

The Primacy of the Liturgy

11.   History shows that, in certain epochs, the life of faith is sustained by the forms and practices of piety, which the faithful have often felt more deeply and actively than the liturgical celebrations. Indeed, "every liturgical celebration, because it is an action of Christ the Priest and of his Body, which is the Church, is a sacred action surpassing all others. No other action of the Church can equal its efficacy by the same title or to the same degree."[16] Hence, the ambivalence that the Liturgy is not "popular" must be overcome. The liturgical renewal of the Council set out to promote the participation of the people in the celebration of the Liturgy, at certain times and places (through hymns, active participation, and lay ministries), which had previously given rise to forms of prayer alternative to, or substitutive of, the liturgical action itself.

The faithful should be made conscious of the preeminence of the Liturgy over any other possible form of legitimate Christian prayer. While sacramental actions are *necessary* to life in Christ, the various forms of popular piety are properly *optional*. Such is clearly proven by the Church's precept which obliges attendance at Sunday Mass. No such obligation, however, has obtained with regard to pious exercises, notwithstanding their worthiness or their widespread diffusion.

---

14. John Paul II, Homily at the celebration of the Word in La Serena (Chile), 2, in *Insegnamenti di Giovanni Paolo II*, X/1 (1987), Libreria Editrice Vaticana, Città del Vaticano 1988, p. 1078.

15. Paul VI, Apostolic Exhortation *Evangelii nuntiandi*, 48.

16. SC 7.

Such, however, may be assumed as obligations by a community or by individual members of the faithful.

The foregoing requires that the formation of priests and of the faithful give preeminence to liturgical prayer and to the liturgical year over any other form of devotion. However, this necessary preeminence is not to be interpreted in exclusive terms, nor in terms of opposition or marginalization.

Evaluation and Renewal

12.   The optional nature of pious exercises should in no way be taken to imply an under estimation or even disrespect for such practices. The way forward in this area requires a correct and wise appreciation of the many riches of popular piety, of the potentiality of these same riches and of the commitment to the Christian life which they inspire.

The Gospel is the measure against which all expressions of Christian piety—both old and new—must be measured. The task of evaluating devotional exercises and practices, and of purifying them when necessary, must be conducted against this criterion so as to ensure their proper relationship with the Christian mystery. What is said of the Christian Liturgy is also true of popular piety: "it may never incorporate rites permeated by magic, superstition, animism, vendettas or sexual connotations."[17]

Hence, the liturgical renewal willed by the Second Vatican Council must also inspire a correct evaluation and renewal of pious exercises and devotional practices. Popular piety should be permeated by: a *biblical* spirit, since it is impossible to imagine a Christian prayer without direct or indirect reference to Sacred Scripture; a *liturgical* spirit if it is to dispose properly for or echo the mysteries celebrated in the liturgical actions; an *ecumenical* spirit, in consideration of the sensibilities and traditions of other Christians without, however, being restricted by inappropriate inhibitions; an *anthropological* spirit which both conserves symbols and expressions of importance or significance for a given nation while eschewing senseless archaicisms, and which strives to dialogue in terms redolent with contemporary sensibility. To be successful, such a renewal must be imbued with a pedagogical awareness and realized gradually, always taking into consideration time and particular circumstances.

Distinct from and in harmony with the Liturgy

13.   The objective difference between pious exercises and devotional practices should always be clear in expressions of worship. Hence, the formulae proper to pious exercises should not be commingled with the liturgical actions. Acts of devotion and piety are external to the celebration of the Holy Eucharist, and of the other sacraments.

On the one hand, a superimposing of pious and devotional practices on the Liturgy so as to differentiate their language, rhythm, course, and theological

---

17. Congregation for Divine Worship and the Discipline of the Sacraments, IV Instruction on the correct application of the Conciliar Constitution on the Sacred Liturgy (nn. 37–40) *Varietates legitimae*, 48.

emphasis from those of the corresponding liturgical action, must be avoided, while any form of competition with or opposition to the liturgical actions, where such exists, must also be resolved. Thus, precedence must always be given to Sunday, Solemnities, and to the liturgical seasons and days.

Since, on the other hand, pious practices must conserve their proper style, simplicity and language, attempts to impose forms of "liturgical celebration" on them are always to be avoided.

THE LANGUAGE OF POPULAR PIETY

14. While conserving its simplicity and spontaneity, the verbal and gestural language of popular piety should be careful to ensure the transmission of the truth of the faith together with the greatness of the Christian mysteries.

Gestures

15. Popular piety is characterized by a great variety and richness of bodily, gestural and symbolic expressions: kissing or touching images, places, relics and sacred objects; pilgrimages, processions; going bare-footed or on one's knees; kneeling and prostrating; wearing medals and badges. . . . These and similar expressions, handed down from father to son, are direct and simple ways of giving external expression to the heart and to one's commitment to live the Christian life. Without this interior aspect, symbolic gesture runs the risk of degenerating into empty customs or mere superstitions, in the worst cases.

Texts and Formulae

16. While drawn up in terms less exacting than those employed for the prayers of the Liturgy, devotional prayers and formulae should be inspired, nonetheless, by Sacred Scripture, the Liturgy, the Fathers of the Church and the Magisterium, and concord with the Church's faith. The established public prayers attached to pious devotions and the various acts associated with pious exercises must always be approved by the local Ordinary.[18]

Song and Music

17. Song, a natural expression of the soul of any nation, plays an important role in popular piety.[19] The conservation of the received corpus of traditional songs must be linked with a biblical and ecclesial spirit which is open to the possibility, where necessary, of their revision or to the composition of new songs.

Among some peoples, song is instinctively linked with hand-clapping, rhythmic corporeal movements and even dance. Such are external forms of interior sentiment and are part of popular traditions, especially on occasions such as patronal feasts. Clearly, such should be genuine expressions of communal prayer and not merely theatrical spectacles. The fact of their prevalence in one area, however, should not be regarded as a reason for their promotion in other areas, especially where they would not be spontaneous.

---

18. Cf. CIC, can 826, §3.
19. Cf. SC 118.

Sacred Images

18.   The use of sacred images is of major importance in the whole area of popular piety, since culturally and artistically they assist the faithful in encountering the mysteries of the Christian faith. Indeed, the veneration of sacred images belongs to the very nature of Catholic piety. Such is clear from its artistic patrimony, which can be seen in many churches and sanctuaries, and to which popular devotion has often contributed.

Here, the principles apply which govern the liturgical use of images of Christ, Our Lady, the Saints. These have been traditionally asserted and defended by the Church in the knowledge that "the honor rendered to the image is directed to the person represented."[20] The necessary rigor which has to be applied in drawing up the iconographic scheme of churches[21]—in matters relating to the truths of the faith and their hierarchy, beauty and quality—must also be applied to images and objects destined for private and personal devotion.

So as to ensure that the iconography used in sacred places is not left to private initiatives, those with responsibility for churches and oratories should safeguard the dignity, beauty and quality of those sacred images exposed for public veneration. Likewise, they should avoid the de facto imposition on the community of pictures or statues inspired by the private devotion of individuals.[22]

The Bishops, therefore, and the rectors of sanctuaries are to ensure that the sacred images produced for the use of the faithful, either in their homes or on their persons, or those borne aloft on their shoulders, are not reduced to banalities, nor risk giving rise to error.

Sacred Places

19.   Apart from the *church*, sanctuaries—which are sometimes not churches—afford important opportunities for the expression of popular piety, which are often marked by particular devotional forms and practices, among which the most significant is that of pilgrimage. Together with these sacred places, which are clearly reserved for public and private prayer, others exist which are often not less important: e.g., homes, places of life and work. On certain occasions even the streets and squares can become places facilitating the manifestation of the faith.

Sacred Times

20.   The rhythm associated with the change from day to night, from one month to another, or of the seasons is often associated with various forms of popular piety. Such can also be true of particular days recalling joyous or tragic personal or community events. Above all, the "the feast days," with their preparations for various religious manifestations, have contributed much in forging the traditions peculiar to a given community.

---

20. Cf. Council of Nicea II, *Definitio de sacris imaginibus* (October 23, 787) in DS 601; Council of Trent *Decretum de invocatione, veneratione,et reliquiis Sanctorum, et sacris imaginibus* (December 3, 1563), in DS 1823–1825.

21. Cf. SC 124–125.

22. Cf. CIC, can 1188.

21.   Manifestations of popular piety are subject to the jurisdiction of the local Ordinary. It is for him to regulate such manifestations, to encourage them as a means of assisting the faithful in living the Christian life, and to purify and evangelize them where necessary. He is also to ensure that they do not substitute for the Liturgy nor become part of the liturgical celebrations.[23] The local ordinary also approves the prayers and formulae associated with acts of public piety and devotional practices.[24] The dispositions given by a particular local Ordinary for the territory of his jurisdiction are for the particular Church entrusted to his pastoral care.

Hence, the faithful—both clerics and laity, either as groups or individuals, may not publically promote prayers, formulae or private initiatives without the permission of the ordinary.

In accordance with the Apostolic Constitution *Pastor Bonus*, n. 70, it is the competence of the Congregation for Divine Worship and the Discipline of the Sacraments to assist the Bishops in matters relating to prayers and devotional practices of the Christian people, as well as to issue dispositions in those cases surpassing the bounds of a particular Church, and in imposing subsidiary provisions.

PART ONE

EMERGING TRENDS: HISTORY, MAGISTERIUM AND THEOLOGY

Chapter One
LITURGY AND POPULAR PIETY IN A HISTORICAL PERSPECTIVE

LITURGY AND POPULAR PIETY THROUGHOUT THE CENTURIES

22.   The relationship between Liturgy and popular piety is ancient. It is therefore necessary to begin by surveying, even rapidly, how this relationship has been experienced down through the centuries, since it will often help to resolve contemporary difficulties.

Christian antiquity

23.   The Apostolic and post-apostolic periods are marked by a profound fusion of the cultic realities which are now called Liturgy and popular piety. For the earliest Christian communities, Christ alone (cf. Col 2:16) was the most important cultic reality, together with his life-giving word (cf. Jn 6:63), his commandment of reciprocal charity (cf. Jn 13:34), and the ritual actions which he commanded in his memory (cf. 1 Cor 11:24–26). Everything else—days and

---

23. Cf. John Paul II, Apostolic Letter *Vicesimus quintus annus,* 18; Congregation for Divine Worship and the Discipline of the Sacraments, IV Instruction for the correct application of the conciliar Constitution on the Sacred Liturgy (nn. 37–40) *Varietates legitimae,* 45.
24. Cf. CIC, can 826, §3.

months, seasons and years, feasts, new moons, food and drink . . . (cf. Gal 4:10; Col 2:16–19)—was of secondary importance.

Nevertheless, the signs of personal piety are already to be found among the first generation of Christians. Inspired by the Jewish tradition, they recommended following the example of incessant prayer of Jesus and St. Paul (cf. Lk 18:1; Rom 12:12; 1 Thes 5:17), and of beginning and ending all things with an act of thanksgiving (cf. 1 Cor 10:31; 1 Thes 2:13; Col 3:17). The pious Israelite began the day praising and giving thanks to God. In the same spirit, he gave thanks for all his actions during the day. Hence, every joyful or sorrowful occasion gave rise to an expression of praise, entreaty, or repentance. The Gospels and the writings of the New Testament contain invocations of Jesus, signs of christological devotion, which were repeated spontaneously by the faithful outside of the context of Liturgy. It must be recalled that it was a common usage of the faithful to use biblical phrases such as: "Jesus, Son of David, have mercy on me;" "Lord if you wish, you can heal me;" "Jesus, remember me when you come into your kingdom;" "My Lord and my God;" "Lord Jesus, receive my spirit." Innumerable prayers to Christ have been developed by the faithful of every generation on the basis this piety.

Until the second century, expressions of popular piety, whether deriving from Jewish, Greco-Roman or other cultures, spontaneously came together in the Liturgy. It has already been noted, for example, that the *Traditio Apostolica* contains elements deriving from popular sources.[25]

The cult of martyrs, which was of great importance for the local Churches, preserves traces of popular usages connected with the memory of the dead.[26] Some of the earliest forms of veneration of the Blessed Virgin Mary[27] also reflect popular piety, among them the *Sub tuum praesidium* and the Marian iconography of the catacombs of St. Priscilla in Rome.

While always most vigilant with regard to interior conditions and the prerequisites for a dignified celebration of the sacred mysteries (cf. 1 Cor 11:17–32), the Church has never hesitated in incorporating into the liturgical rites forms drawn from individual, domestic and community piety.

In this period Liturgy and popular piety, either conceptually or pastorally, did not oppose each other. Both concurred harmoniously in celebrating the one

---

25. The following examples can be traced to a popular context: the *Benedictio fructuum* (n. 32) in A. Botte (ed.) *La Tradition apostolicque de saint Hippolyte. Essai de reconstruction*, Aschendorff, Meunster Westfalen, ed. 1989, pp. 18, 78.

26. Some customs connected with the cult of the martyrs almost certainly derive from popular practices: lamps placed at their tombs; wreathes of flowers and leaves which lent a festive note to sacred places; fragrant unguents placed on the tombs of the martyrs; various objects, especially cloths called *brandae, palliola, nomina* touched to the tombs of the martyrs were regarded as precious, authentic relics; the custom of the *refrigerium* at the tombs of the martyrs.

27. The famous *De Nativitate Mariae* (third century), also known as the *Protoevangelium Iacobi*, and numerous accounts of the *De dormitione Mariae* of the second century, all bear witness to early Christian devotion to the Mother of God. According to scholars, these writings refer to many popular traditions which had a significant influence on the development of Marian devotion.

mystery of Christ, considered as a whole, and in sustaining the supernatural and moral life of the disciples of the Lord.

24.   In the fourth century, given the new politico-social situation of the Church, the question of the relationship between liturgy and popular piety begins to be raised consciously in terms of adaptation and inculturation rather than solely in terms of spontaneous convergence.

The local Churches, guided by clear pastoral and evangelizing principles, did not hesitate to absorb into the Liturgy certain purified solemn and festive cultic elements deriving from the pagan world. These were regarded as capable of moving the minds and imaginations of the people who felt drawn towards them. Such forms, now placed at the service of the mystery of worship, were seen as neither contrary to the Gospel nor to the purity of true Christian worship. Rather, there was a realization that only in the worship of Christ, true God and true Savior, could many cultic expressions, previously attributed to false gods and false Saviors, become true cultic expressions, even though these had derived from man's deepest religious sense.

25.   In the fourth and fifth centuries, a greater sense of the sacredness of times and places begins to emerge. Many of the local Churches, in addition to their recollection of the New Testament data concerning the *dies Domini*, the Easter festival and fasting (cf. Mk 2:18–22), began to reserve particular days for the celebration of Christ's salvific mysteries (Epiphany, Christmas and Ascension), or to honor the memory of the martyrs on their *dies natalis*, or to commemorate the passing of their Pastors on the anniversary of their *dies depositionis*, or to celebrate the sacraments, or to make a solemn undertaking in life. With regard to the socialization of the place in which the community is called to celebrate the divine mysteries and give praise to the Lord, it must be noted that many of these had been transformed from places of pagan worship or profane use and dedicated exclusively to divine worship. They became, often simply by their architectural arrangements, a reflection of the mystery of Christ and an image of the celebrating Church.

26.   During this period, the formation of various liturgical families, with their consequent differences, matured. The more important metropolitan Churches now celebrate the one worship of the Lord with their own cultural and popular forms which developed from differences of language, theological traditions, spiritual sensibilities, and social contexts. This process gave rise to the progressive development of liturgical systems with their own proper styles of celebration and agglomeration of texts and rites. It is not insignificant to note that even during this golden age for the formation of the liturgical rites, popular elements are also to be found in those rites.

On the other hand, bishops and regional synods began to establish norms for the organization of worship. They became vigilant with regard to the doctrinal correctness of the liturgical texts and to their formal beauty, as well as with regard to the ritual sequences.[28] Such interventions established a liturgical order with fixed forms which inevitably extinguished the original liturgical creativity, which had not been completely arbitrary. Some scholars regard these developments as one of the sources of the future proliferation of texts destined for private and popular piety.

27.   Mention must be made of the pontificate of the great pastor and liturgist Pope St. Gregory VII (590–604), since it is regarded as an exemplary reference point for any fruitful relationship between the Liturgy and popular piety. Through the organization of processions, stations and rogations, Gregory the Great undertook a major liturgical reform which sought to offer the Roman people structures which resonated with popular sensibilities while, at the same time, remaining securely based on the celebration of the divine mysteries. He gave wise directives to ensure that the conversion of new nations did not happen without regard for their own cultural traditions. Indeed, the Liturgy itself could be enriched by new legitimate cultic expressions and the noble expressions of artistic genius harmonized with more humble popular sensibilities. He established a sense of unity in Christian worship by anchoring it firmly in the celebration of Easter, even if other elements of the one mystery of Salvation (Christmas, Epiphany, and Ascension) were also celebrated and the memorials of the Saints expanded.

The Middle Ages

28.   Among the main concerns of the Oriental Christian Churches, especially the Byzantine Church, of the Middle Ages, mention can be made of both phases of the struggles against the iconoclast heresy (725–787 and 815–843) which was a watershed for the Liturgy. It was also a period of classical commentaries on the Eucharistic Liturgy and on the iconography for buildings set aside for worship.

In the liturgical field, there was a noticeable increase in the Church's iconographical patrimony and in her sacred rites which assumed a definitive form. The Liturgy reflected the symbolic vision of the universe and a sacral hierarchical vision of the world. In this vision, we have the coalescence of all orders of Christian society, the ideals and structures of monasticism, popular aspirations, the intuitions of the mystics and the precepts of the ascetics.

With the decree *De sacris imaginibus* of the Second Council of Nicea (787)[29] and the resolution of the iconoclastic controversy in the "Triumph of Orthodoxy" (843), iconography, having been given doctrinal legitimacy, developed and organized its definitive form. The icon, hieratic and pregnant with symbolic power, itself became part of the celebration of the Liturgy, reflecting, as it did, the mys-

---

28. "[Placuit] ut nemo in precibus vel Patrem, vel pro Filio, vel Filium pro Patre nominet. Et cum altari assistitur, semper ad patrem dirigatur oratio. Et quicumque sibi preces aliunde describit, non eis utatur, nisi prius cum instructioribus fratribus contulerit." Third Council of Carthage, can. 23, in I. D. Mansi, *Sacrorum Conciliorum nova et amplissima collectio*, III, Florentiae 1759, col. 884; "Placuit etiam hoc, ut preces quae probatae fuerint in concilio celebrentur, sive praefationes sive commendationes, seu manus impositiones, ab omnibus celebrentur, nec aliae omnino contra fidem praeferantur: sed quaecumque a prudentioribus fuerint collectae, dicantur." *Codex canonum Ecclesiae Africae*, can. 103 (ibid., col 807).

29. In DS 600–603.

tery celebrated and retaining something of its permanent presence which was exposed for the veneration of the faithful.

In the West, the High Middle Ages saw the formation of new cultures, and political and civil institution deriving from the encounter of Christianity, already by the fifth century, with peoples such as the Celts, the Visigoths, the Anglo-Saxons, and the Franco-Germans.

Between the seventh and the fifteenth century, a decisive differentiation between Liturgy and popular piety began to emerge which gradually became more pronounced, ending eventually in a dualism of celebration. Parallel with the Liturgy, celebrated in Latin, a communitarian popular piety celebrated in the vernacular emerged.

30.   The following may be counted among the reasons for the development of this dualism:

- the idea that the Liturgy was the competence of clerics since the laity were no more than spectators at the Liturgy;

- the marked distinction of roles in Christian society—clerics, monks, and laity—gave rise to different styles and forms of prayer;

- in Liturgy and iconography, the distinct and particular consideration given to the various aspects of the one mystery of Christ, while expressing a devotion for the life and work of our Lord, failed to facilitate an explicit realization of the centrality of the Paschal mystery and encouraged a multiplicity of particular times and forms of celebration of a distinctively popular tenor;

- lack of a sufficient knowledge of the Scriptures on the part, not only of the laity, but of many clerics and religious, made access to an understanding of the structure and symbolic language of the Liturgy difficult;

- the diffusion of apocryphal literature containing many stories of miracles and episodic anecdotes, on the other hand, had a significant influence on iconography which, touching the imagination of the faithful, naturally attracted their attention;

- the practical absence of any form of homiletic preaching, the disappearance of mystagogical preaching, and poor catechetical formation, rendered the celebration of the Liturgy closed to the understanding and active participation of the faithful who turned to alternative cultic times and forms;

- a tendency to allegory, excessively encroaching on the meaning of the liturgical texts and rites, often deviated the faithful from an understanding of the true nature of the Liturgy;

- the discovery of expressive, popular forms and structures unconsciously redrafted the Liturgy which, from many perspectives, had become increasingly incomprehensible and distant from the people.

31.   The Middle Ages saw the emergence and development of many spiritual movements and associations of different ecclesiastical and juridical form. Their life and activities had notable consequences for the relationship between Liturgy and popular piety.

The new religious orders of evangelical and apostolic life devoted their efforts to preaching, and adopted simpler liturgical forms in comparison to those found in the monasteries. These liturgical forms were often close to the people and to their expressive forms. On the other hand, they also developed and promoted pious exercises that encapsulated their charism, and diffused them among the people.

The emergence of the Confraternities, with their religious and charitable objectives, and of the lay corporations with their professional interests, gave rise to a certain popular liturgical activity. These often erected chapels for their religious needs, chose Patrons and celebrated their feast days. Not infrequently, they compiled the *officia parva* and other prayers for the use of their members. These frequently reflected the influence of the Liturgy as well as containing elements drawn from popular piety.

The various schools of spirituality that had arisen during the Middle Ages became an important reference point for ecclesial life. They inspired existential attitudes and a multiplicity of ways of interpreting life in Christ and in the Holy Spirit. Such interpretations exercised considerable influence on the choice of celebration (e.g. episodes from the Passion of Christ) and were the basis of many pious exercises.

Civil society, constituted ideally as a *societas Christiana*, modeled many of its structures on ecclesiastical usage and measured itself according to the rhythms of liturgical life. An example of this is to be found in the ringing of bells in the evening which called the peasants from the fields and simultaneously signaled the *Angelus*.

32.   Throughout the Middle Ages many forms of popular piety gradually emerged or developed. Many of these have been handed down to our times:

- the organization of sacred performances depicting the mysteries celebrated during the liturgical year, especially those surrounding the salvific events of Christ's birth, his passion, death and resurrection;

- the participation of the faithful was encouraged by the emergence of poetry in the vernacular which was widely used in popular piety;

- as a parallel, or even an alternative to many liturgical expressions, several devotional forms appeared; for example, various forms of Eucharistic adoration served to compensate for the rarity with which Holy Communion was received; in the Late Middle Ages, the rosary tended to substitute for the psalter; among the faithful, the pious exercises of Good Friday became a substitute for the Liturgy proper to that day;

- the growth in popular forms of devotion to Our Lady and the Saints: pilgrimages to the Holy Land, and to the tombs of the Apostles and martyrs, veneration of relics, litanies, and suffrage for the dead;

- the considerable development of the rites of blessing which, together with Christian elements, also reflected a certain response to a naturalistic sensibility as well to popular pre-Christian beliefs and practices;

- nucleuses of "sacred times" based on popular practices were constituted. These were often marginal to the rhythm of the liturgical year: sacred or profane fair days, tridua, octaves, novenas, months devoted to particular popular devotions.

33. In the Middle Ages, the relationship between Liturgy and popular piety is constant and complex, but a dual movement can be detected in that same relationship: the Liturgy inspired and nourished various expressions of popular piety; and several forms of popular piety were assumed by, and integrated into the Liturgy. This is especially true with regard to the rites of consecration of persons, the assumption of personal obligations, the dedication of places, the institution of feasts and to the various blessings.

A dualism, however, prevailed between Liturgy and popular piety. Towards the end of the Middles Ages, both, however, went through a period of crisis. Because of the collapse of cultic unity, secondary elements in the Liturgy acquired an excessive relevance to the detriment of its central elements. In popular piety, because of the lack of adequate catechesis, deviations and exaggerations threatened the correct expressions of Christian worship.

The Modern Period

34. At the dawn of the modern period, a balanced relationship between Liturgy and popular piety did not seem any more likely. The *devotio moderna* of the late fifteenth century was popular with many great spiritual masters and was widespread among clerics and cultivated laymen. It promoted the development of meditative and affective pious exercises based principally on the humanity of Christ—the mysteries of his infancy, his hidden life, his Passion and death. However, the primacy accorded to contemplation, the importance attributed to subjectivity and a certain ascetical pragmatism exalting human endeavor ensured that Liturgy no longer appeared as the primary source of the Christian life in the eyes of men and women advanced in the spiritual life.

35. The *De Imitatione Christi* is regarded as a typical expression of the *devotio moderna*. It has exercised an extraordinary and beneficial influence on many of the Lord's disciples in their quest for Christian perfection. The *De Imitatione Christi* orients the faithful towards a certain type of individual piety which accentuates detachment from the world and the invitation to hear the Master's voice interiorly. Less attention is devoted to the communitarian and ecclesial aspects of prayer and to liturgical spirituality.

Many excellent pious exercises are to be found among those who cultivated the *devotio moderna*, as well as cultic expressions deriving from sincerely devout persons. A full appreciation of the celebration of the Liturgy is not, however, always to be found in such circles.

36.   From the end of the fifteenth to the beginning of the sixteenth century, the discovery of Africa, America and the Far East caused the question of the relationship between Liturgy and popular piety to be posed in new terms.

While the work of evangelizing and catechizing countries distant from the cultural and cultic center of the Roman Rite was certainly accomplished through preaching the Word and celebrating the sacraments (cf. Mt 28:19), it also came about through the pious exercises popularized by the missionaries.

Pious exercises became a means of transmitting the Gospel message and, following conversion, of preserving the Christian faith. By virtue of the norms designed to preserve the Roman Rite, there were few reciprocal influences between the Liturgy and the autochthonous cultures. In Paraguay, the *Reductiones* are a rare example of this. The encounter with these cultures, however, was easily facilitated in the field of popular piety.

37.   Among those most concerned for the reform of the Church at beginning of the sixteenth century, mention must be of two Camoldelesi monks, Paolo Giustiniani and Pietro Querini, authors of the famous *Libellus ad Leonem X*[30] which set out important principles for the revitalization of the Liturgy so as to open its treasures to the entire People of God. They advocated biblical instruction for the clergy and religious, the adoption of the vernacular in the celebration of the divine mysteries and the reform of the liturgical books. They also advocated the elimination of spurious elements deriving from erroneous popular piety, and the promotion of catechesis so as to make the faithful aware of the importance of the Liturgy.

38.   Shortly after the close of the fifth Lateran Council (March 6, 1517), which had made provisions for the instruction of youth in the Liturgy,[31] the crisis leading to the rise of Protestantism arose. Its supporters raised many objections to the Catholic doctrine on the sacraments, to the Church's worship, and to popular piety.

The Council of Trent (1545–1563), convoked to resolve the situation facing the People of God as a result of the spread of Protestantism, addressed questions relating to the Liturgy and popular piety from the doctrinal and cultic perspective,[32] at all three of its phases. Because of the historical context and the doctrinal

---

30. Text in *Annales Camaldulenses*, IX, Venice 1773, coll. 612–719.

31. Cf. Fifth Lateran Council, [*Bulla reformationis Curiae*] in *Conciliorum Oecumenicorum Decreta*, edited by the Instituto per le scienze religiose di Bologna, Edizioni Dehoniane, Bologna 1991, p. 625.

32. The *Decretum de sacramentis* (DS 1600–1630) and the *Decretum de ss. Eucharistia* (DS 1635–1650), the discussions leading to the *Decretum de sacramento paenitentiae* (DS 1667–1693), the *De doctrina de sacramento extremae unctionis* (DS 1694–1700), the *Docrina de communione sub utraque specie et parvulorum* (DS 1725–1730), the *Doctrina de ss. Missae sacrificio* (DS 1738–1750) dealing with essential matters of faith on the Catholic doctrine of the Eucharist as a sacrifice, and on points relating to its ritual celebration, the *Decretum super petitione concessionis calicis* (DS 1760), the *Doctrina de sacramento ordinis* (DS 1763–1770), *Doctrina de sacramento matrimonii* (DS 1797–1800), the *Decretum de Purgatorio* (Ds 1820), the *Decretum de invocatione, veneratione, et reliquiis Sanctorum, et sacris imaginibus* (DS 1821–1825), have had wide application in the field of popular piety.

nature of the matters dealt with by the Council, the liturgical and sacramental questions placed before the Council were answered predominantly from a doctrinal perspective. Errors were denounced and abuses condemned. The Church's faith and liturgical tradition were defended. The decree *De reformatione generali*[33] proposed a pastoral program, whose activation was entrusted to the Holy See and to the Bishops, which demonstrated concern for the problems arising from the liturgical instruction of the people.

39. In conformity with the dispositions of the Council, synods were held in many of the ecclesiastical provinces. These often demonstrated a concern to bring the faithful to an active participation in the celebration of the divine mysteries. Simultaneously, the Roman Pontiffs began a vast program of liturgical reform. The Roman Calendar and the liturgical books of the Roman Rite[34] were revised in the relatively short space of time between 1568 and 1614. In 1588 the Sacred Congregation of Rites was established to promote and correctly order the liturgical celebrations of the Roman Church.[35] The *Catechismus ad Parochos* fulfilled the provision of pastoral and liturgical formation.

40. The reform of the Council of Trent brought many advantages for the Liturgy. There was a return to the "ancient norm of the Fathers"[36] in many of the Church's rites, notwithstanding the relatively limited scientific knowledge of the period then available. Elements and impositions extraneous to the Liturgy or excessively connected with popular sensibilities were eliminated. The doctrinal content of the liturgical texts was subjected to examination to ensure that they reflected the faith in its purity. The Roman Liturgy acquired a notable ritual unity, dignity and beauty.

The reform, however, had a number of indirect negative consequences: the Liturgy seemed to acquire a certain fixed state which derived from the rubrics regulating it rather than from its nature. In its active subject, it seemed to become almost exclusively hierarchical, which reinforced the existing dualism between Liturgy and popular piety.

41. The Catholic reform, with its positive concern to promote a doctrinal, moral and institutional reform of the Church and to counteract the spread of Protestantism, in a certain sense endorsed the complex cultural phenomenon of the Baroque. This, in turn, exercised a considerable influence on the literary, artistic and musical expressions of Catholic piety.

---

33. In *Conciliorum Oecumenicorum Decreta*, cit., pp. 784–796.

34. Pius V published the *Brevarium Romanum ex decreto SS. Concilii restitutum* on July 9, 1568 with the Bull *Quod a nobis*, the *Missale Rmanum ex decreto sacrosancti Concilii tridentini restitutum* with the Bull *Quo primum tempore* of July 14, 1570; Paul V envisaged a reform of the liturgical books when he promulagted the *Rituale Romanum* on June 16, 1614 with the Apostolic Letters *Apostolicae Sedi*.

35. The *Sacra Congregatio Rituum* was founded by Sixtus V on January 22, 1588 with the Apostolic Constitution *Immensa aeterni Dei*.

36. In the Bull promulgating the *Missale Romanum* explicit reference it is explicitly stated that the experts engaged by the Apostolic See "ad pristinam Missale ipsum sanctorum Patrum normam ac ritum restituerunt."

In the post-Tridentine period, the relationship between Liturgy and popular piety acquires some new aspects: the Liturgy entered a static period of substantial uniformity while popular piety entered a period of extraordinary development.

While careful to establish certain limits, determined by the need for vigilance with regard to the exuberant or the fantastic, the Catholic reform promoted the creation and diffusion of pious exercises which were seen as an important means of defending the Catholic faith and of nourishing the piety of the faithful. The rise of Confraternities devoted to the mysteries of the Passion of Our Lord, as well as those of the Blessed Virgin Mary and the Saints are good examples. These usually had the triple purpose of penance, formation of the laity and works of charity. Many beautiful images, full of sentiment, draw their origins from this form of popular piety and still continue to nourish the faith and religious experience of the faithful.

The "popular missions" emerged at this time and contributed greatly to the spread of the pious exercises. Liturgy and popular piety coexist in these exercises, even if somewhat imbalanced at times. The parochial missions set out to encourage the faithful to approach the Sacrament of Penance and to receive Holy Communion. They regarded pious exercises as a means of inducing conversion and of assuring popular participation in an act of worship.

Pious exercises were frequently collected and organized into prayer manuals. Reinforced by due ecclesiastical approval, such became true and proper aids to worship for the various times of the day, month and year, as well as for innumerable circumstances that might arise in life.

The relationship between Liturgy and popular piety during the period of the Catholic Reform cannot be seen simply in contrasting terms of stability and development. Anomalies also existed: pious exercises sometimes took place within the liturgical actions and were superimposed on those same actions. In pastoral practice, they were sometimes more important than the Liturgy. These situations accentuated a detachment from Sacred Scripture and lacked a sufficient emphasis on the centrality of the Paschal mystery of Christ, foundation and summit of all Christian worship, and its privileged expression in Sunday.

42.   The age of enlightenment further delineated the separation of "the religion of the learned" which was potentially close to the Liturgy, and the "religion of the simple people" which, of its very nature, was closer to popular piety. Both the "learned" and the "simple people," however, shared the same religious practices. The "learned" promoted a religious practice based on knowledge and the enlightenment of the intelligence and eschewed popular piety which they regarded as superstitious and fanatical.

The aristocratic sense which permeated many aspects of culture had its influence on the Liturgy. The encyclopedic character of knowledge, coupled with a critical sense and an interest in research, led to the publication of many of the liturgical sources. The ascetical concerns of some movements, often influenced by Jansenism, fuelled a call for a return to the purity of the Liturgy of antiquity. While certainly redolent of the cultural climate, the renewal of interest in the

Liturgy was fuelled by a pastoral concern for the clergy and laity, especially from the seventeenth century in France.

In many areas of its pastoral concern, the Church devoted its attention to popular piety. There was an intensification of that form of apostolic activity which tended to integrate, to some degree, the Liturgy and popular piety. Hence, preaching was encouraged at significant liturgical times, such as Advent and on Sundays when adult catechesis was provided. Such preaching aimed at the conversion of the hearts and morals of the faithful, and encouraged them to approach the Sacrament of Penance, attend Sunday Mass regularly, and to demonstrate the importance of the Sacrament of the Anointing of the Sick and Viaticum.

Popular piety, which had been effective in stemming the negative influences of Protestantism, now became an effective antidote to the corrosiveness of rationalism and to the baleful consequences of Jansenism within the Church. It emerged strengthened and enriched from this task and from the extensive development of the parish missions. Popular piety emphasized certain aspects of the Christian mystery in a new way, for example, the Sacred Heart of Jesus, and new "days," such as the "first Friday of the month," gained importance in the piety of the faithful.

With regard to the eighteenth century, mention must be made of the work of Ludovico Antonio Muratori who combined erudition with notable pastoral activity. In his famous work, *Della regolata devozione dei cristiani*, he advocated a form of religiosity based on the Liturgy and the Scriptures that eschewed all attachment to superstition and magic. The work of Benedict XIV (Prospero Lambertini) was also significant, especially his authorization of the use of the Bible in the vernacular.

43.   The Catholic Reform strengthened the structure and unity of the Roman Rite. Given the notable missionary expansion of the eighteenth century, the Reform spread its proper Liturgy and organizational structure among the peoples to whom the Gospel message was preached.

In the missionary territories of the eighteenth century, the relationship between Liturgy and popular piety was framed in terms similar to, but more accentuated than, those already seen in the sixteenth and seventeenth centuries:

- the Liturgy retained a Roman character and hence remained, at least partially, extraneous to autochthonous culture. The question of inculturation was practically never raised, partly because of the fear of negative consequence for the faith. In this respect, however, mention must be made of the efforts of Matteo Rici in relation to the question of the Chinese rites, and those of Roberto de' Nobili on the question of the Indian rites;

- popular piety, on the one hand, was subject to the danger of religious syncretism, especially where evangelization was not deeply rooted; while on the other, it became more autonomous and mature: it was not limited to reproducing the pious practices promoted by the missionaries, rather it created other forms of pious exercises that reflected the character of the local culture.

The Contemporary Period

44. Following the French revolution with its objective of eradicating the Christian faith and its overt hostility to Christian worship, the nineteenth century witnessed an important liturgical revival.

This was proceeded by the development of a vigorous ecclesiology which saw the Church not only in terms of a hierarchical society but also as the People of God and as a worshipping community. Besides the revival of ecclesiology, mention must also be made of the flowering of biblical and patristic studies, as well as the ecclesial and ecumenical concerns of men such as Antonio Rosmini (+1855) and John Henry Newman (+1890).

The history of the renaissance of liturgical worship reserves a special place for Dom Prosper Guéranger (+1875), who restored the monastic life in France and founded the abbey of Solesmes. His conception of the Liturgy is permeated by a love for the Church and for tradition. The Roman Rite, he maintained in his writings on Liturgy, was indispensable for unity and, hence, he opposed autochthonous forms of liturgical expression. The liturgical renewal which he promoted has the distinct advantage of not having been an academic movement. Rather, it aimed at making the Liturgy an expression of worship in which the entire people of God participated.

45. The revival of the Liturgy was not the sole activity of the nineteenth century. Independently of that revival, popular piety experienced significant growth. The revival of liturgical song coincided with the development of many popular hymns, the widespread use of liturgical aids such as bilingual missals for the use of the faithful, and a proliferation of devotional booklets.

The culture of Romanticism rediscovered man's religious sense and promoted the quest for, and understanding of, the elements of popular piety, as well as emphasizing their importance in worship.

The nineteenth century experienced a phenomenon of crucial significance: expressions of local cult arising from popular initiatives and often associated with prodigious events such as miracles and apparitions. Gradually, these received official approval as well as the favor and protection of the ecclesial authorities, and were eventually assumed into the Liturgy. Several Marian sanctuaries and centers of pilgrimages, and of Eucharistic and penitential Liturgies as well as Marian centers associated with popular piety, are all emblematic of this phenomenon.

While the relationship between popular piety and the Liturgy in the nineteenth century must be seen against the background of a liturgical revival and an ever increasing expansion of popular piety, it has to be noted that that same relationship was affected by the negative influence of an accentuated superimposition of pious exercises on the liturgical actions, a phenomenon already evident during the period of the Catholic Reform.

46. At the outset of the twentieth century, St. Pope Pius X (1903–1914) proposed bringing the Liturgy closer to the people, thereby "popularizing" it. He maintained that the faithful assimilated the "true Christian spirit" by drawing from its "primary and indispensable source, which is active participation in the most holy mysteries and from the solemn public prayer of the Church."[37] In this way, St. Pope Pius X gave authoritative recognition to the objective superiority of the Liturgy over all other forms of piety; dispelled any confusion between Liturgy and popular piety, indirectly clarified the distinction between both and opened the way for a proper understanding of the relationship that must obtain between them.

Thus was born the liturgical movement which was destined to exercise a prominent influence on the Church of the twentieth century, by virtue of the contribution of many eminent men, noted for their learning, piety and commitment, and in which the Supreme Pontiffs recognized the promptings of the Spirit.[38] The ultimate aim of the liturgical movement was pastoral in nature,[39] namely, to encourage in the faithful a knowledge of, and love for, the divine mysteries and to restore to them the idea that these same mysteries belong to a priestly people (cf. 1 Pt 2:5).

In the context of the liturgical movement, it is easy to understand why some of its exponents assumed a diffident attitude to popular piety and identified it as one of the causes leading to the degeneration of the Liturgy. They faced many of the abuses deriving from the superimposition of pious exercises on the Liturgy as well as instances where the Liturgy was displaced by acts of popular worship. In their efforts to restore the purity of divine worship, they took as their ideal the Liturgy of the early centuries of the Church, and consequently radically rejected any form of popular piety deriving from the Middles Ages or the post-Tridentine period.

This rejection, however, failed to take sufficient account of the fact that these forms of popular piety, which were often approved and recommended by the Church, had sustained the spiritual life of the faithful and produced unequalled spiritual fruits. It also failed to acknowledge that popular piety had made a significant contribution to safeguarding and preserving the faith, and to the diffusion of the Christian message. Thus, Pope Pius XII, in his encyclical *Mediator Dei* of November 21, 1947,[40] with which he assumed leadership of the liturgical movement, issued a defense of pious exercises which, to a certain extent, had become synonymous with Catholic piety in recent centuries.

The Constitution *Sacrosanctum Concilium* of the Second Vatican Council finally defined, in proper terms, the relationship obtaining between the Liturgy and

---

37. Motu proprio *Tra le sollecitudini* (November 22, 1903), in *Pii X Pontificis Maximi Acta*, I, Akademische Druck-u. Verlagsanstalt, Graz 1971, p. 77.

38. Cf. Pius XII, Allocution to the participants of the first International Congress on Pastoral Liturgy, Assisi-Rome, (September 22, 1956), in AAS 48 (1956), 712; SC 43.

39. Among those involved with the movement mention must be made of Lambert Beauduin (+1960), Odo Casel (+1948), Pius Parsch (+1954), Bernard Botte (+1960), Romano Guardini (+1968), Josef A. Jungmann (+1975), Cipriano Vagaggini (+1999), Aimé-Georges Martimort (+2000).

40. In AAS 39 (1947), 521–600.

popular piety, by declaring the unquestionable primacy of the Sacred Liturgy and the subordination to it of pious exercises, while emphasizing their validity.[41]

47.   From the foregoing historical outline, it is clear that the question of the relationship between Liturgy and popular piety is not an exclusively contemporary one. Albeit from different perspectives and in changing terms, the question has constantly arisen. It is now time to draw some conclusions from history so as to address the frequently and urgently asked pastoral questions which arise today.

Historical considerations: the causes of imbalances

48.   History principally shows that the correct relationship between Liturgy and popular piety begins to be distorted with the attenuation among the faithful of certain values essential to the Liturgy itself. The following may be numbered among the causes giving rise to this:

- a weakened awareness or indeed a diminished sense of the Paschal mystery, and of its centrality for the history of salvation, of which the Liturgy is an actualization. Such inevitably occurs when the piety of the faithful, unconscious of the "hierarchy of truths," imperceptibly turns towards other salvific mysteries in the life of Christ, of the Blessed Virgin Mary or indeed of the Angels and Saints;

- a weakening of a sense of the universal priesthood in virtue of which the faithful offer "spiritual sacrifices pleasing to God, through Jesus Christ" (1 Pt 2:5; Rom 12:1), and, according to their condition, participate fully in the Church's worship. This is often accompanied by the phenomenon of a Liturgy dominated by clerics who also perform the functions not reserved to them and which, in turn, causes the faithful to have recourse to pious exercises through which they feel a sense of becoming active participants;

- lack of knowledge of the language proper to the Liturgy—as well as its signs, symbols and symbolic gestures—causing the meaning of the celebration to escape the greater understanding of the faithful. Such can engender a sense of being extraneous to the liturgical action, and hence are easily attracted to pious exercises whose language more easily approaches their own cultural formation, or because certain forms of devotions respond more obviously to daily life.

49.   Each of these factors, and both in certain cases, not infrequently produces imbalances in the relationship between the Liturgy and popular piety, to the former's detriment and the latter's impoverishment. These should therefore be corrected through careful and persistent catechetical and pastoral work.

Conversely, the liturgical renewal and the heightened liturgical sense of the faithful have often recontextualized popular piety in its relationship with the

---

41. Cf. SC 7, 10, 13.

Liturgy. Such should be regarded as a positive development and in conformity with the most profound orientation of Christian piety.

The Sacred Constitution on the Liturgy

50.   The relationship between the Liturgy and popular piety, in our times, must be approached primarily from the perspective of the directives contained in the constitution *Sacrosactum Concilium*, which seek to establish a harmonious relationship between both of these expressions of piety, in which popular piety is objectively subordinated to, and directed towards, the Liturgy.[42]

Thus, it is important that the question of the relationship between popular piety and the Liturgy not be posed in terms of contradiction, equality or, indeed, of substitution. A realization of the primordial importance of the Liturgy, and the quest for its most authentic expressions, should never lead to neglect of the reality of popular piety, or to a lack of appreciation for it, nor any position that would regard it as superfluous to the Church's worship or even injurious to it.

Lack of consideration for popular piety, or disrespect for it, often betrays an inadequate understanding of certain ecclesial realities and is not infrequently the product not so much of the doctrine of the faith, but of some ideologically inspired prejudice. These give rise to attitudes which:

- refuse to accept that popular piety itself is an ecclesial reality prompted and guided by the Holy Spirit;[43]

- do not take sufficient account of the fruits of grace and sanctity which popular piety has produced, and continues to produce, within the ecclesial body;

- not infrequently reflect a quest for an illusory "pure Liturgy," which, while not considering the subjective criteria used to determine purity, belongs more to the realm of ideal aspiration than to historical reality;

- and confound, "sense," that noble component of the soul that legitimately permeates many expressions of liturgical and popular piety, and its degenerate form which is "sentimentality."

51.   In the relationship between the Liturgy and popular piety, the opposite phenomenon is also encountered—the importance of popular piety is overestimated practically to the detriment of the Church's Liturgy.

It has to be said that where such happens, either because of particular circumstances or of a theoretical choice, pastoral deviations emerge. The Liturgy is no longer the "summit towards which the activity of the Church is directed; [and] . . . the fount from which all her power flows."[44] Rather it becomes a cultic expression extraneous to the comprehension and sensibility of the people

---

42. Cf. SC 13.

43. Cf. John Paul II, Homily at the Celebration of the Word in La Serena (Chile), 2, in *Insegnamenti di Giovanni Paolo II*, X/1 (1987), cit., p. 1078.

44. SC 10.

which is destined to be neglected, relegated to a secondary role or even become reserved to particular groups.

52.   The laudable idea of making Christian worship more accessible to contemporary man, especially to those insufficiently catechized, should not lead to either a theoretical or practical underestimation of the primary and fundamental expression of liturgical worship, notwithstanding the acknowledged difficulties arising from specific cultures in assimilating certain elements and structures of the Liturgy. In some instances, rather than seeking to resolve such difficulties with patience and farsightedness, recourse is sometimes made to simplistic solutions.

53.   In those instances where the liturgical actions have been superseded by popular piety comments, such as the following, are often heard:

- popular piety is sufficient for the free and spontaneous celebration of "Life" and its multiplicity of expressions; Liturgy, on the other hand, centered at it is on the "Mystery of Christ" is essentially anemic, repetitive, formalistic and inhibits spontaneity;

- the Liturgy fails to involve the total being, both corporeal and spiritual, of each member of the faithful; popular piety, because it speaks directly to man, involves his body, heart and mind;

- popular piety is an authentic and real locus for the life of prayer: through pious exercises the faithful truly dialogue with the Lord, in terms which they fully understand and regard as their own; the Liturgy, however, places words on their lips that are not their own or alien to their level of culture, and thereby becomes a hindrance to prayer rather than a means;

- the ritual with which popular piety is expressed is one which is received and accepted by the faithful because of its correspondence between their cultural expectations and ritual language; the ritual proper to the Liturgy is impenetrable because its various expressive forms derive from different cultural sources widely removed from those of the faithful.

54.   In an exaggerated and dialectic way, such views reflect the divergence that undeniably exists between the Liturgy and popular piety in some cultural ambits.

Where such views are held, they inevitably indicate that an authentic understanding of the Christian Liturgy has been seriously compromised, or even evacuated of its essential meaning.

Against such views, it is always necessary to quote the grave and well pondered words of last ecumenical Council: "every Liturgical celebration, because it is an action of Christ the Priest and of his Body, which is the Church, is a sacred action surpassing all others. No other action of the Church can equal its efficacy by the same title and to the same degree."[45]

---

45. SC 7.

55.   Any unilateral exaltation of popular piety which fails to take account of the Liturgy, is inconsistent with the fact that the essential elements of the Liturgy derive from the will of Christ himself, and is unable to emphasize its indispensable soteriological and doxological importance. Following the Lord's ascension to the glory of the Father, and the descent of the Holy Spirit, the perfect glorification of God and the salvation of man comes about primarily through the celebration of the liturgy,[46] which requires an adherence of faith, and brings the believer to participate in the fundamental salvific event: the Passion, Death and Resurrection of Christ (cf. Rom 6:2–6; 1 Cor 11:23–26).

The Church's understanding of her mystery, and her worshipping and saving actions, constantly affirms that it is through "the Liturgy . . . especially in the divine sacrifice of the Eucharist, [that] 'the work of our redemption is accomplished.'"[47] This affirmation, however, does not deny the importance of other forms of piety.

56.   Theoretical or practical contempt for the Liturgy inevitably leads to a clouding of the Christian understanding of the mystery of God, Who has mercifully deigned to look down on fallen man and bring him to Himself through the incarnation of His Son and the gift of the Holy Spirit. Such fails to perceive the significance of salvation history and the relationship between Old and New Testaments. It underestimates the saving Word of God which sustains the Liturgy, and to which the Liturgy always refers. Such a disposition attenuates in the faithful any realization of the importance of the work of Christ our only Savior who is the Son of God and the Son of the Blessed Virgin Mary. Eventually, it leads to a loss of the *sensus Ecclesiae*.

57.   Any exclusive promotion of popular piety, which should always be seen in terms of the Christian faith,[48] can encourage a process that eventually leads the faithful away from Christian revelation and encourages the undue or distorted use of elements drawn from cosmic or natural religions. It can also give rise to the introduction into Christian worship of elements taken from pre-Christian beliefs, or that are merely cultural, national or ethnic psychological expressions. Likewise, the illusion can be created that the transcendent can be reached through unpurified religious experiences,[49] thereby promoting the notion that salvation can be achieved through man's own personal efforts (the constant danger of Pelagianism should never be forgotten), thereby compromising any authentic Christian understanding of salvation as a gratuitous gift of God. Indeed, the role of secondary mediators, such as the Blessed Virgin Mary, the Angels and Saints, or even national saints, can surpass that of the Lord Jesus Christ, the one Mediator, in the minds of the faithful.

---

46. Cf. SC 5–7.

47. SC 2.

48. Cf. supra n. 9.

49. Cf. Congregation for the Doctrine of the Faith, *Lettera "Orationis forma" ai Vescovi della Chiesa cattolica su alcuni aspetti della meditazione Cristiana* (October 15, 1989): AAS 82 (1990) 362–379.

58.   The Liturgy and popular piety, while not conterminous, remain two legit-imate expressions of Christian worship. While not opposed to each other, nei-ther are they to be regarded as equiparate to each other. Rather, they are to be seen in harmony with each in accordance with the Council's liturgical consti-tution: "The popular devotions of the Christian people . . . should accord with the sacred Liturgy . . . [and] in some way derive from it, and lead people to it, since in fact the Liturgy by its very nature is far superior to any of them."[50]

Hence, the Liturgy and popular piety are two forms of worship which are in mutual and fruitful relationship with each other. In this relationship, however, the Liturgy remains the primary reference point so as "clearly and prudently to channel the yearnings of prayer and the charismatic life"[51] which are found in popular piety. For its part, popular piety, because of its symbolic and expressive qualities, can often provide the Liturgy with important insights for incultura-tion and stimulate an effective dynamic creativity.[52]

Importance of Formation

59.   In the light of the foregoing, it would seem that the formation of both clergy and laity affords a means of resolving many of the reasons underlying the imbal-ances between the Liturgy and popular piety. Together with the necessary formation in Liturgy, which is a long-term process, provision should also be made to complement it by rediscovering and exploring formation in popular piety,[53] especially in view of the latter's importance for the enrichment of the spiritual life.[54]

Since "the spiritual life . . . is not limited solely to participation in the liturgy,"[55] restricting the formation of those involved in assisting spiritual growth exclu-sively to the Liturgy seems inadequate. Moreover, liturgical action, often reduced to participation at the Eucharist, cannot permeate a life lacking in personal prayer or in those qualities communicated by the traditional devotional forms of the Christian people. Current interest in oriental "religious" practices, under various guises, clearly indicates a quest for a spirituality of life, suffering, and sharing. The postconciliar generation—depending on the country—often has never experienced the devotional practices of previous generations. Clearly, cat-echesis and educational efforts cannot overlook the patrimony of popular piety when proposing models for the spiritual life, especially those pious exercises commended by the Church's Magisterium.

---

50. SC 13.

51. III Conferencia General del Episcopado Latino-Americano, *Documento de Puebla*, 465 e.

52. Ibid.

53. Cf. John Paul II, Apostolic Letter *Vicesimus Quintus Annus*, 15.

54. John Paul II, Message to the Plenary meeting of the Congregation for Divine Worship and the Discipline of the Sacraments (September 21, 2001), having reiterated the indispensable centrality of the Liturgy in the Church's life, he said "popular piety, although not always concurring with it, has its natural climax in the celebration of the Liturgy, and should ideally be oriented towards it. This should be clearly shown by appropriate catechesis" in *Notitiae* 37 (2001), 403. Cf. also Congregation for the Clergy, *General Catechetical Directory*, cit., 195–196.

55. SC 12.

60.   Reference has already been made to the Magisterium of the Second Vatican Council, and to that of the Roman Pontiffs and the bishops, on the subject of popular piety.[56] At this point, it seems opportune to provide an organized synthesis of this material so as to facilitate a common doctrinal orientation for popular piety and to encourage a consistent pastoral approach to it.

VALUES IN POPULAR PIETY

61.   Popular piety, according to the Magisterium, is a living reality in and of the Church. Its source is the constant presence of the Spirit of God in the ecclesial community; the mystery of Christ Our Savior is its reference point, the glory of God and the salvation of man its object, its historical moment "the joyous encounter of the work of evangelization and culture."[57] On several occasions, the Magisterium has expressed its esteem for popular piety and its various manifestations, admonishing those who ignore it, or overlook it, or even distain it, to adopt a more positive attitude towards it, taking due note of its many values.[58] Indeed, the Magisterium sees popular piety as "a true treasure of the People of God."[59]

The Magisterium's esteem for popular piety is principally motivated by the values which it incorporates.

Popular piety has an innate sense of the sacred and the transcendent, manifests a genuine thirst for God and "an acute sense of God's deepest attributes: fatherhood, providence, constant and loving presence,"[60] and mercy.[61]

The documents of the Magisterium highlight certain interior dispositions and virtues particularly consonant with popular piety and which, in turn, are prompted and nourished by it: patience and "Christian resignation in the face of irremediable situations;"[62] trusting abandonment to God; the capacity to bear sufferings and to perceive the cross in everyday life;"[63] a genuine desire to please the Lord and to do reparation and penance for the offences offered to Him; detachment from material things; solidarity with, and openness to, others; "a sense of friendliness, charity and family unity."[64]

---

56. Cf. supra n. 2.

57. John Paul II, Homily given at the shrine of the Virgin Mary of "Zapopang," 2, in *AAS*, 71 (1979) 228.

58. Cf. Paul VI, Apostolic Exhortation *Marialis cultus*, 31; John Paul II, Allocution to the Bishops of Basilicata and Apulia, *ad Limina* visit, 4, in AAS 74 (1982), 211–213.

59. John Paul II, Homily given at the Celebration of the Word in La Serena (Chile), 2, in *Insegnamenti di Giovanni Paolo II*, X/1 (1987), cit., p. 1078.

60. Cf. Paul VI, Apostolic Exhortation *Evangelii nuntiandi*, 48.

61. Cf. John Paul II, Apostolic Exhortation *Catechesi tradendae*, 54.

62. III Conferencia General del Episcopado Latino-Americano, *Documento de Puuebla*, 913.

63. Paul VI, Apostolic Exhortation *Evangelii nuntiandi* 48.

64. III Conferencia General del Episcopado Latino-Americano, *Documento de Puebla*, 913.

62.   Popular piety can easily direct its attention to the Son of God who, for love of mankind, became a poor, small child, born of a simple humble woman. Likewise, it has a particular sensibility for the mystery of the Passion and death of Christ.[65]

Contemplation of the mystery of the afterlife is an important feature of popular piety, as is its interest in communion with the Saints in Heaven, the Blessed Virgin Mary, the Angels, and suffrage for the souls of the dead.

63.   That harmonious fusion or the Gospel message with a particular culture, which is often found in popular piety, is a further reason for the Magisterium's esteem of popular piety. In genuine forms of popular piety, the Gospel message assimilates expressive forms particular to a given culture while also permeating the consciousness of that culture with the content of the Gospel, and its idea of life and death, and of man's freedom, mission and destiny.

The transmission of this cultural heritage from father to son, from generation to generation, also implies the transmission of Christian principles. In some cases, this fusion goes so deep that elements proper to the Christian faith become integral elements of the cultural identity of particular nations.[66] Devotion to the Mother of the God would be an example of this.

64.   The Magisterium also highlights the importance of popular piety for the faith-life of the People of God, for the conservation of the faith itself and in inspiring new efforts at evangelization.

It is impossible to overlook "those devotions practiced in certain regions by the faithful with fervor and a moving purity of intention;"[67] that authentic popular piety "in virtue of its essentially Catholic roots, is an antidote to the sects and a guarantee of fidelity to the message of salvation;"[68] that popular piety has been a providential means of preserving the faith in situations where Christians have been deprived of pastoral care; that in areas in which evangelization has been deficient, "the people for the most part express their faith primarily through popular piety;"[69] that popular piety is an important and indispensable "starting point in deepening the faith of the people and in bringing it to maturity."[70]

DEVIATIONS IN POPULAR PIETY

65.   While the Magisterium highlights the undeniable qualities of popular piety, it does not hesitate to point out dangers which can affect it: lack of a sufficient

---

65. Cf. Ibid., 912.

66. Cf. John Paul II, Homily given at the shrine of the Virgin Mary of "Zapopan," 2, in AAS 71 (1979), 228–229; III Conferencia General del Episcopado Latino-Americano, *Documento de Puebla*, 283.

67. John Paul II, Apostolic Exhortation *Catechesi tradendae*, 54.

68. John Paul II, Discourse at the inauguration of the IV General Conference of the Latin-American Bishops, Santo Domingo, (October 12, 1992), 12: *Insegnamenti di Giovanni Paolo II*, XV/2, Libreria Editrice Vaticana, Città del Vaticano 1994, p. 323.

69. III Conferencia General del Episcopado Latino-Americano, *Documento de Puebla*, 913.

70. Ibid., 960.

number of Christian elements such as the salvific significance of the Resurrection of Christ, an awareness of belonging to the Church, the person and action of the Holy Spirit; a disproportionate interest between the Saints and the absolute sovereignty of Jesus Christ and his mysteries; lack of direct contact with Sacred Scripture; isolation from the Church's sacramental life; a dichotomy between worship and the duties of Christian life; a utilitarian view of some forms of popular piety; the use of "signs, gestures and formulae, which sometimes become excessively important or even theatrical;"[71] and in certain instances, the risk of "promoting sects, or even superstition, magic, fatalism or oppression."[72]

66.   In its attempts to remedy such defects in popular piety, the contemporary Magisterium has insistently stressed the need to "evangelize" popular piety,[73] and sees it in relation to the Gospel which "will progressively free it from its defects; purify it, consolidate it and clarify that which is ambiguous by referring it of the contents of faith, hope and charity."[74]

Pastoral sensibility recommends that the work of "evangelizing" popular piety should proceed patiently, tolerantly, and with great prudence, following the methodology adopted by the Church throughout the centuries in matters relating to inculturation of the Christian faith, the Sacred Liturgy[75] and those inherent in popular piety.

THE SUBJECT OF POPULAR PIETY

67.   The Church's Magisterium, mindful that "the spiritual life . . . is not limited solely to participation in the liturgy" and that "the Christian . . . must enter into his bedroom to pray to his Father in secret," indeed, "according to the teaching of the apostle, he must pray without ceasing,"[76] holds that the subject of the various forms of prayer is every Christian—clerics, religious and laity—both privately when moved by the Spirit of Christ, and when praying with the community in groups of different origins and types.[77]

68.   Pope John Paul II has shown how the family can be a subject of popular piety. The exhortation *Familiaris consortio*, having praised the family as the

---

71. John Paul II, Allocution to the Conference of the Bishops of the Abruzzi and the Molise, *ad Limina* visit, 3, in AAS 78 (1986), 1140.

72. John Paul II, Discourse at Popayan (Columbia), in *Insegnamenti di Giovanni Paolo II*, IX/2 (1986), Libreria Editrice Vaticana, Città del Vaticano 1986, p. 115.

73. Cf. John Paul II, Apostolic Letter *Vicesimus quintus annus*, 18; Allocution to the Conference of the Bishops of the Abruzzi and the Molise, *ad Limina* visit, 6, in AAS 78 (1986), 1142; III Conferencia General del Episcopado Latino-Americano, *Document de Puebla*, 458–459; Congregation for Divine Worship and the Discipline of the Sacraments, Circular letter, *Orientamenti e proposte per la celebrazione dell'anno mariano* (April 3, 1987), 68.

74. John Paul II, Allocution to the Conference of the Bishops of the Abruzzi and the Molise *ad Limina* visit, 6, in AAS 78 (1986), 1142.

75. Cf. Congregation for Divine Worship and the Discipline of the Sacraments, IV Instruction for the correct application of the conciliar Constitution on the Liturgy (nn. 37–40) *Varietates legitimae*, 9–20.

76. SC 12.

77. Cf. *Institutio generalis de Liturgia Horarum*, 9.

domestic sanctuary of the Church, emphasizes that "as preparation for worship celebrated in church,[78] and as its prolongation in the home, the Christian family makes use of prayer, which presents a variety of forms. While this variety testifies to the extraordinary riches with which the Spirit vivifies Christian prayer, it serves also the various needs and life situations of those who turn to the Lord in prayer." It also observes that "apart from morning and evening prayers, certain prayers are to be expressly encouraged . . . such as reading and meditating on the word of God, preparation for the reception of the sacraments, devotion and consecration to the Sacred Heart of Jesus, the various forms of the veneration of the Blessed Virgin Mary, grace before and after meals, and observance of popular devotions."[79]

69.   Equally important subjects of popular piety are the confraternities and other pious associations of the faithful. In addition to their charitable and social endeavors, they have an institutional commitment to foster Christian cult, in relation to the Trinity, to Christ in his mysteries, to the Blessed Virgin Mary, to the Angels and Saints, in relation to the Beati, and in promoting suffrage for the souls of the faithful departed.

The Confraternities often observe, side by side with the liturgical calendar, their own proper calendars which indicate particular feasts, offices, novenas, septenaria, tridua, penitential days, processions, pilgrimages, and those days on which specific works of mercy are to be done. They also have their own devotional books and insignia such as medals, habits, cinctures, and even their own places of worship and cemeteries.

The Church recognizes the confraternities and grants juridical personality to them,[80] approves their statutes and fosters their cultic ends and activities. They should, however, avoid conflict and isolation by prudent involvement in parochial and diocesan life.

PIOUS EXERCISES

70.   Pious exercises are typical expressions of popular piety. In origin and content, in language and style, in usage and subject, they greatly differ among each other. The Second Vatican Council gave consideration to pious exercises, reiterating that they were highly to be recommended,[81] and indicated those criteria which authenticate their legitimacy and validity.

71.   In the light of the nature and of the characteristics proper to Christian worship, pious exercises clearly must conform to the doctrine, legal discipline and norms of the Church.[82] Moreover, they should be in harmony with the Sacred

---

78. With reference to the Liturgy note should also be made of the recommendation contained in the *Institutio generalis de Liturgia Horarum*, 27: "It is a laudable thing for the family, the domestic sanctuary, where possible, to celebrate in addition to the usual prayers, some parts of the Liturgy of the Hours so as to draw closer to the Church."

79. John Paul II, Apostolic Exhortation *Familiaris consortio*, 61.

80. Cf. CIC, can. 301 and can. 312.

81. Cf. SC 13; LG 67.

82. Cf. SC 13.

Liturgy, take into account the seasons of the liturgical calendar, in so far as possible, and encourage "conscious, active participation in the prayer of the Church."[83]

72.   Pious exercises are part of Christian worship. The Church has always been attentive to ensure that God is glorified worthily through them, and that man derives spiritual benefit from them and is encouraged to the live the Christian life.

The actions of Pastors in relation to pious exercises have been many. They have recommended and encouraged them, or guided and corrected them or simply tolerated them. Among the myriad of pious exercises, some must be mentioned, especially those erected by the Apostolic See, or which have been recommended by the same Apostolic See throughout the ages.[84] Mention must also be made of the pious exercises of the particular Churches "that are undertaken by order of the bishops according to customs or books lawfully approved;"[85] of the pious exercises that are practiced in accordance with the particular law or tradition of certain religious families, or confraternities, or other pious associations of the faithful, since such have often received the explicit approbation of the Church; and of the pious exercises practiced personally or in the home.

Some pious exercises which grew up among the community of the faithful and have received the approbation of the Magisterium,[86] also enjoy the concession of indulgences.[87]

LITURGY AND PIOUS EXERCISES

73.   The Church's teaching on the relationship of Liturgy and pious exercises may be summarized as follows: the Sacred Liturgy, in virtue of its very nature, is by far superior to pious exercises,[88] and hence pastoral praxis must always accord to the Sacred Liturgy "that preeminent position proper to it in relation to pious exercises;"[89] Liturgy and pious exercises must coexist in accordance with the hierarchy of values and the nature specific to both of these cultic expressions.[90]

74.   Careful attention to these principles should lead to a real effort to harmonize, in so far as possible, pious exercises with the rhythm and demands of the Liturgy, thereby avoiding any "mixture or admixture of these two forms of piety."[91] This in turn ensures that no hybrid, or confused forms, emerge from mixing Liturgy and pious exercises, not that the latter, contrary to the mind of

---

83. John Paul II, Homily at the Celebration of the Word in La Serena (Chile), 2, in *Insegnamenti di Giovanni Paolo II*, X/1 (1987), cit., p. 1079.

84. Cf. SC 13.

85. SC 13.

86. Cf. CIC can. 23.

87. Cf., EI, *Aliae concessiones*, 54.

88. Cf. SC 7.

89. Congregation for Divine Worship and the Discipline of the Sacraments, Circular letter *Orientamenti e proposte per la celebrazione dell'Anno mariano*, 54.

90. Cf. Paul VI, Apostolic Exhortation *Marialis cultus*, 31, 48.

91. The Italian Episcopal Conference, Episcopal Commission for the Liturgy, pastoral note *Il rinnovamento liturgico in Italia* (September 23, 1983), 18, in *Enchiridion CEI*, 3, Edizioni Dehoniane, Bologna 1986, p. 886.

the Church, are eliminated, often leaving an unfilled void to the great detriment of the faithful.[92]

75.   The Apostolic See has not failed to indicate those theological, pastoral, historical, and literary principles by which a renewal of pious exercises is to be effected.[93] It has also signaled the manner in which they should reflect a biblical and liturgical spirit, as well as an ecumenical one. The criteria established by the Holy See emphasize how the essential nucleus of the various pious exercises is to be identified by means of a historical investigation, and also reflect something of contemporary spirituality. Pious exercises are also required to take due account of the implications of a healthy anthropology. They should respect the culture and expressive style of the peoples who use them without, however, losing those traditional elements that are rooted in popular customs.

Chapter Three
THEOLOGICAL PRINCIPLES FOR AN EVALUATION
AND RENEWAL OF POPULAR PIETY

THE LIFE OF WORSHIP: COMMUNION WITH THE FATHER, THROUGH CHRIST, IN THE HOLY SPIRIT

76.   In the history or revelation, man's salvation is constantly presented as a free gift of God, flowing from His mercy, given in sovereign freedom and total gratuity. The entire complex of events and words through which the plan of salvation is revealed and actualized,[94] takes the form of a continuous dialogue between God and man. God takes the initiative, and man is asked for an attitude of listening in faith, and a response in "obedience to faith" (Rom 1:5; 16:26).

The Covenant stipulated on Sinai between God and His chosen people (cf. Ex 19–24) is a singularly important event in this salvific dialogue, and makes the latter a "possession" of the Lord, a "kingdom of priests and a holy people" (Ex 19:6). Israel, although not always faithful to the Covenant, finds in it inspiration and the power to model its life of God Himself (cf. Lk 11:44–45; 19:2), and the content of that life on His Word.

Israel's worship and prayer are directed towards the commemoration of the *mirabilia Dei*, or God's saving interventions in history, so as to conserve a lively veneration of the events in which God's promises were realized, since these are the constant point of reference both for reflection on the faith and for the life of prayer.

77.   In accordance with His eternal plan, "at various times in the past and in various different ways, God spoke to our ancestors through the prophets, but in

---

92. Cf. Apostolic Exhortation *Marialis cultus*, 31; III Conferencia General del Episcopado Latino-Americano, *Documento de Puebla*, 915.

93. Cf. Sacred Congregation for Bishops, *Directorium de pastorali ministerio Episcoporum*, cit., 91; Paul VI, Apostolic Exhortation *Marialis cultus*, 24–38.

94. Cf. Second Vatican Council, Constitution *Dei Verbum*, 2.

our own times, these last days, He has spoken to us through His Son, the Son that He has appointed to inherit everything and though whom he made everything there is" (Heb 1:1–2). The mystery of Christ, especially his Passover of death and Resurrection, is the full and definitive revelation and realization of God's salvific promises. Since Jesus is the "only Son of God (Jn 3:18), he is the one in whom God has given us all things without reserve" (cf. Rom 8:32; Jn 3:16). Hence, the person and works of Christ are the essential reference point for the faith and prayer life of the people of God. In him we find the Teacher of truth (cf. Mt 22:16), the faithful Witness (Rev 1:5), the High Priest (cf. Heb 4:14), the Pastor of our souls (cf. 1 Pt 2:25), and the one, perfect Mediator (cf. 1 Tim 2:5; Heb 8:6; 9:15; 12:24). Through him, man comes to God (cf. Jn 14:6), the Church's praise and supplication rise up to God, and all of divine gifts are given to man.

In Baptism, we are buried with Christ and rise with him (cf. Col 2:12; Rom 6:4), we are freed from the dominion of the flesh and introduced to that of the Spirit (cf. Rom 8:9), and we are called to a state of perfection whose fullness is in Christ (cf. Eph 4:13). We have a model in Christ of a life whose every moment was lived in hearing the word of the Father, and in acceptance of His will. Christ's life is lived as a constant "fiat" to the will of God: "My food is to do the will of the one who sent me" (Jn 4:34).

Christ, therefore, is the perfect model of filial piety and of unceasing dialogue with the Father. He is the model of the constant quest for that vital, intimate, and trusting contact with God which enlightens, guides and directs all of man's life.

78.   In the life of communion with the Father, the faithful are guided by the Spirit (cf. Rom 8:14) who has been given progressively to transform them in Christ. He pours out to them "the spirit of adopted sons," by which they assimilate the filial disposition of Christ (cf. Rom 8:15–17), and his sentiments (cf. Phil 2:5). He makes present the teaching of Christ to the faithful (cf. Jn 14:26; 16:13–25) so that they may interpret the events of life in its light. He brings them to a knowledge of the depths of God (cf. 1 Cor 2:10) and enables them to transform their lives into a "holy sacrifice" (Rom 12:1). He sustains them in rejection and in the trials that must be faced during the process of transforming themselves in Christ. The Spirit is given to sustain, nourish and direct their prayer: "The Spirit too comes to help us in our weakness. For when we cannot choose words in order to pray properly, the Spirit himself expresses our plea in a way that could never be put into words, and God who knows everything in our hearts knows perfectly well what he means, and that the pleas of the saints expressed by the Spirit are according to the mind of God" (Rom 8:26–27).

Christian worship originates in, and draws impetus from, the Spirit. That same worship begins, and is brought to completion, in the Spirit. It can therefore be concluded that without the Spirit of Christ there can be neither authentic liturgical worship, nor genuine expressions of popular piety.

79.   From the principles already outlined above, popular piety should always be formed as a moment of the dialogue between God and man, through Christ in the Holy Spirit. Despite some deficiencies—such as confusion between God the Father and Jesus Christ—popular piety does bare a Trinitarian mark.

Popular piety, indeed, is especially susceptible to the mystery of God's paternity and arouses a sense of awe for His goodness, power and wisdom. It rejoices in the beauty of creation and gives thanks to God for it. Popular piety can express an awareness of the justice and mercy of God the Father, and of His care for the poor and lowly, and it can proclaim that He commends the good and rewards those who live properly and honestly, while abhorring evil and casting away from Himself those who obstinately follow the path of hatred, violence, injustice and deceit.

Popular piety can easily concentrate on the person of Christ, Son of God and Savior of mankind. It can movingly recount the birth of Christ and intuit the immense love released by the child Jesus, true God and true man, a true brother in poverty and persecution from the moment of his birth. Innumerable scenes from the public life of Christ, the Good Shepherd who reaches out to sinners and publicans, the Miracle-worker healing the sick and helping the poor, or the Teacher proclaiming the truth, can be represented in popular piety. Above all it has the capacity to contemplate the mysteries of Christ's Passion because in them it can perceive Christ's boundless love and the extent of his solidarity with human suffering: Jesus betrayed and abandoned, scourged and crowned with thorns, crucified between thieves, taken down from the cross and buried in the earth, and mourned by his friends and disciples.

Popular piety is also consciously aware of the person of the Holy Spirit in the mystery of God. It professes that "through the Holy Spirit" the Son of God "became incarnate of Virgin Mary and was made man"[95] and that the Spirit was poured out to the Apostles at the beginning of the Church (cf. Acts 2:1–13). Popular piety is especially conscious that the power of the Spirit of God, whose seal is placed on all Christians in the Sacrament of Confirmation, is alive in all of the Church's sacraments; that baptism is conferred, sins forgiven, and the Holy Eucharist begun "in the name of the Father, and of the Son, and of the Holy Spirit;" and that all prayer in the Christian community, and the invocation of divine blessing on mankind and all creatures, is done in the name of the three Divine Persons.

80.   Reference to the Most Blessed Trinity, while seminally present in popular piety, is an element requiring further emphasis. The following points offer an outline of how that might be done:

- The faithful require instruction on the character of Christian prayer, which is directed to the Father, through the mediation of the Son, in the power of the Holy Spirit.

- The formulae used in popular piety should give greater emphasis to the person and action of the Holy Spirit. The lack of a "name" for the Spirit of God and the custom of not representing him anthropomorphically have contributed to a certain absence of the Holy Spirit in the texts and formulae of popular piety, while not overlooking the role of music and gestures in expressing our relationship with the Holy Spirit. This lacuna,

---

95. DS 150; *Missale Romanum, Ordo Missae, Symbolum Nicaeno-Constantinopolitanum.*

however, can be overcome by the evangelization of popular piety, as the Magisterium has already recommended on several occasions.

- It is also necessary for popular piety to emphasize the primary and basic importance of the Resurrection of Christ. The loving devotion for the suffering of Christ, often demonstrated by popular piety, should also be completed by setting it in the context of his glorification so as to give integral expression to the salvific plan of God as revealed in Christ, and allow for its inextricable link with his Paschal mystery. Only in this manner can the authentic face of Christianity be seen with its victory over death and its celebration of him who is "God of the living and not of the dead" (Mt 22:32), of Christ, the living one, who was dead but now lives forever (cf. Rev 1:28) and of the Spirit "who is Lord and giver of life."[96]

- Finally, devotion to the Passion of Christ should lead the faithful to a full and conscious participation in the Eucharist, in which the Body of Christ, sacrificed for our sake (cf. 1 Cor 11:24) is given as food; and in which the Blood of Christ, shed on the cross in the new and eternal Covenant and for the remission of sin, is given to drink. Such participation has its highest and most significant moment in the celebration of the Paschal Triduum, apex of the liturgical year, and in the Sunday celebration of the Sacred Mysteries.

THE CHURCH: WORSHIPPING COMMUNITY

81.   The Church, "gathered in the name of the Father, and of the Son, and of the Holy Spirit,"[97] is a worshipping community. By command of her Lord and Founder, the Church effects many acts of worship whose object is the glory of God and the sanctification of man.[98] In different ways and in different measure, these are all celebrations of the Paschal Mystery of Christ, and aimed at realizing the divine will to gather the scattered children [of the Father] into the unity of a single nation.

In her ritual actions, the Church proclaims the Gospel of salvation and announces the Death and Resurrection of Christ, and actualizes the work of his salvation in sacred signs. In the Eucharist she celebrates the memorial of his blessed Passion, his glorious Resurrection, and Ascension. In the celebration of the other sacraments she draws from the gifts of the Holy Spirit which flow from the Cross of our Savior. The Church glorifies the Father in psalms and hymns for the wonders that He has accomplished in the death and exaltation of Christ His Son, and supplicates that the saving mystery of Easter might reach all mankind. With the sacramentals which have been instituted to assist the faithful at various times and in various situations, she prays that their activity might be directed and enlightened by the Spirit of Easter.

---

96. Ibid.

97. St. Cyprian, *De oratione dominica*, 23:CSEL 3/1, Vindobonae 1868, p. 285.

98. Cf. SC 5–7.

82.   The celebration of the Liturgy, however, does not exhaust the Church's divine worship. Following the example and the teaching of the Lord, the disciples of Christ pray in the seclusion of their rooms (cf. Mt 6:6), they gather to pray according to forms created by men and women of great religious experience, who have encouraged the faithful and oriented their piety towards specific aspects of the mystery of Christ. They also pray according to structures which have emerged practically spontaneously from the collective Christian consciousness, in which the demands of popular culture harmoniously convey the essential data of the Gospel message.

83.   Authentic forms of popular piety are also fruits of the Holy Spirit and must always be regarded as expressions of the Church's piety. They are used by the faithful who are in communion with the Church, who accept her faith and who are docile to her discipline of worship. Indeed, many forms of popular piety have been approved and recommended by the Church herself.[99]

84.   Popular piety, as an expression of ecclesial piety, is subject to the general discipline of Christian worship and to the Church's pastoral authority which exercises a role of discernment and authentification in relation to it. The Church renews popular piety by placing it in fertile contact with the revealed Word, tradition and the Sacred Liturgy itself.

On the other hand, expressions of popular piety must always be open to the "ecclesiological principle" of Christian worship. In this way:

- popular piety can have a correct understanding of the relationship between the particular Church and the universal Church. When popular piety concentrates on local or immediate issues, it risks closing itself to universal values and to ecclesiological perspectives;

- the veneration of the Blessed Virgin Mary, of the Angels and Saints, and suffrage for the dead, should be set in the vast context of the relationship between the heavenly Church and the pilgrim Church on earth;

- the relationship between *ministry* and *charism* should be properly understood, while the former is necessary for divine worship, the latter is frequently found in manifestations of popular piety.

COMMON PRIESTHOOD AND POPULAR PIETY

85.   Through the sacraments of Christian initiation, the faithful become part of the Church, a prophetic, priestly and royal people called to worship God in spirit and in truth (cf. Jn 4:23). The Church exercises this task through Christ in the Holy Spirit, not only in the Sacred Liturgy, especially in the celebration of the Holy Eucharist, but also in other forms of the Christian life, among which are numbered the various forms of popular piety. The Holy Spirit confers the ability to offer sacrifices of praise to God, to offer prayer and entreaty to Him, so as to make of one's life "a living and holy sacrifice, pleasing to God" (Rom 12:1; Heb 12:28).

---

99. Cf. SC 13; LG 67.

86. On this priestly basis, popular piety assists the faithful in persevering in prayer and in praising God the Father, in witnessing to Christ (cf. Acts 2:42–47), and in sustaining their vigilance until He comes again in glory. It also justifies our hope, in the Holy Spirit, of life eternal (cf. 1 Pt 3:15) and conserves important aspects of a specific cultic context, and, in different ways and in varying degrees, expresses those ecclesial values which arise and develop within the mystical Body of Christ.

87. The Word of God, as transmitted by Sacred Scripture, as conserved and proposed by the Magisterium of the Church, and as celebrated in the Sacred Liturgy, is the privileged and indispensable instrument of the Holy Spirit in the faithful's worship.

Since the Church is built on, and grows through, listening to the Word of God, the Christian faithful should acquire a familiarity with Sacred Scripture and be imbued with its spirit,[100] so as to be able to translate the meaning of popular piety into terms worthy of, and consonant with, the data of the faith, and render a sense of that devotion that comes from God, who saves, regenerates and sanctifies.

The Bible offers an inexhaustible source of inspiration to popular piety, as well as unrivalled forms of prayer and thematic subjects. Constant reference to Sacred Scripture is also a means and a criterion for curbing exuberant forms of piety frequently influenced by popular religion, which give rise to ambiguous or even erroneous expressions of piety.

88. Prayer should "accompany the reading of Sacred Scripture, so that a dialogue takes place between God and man."[101] Thus, it is highly recommended that the various forms of popular piety normally include biblical texts, opportunely chosen and duly provided with a commentary.

89. In this respect, the models used in liturgical celebrations can be most useful, since they always contain a text taken from Sacred Scripture, variously chosen for different types of celebration. However, since the different expressions of popular piety already exhibit a legitimate structural and expressional diversity, the disposition of the various biblical pericopes need not necessarily be followed in the same ritual structure with which the Word of God is proclaimed in the Sacred Liturgy.

In any event, the liturgical model can serve as a touchstone for popular piety, against which a correct scale of values can be developed, whose first concern is hearing God when He speaks. It encourages popular piety to discover the harmony between the Old and New Testaments and to interpret one in the light of the other. From its centuries-long experience, the liturgical model also provides

---

100. Cf. Second Vatican Council, Constitution *Dei Verbum*, 25.
101. Ibid.

praiseworthy solutions for the correct application of the biblical message and provides a valid criterion to judge the authenticity of prayer.

In choosing biblical texts, it is always desirable to take short texts that are easily memorized, incisive, and easily understood, even if difficult to actualize. Certain forms of popular piety, such as the *Via Crucis* and the Rosary, encourage the use of Sacred Scripture, which can easily be related to particular prayers or gestures that have been learned by heart, especially those biblical passages recounting the life of Christ which are easily remembered.

POPULAR PIETY AND PRIVATE REVELATION

90. Popular piety has always been interested in extraordinary happenings and events that are not infrequently connected with private revelations. While not confined to Marian piety alone, this phenomenon is particularly involved with "apparitions" and "messages." In this regard, it is useful to recall what the *Catechism of the Catholic Church* says about private revelation: "Throughout the ages, there have been so-called private revelations, some of which have been recognized by the authority of the Church. They do not belong, however, to the deposit of faith. It is not their role to improve or complete Christ's definitive Revelation, but to help live more fully by it in a certain period of history. Guided by the Magisterium of the Church, the *sensus fidelium* knows how to discern and welcome in these revelations whatever constitutes an authentic call of Christ or his saints to the Church" (n. 67).[102]

INCULTURATION AND POPULAR PIETY

91. Popular piety is naturally marked by historical and cultural factors. The sheer variety of its expressions is an indicator of that fact. It reflects forms of popular piety that have arisen and been accepted in many particular Churches throughout the ages, and are a sure sign of the extent to which the faith has taken root in the hearts of particular peoples, and of its influence on the daily lives of the faithful. Indeed, "popular piety is the first and most fundamental form of the faith's 'inculturation,' and should be continually guided and oriented by the Liturgy, which, in its turn, nourishes the faith though the heart."[103] The encounter between the innovative dynamism of the Gospel message, and the various elements of a given culture, is affirmed in popular piety."[104]

---

102. On this question see J. Ratzinger, *Commento teologico*, in Congregazione per la Dottrina della Fede, *Il messaggio di Fatima*, Libreria Editrice Vaticana, Città del Vaticano 2000, pp. 32–44.
103. Ibid., p.35.
104. Cf. "Pontifical Council for Culture, *Per una Pastorale della Cultura*, Libreria Editrice Vaticana 1999, 28: popular piety remains one of the principal expressions of a true inculturation of the faith because in it faith and liturgy harmonize, as well as sentiment and the arts, while affirming a consciousness of a proper identity through local traditions. Thus, 'America, which historically has been, and still is, a melting-pot of peoples, has recognized in the *mestiza* face of the Virgin of Tepeyac, *in Blessed Mary of Guadalupe, an impressive example of a perfectly inculturated evangelization . . .' (Ecclesia in America*, n. 11). Popular piety allows a people to express its faith, its relationship with God and Providence, with Our Lady and the Saints, with neighbors, with the dead, with creation and strengthens membership of the Church."

92.   The adaptation or inculturation of a particular pious exercise should not present special difficulties at the level of language, musical and artistic forms, or even of adopting certain gestures. While at one level pious exercises do not concentrate on the essential elements of the sacramental life, at another, it has to be remembered, they are in many cases popular in origin and come directly from the people, and have been formulated in the language of the people, within the framework of the Catholic faith.

The fact that pious exercises and devotions express popular sentiment does not, however, authorize personalistic or subjective approaches to this material. With due respect for the competence proper to local Ordinaries or the Major Superiors of religious orders in cases involving devotions connected with their Orders, the Conference of Bishops should decide in matters relating to pious exercises widely diffused in a particular country or in a vast region.

Great vigilance and a deep sense of discernment are required to ensure that ideas contrary to the Christian faith, or forms of worship vitiated by syncretism, are not insinuated into pious exercises though various forms of language.

It is especially necessary to ensure that those pious exercises undergoing adaptation or inculturation retain their identity and their essential characteristics. In this regard, particular attention must always be given to their historical origin and to the doctrinal and cultic elements by which they are constituted.

With regard to the question of assuming certain elements from popular piety in the process of inculturating the Liturgy, reference should be made to the relative Instruction already published on the subject by this Dicastery.[105]

PART TWO

GUIDELINES FOR THE HARMONIZATION OF POPULAR PIETY WITH THE LITURGY

Foreward

93.   The following guidelines on the relationship between popular piety and the Sacred Liturgy are offered to facilitate the translation into concrete pastoral action of those principles outlined above, so as ensure consistency and fruitfulness in pastoral activity. While mentioning the most common pious exercises and devotional practices, the following exposition does not contain an exhaustive account of every possible local form of popular piety or devotional practice. Given the affinity of the material, and the fact that it sometimes falls into categories that are not clearly defined, some mention will be made of the pastoral care of the Liturgy.

------

105. Cf. Congregation for Divine Worship and the Discipline of the Sacraments, IV Instruction for the Correct Application of the Conciliar Constitution on the Sacred Liturgy (nn. 37–40) *Varietates legitimae*, 45.

The following exposition contains five chapters:

- chapter *four*, on the question of the Liturgical Year, seen from the prospect of the desirability of harmonizing its celebrations with popular piety;

- chapter *five*, on the veneration of the Holy Mother of God, which occupies a singular position both in the Liturgy and popular devotion;

- chapter *six*, on the cult of the Saints and Beati, which also occupies a significant place in the Liturgy and in the devotion of the faithful;

- chapter *seven*, on suffrage for the dead, which occurs in various forms in the Church's worship;

- chapter *eight*, on shrines and pilgrimages; places and expressions characteristic of popular piety, and their liturgical implications.

While referring to very diverse situations, and to the multiplicity of types and forms found in pious exercises, the following text has been developed in constant reference to a number of fundamental presuppositions: the superiority of the Liturgy in respect to other forms of cult;[106] the dignity and legitimacy of popular piety;[107] the pastoral need to avoid any opposition between the Liturgy and popular piety, insurance that their various forms are not confused, so as to eschew the development of hybrid celebrations.[108]

Chapter Four
THE LITURGICAL YEAR AND POPULAR PIETY

94.   The liturgical year is the temporal structure within which the Church celebrates the holy mysteries of Christ: "From the Incarnation and the Nativity to the Ascension, to Pentecost and to the wait in joyful hope for the Lord's coming."[109]

In the liturgical year, "the celebration of the Paschal Mystery . . . is the most privileged moment in the daily, weekly and annual celebration of Christian worship."[110] Consequently, the priority of the Liturgical year over any other devotional form or practice must be regarded as a touchstone for the relationship between Liturgy and popular piety.

SUNDAY

95.   Since the "Lord's day" is the "primordial feast" and "basis and center of the liturgical year,"[111] it cannot be subordinated to popular piety. Hence, pious

---

106. Cf. SC 7, 13.
107. Cf. supra nn. 61–64.
108. Cf. supra n. 74.
109. SC 102.
110. Paul VI, Apostolic Letter *Mysterii paschalis*, in AAS 61 (1969), 222.
111. SC 106; *Calendarium Romanum* ex decreto Sacrosancti Oecumenici Concilii Vaticani II instauratum auctoritate Pauli PP. VI promulgatum, Typis Polyglotis Vaticanis 1969, *Normae universales*, 4.

exercises whose main chronological reference point is Sunday should not be encouraged.

For the pastoral good of the faithful, it is, however, licit to take up on the Sundays "per annum" those celebrations of the Lord, or in honor of the Blessed Virgin Mary or the Saints which occur during the week and which are particularly significant in popular piety, provided that they have precedence over Sundays in the tables published with the Roman calendar.[112]

Given that popular or cultural traditions can sometimes be invasive of the Sunday celebration and deprive it of its Christian character, "There is a need for special pastoral attention to the many situations where there is a risk that the popular and cultural traditions of a region may intrude upon the celebration of Sundays and other liturgical feast days, mingling the spirit of genuine Christian faith with elements which are foreign to it and may distort it. In such cases, catechesis and well-chosen pastoral initiatives need to clarify these situations, eliminating all that is incompatible with the Gospel of Christ. At the same time, it should not be forgotten that these traditions—and, by analogy, some recent cultural initiatives in civil society—often embody values which are not difficult to integrate with the demands of faith. It rests with the discernment of Pastors to preserve the genuine values found in the culture of a particular social context and especially in popular piety, so that liturgical celebration—above all on Sundays and holy days—does not suffer but rather may actually benefit."[113]

IN ADVENT

96.   Advent is a time of waiting, conversion and of hope:

- waiting—memory of the first, humble coming of the Lord in our mortal flesh; waiting—supplication for his final, glorious coming as Lord of History and universal Judge;

- conversion, to which the Liturgy at this time often refers quoting the prophets, especially John the Baptist, "Repent for the kingdom of heaven is at hand" (Mt 3:2);

- joyful hope that the salvation already accomplished by Christ (cf. Rom 8:24–25) and the reality of grace in the world, will mature and reach their fullness, thereby granting us what is promised by faith, and "we shall become like him for we shall see him as he really is" (Jn 3:2).

97.   Popular piety is particularly sensitive to Advent, especially when seen as the memory of the preparation for the coming of the Messiah. The Christian people are deeply conscious of the long period of expectation that preceded the birth of our Savior. The faithful know that God sustained Israel's hope in the coming of the Messiah by the prophets.

Popular piety is not unaware of this extraordinary event. Indeed, it is awestruck at the prospect of the God of glory taking flesh in the womb of the humble and

---

112. Cf. ibid., 58.
113. John Paul II, Apostolic Letter, *Dies Domini* (May 31, 1998), 80.

lowly Virgin Mary. The faithful are particularly sensitive to the difficulties faced by the Virgin Mary during her pregnancy, and are deeply moved by the fact that there was no room at the inn for Joseph and Mary, just as she was about to give birth to the Christ child (cf. Lk 2:7).

Various expressions of popular piety connected with Advent have emerged throughout the centuries. These have sustained the faith of the people, and from one generation to the next, they have conserved many valuable aspects of the liturgical season of Advent.

The Advent Wreath

98.   Placing four candles on green fronds has become a symbol of Advent in many Christian home, especially in the Germanic countries and in North America.

The Advent wreath, with the progressive lighting of its four candles, Sunday after Sunday, until the Solemnity of Christmas, is a recollection of the various stages of salvation history prior to Christ's coming and a symbol of the prophetic light gradually illuminating the long night prior to the rising of the Sun of justice (cf. Ml 3:20; Lk 1:78).

Advent processions

99.   In many regions, various kinds of processions are held in Advent, publicly to announce the imminent birth of the Savior (the "day star" in some Italian processions), or to represent the journey to Bethlehem of Joseph and Mary and their search for a place in which Jesus would be born (the *posadas* in the Hispanic and Latin American tradition).

The Winter Interstice

100.   Advent is celebrated during the Winter interstice in the northern hemisphere. This indicate a change of seasons and a moment of rest in many spheres of human endeavor. Popular piety is extremely sensitive to the vital cycle of nature. While the Winter interstice is celebrated, the seed lays in the ground waiting for the light and heat of the sun, which begins its ascent with the Winter solstice, and eventually causes it to germinate.

In those areas where popular piety has given rise to the celebration of the changing season, such expressions should be conserved and used as a time to pray the Lord, to reflect on the meaning of human work, which is a collaboration with the creative work of God, a self-realization of the person, service to the common good, and an actualization of the plan of redemption.[114]

The Blessed Virgin Mary and Advent

The Liturgy frequently celebrates the Blessed Virgin Mary in an exemplary way during the season of Advent.[115] It recalls the women of the Old Testament who prefigured and prophesied her mission; it exalts her faith and the humility with which she promptly and totally submitted to God's plan of salvation; it high-

---

114. Cf. Second Vatican Council, Constitution *Gaudium et spes*, 34, 35, 67.
115. Cf. Paul VI, Apostolic Exhortation *Marialis cultus*, 4.

lights her presence in the events of grace preceding the birth of the Savior. Popular piety also devotes particular attention to the Blessed Virgin Mary during Advent, as is evident from the many pious exercised practiced at this time, especially the novena of the Immaculate Conception and of Christmas.

However, the significance of Advent, "that time which is particularly apt for the cult of the Mother of God,"[116] is such that it cannot be represented merely as a "Marian month."

In the calendars of the Oriental Churches, the period of preparation for the celebration of the manifestation (Advent) of divine salvation (Theophany) in the mysteries of Christmas-Epiphany of the Only Son of God, is markedly Marian in character. Attention is concentrated on preparation for the Lord's coming in the *Deipara*. For the Orientals, all Marian mysteries are Christological mysteries, since they refer to the mystery of our salvation in Christ. In the Coptic rite, the Lauds of the Virgin Mary are sung in the *Theotokia*. Among the Syrians, Advent is referred to as the *Subbara* or Annunciation, so as to highlight its Marian character. The Byzantine Rite prepares for Christmas with a whole series of Marian feasts and rituals.

102. The Feast of the Immaculate Conception, which is profoundly influential among the faithful, is an occasion for many displays of popular piety and especially for the novena of the Immaculate Conception. There can be no doubt that the feast of the pure and sinless Conception of the Virgin Mary, which is a fundamental preparation for the Lord's coming into the world, harmonizes perfectly with many of the salient themes of Advent. This feast also makes reference to the long messianic waiting for the Savior's birth and recalls events and prophecies from the Old Testament, which are also used in the Liturgy of Advent.

The novena of the Immaculate Conception, wherever it is celebrated, should highlight the prophetical texts which begin with Genesis 3:15, and end in Gabriel's salutation of the one who is "full of grace" (Lk 1:31-33).

The approach of Christmas is celebrated throughout the American continent with many displays of popular piety, centered on the feast of Our Lady of Guadalupe (December 12), which dispose the faithful to receive the Savior at his birth. Mary, who was "intimately united with the birth of the Church in America, became the radiant Star illuminating the proclamation of Christ the Savior to the sons of these nations."[117]

The Christmas Novena

103. The Christmas novena began as a means of communicating the riches of the Liturgy to the faithful who were unable easily to grasp it. It has played a very effective role and can continue to play such a role. At the same time, in current conditions where the faithful have easier access to the Liturgy, it would seem desirable that vespers from the 17–23 of December should be more solemn by adopting the use of the "major antiphons," and by inviting the faithful to

---

116. Ibid.

117. John Paul II, Discourse at the Angelus of January 24, 1999, Mexico City.

participate at the celebration. Such a celebration, held either before or after which the popular devotions to which the faithful are particularly attached, would be an ideal "Christmas novena," in full conformity with the Liturgy and mindful of the needs of the faithful. Some elements, such as the homily, the use of incense, and the intercessions, could also be expanded within the celebration of Vespers.

The Crib

104. As is well known, in addition to the representations of the crib found in churches since antiquity, the custom of building cribs in the home was widely promoted from the thirteenth century, influenced undoubtedly by St. Francis of Assisi's crib in Greccio. Their preparation, in which children play a significant role, is an occasion for the members of the family to come into contact with the mystery of Christmas, as they gather for a moment of prayer or to read the biblical accounts of the Lord's birth.

Popular piety and the spirit of Advent

105. Popular piety, because of its intuitive understanding of the Christian mystery, can contribute effectively to the conservation of many of the values of Advent, which are not infrequently threatened by the commercialization of Christmas and consumer superficiality.

Popular piety perceives that it is impossible to celebrate the Lord's birth except in an atmosphere of sobriety and joyous simplicity and of concern for the poor and marginalized. The expectation of the Lord's birth makes us sensitive to the value of life and the duties to respect and defend it from conception. Popular piety intuitively understands that it is not possible coherently to celebrate the birth of him "who saves his people from their sins" without some effort to overcome sin in one's own life, while waiting vigilantly for Him who will return at the end of time.

CHRISTMASTIDE

106. During Christmastide, the Church celebrates the mystery of the Lord's manifestation: his humble birth in Bethlehem which was made known to the shepherds, the first of Israel to welcome the Savior; the Epiphany to the three wise men who had "come from the East" (Mt 2:1), the first of the Gentiles who recognized and adored Christ the Messiah in the child of Bethlehem; the theophany at the river Jordan in which the Father declares that Jesus is His "well-beloved Son" (Mt 3:17) at the outset of his messianic mission; the miracle of Cana in which Jesus "manifested his glory and his disciples believed in him" (Jn 2:11).

107. In addition to these celebrations recalling the primary meaning of Christmas, there are also other celebrations closely connected with the mystery of the Lord's manifestation: the martyrdom of the Holy Innocents (December 28) whose blood was shed because of hatred for Jesus and because of Herod's rejection of his lordship; the memorial of the Holy Name of Jesus, January 13; the feast of the Holy Family (Sunday in the octave of Christmas) celebrating the holy family in which Jesus "grew in wisdom and grace before God and men" (Lk 2:52); the solemnity of the 1st of January which recalls the divine, virginal and salvific motherhood

of the Blessed Virgin Mary; and, although outside of Christmastide, the feast of the Presentation of the Lord (February 2), celebrating the encounter between the Messiah and his people, represented by Simeon and Anna, and the prophecy of Simeon.

108. Much of the richness and complexity of the mystery of the Lord's manifestation is reflected in displays of popular piety, which is especially sensitive to the childhood of Christ which reveals his love for us. Popular piety intuitively grasps:

- the importance of the "spirituality of gift," which is proper to Christmas: "a child is born for us, a son is *given* to us" (cf. Is 9:5), a gift expressing the infinite love of God, who "so loved the world that he gave his only Son" (Jn 3:16);

- the message of solidarity conveyed by the event of Christmas: solidarity with sinful man, for whom, in Christ, God became man "for us men and for our salvation;"[118] solidarity with the poor, because the Son of God "who was rich but became poor for your sake, to make you rich out of your poverty" (2 Cor 8:9);

- the sacredness of human life and the wonderful event that is every birth, since the Word of life came amongst men and was made visible through his birth of the Virgin Mary (cf. 1 Jn 1:2);

- the messianic joy and peace to which man has aspired in every age: the Angels announce the birth of the Savior of the world to the shepherds, the "Prince of Peace" (Is 9:5) and proclaim "peace on earth to men of good will" (Lk 2:14);

- the spirit of simplicity and poverty, humility and trust in God, suggested by the events surrounding the birth of Christ.

Popular piety, precisely because it can intuit the values inherent in the mystery of Christ's birth, is called upon to cooperate in preserving the memory of the manifestation of the Lord, so as to ensure that the strong religious tradition surrounding Christmas is not secularized by consumerism or the infiltration of various forms of neo-paganism.

Christmas Eve

109. In the space of time between the first Vespers of Christmas and Midnight Mass, both the tradition of Christmas carols, which are potent means of conveying the Christmas message of peace and joy, and popular piety propose certain forms of payers, differing from country to country, which should be cherished and, where necessary, made consonant with the celebration of the Liturgy: These would include:

- "live cribs" and the inauguration of the crib in the homes of the faithful, which is an opportunity for family prayer: this prayer should include a reading of St. Luke's account of the birth of Christ, the typical Christmas

---

118. DS 150; *Missale Romanum, Ordo Missae, Symbolum Nicaeno-Constantinopolitanum.*

carols, as well as prayers of petition and praise, especially those of children who are the protagonists in such family moments;

- the inauguration of the Christmas tree. This event also offers an opportunity for family prayer. Apart from its historical origins, the Christmas tress has become a potent symbol today and is very diffuse amongst Christians; it evokes both the tree planted in the center of Eden (Gn 2:9), and the tree of the Cross, which lends it a Christological significance: Christ is the true tree of life, born of human stock, of the Virgin Mary, the tree which is always green and productive. In the Nordic countries, the tree is decorated with apples and hosts. "Gifts" can be added; but among the gifts placed under the tree, something should be included for the poor, since they belong to every Christian family;

- the Christmas supper. The Christian family, which traditionally blesses the table and gives thanks to the Lord for the gift of food, performs this ceremony with greater intensity at the Christmas supper which gives potent concrete expression to the joy of family ties.

110. Where possible, the Church desires that the faithful should prepare for the celebration of Midnight Mass on December 24 with the Office of Readings.[119] Where such is not possible, it may be opportune to arrange a vigil of hymns, readings, and elements drawn from popular piety.

111. At Midnight Mass, an event of major liturgical significance and of strong resonance in popular piety, the following could be given prominence:

- at the beginning of Mass, the proclamation of the Savior's birth according the formula contained in the Roman Martyrology could be made in song;

- the prayer of the faithful should really be universal, and where appropriate, use several languages; and the poor should always be remembered in the presentation of the gifts;

- at the end of Mass, the faithful could be invited to kiss the image of the Child Jesus, which is then placed in a crib erected in the church or somewhere nearby.

The Feast of the Holy Family

112. The feast of the holy family of Jesus, Mary and Joseph (Sunday in the Christmas octave) is a festive occasion particularly suitable for the celebration of rites or moments of prayer proper to the Christian family. The recollection of Joseph, Mary and Jesus' going up to Jerusalem, together with other observant Jewish families, for the celebration of the Passover (cf. Lk 2:41–42), should normally encourage a positive acceptance of the pastoral suggestion that all members of the family attend Mass on this day. This feast day also affords an opportunity for the renewal of our entrustment to the patronage of the Holy

---

119. Cf. *Institutio generalis de Liturgia Horarum*, 215.

Family of Nazareth;[120] the blessing of children as provided in the ritual;[121] and where opportune, for the renewal of marriage vows taken by the spouses on their wedding day, and also for the exchange of promises between those engaged to be married in which they formalize their desire to found a new Christian family.[122]

Outside of the feast, the faithful have frequent recourse to the Holy Family of Nazareth in many of life's circumstances: joining the Association of the Holy Family so as to model their own families on the Holy Family of Nazareth;[123] frequent prayers to entrust themselves to the patronage of the Holy Family and to obtain assistance at the hour of death.[124]

The Feast of the Holy Innocents

113. Since the sixth century, on December 28, the Church has celebrated the memory of those children killed because of Herod's rage against Christ (cf. Mt 2:16–17). Liturgical tradition refers to them as the "Holy Innocents" and regards them as martyrs. Throughout the centuries Christian art, poetry and popular piety have enfolded the memory of the "tender flock of lambs"[125] with sentiments of tenderness and sympathy. These sentiments are also accompanied by a note of indignation against the violence with which they were taken from their mothers' arms and killed.

In our own times, children suffer innumerable forms of violence which threaten their lives, dignity and right to education. On this day, it is appropriate to recall the vast host of children not yet born who have been killed under the cover of laws permitting abortion, which is an abominable crime. Mindful of these specific problems, popular piety in many places has inspired acts of worship as well as displays of charity which provide assistance to pregnant mothers, encourage adoption and the promotion of the education of children.

December 31

114. Popular piety has given rise to many pious exercises connected with December 31. In many parts of the Western world the end of the civil year is celebrated on this day. This anniversary affords an opportunity for the faithful to reflect on "the mystery of time," which passes quickly and inexorably. Such should give rise to a dual feeling: of penance and sorrow for the sins committed during the year and for the lost occasions of grace; and of thanks to God for the graces and blessings He has given during the past year.

These sentiments have given rise to two pious exercises: prolonged exposition of the Blessed Sacrament, which afford an opportunity for the faithful and many

---

120. Cf. *Actus consecrationis familiarum*, in EI, *Aliae concessiones*, 1, p. 50.

121. Cf. *Rituale Romanum, De benedictionibus, Ordo benedictionis filiorum*, Editio Typica, Typis Polyglotis Vaticanis 1985, 174–194.

122. Cf. ibid., *Ordo benedictionis desponsatorum*, 195–204.

123. Erected by Leo XIII through the Apostolic Letter *Neminem fugit* (June 14, 1892) in *Leonis XIII Pontificis Maximi Acta*, XII, Typographia Vaticana, Romae 1893, pp. 149–158: confirmed by John Paul II with the decree of the Pontifical Council for the Laity (November 25, 1987).

124. Cf. EI, *Piae invocationes*, p. 83.

125. Prudentius, *Cathemerinon* XII, 130: CCL 126, Turnholti 1966, p. 69; Liturgia Horarum: *die 28 Decembris, Ss. Innocentium martyrum, Ad Laudes, Hymnus* "Audit tyrannus anxius."

religious communities for silent prayer; and the singing of the *Te Deum* as an act of community praise and thanksgiving to God for the graces received from Him as the year draws to a close.[126]

In some places, especially in monasteries and in associations of the faithful with a particular devotion to the Holy Eucharist, December 31 is marked by a vigil of prayer which concludes with the celebration of the Holy Mass. Such vigils are to be encouraged and should be celebrated in harmony with the liturgical content of the Christmas Octave, and not merely as a reaction to the thoughtless dissipation with which society celebrates the passage from one year to another, but as a vigil offering the new year to the Lord.

The Solemnity of the Holy Mother of God

115. On New Year's Day, the octave day of Christmas, the Church celebrates the Solemnity of the Holy Mother of God. The divine and virginal motherhood of the Blessed Virgin Mary is a singular salvific event: for Our Lady it was the foretaste and cause of her extraordinary glory; for us it is a source of grace and salvation because "through her we have received the Author of life."[127]

The solemnity of the 1 January, an eminently Marian feast, presents an excellent opportunity for liturgical piety to encounter popular piety: the first celebrates this event in a manner proper to it; the second, when duly catechized, lends joy and happiness to the various expressions of praise offered to Our Lady on the birth of her divine Son, to deepen our understanding of many prayers, beginning with that which says: "Holy Mary, Mother of God, pray for us, sinners."

116. In the West, January 1 is an inaugural day marking the beginning of the civil year. The faithful are also involved in the celebrations for the beginning of the new year and exchange "new year" greetings. However, they should try to lend a Christian understanding to this custom making of these greetings an expression of popular piety. The faithful, naturally, realize that the "new year" is placed under the patronage of the Lord, and in exchanging new year greetings they implicitly and explicitly place the New Year under the Lord's dominion, since to him belongs all time (cf. Rev 1:8; 22:13).[128]

A connection between this consciousness and the popular custom of singing the *Veni Creator Spiritus* can easily be made so that on January 1 the faithful can pray that the Spirit may direct their thoughts and actions, and those of the community, during the course of the year.[129]

117. New year greetings also include an expression of hope for a peaceful New Year. This has profound biblical, Christological and incarnational origins. The "quality of peace" has always been invoked throughout history by all men, and especially during violent and destructive times of war.

---

126. Cf. EI, *Aliae concessiones*, 26, p. 71.

127. *Missale Romanum, die 1 Ianuarii, In octava Navitatis Domini, Sollemnitas Sanctae Dei Genetricis Mariae, Collecta.*

128. Cf. ibid., *In Vigilia paschali, Praeparatio cerei.*

129. Cf. EI, *Aliae concessiones*, 26, p. 70.

The Holy See shares the profound aspirations of man for peace. Since 1967, January 1 has been designated "World Day for Peace."

Popular piety has not been oblivious to this initiative of the Holy See. In the light of the new born Prince of Peace, it reserves this day for intense prayer for peace, education towards peace and those values inextricably linked with it, such as liberty, fraternal solidarity, the dignity of the human person, respect for nature, the right to work, the sacredness of human life, and the denunciation of injustices which trouble the conscience of man and threaten peace.

Solemnity of the Lord's Epiphany

118. Many traditions and genuine manifestations of popular piety have been developed in relation to the Solemnity of the Lord's Epiphany, which is of ancient origin and rich in spiritual content. Among such forms of popular piety, mention may be made of:

- the solemn proclamation of Easter and the principal dominical feasts; its revival in many places would be opportune since it served to make the connection between the Epiphany and Easter, and orientate all feasts towards the greatest Christian solemnity;

- the exchange of "Epiphany gifts," which derives from the gifts offered to Jesus by the three kings (cf. Mt 2:11) and more radically from the gift made to mankind by God in the birth of Emmanuel amongst us (cf. Is 7:14; 9:16; Mt 1:23). It is important, however, to ensure that the exchange of gifts on the solemnity of the Epiphany retains a Christian character, indicating that its meaning is evangelical: hence the gifts offered should be a genuine expression of popular piety and free from extravagance, luxury, and waste, all of which are extraneous to the Christian origins of this practice;

- the blessing of homes, on whose lentils are inscribed the Cross of salvation, together with the indication of the year and the initials of the three wise men (C+M+B), which can also be interpreted to mean *Christus mansionem benedicat*, written in blessed chalk; this custom, often accompanied by processions of children accompanied by their parents, expresses the blessing of Christ through the intercession of the three wise men and is an occasion for gathering offerings for charitable and missionary purposes;

- initiatives in solidarity with those who come from afar; whether Christian or not, popular piety has encouraged a sense of solidarity and openness;

- assistance to the work of evangelization; the strong missionary character of the Epiphany has been well understood by popular piety and many initiatives in support of the missions flourish on January 6, especially the "Missionary work of the Holy Child," promoted by the Apostolic See;

- the assignation of Patrons; in many religious communities and confraternities, patron saints are assigned to the members for the coming year.

The Feast of the Baptism of the Lord

119. Closely connected with the salvific events of the Epiphany are the mysteries of the Baptism of the Lord and the manifestation of his glory at the marriage feast of Cana.

Christmastide closes with the Baptism of the Lord. Only in recent times has the feast been rehabilitated, and hence has not given rise to any particular displays of popular piety. However, the feast presents an excellent opportunity for the faithful to be reminded of their rebirth as children of God in Baptism. The rite of *asperges* could be opportunely used at all Masses on this day, and homilies could well concentrate on the symbols associated with Baptism.

The Feast of the Presentation of Our Lord

120. Until 1969, the ancient feast of the presentation of Our Lord,[130] which is of Oriental origin, was known in the West as the feast of the Purification of Our Lady, and closed the Christmas season, forty days after the Lord's birth. This feast has for long been associated with many popular devotional exercises. The faithful:

- gladly participate in the processions commemorating the Lord's entry into the Temple in Jerusalem and his encounter with God, whose house he had come to for the first time, and then with Simeon and Anna. Such processions, which in the West had taken the place of licentious pagan events, always had a penitential character, and were later identified with the blessing of candles which were carried in procession in honor of Christ, "the light to enlighten the Gentiles (Lk 2:32);

- are sensitive to the actions of the Blessed Virgin in presenting her Son in the Temple, and to her submission to the Law of Moses (Lk 12:1-8) in the rite of purification; popular piety sees in the rite of purification the humility of Our Lady and hence, February 2 has long been regarded as a feast for those in humble service.

121. Popular piety is sensitive to the providential and mysterious event that is the Conception and birth of new life. Christian mothers can easily identify with the maternity of Our Lady, the most pure Mother of the Head of the mystical Body—notwithstanding the notable differences in the Virgin's unique Conception and birth. These too are mothers in God's plan and are about to give birth to future members of the Church. From this intuition and a certain *mimesis* of the purification of Our Lady, the rite of purification after birth was developed, some of whose elements reflect negatively on birth.

---

130. Among the Byzantines, this feast is centered on the *Hypapante*, or the Lord's encounter with those whom he has come to save, who are represented by Simeon and Anna, reflecting the canticle *Nunc dimittis* (Lk 2:29–3), which is frequently repeated in the hymns used on this feast: "The Light to enlighten the gentiles and give glory to your people, Israel."

The revised *Rituale Romanum* provides for the blessing of women both before[131] and after birth,[132] this latter only in cases where the mother could not participate at the baptism of her child.

It is a highly desirable thing for mothers and married couples to ask for these blessings, which should be given in accord with the Church's prayer: in a communion of faith and charity in prayer so that pregnancy can be brought to term without difficulty (blessing before birth), and to give thanks to God for the gift of a child (blessing after birth).

122. In some local Churches, certain elements taken from the Gospel account of the Presentation of the Lord (Lk 2:22–40), such as the obedience of Joseph and Mary to the Law of the Lord, the poverty of the holy spouses, the virginity of Our Lady, mark out the 2 February as a special feast for those at the service of the brethren in the various forms of consecrated life.

123. The feast of February 2 still retains a popular character. It is necessary, however, that such should reflect the true Christian significance of the feast. It would not be proper for popular piety in its celebration of this feast to overlook its Christological significance and concentrate exclusively on its Marian aspects. The fact that this feast should be "considered . . . a joint memorial of Son and Mother"[133] would not support such an inversion. The candles kept by the faithful in their homes should be seen as a sign of Christ "the light of the world" and an expression of faith.

LENT

124. Lent precedes and prepares for Easter. It is a time to hear the Word of God, to convert, to prepare for and remember Baptism, to be reconciled with God and one's neighbor, and of more frequent recourse to the "arms of Christian penance:"[134] prayer, fasting and good works (cf. Mt 6:1–6, 16–18).

Popular piety does not easily perceive the mystical aspect of Lent and does not emphasize any of its great themes or values, such a relationship between "the sacrament of forty days" and "the sacraments of Christian initiation," nor the mystery of the "exodus" which is always present in the Lenten journey. Popular piety concentrates on the mysteries of Christ's humanity, and during Lent the faithful pay close attention to the Passion and Death of Our Lord.

125. In the Roman Rite, the beginning of the forty days of penance is marked with the austere symbol of ashes which are used in the Liturgy of Ash Wednesday. The use of ashes is a survival from an ancient rite according to which converted sinners submitted themselves to canonical penance. The act of putting on ashes symbolizes fragility and mortality, and the need to be redeemed by the mercy

---

131. *Rituale Romanum, De Benedictionibus, Ordo benedictionis mulieris ante partum*,cit., 219–231.
132. Ibid., *Ordo benedictionis mulieris post partum*, 236–253.
133. Paul VI, Apostolic Exhortation, *Marialis cultus*, 7.
134. *Missale Romanum, Feria IV Cinerum, Collecta*.

of God. Far from being a merely external act, the Church has retained the use of ashes to symbolize that attitude of internal penance to which all the baptized are called during Lent. The faithful who come to receive ashes should be assisted in perceiving the implicit internal significance of this act, which disposes them towards conversion and renewed Easter commitment.

Notwithstanding the secularization of contemporary society, the Christian faithful, during Lent, are clearly conscious of the need to turn the mind towards those realities which really count, which require Gospel commitment and integrity of life which, through self-denial of those things which are superfluous, are translated into good works and solidarity with the poor and needy.

Those of the faithful who infrequently attend the sacraments of Penance and the Holy Eucharist should be aware of the long ecclesial tradition associating the precept of confessing grave sins and receive Holy Communion at least once during the Lenten season, or preferably during Eastertide.[135]

126. The existing divergence between the liturgical idea of Lent and the outlook of popular piety need not prevent an effective interaction between Liturgy and popular piety during the forty days of Lent.

An example of such interaction is to be seen in fact that popular piety often encourages particular observances on certain days, or special devotional exercises, or apostolic or charitable works which are foreseen and recommended by the Lenten Liturgy. The practice of fasting, characteristic of the Lenten season since antiquity, is an "exercise" which frees the faithful from earthly concerns so as to discover the life that comes from above: "Man does not live on bread alone, but on every word that comes from the mouth of God" (cf. Dt 8:3; Mt 4:4; Lk 4:4; antiphon for the first Sunday of Lent).

Veneration of the Crucified Christ

127. The journey of Lent ends with the Easter Triduum, initiated by the celebration of the *Coena Domini* Mass. During the Triduum, Good Friday, which is dedicated to the celebration of the Lord's Passion, is eminently suited for the "Adoration of the Holy Cross."

Popular piety tends to anticipate the cultic veneration of the Cross. Throughout Lent, every Friday is observed, since very ancient times, as a commemoration of the Lord's Passion and the faithful easily direct their devotions towards the mystery of the Cross.

They contemplate the crucified Savior, they sense more easily the great suffering which Jesus, the Holy and Innocent One, suffered for the salvation of mankind. They understand his love and the effectiveness of his redemptive sacrifice.

128. The various and numerous devotions to the crucified Christ acquire a special significance in those churches dedicated to the mystery of the Cross or where authentic relics of the true cross are venerated. The "invention of the Cross" in the early fourth century, and the subsequent diffusion throughout

---

135. Cf. CIC, canons 989 and 920.

the Church of particles of the true Cross, gave notable impulse to devotion to the Cross.

Devotions to the crucified Crist contain many elements usually found in popular piety: hymns and prayers, acts such as the unveiling and kissing of the Cross, processions and blessing with the Cross. These can lead to the development of pious exercises often containing many valuable formal and material elements.

Devotion to the Cross, however, sometimes requires a certain enlightenment. The faithful should be taught to place the Cross in its essential reference to the Resurrection of Christ: the Cross, the empty tomb, the Death and Resurrection of Christ are indispensable in the Gospel narrative of God's salvific plan. In the Christian faith, the Cross is an expression of the triumph of Christ over the powers of darkness. Hence, it is adorned with precious stones and is a sign of blessing when made upon one's self, or on others or on objects.

129. The Gospel texts of the Passion are especially detailed. Coupled with a tendency in popular piety to isolate specific moments of the narrative, this has induced the faithful to turn their attention to specific aspects of the Passion of Christ, making of them specific devotions: devotion to the "Ecce Homo," Christ despised, "crowned with thorns and clothed in a purple cloak" (Jn 19:5), and shown to the multitude by Pilate; devotion to the five sacred wounds of Christ, especially to the side of Christ from which flowed blood and water for the salvation of mankind (Jn 19:34); devotion to the instruments of the Passion, the pillar at which Christ was scourged, the steps of the Praetorium, the crown of thorns, the nails, the lance that pierced Him; devotion to the Holy Shroud.

Such expressions of piety, often promoted by persons of great sanctity, are legitimate. However, in order to avoid excessive fragmentation in contemplation of the mystery of the Cross, it is always useful to emphasize the whole event of the Passion, as is the case in biblical and patristic tradition.

Reading of the Lord's Passion

130. The Church exhorts the faithful to frequent personal and community reading of the Word of God. Undoubtedly, the account of the Lord's Passion is among the most important pastoral passages in the New Testament. Hence, for the Christian in his last agony, the *Ordo untionis informorum eorumque pastoralis curae* suggests the reading of the Lord's Passion either in its entirety, or at least some pericopes from it.[136]

During Lent, especially on Wednesdays and Fridays, love for our Crucified Savior should move the Christian community to read the account of the Lord's Passion. Such reading, which is doctrinally significant, attracts the attention of the faithful because of its content and because of its narrative form, and inspires true devotion: repentance for sins, since the faithful see that Christ died for the sins of the entire human race, including their own; compassion and solidarity for the Innocent who was unjustly condemned; gratitude for the infinite love of

---

136. Cf. *Rituale Romanum, Ordo unctionis infirmorum eorumque pastoralis curae,* Editio Typica, Typis Polyglotis Vaticanis 1972, nn. 224–229.

Jesus for all the brethren, which was shown by Jesus, the firstborn Son, in his Passion; commitment to imitating his example of meekness, patience, mercy, forgiveness of offenses, abandonment to the Father, which Jesus did willingly and efficaciously in his Passion.

Outside of the liturgical celebration of the Passion, the Gospel narrative can be "dramatized," giving the various parts of the narrative to different persons; or by interspersing it with hymns or moments of silent reflection.

Via Crucis

131. Of all the pious exercises connected with the veneration of the Cross, none is more popular among the faithful than the *Via Crucis*. Through this pious exercise, the faithful movingly follow the final earthly journey of Christ: from the Mount of Olives, where the Lord, "in a small estate called Gethsemane" (Mk 14:32), was taken by anguish (cf. Lk 22:44), to Calvary where he was crucified between two thieves (cf. Lk 23:33), to the garden where he was placed in freshly hewn tomb (Jn 19:40–42).

The love of the Christian faithful for this devotion is amply attested by the numerous *Via Crucis* erected in so many churches, shrines, cloisters, in the countryside, and on mountain pathways where the various stations are very evocative.

132. The *Via Crucis* is a synthesis of various devotions that have arisen since the High Middle Ages: the pilgrimage to the Holy Land during which the faithful devoutly visit the places associated with the Lord's Passion; devotion to the three falls of Christ under the weight of the Cross; devotion to "the dolorous journey of Christ" which consisted in processing from one church to another in memory of Christ's Passion; devotion to the stations of Christ, those places where Christ stopped on his journey to Calvary because obliged to do so by his executioners or exhausted by fatigue, or because moved by compassion to dialogue with those who were present at his Passion.

In its present form, the *Via Crucis*, widely promoted by St. Leonardo da Porto Maurizio (+1751), was approved by the Apostolic See and indulgenced,[137] consists of fourteen stations since the middle of seventeenth century.

133. The Via Crucis is a journey made in the Holy Spirit, that divine fire which burned in the heart of Jesus (cf. Lk 12:49–50) and brought him to Calvary. This is a journey well esteemed by the Church, since it has retained a living memory of the words and gestures of the final earthly days of her Spouse and Lord.

In the Via Crucis, various strands of Christian piety coalesce: the idea of life being a journey or pilgrimage; as a passage from earthly exile to our true home in Heaven; the deep desire to be conformed to the Passion of Christ; the demands of following Christ, which imply that his disciples must follow behind the Master, daily carrying their own crosses (cf. Lk 9:23).

---

137. Cf. EI, *Aliae concessiones*, 13, pp. 59–60.

The Via Crucis is a particularly apt pious exercise for Lent.

134. The following may prove useful suggestions for a fruitful celebration of the *Via Crucis*:

- the traditional form of the *Via Crucis*, with its fourteen stations, is to be retained as the typical form of this pious exercise; from time to time, however, as the occasion warrants, one or other of the traditional stations might possibly be substituted with a reflection on some other aspects of the Gospel account of the journey to Calvary which are traditionally included in the Stations of the Cross;

- alternative forms of the *Via Crucis* have been approved by Apostolic See[138] or publicly used by the Roman Pontiff:[139] these can be regarded as genuine forms of the devotion and may be used as occasion might warrant;

- the *Via Crucis* is a pious devotion connected with the Passion of Christ; it should conclude, however, in such fashion as to leave the faithful with a sense of expectation of the resurrection in faith and hope; following the example of the *Via Crucis* in Jerusalem which ends with a station at the *Anastasis*, the celebration could end with a commemoration of the Lord's resurrection.

135. Innumerable texts exist for the celebration of the *Via Crucis*. Many of them were compiled by pastors who were sincerely interested in this pious exercise and convinced of its spiritual effectiveness. Texts have also been provided by lay authors who were known for their exemplary piety, holiness of life, doctrine and literary qualities.

Bearing in mind whatever instructions might have been established by the bishops in the matter, the choice of texts for the *Via Crucis* should take a count of the condition of those participating in its celebration and the wise pastoral principle of integrating renewal and continuity. It is always preferable to choose texts resonant with the biblical narrative and written in a clear simple style.

The *Via Crucis* in which hymns, silence, procession and reflective pauses are wisely integrated in a balanced manner, contribute significantly to obtaining the spiritual fruits of the pious exercise.

The Via Matris

136. As Christ and Our Lady of Dolors were associated in God's saving plan (Lk 2:34–35), so too they are associated in the Liturgy and popular piety.

As Christ was the "man of sorrows" (Is 53:3) through whom it pleased God to have "reconciled all things through him and for him, everything in heaven and everything on earth, when he made peace by his death on the cross" (Col 1:20),

---

138. Such is true of the "Via Crucis" in the *Libro del Pellegrino* prepared by the Central Committee for the celebration of the Holy Year of 1975.

139. Such as the texts used by Pope John Paul II for the "Via Crucis" at the Colosseum in 1991, 1992, and 1994.

so too, Mary is "the woman of sorrows" whom God associated with his Son as mother and participant in his Passion (socia passionis).

Since the childhood of Christ, the Blessed Virgin Mary's life was entirely lived out under the sign of the sword (cf. Lk 2:35). Christian piety has signaled out seven particular incidents of sorrow in her life, known as the "seven sorrows" of the Blessed Virgin Mary.

Modeled on the *Via Crucis*, the pious exercise of the *Via Matris dolorosae*, or simply the *Via Matris*, developed and was subsequently approved by the Apostolic See.[140] This pious exercise already existed in embryonic form since the sixteenth century, while its present form dates from the nineteenth century. Its fundamental intuition is a reflection on the life of Our Lady from the prophecy of Simeon (cf. Lk 2:34–35), to the death and burial of her Son, in terms of a journey in faith and sorrow: this journey is articulated in seven "stations" corresponding to the "seven dolors" of the Mother of Our Savior.

137.   This pious exercise harmonizes well with certain themes that are proper to the Lenten season. Since the sorrows of Our Lady are caused by the rejection of her Son (cf. Jn 1:11; Lk 2:1–7; 2:34–35; 4:28–29; Mt 26:47–56; Acts 12:1–5), the *Via Matris* constantly and necessarily refers to the mystery of Christ as the suffering servant (cf. Is 52:13–53:12). It also refers to the mystery of the Church: the stations of the *Via Matris* are stages on the journey of faith and sorrow on which the Virgin Mary has preceded the Church, and in which the Church journeys until the end of time.

The highest expression of the *Via Matris* is the *Pietà*, which has been an inexhaustible source of inspiration for Christian art since the Middle Ages.

HOLY WEEK

138.   "In Holy Week, the Church celebrates the mysteries of salvation accomplished by Christ in the last days of the earthly life, beginning with his messianic entry into Jerusalem."[141]

The people are notably involved in the rites of Holy Week. Many of them still bear the traces of their origins in popular piety. It has come about, however, that in the course of the centuries, a form of celebrative parallelism has arisen in the Rites of Holy Week, resulting in two cycles each with its own specific character: one is strictly liturgical, the other is marked by particular pious exercises, especially processions.

This divergence should be oriented towards a correct harmonization of the liturgical celebrations and pious exercises. Indeed, the attention and interest in manifestations of popular piety, traditionally observed among the people, should

---

140. Cf. Leo XIII, Apostolic Letter *Deipare Perdolentis*, in *Leonis XIII Pontificis Maximi Acta*, III, Typographia Vaticana 1884, pp. 220–222.

141. Congregation for Divine Worship, *Lettera circolare sulla preparazione e celebrazione delle feste pasquali* (January 16, 1988), 27.

lead to a correct appreciation of the liturgical actions, which are supported by popular piety.

Palms, olive branches and other fronds

139. "Holy Week begins with Palm Sunday, or 'Passion Sunday,' which unites the royal splendor of Christ with the proclamation of his Passion."[142]

The procession, commemorating Christ's messianic entry into Jerusalem, is joyous and popular in character. The faithful usually keep palm or olive branches, or other greenery which have been blessed on Palm Sunday in their homes or in their work places.

The faithful, however, should be instructed as to the meaning of this celebration so that they might grasp its significance. They should be opportunely reminded that the important thing is participation at the procession and not only the obtaining of palm or olive branches. Palms or olive branches should not be kept as amulets, or for therapeutic or magical reasons to dispel evil spirits or to prevent the damage these cause in the fields or in the homes, all of which can assume a certain superstitious guise.

Palms and olive branches are kept in the home as a witness to faith in Jesus Christ, the messianic king, and in his Paschal Victory.

THE PASCHAL TRIDUUM

140. Every year, the Church celebrates the great mysteries of the redemption of mankind in the "most sacred triduum of the crucifixion, burial and resurrection."[143] The Sacred Triduum extends from the Mass of the Lord's Supper to Vespers on Easter Sunday and is celebrated "in intimate communion with Christ her Spouse."[144]

HOLY THURSDAY

Visiting the Altar of Repose

141. Popular piety is particularly sensitive to the adoration of the Most Blessed Sacrament in the wake of the Mass of the Lord's Supper.[145] Because of a long historical process, whose origins are not entirely clear, the place of repose has traditionally been referred to as a "a holy sepulcher." The faithful go there to venerate Jesus who was placed in a tomb following the crucifixion and in which he remained for some forty hours.

---

142. Ibid., 28.

143. St. Augustine, *Epistula*, 55, 24: CSEL 34/2, Vindobonae 1895, p. 195. Cf. Sacred Congregation for Rites, general decree *Maxima redemptionis nostrae mysteria*, in AAS 47 (1955), 338.

144. Congregation for Divine Worship, *Lettera circolare sulla preparazione e celebrazione delle feste pasquali*, 38.

145. The procession and reposition of the Blessed Sacrament are not done in those churches in which the Lord's Passion are not celebrated on Good Friday: cf. Congregation for Divine Worship, *Lettera circolare sulla preparazione e celebrazione delle feste pasquali*, 54.

It is necessary to instruct the faithful on the meaning of the reposition: it is an austere solemn conservation of the Body of Christ for the community of the faithful which takes part in the liturgy of Good Friday, and for the viaticum of the infirmed.[146] It is an invitation to silent and prolonged adoration of the wondrous sacrament instituted by Jesus on this day.

In reference to the altar of repose, therefore, the term "sepulcher" should be avoided, and its decoration should not have any suggestion of a tomb. The tabernacle on this altar should not be in the form of a tomb or funerary urn. The Blessed Sacrament should be conserved in a closed tabernacle and should not be exposed in a monstrance.[147]

After midnight on Holy Thursday, the adoration should conclude without solemnity, since the day of the Lord's Passion has already begun.[148]

GOOD FRIDAY

Good Friday Procession

142. The Church celebrates the redemptive death of Christ on Good Friday. The Church meditates on the Lord's Passion in the afternoon liturgical action, in which she prays for the salvation of the word, adores the Cross and commemorates her very origin in the sacred wound in Christ's side (cf. Jn 19:34).[149]

In addition to the various forms of popular piety on Good Friday such as the *Via Crucis*, the passion processions are undoubtedly the most important. These correspond, after the fashion of popular piety, to the small procession of friends and disciples who, having taken the body of Jesus down from the Cross, carried it to the place where there "was a tomb hewn in the rock in which no one had yet been buried" (Lk 23:53).

The procession of the "dead Christ" is usually conducted in austere silence, prayer, and the participation of many of the faithful, who intuit much of the significance of the Lord's burial.

143. It is necessary, however, to ensure that such manifestations of popular piety, either by time or the manner in which the faithful are convoked, do not become a surrogate for the liturgical celebrations of Good Friday.

In the pastoral planning of Good Friday primary attention and maximum importance must be given to the solemn liturgical action, and the faithful must be brought to realize that no other exercise can objectively substitute for this liturgical celebration.

---

146. Cf. Congregation for Divine Worship, *Lettera circolare sulla preparazione e celebrazione delle feste pasquali*, 55; Sacred Congregation of Rites, Instruction on Eucharistic cult *Eucharisticum mysterium*, 49, in AAS 59 (1967), 566–567.
147. Cf. Congregation for Divine Worship, *Lettera circolare sulla preparazione e celebrazione delle feste pasquali*, 55.
148. Cf. ibid., 56.
149. Cf. SC 5; St. Augustine, *Ennaratio in Paslmum 138*, 2: CCL 40, Turnholti 1956, p. 1991.

Finally, the integration of the "dead Christ" procession with the solemn liturgical action of Good Friday should be avoided, for such would constitute a distorted celebrative hybrid.

Passion Plays

144. In many countries, passion plays take place during Holy Week, especially on Good Friday. These are often "sacred representations" which can justly be regarded as pious exercises. Indeed, such sacred representations have their origins in the Sacred Liturgy. Some of these plays, which began in the monks' choir, so as to speak, have undergone a progressive dramatization that has taken them outside of the church.

In some places, responsibility for the representations of the Lord's passion has been given over to the Confraternities, whose members have assumed particular responsibilities to live the Christian life. In such representations, actors and spectators are involved in a movement of faith and genuine piety. It is singularly important to ensure that representations of the Lord's Passion do not deviate from this pure line of sincere and gratuitous piety, or take on the characteristics of folk productions, which are not so much manifestations of piety as tourist attractions.

In relation to sacred "representations" it is important to instruct the faithful on the difference between a "representation" which is commemorative, and the "liturgical actions" which are *anamnesis*, or mysterious presence of the redemptive event of the Passion.

Penitential practices leading to self-crucifixion with nails are not to be encouraged.

Our Lady of Dolors

145. Because of its doctrinal and pastoral importance, it is recommended that "the memorial of Our Lady of Dolors"[150] should be recalled. Popular piety, following the Gospel account, emphasizes the association of Mary with the saving Passion her Son (cf. Jn 19:25–27; Lk 2:34f.), and has given rise to many pious exercises, including:

the *Planctus Mariae*, an intense expression of sorrow, often accompanied by literary or musical pieces of a very high quality, in which Our Lady cries not only for the death of her Son, the Innocent, Holy, and Good One, but also for the errors of his people and the sins of mankind;

the *Ora della Desolata*, in which the faithful devoutly keep vigil with the Mother of Our Lord, in her abandonment and profound sorrow following the death of her only Son; they contemplate Our Lady as she receives the dead body of Christ (the *Pietà*) realizing that the sorrow of the world for the Lord's death finds expression in Mary; in her they behold the personification of all mothers throughout the ages who have mourned the loss of a son. This pious exercise, which in some parts of Latin America is called *El Pésame*, should not be limited merely to the

---

150. Congregation for Divine Worship, *Lettera circolare sulla preparazione e celebrazione delle feste pasquali*, 72.

expression of emotion before a sorrowing mother. Rather, with faith in the resurrection, it should assist in understanding the greatness of Christ's redemptive love and his Mother's participation in it.

HOLY SATURDAY

146. "On Holy Saturday, the Church pauses at the Lord's tomb, meditating his Passion and Death, his descent into Hell, and, with prayer and fasting, awaits his resurrection."[151]

Popular piety should not be impervious to the peculiar character of Holy Saturday. The festive customs and practices connected with this day, on which the celebration of the Lord's resurrection was once anticipated, should be reserved for the vigil and for Easter Sunday.

The "Ora della Madre"

147. According to tradition, the entire body of the Church is represented in Mary: she is the *"credentium collectio universa."*[152] Thus, the Blessed Virgin Mary, as she waits near the Lord's tomb, as she is represented in Christian tradition, is an icon of the Virgin Church keeping vigil at the tomb of her Spouse while awaiting the celebration of his resurrection.

The pious exercise of the *Ora di Maria* is inspired by this intuition of the relationship between the Virgin Mary and the Church: while the body of her Son lays in the tomb and his soul has descended to the dead to announce liberation from the shadow of darkness to his ancestors, the Blessed Virgin Mary, foreshadowing and representing the Church, awaits, in faith, the victorious triumph of her Son over death.

EASTER SUNDAY

148. Easter Sunday, the greatest solemnity in the liturgical year, is often associated with many displays of popular piety: these are all cultic expressions which proclaim the new and glorious condition of the risen Christ, and the divine power released from his triumph over sin and death.

The Risen Christ meets his Mother

149. Popular piety intuits a constancy in the relationship between Christ and his mother: in suffering and death and in the joy of the resurrection.

The liturgical affirmation that God replenished the Blessed Virgin Mary with joy in the resurrection of her Son,[153] has been translated and represented, so as to speak, in the pious exercise of the *meeting of the Risen Christ with His Mother*: on Easter morning two processions, one bearing the image of Our Lady of Dolors,

---

151. Ibid., 73.
152. Rupertus di Deutz, *De glorificatione Trinitatis*, VIII, 13: PL 169, 155D.
153. Cf. Liturgia Horarum, *Commune beatae mariae Virginis*, II Vesperae, *Preces*; *Collectio missarum de beata maria Virgine*, I, Formula 15. *Beata Maria Virgo in ressurectione Domini, Praefatio.*

the other that of the Risen Christ, meet each other so as to show that Our Lady was the first, and full participant in the mystery of the Lord's resurrection.

What has already been said in relation to the processions of "the dead Christ" also applies to this pious exercise: the observance of the pious exercise should not acquire greater importance than the liturgical celebration of Easter Sunday nor occasion inappropriate mixing of liturgical expressions with those of popular piety.[154]

Blessing of the Family Table

150. The Easter liturgy is permeated by a sense of newness: nature has been renewed, since Easter coincides with Spring in the Northern hemisphere; fire and water have been renewed; Christian hearts have been renewed through the Sacrament of Penance, and, where possible, through administration of the Sacraments of Christian initiation; the Eucharist is renewed, so as to speak: these are signs and sign-realities of the new life begun by Christ in the resurrection.

Among the pious exercises connected with Easter Sunday, mention must be made of the traditional blessing of eggs, the symbol of life, and the blessing of the family table; this latter, which is a daily habit in many Christian families that should be encouraged,[155] is particularly important on Easter Sunday: the head of the household, or some other member of the household, blesses the festive meal with Easter water which is brought by the faithful from the Easter Vigil.

Visit to the Mother of the Risen Christ

151. At the conclusion of the Easter Vigil, or following the Second Vespers of Easter, a short pious exercise is kept in many places: flowers are blessed and distributed to the faithful as a sign of Easter joy. Some are brought to the image of Our Lady of Dolors, which is then crowned, as the *Regina Caeli* is sung. The faithful, having associated themselves with the sorrows of the Blessed Virgin in the Lord's Passion and Death, now rejoice with her in His resurrection.

While this pious exercise should not be incorporated into the liturgical action, it is completely in harmony with the content of the Paschal Mystery and is a further example of the manner in which popular piety grasps the Blessed Virgin Mary's association with the saving work of her Son.

EASTERTIDE

The Annual Blessing of Family Homes

152. The annual blessing of families takes place in their homes during Eastertide— or at other times of the year. This pastoral practice is highly recommended to parish priests and to their assistant priests since it is greatly appreciated by the faithful and affords a precious occasion to recollect God's constant presence among Christian families. It is also an opportunity to invite the faithful to live

---

154. Cf. supra n. 143.

155. Cf. *Rituale Romanum, De Benedictionibus, Ordo benedictionis mensae*, cit., 782–784, 806–807.

according to the Gospel, and to exhort parents and children to preserve and promote the mystery of being "a domestic church."[156]

The Via Lucis

153. A pious exercise called the *Via Lucis* has developed and spread to many regions in recent years. Following the model of the *Via Crucis*, the faithful process while meditating on the various appearances of Jesus—from his Resurrection to his Ascension—in which he showed his glory to the disciples who awaited the coming of the Holy Spirit (cf. Jn 14:26; 16:13–15; Lk 24:49), strengthened their faith, brought to completion his teaching on the Kingdom and more closely defined the sacramental and hierarchical structure of the Church.

Through the *Via Lucis*, the faithful recall the central event of the faith—the resurrection of Christ—and their discipleship in virtue of Baptism, the paschal sacrament by which they have passed from the darkness of sin to the bright radiance of the light of grace (cf. Col 1:13; Eph 5:8).

For centuries the *Via Crucis* involved the faithful in the first moment of the Easter event, namely the Passion, and helped to fix its most important aspects in their consciousness. Analogously, the *Via Lucis*, when celebrated in fidelity to the Gospel text, can effectively convey a living understanding to the faithful of the second moment of the Pascal event, namely the Lord's Resurrection.

The *Via Lucis* is potentially an excellent pedagogy of the faith, since *"per crucem ad lucem."* Using the metaphor of a journey, the *Via Lucis* moves from the experience of suffering, which in God's plan is part of life, to the hope of arriving at man's true end: liberation, joy and peace, which are essentially paschal values.

The *Via Lucis* is a potential stimulus for the restoration of a "culture of life" which is open to the hope and certitude offered by faith, in a society often characterized by a "culture of death," despair and nihilism.

Devotion to the Divine Mercy

154. In connection with the octave of Easter, recent years have witnessed the development and diffusion of a special devotion to the Divine Mercy based on the writings of Sr. Faustina Kowalska, who was canonized April 30, 2000. It concentrates on the mercy poured forth in Christ's death and resurrection, fount of the Holy Spirit who forgives sins and restores joy at having been redeemed. Since the liturgy of the Second Sunday of Easter or Divine Mercy Sunday—as it is now called[157]—is the natural locus in which to express man's acceptance of the Redeemer's mercy, the faithful should be taught to understand this devotion in the light of the liturgical celebrations of these Easter days. Indeed, "the paschal Christ is the definitive incarnation of mercy, his living sign which is both historico-salvific and eschatological. At the same time, the Easter liturgy

---

156. Cf. ibid., *Ordo benedictionis annuae familiarum in propris domibus*, 68–89.
157. Cf. *Notificazione* of the Congregation for Divine Worship and the Discipline of the Sacraments (May 5, 2000).

places the words of the psalm on our lips: 'I shall sing forever of the Lord's mercy' (Ps 89[88]:2)."[158]

The Pentecost Novena

155. The New Testament tells us that during the period between the Ascension and Pentecost "all . . . joined in continuous prayer, together with several women, including Mary the mother of Jesus, and with his brothers" (Acts 1:14) while they awaited being "clothed with the power from on high" (Lk 24:49). The pious exercise of the Pentecost novena, widely practiced among the faithful, emerged from prayerful reflection on this salvific event.

Indeed, this novena is already present in the Missal and in the Liturgy of the Hours, especially in the second vespers of Pentecost: the biblical and eucological texts, in different ways, recall the disciples' expectation of the Paraclete. Where possible, the Pentecost novena should consist of the solemn celebration of Vespers. Where such is not possible, the novena should try to reflect the liturgical themes of the days from Ascension to the Vigil of Pentecost.

In some places, the week of prayer for the unity of Christians is celebrated at this time.[159]

PENTECOST

Pentecost Sunday

156. Eastertide concludes with Pentecost Sunday, the fiftieth day, and its commemoration of the outpouring of the Holy Spirit on the apostles (cf. Acts 2:1–4), the Church's foundation, and the beginning of its mission to all nations and peoples. The protracted celebration of the vigil Mass has a particular importance in cathedrals and some parishes, since it reflects the intense persevering prayer of the Christian community in imitation of the Apostles united in prayer with Mother of Jesus.[160]

The mystery of Pentecost exhorts us to prayer and commitment to mission and enlightens popular piety, which is a "continued sign of the presence of the Holy Spirit in the Church. He arouses faith, hope and charity in the hearts [of the faithful], and those ecclesial virtues which make popular piety valuable. The same Spirit ennobles the numerous and varied ways of transmitting the Christian message according to the culture and customs of all times and places."[161]

The faithful are well used to invoking the Holy Spirit especially when initiating new undertakings or works or in times of particular difficulties. Often they use formulas taken from the celebration of Pentecost (*Veni Creator Spiritus*,

---

158. John Paul II, Encyclical letter *Dives in misericordia* 8.

159. Cf. Pontifical Council for the Promotion of Christian Unity, *Directoire pour l'application des Principes et des Normes sur l'Oecuménisme* (March 5, 1993), 110: AAS 85 (1993), 1084.

160. Cf. Congregation for Divine Worship *Lettera circolare sulla preparazione e celebrazione delle feste pasquali*, 107; the forms, biblical texts and prayers for the vigil of Pentecost—already published in some editions of the *Missale Romanum*—are to be found in *Notitiae* 24 (1988), 156–159.

161. John Paul II, Homily given at the Celebration of the Word in La Serena (Chile), 2, in *Insegnamenti di Giovanni Paolo II*, X/1 (1987), cit., p. 1078.

Veni Sancte Spiritus)[162] *or short prayers of supplication (Emitte Spiritum tuum et creabuntur)*. The third glorious mystery of the Rosary invites the faithful to meditate on the outpouring of the Holy Spirit. In Confirmation they are conscious of receiving the Spirit of wisdom and counsel to guide and assist them; the Spirit of strength and light to help them make important decisions and to sustain the trials of life. The faithful are also aware that through Baptism their bodies become temples of the Holy Spirit to be respected and honored, even in death, and they know that the body will be raised up on the last day through the power of the Holy Spirit.

While the Holy Spirit gives access to communion with God in prayer, he also prompts us towards service of our neighbor by encountering him, by reconciliation, by witness, by a desire for justice and peace, by renewal of outlook, by social progress and missionary commitment.[163] In some Christian communities, Pentecost is celebrated as a "day of intercession for the missions."[164]

ORDINARY TIME

Solemnity of the Most Holy Trinity

157. The solemnity of the Most Holy Trinity is celebrated on the Sunday after Pentecost. With the growth of devotion to the mystery of God in His Unity and Trinity, John XXII extended the feast of the Holy Trinity to the entire Latin Church in 1334. During the Middle Ages, especially during the Carolingian period, devotion to the Blessed Trinity was a highly important feature of private devotion and inspired several liturgical expressions. These events were influential in the development of certain pious exercises.

In the present context, it would not appear appropriate to mention specific pious exercises connected with popular devotion to the Blessed Trinity, "the central mystery of the faith and of the Christian life."[165] It suffices to recall that every genuine form of popular piety must necessarily refer to God, "the all-powerful Father, His only begotten Son and the Holy Spirit."[166] Such is the mystery of God, as revealed in Christ and through him. Such have been his manifestations in salvation history. The history of salvation "is the history of the revelation of the one true God: Father, Son and Holy Spirit, who reconciles and unites to Himself those who have been freed from sin."[167]

Numerous pious exercises have a Trinitarian character or dimension. Most of them begin with the sign of the cross "in the name of the Father, and of the Son, and of the Holy Spirit," the same formula with which the disciples of Jesus are baptized (cf. Mt 28:19), thereby beginning a life of intimacy with God, as sons of the Father, brothers of Jesus, and temples of the Holy Spirit. Other pious exercises use formulas similar to those found in the Liturgy of the Hours and begin

---

162. Cf. EI, *Aliae concessiones* 26, pp. 70–71.
163. Cf. Gal 5:16, 22; Second Vatican Council, *Ad gentes* 4; *Gaudium et spes*, 26.
164. John Paul II, Encyclical letter *Redemptoris missio*, 78, in AAS 83 (1991), 325.
165. CCC 234.
166. Ibid., 233.
167. ibid., 234.

by giving "Glory to the Father, Son, and Holy Spirit." Some pious exercises end with a blessing given in the name of the three divine Persons. Many of the prayers used in these pious exercises follow the typical liturgical form and are addressed to the "Father, through Christ, in the Holy Spirit," and conserve doxological formulas taken from the Liturgy.

158. Worship, as has been said in the first part of this Directory, is the dialogue of God with man through Christ in the Holy Spirit.[168] A Trinitarian orientation is therefore an essential element in popular piety. It should be clear to the faithful that all pious exercises in honor of the Blessed Virgin May, and of the Angels and Saints have the Father as their final end, from Whom all things come and to Whom all things return; the incarnate, dead and resurrected Son is the only mediator (1 Tm 2:5) apart from whom access to the Father is impossible (cf. Jn 14:6); the Holy Spirit is the only source of grace and sanctification. It is important to avoid any concept of "divinity" which is abstract from the three Divine Persons.

159. Together with the little doxology (*Glory be to the Father, and to the Son, and to the Holy Spirit. . . .*) and the great doxology (*Glory be to God in the highest*), pious exercises addressed directly to the Most Blessed Trinity often include formulas such as the biblical *Trisagion* (*Holy, Holy, Holy*) and also its liturgical form (*Holy God, Holy Strong One, Holy Immortal One, have mercy on us*), especially in the Eastern Churches, in some Western countries as well as among numerous religious orders and congregations.

The liturgical Trisagion is inspired by liturgical hymns and its biblical counterpart. Here mention could be made of the *Sanctus* used in the celebration of the Mass, the *Te Deum*, the *improperia* of Good Friday's Veneration of the Cross, all of which are derived from Isaiah 6:3 and Revelation 4:8. The Trisagion is a pious exercise in which the faithful, united with the Angels, continually glorify God, the Holy, Powerful and Immortal One, while using expressions of praise drawn from Scripture and the Liturgy.

Solemnity of the Body and Blood of Christ
160. The Solemnity of the Body and Blood of Christ is observed on the Thursday following on the solemnity of the Most Blessed Trinity. This feast is both a doctrinal and cultic response to heretical teaching on the mystery of the real presence of Christ in the Eucharist, and the apogee of an ardent devotional movement concentrated on the Sacrament of the Altar. It was extended to the entire Latin Church by Urban IV in 1264.

Popular piety encouraged the process that led to the institution of the feast of *Corpus Christi*, which reciprocally inspired the development of new forms of Eucharistic piety among the people of God.

For centuries, the celebration of *Corpus Christi* remained the principal point of popular piety's concentration on the Eucharist. In the sixteenth and seventeenth centuries, faith, in reaction to various forms of Protestantism, and culture (art,

---

168. Cf. nn. 76–80.

folklore and literature) coalesced in developing lively and significant expressions of Eucharistic devotion in popular piety.

161. Eucharistic devotion, which is so deeply rooted in the Christian faithful, must integrate two basic principles:

- the supreme reference point for Eucharistic devotion is the Lord's Passover; the Pasch as understood by the Fathers, is the feast of Easter, while the Eucharist is before all else the celebration of the Paschal Mystery or of the Passion, Death and Resurrection of Christ;

- all forms of Eucharist devotion must have an intrinsic reference to the Eucharistic Sacrifice, or dispose the faithful for its celebration, or prolong the worship which is essential to that Sacrifice.

Hence, the *Rituale Romanum* states "The faithful, when worshipping Christ present in the Sacrament of the Altar, should recall that this presence comes from the Sacrifice of the Eucharist, and tends towards sacramental and spiritual communion."[169]

162. The *Corpus Christi* procession represents the typical form of a Eucharistic procession. It is a prolongation of the celebration of the Eucharist: immediately after Mass, the Sacred Host, consecrated during the Mass, is borne out of the Church for the Christian faithful "to make public profession of faith and worship of the Most Blessed Sacrament."[170]

The faithful understand and appreciate the values inherent in the procession: they are aware of being "the People of God," journeying with the Lord, and proclaiming faith in him who has become truly "God-amongst-us."

It is necessary however to ensure that the norms governing processions be observed,[171] especially those ensuring respect for the dignity and reverence of the Blessed Sacrament.[172] It is also necessary to ensure that the typical elements of popular piety accompanying the precession, such as the decoration of the streets and windows with flowers and the hymns and prayers used during the procession, truly "lead all to manifest their faith in Christ, and to give praise to the Lord,"[173] and exclude any forms of competition.

163. The Eucharistic procession is normally concluded by a blessing with the Blessed Sacrament. In the specific case of the Corpus Christi procession, the solemn blessing with the Blessed Sacrament concludes the entire celebration: the usual blessing by the priest is replaced by the blessing with the Blessed Sacrament.

---

169. *Rituale Romanum, De sacra communione et de cultu mysterii eucharistici extra Missam,* Editio Typica, Typis Polyglotis Vaticanis 1973, 80.
170. Ibid., 101; cf. CIC, can. 944.
171. Cf. *Rituale Romanum, De sacra communione et de cultu mysterii eucharistici extra Missam,* cit., 101–108.
172. Cf. ibid., 101–102.
173. Ibid., 104.

It is important that the faithful understand that this blessing is not an independent form of Eucharistic piety, but the end of a prolonged act of worship. Hence, liturgical norms prohibit "exposition of the Blessed Sacrament for the purpose of giving the blessing."[174]

Eucharistic Adoration

164. Adoration of the Blessed Sacrament is a form of Eucharistic cult which is particularly widespread in the Church and earnestly recommended to her Pastors and faithful. Its initial form derives from Holy Thursday and the altar of repose, following the celebration of the *Coena Domini* Mass. This adoration is a most apt way of expressing the connection between the celebration of the memorial of the Lord's Sacrifice and his continued presence in the Sacrament of the Altar. The reservation of the Sacred Species, so as to be able to administer Viaticum to the sick at any time, encouraged the practice among the faithful of recollection before the tabernacle and to worship Christ present in the Sacrament.[175]

"Indeed, this worship of adoration has a sound and firm foundation," [109] especially since faith in the Lord's real presence has as its natural consequence the outward and public manifestation of that belief. Therefore, the devotion prompting the faithful to visit the Blessed Sacrament draws them into an ever deeper share in the Paschal Mystery and leads them to respond gratefully to the gift of him who through his humanity constantly pours divine life into the members of his Body. [110] Abiding with Christ the Lord, they enjoy his intimate friendship and pour out their hearts before him for themselves and for those dear to them, and they pray for the peace and salvation of the world. Offering their entire lives with Christ to the Father in the Holy Spirit, they derive from this sublime colloquy an increase of faith, hope, and charity. Thus they foster those right dispositions that enable them with due devotion to celebrate the memorial of the Lord and receive frequently the bread given us by the Father. [176]

165. In adoration of the Blessed Sacrament, which can take different forms, several elements deriving from the Liturgy and from popular piety come together and it is not always easy to determine their limits:[177]

- a simple visit to the Blessed Sacrament: a brief encounter with Christ inspired by faith in the real presence and characterized by silent prayer;

- adoration of the Blessed Sacrament exposed for a period of time in a monstrance or pyx in accordance with liturgical norm;[178]

---

174. Ibid., 81.

175. Cf. Pius XII, Encyclical letter *Mediator Dei*, in AAS 39 (1947), 568–572; Paul VI, Encyclical letter *Mysterium fidei*, in AAS 57 (1965), 769–772; Sacred Congregation of Rites, Instruction *Eucharisticum mysterium*, nn. 49–50, in AAS 59 (1967), 566–567; *Rituale Romanum, De sacra communione et de cultu mycteria eucharistici extra Missam*, cit., 5.

176. Sacred Congregation of Rites, Instruction *Eucharisticum mysterium*, nn. 49–50.

177. On the matter of indulgences attached to Eucharistic adoration and processions, cf. EI, *Aliae concessiones*, 7, pp. 54–55.

178. Cf. *Rituale Romanum, De sacra communione et de cultu mycteria eucharistici extra Missam*, cit., 82–90; CIC, canon 941.

- perpetual adoration or the *Quarantore*, involving an entire religious community, or Eucharistic association, or parish, which is usually an occasion for various expressions of Eucharistic piety.[179]

The faithful should be encouraged to read the Scriptures during these periods of adoration, since they afford an unrivalled source of prayer. Suitable hymns and canticles based on those of the Liturgy of the Hours and the liturgical seasons could also be encouraged, as well as periods of silent prayer and reflection. Gradually, the faithful should be encouraged not to do other devotional exercises during exposition of the Blessed Sacrament.[180] Given the close relationship between Christ and Our Lady, the rosary can always be of assistance in giving prayer a Christological orientation, since it contains meditation of the Incarnation and the Redemption.[181]

The Sacred Heart of Jesus

166. The Church celebrates the Solemnity of the Sacred Heart of Jesus on the Friday following the second Sunday after Pentecost. In addition to the liturgical celebration, many devotional exercises are connected with the Sacred Heart of Jesus. Of all devotions, devotion to the Sacred Heart was, and remains, one of the most widespread and popular in the Church.

Understood in the light of the Scriptures, the term "Sacred Heart of Jesus" denotes the entire mystery of Christ, the totality of his being, and his person considered in its most intimate essential: Son of God, uncreated wisdom; infinite charity, principal of the salvation and sanctification of mankind. The "Sacred Heart" is Christ, the Word Incarnate, Savior, intrinsically containing, in the Spirit, an infinite divine-human love for the Father and for his brothers.

167. The Roman Pontiffs have frequently averted to the scriptural basis of devotion to the Sacred Heart of Jesus.[182]

Jesus, who is one with the Father (cf. Jn 10:30), invites his disciples to live in close communion with him, to model their lives on him and on his teaching. He, in turn, reveals himself as "meek and humble of heart" (Mt 11:29). It can be said that, in a certain sense, devotion to the Sacred Heart of Jesus is a cultic form of the prophetic and evangelic gaze of all Christians on him who was pierced (cf. Jn 19:37; Zec 12:10), the gaze of all Christians on the side of Christ, transfixed

---

179. Cf. CIC, canon 942.

180. Cf. Reply *ad dubium* on n. 62 of the Instruction *Eucharisticum mysterium*, in *Notitiae* 34 (1998), 133–134; concerning the Rosary, see the following note.

181. Cf. Paul VI, Apostolic Exhortation *Marialis cultus*, 46; Letter of the Congregation for Divine Worship and the Discipline of the Sacraments (January 15, 1997), in *Notitiae* 34 (1998), 506–510; see also the rescript of the Apostolic Penitentiary of March 8, 1996, in *Notitiae* 34 (1998), 511.

182. Cf. Leo XIII, Encyclical Letter *Annum sacrum* (May 25, 1889) on the consecration of mankind to the Sacred Heart, in *Leonis XIII Pontificis Maximi Acta*, XIX, Typographia Vaticana, Romae 1900, pp. 71–80; Pius XII, Encyclical Letter *Haurietis aquas*, in AAS 48 (1956), 311–329; Paul VI, Apostolic Letter *Investigabiles divitias Christi* (February 6, 1965), in AAS 57 (1965), 298–301; John Paul II, Message on the Centenary of the Consecration of Mankind to the Sacred Heart of Jesus (June 11, 1999), in *L'Osservatore Romano*, June 12, 1999.

by a lance, and from which flowed blood and water (cf. Jn 19:34), symbols of the "wondrous sacrament of the Church."[183]

The Gospel of St. John recounts the showing of the Lord's hands and his side to the disciples (cf. Jn 20:20), and of his invitation to Thomas to put his hand into his side (cf. Jn 20:27). This event has also had a notable influence on the origin and development of the Church's devotion to the Sacred Heart.

168. These and other texts present Christ as the paschal Lamb, victorious and slain (cf. Rev 5:6). They were objects of much reflection by the Fathers who unveiled their doctrinal richness. They invited the faithful to penetrate the mysteries of Christ by contemplating the wound opened in his side. Augustine writes: "Access is possible: Christ is the door. It was opened for you when his side was opened by the lance. Remember what flowed out from his side: thus, choose where you want to enter Christ. From the side of Christ as he hung dying upon the Cross there flowed out blood and water, when it was pierced by a lance. Your purification is in that water, your redemption is in that blood."[184]

169. Devotion to the Sacred Heart was particularly strong during the Middle Ages. Many renowned for their learning and holiness developed and encouraged the devotion, among them St. Bernard (+1153), St. Bonaventure (+1274), the mystic St. Lutgarda (+1246), St Matilda of Marburg (+1282), the sainted sisters Matilda (+1299) and Gertrude (+1302) of the monastery of Helfta, and Ludolf of Saxony (+1380). These perceived in the Sacred Heart a "refuge" in which to recover, the seat of mercy, the encounter with him who is the source of the Lord's infinite love, the fount from which flows the Holy Spirit, the promised land, and true paradise.

170. In the modern period devotion to the Sacred Heart of Jesus underwent new developments. At a time when Jansenism proclaimed the rigors of divine justice, the devotion to the Sacred Heart of Jesus served as a useful antidote and aroused in the faithful a love for Our Lord and a trust in his infinite mercy symbolized by his Heart. St. Francis de Sales (+1622) adopted humility, gentleness (cf. Mt 11:29) and tender loving mercy, all aspects of the Sacred Heart, as a model for his life and apostolate. The Lord frequently manifested the abundant mercy of his Heart to St. Margaret Mary (+1690); St. John Eudes (+1680) promoted the liturgical cult of the Sacred Heart, while St. Claude de la Colombière (+1682) and St. John Bosco (+1888) and other saints were avid promoters of devotion to the Sacred Heart.

171. Devotions to the Sacred Heart of Jesus are numerous. Some have been explicitly approved and frequently recommended by the Apostolic See. Among these, mention should be made of the following:

- personal consecration, described by Pius XI as "undoubtedly the principal devotional practice used in relation to the Sacred Heart;"[185]

---

183. SC 5; cf. St. Augustine, *Ennaratio in Psalmum 138*, 2: CCL 40, cit., p. 1991.
184. St. Augustine, *Sermo 311*, 3: PL 38, 1415.
185. Pius XI, Encyclical Letter *Miserentissimus redemptor*, in AAS 20 (1928), 167.

- family consecration to the Sacred Heart, in which the family, by virtue of the Sacrament of Holy Matrimony already participating in the mystery of the unity and love of Christ for the Church, is dedicated to Christ so that he might reign in the hearts of all its members;[186]

- the Litany of the Sacred Heart of Jesus, approved for the whole Church in 1891, which is evidently biblical in character and to which many indulgences have been attached;

- the act of reparation, a prayer with which the faithful, mindful of the infinite goodness of Christ, implore mercy for the offences committed in so many ways against his Sacred Heart;[187]

- the pious practice of the first Fridays of the month which derives from the "great promises" made by Jesus to St. Margaret Mary. At a time when sacramental communion was very rare among the faithful, the first Friday devotion contributed significantly to a renewed use of the Sacraments of Penance and of the Holy Eucharist. In our own times, the devotion to the first Fridays, even if practiced correctly, may not always lead to the desired spiritual fruits. Hence, the faithful require constant instruction so that any reduction of the practice to mere credulity, is avoided and an active faith encouraged so that the faithful may undertake their commitment to the Gospel correctly in their lives. They should also be reminded of the absolute preeminence of Sunday, the "primordial feast,"[188] which should be marked by the full participation of the faithful at the celebration of the Holy Mass.

172. Devotion to the Sacred Heart is a wonderful historical expression of the Church's piety for Christ, her Spouse and Lord: it calls for a fundamental attitude of conversion and reparation, of love and gratitude, apostolic commitment and dedication to Christ and his saving work. For these reasons, the devotion is recommended and its renewal encouraged by the Holy See and by the Bishops. Such renewal touches on the devotion's linguistic and iconographic expressions; on consciousness of its biblical origins and its connection with the great mysteries of the faith; on affirming the primacy of the love of God and neighbor as the essential content of the devotion itself.

173. Popular piety tends to associate a devotion with its iconographic expression. This is a normal and positive phenomenon. Inconveniences can sometimes arise: iconographic expressions that no longer respond to the artistic taste of the people can sometimes lead to a diminished appreciation of the devotion's object, independently of its theological basis and its historico-salvific content.

This can sometimes arise with devotion to the Sacred Heart: perhaps certain overly sentimental images which are incapable of giving expression to the devotion's robust theological content or which do not encourage the faithful to approach the mystery of the Sacred Heart of our Savior.

---

186. Cf. EI, *Aliae concessiones*, 1, p. 50.
187. Cf. EI, *Aliae concessiones*, 3, pp. 51–53.
188. SC 106.

Recent times have seen the development of images representing the Sacred Heart of Jesus at the moment of crucifixion, which is the highest expression of the love of Christ. The Sacred Heart is Christ crucified, his side pierced by the lance, with blood and water flowing from it (cf. Jn 19:34).

The Immaculate Heart of Mary

174. The Church celebrates the liturgical memorial of the Immaculate Heart of Mary the day after the Solemnity of the Sacred Heart of Jesus. The contiguity of both celebrations is in itself a liturgical sign of their close connection: the *mysterium* of the Heart of Jesus is projected onto and reverberates in the Heart of His Mother, who is also one of his followers and a disciple. As the Solemnity of the Sacred Heart celebrates the salvific mysteries of Christ in a synthetic manner by reducing them to their fount—the Heart of Jesus—so too the memorial of the Immaculate Heart of Mary is a celebration of the complex visceral relationship of Mary with her Son's work of salvation: from the Incarnation, to his death and resurrection, to the gift of the Holy Spirit.

Following the apparitions at Fatima in 1917, devotion to the Immaculate Heart of Mary became very widespread. On the twenty-fifth anniversary of the apparitions (1942) Pius XII consecrated the Church and the human race to the Immaculate Heart of Mary, and extended the memorial to the entire Church.

In popular piety devotions to the Immaculate Heart of Mary resemble those of the Sacred Heart of Jesus, while bearing in mind the distance between Jesus and his Mother: consecration of individuals and families, of religious communities and nations;[189] reparation for sins through prayer, mortification and alms deeds; the practice of the *First Five Saturdays*.

With regard to receiving Holy Communion of the Five First Saturdays, the same as has been said in relation to the Nine First Fridays can be repeated:[190] overestimation of temporal factors should be overcome in favor of re-contextualizing the reception of Holy Communion within the framework of the Eucharist. This pious practice should be seen as an opportunity to live intensely the paschal Mystery celebrated in the Holy Eucharist, as inspired by the life of the Blessed Virgin Mary.

The Most Precious Blood of Christ

175. Biblical revelation, both in its figurative stage in the Old Testament and in its perfect and fulfilled stage in the New Testament, connects blood very closely with life, and authentically with death, exodus and the Pasch, with the priesthood and sacrificial cult, with redemption and the covenant.

The Old Testament figures associated with blood and its redemptive significance are fulfilled perfectly in Christ, especially in his Passion, Death and Resurrection.

---

189. Among the various consecrations to the Immaculate Heart of Mary, one of the most important is that of Pius XII's consecration of the world to the Immaculate Heart of Mary on October 31, 1942 (cf. AAS 34 [1942], 318), which was renewed by John Paul II, in communion with the bishops of the Church, on March 25, 1984 (cf. *Insegnamenti di Giovanni Paolo II*, VII/1 [1984], Libreria Editrice Vaticana, Città del Vaticano 1984, pp. 774–779).
190. Cf. supra n. 171.

Thus the mystery of the Blood of Christ is to be found at the very center of the faith and of our salvation.

The mystery of the Saving Blood of Christ recalls and refers to:

- the Incarnation of the Word (cf. Jn 1:14) and Christ's becoming a member of the people of the Old Testament through circumcision (Lk 2:21);

- the Biblical image of the Lamb abounds with implication: "The Lamb of God who takes away the sins of the world" (Jn 1:29), in which Isaiah's Suffering Servant image (Is 53) is also to be found, carries upon himself the sins of mankind (cf. Is 53:4–5); the "Paschal Lamb," symbol of Israel's redemption (cf. At 8:31–35; 1 Cor 5:7; 1 Pt 1:18–20);

- the "chalice of the passion" of which Jesus spoke in allusion to his imminent redemptive death, when he asked the sons of Zebedee: "Can you drink this chalice that I must drink?" (Mt 20:22; cf. Mk 10:38) and the chalice of the agony in the garden of olives (cf. Lk 22:42–43) which was accompanied by the Lord's sweating blood (cf. Lk 22:44);

- the Eucharistic chalice, under the form of wine, contains the Blood of the New Covenant poured out for the remission of sins; it is a memorial of the Lord's Pasch (1 Cor 11:25); and the drink of salvation according to the Lord's own words: "he who eats my flesh and drinks my blood shall have life eternal and I shall raise him up on the last day" (Jn 6:54);

- the event of the Lord's death, since by pouring out his Blood on the Cross, Christ reconciled heaven and earth (cf. Col 1:20);

- the lance which transfixed the immolated Lamb, from whose open side flowed blood and water (cf. Jn 19:34), a sign of the redemption that had been achieved, and of the sacramental life of the Church—blood and water, Baptism and Eucharist—symbol of the Church born from the side of Christ dying on the Cross.[191]

176. The Christological titles associated with the *Redeemer* are particularly associated with the mystery of the Blood of Christ: Christ has redeemed us from an ancient slavery by his most precious and innocent Blood (cf. 1 Pt 1:19) and "purifies us of sin" (1 Jn 1:17); *High Priest* "of all blessings to come" since Christ "has entered the sanctuary once and for all, taking with him not the blood of goats and bull calves, but his own blood, having won an eternal redemption for us;" *faithful Witness* vindicating the blood of the martyrs (cf. Rev 6:10) "who were slain on account of the word of God, for witnessing to it" (cf. Rev 6:9); of *King*, who as God, "reigns from the wood of the Cross," which is adorned with the purple of his own Blood; *Spouse* and *Lamb of God* in whose Blood the members of the Church—the Bride—have washed their garments (cf. Rev 7:14; Eph 5:25–27).

177. The extraordinary importance of the saving Blood of Christ has ensured a central place for its memorial in the celebration of this cultic mystery: At the center of the Eucharistic assembly, in which the Church raises up to God in

---

191. Cf. SC 5.

thanksgiving "the cup of blessing" (1 Cor 10:16; cf. Ps 115–116, 13) and offers it to the faithful as a "real communion with the Blood of Christ" (1 Cor 10:16); and throughout the Liturgical Year. The Church celebrates the saving Blood of Christ not only on the Solemnity of the Body and Blood of Christ, but also on many other occasions, such that the cultic remembrance of the Blood of our redemption (cf. 1 Pt 1:18) pervades the entire Liturgical Year. Hence, at Vespers during Christmastide, the Church, addressing Christ, sings: *"Nos quoque, qui sancto tuo redempti sumus sanguine, ob diem natalis tui hymnum novum concinimus."*[192] In the Paschal Triduum, the redemptive significance and efficacy of the Blood of Christ is continuously recalled in adoration. During the adoration of the Cross on Good Friday the Church sings the hymn: *"Mite corpus perforatur, sanguis unde profluit; terra, pontus, astra, mundus quo lavantur flumine,"*[193] and again on Easter Sunday, *"Cuius corpus sanctissimum in ara crucis torridum, sed et cruorem roeseum gustando, Deo vivimus."*[194]

In some places and in certain particular calendars, the feast of the Most Precious Blood of Christ is still observed on July 1. This feast recalls the various titles of the Redeemer.

178. The veneration of the Blood of Christ has passed from the Liturgy into popular piety where it has been widely diffused in numerous forms of devotional practices. Among these mention can be made of the following:

- the *Chaplet of the Most Precious Blood*, in which the seven "effusions of the Blood of Christ," implicitly or explicitly mentioned in the Gospels, are recalled in a series of biblical meditations and devotional prayers: the Blood of the Circumcision, the Blood of the Garden of Gethsemane, the Blood of the Flagellation, the Blood of the Crowning of Thorns, the Blood of the Ascent to Calvary, the Blood flowing from Christ's side pierced by the lance;

- the *Litany of the Blood of Christ*, which clearly traces the line of salvation history through a series of biblical references and passages. In its present form it was approved by Blessed John XXIII on February 24, 1960;[195]

- *Adoration of the Most Precious Blood of Christ* takes a great variety of forms, all of which have a common end: adoration and praise of the Precious Blood of Christ in the Eucharist, thanksgiving for the gift of Redemption, intercession for mercy and pardon; and offering of the Precious Blood of Christ for the good of the Church;

- the *Via Sanguinis:* a recently instituted pious devotion, practiced in many Christian communities, whose anthropological and cultural roots

---

192. Liturgia Horarum, *Tempus Navitatis I, Ad vesperas, Hymnus "Christe, Redemptor omnium."*

193. *Missale Romanum, Feria VI in Passione Domini, Adoratio sanctae crucis, Hymnus "Crux fidelis."*

194. Liturgia Horarum, *Tempus pascale I, Ad Vesperas, Hymnus "Ad cenam Agni providi."* Analogously, in the alternative hymn "O Rex aeterne, Domine:" Tu crucem propter hominem suscipe dignatus es; dedisti tuum sanguinem nostrae salutis pretium.

195. Text in AAS 52 (1960), 412–413; cf. EI, *Aliae concessiones*, 22, p. 68.

are African. In this devotion, the faithful move from place to place, as in the *Via Crucis*, reliving the various moments in which Christ shed his blood for our salvation.

179. Veneration of the Precious Blood of Christ, shed for our salvation, and a realization of its immense significance have produced many iconographical representations which have been approved by the Church. Among these two types can be identified: those representing the Eucharistic cup, containing the Blood of the New Covenant, and those representing the crucified Christ, from whose hands, feet and side flows the Blood of our Salvation. Sometimes, the Blood flows down copiously over the earth, representing a torrent of grace cleansing it of sin; such representations sometimes feature five Angels, each holding a chalice to collect the Blood flowing from the five wounds of Christ; this task is sometimes given to a female figure representing the Church, the spouse of the Lamb.

Assumption of the Blessed Virgin Mary

180. The Solemnity of the Assumption of the Blessed Virgin Mary clearly stands out in Ordinary Time because of its theological importance. This is an ancient memorial of the Mother of God, which signifies and synthesizes many of the truths of the faith. Our Lady assumed into Heaven:

- is "the highest fruit of the redemption,"[196] and a supreme testimony to the breath and efficacy of Christ's salvific work (soteriological significance);

- is a pledge of the future participation of the members of the mystical Body of Christ in the paschal glory of the Risen Christ (Christological aspect);

- is for all mankind "the consoling assurance of the coming of our final hope: that full glorification which is Christ's will also being that of his brethren, since He is of the 'same flesh and blood' (Heb 2:14; cf. Gal 4:49)"[197] (anthropological aspect);

- is the eschatological icon in which the Church joyfully contemplates "that which she herself desires and hopes wholly to be"[198] (ecclesiological aspect);

- is the guarantee of the Lord's fidelity to his promise: he reserves a munificent reward for his humble Servant because of her faithful cooperation with the divine plan, which is a destiny of fullness, happiness, glorification of her immaculate soul, her virginal body, perfect configuration to her Risen Son (Mariological aspect).[199]

---

196. SC 103.
197. Paul VI, Apostolic Exhortation *Marialis cultus, 6.*
198. SC 103.
199. Cf. Paul VI, Apostolic Exhortation *Marialis cultus, 6.*

181. The Assumption of the Blessed Virgin Mary (August 15) is deeply imbedded in popular piety. In many places the feast is synonymous with the person of Our Lady, and is simply referred to as "Our Lady's Day" or as the "Inmaculada" in Spain and Latin America.

In the Germanic countries, the custom of blessing herbs is associated with August 15. This custom, received into the *Rituale Romanum*,[200] represents a clear example of the genuine evangelization of pre-Christian rites and beliefs: one must turn to God, through whose word "the earth produced vegetation: plants bearing seeds in their several kinds, and trees bearing fruit with their seed inside in their several kinds" (Gn 1:12) in order to obtain what was formerly obtained by magic rites; to stem the damages deriving from poisonous herbs, and benefit from the efficacy of curative herbs.

This ancient use came to be associated with the Blessed Virgin Mary, in part because of the biblical images applied to her such as vine, lavender, cypress and lily, partly from seeing her in terms of a sweet smelling flower because of her virtue, and most of all because of Isaiah 11:1, and his reference to the "shoot springing from the side of Jesse," which would bear the blessed fruit of Jesus.

Week of Prayer for Christian Unity

182. At every celebration of the Holy Eucharist, the Church prays for unity and peace,[201] mindful of Jesus' prayer: "May they all be one. Father, may they be one in us, as you are in me and I am in you, so that the world may believe it was you who sent me" (Jn 17:21). The *Missale Romanum* contains three Masses—among those for various needs—"for Christian unity." The same intention is remembered in the intercessions of the Liturgy of the Hours."[202]

In deference to the sensibilities of the "separated brethren,"[203] expressions of popular piety should take into account the principle of ecumenism.[204] Effectively, "change of heart and holiness of life, along with public and private prayer for the unity of Christians, should be regarded as the soul of the whole ecumenical movement, and merits the name 'spiritual ecumenism.'"[205] The encounter of Catholics with Christians from other Churches or ecclesial communities affords a special occasion for common prayer for the grace of Christian unity, to offer to God their common anxieties, to give thanks to God and to implore his assistance. "Common prayer is particularly recommended during the 'Week of Prayer

---

200. Cf. *Rituale Romanum* Pauli V Pontificis Maximi iussu editum . . . SS.mi D. N. Pii Papae XII auctoritate auctum et ordinatum, Editio iuxta Typicam, Desclée, Romae 1952, pp. 444–449.
201. Cf. *Missale Romanum, Ordo Missae*, the prayer *Domine Jesu Christe*, before the sign of peace.
202. See for example: the intercessions at Vespers on Sunday and Monday of the first week, on Wednesday of the third week; and the prayers at Lauds on Wednesday of the fourth week.
203. Cf. Second Vatican Council, Decree *Unitatis redintegratio*, 3.
204. Cf. Paul VI, Apostolic Exhortation *Marialis cultus*, 32–33.
205. Second Vatican Council, Decree *Unitatis redintegratio*, 8.

for Christian Unity' or during the period between Ascension and Pentecost."[206] Prayer for Christian unity also carries several indulgences.[207]

Chapter Five
VENERATION OF THE HOLY MOTHER OF GOD

SOME PRINCIPLES

183. Popular devotion to the Blessed Virgin Mary is an important and universal ecclesial phenomenon. Its expressions are multifarious and its motivation very profound, deriving as it does from the People of God's faith in, and love for, Christ, the Redeemer of mankind, and from an awareness of the salvific mission that God entrusted to Mary of Nazareth, because of which she is mother not only of Our Lord and Savior Jesus Christ, but also of mankind in the order of grace.

Indeed, "the faithful easily understand the vital link uniting Son and Mother. They realize that the Son is God and that she, the Mother, is also their mother. They intuit the immaculate holiness of the Blessed Virgin Mary, and in venerating her as the glorious queen of Heaven, they are absolutely certain that she who is full of mercy intercedes for them. Hence, they confidently have recourse to her patronage. The poorest of the poor feel especially close to her. They know that she, like them, was poor, and greatly suffered in meekness and patience. They can identify with her suffering at the crucifixion and death of her Son, as well as rejoice with her in his resurrection. The faithful joyfully celebrate her feasts, make pilgrimage to her sanctuary, sing hymns in her honor, and make votive offerings to her. They instinctively distrust whoever does not honor her and will not tolerate those who dishonor her."[208]

The Church exhorts all the faithful—sacred minister, religious and laity—to develop a personal and community devotion to the Blessed Virgin Mary through the use of approved and recommended pious exercises.[209] Liturgical worship, notwithstanding its objective and irreplaceable importance, its exemplary efficacy and normative character, does not in fact exhaust all the expressive possibilities of the People of God for devotion to the Holy Mother of God.[210]

184. The relationship between the Liturgy and popular Marian piety should be regulated by the principles and norms already mentioned in this document.[211] In relation to Marian devotion, the Liturgy must be the "exemplary form,"[212] source of inspiration, constant reference point and ultimate goal of Marian devotion.

---

206. Pontifical Council for the Promotion of Christian Unity, *Directoire pour l'application des Principes et des Normes sur l'Oecuménisme* (March 25, 1993), 110: AAS 85 (1993), 1084.
207. Cf. EI, *Aliae concessiones*, 11, p. 58.
208. Congregation for Divine Worship, Circular Letter *Guidelines and Proposals for the Celebration of the Marian Year* (April 3, 1987), 67.
209. Cf. LG 67; Decree *Presbyterorum Ordinis*, 18; Decree *Optatam totius*, 8; Decree *Apostolicam actuositatem*, 4; CIC, canons 76, §2, 5; 663, §2–§4; 246 §3.
210. Cf. CCC 971, 2673–2679.
211. Cf. supra nn. 47–59, 70–75.
212. Cf. Paul VI, Apostolic Exhortation *Marialis cultus*, 1; Congregation for Divine Worship, Circular Letter *Guidelines an proposals for the celebration of the Marian Year*, 7; *Collectio*

185. Here, it will be useful to recall some pronouncements of the Church's Magisterium on Marian devotions. These should always be adhered to when elaborating new pious exercises or in revising those already in use, or simply in activating them in worship."[213] The care and attention of the Pastors of the Church for Marian devotions are due to their importance, since they are both a fruit and an expression of Marian piety among the people and the ecclesial community, and a significant means of promoting the "Marian formation" of the faithful, as well as in determining the manner in which the piety of the faithful for the Blessed Virgin Mary is molded.

186. The fundamental principle of the Magisterium with regard to such pious exercises is that they should be derivative from the "one worship which is rightly called Christian, because it efficaciously originates in Christ, finds full expression in Christ, and through Him, in the Holy Spirit leads to the Father."[214] Hence, Marian devotions, in varying degrees and modes, should:

- give expression to the Trinitarian note which characterizes worship of the God revealed in the New Testament, the Father, Son and Holy Spirit; the pneumatological aspect, since every true form of piety comes from the Spirit and is exercised in the Spirit; the ecclesial character, in virtue of which the faithful are constituted as the holy people of God, gathered in prayer in the Lord's name (cf. Mt 18:20) in the vital Communion of Saints;[215]

- have constant recourse to Sacred Scripture, as understood in Sacred Tradition; not overlook the demands of the ecumenical movement in the Church's profession of faith; consider the anthropological aspects of cultic expressions so as to reflect a true concept of man and a valid response to his needs; highlight the eschatological tension which is essential to the Gospel message; make clear missionary responsibility and the duty of bearing witness, which are incumbent on the Lord's disciples.[216]

TIMES OF PIOUS MARIAN EXERCISES

Celebration of feast

187. Practically all Marian devotions and pious exercises are in some way related to the liturgical feasts of the General Calendar of the Roman Rite or of the particular calendars of dioceses and religious families. Sometimes, a particular devotion antedates the institution of the feast (as is the case with the feast of

---

missarum de beata Maria Virgine, Praenotanda, 9–18.
213. Cf. Paul VI, Apostolic Exhortation *Marialis cultus*, 24.
214. Ibid, *Intro.*
215. Cf. ibid., 25–39; Congregation for Divine Worship, Circular letter *Guidelines and Proposals for the Celebration of the Marian Year*, 8.
216. Cf. Ibid.,8.

the Holy Rosary), in other instances, the feast is much more ancient than the devotion (as with the *Angelus Domini*). This clearly illustrates the relationship between the Liturgy and pious exercises, and the manner in which pious exercises find their culmination in the celebration of the feast. In so far as liturgical, the feast refers to the history of salvation and celebrates a particular aspect of the relationship of the Virgin Mary to the mystery of Christ. The feast, however, must be celebrated in accordance with liturgical norms, and bear in mind the hierarchal difference between "liturgical acts" and associated "pious exercises."[217]

It should not be forgotten that a feast of the Blessed Virgin, in so far as it is popular manifestation, also has important anthropological implications that cannot be overlooked.

Saturdays

188. Saturdays stand out among those days dedicated to the Virgin Mary. These are designated as *memorials of the Blessed Virgin Mary*.[218] This memorial derives from Carolingian times (ninth century), but the reasons for having chosen Saturday for its observance are unknown.[219] While many explanation have been advanced to explain this choice, none is completely satisfactory from the point of view of the history of popular piety.[220]

Prescinding from its historical origins, today the memorial rightly emphasizes certain values "to which contemporary spirituality is more sensitive: it is a remembrance of the maternal example and discipleship of the Blessed Virgin Mary who, strengthened by faith and hope, on that great Saturday on which Our Lord lay in the tomb, was the only one of the disciples to hold vigil in expectation of the Lord's resurrection; it is a prelude and introduction to the celebration of Sunday, the weekly memorial of the Resurrection of Christ; it is a sign that the "Virgin Mary is continuously present and operative in the life of the Church."[221]

Popular piety is also sensitive to the Saturday memorial of the Blessed Virgin Mary. The statutes of many religious communities and associations of the faithful prescribe that special devotion be paid to the Holy Mother of God on Saturdays, sometimes through specified pious exercises composed precisely for Saturdays.[222]

---

217. Cf. n. 232.

218. The *Missale Romanum* contains diverse formularies for the celebration of Mass in honor of the Blessed Virgin Mary on Saturday mornings during "Ordinary Time," the use of which is optional. See also the *Collectio missarum de beata Maria Virgine, Praenotanda*, 34–36; and the *Liturgia Horarum* for Saturdays of "ordinary time" which permits the Office of the Blessed Virgin Mary on Saturdays.

219. Cf. Alcuin, *Le sacramentaire grégorien*, II, ed. J. Deshusses, Editions Universitaires, Fribourg 1988, pp. 25–27 and 45; PL 101, 455–456.

220. Cf. Umberto de Romanis, *De vita regulari*, II, Cap. XXIV, *Quare sabbatum attribuitur Beatae Virgini*, Typis A. Befani, Romae 1889, pp. 72–75.

221. Congregation for Divine Worship, Circular letter *Guidelines and Proposals for the Celebration of the Marian Year*, 5.

222. An example of which is to be found in *Felicitación sabatina a María Inmaculada* composed by Fr. Manuel Garcia Navarro, who subsequently entered the Carthusians (+1903).

189. Since it is a significant moment, a feast day is frequently preceded by a preparatory triduum, septinaria or novena. The "times and modes of popular piety," however, should always correspond to the "times and modes of the Liturgy."

Tridua, septinaria, and novenas can be useful not only for honoring the Blessed Virgin Mary through pious exercises, but also to afford the faithful an adequate vision of the positions she occupies in the mystery of Christ and of the Church, as well as the role she plays in it.

Pious exercises cannot remain indifferent to the results of biblical and theological research on the Mother of Our Savior. These should become a catechetical means of diffusing such information, without however altering their essential nature.

Tridua, septinaria and novenas are truly preparations for the celebration of the various feast days of Our Lady, especially when they encourage the faithful to approach the Sacraments of Penance and Holy Eucharist, and to renew their Christian commitment following the example of Mary, the first and most perfect disciple of Christ.

In some countries, the faithful gather for prayer on the 13th of each month, in honor of the apparitions of Our Lady at Fatima.

Marian Months

190. With regard to the observance of "Marian months," which is widespread in the Latin and Oriental Churches,[223] a number of essential points can be mentioned.[224]

In the West, the practice of observing months dedicated to the Blessed Virgin emerged from a context in which the Liturgy was not always regarded as the normative form of Christian worship. This caused, and continues to cause, some difficulties at a liturgico-pastoral level that should be carefully examined.

191. In relation to the western custom of observing a "Marian month" during the month of May (or in November in some parts of the Southern hemisphere), it would seem opportune to take into account the demands of the Liturgy, the expectations of the faithful, their maturity in the faith, in an eventual study of the problems deriving from the "Marian months" in the overall pastoral activity of the local Church, as might happen, for example, with any suggestion of abolishing the Marian observances during the month of May.

---

223. In the Byzantine rite, the liturgy for the month of August is centered on the solemnity of the Dormition of Our Lady (August 15). Until the twelfth century, it was observed as a "Marian month;" in the Coptic rite the "Marian month" is that of *kiahk*, corresponding approximately to January-February, and is structured in relation to Christmas. In the West the first indications of a Marian month date from the sixteenth century. By the eighteenth century, the Marian month—in its modern sense—is well attested but during this period the pastors of souls concentrate their apostolic efforts—including Penance and the Eucharist—not so much on the Liturgy but on pious exercises, which were much favored by the faithful.
224. Cf. Congregation for Divine Worship, Circular Letter, *Guidelines and Proposals for the Celebration of the Marian Year*, 64–65.

In many cases, the solution for such problems would seem to lay in harmonizing the content of the "Marian months" with the concomitant season of the Liturgical Year. For example, since the month of May largely corresponds with the fifty days of Easter, the pious exercises practiced at this time could emphasize Our Lady's participation in the Paschal mystery (cf. Jn 19:25–27), and the Pentecost event (cf. Acts 1:14) with which the Church begins: Our Lady journeys with the Church having shared in the novum of the Resurrection, under the guidance of the Holy Spirit. The fifty days are also a time for the celebration of the sacraments of Christian initiation and of the mystagogy. The pious exercises connected with the month of May could easily highlight the earthly role played by the glorified Queen of Heaven, here and now, in the celebration of the Sacraments of Baptism, Confirmation and Holy Eucharist.[225]

The directives of *Sacrosanctum Concilium* on the need to orient the "minds of the faithful . . . firstly to the feasts of the Lord, in which the mysteries of salvation are celebrated during the year,"[226] and with which the Blessed Virgin Mary is certainly associated, should be closely followed.

Opportune catechesis should remind the faithful that the weekly Sunday memorial of the Paschal Mystery is "the primordial feast day." Bearing in mind that the four weeks of Advent are an example of a Marian time that has been incorporated harmoniously into the Liturgical Year, the faithful should be assisted in coming to a full appreciation of the numerous references to the Mother of our Savior during this particular period.

PIOUS EXERCISES RECOMMENDED BY THE MAGISTERIUM

192. This is not the place to reproduce the list of Marian exercises approved by the Magisterium. Some, however, should be mentioned, especially the more important ones, so as to make a few suggestions about their practice and emendation.

Prayerfully Hearing the Word of God

193. The Council's call for the "sacred celebration of the word of God" at significant moments throughout the Liturgical Year,[227] can easily find useful application in devotional exercises made in honor of the Mother of the Word Incarnate. This corresponds perfectly with the orientation of Christian piety[228] and reflects the conviction that it is already a worthy way to honor the Blessed Virgin Mary, since it involves acting as she did in relation to the Word of God. She lovingly accepted the Word and treasured it in her heart, meditated on it in her mind and spread it with her lips. She faithfully put it into practice and modeled her life on it.[229]

---

225. For comments on the Blessed Virgin Mary and the Sacraments of Christian initiation cf. ibid., 25–31.
226. SC 108.
227. Cf. SC 35, 4.
228. Cf. Paul VI, Apostolic Exhortation *Marialis cultus*, 30.
229. Cf. ibid., 17; *Collectio missarum de beata Virginis Mariae, Praenotanda ad lectionarium*, 10.

194. "Celebrations of the Word, because of their thematic and structural content, offer many elements of worship which are at the same time genuine expressions of devotion and opportunities for a systematic catechesis on the Blessed Virgin Mary. Experience, however, proves that celebrations of the Word should not assume a predominantly intellectual or didactic character. Through hymns, prayers, and participation of the faithful they should allow for simple and familiar expressions of popular piety which speak directly to the hearts of the faithful."[230]

Angelus Domini

195. The *Angelus Domini* is the traditional form used by the faithful to commemorate the holy annunciation of the angel Gabriel to Mary. It is used three times daily: at dawn, midday and dusk. It is a recollection of the salvific event in which the Word became flesh in the womb of the Virgin Mary, through the power of the Holy Spirit in accordance with the salvific plan of the Father.

The recitation of the *Angelus* is deeply rooted in the piety of the Christian faithful, and strengthened by the example of the Roman Pontiffs. In some places changed social conditions hinder its recitation, but in many other parts every effort should be made to maintain and promote this pious custom and at least the recitation of three *Aves*. The *Angelus* "over the centuries has conserved its value and freshness with its simple structure, biblical character . . . quasi-liturgical rhythm by which the various time of the day are sanctified, and by its openness to the Paschal Mystery."[231]

It is therefore "desirable that on some occasions, especially in religious communities, in shrines dedicated to the Blessed Virgin, and at meetings or conventions, the *Angelus* be solemnly recited by singing the *Ave Maria*, proclaiming the Gospel of the Annunciation"[232] and by the ringing of bells.

Regina Coeli

196. By disposition of Benedict XIV (April 2, 1742), the *Angelus* is replaced with the antiphon *Regina Caeli* during Paschaltide. This antiphon, probably dating from the tenth or eleventh century,[233] happily conjoins the mystery of the Incarnation of the Word (*quem meruisti portare*) with the Paschal event (*resurrexit sicut dixit*). The ecclesial community addresses this antiphon to Mary for the Resurrection of her Son. It adverts to, and depends on, the invitation to joy addressed by Gabriel to the Lord's humble servant who was called to become the Mother of the saving Messiah (*Ave, gratia plena*).

---

230. Congregation for Divine Worship, Circular Letter *Guidelines and Proposals for the Celebration of the Marian Year*, 10.

231. Cf. Paul VI, Apostolic Exhortation *Marialis cultus*, 41.

232. Congregation for Divine Worship, Circular Letter, *Guidelines and Proposals for the Celebration of the Marian year*, 61.

233. The antiphon is found in the twelfth century Antiphonary of the Abbey of San Lupo in Benevento. Cf. R. J. Hesbert (ed.), *Corpus Antiphonalium Officii*, vol. II, Herder, Roma 1965, pp. XX–XXIV; vol. III, Herder, Roma 1968, p. 440.

As with the *Angelus*, the recitation of the *Regina Caeli* could sometimes take a solemn form by singing the antiphon and proclaiming the Gospel of the resurrection.

The Rosary

197. The Rosary, or Psalter of the Blessed Virgin Mary, is one of the most excellent prayers to the Mother of God.[234] Thus, "the Roman Pontiffs have repeatedly exhorted the faithful to the frequent recitation of this biblically inspired prayer which is centered on contemplation of the salvific events of Christ's life, and their close association with the his Virgin Mother. The value and efficacy of this prayer have often been attested by saintly Bishops and those advanced in holiness of life."[235]

The Rosary is essentially a contemplative prayer, which requires "tranquility of rhythm or even a mental lingering which encourages the faithful to meditate on the mysteries of the Lord's life."[236] *Its use is expressly recommended in the formation and spiritual life of clerics and religious.*[237]

198. *The Blessing for Rosary Beads*[238] indicates the Church's esteem for the Rosary. This rite emphasizes the community nature of the Rosary. In the rite, the blessing of rosary beads is followed by the blessing of those who meditate on the mysteries of the life, death and resurrection of Our Lord so as to "establish a perfect harmony between prayer and life."[239]

As indicated in the *Benedictionale*, Rosary beads can be blessed publicly, on occasions such as a pilgrimage to a Marian shrine, a feast of Our Lady, especially that of the Holy Rosary, and at the end of the month of October.[240]

199. With due regard for the nature of the rosary, some suggestions can now be made which could make it more proficuous.

On certain occasions, the recitation of the Rosary could be made more solemn in tone "by introducing those Scriptural passages corresponding with the various mysteries, some parts could be sung, roles could be distributed, and by solemnly opening and closing of prayer."[241]

---

234. Regarding indulgences cf. EI, *Aliae concessiones*, 17, p. 62. For a commentary on the *Ave maria* cf. CCC 2676–2677.

235. Congregation for Divine Worship, Circular Letter *Guidelines and Proposals for the Celebration of the Marian Year*, 62.

236. Paul VI, Apostolic Exhortation *Marialis cultus*, 62.

237. Cf. CIC, canons 246, §3; 276, §2, 5; 663, §4; Congregation for the Clergy, *Directory for the Ministry and Life of Priests*, Libreria Editrice Vaticana, Città del Vaticano 1994, 39.

238. Cf. *Rituale Romanum, de Benedictionibus, Ordo benedictionis coronarum Roasrii*, cit., 1183–1207.

239. Ibid.

240. Cf. ibid.,1183–1184.

241. Congregation for Divine Worship, Circular Letter *Guidelines and Proposals for the Celebration of the Marian Year*, 62, a.

200. Those who recite a third of the Rosary sometimes assign the various mysteries to particular days: joyful (Monday and Thursday), sorrowful (Tuesday and Friday), glorious (Wednesday, Saturday and Sunday).

Where this system is rigidly adhered to, conflict can arise between the content of the mysteries and that of the Liturgy of the day: the recitation of the sorrowful mysteries on Christmas day, should it fall on a Friday. In cases such as this it can be reckoned that "the liturgical character of a given day takes precedence over the usual assignment of a mystery of the Rosary to a given day; the Rosary is such that, on particular days, it can appropriately substitute meditation on a mystery so as to harmonize this pious practice with the liturgical season."[242] Hence, the faithful act correctly when, for example, they contemplate the arrival of the three Kings on the Solemnity of the Epiphany, rather than the finding of Jesus in the Temple. Clearly, such substitutions can only take place after much careful thought, adherence to Sacred Scripture and liturgical propriety.

201. The custom of making an insertion in the recitation of the Hail Mary, which is an ancient one that has not completely disappeared, has often been recommended by the Pastors of the Church since it encourages meditation and the concurrence of mind and lips.[243]

Insertions of this nature would appear particularly suitable for the repetitive and meditative character of the Rosary. It takes the form of a relative clause following the name of Jesus and refers to the mystery being contemplated. The meditation of the Rosary can be helped by the choice of a short clause of a Scriptural and Liturgical nature, fixed for every decade.

202. "In recommending the value and beauty of the Rosary to the faithful, care should be taken to avoid discrediting other forms of prayer, or of overlooking the existence of a diversity of other Marian chaplets which have also been approved by the Church."[244] It is also important to avoid inculcating a sense of guilt in those who do not habitually recite the Rosary: "The Rosary is an excellent prayer, in regard to which, however, the faithful should feel free to recite it, in virtue of its inherent beauty."[245]

Litanies of the Blessed Virgin Mary

203. Litanies are to be found among the prayers to the Blessed Virgin recommended by the Magisterium. These consist in a long series of invocations of Our Lady, which follow in a uniform rhythm, thereby creating a stream of prayer characterized by insistent praise and supplication. The invocations, generally very short, have two parts: the first of praise (*Virgo clemens*), the other of supplication (*Ora pro nobis*).

---

242. Ibid., 62, b.
243. Cf. SC 90.
244. Congregation for Divine Worship, Circular Letter, *Guidelines and Proposals for the Celebration of the Marian Year*, 62, c.
245. Paul VI, Apostolic Exhortation *Marialis cultus*, 55.

The liturgical books contain two Marian litanies:[246] *The Litany of Loreto*, repeatedly recommended by the Roman Pontiffs; and the *Litany for the Coronation of Images of the Blessed Virgin Mary*,[247] which can be an appropriate substitute for the other litany on certain occasions.[248]

From a pastoral perspective, a proliferation of litanies would not seem desirable,[249] just as an excessive restriction on them would not take sufficient account of the spiritual riches of some local churches and religious communities. Hence, the Congregation for Divine Worship and the Discipline of the Sacraments recommends "taking account of some older and newer formulas used in the local Churches or in religious communities which are notable for their structural rigor and the beauty of their invocations."[250] This exhortation, naturally, applies to the specific authorities in the local churches or religious communities.

Following the prescription of Leo XIII that the recitation of the Rosary should be concluded by the Litany of Loreto during the month of October, the false impression has arisen among some of the faithful that the Litany is in some way an appendix to the Rosary. The Litanies are independent acts of worship. They are important acts of homage to the Blessed Virgin Mary, or as processional elements, or form part of a celebration of the Word of God or of other acts of worship.

Consecration and Entrustment to Mary

204. The history of Marian devotion contains many examples of personal or collective acts of "consecration or entrustment to the Blessed Virgin Mary" (*oblatio, servitus, commendatio, dedicatio*). They are reflected in the prayer manuals and statutes of many associations where the formulas and prayers of consecration, or its remembrance, are used.

The Roman Pontiffs have frequently expressed appreciation for the pious practice of "consecration to the Blessed Virgin Mary" and the formulas publicly used by them are well known.[251]

---

246. The Litany of Loreto was first included in the *Rituale Romanum* in 1874, as an appendix. Regarding indulgences connected with it cf. EI, *Aliae concessiones*, 22, p. 68.

247. Cf. *Ordo coronandi imaginem beatae Mariae Virginis*, Editio Typica, Typis Polyglotis Vaticanis 1981, n. 41, pp. 27–29.

248. Cf. Congregation for Divine Worship, Circular Letter *Guidelines and Proposals for the Celebration of the Marian Year*, 63, c.

249. Litanies multiplied in the sixteenth century. Often, they were in poor taste and the results of an informed piety. In 1601, Clement VIII had the Holy Office issue *Quoniam multi* which was intended to curb the excessive and uncontrolled production of litanies. According to the terms of this decree, only the more ancient litanies contained in the Breviary, Missal, Pontifical and Ritual, as well as the Litany of Loreto were approved for the use of the faithful (cf. *Magnum Bullarium Romanum*, III, Lugduni 1656, p. 1609).

250. Congregation for Divine Worship, Circular Letter *Guidelines and Proposals for the Celebration of the Marian Year*, 63, d.

251. See the *Atto di affidamento alla Beata Vergine Maria* pronounced by John Paul II on Sunday, October 8, 2000, together with the Bishops gathered in Rome for the celebration of the Great Jubilee.

Louis Grignon de Montfort is one of the great masters of the spirituality underlying the act of "consecration to Mary." He "proposed to the faithful consecration to Jesus through Mary, as an effective way of living out their baptismal commitment."[252]

Seen in the light of Christ's words (cf. Jn 19:25–27), the act of consecration is a conscious recognition of the singular role of Mary in the Mystery of Christ and of the Church, of the universal and exemplary importance of her witness to the Gospel, of trust in her intercession, and of the efficacy of her patronage, of the many maternal functions she has, since she is a true mother in the order of grace to each and every one of her children.[253]

It should be recalled, however, that the term "consecration" is used here in a broad and non-technical sense: "the expression is used of 'consecrating children to Our Lady,' by which is intended placing children under her protection and asking her maternal blessing for them."[254] Some suggest the use of the alternative terms "entrustment" or "gift." Liturgical theology and the consequent rigorous use of terminology would suggest reserving the term *consecration* for those self-offerings which have God as their object, and which are characterized by totality and perpetuity, which are guaranteed by the Church's intervention and have as their basis the Sacraments of Baptism and Confirmation.

The faithful should be carefully instructed about the practice of consecration to the Blessed Virgin Mary. While such can give the impression of being a solemn and perpetual act, it is, in reality, only analogously a "consecration to God." It springs from a free, personal, mature decision taken in relation to the operation of grace and not from a fleeting emotion. It should be expressed in a correct liturgical manner: to the Father, through Christ in the Holy Spirit, imploring the intercession of the Blessed Virgin Mary, to whom we entrust ourselves completely, so as to keep our baptismal commitments and live as her children. The act of consecration should take place outside of the celebration of the Eucharistic Sacrifice, since it is a devotional act which cannot be assimilated to the Liturgy. It should also be borne in mind that the act of consecration to Mary differs substantially from other forms of liturgical consecration.

The Brown Scapular and other Scapulars

205. The history of Marian piety also includes "devotion" to various scapulars, the most common of which is devotion to the Scapular of Our Lady of Mount Carmel. Its use is truly universal and, undoubtedly, it is one of those pious practices which the Council described as "recommended by the Magisterium throughout the centuries."[255]

---

252. John Paul II, Encyclical Letter, R*edemptoris Mater*, 48.
253. Cf. LG 61; John Paul II, Encyclical Letter, *Redemptoris Mater*, 40–44.
254. Congregation for Divine Worship, Circular letter *Guidelines and Proposals for the Celebration of the Marian Year*, 86.
255. LG 67; cf. Paul VI Letter to Cardinal Silva Henriquez, Papal Legate to the Marian Congress in Santo Domingo, in AAS 57 (1965), 376–379.

The Scapular of Mount Carmel is a reduced form of the religious habit of the Order of the Friars of the Blessed Virgin of Mount Carmel. Its use is very diffuse and often independent of the life and spirituality of the Carmelite family.

The Scapular is an external sign of the filial relationship established between the Blessed Virgin Mary, Mother and Queen of Mount Carmel, and the faithful who entrust themselves totally to her protection, who have recourse to her maternal intercession, who are mindful of the primacy of the spiritual life and the need for prayer.

The Scapular is imposed by a special rite of the Church which describes it as "a reminder that in Baptism we have been clothed in Christ, with the assistance of the Blessed Virgin Mary, solicitous for our conformation to the Word Incarnate, to the praise of the Trinity, we may come to our heavenly home wearing our nuptial garb."[256]

The imposition of the Scapular should be celebrated with "the seriousness of its origins. It should not be improvised. The Scapular should be imposed following a period of preparation during which the faithful are made aware of the nature and ends of the association they are about to join and of the obligations they assume."[257]

Medals

206. The faithful like to wear medals bearing effigies of the Blessed Virgin Mary. These are a witness of faith and a sign of veneration of the Holy Mother of God, as well as of trust in her maternal protection.

The Church blesses such objects of Marian devotion in the belief that "they help to remind the faithful of the love of God, and to increase trust in the Blessed Virgin Mary."[258] The Church also points out that devotion to the Mother of Christ also requires "a coherent witness of life."[259]

Among the various medals of the Blessed Virgin Mary, the most diffuse must be the "Miraculous Medal." Its origins go back to the apparitions in 1830 of Our Lady to St. Catherine Labouré, a humble novice of the Daughters of Charity in Paris. The medal was struck in accordance with the instructions given by Our Lady and has been described as a "Marian microcosm" because of its extraordinary symbolism. It recalls the mystery of Redemption, the love of the Sacred Heart of Jesus and of the Sorrowful Heart of Mary. It signifies the mediatory role of the Blessed Virgin Mary, the mystery of the Church, the relationship between Heaven and earth, this life and eternal life.

---

256. Congregation for Divine Worship, Circular Letter *Guidelines and Proposals for the Celebration of the Marian Year*, 88.

257. *Rituale Romanum, De Benedictionibus, Ordo benedictionis et impositionis scapularis,* cit., 1213.

258. *Rituale Romanum, De benedicionibus, Ordo benedictionis rerum quae ad pietatem et devotionem exercendam destinatur,* cit., 1168.

259. Ibid.

St. Maximilian Kolbe (+1941) and the various movements associated with him, have been especially active in further popularizing the miraculous medal. In 1917 he adopted the miraculous medal as the badge of the "Pious Union of the Militia of the Immaculate Conception" which he founded in Rome while still a young religious of the Conventual Friars Minor.

Like all medals and objects of cult, the Miraculous Medal is never to be regarded as a talisman or lead to any form of blind credulity.[260] The promise of Our Lady that "those who wear the medal will receive great graces," requires a humble and tenacious commitment to the Christian message, faithful and persevering prayer, and a good Christian life.

The "Akathistos" Hymn

207. In the Byzantine tradition, one of the oldest and most revered expressions of Marian devotion is the hymn "Akathistos"—meaning the hymn sung while standing. It is a literary and theological masterpiece, encapsulating in the form of a prayer, the universally held Marian belief of the primitive Church. The hymn is inspired by the Scriptures, the doctrines defined by the Councils of Nicea (325), Ephesus (431), and Chalcedon (451), and reflects the Greek Fathers of the fourth and fifth centuries. It is solemnly celebrated in the Eastern Liturgy on the Fifth Saturday of Lent. The hymn is also sung on many other liturgical occasions and is recommended for the use of the clergy and faithful.

In recent times the Akathistos has been introduced to some communities in the Latin Rite.[261] Some solemn liturgical celebrations of particular ecclesial significance, in the presence of the Pope, have also helped to popularize the use of the hymn in Rome.[262] This very ancient hymn,[263] the mature fruit of the undivided Church's earliest devotion to the Blessed Virgin Mary, constitutes an appeal and invocation for the unity of Christians under the guidance of the Mother of God: "Such richness of praise, accumulated from the various forms of the great tradition of the Church, could help to ensure that she may once again breathe with 'both lungs': the East and the West."[264]

---

260. Cf. LG 67; Paul VI, Apostolic Exhortation *Marialis cultus*, 38; CCC 2111.

261. In addition to the *Akathistos* other prayers deriving from the Oriental traditions have received grants of indulgences: cf. EI *Aliae concessiones*, 23, pp. 68–69.

262. The singing of the *Akathistos* at Santa Maria Maggiore on June 7, 1981 marked the anniversaries of the Councils of Constantinople (381) and Ephesus (431); the hymn was also sung to commemorate the 450th anniversary of the apparitions of Guadalupe in Mexico, December 10–12, 1981. On March 25, 1988, John Paul II presided at Matins in Santa Maria Supra Minerva during which the hymn was sung in the Slavonic Rite. It is again explicitly mentioned among the indulgenced devotions for the Jubilee Year in the Bull *Incarnationis mysterium*. It was sung at Santa Maria Maggiore on December 8, 2000 in Greek, Old Slavonic, Hungarian, Romanian and Arabic at a solemn celebration with the representatives of the Byzantine Catholic Churches at which John Paul II presided.

263. While its author is unknown, modern scholarship tends to place its composition some time after the Council of Chalcedon. A Latin version was written down around 800 by Christopher, Bishop of Venice, which had enormous influence on the piety of the Western middles age. It is associated with Germanus of Constantinople who died in 733.

264. John Paul II, Circular Letter *Redemptoris Mater*, 34.

Chapter Six
VENERATION OF THE SAINTS AND BEATI

Principles

208. The cult of the Saints, especially of the martyrs, is an ancient ecclesial phenomenon, that is rooted in the Scriptures (cf. Acts 7:54–60; Acts 6:9–11; 7:9–17) and the practice of the Church of the first half of the second century.[265] Both Eastern and Western Churches have always venerated the Saints. The Church has strenuously defended and explicated the theological basis of this cult, especially since the rise of Protestantism and its objections to certain aspects of the traditional veneration of the Saints. The connection between the cult of the Saints and the doctrine of the Church has also been clearly illustrated. The cultic expressions, both liturgical and devotional, of the veneration have always be carefully disciplined by the Church, which has always stressed the exemplary testimony to genuine Christian life given by these illustrious disciples of the Lord.

209. When treating of the Liturgical Year, *Sacrosanctum Concilium* effectively illustrates this ecclesial reality and the significance of the veneration of the Saints and *Beati*: "The Church has always included in the annual cycle memorial days of the martyrs and other saints. Raised up to perfection by the manifold grace of God and already in possession of eternal salvation, they sing God's perfect praise in heaven and pray for us. By celebrating their anniversaries, the Church proclaims the achievement of the paschal mystery in the saints who have suffered and who have been glorified with Christ. She proposes them to the faithful as examples who draw all men to the Father through Christ, and through their merits she begs God's favors."[266]

210. A correct understanding of the Church's doctrine on the Saints is only possible in the wider context of the articles of faith concerning:

- the "One, Holy, Catholic and Apostolic Church,[267] Holy because of the presence in the Church of "Jesus Christ who, with the Father and the Holy Spirit, is proclaimed as the "sole Holy One;"[268] because of the incessant action of the Spirit of holiness;[269] and because the Church has been given the necessary means of sanctification. While the Church does have sinners in her midst, she "is endowed already with a sanctity which is real though imperfect;"[270] she is "the Holy People of God,"[271] whose members, according to Scripture, are called "Saints" (cf. Acts 9:13; 1 Cor 6:1; 16:1).

---

265. Cf. St. Eusebius of Caesarea, *Historia ecclesiastica*, V, XV, 42–47: SCh 31, Paris 1952, pp. 189–190.

266. SC 104.

267. DS 150; *Missale Romanum, Ordo Missae, Symbolum Nicaeno-Constantinopolitanum.*

268. John Paul II, Apostolic Constitution, *Divinitus pefctionis magister*, in AAS 75 (1983), 349.

269. Cf. LG 4.

270. Ibid.,48.

271. Ibid., 48.

- the "communion of Saints"[272] through which the Church in heaven, the Church awaiting purification "in the state of Purgatory,"[273] and the pilgrim Church on earth share "in the same love of God and neighbor."[274] Indeed, all who are in Christ and possess his Spirit make up a single Church and are united in him.

- the doctrine of the sole mediation of Christ (cf. 1 Tm 2:3), which does not, however, exclude subordinate mediations, which must always be understood in relation to the all-embracing mediation of Christ.[275]

211. The doctrines of the Church and her Liturgy propose the Saints and *Beati who already contemplate in the "clarity of His unity and trinity"*[276] to the faithful because they are:

- historical witnesses to the universal vocation to holiness; as eminent fruit of the redemption of Christ, they are a poof and record that God calls his children to the perfection of Christ (cf. Eph 4:13; Col 1:28), in all times and among all nations, and from the most varied socio-cultural conditions and states of life;

- illustrious disciples of Christ and therefore models of evangelical life;[277] the church recognizes the heroicness of their virtues in the canonization process and recommends them as models for the faithful;

- citizens of the heavenly Jerusalem who ceaselessly sing the glory and mercy of God; the Paschal passage from this world to the Father has already been accomplished in them;

- intercessors and friends of the faithful who are still on the earthly pilgrimage, because the Saints, already enraptured by the happiness of God, know the needs of their brothers and sisters and accompany them on their pilgrim journey with their prayers and protection;

- patrons of the local churches, of which they were founders (St. Eusebius of Vercelli) or illustrious Pastors (St. Ambrose of Milan); patrons of nations: apostles of their conversion to the Christian faith (St Thomas and St. Bartholomew in India) or expressions of national identity (St. Patrick in the case of Ireland); of corporations and professions (St. Omobono for tailors); in particular circumstances—in childbirth (St. Anne, St. Raimondo Nonato), in death (St. Joseph)—or to obtain specific graces (St. Lucy for the recovery of eyesight) etc.

---

272. *Symbolum Apostolicum,* in DS 19.

273. CCC 1472.

274. LG 49.

275. Cf. Ibid.

276. Council of Florence, *Decretum pro Graecis,* in DS 1305.

277. Cf. *Missale Romanum, Die 1 Novembris Omnium Sanctorum Sollemnitas, Praefatio.*

In thanksgiving to God the Father, the Church professes all this when she proclaims "You give us an example to follow in the lives of your Saints, assistance by their intercession, and a bond of fraternal love in the communion of grace."[278]

212. The ultimate object of veneration of the Saints is the glory of God and the sanctification of man by conforming one's life fully to the divine will and by imitating the virtue of those who were preeminent disciples of the Lord.

Catechesis and other forms of doctrinal instruction should therefore make known to the faithful that: our relationship with the Saints must be seen in the light of the faith and should not obscure the *"cultus latriae* due to God the Father through Christ in the Holy Spirit, but intensify it;" "true cult of the Saints consists not so much in the multiplication of external acts but in intensification of active charity," which translates into commitment to the Christian life.[279]

HOLY ANGELS

213. With the clear and sober language of catechesis, the Church teaches that "the existence of the spiritual, non-corporeal beings that Sacred Scripture usually calls 'angels' is a truth of faith. The witness of Scripture is as clear as the unanimity of Tradition."[280]

Tradition regards the angels as messengers of God, "potent executives of his commands, and ready at the sound of his words" (Ps 103:20. They serve his salvific plan, and are "sent to serve those who will inherit salvation" (Heb 1:14).

214. The faithful are well aware of the numerous interventions of angels in the New and Old Covenants. They closed the gates of the earthly paradise (cf. Gn 3:24), they saved Hagar and her child Ishmael (cf. Gn 21:17), they stayed the hand of Abraham as he was about to sacrifice Isaac (cf. Gn 22:7), they announce prodigious births (cf. Jdt 13:3–7), they protect the footsteps of the just (cf. Ps 91:11), they praise God unceasingly (cf. Is 6:1–4), and they present the prayer of the Saints to God (cf. Rev 8:34). The faithful are also aware of the angel's coming to help Elijah, an exhausted fugitive (cf. 1 Kgs 19:4–8), of Azariah and his companions in the fiery furnace (cf. Dn 3:49–50), and are familiar with the story of Tobias in which Raphael, "one of the seven Angels who stand ever ready to enter the presence of the glory of God" (cf. Tb 12:15), renders many services to Tobit, his son Tobias and his wife Sarah.

The faithful are also conscious of the roles played by the Angels in the life of Jesus: the Angel Gabriel declared to Mary that she would conceive and give birth to the Son of the Most High (cf. Lk 1:26–38), and that an Angel revealed to Joseph the supernatural origin of Mary's conception (cf. Mt 1:18–25); the Angels appear to the shepherds in Bethlehem with the news of great joy of the Savior's birth (cf. Lk 2:8–24); "the Angel of the Lord" protected the infant Jesus when he was threatened by Herod (cf. Mt 2:13–20); the Angels ministered to Jesus in the desert (cf. Mt 4:11) and comforted him in his agony (Lk 22:43), and to the women

278. Ibid., *Praefatio I de Sanctis.*
279. LG 51.
280. CCC 328.

gathered at the tomb, they announced that he had risen (cf. Mk 16:1–8), they appear again at the Ascension, revealing its meaning to the disciples and announcing that "Jesus . . . will come back in the same way as you have seen him go" (Acts 1:11).

The faithful will have well grasped the significance of Jesus' admonition not to despise the least of those who believe in him for "their Angels in heaven are continually in the presence of my Father in heaven" (Mt 10:10), and the consolation of his assurance that "there is rejoicing among the Angels of God over one repentant sinner" (Lk 15:10). The faithful also realize that "the Son of man will come in his glory with all his Angels" (Mt 25:31) to judge the living and the dead, and bring history to a close.

215. The Church, which at its outset was saved and protected by the ministry of Angels, and which constantly experiences their "mysterious and powerful assistance,"[281] venerates these heavenly spirits and has recourse to their prompt intercession.

During the liturgical year, the Church celebrates the role played by the Holy Angels in the events of salvation[282] and commemorates them on specific days: September 29 (feast of the Archangels Michael, Gabriel and Raphael), October 2 (the Guardian Angels). The Church has a votive Mass dedicated to the Holy Angels whose preface proclaims that "the glory of God is reflected in his Angels."[283] In the celebration of the sacred mysteries, the Church associates herself with the angelic hymn and proclaims the thrice holy God (cf. Is 6:3)[284] invoking their assistance so that the Eucharistic sacrifice "may be taken [to your] altar in heaven, in the presence of . . . divine majesty."[285] The office of Lauds is celebrated in their presence (cf. Ps 137:1).[286] The Church entrusts to the ministry of the Holy Angels (cf. Rev 5:8; 8:3) the prayers of the faithful, the contrition of penitents,[287] and the protection of the innocent from the assaults of the Malign One.[288] The Church implores God to send his Angels at the end of the day to protect the faithful as they sleep,[289] prays that the celestial spirits come to the assistance of the faithful in their last agony,[290] and in the rite of

---

281. Ibid., 336.

282. The same is true, for example in the solemnity of Easter and in the solemnities of the Annunciation (March 25), Christmas (December 25), Ascension, the Immaculate Conception (December 8), St. Joseph (March 19), Sts. Peter and Paul (June 29), Assumption (August 15) and All Saints (November 1).

283. *Missale Romanum, Praefatio de Angelis.*

284. Cf. ibid., *Prex eucharistica, Sanctus.*

285. Ibid., *Prex eucharistica I, Supplices te rogamus.*

286. Cf. St. Benedict, *Regula*, 19, 5: CSEL 75, Vindobonae 1960, p. 75.

287. Cf. *Rituale Romanum, Ordo Paenitentiae*, Editio Typica, Typis Polyglotis Vatacanis 1974, 54.

288. Cf. Liturgia Horarum, *Die 2 Octobris, Ss. Angelorum Custodum memoria, Ad Vesperas, Hymnus,* "Custodes hominum psallimus angelos."

289. Cf. ibid., *Ad Completorium post II Vesperas Dominicae et Sollemnitatum, Oratio* "Visita quaesumus."

290. Cf. *Rituale Romanum, Ordo unctionis informorum eorumque patoralis curae*, cit., 147.

obsequies, invokes God to send his Angels to accompany the souls of just into paradise[291] and to watch over their graves.

216. Down through the centuries, the faithful have translated into various devotional exercises the teaching of the faith in relation to the ministry of Angels: the Holy Angels have been adopted as patrons of cities and corporations; great shrines in their honor have developed such as Mont-Saint-Michel in Normandy, San Michele della Chiesa in Piemonte and San Michele Gargano in Apulia, each appointed with specific feast days; hymns and devotions to the Holy Angels have also been composed.

Popular piety encompasses many forms of devotion to the Guardian Angels. St. Basil the Great (+378) taught that "each and every member of the faithful has a Guardian Angel to protect, guard and guide them through life."[292] This ancient teaching was consolidated by biblical and patristic sources and lies behind many forms of piety. St. Bernard of Clairvaux (+1153) was a great master and a notable promoter of devotion to the Guardian Angels. For him, they were a proof "that heaven denies us nothing that assists us," and hence, "these celestial spirits have been placed at our sides to protect us, instruct us and to guide us."[293]

Devotion to the Holy Angels gives rise to a certain form of the Christian life which is characterized by:

- devout gratitude to God for having placed these heavenly spirits of great sanctity and dignity at the service of man;

- an attitude of devotion deriving from the knowledge of living constantly in the presence of the Holy Angels of God;—serenity and confidence in facing difficult situations, since the Lord guides and protects the faithful in the way of justice through the ministry of His Holy Angels. Among the prayers to the Guardian Angels the *Angele Dei*[294] is especially popular, and is often recited by families at morning and evening prayers, or at the recitation of the *Angelus*.

217. Popular devotion to the Holy Angels, which is legitimate and good, can, however, also give rise to possible deviations:

- when, as sometimes can happen, the faithful are taken by the idea that the world is subject to demiurgical struggles, or an incessant battle between good and evil spirits, or Angels and daemons, in which man is left at the mercy of superior forces and over which he is helpless; such cosmologies bear little relation to the true Gospel vision of the struggle to overcome the Devil, which requires moral commitment, a fundamental option for the Gospel, humility and prayer;

---

291. Cf. *Rituale Romanum, Ordo exsequiarum*, Editio Typica, Typis Polyglottis Vaticanis 1969, 50.

292. St. Basil of Caesarea, *Adversus Eunomium III*, 1: PG 29, 656.

293. St. Bernard of Clairvaux, *Sermo XII in Psalmum "Qui habitat,"* 3: *Sancti Bernardi Opera, IV*, Editiones Cistercienses, Romae 1966, p. 459.

294. Cf. EI, *Normae et concessiones*, 18, p. 65.

- when the daily events of life, which have nothing or little to do with our progressive maturing on the journey towards Christ, are read schematically or simplistically, indeed childishly, so as to ascribe all setbacks to the Devil and all success to the Guardian Angels. The practice of assigning names to the Holy Angels should be discouraged, except in the cases of Gabriel, Raphael and Michael whose names are contained in Holy Scripture.

ST. JOSEPH

218. In activating His plan of salvation, God, in His sapient providence, assigned to Joseph of Nazareth, "the just man" (cf. Mt 1:19), and spouse of the Virgin Mary (cf. ibid.; Lk 1:27), a particularly important mission: legally to insert Jesus Christ into the line of David from whom, according to the prophets, the Messiah would be born, and to act as his father and guardian.

In virtue of this mission, St. Joseph features in the mysteries of the infancy of Jesus: God revealed to him that Jesus had been conceived by the Holy Spirit; (cf. Mt 1:20–21); he witnessed the birth of Christ in Bethlehem (cf. Lk 2:6–7), the adoration of the shepherds (cf. Lk 2:15–16), the adoration of the Magi (cf. Mt 2:11); he fulfilled his mission religiously with regard to the rearing of Christ, having had him circumcised according to the discipline of the Covenant of Abraham (Lk 2:21) and in giving him the name of Jesus (Mt 1:21); in accordance with the Law of the Lord, he presented Christ in the Temple and made the offering prescribed for the poor (cf. Lk 2:22–24; Ex 13:2, 12–13), and listened in wonder to the prophecy of Simeon (cf. Lk 2: 25–33); he protected the Mother of Christ and her Son from the persecution of Herod by taking them to Egypt (cf. Mt 2:13–23); together with Mary and Jesus, he went every year to Jerusalem for the Passover, and was distraught at having lost the twelve year old Jesus in the Temple (Lk 2:43–50); he lived in Nazareth and exercised paternal authority over Jesus who was submissive to him (Lk 2:51); he instructed Jesus in the law and in the craft of carpentry.

219. The virtues of St. Joseph have been the object of ecclesial reflection down through the centuries, especially the more recent centuries. Among those virtues the following stand out: faith, with which he fully accepted God's salvific plan; prompt and silent obedience to the will of God; love for and fulfillment of the law, true piety, fortitude in time of trial; chaste love for the Blessed Virgin Mary, a dutiful exercise of his paternal authority, and fruitful reticence.

220. Popular piety has grasped the significance, importance and universality of the patronage of St. Joseph "to whose care God entrusted the beginning of our redemption,"[295] "and his most valuable treasures."[296] The following have been entrusted to the patronage of St. Joseph: the entire Church was placed under the

---

295. *Missale Romanum, Die 19 Martii, Sollemnitas S. Iosephi sponsi beatae Mariae Virginis, Collecta.*
296. Sacred Congregation for Rites, Decree *Quemadmodum Deus*, in *Pii IX Pontificis Maximi Acta*, Pars Prima, vol. 5, Akademische Druck–u. Verlagsanstalt, Graz 1971, p. 282; cf. John Paul II, Apostolic Exhortation *Redemptoris custos*, 1, in AAS 82 (1990), 6.

patronage and protection of this Holy patriarch[297] by the Blessed Pius IX; those who are consecrated to God by celibacy for the sake of the Kingdom of Heaven (cf. Mt 19:12): "in St Joseph they have . . . a type and a protector of chaste integrity;"[298] workers and craftsmen, for whom the carpenter of Nazareth is a singular model;[299] the dying, since pious tradition holds that he was assisted by Mary and Jesus in his last agony.[300]

221. The person and role of St. Joseph is frequently celebrated in the Liturgy, especially in connection with nativity and infancy of Christ: during Advent;[301] Christmastide, especially the feast of the Holy Family, on the Solemnity of St. Joseph (March 19), and on his memorial (May 1).

St. Joseph is also mentioned in the *Communicantes* of the Roman Canon and in the *Litany of the Saints*.[302] The invocation of the Holy Patriarch[303] is suggested in the *Commendation of the Dying*, as well as the community's prayer that the souls of the dead, having left this world, may "be taken to the peace of the new and eternal Jerusalem, and be with Mary, the Mother of God, St. Joseph, and all of the Angels and Saints."[304]

222. St. Joseph plays a prominent part in popular devotion: in numerous popular traditions; the custom of reserving Wednesdays for devotion to St. Joseph, popular at least since the end of the seventeenth century, has generated several pious exercises including that of the *Seven Wednesdays*; in the pious aspirations made by the faithful;"[305] in prayers such as that of Pope Leo XIII, *A te, Beate Ioseph*, which is daily recited by the faithful;"[306] in the Litany of St Joseph, approved by St. Pope Pius X;[307] and in the recitation of the chaplet of St Joseph, recollecting the *Seven agonies and seven joys of St. Joseph*.

223. That the solemnity of St. Joseph (19 March) falls in Lent, when the Church concentrates her attention on preparation for Baptism and the memorial of the

---

297. The declaration of St. Joseph as patron of the universal Church took place on December 8 1870 with the Decree *Quemadmodum Deus* to which reference has already been made.

298. Leo XIII, Encyclical Letter *Quamquam pluries* (August 15, 1889) in *Leonis XIII Pontificis Maximi Acta*, IX, Typographia Vaticana, Romae 1890, p. 180.

299. Cf. Pius XII, *Allocutio ad adscriptos Societatibus Christianis Operariorum Italicorum* (A.C.L.I.) (May 1, 1955), in AAS 47 (1955), 402–407, declaring the institution of the feast of St. Joseph the Worker for the 1 May (cf. Sacred Congregation for Rites, *Decree* [April 24, 1956] in AAS 48 [1956], 237); John Paul II Apostolic Exhortation *Redemptoris custos*, 22–24, in AAS 82 (1990), 26–28.

300. Cf. St. Bernardine of Siena, *De Sancto Joseph sponso beatae Virginis*, art. II, cap. III, in *S. Bernardini Opera omnia*, t. VII, Typis Collegii Sancti Bonaventurae, Ad Claras Aquas 1959, p. 28.

301. Especially on days when the central theme of the liturgy is the genealogy of Our Lord (Mt 1:1–17, December 17) or the angel's message to St. Joseph (Mt 1:20–24, December 18); IV Sunday in Advent (A): both pericopes underline that Jesus is the Messiah, "the Son of David" (Mt 1:1) through Joseph who was of the house of David (cf. Mt 1:20; Lk 1:27, 32).

302. Cf. *Calendarium Romanum, Litanae Sanctorum*, cit., 1969, pp. 33–39.

303. Cf. *Rituale Romanum, Ordo unctionis infirmorum eorumque pastoralis curae*, cit., 143.

304. Ibid., 146.

305. Cf. EI, *Piae invocationes*, p. 83.

306. Cf. EI, *Aliae concessiones*, 19, p. 66.

307. cf. EI, *Aliae concessiones*, 22, p. 68.

Lord's Passion, inevitably gives rise to an attempt to harmonize the Liturgy and popular piety. Hence, the traditional practices of a "month of St. Joseph" should be synchronized with the liturgical Year. Indeed, the liturgical renewal movement attempted to instill among the faithful a realization of the importance of the meaning of Lent. Where the necessary adaptations can be made to the various expressions of popular piety, devotion to St. Joseph should naturally be encouraged among the faithful who should be constantly remained of this "singular example . . . which, surpassing all states of life, should be recommended to the entire Christian community, whatever their condition or rank.[308]

ST. JOHN THE BAPTIST

224. St. John the Baptist, the son of Zachary and Elizabeth, straddles the both Old and New Testaments. His parents were reckoned as "just before God" (Lk 1:6). John the Baptist is a major figure in the history of salvation. While in his mother's womb, he recognized the Savior, as he was borne in his mother's womb (cf. Lk 1:39–45); his birth was accompanied by great signs (cf. Lk 1:57–66); he retired to the desert where he led a life of austerity and penance (cf. Lk 1:80; Mt 3:4); "Prophet of the Most High" (Lk 1:76), the word of God descended on him (Lk 3:2); "he went through the whole of the Jordan district proclaiming a baptism of repentance for the forgiveness of sins" (Lk 3:3); like the new Elijah, humble and strong, he prepared his people to receive the Lord (cf. Lk 1:17); in accordance with God's saving plan, he baptized the Savior of the World in the waters of the Jordan (cf. Mt 3:13–16); to his disciples, he showed that Jesus was "the Lamb of God" (Jn 1:29), "the Son of God" (Jn 1:34), the Bridegroom of the new messianic community (cf. Jn 3:28–30); he was imprisoned and decapitated by Herod for his heroic witness to the truth (cf. Mk 6:14–29), thereby becoming the Precursor of the Lord's own violent death, as he had been in his prodigious birth and prophetic preaching. Jesus praised him by attributing to him the glorious phrase "of all children born to women, there is no one greater than John" (Lk 7:28).

225. The cult of St. John the Baptist has been present in the Christian Church since ancient times. From a very early date, it acquired popular forms and connotations. In addition to the celebration of his death (August 29), of all the Saints he is the only one whose birth is also celebrated (June 24)—as with Christ and the Blessed Virgin Mary.

In virtue of having baptized Jesus in the Jordan, many baptisteries are dedicated to him and his image as "baptizer" is to be found close to many baptismal founts. He is the patron Saint of those condemned to death or who have been imprisoned for the witness to the faith, in virtue of the harsh prison which he endured and of the death which he encountered.

In all probability, the date of John the Baptist's birth (June 24) was fixed in relation to that of Christ (December 25): according to what was said by the Angel Gabriel, when Mary conceived Our Savior, Elizabeth had already been with child for six months (cf. Lk 1:26, 36). The date of 24 June is also linked to the solar cycle of the Northern hemisphere. The feast is celebrated as the Sun, turning

---

308. John Paul II, Apostolic Exhortation *Redemptoris custos*, 1, in AAS 82 (1990), 31.

towards the South of the zodiac, begins to decline: a phenomenon that was taken to symbolize John the Baptist who said in relation to Jesus: *"illum oportet crescere, me autem minui"* (Jn 3:30).

John's mission of witnessing to the light (cf. Jn 1:7) lies at the origin of the custom of blessing bonfires on St John's Eve—or at least gave a Christian significance to the practice. The Church blesses such fires, praying God that the faithful may overcome the darkness of the world and reach the "indefectible light" of God.[309]

CULT DUE TO THE SAINTS AND TO THE *BEATI*

226. The reciprocal influence of Liturgy and popular piety is particularly noticeable in the various forms of cult given to the saints and to the Beati. Here, it would seem opportune to recall, however briefly, the principal forms of the Church's veneration of the Saints in the Liturgy: these should enlighten and guide expressions of popular piety.

Celebration of Saints

227. The celebration of a feast in honor of a Saint—and what is said in this regard also applies to the *Beati, servatis servandis*—is undoubtedly the most eminent expression of cult that the ecclesial community can give: in many cases it implicitly involves the celebration of the Holy Eucharist. Determining a day for such an observance is a relevant, and sometimes complicated, cultic event, in which various historical, liturgical, and cultic factors cannot always be easily accommodated.

In the Roman Church and in other local Churches, the celebration of the memorial of the martyrs on the anniversary of their passion (their assimilation with Christ and heavenly birth),[310] the recollection of the *Ecclesiae conditor* or of other saintly Bishops who ruled these sees, the memorial of Confessors for the faith or of anniversaries such as the dedication of the Cathedral, progressively gave rise to the development of local calendars, which kept the date and place of the deaths of particular Saints, or groups of Saints.

The martyrologies quickly evolved from the local calendars: the Syriac Martyrology (fifth century), the *Martyrologium Hieronymianum* (sixth century), the Martyrology of Bede (eighth century), the Martyrology of Lyons (ninth century), the Martyrology of Usardo (ninth century) and that of Adon (ninth century).

On January 14, 1584, Gregory XIII promulgated the *editio typica* of the *Martyrologium Romanum* for liturgical use. On June 29, 2001, John Paul II

---

309. Cf. *Rituale Romanum* Pauli V Pontificis Maximi iussu editum . . . Pii XII auctoritate ordinatum et auctum, Tit. IX, cap. III, 13: *Benedictio rogi in Vigilia Navitatis S. Ioannis Baptistae.*

310. The tradition of the "dies natalis" or date of death of the martyrs. This usage dates at least from the fifth century. Cf. St. Augustine, *Sermo* 310, 1: PL 38, 1412–1413.

promulgated the first postconciliar revision of the *Martyrologium Romanum*.[311] The revision was based on the Roman tradition and incorporated the dates of many historical martyrdoms, and collects the names of many Saints and *Beati*. The *Martyrologium Romanum* bears witness to the extraordinary wealth of sanctity which the Spirit of the Lord has raised up in the Church in different places, and at different times in her history.

228. The development of the *Calendarium Romanum*, which indicates the date and grade of the celebrations in honor of the Saints, is closely related to the history of the *Martyrologium Romanum*.

In accordance with the desire of the Second Vatican Council, the present *Calendarium Romanum*[312] contains only those memorials of the "Saints of a truly universal importance,"[313] and leaves mention of other Saints to the particular calendars of a given nation, region, diocese or religious family.

It would seem convenient to recall, at this point, the reasons leading to the reduction in the number of commemorations in the *Calendarium Romanum* so as to translate it into pastoral praxis: the reduction was made because "the feasts of the Saints may not take precedence over commemorations of the mysteries of salvation."[314] Throughout the centuries, "the multiplication of feasts, vigils, and octaves, and the growing complexity of the various parts of the liturgical year" often "led the faithful to observe particular devotions so that the impression was given of their detaching themselves from the fundamental mysteries of divine redemption."[315]

229. From the foregoing reflection on the origin and development of the *Calendarium Romanum Generale* a number of useful pastoral inferences can be made:

- it is necessary to instruct the faithful on the links between the feasts of the Saints and the commemoration of the mystery of salvation of Christ. The *raison d'etre* for the feasts of the Saints is to highlight concrete realizations of the saving plan of God and "to proclaim the marvels of Christ in his servants;"[316] the feasts accorded to the Saints, the members of the Body of Christ, are ultimately feasts of the Head who is Christ;

- it is always useful to teach the faithful to realize the importance and significance of the feasts of those Saints who have had a particular mission in the history of Salvation, or a singular relationship with Christ such as St. John the Baptist (June 24), St. Joseph (March 19), Sts. Peter

---

311. *Martyrologium Romanum* ex decreto Sacrosancti Oecumenici Concilii Vaticani Secundi instauratum auctoritate Ioannis Pauli PP. II promulgatum, Editio Typica, Typiis Vaticanis 2001.
312. The *Calendarium Romanum* was published by Paul VI on February 14, 1969, with the Apostolic Letter *Mysterii paschalis*, in AAS 61 (1969), 222–226.
313. SC 111.
314. Ibid.
315. Paul VI, Apostolic Letter *Mysterii paschalis*, 1, in AAS 61 (1969), 222.
316. SC 111.

and Paul (June 29), the Apostles and Evangelists, St. Mary Magdalen (July 22), St. Martha (July 29) and St. Stephen (December 26);

- it is also important to exhort the faithful to have a particular devotion to the Saints who have had an important role in the particular Churches, for example, the Patrons of a particular Church or those who first proclaimed the Gospel to the original community;
- finally, it is useful to explain the notion of the "universality" of the Saints inscribed in the *Calendarium Romanum Generale* to the faithful, as well as the significance of the grades with which their feasts are observed: solemnity, feast and memorial (obligatory or optional).

Feast Days

230. Both the Liturgy and popular piety attach great importance to the feast days assigned to the Saints. The "Saint's day" is marked with numerous cultic displays, some liturgical, others deriving from popular piety. Such cultic expressions can sometimes conflict.

Conflicts of this nature must be resolved by application of the norms contained in the *Missale Romanum* and in the *Calendarium Romanum Generale* on the grades assigned to the celebration of Saints and Beati. In this, account must be taken of the their relationship with a particular Christian community (principal Patron of a place, Title of a Church, Founder of a religious family, or their Principal Patron); the conditions governing the transfer of certain feasts to the subsequent Sunday, and of norms on the celebration of the feasts of Saints at certain particular times during the liturgical year.[317]

The aforementioned norms should be respected not only from a sense of respect for the liturgical authority of the Apostolic See, but above all from a sense of reverence for the mystery of Christ and a desire to promote the spirit of the Liturgy.

It is especially necessary to ensure that the reasons which have led to the transfer of some feasts, for example from Lent to Ordinary Time, are not nullified in pastoral practice: following the liturgical celebration of the Saint on the new date while continuing to observe the old date in popular piety. Such practices not only severely affect the harmony that should obtain between the Liturgy and popular piety, but also create duplication, confusion and disorder.

231. It is always necessary to ensure that the feast days of the Saints are carefully prepared both liturgically and pastorally.

Such requires a correct presentation of the objectives of the cult of the Saints, i.e. the glorification of God "in His Saints,"[318] a commitment to live the Christian life following the example of Christ, of whose mystical Body the Saints are pre-eminent members.

---

317. Cf. *Calendarium Romanum*, cit., *Normae universales*, 58–59; S.Congregation for Divine Worship, Instruction *De Calendariis particularibus*, 8–12, in AAS 62 (1970), 653–654.
318. Liturgia Horarum, *Commune Sanctorum virorum, Ad Invitatorium.*

It is also necessary to represent the figure of the Saint in a correct manner. Bearing in mind the prospect of contemporary society, this presentation should not only contain an account of the legendary events associated with the Saint, or of his thaumaturgic powers, but should also include an evaluation of his significance for the Christian life, the greatness of his sanctity, the effectiveness of his Christian witness, and of the manner in which his particular charism has enriched the Church.

232. A "Saint's day" also has an anthropological significance: it is a feast day. The feast also echoes man's vital needs, and is deeply rooted in his longing for the transcendent. The feast, with its manifestations of joy and rejoicing, is an affirmation of the value of life and creation. The feast is also an expression of integral freedom and of man's tendency towards true happiness, with its interruption of daily routine, formal conventions, and of the need to earn a living. As a cultural expression, the feast highlights the particular genius of a certain people and their cultural characteristics, and their true folk customs. As a social moment, the feast is an occasion to strengthen family relations and to make new contacts.

233. From a religious and anthropological perspective, several elements serve to undermine the genuine nature of the "Saint's day."

In a religious perspective, the "Saint's feast" of the "patronal feast" of the parish, when emptied of the Christian content that lies at its origin—the honor given to Christ in one of his members—becomes a mere popular observance or a social occasion, serving, in the best instances, as little other than a social occasion for the members of a particular community.

In an anthropological perspective, "to celebrate," not infrequently, is defined by the behavior assumed by particular individuals or groups which can be widely at variance with the true significance of the feast. To celebrate a feast is to allow man to participate in God's lordship over creation, and in His active "rest," rather than in any form of laziness. It is an expression of simple joy, rather than unlimited selfishness. It is an expression of true liberty rather than an occasion for ambiguous amusement which creates new and more subtle forms of enslavement. It can safely be said that: transgressions of the norms for ethical behavior not only contradict the law of the Lord, but also injure the anthropological fiber of celebration.

Celebration of the Eucharist

234. The celebration of the feast of a Saint or *Beatus* is not the only manner in which the Saints are present in the liturgy. The celebration of the Eucharist is the singular moment of communion with the Saints in heaven.

In the Liturgy of the Word, the Old Testament readings frequently refer to the great Patriarchs and prophets, and to other persons distinguished by their virtue and by their love for the law of the Lord. The New Testament recounts the deeds of the Apostles and other Saints who enjoyed the Lord's friendship. The lives of the Saints sometimes reflect the Gospel so closely that their very personality becomes apparent from merely reading the pages.

The relationship between Sacred Scripture and Christian hagiography, in the context of the celebration of the Eucharist, has given rise to the composition of a number of Commons which provide a synopsis of a particular biblical text which illustrates the lives of the Saints. With regard to this relationship, it has been said that Sacred Scripture orients and indicates the journey of the Saints to perfect charity. The Saints, in turn, become a living exegesis of the Word.

Reference is made to the Saints at various points during the celebration of the Eucharist. The Canon mentions "the gifts of your servant Abel, the sacrifice of Abraham our father in faith and the bread and wine offered by your priest Melchizedek."[319] The same Eucharistic prayer becomes an occasion to express our communion with the Saints, by venerating their memory and pleading for their intercession, since "in union with the whole Church, we honor Mary, the Virgin Mother of God, we honor Joseph her husband, the Apostles and martyrs: Peter and Paul, Andrew . . . and all the Saints, may their prayers and intercession gain us your constant help and protection."[320]

The Litany of the Saints

235. The Litany of the Saints has been used in the Roman Church since the seventh century.[321] Its liturgical structure is subtle, simple and popular. Through the litany, the Church invokes the Saints on certain great sacramental occasions and on other occasions when her imploration is intensified: at the Easter vigil, before blessing the Baptismal fount; in the celebration of the Sacrament of Baptism; in conferring Sacred Orders of the episcopate, priesthood and deaconate; in the rite for the consecration of virgins and of religious profession; in the rite of dedication of a church and consecration of an altar; at rogation; at the stational Masses and penitential processions; when casting out the Devil during the rite of exorcism; and in entrusting the dying to the mercy of God.

The Litanies of the Saints contain elements deriving from both the liturgical tradition and from popular piety. They are expressions of the Church's confidence in the intercession of the Saints and an experience of the communion between the Church of the heavenly Jerusalem and the Church on her earthly pilgrim journey. The names of the *Beati* that have been inscribed in the calendars of particular Churches or religious institutes may be invoked in the litanies of the Saints.[322] Clearly, the names of those whose cult has not received ecclesial recognition should not be used in the litanies.

The Relics of the Saints

236. The Second Vatican Council recalls that "the Saints have been traditionally honored in the Church, and their authentic relics and images held in

---

319. *Missale Romanum, Prex eucharistica I, Supra quae propitio.*

320. Ibid., *Communicantes.* Provision is made for a memorial of the Saint or patron of the day in *Prex eucharistica III.*

321. Cf. *Ordo Romanus* in A. Andrieu (ed.), *Les "Ordines Romani" du Haut Moyen-Age*, III, Spicilegium Sacrum Lovaniense, Lovain 1951, p. 249. For indulgences cf. EI, *Aliae concessiones*, 22, p. 68.

322. Cf. Congregation for Divine Worship and the Discipline of the Sacraments, *Notificatio de cultu Beatorum*, 13, in *Notitiae* 35 (1999), 446.

veneration."[323] The term "relics of the Saints" principally signifies the bodies—or notable parts of the bodies—of the Saints who, as distinguished members of Christ's mystical Body and as Temples of the Holy Spirit (cf. 1 Cor 3:16; 6:19; 2 Cor 6:16)[324] in virtue of their heroic sanctity, now dwell in Heaven, but who once lived on earth. Objects which belonged to the Saints, such as personal objects, clothes and manuscripts are also considered relics, as are objects which have touched their bodies or tombs such as oils, cloths, and images.

237. The *Missale Romanum* reaffirms the validity "of placing the relics of the Saints under an altar that is to be dedicated, even when not those of the martyrs."[325] This usage signifies that the sacrifice of the members has its origin in the Sacrifice of the altar,[326] as well as symbolizing the communion with the Sacrifice of Christ of the entire Church, which is called to witness, even to the point of death, fidelity to her Lord and Spouse.

Many popular usages have been associated with this eminently liturgical cultic expression. The faithful deeply revere the relics of the Saints. An adequate pastoral instruction of the faithful about the use of relics will not overlook:

- ensuring the authenticity of the relics exposed for the veneration of the faithful; where doubtful relics have been exposed for the veneration of the faithful, they should be discreetly withdrawn with due pastoral prudence;[327]

- preventing undue dispersal of relics into small pieces, since such a practice is not consonant with due respect for the human body; the liturgical norms stipulate that relics must be "of a sufficient size as make clear that they are parts of the human body;"[328]

- admonishing the faithful to resist the temptation to form collections of relics; in the past this practice has had some deplorable consequences;

- preventing any possibility of fraud, trafficking,[329] or superstition.

The various forms of popular veneration of the relics of the Saints, such as kissing, decorations with lights and flowers, bearing them in processions, in no way exclude the possibility of taking the relics of the Saints to the sick and dying, to comfort them or use the intercession of the Saint to ask for healing. Such should be conducted with great dignity and be motivated by faith. The relics of

---

323. SC 111; cf. the Council of Trent, *Decretum de invocatione, veneratione et reliquiis Sanctorum, et sacris imaginibus* (December 3, 1563), in DS 1822.

324. Cf. ibid.

325. *Institutio generalis Missalis Romani*, 302.

326. Cf. *Pontificale Romanum, Ordo dedicationis ecclesiae et altaris*, Editio Typica, Typis Polyglotis Vaticanis 1977, cap. IV, *Praenotanda*, 5.

327. Cf. ibid., cap. II, *Praenotanda*, 5.

328. Ibid.

329. Cf. CIC, can. 1190.

the Saints should not be exposed on the mensa of the altar, since this is reserved for the Body and Blood of the King of Martyrs.[330]

Sacred Images

238. The Second Council of Nicea, "following the divinely inspired teaching of our Holy Fathers and the tradition of the Catholic Church," vigorously defended the veneration of the images of the Saints: "we order with ever rigor and exactitude that, similar to the depictions of the precious and vivifying Cross of our redemption, the sacred images to be used for veneration are to be depicted in mosaic or any other suitable material, and exposed in the holy churches of God, on their furnishings, vestments, on their walls, as well as in the homes of the faithful and in the streets, be they images of Our Lord God and Savior Jesus Christ, or of Our Immaculate Lady, the holy Mother of God, or of the Angels, the Saints and the just."[331]

The Fathers of Nicea see the basis for the use of sacred images in the mystery of the Incarnation of Christ, "the image of the invisible God" (Col 1:15): "the Incarnation of the Son of God initiated a new 'economy' of images."[332]

239. The veneration of sacred images, whether paintings, statues, bas reliefs or other representations, apart from being a liturgical phenomenon, is an important aspect of popular piety: the faithful pray before sacred images, both in churches and in their homes. They decorate them with flowers, lights, and jewels; they pay respect to them in various ways, carrying them in procession, hanging *ex votos* near them in thanksgiving; they place them in shrines in the fields and along the roads.

Veneration of sacred images requires theological guidance if it is to avoid certain abuses. It is therefore necessary that the faithful be constantly reminded of the doctrine of the Church on the veneration of sacred images, as exemplified in the ecumenical Councils,[333] and in the *Catechism of the Catholic Church*.[334]

240. According to the teaching of the Church, sacred images are:

- iconographical transcriptions of the Gospel message, in which image and revealed word are mutually clarified; ecclesiastical tradition requires that images conform "to the letter of the Gospel message;"[335]

---

330. Cf. St. Ambrose, *Epistula LXXVII* (Maur. 22), 13: CSEL 82/3, Vindobonae 1982, pp. 134–135; *Pontificale Romanum, Ordo dedicationis ecclesiae et altaris*, cit., cap. IV, *Praenotanda*, 10.

331. Second Council of Nicea, *Definitio de sacris imaginibus* (October 23, 787), in DS 600.

332. CCC 1161.

333. Cf. Council of Nicea II, *Definitio de sacris imaginibus* (October 23, 787) in DS 600–603; Council of Trent *Decretum de invocatione, veneratione et reliquiis Sanctorum et sacris imaginibus* (December 3, 1562), in DS 1821–1825; SC 111.

334. Cf. CCC nn. 1159–1162.

335. Council of Nicea II, *Definitio de sacris imaginibus*, in *Conciliorum Oecumeniorum Decreta*, cit., p. 135 (not contained in DS).

- sacred signs which, in common with all liturgical signs, ultimately refer to Christ; images of the Saints "signify Christ who is glorified in them;"[336]

- memorials of our brethren who are Saints, and who "continue to participate in the salvation of the world, and to whom we are united, above all in sacramental celebrations;"[337]

- an assistance in prayer: contemplation of the sacred images facilitates supplication and prompts us to give glory to God for the marvels done by his grace working in the Saints;—a stimulus to their imitation because "the more the eye rests on these sacred images, the more the recollection of those whom they depict grows vivid in the contemplative beholder;"[338] the faithful tend to imprint on their hearts what they contemplate with the eye: "a true image of the new man," transformed in Christ, through the power of the Holy Spirit, and in fidelity to his proper vocation;

- and a form of catechesis, because "through the history of the mysteries of our redemption, expressed in pictures and other media, the faithful are instructed and confirmed in the faith, since they are afforded the means of meditating constantly on the articles of faith."[339]

241. It is necessary for the faithful to understand the relative nature of the cult of images. The image is not venerated in itself. Rather, that which it represents is venerated. Thus, sacred images "are given due honor and veneration, not because there are believed to contain some divinity or power justifying such cult, nor because something has to be requested of an image, nor because trust is reposed in them, as the pagans used to do with idols, but because the honor given to sacred images is given to the prototypes whom they represent."[340]

242. In the light of the foregoing, the faithful should be careful not to fall into the error of raising sacred images to the level of paragons. The fact that some sacred images are the object of such devotion that they have become embodiments of the religious culture of nations or cities or particular groups, should be explained in the light of the grace which is at the basis of the veneration accorded them, and of the historical and social circumstances of the history surrounding them. It is good that a people should recall such events, to strengthen its faith, glorify God, conserve its cultural identity, and pray incessantly with confidence to the Lord who, according to his own words (cf. Mt. 7:7; Lk 11:9; Mk 11:24), is always prepared to hear them; thereby causing an increase of charity and hope, and the growth of the spiritual life of the Christian faithful.

243. By their very nature, sacred images belong to the realm of sacred signs and to the realm of art. These "are often works of art infused with innate religious

---

336. CCC 1161.

337. Ibid.

338. Council of Nicea II, *Definitio de sacris imaginibus*, in DS 601.

339. Council of Trent, *Decretum de sacris invocatione, veneratione et reliquiis Sanctorum, et sacris imaginibus*, in DS 1824.

340. Ibid., 1823.

feeling, and seem almost to reflect that beauty that comes from God and that leads to God."[341] The primary function of sacred images is not, however, to evince aesthetic pleasure but to dispose towards Mystery. Sometimes, the artistic aspects of an image can assume a disproportionate importance, seeing the image as an "artistic" theme, rather conveying a spiritual message.

The production of sacred images in the West is not governed by strict canons that have been in place for centuries, as is the case in the Eastern Church. This does not imply that the Latin Church has overlooked or neglected its oversight of sacred images: the exposition of images contrary to the faith, or indecorous images, or images likely to lead the faithful into error, or images deriving from a disincarnate abstraction or dehumanizing images, have been prohibited on numerous occasions. Some images are examples of anthropocentric humanism rather than reflections of a genuine spirituality. The tendency to remove sacred images from sacred places is to be strongly condemned, since this is detrimental for the piety of the Christian faithful.

Popular piety encourages sacred images which reflect the characteristics of particular cultures; realistic representations in which the saints are clearly identifiable, or which evidently depict specific junctures in human life: birth, suffering, marriage, work, death. Efforts should be made, however, to ensure that popular religious art does not degenerate into mere oleography: in the Liturgy, there is a correlation between iconography and art, and the Christian art of specific cultural epochs.

244. The Church blesses sacred images because of their cultic significance. This is especially true of the images of the Saints which are destined for public veneration,[342] when she prays that, guided by a particular Saint, "we may progress in following the footsteps of Christ, so that the perfect man may be formed in us to the full measure of Christ."[343] The Church has published norms for the exposition of sacred images in churches and other sacred places which are to be diligently observed.[344] No statue or image is to be exposed on the table of an altar. Neither are the relics of the Saints to be exposed on the table of an altar.[345] It is for the local ordinary to ensure that inappropriate images or those leading to error or superstition are not exposed for the veneration of the faithful.

Processions

245. Processions are cultic expressions of a universal character and have multiple social and religious significance. In them, the relationship between Liturgy and popular piety is especially important. Inspired by biblical examples (cf. Es 14:8–31; 2 Sam 6:12–19; 1 Cor 15:25–16:3), the Church has instituted a number of liturgical processions which have differing emphases:

---

341. *Rituale Romanum, De Benedictionibus, Ordo as benedicendas imagines quae fidelium venerationi publicae exhibentur*, cit., 985.
342. Cf. *Rituale Romanum, De Benedictionibus, Ordo benedictionis imaginis Sanctorum*, cit., 1018–1031.
343. Ibid., 1027.
344. Cf. CIC, can. 1188; *Institutio generalis Missalis Romani*, 318.
345. Cf. *Pontificale Romanum, Ordo dedicationis ecclesiae et altaris*, cit., cap. IV, *Praenotanda*, 10.

- some recall salvific events in the life of Christ, among them: the procession on February 2, commemorating the Lord's presentation in the Temple (cf. Lk 2:22–38); Palm Sunday, in evocation of the Lord's messianic entry into Jerusalem (cf. Mt 21:1–10; Mk 11:1–11; Lk 19:28–38; Jn 12:12–16); the procession at the Easter Vigil commemorating the Lord's passage from the darkness of the tomb to the glory of the Resurrection, synthesizing and surpassing everything that had happened in the Old Testament, and standing as a necessary prelude to the sacramental "passages" accomplished in the disciples of Christ, especially in the celebration of Baptism and in the rite of exequies;

- others are votive processions, such as the Eucharistic procession on the feast of Corpus Christi: the Blessed Sacrament passing through the streets arouses sentiments of gratitude and thanksgiving in the minds and hearts of the faithful, it arouses in them faith-adoration and is a source of grace and blessing (Acts 10:38);[346] the rogation processions, whose dates are to be established by the respective Conferences of Bishops, are both public implorations of God's blessing on the fields and on man's work, and penitential in character; the procession to the cemeteries on 2 November are commemorations of the faithful departed;

- others again are required by certain liturgical actions, such as: the stational processions during Lent, at which the worshipping community leaves from the established gathering point (collectio) for the church of the statio; the procession for the reception at the parish churches of the Holy Oils blessed on Holy Thursday; the procession for the veneration of the Cross on Good Friday; the procession of the baptized at the Vespers of Easter Sunday, during which psalms and canticles are sung on the way to the baptistery;[347] the processions associated with the celebration of the Holy Eucharist, such as the entrance of the Sacred Ministers, the proclamation of the Gospel, the presentation of the gifts, the communion with the Body of Christ; the procession carrying the Viaticum to the sick, where still practiced; funeral corteges accompanying the bodies of the faithful departed from their homes to the church, and from the church to the cemetery; the procession for the translation of relics.

246. From the Middle Ages, votive processions acquired a particular importance in popular piety, and reached their apogee during the age of the Baroque. The Patron Saints of a city, or streets, or guild were honored by carrying their relics, or image, or effigy in procession.

In their true form, processions are a manifestation of the faith of the people. They often have cultural connotations and are capable of reawakening the religious sense of the people. From the perspective of the Christian's faith, votive processions, like other pious exercises, are exposed to certain risks: the precedence of devotions over the sacraments, which are relegated to second place, of external

---

346. Cf. *Rituale Romanum, De sacra communione et de cultu Mysterii eucharistici extra Missam*, cit., 101; CIC, can. 944; supra note 162.
347. *Institutio generalis de Liturgia Horarum*, 213.

displays over interior disposition; regarding the procession as the apogee of a feast; the impression given to some of the less competently instructed of the faithful that Christianity is merely a "religion of Saints;" the degeneration of the procession itself from a manifestation of faith to a mere spectacle or a purely secular parade.

247. To preserve the character of processions as manifestations of faith, it is necessary for the faithful to be carefully instructed on their theological, liturgical and anthropological aspects.

From a theological perspective, it is important to emphasize that a procession is a sign of the Church's condition, the pilgrimage of the People of God, with Christ and after Christ, aware that in this world it has no lasting dwelling. Through the streets of this earth it moves towards the heavenly Jerusalem. It is also a sign of the witness to the faith that every Christian community is obliged to give to the Lord in the structures of civil society. It is also a sign of the Church's missionary task which reaches back to her origins and the Lord's command (cf. Mt 28:19–20), which sent her to proclaim the Gospel message of salvation.

From a liturgical point of view, processions, even those of a popular tenor, should be oriented towards the Liturgy. The journey from church to church should be presented as the journey of the community living in this world towards the community living in Heaven. Such processions should be conducted under ecclesiastical supervision so as to avoid anything unsuitable or degenerative. They should begin with a moment of prayer during which the Word of God should be proclaimed. Hymns and canticles should be sung and instrumental music can also be used. Lighted candles or lamps should be carried by the faithful during the procession. Pauses should be arranged along the way so as to provide for alternative paces, bearing in mind that such also reflects the journey of life. The procession should conclude with a doxology to God, source of all sanctity, and with a blessing given by a Bishop, Priest or Deacon.

From an anthropological perspective, the procession should make it evident that it is "a commonly undertaken journey." The participants join in the same atmosphere of prayer and are united in singing, and concentrated on arriving at the same goal. Thus the faithful feel united with each other, and intent in giving concrete expression to their Christian commitment throughout the journey of life.

Chapter Seven
SUFFRAGE FOR THE DEAD

FAITH IN THE RESURRECTION OF THE DEAD

248. "It is in regard to death that man's condition is most shrouded in doubt."[348] However, faith in Christ changes that doubt into the certainty of life without end. Christ has told us that he came from the Father "so that whosoever believes in him might not die but have eternal life" (Jn 3:16). Again he says, "it is my

---

348. Second Vatican Council, Constitution *Gaudium et spes* 18.

Father's will that whoever sees the Son and believes in him shall have eternal life; and I shall raise him up on the last day."[349]

Based on the Word of God, the Christian firmly believes and hopes that "just as Christ is truly risen from the dead and lives for ever, so after death the righteous will live for ever with the risen Christ and he will raise them up on the last day."[350]

249. Belief in the resurrection of the dead is an essential part of Christian revelation. It implies a particular understanding of the ineluctable mystery of death.

Death is the end of earthy life, but "not of our existence"[351] since the soul is immortal. "Our lives are measured by time, in the course of which we change, grow old and, as with all living beings on earth, death seems like the normal end of life."[352] Seen from the perspective of the faith, "death is the end of man's earthly pilgrimage, of the time of grace and mercy which God offers him so as to work out his earthly life in keeping with the divine plan, and to decide his ultimate destiny."[353]

In one light death can seem natural, in another it can be seen as "the wages of sin" (Rom 6:23). Authentically interpreting the meaning of Scripture (cf. Jn 2:17; 3:3; 3:19; Wis 1:13; Rom 5:12; 6:23), the Church teaches that "death entered the world on account of man's sin."[354]

Jesus, the Son of God, "born of a woman and subject to the law" (Gal 4:4) underwent death which is part of the human condition; despite his anguish in the face of death (Mk 14:33–34; Heb 5:7–8), "he accepted it in an act of complete and free submission to his Father's will. The obedience of Jesus has transformed the curse of death into a blessing."[355]

Death is the passage to the fullness of true life. The Church, subverting the logic of this world, calls the Christian's day of death his *dies natalis*, the day of his heavenly birth, where "there will be no more death, and no more mourning or sadness [for] the world of the past has gone" (Rev 21:4). Death is the prolongation, in a new way, of life as the Liturgy says: "For your faithful, O Lord, life has changed not ended; while our earthly dwelling is destroyed, a new and eternal dwelling is prepared for us in Heaven."[356]

The death of a Christian is an event of grace, having, as it does, a positive value and significance in Christ and through Christ. Scripture teaches that: "Life to me, of course, life is Christ, but then death would bring me something more" (Phil 1:21); here is a saying you can rely on: "if we have died with him, then we shall live with him" (2 Tm 2:11).

---

349. DS 150: *Missale Romanum, Ordo Missae, Symbolum Nicaeno-Constantinopolitanum.*
350. CCC 989.
351. St. Ambrose, *De excessu fratris*, I, 70: CSEL 73, Vindobonae 1955, p. 245.
352. CCC 1007.
353. Ibid.,1013.
354. Ibid., 1008; cf. Council of Trent, *Decretum de peccato originali* (June 17, 1546), in DS 1511.
355. CCC 1009.
356. *Missale Romanum, Praefatio defunctorum*, I.

250. According to the faith of the Church, "to die in Christ" begins at Baptism. In Baptism, the Lord's disciples sacramentally die in Christ so as to live a new life. If the disciples die in the grace of Christ, physical death seals that "dying with Christ," and consummates it by incorporating them fully and definitively into Christ the Redeemer.

The Church's prayer of suffrage for the souls of the faithful departed implores eternal life not only for the disciples of Christ who have died in his peace, but for the dead whose faith is known to God.[357]

THE MEANING OF SUFFRAGE

251. The just encounter God in death. He calls them to himself so as to share eternal life with them. No one, however, can be received into God's friendship and intimacy without having been purified of the consequences of personal sin. "The Church gives the name Purgatory to this final purification of the elect, which is entirely different from the punishment of the damned. The Church formulated her doctrine of faith on Purgatory especially at the Councils of Florence and Trent."[358]

Hence derives the pious custom of suffrage for the souls of the faithful departed, which is an urgent supplication of God to have mercy on the souls of the dead, to purify them by the fire of His charity, and to bring them to His kingdom of light and life. This suffrage is a cultic expression of faith in the communion of saints. Indeed, "the Church in its pilgrim members, from the very earliest days of the Christian religion, has honored with great respect the memory of the dead; and 'because it is a holy and a wholesome thought to pray for the dead that they may be loosed from their sins' (2 Mc 12:46) she offers her suffrages for them."[359] These consist, primarily, in the celebration of the holy sacrifice of the Eucharist,[360] and in other pious exercises, such as prayers for the dead, alms deeds, works of mercy,[361] and the application of indulgences to the souls of the faithful departed.[362]

CHRISTIAN EXEQUIES

252. The Roman Liturgy, like other Latin and Oriental Liturgies, contains many and varied forms of suffrage for the dead.

The rite of Christian exequies consists traditionally of three parts. Because of the profoundly changed circumstances of life in the greater urban conurbations,

---

357. Cf. ibid., *Prex eucharistica IV, Commemoratio pro defunctis*.

358. CCC 1031; cf. DS 1304; 1820; 1580.

359. LG 50.

360. Second Council of Lyons, *Professio fidei Michaelis Paleologi* (Iuly 6, 1274), in DS 856: St. Cyprian, *Epistula* I, 2: CSEL 3/2, Vindobonae 1871, pp. 466–467; St. Augustine, *Confessiones*, IX, 12, 32: CSEL 33/1, Vindobonae 1896, pp. 221–222.

361. Cf. St. Augustine, *De curis pro mortuis gerenda*, 6: CSEL 41, Vindobonae 1900, pp. 629–631; St. John Christosom, *Homilia in primam ad Corinthios*, 41, 5: PG 61, 494–495; CCC1032.

362. Cf. EI, *Normae de Indulgentiis*, 3, p. 21; *Aliae concessiones*, 29, pp. 74–75.

these are often reduced to two or even only one part. The rite of Christian exequies are:[363]

- *prayer vigil* at the home of the deceased, or somewhere else as circumstances permit, during which family, friends and members of the Christian community gather to pray to God in suffrage, to hear the "the words of life eternal," and in their light, to see beyond this world by contemplating the risen Christ in faith; to comfort those who mourn the deceased; and to express Christian solidarity in accordance with the words of the Apostle "be sad with those in sorrow" (Rom 12:15);[364]

- *the celebration of the Holy Eucharist*, which is highly desirable when possible. In the celebration of the Holy Eucharist, the Christian community listens to "the word of God which proclaims the Paschal Mystery, assures us of the hope of meeting again in the Kingdom of God, enlivens our devotion to the dead and exhorts us to witness through a truly Christian life."[365] The celebrant comments on the word of God in his homily, "avoiding any form of funerary eulogy."[366] In the Holy Eucharist, "the Church expresses her efficacious communion with the departed: offering to the Father in the Holy Spirit the sacrifice of the death and Resurrection of Christ; she asks Him to purify His child of his sins and their consequences, and to admit him to the Paschal fullness of the table of the kingdom."[367] A profound reading of the requiem Mass allows us to see how the Liturgy has made of the Holy Eucharist, that eschatological banquet, the true Christian *refrigerium* for the deceased;

- the *Rite of committal, the funeral cortege, and burial*; at the committal, the deceased is commended to God, "the final commendation by which the Christian community says farewell to one of its members before his body is buried."[368] In the funeral cortege, mother Church, who has sacramentally borne all Christians in her womb during their earthly pilgrimage, now accompanies the body of the deceased to his place of rest, while he awaits the resurrection (cf. 1 Cor 15:42–44).

253. Every stage of the rite of obsequies should be conducted with the greatest dignity and religious sensibility. Hence, it is necessary for: the body of the deceased, which was the Temple of the Holy Spirit, to be treated with the utmost respect; funeral furnishings should be decorous and free of all ostentation; the liturgical signs, the cross, the paschal candle, the holy water and the incense, should all be used with the utmost propriety.

---

363. Cf. *Rituale Romanum, Ordo exsequiarum*, cit., *Praenotanda*, 4.

364. This vigil, which is still called a "wake" in English-speaking countries, is an act of faith in the resurrection, even though it may have lost all theological and historical significance, and an imitation of the women in the Gospel who came to anoint the body of Christ, and became the first witnesses of the resurrection.

365. *Rituale Romanum, Ordo exsequiarum*, cit., *Praenotanda*, 11.

366. Ibid., 41.

367. CCC 1689.

368. *Rituale Romanum, Ordo exsequiarum*, cit., *Praenotanda*, 10.

254. Christian piety has always regarded burial as the model for the faithful to follow since it clearly displays how death signifies the total destruction of the body. The practice eschews meanings that can be associated with mummification or embalming or even with cremation. Burial recalls the earth from which man comes (cf. Gn 2:6) and to which he returns (cf. Gn 3:9; Sir 17:1), and also recalls the burial of Christ, the grain which, fallen on the earth, brought forth fruit in plenty (cf. Jn 12:24).

Cremation is also a contemporary phenomenon in virtue of the changed circumstances of life. In this regard, ecclesiastical discipline states: "Christian obsequies may be conceded to those who have chosen to have their bodies cremated, provided that such choice was not motivated by anything contrary to Christian doctrine."[369] In relation to such a decision, the faithful should be exhorted not to keep the ashes of the dead in their homes, but to bury them in the usual manner, until God shall raise up those who rest in the earth, and until the sea gives up its dead (cf. Rev 20:13).

OTHER SUFFRAGE

255. The Church offers the sacrifice of the Holy Eucharist for the dead not only on the occasion of their funerals, but also on the third, seventh, and thirtieth day following their deaths, as well as on their anniversaries. The celebration of the Mass in suffrage for the souls of the faithful departed is the Christian way of recalling and prolonging, in the Lord, that communion with those who have crossed the threshold of death. On November 2, the Church incessantly offers the holy sacrifice of the Mass for the souls of all the faithful departed and prays the Liturgy of the Hours for them.

The Church daily supplicates and implores the Lord, in the celebration of the Mass and at Vespers, that "the faithful who have gone before us marked with the sign of faith . . . may be given light, happiness and peace."[370]

It is important to instruct the faithful in the light of the celebration of the sacrifice of the Eucharist, in which the Church prays that all of the faithful departed, of whatever place or time, will be brought to the glory of the risen Lord, so as to avoid possessive or particular ideas that relate the Mass only to one's "own" dead.[371] The celebration of Mass in suffrage for the dead also presents an important opportunity for catechesis on the last things.

THE MEMORIAL OF THE DEAD IN POPULAR PIETY

256. As with the Liturgy, popular piety pays particular attention to the memory of the dead and carefully raises up to God prayers in suffrage for them.

In matters relating to the "memorial of the dead," great pastoral prudence and tact must always be employed in addressing the relationship between Liturgy

---

369. Ibid., 15; Supreme Congregation of the Holy Office, Instruction, *De cadaverum crematione*, 2–3, in AAS 56 (1964), 822–823; CIC, can. 1184, 5, § 1, 2.

370. *Missale Romanum, Prex eucharistica I, Commemoratio pro defunctis.*

371. Regarding Masses for the dead cf. *Institutio generalis Missalis Romani*, 355.

and popular piety, both in its doctrinal aspect and in harmonizing the liturgical actions and pious exercises.

257. It is always necessary to ensure that popular piety is inspired by the principles of the Christian faith. Thus, they should be made aware of the paschal meaning of the death undergone by those who have received Baptism and who have been incorporated into the mystery of the death and resurrection of Christ (cf. Rom 6:3–10); the immortality of the soul (cf. Lk 23:43); the communion of Saints, through which "union with those who are still on their pilgrim journey with the faithful who repose in Christ is not in the least broken, but strengthened by a communion of spiritual goods, as constantly taught by the Church:"[372] "our prayer for them is capable not only of helping them, but also of making their intercession for us effective;"[373] the resurrection of the body; the glorious coming of Christ, who will "judge the living and the dead;"[374] the reward given to each according to his deeds; life eternal.

Deeply rooted cultural elements connoting particular anthropological concepts are to be found among the customs and usages connected with the "cult of the dead" among some peoples. These often spring from a desire to prolong family and social links with the departed. Great caution must be used in examining and evaluating these customs. Care should be taken to ensure that they are not contrary to the Gospel. Likewise, care should be taken to ensure that they cannot be interpreted as pagan residues.

258. In matters relating to doctrine, the following are to be avoided:

- the invocation of the dead in practices involving divination;

- the interpretation or attribution of imaginary effects to dreams relating to the dead, which often arises from fear;

- any suggestion of a belief in reincarnation;

- the danger of denying the immortality of the soul or of detaching death from the resurrection, so as to make the Christian religion seem like a religion of the dead;

- the application of spacio-temporal categories to the dead.

259. "Hiding death and its signs" is widespread in contemporary society and prone to the difficulties arising from doctrinal and pastoral error.

Doctors, nurses, and relatives frequently believe that they have a duty to hide the fact of imminent death from the sick who, because of increasing hospitalization, almost always die outside of the home.

It has been frequently said that the great cities of the living have no place for the dead: buildings containing tiny flats cannot house a space in which to hold a vigil for the dead; traffic congestion prevents funeral corteges because they

---

372. LG 49.

373. CCC 958.

374. DS 150; *Missale Romanum, Ordo Missae, Symbolum Nicaeno-Constantinopolitanum.*

block the traffic; cemeteries, which once surrounded the local church and were truly "holy ground" and indicated the link between Christ and the dead, are now located at some distance outside of the towns and cities, since urban planning no longer includes the provision of cemeteries.

Modern society refuses to accept the "visibility of death," and hence tries to conceal its presence. In some places, recourse is even made to conserving the bodies of the dead by chemical means in an effort to prolong the appearance of life.

The Christian, who must be conscious of and familiar with the idea of death, cannot interiorly accept the phenomenon of the "intolerance of the dead," which deprives the dead of all acceptance in the city of the living. Neither can he refuse to acknowledge the signs of death, especially when intolerance and rejection encourage a flight from reality, or a materialist cosmology, devoid of hope and alien to belief in the death and resurrection of Christ.

The Christian is obliged to oppose all forms of "commercialization of the dead," which exploit the emotions of the faithful in pursuit of unbridled and shameful commercial profit.

260. In accordance with time, place and tradition, popular devotions to the dead take on a multitude of forms:

- the novena for the dead in preparation for the 2 November, and the octave prolonging it, should be celebrated in accordance with liturgical norms;

- visits to the cemetery; in some places this is done in a community manner on November 2, at the end of the parochial mission, when the parish priest takes possession of the parish; visiting the cemetery can also be done privately, when the faithful go to the graves of their own families to maintain them or decorate them with flowers and lamps. Such visits should be seen as deriving from the bonds existing between the living and the dead and not from any form of obligation, non-fulfillment of which involves a superstitious fear;

- membership of a confraternity or other pious association whose objects include "burial of the dead" in the light of the Christian vision of death, praying for the dead, and providing support for the relatives of the dead;

- suffrage for the dead through alms deeds, works of mercy, fasting, applying indulgences, and especially prayers, such as the *De profundis*, and the formula *Requiem aeternam*, which often accompanies the recitation of the *Angelus*, the rosary, and at prayers before and after meals.

Chapter Eight
SHRINES AND PILGRIMAGES

261. The relationship between the Liturgy and popular piety is probably most evident at shrines. These are often dedicated to the Holy Trinity, to Christ our Savior, to the Blessed Virgin Mary, to the Saints or *Beati*. "At shrines more abundant means of salvation are to be provided for the faithful; the word of God is

to be carefully proclaimed; liturgical life is to be appropriately fostered especially through the celebration of the Eucharist and penance; and approved forms of popular piety are to be fostered."[375]

Pilgrimage is closely connected with shines, and is itself an expression of popular piety.

Even though weakened by the effects of secularism, interest in shrines and pilgrimage remains high among the faithful.

In view of the object of this Directory, it would seem appropriate to offer some guidelines for the pastoral activities of shrines, and for pilgrimages so that they may be conducted in accordance with a correct understanding of the relationship between Liturgy and popular piety.

THE SHRINE

Principles

262. In accordance with Christian revelation, the risen Christ is the supreme and definitive sanctuary (cf. Jn 2:18–21; Rev 21:22) around which the community of the disciples gathers. In turn, that community is the new dwelling place of the Lord (cf. 1 Pt 2:5; Eph 2:19–22).

Theologically, a shrine, which often derives from popular piety, is a sign of the active and saving presence of the Lord in history, and a place of respite in which the people of God, on its journey to the heavenly City (cf. Heb 13:14), can renew its strength for the pilgrim journey.[376]

263. Shrines, like churches, have enormous symbolic value: they are icons "of the dwelling place of God among men" (Rev 21:3) and allude to "the mystery of the Temple" which was fulfilled in the Body of Christ (cf. Jn 1:14; 2:21), in the ecclesial community (cf. 1 Pt 2:5) of the faithful (cf. 1 Cor 3:16–17; 6:19; 2 Cor 6:16).

To the faithful, shrines represent:

- a memorial to an original extraordinary event which has given rise to persistent devotion, or a witness to the piety and gratitude of a people that has received many benefits;

- privileged places of divine assistance and of the intercession of Blessed Virgin Mary, the Saints or the *Beati*, in virtue of the frequent signs of mercy that have been shown in them;

- signs of cosmic harmony and reflections of divine beauty because of their physical positioning which is often elevated, solitary and austere;

---

375. CIC, can 1234, §1.
376. Cf. Pontifical Council for the Pastoral Care of Migrants and Itinerants, *The Shrine, Memory, Presence and Prophecy of the Living God* (May 8, 1999), Libreria Editrice Vaticana, Città del Vaticano 1999.

- a call to conversion because of what is preached in them, an invitation to redouble the life of charity and the works of mercy, and an exhortation to follow Christ;

- places dedicated to consolidating the faith, to growth in grace, refuge and consolation in affliction, by virtue of the sacramental life practiced in them;

- particular interpretations and prolongations of the Word of God by virtue of the Gospel message proclaimed in them;

- an encouragement to cultivate an eschatological outlook, a sense of transcendence and to learn to direct their earthly footsteps towards the sanctuary of Heaven (cf. Heb 9:11; Rev 21:3).

"Christian shrines have always been, and continue to be, signs of God, and of His intervention in history. Each one of them is a memorial to the Incarnation and to the Redemption."[377]

CANONICAL RECOGNITION

264. "The term shrine signifies a church or other sacred place to which the faithful make pilgrimages for a particular pious reason with the approval of the local ordinary."[378]

A prior condition for the canonical recognition of a diocesan, national or international shrine is the respective approval of the diocesan bishop, the Conference of Bishops, or the Holy See. Canonical approval is an official recognition of a sacred place and for the specific purpose of receiving the pilgrimages of the people of God which go there to worship the Father, profess the faith, and to be reconciled with God, the Church and one's neighbor, and to implore the intercession of the Mother of God or one of the Saints.

It should not be overlooked, however, that many other places, often humble little churches in the cities or in the countryside, locally fulfill the same functions as shrines, even without canonical recognition. These also form part of the "topography" of the faith and of the popular piety of the people of God,[379] of a particular community living in a specific geographical area, on its journey towards the heavenly Jerusalem in faith (Rev 21).

THE SHRINE AS PLACE OF CULTIC CELEBRATION

265. Shrines have an important cultic function. The faithful visit shrines to participate in the liturgical celebrations and the various pious exercises practiced there. This fact, however, should not cause the faithful to overlook the Gospel teaching according to which no specific place is decisive for authentic worship of the Lord (Cf. Jn 4:20–24).

---

377. John Paul II, *Allocution to the rectors of French Shrines* in *Insegnamenti di Giovanni Paolo II*, IV/I (1981), Libreria Editrice Vaticana, Città del Vaticano 1981, p. 138.

378. CIC, can 1230. For the concession of indulgences see EI, *Aliae concessiones*, 33, §1, 4E, p. 77.

379. Cf. John Paul II, Encyclical Letter *Redemptoris Mater*, 28.

Exemplary liturgical celebration

266. Those in charge of shrines should ensure that the quality of the liturgy celebrated at the shrines is exemplary: "Among the functions ascribed to sanctuaries, and confirmed by the Code of Canon Law, is that of fostering the Liturgy. This is not to be understood as increasing the number of liturgical celebrations, but in terms of improving the quality of liturgical celebration. The rectors of sanctuaries should be aware of their responsibility to ensure that this goal is reached. They should realize that the faithful who come to a shrine from diverse places should be able to return comforted in spirit, and edified by the liturgical celebrations: by their capacity to communicate the message of salvation, by the noble simplicity of their ritual expression, and by the faithful observance of the liturgical norms. Rectors of shrines are well aware that the effects of exemplary liturgical celebration are not limited to the liturgical actions celebrated in shrines: both priests and pilgrims take back to their own places the strong cultic impressions that they have experienced in shrines."[380]

Celebration of the Sacrament of Penance

267. For many of the faithful, a visit to a shrine is a propitious occasion on which to avail of the Sacrament of Penance. It is, however, necessary to encourage the various constitutive elements of the Sacrament of Penance:

- *the place of celebration*: in addition to the traditional confessionals located in the church, it is desirable that a confessional chapel be provided for the celebration of the Sacrament of Penance and in which space is available for community preparation, and for penitential celebrations. These should always respect the canonical norms relating to the Sacrament of Penance as well as the privacy which is needed for confession. It should also provide some possibility for dialogue with the confessor.

- *preparation for the Sacrament*: sometimes, the faithful require assistance in preparing for confession, especially in directing the mind and heart to God through a sincere conversion, "since the essence of Penance consists of this."[381] The *Ordo Paenitentiae*[382] provides for celebrations designed to assist preparation for confession through a fruitful celebration of the Word of God; or at least some form of suitable preparatory material being placed at the disposal of the faithful, so as to prepare them not only for the confession of sins, but also for a sincere amendment of life.

- choice of the *ritual action*, to lead the faithful to discover the ecclesial nature of Penance; in this respect *the Rite for the reconciliation of several penitents with individual confession and absolution* (the second rite of Penance), properly prepared and conducted, should not be exceptional,

---

380. Congregation for Divine Worship, Circular Letter *Orientations and Proposals for the Celebration of the Marian Year*, 75.
381. *Rituale Romanum, Ordo Paenitentiae*, cit., 6 a.
382. Cf. Ibid, *Appendix II, Specimina celebrationum panitentialium*, 1–73.

but a normal celebration of the Sacrament of Penance especially at particular times of the Liturgical Year. Indeed, "communal celebration manifests more clearly the ecclesial nature of penance."[383] Reconciliation without individual confession and absolution is a completely exceptional and extraordinary form of the Sacrament of Penance, and may not be considered interchangeable with the ordinary form of the Sacrament. The use of general absolution cannot be justified solely by the presence of great numbers of the faithful, as happens on feast days and pilgrimages.[384]

Celebration of the Eucharist

268. "The celebration of the Eucharist is the climax and pivot of all pastoral activity in shrines."[385] Great care should be devoted to the celebration of the Eucharist so that its exemplary celebration may lead the faithful to a deep encounter with Christ.

It can happen that different groups wish to celebrate the Eucharist at the same time. This practice is not consistent with the ecclesial dimension of the Eucharistic mystery, in that the celebration of the Eucharist, rather than being an expression of fraternity, becomes and expression of individualism which fails to reflect the communion and universality of the Church.

A simple reflection on the nature of the Eucharistic celebration, "sacrament of holiness, sign of unity, and bond of charity,"[386] should be sufficient to persuade priests who lead pilgrim groups to celebrate the Eucharist with other groups of the same language. On occasions when pilgrims come together from different countries, it is important that the Creed and the Our Father be sung in Latin using the simpler melodies.[387] Such celebrations offer a truer image of the Church and of the Eucharist, and afford the faithful an opportunity for mutual encounter and reciprocal enrichment.

Anointing of the Sick

269. The *Ordo unctionis infirmorum cumque pastoralis curae* provides for the communal celebration of the Anointing of the Sick, especially on the occasion of a pilgrimage to a shrine.[388] Such is perfectly in accord with the nature of the Sacrament: obviously, where the imploration of the Lord's mercy is more intense, there too will the maternal solicitude of the Church be more sought by her children who, through sickness or old age, begin to be in danger of death.[389]

The Rite is to be conducted in accordance with the stipulations of the *Ordo*. "When several priests are available, each priest lays on hands and administers

---

383. Ibid., *Praenotanda*, 22.
384. Cf. CIC, can. 961, §2.
385. *Collectio missarum de Beata Maria Virgine, Praenotanda*, 30.
386. SC 47.
387. Cf. *Institutio generalis Missalis Romani*, 41.
388. Cf. n. 83.
389. Cf. CIC, can. 1004.

the anointing with the formula to each sick person in the group; the prayers, however, are to be recited by the principal celebrant."[390]

Celebration of the Other Sacraments

270. In addition to the celebration of the Sacraments of Penance, Holy Eucharist, and the Anointing of the Sick, the other sacraments are occasionally celebrated. This requires particular care on the part of the rectors of shrines to ensure that the dispositions of the local bishop are observed and that additionally:

- they seek to build a genuine understanding and develop a fruitful collaboration between shrine and parish community;

- they consider the nature of every sacrament; for example, since the Sacraments of Christian initiation require preparation and effect the insertion of the Baptized into a particular ecclesial community, they should normally be received in the parish;

- they should ensure that the celebration of every sacrament has been preceded by adequate preparation: the rectors of shrines may not proceed to the marriage of any couple unless they shall have obtained the permission of the Ordinary or the parish priest;[391]

- they should evaluate carefully the multiple and unpredictable circumstances that can arise, and for which it is not always possible to establish norms.

Celebrating the Liturgy of the Hours

271. A visit to a shrine, which is always a special occasion of private and community prayer, affords a valuable opportunity to assist the faithful in appreciating the beauty of the Liturgy of the Hours, and to allow them to participate in the daily praise which the Church, on her earthly pilgrimage, raises up to the Father, through Christ in the Holy Spirit.[392]

Rectors of shrines, therefore, are to make provision for the worthy and opportune celebration of the Liturgy of the Hours, especially Morning and Evening prayer, in the liturgical programs proposed for pilgrims. In this respect, a votive office connected with the shrine could be used either in whole or part.[393]

During the course of the pilgrimage to a shrine, priests will ensure that some hour of the Divine Office is recited by the faithful.

Sacramentals

272. From earliest times, the Church is familiar with the practice of blessing people, places, food, and other objects. In our times, the custom of blessings presents some delicate concerns because of ancient practices or customs deeply rooted amongst the faithful. The question is obviously more pertinent in shrines

---

390. *Rituale Romanum, Ordo unctionis infirmorum eorumque pastoralis curae*, cit., 90.
391. Cf. CIC, can. 1115.
392. Cf. *Institutio Generalis de Liturgia Horarum*, 27.
393. Cf. ibid., 245.

where the faithful come to implore the graces and assistance of the Lord through the intercession of Our Lady of Mercy, or of the Saints, and request the most varied of blessings. Correct pastoral practice in dispensing blessings demands that the rectors of shrines:

- proceed gradually and prudently in applying the principles contained in the *Rituale Romanum*,[394] which are based on the fundamental principle that a blessing is an authentic expression of faith in God, the giver of all good things;

- give due importance— where possible—to the two elements which constitute the "typical structure" of a blessing: proclamation of the Word of God which makes sense of the sacred sign, and the prayer with which the Church praises God and implores his assistance,[395] as recalled when the ordained minister makes the sign of the cross;

- give precedence to community celebrations over individual or private celebrations and to educate the faithful to active and conscious participation.[396]

273. It is, therefore, desirable that the rectors of shrines provide for the celebration of blessings at specific times during the day,[397] especially during those periods when there is a notable increase in the number of pilgrims. From these celebrations, which should be marked by dignity and authenticity, the faithful should be able to grasp the true meaning of a blessing, and the importance of commitment to observing the commandments of God, which is "implied by asking for a blessing."[398]

SHRINES AS PLACES OF EVANGELIZATION

274. Innumerable centers of social communications broadcast news and messages of all kinds every day of the week. A shrine, however, is a place for the proclamation of a message of life: the "Gospel of God" (Mk 1:14; Rom 1:1), or the "Gospel of Jesus Christ" (Mk 1:1), that is the good news coming from God about Jesus Christ: he is the Savior of all mankind, by whose death and resurrection heaven and earth have been reconciled for ever.

The fundamental points of that message must be proposed, either directly or indirectly, to the faithful who make pilgrimage to shrines: the program outlined in the Sermon on the Mount; the joyful proclamation of the goodness and fatherhood of God and of His loving providence; the commandment of love; the salvific significance of the Cross; the transcendent end of human life.

---

394. Cf. *Rituale Romanum, De Benedictionibus*, cit., *Praenotanda*, 1–34.

395. Cf. ibid., 22–24.

396. Cf. ibid., 24 a.

397. Cf. ibid., 30.

398. Cf. *ibid.*, 15.

Many shrines are effective places for the proclamation of the Gospel: in the most varied of ways the message of Christ is transmitted to the faithful as a call to conversion and an invitation to follow Christ, as an exhortation to perseverance, as a reminder of the demands of justice, as a word of consolation and peace.

The fact should not be overlooked that many shrines support the missions *ad gentes* in various ways and fulfill an important role of evangelization in the Church.

SHRINES AS CHARITABLE CENTERS

275. The exemplary role of shrines is also expressed through charity. Every shrine in so far as it celebrates the merciful presence of the Lord, the example and the intercession of the Blessed Virgin Mary and the Saints, "is in itself a hearth radiating the light and warmth of charity."[399] In common parlance and in the language of the poor "charity is love expressed in the name of God."[400] It finds concrete expression in hospitality and mercy, solidarity and sharing, assistance and giving.

Many shrines are centers mediating the love of God and fraternal charity on the one hand, and the needs of mankind on the other. This is made possible by the generosity of the faithful and the zeal of those responsible for the shrines. The charity of Christ flourishes in these sanctuaries which seem to be an extension of the maternal solicitude of Our Lady and of the compassionate presence of the Saints expressed:

- in the creation and development of permanent centers of social assistance such as hospitals, educational institutions for needy children, and in the provision of homes for the aged;

- "in the hospitality extended to pilgrims, especially the poor, to whom the opportunity for rest and shelter should be offered, in so far as possible;

- in the solicitude shown to the old, the sick, the handicapped, to whom particular attention is always given, especially in reserving for them the best places in the shrine: without isolating them from the other pilgrims, celebrations should be made available at convenient times, taking into account their ability to participate at them; effective collaboration should also exist between the shrines and those who generously provide for transport;

- in availability and service to all who come to shrines: educated and uneducated members of the faithful, poor and rich, locals and strangers."[401]

---

399. Central Committee for the Marian Year, *Marian Sanctuaries*, 4 (Circular Letter October 7, 1987).
400. Ibid.
401. Congregation for Divine Worship, Circular Letter, *Orientations and proposals for the Celebration of the Marian Year*, 76.

276. Shrines are often of cultural or heritage significance in themselves. They synthesize numerous expressions of popular culture: historical and artistic monuments, particular linguistic and literary forms, or even musical compositions.

In this perspective, shrines can often play an important role in the definition of the cultural identity of a nation. Since a shrine can produce a harmonious synthesis between grace and nature, piety and art, it can also be presented as an example of the *via pulchritudinis* for the contemplation of the beauty of God, of the mystery of the *Tota pulchra*, and of the wonderful accomplishment of the Saints.

The tendency to promote shrines as "cultural centers" must also be acknowledged. Such efforts include the organization of courses and lectures, from which important publications can derive, as well as the production of sacred "representations," concerts and other artistic and literary activities.

The cultural activities of a shrine are undertaken as collateral initiatives in support of human development. They are secondary to the shrine's principal functions as a place of divine worship, of evangelization and charity. The rectors of shrines will therefore ensure that the cultic functions of such places will not be superseded by any cultural activities taking place in them.

SANCTUARIES AND ECUMENICAL COMMITMENT

277. The shrine, as a place of proclamation of the Word, of call to conversion, of intercession, of intense liturgical life, and of charitable works, is, to a certain extent, a "spiritual benefit" shared with our brothers and sisters not in full communion with the Catholic Church, in accord with the norms of the *Ecumenical Directory*.[402]

In this sense, the shrine is called to be a place of ecumenical commitment, fully aware of the grave and urgent need for the unity of those who believe in Christ, the one Lord and Savior.

Rectors of shrines will therefore make pilgrims aware of that "spiritual ecumenism" of which *Unitatis redintegratio*[403] and the *Directory on Ecumenism*[404] speak, and which should be constantly remembered by the faithful in their prayers, in the celebration of the Eucharist and in their daily lives.[405] Prayers for Christian unity should therefore be intensified in shrines especially during the week of prayer for Christian unity, as well as on the solemnities of the Ascension and Pentecost, in which we remember the community of Jerusalem united in prayer while awaiting the coming of the Holy Spirit to confirm their unity and their universal mission.[406]

---

402. Cf. Pontifical Council for the Promotion of Christian Unity, *Directoire pour l'application des Principes et des Normes sur L'Oecuménisme* (March 25, 1993): AAS 85 (1993), 1039–1119.
403. N. 8.
404. N. 25, in AAS 85 (1993), 1049.
405. Cf. ibid., n. 27, p. 1049.
406. cf. ibid., n. 110, p. 1084.

Were the opportunity to arise, the rectors of shrines should encourage prayer meetings for Christians from various confessions from time to time. These meetings should be carefully and collaboratively prepared. The Word of God should be preeminent in them and they should include prayers drawn from the various Christian denominations.

In certain circumstances, and by way of exception, attention may be given to persons of different religions: some shrines, indeed, are visited by non-Christians who go there because of the values inherent in Christianity. All acts of worship taking place in a shrine must always be clearly consistent with the Catholic faith, without ever attempting to obfuscate anything of the content of the Church's faith.

278. Ecumenical endeavors in shrines dedicated to Our Lady pose special considerations. At a supernatural level, Our Lady, who gave birth to our Savior and was the first and perfect disciple, played an important role in promoting unity and concord among the disciples of the Lord. Hence the Church refers to her as the *Mater unitatis*.[407] At the historical level, different interpretations of her role in the history of salvation have provoked divisions among Christians. On the other hand, it must be recognized that the Marian role is beginning to bear fruit in ecumenical dialogue.

PILGRIMAGE

279. Pilgrimage is a universal religious experience and a typical expression of popular piety.[408] It is invariably connected with a shrine, for which it is an indispensable component.[409] Pilgrims needs shrines, and shrines need pilgrims.

BIBLICAL PILGRIMAGE

280. In the Bible, pilgrimage, with its religious symbolism, goes back as far as that of the Patriarchs Abraham, Isaac and Jacob to Sichem (cf. Gn 12:6–7; 33:18–20), Bethel (cf. Gn 28:10–22; 35:1–15) and Mamre (Gn 13:18; 18:1–15) where God showed himself to them and made a commitment to give them the "promised land."

For the tribes of Israel delivered from Egypt, Sinai, the mountain on which God revealed himself to Moses (cf. Ex 19–20) became a sacred place and the crossing

---

407. Cf. *Collectio missarum de Beata Maria Virgine*, Form. 38: "Sancta Maria Mater Unitatis;" St. Augustine, *Sermo* 192, 2: PL 38, 1013; Paul VI, Homily on the Feast of the Presentation of Our Lord in the Temple, (February 2, 1965), in *Insegnamenti di Paolo VI*, III (1965), Tipografia Polyglotta Vaticana, Città del Vaticano 1966, p. 68; John Paul II, Homily at the Shrine of Jasna Gora (June 4, 1979) in *Insegnamenti di Giovanni Paolo II*, II/1 (1979), Libreria Editrice Vaticana, Città del Vaticano 1979, p. 1418; Angelus discourse (June 12, 1988) in *Insegnamenti di Giovanni Paolo II*, XI/2 (1988), Libreria Editrice Vaticana, Città del Vaticano 1989, p. 1997.

408. Cf. Pontifical Council for Migrants and Itinerants, *Pilgrimage in the Great Jubilee of 2000* (April 25, 1998), Libreria Editrice Vaticana, Città del Vaticano, 1998.

409. According to the Code of Canon Law, the frequency of pilgrimages is an integral element of the concept of shrine: "The term shrine signifies a church or other place to which the faithful make pilgrimages for a particular pious reason with the approval of the local ordinary" (can. 1230).

of the desert became a journey to the promised land: the journey had God's blessing, the Ark (Num 9:15–23) and the Tabernacle (cf. 2 Sam 7:6) symbolized the presence of God among his people, leading them and protecting them by the Cloud (cf. Num 9:15–23).

When Jerusalem became the place of the Temple and the Ark, it became a city-shrine for the Jews and the object of their "holy journey" (Ps 84:6), in which the pilgrim encountered "cries of joy and praise and an exultant throng" (Ps 42:5), and appeared in his presence in "God's house" (cf. Ps 84:6–8).[410]

The men of Israel were obliged to present themselves before the Lord three times each year (cf. Ex 23:17), in the Temple in Jerusalem: this gave rise to the pilgrimage to the Temple on the feast of the Pasch, of the feast of weeks (Pentecost) and of tents; every religious family, such as that of Jesus (cf. Lk 2:41), went to Jerusalem for these feast of the Passover. Jesus went on pilgrimage to Jerusalem during his public ministry (cf. Jn 11:55–56); St. Luke presents the saving mission of Jesus as a mystic pilgrimage (cf. Lk 9:51–19:45) whose object is Jerusalem, the messianic city, the place of his sacrifice and of his exodus to the Father: "I came from the Father and have come into the world and now I leave the world to go to the Father" (Jn 16:28). The Church began her missionary journey during a gathering of pilgrims in Jerusalem when "there were devout men in Jerusalem from every nation under the heavens" (Acts 2:5) to celebrate Pentecost.

CHRISTIAN PILGRIMAGE

281. When Jesus accomplished in himself the mystery of the Temple (cf. Jn 2:22–23) and had passed from this world to the Father (cf. Jn 13:1), thereby going through the definitive exodus in his own person, no pilgrimage was binding any longer on his disciples: their entire lives now become a pilgrimage towards the sanctuary of heaven and the Church is seen as an "earthly pilgrimage."[411]

The Church, however, because of the harmony between her teaching and the spiritual values inherent in pilgrimage, has not only regarded pilgrimage as a legitimate form of piety but has encouraged it throughout her history.

282. With a few exceptions, pilgrimage did not form part of the cultic life of the Church for the first three centuries of her history: the Church feared contamination from the religious practices of Judaism and paganism, where pilgrimage was much practiced.

During this period, however, the basis was laid for a revival of the practice of pilgrimage with a Christian character: the cult of the martyrs, to whose tombs many of the faithful went to venerate the mortal remains of these outstanding witnesses to Christ, logically and gradually became a successor to the "pious visit" and to the "votive pilgrimage."

---

410. The significance of the pilgrimage is borne out in the "canticles of ascent," psalms 120–134, used by those going up to Jerusalem. In their Christian interpretation, these express the Church's joy as she journeys on her earthly pilgrimage to the heavenly Jerusalem.
411. *Missale Romanum, Prex eucharistica III, Intercessiones.*

283. In the Constantinian era, following the rediscovery of the places associated with the Passion of Our Lord and the of the relics of the Passion, Christian pilgrimage made significant progress: pilgrimage to Palestine was especially important in this regard, since its holy places, starting with Jerusalem made it a "Holy Land." Contemporary accounts make this clear, as can be seen in the fourth century *Itenerarium Burdigalense* and the *Itenerarium Egeriae*.

Basilicas were built on the site of the "holy places": the *Anastasis* on the Holy Sepulchre, the *Martyrium* on Mount Calvary, and quickly became places of pilgrimage. The sites associated with the infancy and public life of Christ also became places of pilgrimage. Pilgrimages began to be made to some of the site associated with the Old testament, such as Mount Sinai.

284. The Middle Ages were the golden age of pilgrimage. Apart from their strictly religious function, they played an extraordinary part in the development of Western Christianity, the amalgamation of various nations, and the interchange of ideas and values from every European civilization.

There were numerous places of pilgrimage. Jerusalem, despite its occupation by the Muslims, still remained a great spiritual attraction for the faithful, and gave rise to the Crusades, whose purpose was to make Jerusalem accessible to the faithful who wished to visit the Holy Sepulchre. Numerous pilgrims flocked to venerate the instruments of the Passion: the tunic, the holy towel of Veronica, the holy stairs, and the holy shroud. Pilgrims came to Rome to venerate the tombs of the Apostles Peter and Paul (*ad Limina Apsotolorum*), the catacombs and basilicas, in recognition of the service rendered to the universal Church by the successor of Peter. The shrine of Santiago de Compostela from the ninth to the sixteenth centuries was frequented by countless pilgrims. They came on foot from various countries and reflect an idea of pilgrimage that is at once religious, social, and charitable. The tomb of St. Martin of Tours was another important center of pilgrimage, as was Canterbury, the place of the martyrdom of St. Thomas à Becket. These places of pilgrimage had enormous influence throughout Europe. Monte Gargano in Apulia, San Michele della Chiesa in the Piemonte, and Mont St. Michel in Normandy, all dedicated to St. Michael the Archangel, were important pilgrim centers, as were Walsingham, Rocamadour and Loreto.

285. Pilgrimage declined in the modern period because of changed cultural circumstances, the events surrounding the Protestant movement and also because of the influence of the enlightenment: the journey to a distant country become "a spiritual journey," or an "interior journey," or a "symbolic procession" reduced a short walk as in the case of the *via Crucis*.

The second half of the nineteenth century saw a revival of pilgrimage, but in a much changed form: the goal of such pilgrimage becomes a particular shrine which embodies the faith or cultural identity of specific nations: shrines can mentioned in this context such as Altoeting, Antipolo, Aparecida, Assisi, Caacupé, Coromoto, Czestochowa, Ernakilam-Angamaly, Fatima, Guadalupe, Kevelaer, Knock, La Vang, Loreto, Lourdes, Mariazell, Marienberg, Montevergine, Montserrat,

Nagasaki, Namugongo, Padova, Pompei, San Giovanni Rotondo, Washington, Yamoussoukro etc.

286. Despite change, pilgrimage has maintained the essential traits of its spirituality throughout the ages, down to our own time.

Eschatological Dimension. The original and essential quality of pilgrimage: a pilgrimage, or "journey to a shrine," is both a moment in and parable of, our journey towards the Kingdom; it affords an opportunity for the Christian to take greater stock of his eschatological destiny as *homo viator*: journeying between the obscurity of the faith and the thirst for the vision of clarity, tribulation and the desire for everlasting life, the weariness of the journey and the rest awaiting, between exile and homeland, between frenetic activity and contemplation.[412]

The exodus event, Israel's journey towards the promised land, is also reflected in the spirituality of pilgrimage: the pilgrim is well aware that "there is no eternal city for us in this life" (Heb 14:14), and that beyond the immediate objective of a particular shrine and across the desert of life, we find our true Promised Land, in heaven. *Penitential dimension.* Pilgrimage is also a journey of conversion: in journeying towards a shrine the pilgrim moves from a realization of his own sinfulness and of his attachment to ephemeral and unnecessary things to interior freedom and an understanding of the deeper meaning of life. As has already been said, a visit to a shrine can be a propitious occasion for the faithful and is often undertaken in order to avail of the Sacrament of Penance.[413] In the past—as in our own times—pilgrimage itself has been seen as a penitential act.

When the pilgrim returns from a genuine pilgrimage, he does so with the intention of "amending his life," and ordering it more closely to God, and to live in a more transcendent way.

Festive dimension. The penitential aspect of pilgrimage is complemented by a festive aspect: the festive dimension also lies at the heart of pilgrimage, and arises from many anthropological reasons.

The joy of a Christian pilgrimage is a continuation of the joy experienced on Israel's pious pilgrimage to Jerusalem: "I rejoiced when I heard them say: 'let us go up to God's house'" (Ps 122:1); pilgrimage can be a break from the monotony of daily routine; it can be an alleviation of the burdens of every day life, especially for the poor whose lot is heavy; it is an occasion to give expression to Christian fraternity, in moments of friendship meeting each other, and spontaneity which can sometimes be repressed.

Worship dimension. Pilgrimage is essentially an act of worship: a pilgrim goes to a shrine to encounter God, to be in His presence, and to offer Him adoration in worship, and to open his heart to Him.

---

412. Cf. St. Augustine, *Tractatus CXXIV In Iohannis Evangelium*, 5: CCL 36, Turnholti 1954, p. 685.
413. Cf., supra n. 267.

During his visit to the shrine, the pilgrim completes many acts of worship which are properly Liturgical or drawn from popular piety. He performs different kind of prayers: prayers of *praise and adoration* to the Lord for his goodness and holiness; prayers of *thanksgiving* for the gifts he has given; prayers *in discharge of a vow*; prayers *imploring the graces* necessary in life; prayers *asking for forgiveness* of sins committed.

Frequently, the pilgrim's prayers are directed to Our Lady, or to the Angels and Saints who are regarded as powerful intercessors with God. The icons venerated at pilgrim shrines are signs of the presence of the Mother of God and the Saints who surround the Lord in his glory, "living for ever to intercede for us" (Heb 7:25), and always present in the community gathered in his name (cf. Mt 18:20; 28:20). Sacred images, whether of Christ, his Mother, the Angels and Saints, are signs of the divine presence and of God's provident love; they bear witness to the prayers of generations raised up to God in supplication, to the sighs of the afflicted, and to the thankful joy of those who have received grace and mercy.

Apostolic dimension. The pilgrim's journey, in a certain sense, recalls the journey of Christ and his disciples as they travelled throughout Palestine to announce the Gospel of salvation. In this perspective, pilgrimage is a proclamation of faith in which pilgrims become "errant heralds of Christ."[414]

Dimension of communion. The pilgrim who journeys to a shrine is in a communion of faith and charity not only with those who accompany him on the "sacred journey" (cf. Ps 84:6), but with the Lord himself who accompanies him as he once accompanied the disciples on the road to Emmaus (cf. Lk 24:13–35). He travels with his own community and through that community, he journeys with the Church in heaven and on earth. He travels with all of the faithful who have prayed at that shrine down through the centuries. He appreciates the natural beauty which surrounds the shrine and which he is moved to respect. The pilgrim journeys with mankind whose sufferings and hopes are so clearly evident at the shrine, especially as represented through art.

CONDUCTING A PILGRIMAGE

287. As the shrine is a place of prayer, a pilgrimage is a journey of prayer. Each stage of the pilgrim journey should be marked by prayer and the Word of God should be its light and its guide, its food and its sustenance.

The success of a pilgrimage, seen as an act of worship, and of the spiritual fruits deriving from it, require careful planning of the various celebrations that will take place during the pilgrimage, and adequate highlighting of their various phases.

The beginning of the pilgrimage should be an occasion of prayer, preferably in the parish church or in some other suitable church, with the celebration of the

---

414. Second Vatican Council, Decree *Apostolicam actuositatem*, 14.

Holy Eucharist or a part of the Liturgy of the Hours,[415] or with a special blessing for pilgrims.[416]

The *final* stage of the pilgrimage should be characterized by intense prayer. It should preferably be traveled on foot in processional form, and interspersed with prayer, hymns and pauses at the shrines marking the route to the sanctuary.

The *reception* of the pilgrims could be a suitable moment for a "threshold liturgy," placing the pilgrims and the keepers of the shrine in a perfect context of faith; where possible, the latter should join with the pilgrims in the final phase of the pilgrim journey.

The *time* spent in the sanctuary constitutes the most important part of the pilgrimage and should be marked by a commitment to conversion, ratified by reception of the Sacrament of Penance; by private prayer of thanksgiving, supplication, or of intercession, in accordance with the nature of the shrine or the objectives of the pilgrimage; by celebration of the Holy Eucharist, which is the climax of the pilgrimage.[417]

The *conclusion* of the pilgrimage should be marked by a moment of prayer, either in the shrine itself or at the church from which the pilgrimage departed.[418] The pilgrims should give thanks to God for the gift of the pilgrimage and ask the Lord for his assistance in living out the Christian vocation more generously when they return to their homes.

From antiquity, pilgrims have always brought home souvenirs of their pilgrimage, in recollection of the shrine that they had visited. Care should be taken to ensure that objects, images, and books available in shrines transmit authentically the spirit of the shrine. Care should also be taken to ensure that shops or stalls are not set up within the sacred space of the sanctuary, and that even the appearance of commerce be excluded.

CONCLUSION

288. Both parts of this Directory contain many directives, proposals, and guidelines to encourage and clarify popular piety and religiosity, and to harmonize it with the Liturgy.

In referring to specific traditions and diverse circumstances, the Directory wishes to set forth some basic presuppositions, to reiterate various directives, and to make some suggestions so as to promote fruitful pastoral activity.

---

415. Cf. *Rituale Romanum, De Benedictionibus, Ordo ad benedicendos peregrinos*, cit., 407.
416. Cf. ibid., 409–419.
417. Cf. supra nn. 265–273.
418. Cf. *Rituale Romanum, De benedictionibus, Ordo benedictionis peregrinorum ante vel post reditum*, cit., 420–430.

With the assistance of their collaborators, especially of the rectors of shrines, it is for the Bishops to establish norms and practical guidelines in relation to this matter, taking into account local traditions and particular manifestations of popular piety and religiosity.

MARIALIS CULTUS
FOR THE RIGHT ORDERING AND DEVELOPMENT OF DEVOTION TO THE BLESSED VIRGIN MARY

APOSTOLIC EXHORTATION
POPE PAUL VI
FEBRUARY 2, 1974

AN OVERVIEW OF *MARIALIS CULTUS*
Michael R. Prendergast

Michael R. Prendergast

AN INTRODUCTION TO *MARIALIS CULTUS*

Pope Paul VI issued his apostolic exhortation, *Marialis cultus* (MarCult), on February 2, 1974.[1] Rejoicing in the work accomplished by the Church in the "improvement of divine worship . . . restored according to the principles and norms"[2] of the *Constitution on the Sacred Liturgy*, the Holy Father addresses his exhortation to his fellow bishops and to the people of God. He encourages that the Church "venerates with special love Mary the most holy Mother of God" as well as the venerable tradition of keeping the "memory of the martyrs and the other saints."[3]

Rooted in the theology of the Second Vatican Council, *Marialis cultus* was heavily influenced by article 103 of CSL, which emphasizes the "special love" the Church has for Mary and the "inseparable bond" between Mary and her Son's saving work. These themes occur repeatedly in *Marialis cultus*.

Marialis cultus was also influenced by *Lumen gentium*, chapter 8. In this chapter, entitled, "Our Lady," the Council fathers uphold "the cult, especially the liturgical cult, of the Blessed Virgin Mary" . . . and speak of the . . . "filial love towards our mother and the imitation of her virtues."[4] However, "The Council's theology of Mary is based primarily on the biblical narrative of her relation to Christ and his Church, whereas *Marialis cultus* uses more personalist language to rekindle and deepen the memory of Mary."[5]

Marialis cultus is not focused upon the *person* of Mary, but focuses rather on the way in which the *Church* celebrates Marian liturgies and devotions.[6] The document, which took four years to prepare, was a response to "the Marian crisis" of the time—the question and concern that Marian devotion was incompatible with the theology and liturgical practice of the post-Conciliar Church. Pope Paul VI sought to restore the Marian devotion of the faithful while main-

---

1. February 2 is the Feast of the Presentation of the Lord. The name of and promulgation of the document on this feast is significant. Prior to the Second Vatican Council, February 2 was the Feast of the Purification of the Blessed Virgin Mary. This Marian feast was linked to the Jewish rite of purification of the mother that was performed according to Mosaic law forty days after the birth of a male child (see Leviticus 12:2–6). With the post-Conciliar reform of the General Roman Calendar, the name was changed to the Feast of the Presentation of the Lord; thus, shifting the Marian focus of this liturgical observance to a Christocentric focus.

2. *Marialis cultus* (MarCult), introduction.

3. Ibid.; quoting the *Constitution on the Sacred Liturgy*, 103.

4. *Lumen gentium* (LG), 67.

5. John G. Roten, SM, "Memory and Mission: A Theological Reflection on Mary in the Paschal Mysteries," *Marian Studies* 42 (1991): 86.

6. Marilogist, John G. Roten, notes that "*Lumen Gentium* and *Marialis Cultus* are significantly the same: they both attempt to retrieve the living memory of Mary. *Lumen Gentium* concentrates on knowing the *memoria*; [whereas] *Marialis Cultus* concentrates on the *memoria* itself, that is, on how it can be reached in and through her." See Roten, p. 86.

taining the theology presented in the Conciliar documents. The introductory paragraphs of *Marialis cultus* place the initial reforms of the Second Vatican Council within an affirmative perspective while at the same time it seeks to promote a systematic renewal with "vigilant solicitude."[7]

PART ONE: DEVOTION TO THE BLESSED VIRGIN MARY IN THE LITURGY

Marialis cultus is divided into three major parts. Part I discusses the role of the Blessed Virgin in the reformed liturgy of the Second Vatican Council. In the first section of part I, Pope Paul VI notes that the reformed General Roman Calendar "makes it possible in a more organized and closely-knit fashion to include the commemoration of Christ's Mother in the annual cycle of the mysteries of her Son."[8] The post-Conciliar liturgical reform decreased the number of Marian celebrations. Before the General Roman Calendar was revised in 1969, the Missal of 1570 included twenty-two Marian celebrations and feasts and immediately after the reform of the Calendar, the 1973 Missal of Paul VI included only fourteen Marian celebrations—four solemnities, three feasts, five memorials, and two optional memorials.[9] In 1986 the Congregation for Divine Worship and the Discipline of the Sacraments (CDWDS) published a collection of forty-six formularies for Marian Masses. These formularies were since updated with the new edition of the Missal.

Marialis cultus provides particular recommendations for honoring Mary during particular times of the liturgical year. For example, Paul VI recommended that Advent was "particularly suited to devotion ot the Mother of the Lord."[10] Paul VI names January 1, the solemnity of Mary's divine motherhood, as the World Day of Peace.[11] He implores the Church to pray to God through the intercession of the Queen of Peace for the priceless gift of peace. These are just some examples provided in the document regarding the role of Mary during the liturgical year.

The document continues with a list of the memorials and feasts "in which the Blessed Virgin [is] closely associated with her Son."[12] These include the Nativity of Mary (September 8); the Visitation (May 31), Our Lady of Sorrows (September 15); Our Lady of Lourdes (February 11); Dedication of St. Mary Major (August 5); Our Lady of Mount Carmel (July 16), and Our Lady of the Rosary (October 7).

---

7. MarCult, introduction.

8. Ibid., 2.

9. Prior to the reform of the liturgical calendar, a Memorial of the Seven Sorrows of the Blessed Virgin Mary was celebrated on September 15 and on the final Friday of Lent. Following the Second Vatican Council, these two memorials were combined into one observance, the [optional] Memorial of Our Lady of Sorrows celebrated on September 15. The reform of the liturgical calendar also changed the names of the Feast of the Purification of the Blessed Virgin Mary (February 2; see also footnote 1) to the Feast of the Presentation of the Lord and the Feast of the Annunciation of the Blessed Virgin Mary to the Solemnity of the Annunciation of the Lord (March 25), thus, changing the categorical distinction of these observances as "Feasts of the Lord" rather than "Feasts of Mary." These changes account for the numeric change of twenty-two to fourteen Marian liturgical observances.

10. MarCult, 4.

11. See ibid., 5.

12. Ibid., 7–8.

In the second section of part I, the Blessed Virgin is presented as the model of the Church in divine worship—a model of the spiritual attitude with which the Church celebrates and lives the divine mysteries."[13] *Lumen gentium* refers to Mary as "advocate, helper, benefactress and mediatrix," which "neither takes away anything from, nor adds anything to, the dignity and efficacy of Christ the one Mediator."[14] Mary is a Virgin who listens;[15] a Virgin who prays;[16] a Virgin who is mother;[17] a Virgin who makes her offering to God;[18] a mother who is the teacher of devotion;[19] and a model of the "Church's work of charity.[20] *Marialis cultus* demonstrates a clear "exhortation" to all the Church "that the cult, especially th eliturgical cult, of the Blessed Virgin Mary be generously fostered."[21]

THE RENEWAL OF DEVOTION TO MARY

Regarding to Marian devotion, the principles and guidelines for renewal also affect the catechetical process. Section one of part II of *Marialis cultus* treats the Trinitarian, Christological, and ecclesial aspects of devotion to Mary.[22] Here the document clearly specifies that "exercises of piety directed towards the Virgin Mary should clearly express the Trinitarian and Christological note that is intrinsic an essential to them" and "in the expressions of devotion to the Virgin the Christological aspect should have particular prominence."[23] Thus, any homage given "to the Queen becomes honor rendered to the King."[24] The link or relationship to Christ must always be evident with all forms of Marian piety and veneration.

Marialis cultus 26 and 27 focus on the influence of the Holy Spirit in the life of Mary. The Paraclete had a profound role in the life of the Virgin of Nazareth and is seen as "a culminating moment of the Spirit's action in the history of salvation."[25] Since the early days of the Church Mary was "fashioned by the Holy Spirit into a new kind of substance and a new creature."[26] Paul VI encourages pastors and theologians to "meditate more deeply on the working of the Holy Spirit in the history of salvation, and to ensure that Christian spiritual writings give due prominence to his life-giving action."[27] Paul VI comments on the importance of the role of Mary in the Byzantine Rite in which "on the central door of the iconostasis there is a representation of the Annunciation and in

---

13. Ibid., 16.
14. LG, 62.
15. MarCult., 17.
16. Ibid., 18.
17. Ibid., 20.
18. Ibid.
19. Ibid., 21.
20. MarCult., 20.
21. MarCult, 23; quoting *Lumen gentium*, 67.
22. See ibid., 25–28.
23. Ibid., 25.
24. Ibid.
25. Ibid., 26.
26. Ibid.
27. Ibid., 27.

the apse an image of the glorious Theotokos."[28] He provides the beautiful image of how "the assent of the humble handmaid of the Lord" enables humanity to begin "its return to God and sees in the glory of the all-holy Virgin the goal towards which it is journeying."[29]

Section two of part II presents four guidelines for devotion to Mary. These guidelines or considerations—biblical, liturgical, ecumenical, and anthropological—provide the lens through which all catechesis and the teaching of Marian doctrine must be situated.

BIBLICAL CONSIDERATION

Paul VI emphasizes that "every form of worship should have a biblical imprint"[30] and so devotion to Mary must take its source and inspiration from the Sacred Scriptures—texts, chants, and symbols. In doing so, Marian devotion points to a Christocentric form of worship and piety.

LITURGICAL CONSIDERATION

Marialis cultus was issued almost eleven years after the promulgation of CSL. During this time, some were emphasizing the liturgical rites to the point of suppressing popular devotions. Paul VI reiterates CSL 13, in that "it is necessary . . . that such devotions with consideration for the liturgical seasons should be so arranged as to be in harmony with the sacred liturgy. They should somehow derive their inspiration from it, and because of its preeminence they should orient the Christian people towards it."[31] He reminds the Church of the danger of those who reject popular devotions as well as those who do not follow "wholesome liturgical and pastoral criteria, mix practices of piety and liturgical acts in hybrid celebrations."[32] The Holy Father is discouraging these erroneous practices.

ECUMENICAL CONSIDERATIONS

The pope also raises the issue of devotion to the Virgin Mary in relationship to the unity of Christians. Many differences exist between Roman Catholics and other ecclesial communities, especially regarding to the role of Mary in salvation history. The pope prays "that devotion to the humble handmaid of the Lord . . . will become . . . not an obstacle but a path and a rallying point for the union of all who believe in Christ."[33]

ANTHROPOLOGICAL CONSIDERATIONS

What follows are three extraordinary articles on the veneration of Mary emphasizing that "close attention [must be given] to certain findings of the human

---

28. Ibid., 28.
29. Ibid.
30. Ibid., 30.
31. Ibid., 31.
32. Ibid., 31.
33. Ibid., 33.

sciences."[34] The pope recognizes the contributions women are making in society; however, as a result some perceive venerating Mary as problematic. Many women were now taking roles outside of the home with responsibilities previously assumed by men. As such, they had a difficult time relating to Mary.[35] Paul VI encourages Marian veneration, upholding her as one whose life was "is worthy of imitation because she was the first and the most perfect of Christ's disicples."[36] Paul VI is quite pastoral in stating that the Church "does not bind herself to any particular expression of an individual cultural epoch or to the particular anthropological ideas underlying such expressions."[37] Therefore, Paul appears sensitive to both the past and the prevailing mores of the world in the 1970s.

In concluding this section, Paul VI encourages devotions to be constant with sound doctrine and he discourages any practices that rely on "external practices" or that "are not in harmony with the Catholic Faith."[38] Devotion to Mary should be pure and selfless.[39]

PART III: THE *ANGELUS* AND THE ROSARY

The *Angelus* is a prayer reflecting on the Incarnation and Mary's *fiat*. At the time this document was issued, recitation of the *Angelus* had begun to disappear. The pope found no need to revise the prayer because of its simple and biblical content. Rather, he exhorts the faithful to continue this "traditional recitation wherever and whenever possible."[40]

Paul VI devotes fourteen articles to the Rosary. He notes that the Rosary is suitable "for fostering contemplative prayer—prayer of both praise and petition . . . recalled its intrinsic effectiveness for promoting Christian life and apostolic commitment."[41] It is a devotion rooted in the Sacred Scriptures, specifically centered upon the Gospel texts on the "mystery of the redemptive Incarnation" and "a prayer with a clearly Christological orientation."[42] The Holy Father stresses the importance of contemplation and notes without it the "Rosary is a body without a soul, and its recitation is in danger of being a mechanical repetition of formulas."[43] The Holy Father again reiterates CSL and cautions that the "pious practice of the Rosary must be neither set in opposition to one another [the liturgy] nor as being seen as identical [to the liturgy]."[44] Paul VI clearly stares "it is a mistake to recite the Rosary during the celebration of the liturgy"[45] and he laments this practice still persists in certain places. Paul VI strongly recommends

---

34. Ibid., 34.
35. See ibid.
36. Ibid., 35.
37. Ibid., 36.
38. See ibid., 38.
39. See ibid.
40. Ibid., 41.
41. Ibid., 42.
42. Ibid., 46.
43. Ibid., 47.
44. Ibid., 48.
45. Ibid.

"the recitation of the family Rosary" and refers to the family as the "vital cell of society, [which] 'shows itself to be the domestic sanctuary of the Church through the mutual affection of its members and the common prayer they offer to God.'"[46]

CONCLUSION

The conclusion to *Marialis cultus* discusses the theological and pastoral value of devotion to the Blessed Virgin and encourages Marian devotion within the pastoral catechetical process, especially regarding to liturgical catechesis, in a manner that is harmonious with theological and liturgical reforms of the Second Vatican Council. *Marialis cultus* is an exhortation that upholds the principles of the *Constitution on the Sacred Liturgy* and contextualizes the role of devotion to the Blessed Virgin Mary in the postconciliar era. With confidence, joy, and hope let us call on the Blessed Virgin Mary and implore her intercession, before her Son, on behalf of the whole Body of Christ.

---

46. Ibid., 52; quoting LG, 11.

OUTLINE

APOSTOLIC EXHORTATION
OF HIS HOLINESS PAUL VI

MARIALIS CULTUS

FOR THE RIGHT ORDERING AND DEVELOPMENT
OF DEVOTION TO THE BLESSED VIRGIN MARY

To All Bishops in Peace and Communion
with the Apostolic See
February 2, 1974

INTRODUCTION

OCCASION AND PURPOSE OF THE DOCUMENT
DIVISION OF THE TREATISE

Venerable Brothers:

Health and the Apostolic Blessing

From the moment when we were called to the See of Peter, we have constantly striven to enhance devotion to the Blessed Virgin Mary, not only with the intention of interpreting the sentiments of the Church and our own personal inclination but also because, as is well known, this devotion forms a very noble part of the whole sphere of that sacred worship in which there intermingle the highest expressions of wisdom and of religion[1] and which is therefore the primary task of the People of God.

Precisely with a view to this task, we have always favored and encouraged the great work of liturgical reform promoted by the Second Vatican Ecumenical Council, and it has certainly come about not without a particular design of divine Providence that the first conciliar document which together with the venerable Fathers we approved and signed *in Spiritu Sancto* was the Constitution *Sacrosanctum Concilium*. The purpose of this document was precisely to restore and enhance the liturgy and to make more fruitful the participation of the faithful in the sacred mysteries.[2] From that time onwards, many acts of our pontificate have

---

1. Cf. Lactantius, *Divinae institutiones* IV, 3, 6–10: CSEL 19 p. 279.
2. Cf. Second Vatican Council, Constitution on the Sacred Liturgy, *Sacrosanctum Concilium*, 1–3, 11, 21, 48; AAS 56 (1964), pp. 97–98, 102–103, 105–106, 113.

been directed towards the improvement of divine worship, as is demonstrated by the fact that we have promulgated in these recent years numerous books of the Roman Rite, restored according to the principles and norms of the same Council. For this we profoundly thank the Lord, the giver of all good things, and we are grateful to the episcopal conferences and individual bishops who in various ways have collaborated with us in the preparation of these books.

We contemplate with joy and gratitude the work so far accomplished and the first positive results of the liturgical renewal, destined as they are to increase as this renewal comes to be understood in its basic purposes and correctly applied. At the same time we do not cease with vigilant solicitude to concern ourself with whatever can give orderly fulfillment to the renewal of the worship with which the Church in spirit and truth (cf. Jn 4:24) adores the Father and the Son and the Holy Spirit, "venerates with special love Mary the most holy Mother of God"[3] and honors with religious devotion the memory of the martyrs and the other saints.

The development, desired by us, of devotion to the Blessed Virgin Mary is an indication of the Church's genuine piety. This devotion fits—as we have indicated above—into the only worship that is rightly called "Christian," because it takes its origin and effectiveness from Christ, finds its complete expression in Christ, and leads through Christ in the Spirit to the Father. In the sphere of worship this devotion necessarily reflects God's redemptive plan, in which a special form of veneration is appropriate to the singular place which Mary occupies in that plan.[4] Indeed every authentic development of Christian worship is necessarily followed by a fitting increase of veneration for the Mother of the Lord. Moreover, the history of piety shows how "the various forms of devotion towards the Mother of God that the Church has approved within the limits of wholesome and orthodox doctrine"[5] have developed in harmonious subordination to the worship of Christ, and have gravitated towards this worship as to their natural and necessary point of reference. The same is happening in our own time. The Church's reflection today on the mystery of Christ and on her own nature has led her to find at the root of the former and as a culmination of the latter the same figure of a woman: the Virgin Mary, the Mother of Christ and the Mother of the Church. And the increased knowledge of Mary's mission has become joyful veneration of her and adoring respect for the wise plan of God, who has placed within His family (the Church), as in every home, the figure of a Woman, who in a hidden manner and in a spirit of service watches over that family "and carefully looks after it until the glorious day of the Lord."[6]

In our time, the changes that have occurred in social behavior, people's sensibilities, manners of expression in art and letters and in the forms of social communication have also influenced the manifestations of religious sentiment.

---

3. Second Vatican Council, Constitution on the Sacred Liturgy, *Sacrosanctum Concilium*, 103: AAS 56 (1964), p. 125.

4. Cf. Second Vatican Council, Dogmatic Constitution on the Church, *Lumen gentium*, 66: AAS 57 (1965), p. 65.

5. Ibid.

6. Votive Mass of the Blessed Virgin Mary, Mother of the Church, Preface.

Certain practices of piety that not long ago seemed suitable for expressing the religious sentiment of individuals and of Christian communities seem today inadequate or unsuitable because they are linked with social and cultural patterns of the past. On the other hand in many places people are seeking new ways of expressing the unchangeable relationship of creatures with their Creator, of children with their Father. In some people this may cause temporary confusion. But anyone who, with trust in God reflects upon these phenomena discovers that many tendencies of modern piety (for example, the interiorization of religious sentiment) are meant to play their part in the development of Christian piety in general and devotion to the Blessed Virgin in particular. Thus our own time, faithfully attentive to tradition and to the progress of theology and the sciences, will make its contribution of praise to her whom, according to her own prophetical words, all generations will call blessed (cf. Lk 1:48).

We therefore judge it in keeping with our apostolic service, venerable Brothers, to deal, in a sort of dialogue, with a number of themes connected with the place that the Blessed Virgin occupies in the Church's worship. These themes have already been partly touched upon by the Second Vatican Council[7] and also by ourself,[8] but it is useful to return to them in order to remove doubts and, especially, to help the development of that devotion to the Blessed Virgin which in the Church is motivated by the Word of God and practiced in the Spirit of Christ.

We therefore wish to dwell upon a number of questions concerning the relationship between the sacred liturgy and devotion to the Blessed Virgin (I), to offer considerations and directives suitable for favoring the development of that devotion (II) and finally to put forward a number of reflections intended to encourage the restoration, in a dynamic and more informed manner, of the recitation of the Rosary, the practice of which was so strongly recommended by our predecessors and is so widely diffused among the Christian people (III).

PART ONE

DEVOTION TO THE BLESSED VIRGIN MARY IN THE LITURGY

1. As we prepare to discuss the place which the Blessed Virgin Mary occupies in Christian worship, we must first turn our attention to the sacred liturgy. In addition to its rich doctrinal content, the liturgy has an incomparable pastoral effectiveness and a recognized exemplary conduct for the other forms of worship. We would have liked to take into consideration the various liturgies of the East and the West, but for the purpose of this document we shall dwell almost exclusively on the books of the Roman Rite. In fact, in accordance with the practical norms issued by the Second Vatican Council,[9] it is this Rite alone which

---

7. Cf. Second Vatican Council, Dogmatic Constitution on the Church, *Lumen gentium* 66–67: AAS 57 (1965), pp. 65–66, Constitution on the Sacred Liturgy, *Sacrosanctum Concilium*, 103: AAS 56 (1964), p. 125.

8. Apostolic Exhortation, *Signum magnum*: AAS 59 (1967), pp. 465–475.

9. Cf. Second Vatican Council, Constitution on the Sacred Liturgy, *Sacrosanctum Concilium*, 3: AAS 56 (1964), p 98.

has been the object of profound renewal. This is true also in regard to expressions of veneration for Mary. This Rite therefore deserves to be carefully considered and evaluated.

SECTION ONE

THE BLESSED VIRGIN IN THE REVISED ROMAN LITURGY

2. The reform of the Roman liturgy presupposed a careful restoration of its General Calendar. This Calendar is arranged in such a way as to give fitting prominence to the celebration on appropriate days of the work of salvation. It distributes throughout the year the whole mastery of Christ, from the Incarnation to the expectation of His return in glory,[10] and thus makes it possible in a more organic and closely-knit fashion to include the commemoration of Christ's Mother in the annual cycle of the mysteries of her Son.

3. For example, during Advent there are many liturgical references to Mary besides the Solemnity of December 8, which is a joint celebration of the Immaculate Conception of Mary, of the basic preparation (cf. Is 11:1, 10) for the coming of the Savior and of the happy beginning of the Church without spot or wrinkle.[11] Such liturgical references are found especially on the days from December 17 to 24, and more particularly on the Sunday before Christmas, which recalls the ancient prophecies concerning the Virgin Mother and the Messiah[12] and includes readings from the Gospel concerning the imminent birth of Christ and His precursor.[13]

4. In this way the faithful, living in the liturgy the spirit of Advent, by thinking about the inexpressible love with which the Virgin Mother awaited her Son,[14] are invited to take her as a model and to prepare themselves to meet the Savior who is to come. They must be "vigilant in prayer and joyful in . . . praise."[15] We would also remark that the Advent liturgy, by linking the awaiting of the Messiah and the awaiting of the glorious return of Christ with the admirable commemoration of His Mother, presents a happy balance in worship. This balance can be taken as a norm for preventing any tendency (as has happened at times in certain forms of popular piety) to separate devotion to the Blessed Virgin from its necessary point of reference—Christ. It also ensures that this season,

---

10. Cf. Second Vatican Council, ibid., 102: AAS 56 (1954), p. 125.

11. Cf. Roman Missal restored by Decree of the Sacred Ecumenical Second Vatican Council, promulgated by authority of Pope Paul VI typical edition, MCMLXX, December 8, Preface.

12. Roman Missal, restored by Decree of the Sacred Ecumenical Second Vatican Council promulgated by authority of Pope Paul VI, *Ordo Lectionum Missae*, typical edition MCMLXIX. p. 8, First Reading (Year A: Is 7:10–14: "Behold a Virgin shall conceive;" Year B: 2 Sam 7:1–15; 8b–11, 16: "The throne of David shall be established for ever before the face of the Lord;" Year C: Mic 5:2a [Heb 1–4a]: "Out of you will be born for me the one who is to rule over Israel").

13. Ibid., p. 8, Gospel (Year A: Mt 1:18–24: "Jesus is born of Mary who was espoused to Joseph, the son of David;" Year B: Lk 1:26–38: "You are to conceive and bear a son;" Year C: Lk 1:39–45: "Why should I be honored with a visit from the Mother of my Lord?").

14. Cf. Roman Missal Advent Preface, II.

15. Roman Missal, ibid.

as liturgy experts have noted, should be considered as a time particularly suited to devotion to the Mother of the Lord. This is an orientation that we confirm and which we hope to see accepted and followed everywhere.

5.   The Christmas season is a prolonged commemoration of the divine, virginal and salvific motherhood of her whose "inviolate virginity brought the Savior into the world."[16] In fact, on the Solemnity of the Birth of Christ the Church both adores the Savior and venerates His glorious Mother. On the Epiphany, when she celebrates the universal call to salvation, the Church contemplates the Blessed Virgin, the true Seat of Wisdom and true Mother of the King, who presents to the Wise Men, for their adoration, the Redeemer of all peoples (cf. Mt 2:11). On the Feast of the Holy Family of Jesus, Mary and Joseph (the Sunday within the octave of Christmas) the Church meditates with profound reverence upon the holy life led in the house at Nazareth by Jesus, the Son of God and Son of Man, Mary his Mother, and Joseph the just man (cf. Mt 1:19).

In the revised ordering of the Christmas period it seems to us that the attention of all should be directed towards the restored Solemnity of Mary the Holy Mother of God. This celebration, placed on January 1 in conformity with the ancient indication of the liturgy of the City of Rome, is meant to commemorate the part played by Mary in this mystery of salvation. It is meant also to exalt the singular dignity which this mystery brings to the "holy Mother . . . through whom we were found worthy to receive the Author of life."[17] It is likewise a fitting occasion for renewing adoration of the newborn Prince of Peace, for listening once more to the glad tidings of the angels (cf. Lk 2:14), and for imploring from God, through the Queen of Peace, the supreme gift of peace. It is for this reason that, in the happy concurrence of the Octave of Christmas and the first day of the year, we have instituted the World Day of Peace, an occasion that is gaining increasing support and already bringing forth fruits of peace in the hearts of many.

6.   To the two solemnities already mentioned (the Immaculate Conception and the Divine Motherhood) should be added the ancient and venerable celebrations of March 25 and August 15.

For the Solemnity of the Incarnation of the Word, in the Roman Calendar the ancient title—the Annunciation of the Lord—has been deliberately restored, but the feast was and is a joint one of Christ and of the Blessed Virgin: of the Word, who becomes Son of Mary (Mk 6:3), and of the Virgin, who becomes Mother of God. With regard to Christ, the East and the West, in the inexhaustible riches of their liturgies, celebrate this solemnity as the commemoration of the salvific "fiat" of the Incarnate Word, who, entering the world, said: "God, here I am! I am coming to obey Your will" (cf. Heb 10:7; Ps 39:8-9). They commemorate it as the beginning of the redemption and of the indissoluble and wedded union of the divine nature with human nature in the one Person of the Word. With regard to Mary, these liturgies celebrate it as a feast of the new Eve,

---

16. Roman Missal, Eucharistic Prayer I, *Communicantes* for Christmas and its octave.

17. Roman Missal, January 1, Entry antiphon and Collect.

the obedient and faithful virgin, who with her generous "fiat" (cf. Lk 1:38) became through the working of the Spirit the Mother of God, but also the true Mother of the living, and, by receiving into her womb the one Mediator (cf. 1 Tm 2:5), became the true Ark of the Covenant and true Temple of God. These liturgies celebrate it as a culminating moment in the salvific dialogue between God and man, and as a commemoration of the Blessed Virgin's free consent and cooperation in the plan of redemption.

The solemnity of August 15 celebrates the glorious Assumption of Mary into heaven. It is a feast of her destiny of fullness and blessedness, of the glorification of her immaculate soul and of her virginal body, of her perfect configuration to the Risen Christ; a feast that sets before the eyes of the Church and of all mankind the image and the consoling proof of the fulfillment of their final hope, namely, that this full glorification is the destiny of all those whom Christ has made his brothers, having "flesh and blood in common with them" (Heb 2:14; cf. Gal 4:4). The Solemnity of the Assumption is prolonged in the celebration of the Queenship of the Blessed Virgin Mary, which occurs seven days later. On this occasion we contemplate her who, seated beside the King of ages, shines forth as Queen and intercedes as Mother.[18] These four solemnities therefore, mark with the highest liturgical rank the main dogmatic truths concerning the handmaid of the Lord.

7.   After the solemnities just mentioned, particular consideration must be given to those celebrations that commemorate salvific events in which the Blessed Virgin was closely associated with her Son. Such are the feasts of the Nativity of Our Lady (September 8), "the hope of the entire world and the dawn of salvation"[19]; and the Visitation (May 31), in which the liturgy recalls the "Blessed Virgin Mary carrying her Son within her,"[20] and visiting Elizabeth to offer charitable assistance and to proclaim the mercy of God the Savior.[21] Then there is the commemoration of Our Lady of Sorrows (September 15), a fitting occasion for reliving a decisive moment in the history of salvation and for venerating, together with the Son "lifted up on the cross, his suffering Mother."[22]

The feast of February 2, which has been given back its ancient name, the Presentation of the Lord, should also be considered as a joint commemoration of the Son and of the Mother, if we are fully to appreciate its rich content. It is the celebration of a mystery of salvation accomplished by Christ, a mystery with which the Blessed Virgin was intimately associated as the Mother of the Suffering Servant of Yahweh, as the one who performs a mission belonging to ancient Israel, and as the model for the new People of God, which is ever being tested in its faith and hope by suffering and persecution (cf. Lk 2:21–35).

8.   The restored Roman Calendar gives particular prominence to the celebrations listed above, but it also includes other kinds of commemorations connected

---

18. Cf. Roman Missal, August 22. Collect.

19. Roman Missal, September 8, Prayer after Communion.

20. Roman Missal, May 31, Collect.

21. Cf. ibid., Collect and Prayer over the gifts.

22. Cf. Roman Missal, September 15, Collect.

with local devotions and which have acquired a wider popularity and interest (e.g., February 11, Our Lady of Lourdes; August 5, the Dedication of the Basilica of St. Mary Major). Then there are others, originally celebrated by particular religious families but which today, by reason of the popularity they have gained, can truly be considered ecclesial (e.g., July 16, Our Lady of Mount Carmel; October 7, Our Lady of the Rosary). There are still others which, apart from their apocryphal content, present lofty and exemplary values and carry on venerable traditions having their origin especially in the East (e.g., the Immaculate Heart of the Blessed Virgin, celebrated on the Saturday following the second Sunday after Pentecost).

9. Nor must one forget that the General Roman Calendar does not include all celebrations in honor of the Blessed Virgin. Rather, it is for individual Calendars to include, with fidelity to liturgical norms but with sincere endorsement, the Marian feasts proper to the different local Churches. Lastly, it should be noted that frequent commemorations of the Blessed Virgin are possible through the use of the Saturday Masses of our Lady. This is an ancient and simple commemoration and one that is made very adaptable and varied by the flexibility of the modern Calendar and the number of formulas provided by the Missal.

10. In this Apostolic Exhortation we do not intend to examine the whole content of the new Roman Missal. But by reason of the work of evaluation that we have undertaken to carry out in regard to the revised books of the Roman Rite,[23] we would like to mention some of the aspects and themes of the Missal. In the first place, we are pleased to note how the Eucharistic Prayers of the Missal, in admirable harmony with the Eastern liturgies,[24] contain a significant commemoration of the Blessed Virgin. For example, the ancient Roman Canon, which commemorates the Mother of the Lord in terms full of doctrine and devotional inspiration: "In union with the whole Church we honor Mary, the ever-virgin Mother of Jesus Christ our Lord and God." In a similar way the recent Eucharistic Prayer III expresses with intense supplication the desire of those praying to share with the Mother the inheritance of sons: "May he make us an everlasting gift to you (the Father) and enable us to share in the inheritance of your saints, with Mary, the Virgin Mother of God." This daily commemoration, by reason of its place at the heart of the divine Sacrifice, should be considered a particularly expressive form of the veneration that the Church pays to the "Blessed of the Most High" (cf. Lk 1:28).

11. As we examine the texts of the revised Missal we see how the great Marian themes of the Roman prayerbook have been accepted in perfect doctrinal continuity with the past. Thus, for example, we have the themes of Mary's Immaculate Conception and fullness of grace, the divine motherhood, the unblemished and fruitful virginity, the Temple of the Holy Spirit, Mary's cooperation in the work

---

23. Cf. 1, p. 15.

24. From among the many anaphoras cf. the following which are held In special honour by the Eastern rites: *Anaphora Marci Evangelistae: Prex Eucharistica*, ed. A. Hanggi-I, Pahl, Fribourg Editions Universitaires, 1968, p. 107; *Anaphora Iacobi fratris Domini graeca*, ibid., p. 257; *Anaphora Ioannis Chrysostomi*, ibid., p. 229.

of her Son, her exemplary sanctity, merciful intercession, Assumption into heaven, maternal Queenship and many other themes. We also see how other themes, in a certain sense new ones, have been introduced in equally perfect harmony with the theological developments of the present day. Thus, for example, we have the theme of Mary and the Church, which has been inserted into the texts of the Missal in a variety of aspects, a variety that matches the many and varied relations that exist between the Mother of Christ and the Church. For example, in the celebration of the Immaculate Conception which texts recognize the beginning of the Church, the spotless Bride of Christ.[25] In the Assumption they recognize the beginning that has already been made and the image of what, for the whole Church, must still come to pass.[26] In the mystery of Mary's motherhood they confess that she is the Mother of the Head and of the members—the holy Mother of God and therefore the provident Mother of the Church.[27]

When the liturgy turns its gaze either to the primitive Church or to the Church of our own days it always finds Mary. In the primitive Church she is seen praying with the apostles;[28] in our own day she is actively present, and the Church desires to live the mystery of Christ with her: "Grant that your Church which with Mary shared Christ's passion may be worthy to share also in his resurrection."[29] She is also seen represented as a voice of praise in unison with which the Church wishes to give glory to God: ". . . with her [Mary] may we always praise you."[30] And since the liturgy is worship that requires as way of living consistent with it, it asks that devotion to the Blessed Virgin should become a concrete and deeply-felt love for the Church, as is wonderfully expressed in the prayer after Communion in the Mass of September: ". . . that as we recall the sufferings shared by the Blessed Virgin Mary, we may with the Church fulfill in ourselves what is lacking in the sufferings of Christ."

12.   The Lectionary is one of the books of the Roman Rite that has greatly benefited from the postconciliar reform, by reason both of its added texts and of the intrinsic value of these texts, which contain the ever-living and efficacious word of God (cf. Heb 4:12). This rich collection of biblical texts has made it possible to arrange the whole history of salvation in an orderly three-year cycle and to set forth more completely the mystery of Christ. The logical consequence has been that the Lectionary contains a larger number of Old and New Testament readings concerning the Blessed Virgin.[31] This numerical increase has not

---

25. Cf. Roman Missal, December 8, Preface.

26. Cf. Roman Missal, August 15, Preface.

27. Cf. Roman Missal, January 1, Prayer after Communion.

28. Cf. Roman Missal, Common of the Blessed Virgin Mary, 6, Paschaltide, Collect.

29. Roman Missal, September 15, Collect.

30. Roman Missal, 31 Mary Collect. On the same lines is the Preface of the Blessed Virgin Mary II: "We do well . . . in celebrating the memory of the Virgin Mary . . . to glorify your love for us in the words of her song of thanksgiving."

31. Cf. Lectionary, III Sunday of Advent (Year C: Zeph 3:14–18a): IV Sunday of Advent (cf. above footnote 12); Sunday within the octave of Christmas (Year A: Mt 2:13–15; Year B: Lk 2:22–40; Year C: Lk 2:41–52); II Sunday after Christmas (Jn 1:1–18); VII Sunday after Easter (Year A: Acts 1:12–14): II Sunday of the Year C: Jn 1:1–12); X Sunday of the Year (Year B: Gen 3:9–15); XIV Sunday of the Year (Year B: Mk 6:1–6).

however been based on random choice: only those readings have been accepted which in different ways and degrees can be considered Marian, either from the evidence of their content or from the results of careful exegesis, supported by the teachings of the magisterium or by solid Tradition. It is also right to observe that these readings occur not only on feasts of the Blessed Virgin but are read on many other occasions, for example on certain Sundays during the liturgical year, in the celebration of rites that deeply concern the Christian's sacramental life and the choices confronting him,[32] as also in the joyful or sad experiences of his life on earth.[33]

13.   The Liturgy of the Hours, the revised book of the Office, also contains outstanding examples of devotion to the Mother of the Lord. These are to be found in the hymns—which include several masterpieces of universal literature, such as Dante's sublime prayer to the Blessed Virgin[34]—and in the antiphons that complete the daily Office. To these lyrical invocations there has been added the well-known prayer *Sub tuum praesidium*, venerable for its antiquity and admirable for its content. Other examples occur in the prayers of intercession at Lauds and Vespers, prayers which frequently express trusting recourse to the Mother of mercy. Finally there are selections from the vast treasury of writings on our Lady composed by authors of the first Christian centuries, of the Middle Ages and of modern times.

14.   The commemoration of the Blessed Virgin occurs often in the Missal, the Lectionary and the Liturgy of the Hours—the hinges of the liturgical prayer of the Roman Rite. In the other revised liturgical books also expressions of love and suppliant veneration addressed to the Theotokos are not lacking. Thus the Church invokes her, the Mother of grace, before immersing candidates in the saving waters of baptism;[35] the Church invokes her intercession for mothers who, full of gratitude for the gift of motherhood, come to church to express their joy;[36] the Church holds her up as a model to those who follow Christ by embracing the religious life[37] or who receive the Consecration of Virgins.[38] For these people the Church asks Mary's motherly assistance.[39] The Church prays fervently to Mary on behalf of her children who have come to the hour of their

---

32. Cf. Lectionary, the catechumenate and baptism of adults: the Lord's Prayer (Second Reading, 2, Gal. 4:47); Christian initiation outside the Easter Vigil (Gospel, 7, Jn 1:1–5; 9–16; 16–18); Nuptial Mass (Gospel, 7, Jn 2:1–11); consecration of Virgins and religious profession (First Reading, 7, Is 61:9–11; Gospel, 6, Mk 3:31–35; Lk 1:26–38 [cf. *Ordo consecrationis virginum* 130; *Ordo professionis religiosae, pars altera*, 145]).

33. Cf. Lectionary, For refugees and exiles (Gospel, 1, Mt 2:13–15; 19–23); In thanksgiving (First Reading, 4, Zeph 3:14–15).

34. Cf. *La Divina Commedia, Paradiso* XXXIII, 1–9; cf. Liturgy of the Hours, remembrance of Our Lady on Saturdays, Office of Reading Hymn.

35. *Ordo baptismi parvulorum*, 48: *Ordo initiationis christiana adultorum*, 214.

36. Cf. *Rituale Romanum*, Tit. VII, cap. III, *De benedictione mulieris post partum*.

37. Cf. *Ordo professionis religiosae*, Pars prior, 57 and 67.

38. Cf. *Ordo consecrationis virginum*, 16.

39. Cf. *Ordo professionis religiosae*, Pars prior, 62 and 142; Pars altera, 67 and 158; *Ordo consecrationis virginum*, 18 and 20.

death.[40] The Church asks Mary's intercession for those who have closed their eyes to the light of this world and appeared before Christ, the eternal Light;"[41] and the Church, through Mary's prayers, invokes comfort upon those who in sorrow mourn with faith the departure of their loved ones.[42]

15.   The examination of the revised liturgical books leads us to the comforting observation that the postconciliar renewal has, as was previously desired by the liturgical movement, properly considered the Blessed Virgin in the mystery of Christ, and, in harmony with tradition, has recognized the singular place that belongs to her in Christian worship as the holy Mother of God and the worthy Associate of the Redeemer.

It could not have been otherwise. If one studies the history of Christian worship, in fact, one notes that both in the East and in the West the highest and purest expressions of devotion to the Blessed Virgin have sprung from the liturgy or have been incorporated into it.

We wish to emphasize the fact that the veneration which the universal Church today accords to blessed Mary is a derivation from and an extension and unceasing increase of the devotion that the Church of every age has paid to her, with careful attention to truth and with an ever watchful nobility of expression. From perennial Tradition kept alive by reason of the uninterrupted presence of the Spirit and continual attention to the Word, the Church of our time draws motives, arguments and incentives for the veneration that she pays to the Blessed Virgin. And the liturgy, which receives approval and strength from the Magisterium, is a most lofty expression and an evident proof of this living Tradition.

SECTION TWO

THE BLESSED VIRGIN AS THE MODEL OF THE CHURCH IN DIVINE WORSHIP

16.   In accordance with some of the guidelines of the Council's teaching on Mary and the Church, we now wish to examine more closely a particular aspect of the relationship between Mary and the liturgy—namely, Mary as a model of the spiritual attitude with which the Church celebrates and lives the divine mysteries. That the Blessed Virgin is an exemplar in this field derives from the fact that she is recognized as a most excellent exemplar of the Church in the order of faith, charity and perfect union with Christ,[43] that is, of that interior disposition with which the Church, the beloved spouse, closely associated with her Lord, invokes Christ and through him worships the eternal Father.[44]

---

40. Cf. *Ordo unctionis infirmorum eorumque pastoralis curae*, 143, 146, 147, 150.

41. Cf. Roman Missal, Masses for the Dead, for dead brothers and sisters, relations and benefactors, Collect.

42. Cf. *Ordo exsequiarum*, 226.

43. Cf. Second Vatican Council, Dogmatic Constitution on the Church, *Lumen gentium*, 63: AAS 57 (1965), p. 64.

44. Cf. Second Vatican Council, Constitution on the Sacred Liturgy, *Sacrosanctum Concilium*, 7: AAS 56 (1964), pp. 100–101.

17.   Mary is the attentive Virgin, who receives the word of God with faith, that faith which in her case was the gateway and path to divine motherhood, for, as Saint Augustine realized, "Blessed Mary by believing conceived Him (Jesus) whom believing she brought forth."[45] In fact, when she received from the angel the answer to her doubt (cf. Lk 1:34–37), "full of faith, and conceiving Christ in her mind before conceiving Him in her womb, she said, 'I am the handmaid of the Lord, let what you have said be done to me' (Lk 1:38)."[46] It was faith that was for her the cause of blessedness and certainty in the fulfillment of the promise: "Blessed is she who believed that the promise made her by the Lord would be fulfilled" (Lk 1:45). Similarly, it was faith with which she, who played a part in the Incarnation and was a unique witness to it, thinking back on the events of the infancy of Christ, meditated upon these events in her heart (cf. Lk 2:19, 51). The Church also acts in this way, especially in the liturgy, when with faith she listens, accepts, proclaims and venerates the word of God, distributes it to the faithful as the bread of life[47] and in the light of that word examines the signs of the times and interprets and lives the events of history.

18.   Mary is also the Virgin in prayer. She appears as such in the visit to the mother of the precursor, when she pours out her soul in expressions glorifying God, and expressions of humility, faith and hope. This prayer is the Magnificat (cf. Lk 1:46–55), Mary's prayer par excellence, the song of the messianic times in which there mingles the joy of the ancient and the new Israel. As St. Irenaeus seems to suggest, it is in Mary's canticle that there was heard once more the rejoicing of Abraham who foresaw the Messiah (cf. Jn 8:56)[48] and there rang out in prophetic anticipation the voice of the Church: "In her exultation Mary prophetically declared in the name of the Church: 'My soul proclaims the glory of the Lord. . . .'"[49] And in fact Mary's hymn has spread far and wide and has become the prayer of the whole Church in all ages.

At Cana, Mary appears once more as the Virgin in prayer: when she tactfully told her Son of a temporal need she also obtained an effect of grace, namely, that Jesus, in working the first of His "signs," confirmed His disciples' faith in Him (cf. Jn 2:1–12).

Likewise, the last description of Mary's life presents her as praying. The apostles "joined in continuous prayer, together with several women, including Mary the mother of Jesus, and with his brothers" (Acts 1:14). We have here the prayerful presence of Mary in the early Church and in the Church throughout all ages, for, having been assumed into heaven, she has not abandoned her mission of intercession and salvation.[50] The title Virgin in prayer also fits the Church, which

---

45. *Sermo* 215, 4: PL 38, 1074.

46. Ibid.

47. Cf. Second Vatican Council, Dogmatic Constitution on Divine Revelation, *Dei Verbum*, 21: AAS 58 (1966), pp. 827–828.

48. Cf. *Adversus haereses* IV, 7, 1: PG 7, 1, 990–991: S Ch. 100, t. II, pp. 454–458.

49. Cf. *Adversus haereses* III, 10, 2: PG 7, 1, 873: S Ch. 34, p. 164.

50. Cf. Second Vatican Council, Dogmatic Constitution on the Church, *Lumen gentium*, 62: AAS 57 (1965), p. 63.

day by day presents to the Father the needs of her children, "praises the Lord unceasingly and intercedes for the salvation of the world."[51]

19.   Mary is also the Virgin-Mother—she who "believing and obeying . . . brought forth on earth the Father's Son. This she did, not knowing man but overshadowed by the Holy Spirit."[52] This was a miraculous motherhood, set up by God as the type and exemplar of the fruitfulness of the Virgin-Church, which "becomes herself a mother. . . . For by her preaching and by baptism she brings forth to a new and immortal life children who are conceived by the power of the Holy Spirit and born of God."[53] The ancient Fathers rightly taught that the Church prolongs in the sacrament of Baptism the virginal motherhood of Mary. Among such references we like to recall that of our illustrious predecessor, Saint Leo the Great, who in a Christmas homily says: "The origin which (Christ took in the womb of the Virgin he has given to the baptismal font: he has given to water what he had given to his Mother—the power of the Most High and the overshadowing of the Holy Spirit (cf. Lk 1:35), which was responsible for Mary's bringing forth the Savior, has the same effect, so that water may regenerate the believer."[54] If we wished to go to liturgical sources, we could quote the beautiful *Illatio* of the Mozarabic liturgy: "The former [Mary] carried Life in her womb; the latter [the Church] bears Life in the waters of baptism. In Mary's members Christ was formed; in the waters of the Church Christ is put on."[55]

20.   Mary is, finally, the Virgin presenting offerings. In the episode of the Presentation of Jesus in the Temple (cf. Lk 2:22–35), the Church, guided by the Spirit, has detected, over and above the fulfillment of the laws regarding the offering of the firstborn (cf. Ex 13:11–16) and the purification of the mother (cf. Lv 12:6–8), a mystery of salvation related to the history of salvation. That is, she has noted the continuity of the fundamental offering that the Incarnate Word made to the Father when He entered the world (cf. Heb 15:5–7). The Church has seen the universal nature of salvation proclaimed, for Simeon, greeting in the Child the light to enlighten the peoples and the glory of the people Israel (cf. Lk 2:32), recognized in Him the Messiah, the Savior of all. The Church has understood the prophetic reference to the Passion of Christ: the fact that Simeon's words, which linked in one prophecy the Son as "the sign of contradiction" (Lk 2:34) and the Mother, whose soul would be pierced by a sword (cf. Lk 2:35), came true on Calvary. A mystery of salvation, therefore, that in its various aspects orients the episode of the Presentation in the Temple to the salvific event of the cross. But the Church herself, in particular from the Middle Ages onwards, has detected in the heart of the Virgin taking her Son to Jerusalem to present

---

51. Second Vatican Council, Constitution on the Sacred Liturgy, *Sacrosanctum Concilium*, 83: AAS 56 (1964), p. 121.

52. Second Vatican Council, Dogmatic Constitution on the Church, *Lumen gentium*, 63: AAS 57 (1965), p. 64.

53. Ibid., 64: AAS 57 (1965), p. 64.

54. *Tractatus XXV (In Nativitate Domini)*, 5: CCL 138, p. 123; S. Ch. 22 bis, p. 132; cf. also *Tractatus XXIX* In *(In Nativitate Domini)* 1: CCL ibid., p. 147; S. Ch. ibid., p. 178; *Tractatus LXIII (De Passione Domini)*, 6: CCL ibid., p. 386; S. Ch. 74, p. 82.

55. M. Ferotin, *Le Liber Mozarabicus Sacramentorum*, col. 56.

him to the Lord (cf. Lk 2:22) a desire to make an offering, a desire that exceeds the ordinary meaning of the rite. A witness to this intuition is found in the loving prayer of Saint Bernard "Offer your Son, holy Virgin, and present to the Lord the blessed fruit of your womb. Offer for the reconciliation of us all the holy Victim which is pleasing to God."[56]

This union of the Mother and the Son in the work of redemption[57] reaches its climax on Calvary, where Christ "offered himself as the perfect sacrifice to God" (Heb 9:14) and where Mary stood by the cross (cf. Jn 19:25), "suffering grievously with her only-begotten Son. There she united herself with a maternal heart to His sacrifice, and lovingly consented to the immolation of this victim which she herself had brought forth"[58] and also was "offering to the eternal Father."[59] To perpetuate down the centuries the Sacrifice of the Cross, the divine Savior instituted the Eucharistic sacrifice, the memorial of his death and resurrection, and entrusted it to his spouse the Church,[60] which, especially on Sundays, calls the faithful together to celebrate the Passover of the Lord until he comes again.[61] This the Church does in union with the saints in heaven and in particular with the Blessed Virgin,[62] whose burning charity and unshakable faith she imitates.

21.   Mary is not only an example for the whole Church in the exercise of divine worship but is also, clearly, a teacher of the spiritual life for individual Christians. The faithful at a very early date began to look to Mary and to imitate her in making their lives an act of worship of God and making their worship a commitment of their lives. As early as the fourth century, St. Ambrose, speaking to the people, expressed the hope that each of them would have the spirit of Mary in order to glory God: "May the heart of Mary be in each Christian to proclaim the greatness of the Lord; may her spirit be in everyone to exult in God."[63] But Mary is above all the example of that worship that consists in making one's life an offering to God. This is an ancient and ever new doctrine that each individual can hear again by heeding the Church's teaching, but also by heeding the very voice of the Virgin as she, anticipating in herself the wonderful petition of the Lord's Prayer—"Your will be done" (Mt 6:10)—replied to God's messenger: "I am the handmaid of the Lord. Let what you have said be done to me" (Lk 1:38).

---

56. *In Purificatione B. Mariae, Sermo III*, 2: PL 183, 370; *Sancti Bernardi Opera*, ed. J. Leclercq-H. Rochais , vol. IV, Rome 1966, p. 342.

57. Cf. Second Vatican Council Dogmatic Constitution on the Church, *Lumen gentium* 57: AAS 57 (1965), p. 61.

58. Ibid., 58: AAS 57 (1965), p. 61.

59. Cf. Pius XII Encyclical Letter *Mystici Corporis*: AAS 35 (1943), p. 247.

60. Cf. Second Vatican Council, Constitution on the Sacred Liturgy, *Sacrosanctum Concilium*, 47: AAS 56 (1964), p. 113.

61. Ibid., 102, 106: AAS 56 (1964), p. 125, 126.

62. ". . . deign to remember all who have been pleasing to you throughout the ages, the holy Fathers, the Patriarchs, Prophets, Apostles . . . and the holy and glorious Mother of God and all the saints . . . may they remember our misery and poverty, and together with us may they offer you this great and unbloody sacrifice": Anaphora *Iacobi fratris Domini syriaca: Prex Eucharistica*, ed. A. Hänggi-I. Pahl, Fribourg, Editions Universitaires, 1968, p. 274.

63. *Expositio Evangelii secundum Lucam*, II 26: CSEL 32, IV, p. 55; S. Ch. 45, pp. 83–84.

And Mary's "yes" is for all Christians a lesson and example of obedience to the will of the Father, which is the way and means of one's own sanctification.

22.   It is also important to note how the Church expresses in various effective attitudes of devotion the many relationships that bind her to Mary: in profound veneration, when she reflects on the singular dignity of the Virgin who, through the action of the Holy Spirit has become Mother of the Incarnate Word; in burning love, when she considers the spiritual motherhood of Mary towards all members of the Mystical Body; in trusting invocation, when she experiences the intercession of her advocate and helper;[64] in loving service, when she sees in the humble handmaid of the Lord the queen of mercy and the mother of grace; in the zealots' imitation, when she contemplates the holiness and virtues of her who is "full of grace" (Lk 1:28); in profound wonder, when she sees in her, "as in a faultless model, that which she herself wholly desires and hopes to be;"[65] in attentive study, when she recognizes in the associate of the Redeemer, who already shares fully in the fruits of the Paschal Mystery, the prophetic fulfillment of her own future, until the day on which, when she has been purified of every spot and wrinkle (cf. Eph 5:27), she will become like a bride arrayed for the bridegroom, Jesus Christ (cf. Rev 21:2).

23.   Therefore, venerable Brothers, as we consider the piety that the liturgical Tradition of the universal Church and the renewed Roman Rite expresses towards the holy Mother of God, and as we remember that the liturgy through its preeminent value as worship constitutes the golden norm for Christian piety, and finally as we observe how the Church when she celebrates the sacred mysteries assumes an attitude of faith and love similar to that of the Virgin, we realize the rightness of the exhortation that the Second Vatican Council addresses to all the children of the Church, namely "that the cult, especially the liturgical cult, of the Blessed Virgin be generously fostered."[66] This is an exhortation that we would like to see accepted everywhere without reservation and put into zealous practice.

PART TWO

THE RENEWAL OF DEVOTION TO MARY

24.   The Second Vatican Council also exhorts us to promote other forms of piety side by side with liturgical worship, especially those recommended by the Magisterium.[67] However, as is well known, the piety of the faithful and their veneration of the Mother of God has taken on many forms according to circumstances of time and place, the different sensibilities of peoples and their different

---

64. Cf. Second Vatican Council, Dogmatic Constitution on the Church, *Lumen gentium*, 62: AAS 57 (1965), p. 63.

65. Cf. Second Vatican Council, Constitution on the Sacred Liturgy, *Sacrosanctum Concilium*, 103: AAS 56 (1964), pp. 125.

66. Cf. Second Vatican Council, Dogmatic Constitution on the Church, *Lumen gentium* 67: AAS 57 (1965), p. 65–66.

67. Cf. ibid.

cultural traditions. Hence it is that the forms in which this devotion is expressed, being subject to the ravages of time, show the need for a renewal that will permit them to substitute elements that are transient, to emphasize the elements that are ever new and to incorporate the doctrinal data obtained from theological reflection and the proposals of the Church's magisterium. This shows the need for episcopal conferences, local churches, religious families and communities of the faithful to promote a genuine creative activity and at the same time to proceed to a careful revision of expressions and exercises of piety directed towards the Blessed Virgin. We would like this revision to be respectful of wholesome tradition and open to the legitimate requests of the people of our time. It seems fitting therefore, venerable Brothers, to put forward some principles for action in this field.

SECTION ONE

TRINITARIAN, CHRISTOLOGICAL AND ECCLESIAL ASPECTS OF DEVOTION TO THE BLESSED VIRGIN

25.   In the first place it is supremely fitting that exercises of piety directed towards the Virgin Mary should clearly express the Trinitarian and Christological note that is intrinsic and essential to them. Christian worship, in fact, is of itself worship offered to the Father and to the Son and to the Holy Spirit, or, as the liturgy puts it, to the Father through Christ in the Spirit. From this point of view worship is rightly extended, though in a substantially different way, first and foremost and in a special manner, to the Mother of the Lord and then to the saints, in whom the Church proclaims the Paschal Mystery, for they have suffered with Christ and have been glorified with Him.[68] In the Virgin Mary everything is relative to Christ and dependent upon Him. It was with a view to Christ that God the Father from all eternity chose her to be the all-holy Mother and adorned her with gifts of the Spirit granted to no one else. Certainly genuine Christian piety has never failed to highlight the indissoluble link and essential relationship of the Virgin to the divine Savior.[69] Yet it seems to us particularly in conformity with the spiritual orientation of our time, which is dominated and absorbed by the "question of Christ,"[70] that in the expressions of devotion to the Virgin the Christological aspect should have particular prominence. It likewise seems to us fitting that these expressions of devotion should reflect God's plan, which laid down "with one single decree the origin of Mary and the Incarnation of the divine Wisdom."[71] This will without doubt contribute to making piety towards the Mother of Jesus more solid, and to making it an effective

---

68. Cf. Second Vatican Council, Constitution on the Sacred Liturgy, *Sacrosanctum Concilium*, 104: AAS 56 (1964), pp. 125–126.

69. Cf. Second Vatican Council, Dogmatic Constitution on the Church, *Lumen gentium*, 66: AAS 57 (1965), p. 65.

70. Cf. Paul VI, Talk of April 24, 1970, in the church of Our Lady of Bonaria in Cagliari: AAS 62 (1970), p. 300.

71. Pius IX, Apostolic Letter *Ineffabilis Deus: Pii IX Pontificis Maximi Acta*, I, 1, Rome 1854, p. 599. Cf. also V. Sardi, *La solenne definizione del dogma dell'Immacolato concepimento di Maria Santissima, Atti e documenti . . .* , Rome 1904–1905, vol. II, p. 302.

instrument for attaining to full "knowledge of the Son of God, until we become the perfect man, fully mature with the fullness of Christ himself" (Eph 4:13). It will also contribute to increasing the worship due to Christ Himself, since, according to the perennial mind of the Church authoritatively repeated in our own day,[72] "what is given to the handmaid is referred to the Lord; thus what is given to the Mother redounds to the Son; . . . and thus what is given as humble tribute to the Queen becomes honor rendered to the King."[73]

26.   It seems to us useful to add to this mention of the Christological orientation of devotion to the Blessed Virgin a reminder of the fittingness of giving prominence in this devotion to one of the essential facts of the Faith: the Person and work of the Holy Spirit. Theological reflection and the liturgy have in fact noted how the sanctifying intervention of the Spirit in the Virgin of Nazareth was a culminating moment of the Spirit's action in the history of salvation. Thus, for example, some Fathers and writers of the Church attributed to the work of the Spirit the original holiness of Mary, who was as it were "fashioned by the Holy Spirit into a kind of new substance and new creature."[74] Reflecting on the Gospel texts—"The Holy Spirit will come upon you and the power of the Most High will cover you with his shadow" (Lk 1:35) and "[Mary] was found to be with child through the Holy Spirit. . . . She has conceived what is in her by the Holy Spirit" (Mt 1:18, 20)—they saw in the Spirit's intervention an action that consecrated and made fruitful Mary's virginity[75] and transformed her into the "Abode of the King" or "Bridal Chamber of the Word,"[76] the "Temple" or "Tabernacle of the Lord,"[77] the "Ark of the Covenant" or "the Ark of Holiness,"[78] titles rich in biblical echoes. Examining more deeply still the mystery of the Incarnation, they saw in the mysterious relationship between the Spirit and Mary an aspect redolent of marriage, poetically portrayed by Prudentius: "The

---

72. Cf. Second Vatican Council, Dogmatic Constitution on the Church, *Lumen gentium*, 66: AAS 57 (1965), p. 65.

73. S. Ildephonsus, *De viginitate perpetua sanctae Mariae*, chapter XII: PL 96, 108.

74. Cf. Second Vatican Council, Dogmatic Constitution on the Church, *Lumen gentium*, 56: AAS 57 (1965), p. 60 and the authors mentioned in note 176 of the document.

75. Cf. St Ambrose, *De Spiritu Sancto II*, 37–38: CSEL 79, pp. 100–101; Cassian, *De incarnatione Domini II*, chapter II: CSEL 17, pp. 247–249; St. Bede, *Homilia* 1, 3: CCL 122, p. 18 and p. 20.

76. Cf. St Ambrose, *De institutione virginis*, chapter XII, 79: PL 16 (ed. 1880), 339; *Epistula 30*, 3 and *Epistula 42*, 7: ibid., 1107 and 1175; *Expositio evangelii secundum Lucam X*, 132. S. Ch. 52, p. 200; S. Proclus of Constantinople, *Oratio I*, 1 and *Oratio V*, 3: PG 65, 681 and 720; St. Basil of Seleucia, *Oratio XXXIX*, 3: PG 85, 433; St. Andrew of Crete, Oratio IV: PG 97, 868; St Germanus of Constantinople, *Oratio IIII*, 15: PG 98, 305.

77. Cf. St. Jerome, *Adversus Iovinianum* I, 33: PL 23, 267; St Ambrose, *Epistula 63*, 33: PL 16 (ed. 1880), 1249; *De institutione virginis*, chapter XVII, 105: ibid., 346; *De Spiritu Sancto III*, 79–80: CSEL 79, pp. 182–183; Sedulius, Hymn "A solis ortus cardine," verses 13–14 CSEL 10, p. 164; *Hymnus Acathistos*, Str. 23; ed. I. B. Pitra, *Analecta Sacra*, I, p. 261; St Produs of Constantanople, *Oratio I*, 3: PG 65, 648; *Oratio II*, 6: ibid., 700; St Basil of Seleucia, *Oratio IV*, *In Nativitatem B. Mariae*: PG 97, 868; St John Damascene, *Oratio IV*, 10: PG 96, 677.

78. Cf. Severus of Antioch, *Homilia* 57: PO 8, pp. 357–358; Hesychius of Jerusalem, *Homilia de sancta Maria Deipara*: PG 93, 1464; Chrysippus of Jerusalem, *Oratio in sanctam Mariam Deiparam*, 2 PO 19, p. 338: St Andrew of Crete, *Oratio V*: PG 97, 896; St John Damascene, *Oratio VI*, 6: PG 96, 972.

unwed Virgin espoused the Spirit,"[79] and they called her the "Temple of the Holy Spirit,"[80] an expression that emphasizes the sacred character of the Virgin, now the permanent dwelling of the Spirit of God. Delving deeply into the doctrine of the Paraclete, they saw that from Him as from a spring there flowed forth the fullness of grace (cf. Lk 1:28) and the abundance of gifts that adorned her. Thus they attributed to the Spirit the faith, hope and charity that animated the Virgin's heart, the strength that sustained her acceptance of the will of God, and the vigor that upheld her in her suffering at the foot of the cross.[81] In Mary's prophetic canticle (cf. Lk 1:46–55) they saw a special working of the Spirit who had spoken through the mouths of the prophets.[82] Considering, finally, the presence of the Mother of Jesus in the Upper Room, where the Spirit came down upon the infant Church (cf. Acts 1:12–14; 2:1–4), they enriched with new developments the ancient theme of Mary and the Church.[83] Above all they had recourse to the Virgin's intercession in order to obtain from the Spirit the capacity for engendering Christ in their own soul, as is attested to by Saint Ildephonsus in a prayer of supplication, amazing in its doctrine and prayerful power: "I beg you, holy Virgin, that I may have Jesus from the Holy Spirit, by whom you brought Jesus forth. May my soul receive Jesus through the Holy Spirit by whom your flesh conceived Jesus. . . . May I love Jesus in the Holy Spirit in whom you adore Jesus as Lord and gaze upon Him as your Son."[84]

27.   It is sometimes said that many spiritual writings today do not sufficiently reflect the whole doctrine concerning the Holy Spirit. It is the task of specialists to verify and weigh the truth of this assertion, but it is our task to exhort everyone, especially those in the pastoral ministry and also theologians, to meditate more deeply on the working of the Holy Spirit in the history of salvation, and to ensure that Christian spiritual writings give due prominence to His life-giving action. Such a study will bring out in particular the hidden relationship

---

79. *Liber Apotheosis*, verses 571–572: CCL 126, p. 97.

80. Cf. S. Isidore, *De ortu et obitu Patrum*, chapter LXVII, 111: PL 83, 148: St Ildephonsus, *De virginitate perpetua sanctae Mariae*, chapter X: PL 96, 95; St Bernard, *In Assumptione B. Virginis Mariae: Sermo IV*, 4: PL 183, 428; *In Nativitate B. Virginis Mariae*: ibid., 442; St Peter Damien, *Carmina sacra et preces II, Oratio ad Deum Filium*: PL 145, 921; Antiphon "Beata Dei Genetrix Maria": *Corpus antiphonalium officii*, ed. R.J. Hesbert, Rome 1970, vol. IV, n. 6314, p. 80.

81. Cf. Paulus Diaconus, *Homilia I, In Assumptione B. Mariae Virginis:* PL 95, 1567: *De Assumptione sanctae Mariae Virginis;* Paschasio Radherto trib., 31, 42, 57, 83: ed. A. Ripberger, in "Spicilegium Friburgense," 9, 1962, pp. 72, 76, 84, 96–97; Eadmer of Canterbury, *De excellentia Virginis Mariae*, chapters IV–V: PL 159, 562–567; St Bernard, *In laudibus Virginis Matris, Homilia IV*, 3: *Sancti Bernardi Opera*, ed. J Leclercq-H. Rochais, IV, Rome 1966, pp. 49–50.

82. Cf. Origen, *In Lucam Homilia VII*, 3: PG 13, 1817; S. Ch. 87, p. 156; St Cyril of Alexandria, *Commentarius in Aggaeum prophetam*, chapter XIX: PG 71, 1060; St Ambrose, *De fide IV 9*, 113–114: CSEL 78, pp. 197–198; *Expositio evangelii secundum Lucam I; 23 and 27–28*: CSEL 32, IV, pp. 53–54 and 55–56; Severianus Gabalensis, *In mundi creationem, Oratio VI*, 10: PG 56, 497–498;" Antipater of Bostra, *Homilia in Sanctissimae Deiparae Annuntiationem*, 16; PG 85, 1785.

83. Cf. Eadmer of Canterbury, *De excellentia Virginis Mariae*, chapter VII: PL 159, 571; St Amedeus of Lausanne, *De Maria Virgini Matre, Homilia VII:* PL 188, 1337; S. Ch. 72, p. 184.

84. *De virginitate perpetua sanctae Mariae*, chapter XII: PL 96, 106.

between the Spirit of God and the Virgin of Nazareth, and show the influence they exert on the Church. From a more profound meditation on the truths of the Faith will flow a more vital piety.

28.   It is also necessary that exercises of piety with which the faithful honor the Mother of the Lord should clearly show the place she occupies in the Church: "the highest place and the closest to us after Christ."[85] The liturgical buildings of Byzantine rite, both in the architectural structure itself and in the use of images, show clearly Mary's place in the Church. On the central door of the iconostasis there is a representation of the Annunciation and in the apse an image of the glorious Theotokos. In this way one perceives how through the assent of the humble handmaid of the Lord mankind begins its return to God and sees in the glory of the all-holy Virgin the goal towards which it is journeying. The symbolism by which a church building demonstrates Mary's place in the mystery of the Church is full of significance and gives grounds for hoping that the different forms of devotion to the Blessed Virgin may everywhere be open to ecclesial perspectives.

The faithful will be able to appreciate more easily Mary's mission in the mystery of the Church and her preeminent place in the communion of saints if attention is drawn to the Second Vatican Council's references to the fundamental concepts of the nature of the Church as the Family of God, the People of God, the Kingdom of God and the Mystical Body of Christ.[86] This will also bring the faithful to a deeper realization of the brotherhood which unites all of them as sons and daughters of the Virgin Mary, "who with a mother's love has cooperated in their rebirth and spiritual formation,"[87] and as sons and daughters of the Church, since "we are born from the Church's womb, we are nurtured by the Church's milk, we are given life by the Church's Spirit."[88] They will also realize that both the Church and Mary collaborate to give birth to the Mystical Body of Christ since "both of them are the Mother of Christ, but neither brings forth the whole (body) independently of the other."[89] Similarly the faithful will appreciate more clearly that the action of the Church in the world can be likened to an extension of Mary's concern. The active love she showed at Nazareth, in the house of Elizabeth, at Cana and on Golgotha—all salvific episodes having vast ecclesial importance—finds its extension in the Church's maternal concern that all men should come to knowledge of the truth (cf. 1 Tm 2:4), in the Church's concern for people in lowly circumstances and for the poor and weak, and in her constant commitment to peace and social harmony, as well as in her untiring efforts to ensure that all men will share in the salvation which was merited for them by Christ's death. Thus love for the Church will become love for Mary, and vice versa, since the one cannot exist without the other, as St. Chromatius

---

85. Second Vatican Council, Dogmatic Constitution on the Church, *Lumen gentium*, 54: AAS 57 (1965), p. 59. Cf. Paulus VI, *Allocutio ad Patres Conciliares habita, altera exacta Concilii Oecumenici Vaticani Secundi Sessione*, December 4, 1963: AAS 56 (1964), p. 37.

86. Second Vatican Council, Dogmatic Constitution on the Church, *Lumen gentium*, 6, 7–8, 9–11: AAS 57 (1965), pp. 8–9, 9–12, 12–21.

87. Ibid., 63: AAS 57 (1965) p. 64.

88. St. Cyprian, *De Catholicae Ecclesiae unitate*, 5: CSEL 3, p. 214.

89. Isaac de Stella, *Sermo LI, In Assumptione B. Mariae*: PL 194, 1863.

of Aquileia observed with keen discernment: "The Church was united . . . in the Upper Room with Mary the Mother of Jesus and with his brethren. The Church therefore cannot be referred to as such unless it includes Mary the Mother of our Lord, together with his brethren."[90] In conclusion, therefore, we repeat that devotion to the Blessed Virgin must explicitly show its intrinsic and ecclesiological content: thus it will be enabled to revise its forms and texts in a fitting way.

SECTION TWO

FOUR GUIDELINES FOR DEVOTION TO THE BLESSED VIRGIN: BIBLICAL, LITURGICAL, ECUMENICAL AND ANTHROPOLOGICAL

29.   The above considerations spring from an examination of the Virgin Mary's relationship with God—the Father and the Son and the Holy Spirit—and with the Church. Following the path traced by conciliar teaching,[91] we wish to add some further guidelines from Scripture, liturgy, ecumenism and anthropology. These are to be borne in mind in any revision of exercises of piety or in the creation of new ones, in order to emphasize and accentuate the bond which unites us to her who is the Mother of Christ and our Mother in the communion of saints.

30.   Today it is recognized as a general need of Christian piety that every form of worship should have a biblical imprint. The progress made in biblical studies, the increasing dissemination of the Sacred Scriptures, and above all the example of Tradition and the interior action of the Holy Spirit are tending to cause the modern Christian to use the Bible ever increasingly as the basic prayerbook, and to draw from it genuine inspiration and unsurpassable examples. Devotion to the Blessed Virgin cannot be exempt from this general orientation of Christian piety;[92] indeed it should draw inspiration in a special way from this orientation in order to gain new vigor and sure help. In its wonderful presentation of God's plan for man's salvation, the Bible is replete with the mystery of the Savior, and from Genesis to the Book of Revelation, also contains clear references to her who was the Mother and associate of the Savior. We would not, however, wish this biblical imprint to be merely a diligent use of texts and symbols skillfully selected from the Sacred Scriptures. More than this is necessary. What is needed is that texts of prayers and chants should draw their inspiration and their wording from the Bible, and above all that devotion to the Virgin should be imbued with the great themes of the Christian message. This will ensure that, as they venerate the Seat of Wisdom, the faithful in their turn will be enlightened by the divine word, and be inspired to live their lives in accordance with the precepts of Incarnate Wisdom.

---

90. *Sermo XXX*, I: S. Ch. 164, p. 134.

91. Cf. Second Vatican Council, Dogmatic Constitution on the Church, *Lumen gentium*, 66–69: AAS 57 (1965), pp. 65–67.

92. Cf. Second Vatican Council, Dogmatic Constitution on Divine Revelation, *Dei Verbum*, 25: AAS 58 (1966), pp. 829–830.

31.   We have already spoken of the veneration which the Church gives to the Mother of God in the celebration of the sacred liturgy. However, speaking of the other forms of devotion and of the criteria on which they should be based we wish to recall the norm laid down in the Constitution *Sacrosanctum concilium*. This document, while wholeheartedly approving of the practices of piety of the Christian people, goes on to say: ". . . it is necessary however that such devotions with consideration for the liturgical seasons should be so arranged as to be in harmony with the sacred liturgy. They should somehow derive their inspiration from it, and because of its preeminence they should orient the Christian people towards it."[93] Although this is a wise and clear rule, its application is not an easy matter, especially in regard to Marian devotions, which are so varied in their formal expressions. What is needed on the part of the leaders of the local communities is effort, pastoral sensitivity and perseverance, while the faithful on their part must show a willingness to accept guidelines and ideas drawn from the true nature of Christian worship; this sometimes makes it necessary to change longstanding customs wherein the real nature of this Christian worship has become somewhat obscured.

In this context we wish to mention two attitudes which in pastoral practice could nullify the norm of the Second Vatican Council. In the first place there are certain persons concerned with the care of souls who scorn a priori devotions of piety which, in their correct forms, have been recommended by the Magisterium, who leave them aside and in this way create a vacuum which they do not fill. They forget that the Council has said that devotions of piety should harmonize with the liturgy, not be suppressed. Secondly there are those who, without wholesome liturgical and pastoral criteria, mix practices of piety and liturgical acts in hybrid celebrations. It sometimes happens that novenas or similar practices of piety are inserted into the very celebration of the Eucharistic Sacrifice. This creates the danger that the Lord's Memorial Rite, instead of being the culmination of the meeting of the Christian community, becomes the occasion, as it were, for devotional practices. For those who act in this way we wish to recall the rule laid down by the Council prescribing that exercises of piety should be harmonized with the liturgy not merged into it. Wise pastoral action should, on the one hand, point out and emphasize the proper nature of the liturgical acts, while on the other hand it should enhance the value of practices of piety in order to adapt them to the needs of individual communities in the Church and to make them valuable aids to the liturgy.

32.   Because of its ecclesial character, devotion to the Blessed Virgin reflects the preoccupations of the Church herself. Among these especially in our day is her anxiety for the reestablishment of Christian unity. In this way devotion to the Mother of the Lord is in accord with the deep desires and aims of the ecumenical movement, that is, it acquires an ecumenical aspect. This is so for a number of reasons.

---

93. Op cit., 13: AAS 56 (1964), p. 103.

In the first place, in venerating with particular love the glorious Theotokos and in acclaiming her as the "Hope of Christians,"[94] Catholics unite themselves with their brethren of the Orthodox Churches, in which devotion to the Blessed Virgin finds its expression in a beautiful lyricism and in solid doctrine. Catholics are also united with Anglicans, whose classical theologians have already drawn attention to the sound scriptural basis for devotion to the Mother of our Lord, while those of the present day increasingly underline the importance of Mary's place in the Christian life. Praising God with the very words of the Virgin (cf. Lk 1:46–55), they are united, too, with their brethren in the Churches of the Reform, where love for the Sacred Scriptures flourishes.

For Catholics, devotion to the Mother of Christ and Mother of Christians is also a natural and frequent opportunity for seeking her intercession with her Son in order to obtain the union of all the baptized within a single People of God.[95] Yet again, the ecumenical aspect of Marian devotion is shown in the Catholic Church's desire that, without in any way detracting from the unique character of this devotion,[96] every care should be taken to avoid any exaggeration which could mislead other Christian brethren about the true doctrine of the Catholic Church.[97] Similarly, the Church desires that any manifestation of cult which is opposed to correct Catholic practice should be eliminated.

Finally, since it is natural that in true devotion to the Blessed Virgin "the Son should be duly known, loved and glorified . . . when the Mother is honored,"[98] such devotion is an approach to Christ, the source and center of ecclesiastical communion, in which all who openly confess that He is God and Lord, Savior and sole Mediator (cf. 1 Tm 2:5) are called to be one, with one another, with Christ and with the Father in the unity of the Holy Spirit.[99]

33.   We realize that there exist important differences between the thought of many of our brethren in other Churches and ecclesial communities and the Catholic doctrine on "Mary's role in the work of salvation."[100] In consequence there are likewise differences of opinion on the devotion which should be shown to her. Nevertheless, since it is the same power of the Most High which overshadowed the Virgin of Nazareth (cf. Lk 1:35) and which today is at work within the ecumenical movement and making it fruitful, we wish to express our confidence that devotion to the humble handmaid of the Lord, in whom the Almighty

94. Cf. *Officium magni canonis paracletici*, *Magnum Orologion*, Athens 1963, p. 558: passim in liturgical canons and prayers: cf. Sophronius Eustradiadou, *Theotokarion*, Chennevières-su-Marne 1931, pp. 9, 19.

95. Cf. Second Vatican Council, Dogmatic Constitution on the Church, *Lumen gentium*, 69: AAS 57 (1965), pp. 66–67.

96. Cf. ibid., 66: AAS 57 (1965), p. 65; Constitution on the Sacred Liturgy, *Sacrosanctum Concilium*, 103: AAS 56 (1964), p. 125.

97. Second Vatican Council, Dogmatic Constitution on the Church, *Lumen gentium*, 67: AAS 57 (1965), pp. 65–66.

98. Ibid., 66: AAS 57 (1965), p. 65.

99. Cf. Paul VI, Address in the Vatican Basilica to the Fathers of the Council, November 21, 1964: AAS 56 (1964), p. 1017.

100. Second Vatican Council, Decree on Ecumenism, *Unitatis redintegratio*, 20: AAS 57 (1965), p. 105.

has done great things (cf. Lk 1:49), will become, even if only slowly, not an obstacle but a path and a rallying point for the union of all who believe in Christ. We are glad to see that, in fact, a better understanding of Mary's place in the mystery of Christ and of the Church on the part also of our separated brethren is smoothing the path to union. Just as at Cana the Blessed Virgin's intervention resulted in Christ's performing His first miracle (cf. Jn 2:1–12), so today her intercession can help to bring to realization the time when the disciples of Christ will again find full communion in faith. This hope of ours is strengthened by a remark of our predecessor Leo XIII, who wrote that the cause of Christian unity "properly pertains to the role of Mary's spiritual motherhood. For Mary did not and cannot engender those who belong to Christ, except in one faith and one love: for 'Is Christ divided?' (1 Cor. 1:13) We must all live together the life of Christ, so that in one and the same body 'we may bear fruit for God' (Rom 7:4)."[101]

34.   Devotion to the Blessed Virgin must also pay close attention to certain findings of the human sciences. This will help to eliminate one of the causes of the difficulties experienced in devotion to the Mother of the Lord, namely, the discrepancy existing between some aspects of this devotion and modern anthropological discoveries and the profound changes which have occurred in the psycho-sociological field in which modern man lives and works. The picture of the Blessed Virgin presented in a certain type of devotional literature cannot easily be reconciled with today's lifestyle, especially the way women live today. In the home, woman's equality and co-responsibility with man in the running of the family are being justly recognized by laws and the evolution of customs. In the sphere of politics women have in many countries gained a position in public life equal to that of men. In the social field women are at work in a whole range of different employments, getting further away every day from the restricted surroundings of the home. In the cultural field new possibilities are opening up for women in scientific research and intellectual activities.

In consequence of these phenomena some people are becoming disenchanted with devotion to the Blessed Virgin and finding it difficult to take as an example Mary of Nazareth because the horizons of her life, so they say, seem rather restricted in comparison with the vast spheres of activity open to mankind today. In this regard we exhort theologians, those responsible for the local Christian communities and the faithful themselves to examine these difficulties with due care. At the same time we wish to take the opportunity of offering our own contribution to their solution by making a few observations.

35.   First, the Virgin Mary has always been proposed to the faithful by the Church as an example to be imitated, not precisely in the type of life she led, and much less for the socio-cultural background in which she lived and which today scarcely exists anywhere. She is held up as an example to the faithful rather for the way in which, in her own particular life, she fully and responsibly accepted the will of God (cf. Lk 1:38), because she heard the word of God and acted on it, and because charity and a spirit of service were the driving force of her actions. She is worthy of imitation because she was the first and the

---

101. Encyclical Letter, *Adiutricem Populi*: AAS 28 (1895–1896), p. 135.

most perfect of Christ's disciples. All of this has a permanent and universal exemplary value.

36.   Secondly, we would like to point out that the difficulties alluded to above are closely related to certain aspects of the image of Mary found in popular writings. They are not connected with the Gospel image of Mary nor with the doctrinal data which have been made explicit through a slow and conscientious process of drawing from Revelation. It should be considered quite normal for succeeding generations of Christians in differing sociocultural contexts to have expressed their sentiments about the Mother of Jesus in a way and manner which reflected their own age. In contemplating Mary and her mission these different generations of Christians, looking on her as the New Woman and perfect Christian, found in her as a virgin, wife and mother the outstanding type of womanhood and the preeminent exemplar of life lived in accordance with the Gospels and summing up the most characteristic situations in the life of a woman. When the Church considers the long history of Marian devotion she rejoices at the continuity of the element of cult which it shows, but she does not bind herself to any particular expression of an individual cultural epoch or to the particular anthropological ideas underlying such expressions. The Church understands that certain outward religious expressions, while perfectly valid in themselves, may be less suitable to men and women of different ages and cultures.

37.   Finally, we wish to point out that our own time, no less than former times, is called upon to verify its knowledge of reality with the word of God, and, keeping to the matter at present under consideration, to compare its anthropological ideas and the problems springing therefrom with the figure of the Virgin Mary as presented by the Gospel. The reading of the divine Scriptures, carried out under the guidance of the Holy Spirit, and with the discoveries of the human sciences and the different situations in the world today being taken into account, will help us to see how Mary can be considered a mirror of the expectations of the men and women of our time. Thus, the modern woman, anxious to participate with decision-making power in the affairs of the community, will contemplate with intimate joy Mary who, taken into dialogue with God, gives her active and responsible consent,[102] not to the solution of a contingent problem, but to that "event of world importance," as the Incarnation of the Word has been rightly called.[103] The modern woman will appreciate that Mary's choice of the state of virginity, which in God's plan prepared her for the mystery of the Incarnation, was not a rejection of any of the values of the married state but a courageous choice which she made in order to consecrate herself totally to the love of God. The modern woman will note with pleasant surprise that Mary of Nazareth, while completely devoted to the will of God, was far from being a timidly submissive woman or one whose piety was repellent to others; on the contrary, she was a woman who did not hesitate to proclaim that God vindicates the humble and the oppressed, and removes the powerful people of this world from their privileged positions (cf. Lk 1:51–53). The modern woman will recognize in Mary,

102. Second Vatican Council, Dogmatic Constitution on the Church, *Lumen gentium*, 56: AAS 57 (1965), p. 60.
103. Cf. St Peter Chrysologus, *Sermo CXLIII*: PL 52, 583.

who "stands out among the poor and humble of the Lord,"[104] a woman of strength, who experienced poverty and suffering, flight and exile (cf. Mt 2:13–23). These are situations that cannot escape the attention of those who wish to support, with the Gospel spirit, the liberating energies of man and of society. And Mary will appear not as a Mother exclusively concerned with her own divine Son, but rather as a woman whose action helped to strengthen the apostolic community's faith in Christ (cf. Jn 2:1–12), and whose maternal role was extended and became universal on Calvary.[105] These are but examples, but examples which show clearly that the figure of the Blessed Virgin does not disillusion any of the profound expectations of the men and women of our time but offers them the perfect model of the disciple of the Lord: the disciple who builds up the earthly and temporal city while being a diligent pilgrim towards the heavenly and eternal city; the disciple who works for that justice which sets free the oppressed and for that charity which assists the needy; but above all, the disciple who is the active witness of that love which builds up Christ in people's hearts.

38.   Having offered these directives, which are intended to favor the harmonious development of devotion to the Mother of the Lord, we consider it opportune to draw attention to certain attitudes of piety which are incorrect. The Second Vatican Council has already authoritatively denounced both the exaggeration of content and form which even falsifies doctrine and likewise the small-mindedness which obscures the figure and mission of Mary. The Council has also denounced certain devotional deviations, such as vain credulity, which substitutes reliance on merely external practices for serious commitment. Another deviation is sterile and ephemeral sentimentality, so alien to the spirit of the Gospel that demands persevering and practical action.[106] We reaffirm the Council's reprobation of such attitudes and practices. They are not in harmony with the Catholic Faith and therefore they must have no place in Catholic worship. Careful defense against these errors and deviations will render devotion to the Blessed Virgin more vigorous and more authentic. It will make this devotion solidly based, with the consequence that study of the sources of Revelation and attention to the documents of the Magisterium will prevail over the exaggerated search for novelties or extraordinary phenomena. It will ensure that this devotion is objective in its historical seeing, and for this reason everything that is obviously legendary or false must be eliminated. It will ensure that this devotion matches its doctrinal content—hence the necessity of avoiding a one-sided presentation of the figure of Mary, which by overstressing one element compromises the overall picture given by the Gospel. It will make this devotion clear in its motivation; hence every unworthy self-interest is to be carefully banned from the area of what is sacred.

104. Second Vatican Council, Dogmatic Constitution on the Church, *Lumen gentium*, 55: AAS 57 (1965), pp. 59–60.
105. Cf. Paul VI Apostolic Constitution, *Signum Magnum*, I: AAS 59 (1967), pp. 467–468; Roman Missal, September 15, Prayer over the gifts.
106. Second Vatican Council, Dogmatic Constitution on the Church, *Lumen gentium*, 67: AAS 57 (1965), pp. 65–66.

39.   Finally, insofar as it may be necessary we would like to repeat that the ultimate purpose of devotion to the Blessed Virgin is to glorify God and to lead Christians to commit themselves to a life which is in absolute conformity with His will. When the children of the Church unite their voices with the voice of the unknown woman in the Gospel and glorify the Mother of Jesus by saying to Him: "Blessed is the womb that bore you and the breasts that you sucked" (Lk 11:27), they will be led to ponder the Divine Master's serious reply: "Blessed rather are those who hear the word of God and keep it!" (Lk 11:28). While it is true that this reply is in itself lively praise of Mary, as various Fathers of the Church interpreted it[107] and the Second Vatican Council has confirmed,[108] it is also an admonition to us to live our lives in accordance with God's command-ments. It is also an echo of other words of the Savior: "Not every one who says to me 'Lord, Lord,' will enter the kingdom of heaven, but he who does the will of my Father who is in heaven" (Mt 7:21); and again: "You are my friends if you do what I command you" (Jn 15:14).

PART THREE

OBSERVATIONS ON TWO EXERCISES OF PIETY: THE ANGELUS AND THE ROSARY

40.   We have indicated a number of principles which can help to give fresh vigor to devotion to the Mother of the Lord. It is now up to episcopal conferences, to those in charge of local communities and to the various religious congregations prudently to revise practices and exercises of piety in honor of the Blessed Virgin, and to encourage the creative impulse of those who through genuine religious inspiration or pastoral sensitivity wish to establish new forms of piety. For dif-ferent reasons we nevertheless feel it is opportune to consider here two practices which are widespread in the West, and with which this Apostolic See has con-cerned itself on various occasions: the Angelus and the Rosary.

THE ANGELUS

41.   What we have to say about the Angelus is meant to be only a simple but earnest exhortation to continue its traditional recitation wherever and whenever possible. The Angelus does not need to be revised, because of its simple struc-ture, its biblical character, its historical origin which links it to the prayer for peace and safety, and its quasi-liturgical rhythm which sanctifies different moments during the day, and because it reminds us of the Paschal Mystery, in which recalling the Incarnation of the Son of God we pray that we may be led "through his passion and cross to the glory of his resurrection."[109] These factors ensure that the Angelus, despite the passing of centuries, retains an unaltered

---

107. St Augustine, *In Iohannis Evangelium, Tractatus X*, 3; CCL 36, pp. 101–102; Epistula 243, *Ad Laetum*, 9: CSEL 57, pp. 575–576; St Bede, *In Lucae Evangelium expositio*, IV, XI, 28: CCL 120, p. 237; *Homilia I*, 4: CCL 122, pp. 26–27.

108. Second Vatican Council, Dogmatic Constitution on the Church, *Lumen gentium*, 58: AAS 57 (1965), p. 61.

109. Roman Missal, IV Sunday of Advent, Collect. Similarly the Collect of March 25, which may be used in place of the previous one in the recitation of the Angelus.

value and an intact freshness. It is true that certain customs traditionally linked with the recitation of the Angelus have disappeared or can continue only with difficulty in modern life. But these are marginal elements. The value of contemplation on the mystery of the Incarnation of the Word, of the greeting to the Virgin, and of recourse to her merciful intercession remains unchanged. And despite the changed conditions of the times, for the majority of people there remain unaltered the characteristic periods of the day—morning, noon and evening—which mark the periods of their activity and constitute an invitation to pause in prayer.

THE ROSARY

42.   We wish now, venerable Brothers, to dwell for a moment on the renewal of the pious practice which has been called "the compendium of the entire Gospel"[110]: the Rosary. To this our predecessors have devoted close attention and care. On many occasions they have recommended its frequent recitation, encouraged its diffusion, explained its nature, recognized its suitability for fostering contemplative prayer—prayer of both praise and petition—and recalled its intrinsic effectiveness for promoting Christian life and apostolic commitment.

We, too, from the first general audience of our pontificate on July 13, 1963, have shown our great esteem for the pious practice of the Rosary.[111] Since that time we have underlined its value on many different occasions, some ordinary, some grave. Thus, at a moment of anguish and uncertainty, we published the Letter *Christi Matri* (September 15, 1966), in order to obtain prayers to Our Lady of the Rosary and to implore from God the supreme benefit of peace.[112] "We renewed this appeal in our Apostolic Exhortation *Recurrens mensis October* (October 7, 1969), in which we also commemorated the fourth centenary of the Apostolic Letter *Consueverunt Romani pontifices* of our predecessor Saint Pius V, who in that document explained and in a certain sense established the traditional form of the Rosary.[113]

43.   Our assiduous and affectionate interest in the Rosary has led us to follow very attentively the numerous meetings which in recent years have been devoted to the pastoral role of the Rosary in the modern world, meetings arranged by associations and individuals profoundly attached to the Rosary and attended by bishops, priests, religious and lay people of proven experience and recognized ecclesial awareness. Among these people special mention should be made of the sons of Saint Dominic, by tradition the guardians and promoters of this very salutary practice. Parallel with such meetings has been the research work of historians, work aimed not at defining in a sort of archaeological fashion the primitive form of the Rosary but at uncovering the original inspiration and driving force behind it and its essential structure. The fundamental characteristics

---

110. Pius XII, Letter to the Archbishop of Manila, "Philippinas Insulas": AAS 38 (1946), p. 419.
111. Discourse to the participants in the III Dominican International Rosary Congress: *Insegnamenti di Paolo VI*, 1, (1963) pp. 463–464.
112. In AAS 58 (1966), pp. 745–749.
113. In AAS 61 (1969), pp. 649–654.

of the Rosary, its essential elements and their mutual relationship have all emerged more clearly from these congresses and from the research carried out.

44.   Thus, for instance, the Gospel inspiration of the Rosary has appeared more clearly: the Rosary draws from the Gospel the presentation of the mysteries and its main formulas. As it moves from the angel's joyful greeting and the Virgin's pious assent, the Rosary takes its inspiration from the Gospel to suggest the attitude with which the faithful should recite it. In the harmonious succession of Hail Marys the Rosary puts before us once more a fundamental mystery of the Gospel—the Incarnation of the Word, contemplated at the decisive moment of the Annunciation to Mary. The Rosary is thus a Gospel prayer, as pastors and scholars like to define it, more today perhaps than in the past.

45.   It has also been more easily seen how the orderly and gradual unfolding of the Rosary reflects the very way in which the Word of God, mercifully entering into human affairs, brought about the Redemption. The Rosary considers in harmonious succession the principal salvific events accomplished in Christ, from His virginal conception and the mysteries of His childhood to the culminating moments of the Passover—the blessed passion and the glorious resurrection—and to the effects of this on the infant Church on the day of Pentecost, and on the Virgin Mary when at the end of her earthly life she was assumed body and soul into her heavenly home. It has also been observed that the division of the mysteries of the Rosary into three parts not only adheres strictly to the chronological order of the facts but above all reflects the plan of the original proclamation of the Faith and sets forth once more the mystery of Christ in the very way in which it is seen by Saint Paul in the celebrated "hymn" of the Letter to the Philippians—kenosis, death and exaltation (cf. 2:6–11).

46.   As a Gospel prayer, centered on the mystery of the redemptive Incarnation, the Rosary is therefore a prayer with a clearly Christological orientation. Its most characteristic element, in fact, the litany-like succession of Hail Marys, becomes in itself an unceasing praise of Christ, who is the ultimate object both of the angel's announcement and of the greeting of the mother of John the Baptist: "Blessed is the fruit of your womb" (Lk 1:42). We would go further and say that the succession of Hail Marys constitutes the warp on which is woven the contemplation of the mysteries. The Jesus that each Hail Mary recalls is the same Jesus whom the succession of the mysteries proposes to us—now as the Son of God, now as the Son of the Virgin—at his birth in a stable at Bethlehem, at his presentation by his Mother in the Temple, as a youth full of zeal for his Father's affairs, as the Redeemer in agony in the garden, scourged and crowned with thorns, carrying the cross and dying on Calvary, risen from the dead and ascended to the glory of the Father to send forth the gift of the Spirit. As is well known, at one time there was a custom, still preserved in certain places, of adding to the name of Jesus in each Hail Mary reference to the mystery being contemplated. And this was done precisely in order to help contemplation and to make the mind and the voice act in unison.

47.   There has also been felt with greater urgency the need to point out once more the importance of a further essential element in the Rosary, in addition

to the value of the elements of praise and petition, namely the element of contemplation. Without this the Rosary is a body without a soul, and its recitation is in danger of becoming a mechanical repetition of formulas and of going counter to the warning of Christ: "And in praying do not heap up empty phrases as the Gentiles do; for they think that they will be heard for their many words" (Mt 6:7). By its nature the recitation of the Rosary calls for a quiet rhythm and a lingering pace, helping the individual to meditate on the mysteries of the Lord's life as seen through the eyes of her who was closest to the Lord. In this way the unfathomable riches of these mysteries are unfolded.

48.   Finally, as a result of modern reflection the relationships between the liturgy and the Rosary have been more clearly understood. On the one hand it has been emphasized that the Rosary is, as it were, a branch sprung from the ancient trunk of the Christian liturgy, the Psalter of the Blessed Virgin, whereby the humble were associated in the Church's hymn of praise and universal intercession. On the other hand it has been noted that this development occurred at a time—the last period of the Middle Ages—when the liturgical spirit was in decline and the faithful were turning from the liturgy towards a devotion to Christ's humanity and to the Blessed Virgin Mary, a devotion favoring a certain external sentiment of piety. Not many years ago some people began to express the desire to see the Rosary included among the rites of the liturgy, while other people, anxious to avoid repetition of former pastoral mistakes, unjustifiably disregarded the Rosary. Today the problem can easily be solved in the light of the principles of the Constitution *Sacrosanctum Concilium*. Liturgical celebrations and the pious practice of the Rosary must be neither set in opposition to one another nor considered as being identical.[114] The more an expression of prayer preserves its own true nature and individual characteristics, the more fruitful it becomes. Once the preeminent value of liturgical rites has been reaffirmed it will not be difficult to appreciate the fact that the Rosary is a practice of piety which easily harmonizes with the liturgy. In fact, like the liturgy, it is of a community nature, draws its inspiration from Sacred Scripture and is oriented towards the mystery of Christ. The commemoration in the liturgy and the contemplative remembrance proper to the Rosary, although existing on essentially different planes of reality, have as their object the same salvific events wrought by Christ. The former presents new, under the veil of signs and operative in a hidden way, the great mysteries of our Redemption. The latter, by means of devout contemplation, recalls these same mysteries to the mind of the person praying and stimulates the will to draw from them the norms of living. Once this substantial difference has been established, it is not difficult to understand that the Rosary is an exercise of piety that draws its motivating force from the liturgy and leads naturally back to it, if practiced in conformity with its original inspiration. It does not, however, become part of the liturgy. In fact, meditation on the mysteries of the Rosary, by familiarizing the hearts and minds of the faithful with the mysteries of Christ, can be an excellent preparation for the creation of those same mysteries in the liturgical action and an also become a continuing echo thereof. However, it is a mistake to recite the Rosary during

114. Cf. 13: AAS 56 (1964), pp. 103.

the celebration of the liturgy, though unfortunately this practice still persists here and there.

49.   The Rosary of the Blessed Virgin Mary, according to the tradition accepted by our predecessor St. Pius V and authoritatively taught by him, consists of various elements disposed in an organic fashion:

a) Contemplation in communion with Mary, of a series of mysteries of salvation, wisely distributed into three cycles. These mysteries express the joy of the messianic times, the salvific suffering of Christ and the glory of the Risen Lord which fills the Church. This contemplation by its very nature encourages practical reflection and provides stimulating norms for living.

b) The Lord's Prayer, or Our Father, which by reason of its immense value is at the basis of Christian prayer and ennobles that prayer in its various expressions.

c) The litany-like succession of the Hail Mary, which is made up of the angel's greeting to the Virgin (cf. Lk 1:28), and of Elizabeth's greeting (cf. Lk 1:42), followed by the ecclesial supplication, Holy Mary. The continued series of Hail Marys is the special characteristic of the Rosary, and their number, in the full and typical number of one hundred and fifty, presents a certain analogy with the Psalter and is an element that goes back to the very origin of the exercise of piety. But this number, divided, according to a well-tried custom, into decades attached to the individual mysteries, is distributed in the three cycles already mentioned, thus giving rise to the Rosary of fifty Hail Marys as we know it. This latter has entered into use as the normal measure of the pious exercise and as such has been adopted by popular piety and approved by papal authority, which also enriched it with numerous indulgences.

d) The doxology Glory be to the Father which, in conformity with an orientation common to Christian piety concludes the prayer with the glorifying of God who is one and three, from whom, through whom and in whom all things have their being (cf. Rom 11:36).

50.   These are the elements of the Rosary. Each has its own particular character which, wisely understood and appreciated, should be reflected in the recitation in order that the Rosary may express all its richness and variety. Thus the recitation will be grave and suppliant during the Lord's Prayer, lyrical and full of praise during the tranquil succession of Hail Marys, contemplative in the recollected meditation on the mysteries and full of adoration during the doxology. This applies to all the ways in which the Rosary is usually recited: privately, in intimate recollection with the Lord; in community, in the family or in groups of the faithful gathered together to ensure the special presence of the Lord (cf. Mt 18:20); or publicly, in assemblies to which the ecclesial community is invited.

51. In recent times certain exercises of piety have been created which take their inspiration from the Rosary. Among such exercises we wish to draw attention to and recommend those which insert into the ordinary celebration of the word of God some elements of the Rosary, such as meditation on the mysteries and litany-like repetition of the angel's greeting to Mary. In this way these elements gain in importance, since they are found in the context of Bible readings, illustrated with a homily, accompanied by silent pauses and emphasized with song. We are happy to know that such practices have helped to promote a more complete understanding of the spiritual riches of the Rosary itself and have served to restore esteem for its recitation among youth associations and movements.

52. We now desire, as a continuation of the thought of our predecessors, to recommend strongly the recitation of the family Rosary. The Second Vatican Council has pointed out how the family, the primary and vital cell of society, "shows itself to be the domestic sanctuary of the Church through the mutual affection of its members and the common prayer they offer to God."[115] The Christian family is thus seen to be a "domestic Church"[116] if its members, each according to his proper place and tasks, all together promote justice, practice works of mercy, devote themselves to helping their brethren, take part in the apostolate of the wider local community and play their part in its liturgical worship.[117] This will be all the more true if together they offer up prayers to God. If this element of common prayer were missing, the family would lack its very character as a domestic Church. Thus there must logically follow a concrete effort to reinstate communal prayer in family life if there is to be a restoration of the theological concept of the family as the domestic Church.

53. In accordance with the directives of the Council the *Institutio Generalis de Liturgia Horarum* rightly numbers the family among the groups in which the Divine Office can suitably be celebrated in community: "It is fitting . . . that the family, as a domestic sanctuary of the Church, should not only offer prayers to God in common, but also, according to circumstances, should recite parts of the Liturgy of the Hours, in order to be more intimately linked with the Church."[118] No avenue should be left unexplored to ensure that this clear and practical recommendation finds within Christian families growing and joyful acceptance.

54. But there is no doubt that, after the celebration of the Liturgy of the Hours, the high point which family prayer can reach, the Rosary should be considered as one of the best and most efficacious prayers in common that the Christian family is invited to recite. We like to think, and sincerely hope, that when the family gathering becomes a time of prayer, the Rosary is a frequent and favored manner of praying. We are well aware that the changed conditions of life today

---

115. Decree on the Lay Apostolate, *Apostolicam actuositatem*, 11: AAS 58 (1966), p. 848.

116. Second Vatican Council, Dogmatic Constitution on the Church, *Lumen gentium*, 11: AAS 57 (1965), p. 16.

117. Cf. Second Vatican Council, Decree on the Lay Apostolate, *Apostolicam actuositatem*, 11: AAS 58 (1966), p. 848.

118. Op. cit., 27.

do not make family gatherings easy, and that even when such a gathering is possible many circumstances make it difficult to turn it into an occasion of prayer. There is no doubt of the difficulty. But it is characteristic of the Christian in his manner of life not to give in to circumstances but to overcome them, not to succumb but to make an effort. Families which want to live in full measure the vocation and spirituality proper to the Christian family must therefore devote all their energies to overcoming the pressures that hinder family gatherings and prayer in common.

55.   In concluding these observations, which give proof of the concern and esteem which the Apostolic See has for the Rosary of the Blessed Virgin, we desire at the same time to recommend that this very worthy devotion should not be propagated in a way that is too one-sided or exclusive. The Rosary is an excellent prayer, but the faithful should feel serenely free in its regard. They should be drawn to its calm recitation by its intrinsic appeal.

CONCLUSION

THEOLOGICAL AND PASTORAL VALUE OF DEVOTION TO THE BLESSED VIRGIN

56.   Venerable Brothers, as we come to the end of this our Apostolic Exhortation we wish to sum up and emphasize the theological value of devotion to the Blessed Virgin and to recall briefly its pastoral effectiveness for renewing the Christian way of life.

The Church's devotion to the Blessed Virgin is an intrinsic element of Christian worship. The honor which the Church has always and everywhere shown to the Mother of the Lord, from the blessing with which Elizabeth greeted Mary (cf. Lk 1:42–45) right up to the expressions of praise and petition used today, is a very strong witness to the Church's norm of prayer and an invitation to become more deeply conscious of her norm of faith. And the converse is likewise true. The Church's norm of faith requires that her norm of prayer should everywhere blossom forth with regard to the Mother of Christ. Such devotion to the Blessed Virgin is firmly rooted in the revealed word and has solid dogmatic foundations. It is based on the singular dignity of Mary, "Mother of the Son of God, and therefore beloved daughter of the Father and Temple of the Holy Spirit—Mary, who, because of this extraordinary grace, is far greater than any other creature on earth or in heaven."[119] This devotion takes into account the part she played at decisive moments in the history of the salvation which her Son accomplished, and her holiness, already full at her Immaculate Conception yet increasing all the time as she obeyed the will of the Father and accepted the path of suffering (cf. Lk 2:34–35, 41–52; Jn 19:25–27), growing constantly in faith, hope and charity. Devotion to Mary recalls too her mission and the special position she holds within the People of God, of which she is the preeminent member, a shining example and the loving Mother; it recalls her unceasing and efficacious intercession which, although she is assumed into heaven, draws her close to those

---

119. Second Vatican Council, Dogmatic Constitution on the Church, *Lumen gentium*, 53: AAS 57 (1965), pp. 58–59.

who ask her help, including those who do not realize that they are her children. It recalls Mary's glory which ennobles the whole of mankind, as the outstanding phrase of Dante recalls: "You have so ennobled human nature that its very Creator did not disdain to share in it."[120] Mary, in fact, is one of our race, a true daughter of Eve—though free of that mother's sin—and truly our sister, who as a poor and humble woman fully shared our lot.

We would add further that devotion to the Blessed Virgin finds its ultimate justification in the unfathomable and free will of God who, being eternal and divine charity (cf. 1 Jn 4:7–8, 16), accomplishes all things according to a loving design. He loved her and did great things for her (cf. Lk 1:49). He loved her for his own sake, and he loved her for our sake, too; he gave her to himself and he gave her also to us.

57.   Christ is the only way to the Father (cf. Jn 14:4–11), and the ultimate example to whom the disciple must conform his own conduct (cf. Jn 13:15), to the extent of sharing Christ's sentiments (cf. Phil 2:5), living His life and possessing his Spirit (cf. Gal 2 20; Rom 8:10–11). The Church has always taught this and nothing in pastoral activity should obscure this doctrine. But the Church, taught by the Holy Spirit and benefiting from centuries of experience, recognizes that devotion to the Blessed Virgin, subordinated to worship of the divine Savior and in connection with it, also has a great pastoral effectiveness and constitutes a force for renewing Christian living. It is easy to see the reason for this effectiveness: Mary's many-sided mission to the People of God is a supernatural reality which operates and bears fruit within the body of the Church. One finds cause for joy in considering the different aspects of this mission, and seeing how each of these aspects with its individual effectiveness is directed towards the same end, namely, producing in the children the spiritual characteristics of the firstborn Son. The Virgin's maternal intercession, her exemplary holiness and the divine grace which is in her become for the human race a reason for divine hope.

The Blessed Virgin's role as Mother leads the People of God to turn with filial confidence to her who is ever ready to listen with a mother's affection and efficacious assistance.[121] Thus the People of God have learned to call on her as the Consoler of the afflicted, the Health of the sick, and the Refuge of sinners, that they may find comfort in tribulation, relief in sickness and liberating strength in guilt. For she, who is free from sin, leads her children to combat sin with energy and resoluteness.[122] This liberation from sin and evil (cf. Mt 6:13)—it must be repeated—is the necessary premise for any renewal of Christian living.

The Blessed Virgin's exemplary holiness encourages the faithful to "raise their eyes to Mary who shines forth before the whole community of the elect as a model of the virtues."[123] It is a question of solid, evangelical virtues: faith and the docile acceptance of the Word of God (cf. Lk 1:26–38, 1:45, 11:27–28; Jn 2:5);

---

120. *La Divina Commedia, Paradiso XXXIII*, 4–6.
121. Cf. Second Vatican Council, Dogmatic Constitution on the Church, *Lumen gentium*, 60–63: AAS 57 (1965), pp. 62–64.
122. Cf. ibid., 65: AAS 57 (1965), pp. 64–65.
123. Ibid., 65: AAS 57 (1965), p. 64.

generous obedience (cf Lk 1:38); genuine humility (cf. Lk 1:48); solicitous charity (cf. Lk 1:39–56); profound wisdom (cf. Lk 1:29, 34; 2:19, 33:51); worship of God manifested in alacrity in the fulfillment of religious duties (cf. Lk 2:21–41), in gratitude for gifts received (cf. Lk 1:46–49), in her offering in the Temple (cf. Lk 2:22–24) and in her prayer in the midst of the apostolic community (cf. Acts 1:12–14); her fortitude in exile (cf. Mt 2:13–23) and in suffering (cf. Lk 2:34–35, 49; Jn 19:25); her poverty reflecting dignity and trust in God (cf. Lk 1:48, 2:24) her attentive care for her Son, from his humble birth to the ignominy of the cross (cf. Lk 2:1–7; Jn 19:25–27); her delicate forethought (cf. Jn. 2:1–11); her virginal purity (cf. Mt 1:18–25; Lk 1:26–38); her strong and chaste married love. These virtues of the Mother will also adorn her children who steadfastly study her example in order to reflect it in their own lives. And this progress in virtue will appear as the consequence and the already mature fruit of that pastoral zeal which springs from devotion to the Blessed Virgin.

Devotion to the Mother of the Lord becomes for the faithful an opportunity for growing in divine grace, and this is the ultimate aim of all pastoral activity. For it is impossible to honor her who is "full of grace" (Lk 1:28) without thereby honoring in oneself the state of grace, which is friendship with God, communion with him and the indwelling of the Holy Spirit. It is this divine grace which takes possession of the whole man and conforms him to the image of the Son of God (cf. Rom 8:29; Col 1:18). The Catholic Church, endowed with centuries of experience, recognizes in devotion to the Blessed Virgin a powerful aid for man as he strives for fulfillment. Mary, the New Woman, stands at the side of Christ, the New Man, within whose mystery the mystery of man[124] alone finds true light; she is given to it as a pledge and guarantee that God's plan in Christ for the salvation of the whole man has already achieved realization in a creature: in her. Contemplated in the episodes of the Gospels and in the reality which she already possesses in the City of God, the Blessed Virgin Mary offers a calm vision and a reassuring word to modern man, torn as he often is between anguish and hope, defeated by the sense of his own limitations and assailed by limitless aspirations, troubled in his mind and divided in his heart, uncertain before the riddle of death, oppressed by loneliness while yearning for fellowship, a prey to boredom and disgust. She shows forth the victory of hope over anguish, of fellowship over solitude, of peace over anxiety, of joy and beauty over boredom and disgust, of eternal visions over earthly ones, of life over death.

Let the very words that she spoke to the servants at the marriage feast of Cana, "Do whatever he tells you" (Jn 2:5), be a seal on our Exhortation and a further reason in favor of the pastoral value of devotion to the Blessed Virgin as a means of leading men to Christ. Those words, which at first sight were limited to the desire to remedy an embarrassment at the feast, are seen in the context of Saint John's Gospel to reecho the words used by the people of Israel to give approval to the Covenant at Sinai (cf. Ex 19:8, 24:3, 7; Dt 5:27) and to renew their commitments (cf. Jos 24:24; Ezr 10:12; Neh 5:12). And they are words which harmonize

---

124. Cf. Second Vatican Council, Pastoral Constitution on the Church in the Modern World, *Gaudium et spes*, 22: AAS 58 (1966), pp. 1042–1044.

wonderfully with those spoken by the Father at the theophany on Mount Tabor: "Listen to him" (Mt 17:5).

EPILOGUE

58.   Venerable Brothers, we have dealt at length with an integral element of Christian worship: devotion to the Mother of the Lord. This has been called for by the nature of the subject, one which in these recent years has been the object of study and revision and at times the cause of some perplexity. We are consoled to think that the work done by this Apostolic See and by yourselves in order to carry out the norms of the Council—particularly the liturgical reform—is a stepping stone to an ever more lively and adoring worship of God, the Father and the Son and the Holy Spirit, and to an increase of the Christian life of the faithful. We are filled with confidence when we note that the renewed Raman liturgy, also taken as a whole, is a splendid illustration of the Church's devotion to the Blessed Virgin. We are upheld by the hope that the directives issued in order to render this devotion ever more pure and vigorous will be applied with sincerity. We rejoice that the Lord has given us the opportunity of putting forward some points for reflection in order to renew and confirm esteem for the practice of the Rosary. Comfort, confidence, hope and joy are the sentiments which we wish to transform into fervent praise and thanksgiving to the Lord as we unite our voice with that of the Blessed Virgin in accordance with the prayer of the Roman Liturgy.

Dear Brothers, while we express the hope that, thanks to your generous commitment, there will be among the clergy and among the people entrusted to your care a salutary increase of devotion to Mary with undoubted profit for the Church and for society, we cordially impart our special apostolic blessing to yourselves and to all the faithful people to whom you devote your pastoral zeal.

Given in Rome, at Saint Peter's, on the second day of February, the Feast of the Presentation of the Lord, in the year 1974, the eleventh of our Pontificate.

PAULUS PP. VI[125]

---

125. Cf. Roman Missal, May 31, Collect.

ROSARIUM VIRGINIS MARIAE
ON THE MOST HOLY ROSARY

APOSTOLIC LETTER
POPE JOHN PAUL II
OCTOBER 16, 2002

AN OVERVIEW OF
ROSARIUM VIRGINIS MARIAE

Rev. Thomas P. Looney, CSC

"Not only does this prayer not conflict with the Liturgy, *it sustains it*, since it serves as an excellent introduction and a faithful echo of the Liturgy, enabling people to participate fully and interiorly in it and to reap its fruits in their daily lives."
—*Rosarium Virginis Mariae*, 4

On October 16, 2002, Pope John Paul II promulgated the apostolic letter, *Rosarium Virginis Mariae* (RVM). In this letter the pope calls the Catholic faithful to a deeper appreciation of the Rosary as a means of contemplative prayer and proposes the addition of the Luminous Mysteries to the prayer's traditional pattern. In a world that hungers for spirituality and where many Christians find themselves drawn to contemplative methods of prayer espoused in non-Christian religions, John Paul II proposes that the Rosary is a privileged method of contemplation that can enable Christian communities to become "genuine schools of prayer."[1]

Christian contemplation has a Christological focus, an ecclesial context, and an anthropological vision. We, as Christians, look to Christ in the midst of the community of faith to discern the true meaning of our humanity trusting that the power of the Spirit, despite our human weakness, can conform us to Christ. The Rosary embodies each of these dimensions and thereby is a profoundly Christian form of contemplation. Through an examination of the contemplative aspects of the Rosary, this essay will explain how this traditional and loved devotion draws the faithful deeper into the mysteries of Christ as encountered most fully in the liturgical rites of the Church.

THE ROSARY'S CHRISTOLOGICAL FOCUS

The Christological dimension of the Rosary is the strongest emphasis in Pope John Paul II's apostolic letter. The text emphasizes three aspects of the Rosary's Christological focus: its focus on the person of Christ, its scriptural foundation, and its invitation to conform our minds and hearts to the mind and heart of Christ.

Pope John Paul II describes the Rosary as an opportunity to contemplate with Mary "the beauty of the face of Christ" and to experience "the depths of his love."[2] The Rosary is a personal encounter of Christ with and through Mary. It seems that at the heart of the pope's intention in expanding the traditional form of the Rosary to include the Luminous Mysteries is precisely to emphasize that the Rosary is by its very nature a contemplation of the life of Christ. The

---

1. *Rosarium Virginis Mariae* (RVM), 5.
2. Ibid., 1.

Luminous Mysteries proclaim in a profound way that Jesus "is the definitive revelation of God."[3] The ultimate object of contemplation for all the individual mysteries of the Rosary, even the Assumption and Coronation of Mary, is the person of Christ. In the Joyful Mysteries, for example, "Mary leads us to discover the secret of Christian joy, reminding us that Christianity is, first and foremost, *euangelion*, 'good news', which has as its heart and its whole content the person of Jesus Christ, the Word made flesh, the one Saviour of the world."[4]

Even in the great prayer directed to Mary, the *Ave Maria*, the name of Jesus forms and constitutes its center. In fact, in order to emphasize this, the pope recommends the practice of inserting a Christological phrase that amplifies the meaning of the particular mystery being contemplated.[5] The very structure of the beads themselves "converge upon the Crucifix" ever reminding us that "everything begins from him, everything leads towards him, everything, through him, in the Holy Spirit, attains to the Father."[6]

The Rosary's Christological dimension is also emphasized by the pope's assertion that the Rosary is a compendium of the Gospel.[7] John Paul II suggests that the recitation of the Rosary does not supplant the need for a prayerful reading of the Scripture but, in fact, requires and presupposes it.[8] The Rosary leads to a prayerful remembrance of the events of the life, ministry, Death, and Resurrection of Jesus. This relatively short apostolic letter contains over one hundred and fifty references to the Scripture that highlight the value of prayer in the life of the believer and that focus on the events of the life of Jesus. The Rosary is a prayer that reminds the Christian both of the dynamic movement of prayer itself, as well as the foundational events in the life of Jesus of Nazareth.

In order to emphasize the importance of a scriptural basis for the Rosary, the pope suggests that in its communal recitation biblical passages related to the mystery be proclaimed in the assembly for: "No other words can ever match the efficacy of the inspired word."[9]

The Rosary's focus on the person of Christ and its scriptural foundation point to the element that distinguishes Christian contemplation from all other forms, the "disciple's commitment to become conformed ever more fully to his Master (cf. Rom 8:29; Phil 3:10, 12)."[10] In responding to the Spirit's call to conform ourselves to Christ, the taking up of the Rosary is a privileged means of coming to a deeper knowledge of the mind and the heart of Christ. For in praying with Mary we are joined to the human being whose life was most perfectly conformed to Christ. Christians are not only encouraged by her example of absolute fidelity in discipleship, but are blessed with the presence of her maternal affection. Mary's maternal care enables us to engage the Gospel demand of conformity to Christ within the context of friendship.[11] Our relationship with

---

3. Ibid., 19.
4. Ibid., 20.
5. See ibid., 33.
6. Ibid., 36.
7. See ibid., 1.
8. See ibid., 29.
9. Ibid., 30.
10. Ibid., 15.
11. See ibid.

Mary fostered through the Rosary enables us to meet the challenges of the Christian life. Mary continues to proclaim to us the message she proclaimed to the waiters at the wedding feast in Cana: "Do whatever he tells you (Jn 2:5)."[12] United in prayer in the school of Mary, the believer trusts that Mary will continually point us to Christ so that our hearts and minds will be more deeply conformed to the heart and mind of her Son.

THE ROSARY'S ECCLESIAL CONTEXT

In addition to the strong Christological focus attributed to the Rosary, Pope John Paul II emphasizes its ecclesial context. The praying of the Rosary is by its very nature an ecclesial event for it is prayed in the company of Mary, member and Mother of the Church; it leads us to contemplate the truths of faith and to be molded and formed by them; and it prepares us to enter more deeply into the sacred liturgy and to contemplate the fruits of the liturgical celebration.

In this letter Pope John Paul II emphasizes the Marian character of the Church and of the Church's prayer. Since the Church is the community of those who are conformed to Christ by the outpouring of the Holy Spirit, and Mary is the human being most fully conformed to Christ, she is a preeminent member of the Church. And since Mary intercedes for the outpouring of the Holy Spirit on all believers she is *the perfect icon of the motherhood on the Church.*"[13] The Church is the locus of the dispensation of grace. Mary is totally subordinate to Christ for she is a recipient of his redemptive grace, but she also shares a privileged position in the distribution of grace. Mary is both Mother and member of the Church, the fellowship of grace. Pope John Paul II writes, "She who is both the Mother of Christ and a member of the Church, indeed her 'pre-eminent and altogether singular member', is at the same time the 'Mother of the Church.'"[14] Thus, to sit in the school of Mary and to contemplate with her the face of Christ is to be engaged in a profoundly ecclesial action. Since the Lord's Prayer forms the foundation of the Rosary and anchors its Marian and Christological dimensions, even the private recitation of the Rosary is "an ecclesial experience."[15] In particular, it is contemplation of the mystery of Pentecost that "reveals the face of the Church as a family gathered together with Mary, enlivened by the outpouring of the Spirit and ready for the mission of evangelization."[16] The Church's mission of evangelization is nourished as Mary invites us to keep our attention fixed upon her Son. Mary, in fact, sustains the very prayer of the Church itself; a prayer whose initial impetus arises in believers' hearts by the spirit of Christ. It was to her care that the "dying Redeemer entrusted, in the person of the beloved disciple, all the sons and daughters of the Church: 'Woman, behold your son!' (Jn 19:26)."[17]

The Rosary has an essential ecclesial context for its prayerful recitation invites us to contemplate the truths of Christian faith and to be molded and

---

12. Ibid., 21.
13. Ibid., 15.
14. Ibid.
15. Ibid., 32.
16. Ibid., 23.
17. Ibid., 7.

shaped in the power of their remembrance. John Paul II proposes a fundamental Marian perspective on the mysteries of faith. When we attend to the Lord in prayer with Mary "she continues to relate her personal account of the Gospel. *Mary constantly sets before the faithful the 'mysteries' of her Son,* with the desire that the contemplation of those mysteries will release all their saving power."[18] Through the Rosary the truths of Christian faith are called to mind so that believers might be shaped by them: The Incarnation, the Eucharistic mystery, the redemptive suffering of Jesus, and the resurrection of the body, are recalled in reflections based upon the various mysteries. The Church's faith in the fatherhood of God, the Trinity, and the *Theotokos* are recalled in the recitation of the prayers themselves. Each mystery, as well as the prayers recited, has a Christological reference that enables us to grasp the heart of the Christian mystery: "the Mystery of the Word made flesh, in whom 'all the fullness of God dwells bodily' (Col 2:9)."[19] In coming to know the truths of Christ we come to know the deepest truths about ourselves. "Anyone who contemplates Christ through the various stages of his life cannot fail to perceive in him *the truth about man.*"[20]

THE ROSARY'S ANTHROPOLOGICAL VISION

In addition to its Christological focus and ecclesial context, John Paul II emphasizes the anthropological vision at the heart of the Rosary. The Rosary is truly contemplative: It deeply respects all of the dimensions of human personhood; it draws us into the psychological dynamics of the nature of love; it evokes a wide variety of human sentiments; and it provides both a mantra of prayerful recitation as well as the silence that enables believers to encounter Christ in the depth of the soul.

Pope John Paul II emphasizes the manner in which the Rosary respects the truths of the human person both on a theoretical and on a practical level. On the theoretical level, he asserts that it is in the contemplation of the person of Christ that the Lord reveals to us what it means to be truly human. He writes, "Following in the path of Christ, in whom man's path is 'recapitulated', revealed and redeemed, believers come face to face with the image of the true man."[21] On a practical level, Pope John Paul II stresses that the Rosary is a valid method of prayer for, like all true contemplative prayer, "it normally engages the whole person in all his complex psychological, physical and relational reality."[22]

In a very profound way the Rosary enables us to experience the heart of true relationship, the love that God has bestowed upon us in Christ. Its profound calling to mind of the truth and implications of the Incarnation enables believers to grow in appreciation of the unfathomable love of God. The pope states, "In Christ, God has truly assumed a 'heart of flesh'. Not only does God have a divine heart, rich in mercy and in forgiveness, but also a human heart, capable

18. Ibid., 11.
19. Ibid., 24.
20. Ibid., 25.
21. Ibid., 25.
22. Ibid., 27.

of all the stirrings of affection."[23] As we recall in prayer the depths of Christ's affection for us, our prayer becomes more deeply an active love for the Lord who first loved us. To pray the Hail Mary is to be taken up into an "outpouring of that love."[24] To pray the Rosary, prompted by the Spirit, and sustained by Mary's presence, is to be embraced by the dynamics of a divine and a human love.

THE ROSARY AND THE LITURGY

At the heart of this knowledge of the deepest truths about humanity is the realization of the need for salvation. Humans need and long for the saving encounter of the presence of the living God. It is the Church's faith that in the celebration of the liturgy we encounter in a most profound way the presence of Christ in the Spirit that effects salvation—the forgiveness of sin. Although the Rosary is not a liturgical or sacramental encounter, John Paul II, drawing on Pope Paul VI, stresses that its proper recitation not only does "not conflict with the Liturgy, *it sustains it,* since it serves as an excellent introduction and faithful echo of the Liturgy, enabling people to participate fully and interiorly in it and to reap its fruits in their daily lives."[25] John Paul II draws upon the biblical understanding of remembrance expressed by the Hebrew word *zakar* to emphasize the manner in which Spirit-empowered memory makes the gift and offer of salvation present in the moment. In an analogous sense, meditation on the mysteries of the Rosary "in a spirit of faith and love is to be open to the grace which Christ won for us by the mysteries of his life, death and resurrection."[26] While the liturgy is a saving action par excellence, "the Rosary too, as a 'meditation' with Mary on Christ, is a *salutary contemplation.*"[27] Since all genuine prayer is prompted by grace and moves us to encounter with Christ in the Spirit, it becomes a preparation for deeper encounter with Christ in the liturgy and enables us to tap into the fruits of the liturgical celebration in our lives.

The theological context of the Rosary is rooted ultimately in the inherently relational nature of Christian experience. In this letter John Paul II stresses that our relationship with Christ automatically places us in relationship with his Mother, who is both member of the Church with us and Mother of the Church for us. Mary, a symbol of faithful discipleship and of the community of disciples, continues to lead us to Christ. She summons us to "do whatever he tells you,"[28] so that the eschatological goal of the Church may come to completion; a completion that is related to the believer's conformity to Christ's vision for humanity.

In praying the Rosary one gazes with Mary in a loving manner upon the various experiences of the life of her Son and comes to share with her a variety of human emotions. John Paul II describes Mary's gaze as *"a questioning look,"*

---

23. Ibid., 26.
24. Ibid.
25. Ibid., 4.
26. Ibid., 13.
27. Ibid.
28. John 2:5.

"a penetrating gaze," "a look of sorrow," "a gaze radiant with the joy of the resurrection," and the *"gaze afire* with the outpouring of the Spirit."[29] In the praying of the Rosary we may feel perplexed, united with our beloved, completely known, saddened beyond belief, joyful beyond words, or afire with love. In all of these emotions we share something of Mary's experience of her Son. As we bring to our prayer the emotional and psychological truth of our present moment, we may find—either in a commensurate emotion or in one that contradicts our experience—the comfort or challenge, respectively, that we need to live more deeply in Christ.

It is precisely the mantra of the prayerful recitation and the opportunities for silence provided by the Rosary that enable us to see our lives more clearly in relationship to the person of Jesus. Pope John Paul II parallels the offering of the Rosary to the dynamics of the Jesus prayer that so deeply informs Eastern Christian tradition.[30] In the silence of our hearts, informed by the backdrop of the truths of our faith and of the mysteries of Christ's life, we find ourselves attuned to the saving reality of the Father's love for us. In coming to the quiet, we are embraced and empowered by love.

Like all truly Christian contemplation the ultimate object of the Rosary is conformity to the Christ whom we have come to know at the heart of our prayer. As we come to know him more deeply, we are compelled to take up the fruit of his redemptive love and to give our lives to the service of the kingdom he proclaimed.

The contemplative dimension of the Rosary ultimately leads those who pray it to take on the mind and the heart of Christ, to be conformed more deeply to the Good News of the one born in time at the moment of Mary's fiat.

---

29. RVM, 10.
30. See ibid., 5.

OUTLINE

APOSTOLIC LETTER
ROSARIUM VIRGINIS MARIAE

OF THE SUPREME PONTIFF
JOHN PAUL II

TO THE BISHOPS, CLERGY
AND FAITHFUL
ON THE MOST HOLY ROSARY

INTRODUCTION

1.   The Rosary of the Virgin Mary, which gradually took form in the second millennium under the guidance of the Spirit of God, is a prayer loved by countless Saints and encouraged by the Magisterium. Simple yet profound, it still remains, at the dawn of this third millennium, a prayer of great significance, destined to bring forth a harvest of holiness. It blends easily into the spiritual journey of the Christian life, which, after two thousand years, has lost none of the freshness of its beginnings and feels drawn by the Spirit of God to "set out into the deep" (*duc in altum!*) in order once more to proclaim, and even cry out, before the world that Jesus Christ is Lord and Savior, "the way, and the truth and the life" (Jn 14:6), "the goal of human history and the point on which the desires of history and civilization turn."[1]

The Rosary, though clearly Marian in character, is at heart a Christocentric prayer. In the sobriety of its elements, it has all the *depth of the Gospel message in its entirety*, of which it can be said to be a compendium.[2] It is an echo of the prayer of Mary, her perennial *Magnificat* for the work of the redemptive Incarnation which began in her virginal womb. With the Rosary, the Christian people *sits at the school of Mary* and is led to contemplate the beauty of the face of Christ and to experience the depths of his love. Through the Rosary the faithful receive abundant grace, as though from the very hands of the Mother of the Redeemer.

THE POPES AND THE ROSARY

2.   Numerous predecessors of mine attributed great importance to this prayer. Worthy of special note in this regard is Pope Leo XIII who on September 1, 1883

---

1. Pastoral Constitution on the Church in the Modern World *Gaudium et spes*, 45.
2. Pope Paul VI, Apostolic Exhortation *Marialis cultus* (February 2, 1974), 42: AAS 66 (1974), 153.

promulgated the Encyclical *Supremi apostolatus officio*,[3] a document of great worth, the first of his many statements about this prayer, in which he proposed the Rosary as an effective spiritual weapon against the evils afflicting society. Among the more recent Popes who, from the time of the Second Vatican Council, have distinguished themselves in promoting the Rosary I would mention Blessed John XXIII[4] and above all Pope Paul VI, who in his Apostolic Exhortation *Marialis cultus* emphasized, in the spirit of the Second Vatican Council, the Rosary's evangelical character and its Christocentric inspiration. I myself have often encouraged the frequent recitation of the Rosary. From my youthful years this prayer has held an important place in my spiritual life. I was powerfully reminded of this during my recent visit to Poland, and in particular at the Shrine of Kalwaria. The Rosary has accompanied me in moments of joy and in moments of difficulty. To it I have entrusted any number of concerns; in it I have always found comfort. Twenty-four years ago, on October 29, 1978, scarcely two weeks after my election to the See of Peter, I frankly admitted: "The Rosary is my favorite prayer. A marvelous prayer! Marvelous in its simplicity and its depth. . . . It can be said that the Rosary is, in some sense, a prayer-commentary on the final chapter of the Vatican II Constitution *Lumen gentium*, a chapter which discusses the wondrous presence of the Mother of God in the mystery of Christ and the Church. Against the background of the words *Ave Maria* the principal events of the life of Jesus Christ pass before the eyes of the soul. They take shape in the complete series of the joyful, sorrowful and glorious mysteries, and they put us in living communion with Jesus through—we might say—the heart of his Mother. At the same time our heart can embrace in the decades of the Rosary all the events that make up the lives of individuals, families, nations, the Church, and all mankind. Our personal concerns and those of our neighbors, especially those who are closest to us, who are dearest to us. Thus the simple prayer of the Rosary marks the rhythm of human life."[5]

With these words, dear brothers and sisters, I set *the first year of my Pontificate* within the daily rhythm of the Rosary. Today, *as I begin the twenty-fifth year of my service as the Successor of Peter*, I wish to do the same. How many graces have I received in these years from the Blessed Virgin through the Rosary: *Magnificat anima mea Dominum!* I wish to lift up my thanks to the Lord in the words of his Most Holy Mother, under whose protection I have placed my Petrine ministry: *Totus tuus!*

OCTOBER 2002–OCTOBER 2003: THE YEAR OF THE ROSARY

3.   Therefore, in continuity with my reflection in the Apostolic Letter *Novo millennio ineunte*, in which, after the experience of the Jubilee, I invited the people of God to "start afresh from Christ,"[6] I have felt drawn to offer a reflection on the Rosary, as a kind of Marian complement to that Letter and an exhortation

---

3. Cf. *Acta Leonis XIII*, 3 (1884), 280–289.

4. Particularly worthy of note is his Apostolic Epistle on the Rosary *Il religioso convegno* (September 29, 1961): AAS 53 (1961), 641–647.

5. Angelus: *Insegnamenti di Giovanni Paolo II*, I (1978): 75–76.

6. AAS 93 (2001), 285.

to contemplate the face of Christ in union with, and at the school of, his Most Holy Mother. To recite the Rosary is nothing other than to *contemplate with Mary the face of Christ*. As a way of highlighting this invitation, prompted by the forthcoming 120th anniversary of the aforementioned Encyclical of Leo XIII, I desire that during the course of this year the Rosary should be especially emphasized and promoted in the various Christian communities. I therefore proclaim the year from October 2002 to October 2003 *the Year of the Rosary*.

I leave this pastoral proposal to the initiative of each ecclesial community. It is not my intention to encumber but rather to complete and consolidate pastoral programs of the Particular Churches. I am confident that the proposal will find a ready and generous reception. The Rosary, reclaimed in its full meaning, goes to the very heart of Christian life; it offers a familiar yet fruitful spiritual and educational opportunity for personal contemplation, the formation of the People of God, and the new evangelization. I am pleased to reaffirm this also in the joyful remembrance of another anniversary: the fortieth anniversary of the opening of the Second Vatican Ecumenical Council on October 11, 1962, the "great grace" disposed by the Spirit of God for the Church in our time.[7]

OBJECTIONS TO THE ROSARY

4.   The timeliness of this proposal is evident from a number of considerations. First, the urgent need to counter a certain crisis of the Rosary, which in the present historical and theological context can risk being wrongly devalued, and therefore no longer taught to the younger generation. There are some who think that the centrality of the Liturgy, rightly stressed by the Second Vatican Ecumenical Council, necessarily entails giving lesser importance to the Rosary. Yet, as Pope Paul VI made clear, not only does this prayer not conflict with the Liturgy, *it sustains it*, since it serves as an excellent introduction and a faithful echo of the Liturgy, enabling people to participate fully and interiorly in it and to reap its fruits in their daily lives.

Perhaps too, there are some who fear that the Rosary is somehow unecumenical because of its distinctly Marian character. Yet the Rosary clearly belongs to the kind of veneration of the Mother of God described by the Council: a devotion directed to the Christological center of the Christian faith, in such a way that "when the Mother is honored, the Son . . . is duly known, loved and glorified."[8] If properly revitalized, the Rosary is an aid and certainly not a hindrance to ecumenism!

A PATH OF CONTEMPLATION

5.   But the most important reason for strongly encouraging the practice of the Rosary is that it represents a most effective means of fostering among the faithful that *commitment to the contemplation of the Christian mystery* which I

---

7. During the years of preparation for the Council, Pope John XXIII did not fail to encourage the Christian community to recite the Rosary for the success of this ecclesial event: cf. Letter to the Cardinal Vicar (September 28, 1960): AAS 52 (1960), 814–816.

8. Dogmatic Constitution on the Church *Lumen gentium*, 66.

have proposed in the Apostolic Letter *Novo millennio ineunte* as a genuine "training in holiness": "What is needed is a Christian life distinguished above all in the *art of prayer*."[9] Inasmuch as contemporary culture, even amid so many indications to the contrary, has witnessed the flowering of a new call for spirituality, due also to the influence of other religions, it is more urgent than ever that our Christian communities should become "genuine schools of prayer."[10]

The Rosary belongs among the finest and most praiseworthy traditions of Christian contemplation. Developed in the West, it is a typically meditative prayer, corresponding in some way to the "prayer of the heart" or "Jesus prayer" which took root in the soil of the Christian East.

PRAYER FOR PEACE AND FOR THE FAMILY

6.   A number of historical circumstances also make a revival of the Rosary quite timely. First of all, the need to implore from God *the gift of peace*. The Rosary has many times been proposed by my predecessors and myself as a prayer for peace. At the start of a millennium which began with the terrifying attacks of September 11, 2001, a millennium which witnesses every day in numerous parts of the world fresh scenes of bloodshed and violence, to rediscover the Rosary means to immerse oneself in contemplation of the mystery of Christ who "is our peace," since he made "the two of us one, and broke down the dividing wall of hostility" (Eph 2:14). Consequently, one cannot recite the Rosary without feeling caught up in a clear commitment to advancing peace, especially in the land of Jesus, still so sorely afflicted and so close to the heart of every Christian.

A similar need for commitment and prayer arises in relation to another critical contemporary issue: *the family*, the primary cell of society, increasingly menaced by forces of disintegration on both the ideological and practical planes, so as to make us fear for the future of this fundamental and indispensable institution and, with it, for the future of society as a whole. The revival of the Rosary in Christian families, within the context of a broader pastoral ministry to the family, will be an effective aid to countering the devastating effects of this crisis typical of our age.

"BEHOLD, YOUR MOTHER!" (JN 19:27)

7.   Many signs indicate that still today the Blessed Virgin desires to exercise through this same prayer that maternal concern to which the dying Redeemer entrusted, in the person of the beloved disciple, all the sons and daughters of the Church: "Woman, behold your son!" (Jn 19:26). Well-known are the occasions in the nineteenth and the twentieth centuries on which the Mother of Christ made her presence felt and her voice heard, in order to exhort the People of God to this form of contemplative prayer. I would mention in particular, on account of their great influence on the lives of Christians and the authoritative recognition they have received from the Church, the apparitions of Lourdes and of

---

9. No. 32: AAS 93 (2001), 288.

10. Ibid., 33: loc. cit., 289.

Fatima;[11] these shrines continue to be visited by great numbers of pilgrims seeking comfort and hope.

8.   It would be impossible to name all the many Saints who discovered in the Rosary a genuine path to growth in holiness. We need but mention Saint Louis Marie Grignion de Montfort, the author of an excellent work on the Rosary,[12] and, closer to ourselves, Padre Pio of Pietrelcina, whom I recently had the joy of canonizing. As a true apostle of the Rosary, Blessed Bartolo Longo had a special charism. His path to holiness rested on an inspiration heard in the depths of his heart: "Whoever spreads the Rosary is saved!"[13] As a result, he felt called to build a Church dedicated to Our Lady of the Holy Rosary in Pompei, against the background of the ruins of the ancient city, which scarcely heard the proclamation of Christ before being buried in 79 A.D. during an eruption of Mount Vesuvius, only to emerge centuries later from its ashes as a witness to the lights and shadows of classical civilization. By his whole life's work and especially by the practice of the "Fifteen Saturdays," Bartolo Longo promoted the Christocentric and contemplative heart of the Rosary, and received great encouragement and support from Leo XIII, the "Pope of the Rosary."

CHAPTER I
CONTEMPLATING CHRIST WITH MARY

A FACE RADIANT AS THE SUN

9.   "And he was transfigured before them, and his face shone like the sun" (Mt 17:2). The Gospel scene of Christ's transfiguration, in which the three Apostles Peter, James and John appear entranced by the beauty of the Redeemer, can be seen as *an icon of Christian contemplation*. To look upon the face of Christ, to recognize its mystery amid the daily events and the sufferings of his human life, and then to grasp the divine splendor definitively revealed in the Risen Lord, seated in glory at the right hand of the Father: this is the task of every follower of Christ and therefore the task of each one of us. In contemplating Christ's face we become open to receiving the mystery of Trinitarian life, experiencing ever anew the love of the Father and delighting in the joy of the Holy Spirit. Saint Paul's words can then be applied to us: "Beholding the glory of the Lord, we are being changed into his likeness, from one degree of glory to another; for this comes from the Lord who is the Spirit" (2 Cor 3:18).

---

11. It is well-known and bears repeating that private revelations are not the same as public revelation, which is binding on the whole Church. It is the task of the Magisterium to discern and recognize the authenticity and value of private revelations for the piety of the faithful.

12. *The Secret of the Rosary.*

13. Blessed Bartolo Longo, *Storia del Santuario di Pompei*, Pompei, 1990, 59.

10.   The contemplation of Christ has an *incomparable model* in Mary. In a unique way the face of the Son belongs to Mary. It was in her womb that Christ was formed, receiving from her a human resemblance which points to an even greater spiritual closeness. No one has ever devoted himself to the contemplation of the face of Christ as faithfully as Mary. The eyes of her heart already turned to him at the Annunciation, when she conceived him by the power of the Holy Spirit. In the months that followed she began to sense his presence and to picture his features. When at last she gave birth to him in Bethlehem, her eyes were able to gaze tenderly on the face of her Son, as she "wrapped him in swaddling cloths, and laid him in a manger" (Lk 2:7).

Thereafter Mary's gaze, ever filled with adoration and wonder, would never leave him. At times it would be *a questioning look*, as in the episode of the finding in the Temple: "Son, why have you treated us so?" (Lk 2:48); it would always be *a penetrating gaze*, one capable of deeply understanding Jesus, even to the point of perceiving his hidden feelings and anticipating his decisions, as at Cana (cf. Jn 2:5). At other times it would be *a look of sorrow*, especially beneath the Cross, where her vision would still be that of a mother giving birth, for Mary not only shared the passion and death of her Son, she also received the new son given to her in the beloved disciple (cf. Jn 19:26–27). On the morning of Easter hers would be *a gaze radiant with the joy of the Resurrection*, and finally, on the day of Pentecost, *a gaze afire* with the outpouring of the Spirit (cf. Acts 1:14).

MARY'S MEMORIES

11.   Mary lived with her eyes fixed on Christ, treasuring his every word: "She kept all these things, pondering them in her heart" (Lk 2:19; cf. 2:51). The memories of Jesus, impressed upon her heart, were always with her, leading her to reflect on the various moments of her life at her Son's side. In a way those memories were to be the "rosary" which she recited uninterruptedly throughout her earthly life.

Even now, amid the joyful songs of the heavenly Jerusalem, the reasons for her thanksgiving and praise remain unchanged. They inspire her maternal concern for the pilgrim Church, in which she continues to relate her personal account of the Gospel. *Mary constantly sets before the faithful the "mysteries" of her Son*, with the desire that the contemplation of those mysteries will release all their saving power. In the recitation of the Rosary, the Christian community enters into contact with the memories and the contemplative gaze of Mary.

THE ROSARY, A CONTEMPLATIVE PRAYER

12.   The Rosary, precisely because it starts with Mary's own experience, is *an exquisitely contemplative prayer*. Without this contemplative dimension, it would lose its meaning, as Pope Paul VI clearly pointed out: "Without contemplation, the Rosary is a body without a soul, and its recitation runs the risk of becoming a mechanical repetition of formulas, in violation of the admonition of Christ: 'In praying do not heap up empty phrases as the Gentiles do; for they

think they will be heard for their many words' (Mt 6:7). By its nature the recitation of the Rosary calls for a quiet rhythm and a lingering pace, helping the individual to meditate on the mysteries of the Lord's life as seen through the eyes of her who was closest to the Lord. In this way the unfathomable riches of these mysteries are disclosed."[14]

It is worth pausing to consider this profound insight of Paul VI, in order to bring out certain aspects of the Rosary which show that it is really a form of Christocentric contemplation.

REMEMBERING CHRIST WITH MARY

13. Mary's contemplation is above all *a remembering*. We need to understand this word in the biblical sense of remembrance (*zakar*) as a making present of the works brought about by God in the history of salvation. The Bible is an account of saving events culminating in Christ himself. These events not only belong to "yesterday;" *they are also part of the "today" of salvation*. This making present comes about above all in the Liturgy: what God accomplished centuries ago did not only affect the direct witnesses of those events; it continues to affect people in every age with its gift of grace. To some extent this is also true of every other devout approach to those events: to "remember" them in a spirit of faith and love is to be open to the grace which Christ won for us by the mysteries of his life, death and resurrection.

Consequently, while it must be reaffirmed with the Second Vatican Council that the Liturgy, as the exercise of the priestly office of Christ and an act of public worship, is "the summit to which the activity of the Church is directed and the font from which all its power flows,"[15] it is also necessary to recall that the spiritual life "is not limited solely to participation in the liturgy. Christians, while they are called to prayer in common, must also go to their own rooms to pray to their Father in secret (cf. Mt 6:6); indeed, according to the teaching of the Apostle, they must pray without ceasing (cf. 1 Thes 5:17)."[16] The Rosary, in its own particular way, is part of this varied panorama of "ceaseless" prayer. If the Liturgy, as the activity of Christ and the Church, is *a saving action par excellence*, the Rosary too, as a "meditation" with Mary on Christ, is *a salutary contemplation*. By immersing us in the mysteries of the Redeemer's life, it ensures that what he has done and what the liturgy makes present is profoundly assimilated and shapes our existence.

LEARNING CHRIST FROM MARY

14. Christ is the supreme Teacher, the revealer and the one revealed. It is not just a question of learning what he taught but of *"learning him."* In this regard could we have any better teacher than Mary? From the divine standpoint, the Spirit is the interior teacher who leads us to the full truth of Christ (cf. Jn 14:26; 15:26; 16:13). But among creatures no one knows Christ better than Mary; no

---

14. Apostolic Exhortation *Marialis cultus* (February 2, 1974), 47: AAS (1974), 156.
15. Constitution on the Sacred Liturgy *Sacrosanctum Concilium*, 10.
16. Ibid., 12.

one can introduce us to a profound knowledge of his mystery better than his Mother.

The first of the "signs" worked by Jesus—the changing of water into wine at the marriage in Cana—clearly presents Mary in the guise of a teacher, as she urges the servants to do what Jesus commands (cf. Jn 2:5). We can imagine that she would have done likewise for the disciples after Jesus' Ascension, when she joined them in awaiting the Holy Spirit and supported them in their first mission. Contemplating the scenes of the Rosary in union with Mary is a means of learning from her to "read" Christ, to discover his secrets and to understand his message.

This school of Mary is all the more effective if we consider that she teaches by obtaining for us in abundance the gifts of the Holy Spirit, even as she offers us the incomparable example of her own "pilgrimage of faith."[17] As we contemplate each mystery of her Son's life, she invites us to do as she did at the Annunciation: to ask humbly the questions which open us to the light, in order to end with the obedience of faith: "Behold I am the handmaid of the Lord; be it done to me according to your word" (Lk 1:38).

BEING CONFORMED TO CHRIST WITH MARY

15.   Christian spirituality is distinguished by the disciple's commitment to become conformed ever more fully to his Master (cf. Rom 8:29; Phil 3:10, 12). The outpouring of the Holy Spirit in Baptism grafts the believer like a branch onto the vine which is Christ (cf. Jn 15:5) and makes him a member of Christ's mystical Body (cf. 1 Cor 12:12; Rom 12:5). This initial unity, however, calls for a growing assimilation which will increasingly shape the conduct of the disciple in accordance with the "mind" of Christ: "Have this mind among yourselves, which was in Christ Jesus" (Phil 2:5). In the words of the Apostle, we are called "to put on the Lord Jesus Christ" (cf. Rom 13:14; Gal 3:27).

In the spiritual journey of the Rosary, based on the constant contemplation—in Mary's company—of the face of Christ, this demanding ideal of being conformed to him is pursued through an association which could be described in terms of friendship. We are thereby enabled to enter naturally into Christ's life and as it were to share his deepest feelings. In this regard Blessed Bartolo Longo has written: "Just as two friends, frequently in each other's company, tend to develop similar habits, so too, by holding familiar converse with Jesus and the Blessed Virgin, by meditating on the mysteries of the Rosary and by living the same life in Holy Communion, we can become, to the extent of our lowliness, similar to them and can learn from these supreme models a life of humility, poverty, hiddenness, patience and perfection."[18]

In this process of being conformed to Christ in the Rosary, we entrust ourselves in a special way to the maternal care of the Blessed Virgin. She who is both the Mother of Christ and a member of the Church, indeed her "preeminent and

---

17. Second Vatican Ecumenical Council, Dogmatic Constitution on the Church *Lumen gentium*, 58.

18. *I Quindici Sabati del Santissimo Rosario*, 27th ed., Pompei, 1916, 27.

altogether singular member,"[19] is at the same time the "Mother of the Church." As such, she continually brings to birth children for the mystical Body of her Son. She does so through her intercession, imploring upon them the inexhaustible outpouring of the Spirit. Mary is *the perfect icon of the motherhood of the Church.*

The Rosary mystically transports us to Mary's side as she is busy watching over the human growth of Christ in the home of Nazareth. This enables her to train us and to mold us with the same care, until Christ is "fully formed" in us (cf. Gal 4:19). This role of Mary, totally grounded in that of Christ and radically subordinated to it, "in no way obscures or diminishes the unique mediation of Christ, but rather shows its power."[20] This is the luminous principle expressed by the Second Vatican Council which I have so powerfully experienced in my own life and have made the basis of my episcopal motto: *Totus tuus.*[21] The motto is of course inspired by the teaching of Saint Louis Marie Grignion de Montfort, who explained in the following words Mary's role in the process of our configuration to Christ: *"Our entire perfection consists in being conformed, united and consecrated to Jesus Christ.* Hence the most perfect of all devotions is undoubtedly that which conforms, unites and consecrates us most perfectly to Jesus Christ. Now, since Mary is of all creatures the one most conformed to Jesus Christ, it follows that among all devotions that which most consecrates and conforms a soul to our Lord is devotion to Mary, his Holy Mother, and that the more a soul is consecrated to her the more will it be consecrated to Jesus Christ."[22] Never as in the Rosary do the life of Jesus and that of Mary appear so deeply joined. Mary lives only in Christ and for Christ!

PRAYING TO CHRIST WITH MARY

16.   Jesus invited us to turn to God with insistence and the confidence that we will be heard: "Ask, and it will be given to you; seek, and you will find; knock, and it will be opened to you" (Mt 7:7). The basis for this power of prayer is the goodness of the Father, but also the mediation of Christ himself (cf. 1 Jn 2:1) and the working of the Holy Spirit who "intercedes for us" according to the will of God (cf. Rom 8:26–27). For "we do not know how to pray as we ought" (Rom 8:26), and at times we are not heard "because we ask wrongly" (cf. Jas 4:2–3).

In support of the prayer which Christ and the Spirit cause to rise in our hearts, Mary intervenes with her maternal intercession. "The prayer of the Church is sustained by the prayer of Mary."[23] If Jesus, the one Mediator, is the Way of our prayer, then Mary, his purest and most transparent reflection, shows us the Way. "Beginning with Mary's unique cooperation with the working of the Holy Spirit, the Churches developed their prayer to the Holy Mother of God, centering it on

---

19. Second Vatican Ecumenical Council, Dogmatic Constitution on the Church *Lumen gentium*, 53.

20. Ibid., 60.

21. Cf. First Radio Address *Urbi et orbi* (October 17, 1978): AAS 70 (1978), 927.

22. *Treatise on True Devotion to the Blessed Virgin Mary.*

23. *Catechism of the Catholic Church*, 2679.

the person of Christ manifested in his mysteries."[24] At the wedding of Cana the Gospel clearly shows the power of Mary's intercession as she makes known to Jesus the needs of others: "They have no wine" (Jn 2:3).

The Rosary is both meditation and supplication. Insistent prayer to the Mother of God is based on confidence that her maternal intercession can obtain all things from the heart of her Son. She is "all-powerful by grace," to use the bold expression, which needs to be properly understood, of Blessed Bartolo Longo in his *Supplication to Our Lady*.[25] This is a conviction which, beginning with the Gospel, has grown ever more firm in the experience of the Christian people. The supreme poet Dante expresses it marvelously in the lines sung by Saint Bernard: "Lady, thou art so great and so powerful, that whoever desires grace yet does not turn to thee, would have his desire fly without wings."[26] When in the Rosary we plead with Mary, the sanctuary of the Holy Spirit (cf. Lk 1:35), she intercedes for us before the Father who filled her with grace and before the Son born of her womb, praying with us and for us.

PROCLAIMING CHRIST WITH MARY

17.   The Rosary is also *a path of proclamation and increasing knowledge*, in which the mystery of Christ is presented again and again at different levels of the Christian experience. Its form is that of a prayerful and contemplative presentation, capable of forming Christians according to the heart of Christ. When the recitation of the Rosary combines all the elements needed for an effective meditation, especially in its communal celebration in parishes and shrines, it can present *a significant catechetical opportunity* which pastors should use to advantage. In this way too Our Lady of the Rosary continues her work of proclaiming Christ. The history of the Rosary shows how this prayer was used in particular by the Dominicans at a difficult time for the Church due to the spread of heresy. Today we are facing new challenges. Why should we not once more have recourse to the Rosary, with the same faith as those who have gone before us? The Rosary retains all its power and continues to be a valuable pastoral resource for every good evangelizer.

CHAPTER II
MYSTERIES OF CHRIST—MYSTERIES OF HIS MOTHER

THE ROSARY, "A COMPENDIUM OF THE GOSPEL"

18.   The only way to approach the contemplation of Christ's face is by listening in the Spirit to the Father's voice, since "no one knows the Son except the Father" (Mt 11:27). In the region of Caesarea Philippi, Jesus responded to Peter's confession of faith by indicating the source of that clear intuition of his identity:

---

24. Ibid., 2675.

25. The *Supplication to the Queen of the Holy Rosary* was composed by Blessed Bartolo Longo in 1883 in response to the appeal of Pope Leo XIII, made in his first Encyclical on the Rosary, for the spiritual commitment of all Catholics in combating social ills. It is solemnly recited twice yearly, in May and October.

26. *Divina Commedia*, Paradiso XXXIII, 13–15.

"Flesh and blood has not revealed this to you, but my Father who is in heaven" (Mt 16:17). What is needed, then, is a revelation from above. In order to receive that revelation, attentive listening is indispensable: "Only *the experience of silence and prayer* offers the proper setting for the growth and development of a true, faithful and consistent knowledge of that mystery."[27]

The Rosary is one of the traditional paths of Christian prayer directed to the contemplation of Christ's face. Pope Paul VI described it in these words: "As a Gospel prayer, centered on the mystery of the redemptive Incarnation, the Rosary is a prayer with a clearly Christological orientation. Its most characteristic element, in fact, the litany-like succession of *Hail Marys*, becomes in itself an unceasing praise of Christ, who is the ultimate object both of the Angel's announcement and of the greeting of the Mother of John the Baptist: 'Blessed is the fruit of your womb' (Lk 1:42). We would go further and say that the succession of *Hail Marys* constitutes the warp on which is woven the contemplation of the mysteries. The Jesus that each *Hail Mary* recalls is the same Jesus whom the succession of mysteries proposes to us now as the Son of God, now as the Son of the Virgin."[28]

A PROPOSED ADDITION TO THE TRADITIONAL PATTERN

19.   Of the many mysteries of Christ's life, only a few are indicated by the Rosary in the form that has become generally established with the seal of the Church's approval. The selection was determined by the origin of the prayer, which was based on the number 150, the number of the Psalms in the Psalter.

I believe, however, that to bring out fully the Christological depth of the Rosary it would be suitable to make an addition to the traditional pattern which, while left to the freedom of individuals and communities, could broaden it to include *the mysteries of Christ's public ministry between his Baptism and his Passion.* In the course of those mysteries we contemplate important aspects of the person of Christ as the definitive revelation of God. Declared the beloved Son of the Father at the Baptism in the Jordan, Christ is the one who announces the coming of the Kingdom, bears witness to it in his works and proclaims its demands. It is during the years of his public ministry that *the mystery of Christ is most evidently a mystery of light:* "While I am in the world, I am the light of the world" (Jn 9:5).

Consequently, for the Rosary to become more fully a "compendium of the Gospel," it is fitting to add, following reflection on the Incarnation and the hidden life of Christ (*the joyful mysteries*) and before focusing on the sufferings of his Passion (*the sorrowful mysteries*) and the triumph of his Resurrection (*the glorious mysteries*), a meditation on certain particularly significant moments in his public ministry (*the mysteries of light*). This addition of these new mysteries, without prejudice to any essential aspect of the prayer's traditional format, is meant to give it fresh life and to enkindle renewed interest in the Rosary's place within

---

27. John Paul II, Apostolic Letter *Novo millennio ineunte* (January 6, 2001), 20: AAS 93 (2001), 279.

28. Apostolic Exhortation *Marialis cultus* (February 2, 1974), 46: AAS 66 (1974), 155.

Christian spirituality as a true doorway to the depths of the Heart of Christ, ocean of joy and of light, of suffering and of glory.

THE JOYFUL MYSTERIES

20.   The first five decades, the "joyful mysteries," are marked by *the joy radiating from the event of the Incarnation*. This is clear from the very first mystery, the Annunciation, where Gabriel's greeting to the Virgin of Nazareth is linked to an invitation to messianic joy: "Rejoice, Mary." The whole of salvation history, in some sense the entire history of the world, has led up to this greeting. If it is the Father's plan to unite all things in Christ (cf. Eph 1:10), then the whole of the universe is in some way touched by the divine favor with which the Father looks upon Mary and makes her the Mother of his Son. The whole of humanity, in turn, is embraced by the *fiat* with which she readily agrees to the will of God.

Exultation is the keynote of the encounter with Elizabeth, where the sound of Mary's voice and the presence of Christ in her womb cause John to "leap for joy" (cf. Lk 1:44). Gladness also fills the scene in Bethlehem, when the birth of the divine Child, the Savior of the world, is announced by the song of the angels and proclaimed to the shepherds as "news of great joy" (Lk 2:10).

The final two mysteries, while preserving this climate of joy, already point to the drama yet to come. The Presentation in the Temple not only expresses the joy of the Child's consecration and the ecstasy of the aged Simeon; it also records the prophecy that Christ will be a "sign of contradiction" for Israel and that a sword will pierce his mother's heart (cf. Lk 2:34–35). Joy mixed with drama marks the fifth mystery, the finding of the twelve-year-old Jesus in the Temple. Here he appears in his divine wisdom as he listens and raises questions, already in effect one who "teaches." The revelation of his mystery as the Son wholly dedicated to his Father's affairs proclaims the radical nature of the Gospel, in which even the closest of human relationships are challenged by the absolute demands of the Kingdom. Mary and Joseph, fearful and anxious, "did not understand" his words (Lk 2:50).

To meditate upon the "joyful" mysteries, then, is to enter into the ultimate causes and the deepest meaning of Christian joy. It is to focus on the realism of the mystery of the Incarnation and on the obscure foreshadowing of the mystery of the saving Passion. Mary leads us to discover the secret of Christian joy, reminding us that Christianity is, first and foremost, *euangelion*, "good news," which has as its heart and its whole content the person of Jesus Christ, the Word made flesh, the one Savior of the world.

THE MYSTERIES OF LIGHT

21.   Moving on from the infancy and the hidden life in Nazareth to the public life of Jesus, our contemplation brings us to those mysteries which may be called in a special way "mysteries of light." Certainly the whole mystery of Christ is a mystery of light. He is the "light of the world" (Jn 8:12). Yet this truth emerges in a special way during the years of his public life, when he proclaims the Gospel of the Kingdom. In proposing to the Christian community five significant

moments—"luminous" mysteries—during this phase of Christ's life, I think that the following can be fittingly singled out: (1) his Baptism in the Jordan, (2) his self-manifestation at the wedding of Cana, (3) his proclamation of the Kingdom of God, with his call to conversion, (4) his Transfiguration, and finally, (5) his institution of the Eucharist, as the sacramental expression of the Paschal Mystery.

Each of these mysteries is *a revelation of the Kingdom now present in the very person of Jesus.* The Baptism in the Jordan is first of all a mystery of light. Here, as Christ descends into the waters, the innocent one who became "sin" for our sake (cf. 2 Cor 5:21), the heavens open wide and the voice of the Father declares him the beloved Son (cf. Mt 3:17 and parallels), while the Spirit descends on him to invest him with the mission which he is to carry out. Another mystery of light is the first of the signs, given at Cana (cf. Jn 2:1–12), when Christ changes water into wine and opens the hearts of the disciples to faith, thanks to the intervention of Mary, the first among believers. Another mystery of light is the preaching by which Jesus proclaims the coming of the Kingdom of God, calls to conversion (cf. Mk 1:15) and forgives the sins of all who draw near to him in humble trust (cf. Mk 2:3–13; Lk 7:47–48): the inauguration of that ministry of mercy which he continues to exercise until the end of the world, particularly through the Sacrament of Reconciliation which he has entrusted to his Church (cf. Jn 20:22–23). The mystery of light *par excellence* is the Transfiguration, traditionally believed to have taken place on Mount Tabor. The glory of the Godhead shines forth from the face of Christ as the Father commands the astonished Apostles to "listen to him" (cf. Lk 9:35 and parallels) and to prepare to experience with him the agony of the Passion, so as to come with him to the joy of the Resurrection and a life transfigured by the Holy Spirit. A final mystery of light is the institution of the Eucharist, in which Christ offers his body and blood as food under the signs of bread and wine, and testifies "to the end" his love for humanity (Jn 13:1), for whose salvation he will offer himself in sacrifice.

In these mysteries, apart from the miracle at Cana, *the presence of Mary remains in the background.* The Gospels make only the briefest reference to her occasional presence at one moment or other during the preaching of Jesus (cf. Mk 3:31–5; Jn 2:12), and they give no indication that she was present at the Last Supper and the institution of the Eucharist. Yet the role she assumed at Cana in some way accompanies Christ throughout his ministry. The revelation made directly by the Father at the Baptism in the Jordan and echoed by John the Baptist is placed upon Mary's lips at Cana, and it becomes the great maternal counsel which Mary addresses to the Church of every age: "Do whatever he tells you" (Jn 2:5). This counsel is a fitting introduction to the words and signs of Christ's public ministry and it forms the Marian foundation of all the "mysteries of light."

THE SORROWFUL MYSTERIES

22.   The Gospels give great prominence to the sorrowful mysteries of Christ. From the beginning Christian piety, especially during the Lenten devotion of the *Way of the Cross,* has focused on the individual moments of the Passion, realizing that here is found *the culmination of the revelation of God's love* and

the source of our salvation. The Rosary selects certain moments from the Passion, inviting the faithful to contemplate them in their hearts and to relive them. The sequence of meditations begins with Gethsemane, where Christ experiences a moment of great anguish before the will of the Father, against which the weakness of the flesh would be tempted to rebel. There Jesus encounters all the temptations and confronts all the sins of humanity, in order to say to the Father: "Not my will but yours be done" (Lk 22:42 and parallels). This "Yes" of Christ reverses the "No" of our first parents in the Garden of Eden. And the cost of this faithfulness to the Father's will is made clear in the following mysteries; by his scourging, his crowning with thorns, his carrying the Cross and his death on the Cross, the Lord is cast into the most abject suffering: *Ecce homo!*

This abject suffering reveals not only the love of God but also the meaning of man himself.

Ecce homo: the meaning, origin and fulfillment of man is to be found in Christ, the God who humbles himself out of love "even unto death, death on a cross" (Phil 2:8). The sorrowful mysteries help the believer to relive the death of Jesus, to stand at the foot of the Cross beside Mary, to enter with her into the depths of God's love for man and to experience all its life-giving power.

THE GLORIOUS MYSTERIES

23.   "The contemplation of Christ's face cannot stop at the image of the Crucified One. He is the Risen One!"[29] The Rosary has always expressed this knowledge born of faith and invited the believer to pass beyond the darkness of the Passion in order to gaze upon Christ's glory in the Resurrection and Ascension. Contemplating the Risen One, Christians *rediscover the reasons for their own faith* (cf. 1 Cor 15:14) and relive the joy not only of those to whom Christ appeared—the Apostles, Mary Magdalene and the disciples on the road to Emmaus—but also *the joy of Mary*, who must have had an equally intense experience of the new life of her glorified Son. In the Ascension, Christ was raised in glory to the right hand of the Father, while Mary herself would be raised to that same glory in the Assumption, enjoying beforehand, by a unique privilege, the destiny reserved for all the just at the resurrection of the dead. Crowned in glory—as she appears in the last glorious mystery—Mary shines forth as Queen of the Angels and Saints, the anticipation and the supreme realization of the eschatological state of the Church.

At the center of this unfolding sequence of the glory of the Son and the Mother, the Rosary sets before us the third glorious mystery, Pentecost, which reveals the face of the Church as a family gathered together with Mary, enlivened by the powerful outpouring of the Spirit and ready for the mission of evangelization. The contemplation of this scene, like that of the other glorious mysteries, ought to lead the faithful to an ever greater appreciation of their new life in Christ, lived in the heart of the Church, a life of which the scene of Pentecost itself is the great "icon." The glorious mysteries thus lead the faithful to *greater*

---

29. John Paul II, Apostolic Letter *Novo millennio ineunte* (January 6, 2001), 28: AAS 93 (2001), 284.

hope for the eschatological goal towards which they journey as members of the pilgrim People of God in history. This can only impel them to bear courageous witness to that "good news" which gives meaning to their entire existence.

FROM "MYSTERIES" TO THE "MYSTERY": MARY'S WAY

24.   The cycles of meditation proposed by the Holy Rosary are by no means exhaustive, but they do bring to mind what is essential and they awaken in the soul a thirst for a knowledge of Christ continually nourished by the pure source of the Gospel. Every individual event in the life of Christ, as narrated by the Evangelists, is resplendent with the Mystery that surpasses all understanding (cf. Eph 3:19): the Mystery of the Word made flesh, in whom "all the fullness of God dwells bodily" (Col 2:9). For this reason the *Catechism of the Catholic Church* places great emphasis on the mysteries of Christ, pointing out that "everything in the life of Jesus is a sign of his Mystery."[30] The *"duc in altum"* of the Church of the third millennium will be determined by the ability of Christians to enter into the "perfect knowledge of God's mystery, of Christ, in whom are hidden all the treasures of wisdom and knowledge" (Col 2:2–3). The Letter to the Ephesians makes this heartfelt prayer for all the baptized: "May Christ dwell in your hearts through faith, so that you, being rooted and grounded in love, may have power . . . to know the love of Christ which surpasses knowledge, that you may be filled with all the fullness of God" (3:17–19).

The Rosary is at the service of this ideal; it offers the "secret" which leads easily to a profound and inward knowledge of Christ. We might call it *Mary's way*. It is the way of the example of the Virgin of Nazareth, a woman of faith, of silence, of attentive listening. It is also the way of a Marian devotion inspired by knowledge of the inseparable bond between Christ and his Blessed Mother: *the mysteries of Christ* are also in some sense *the mysteries of his Mother*, even when they do not involve her directly, for she lives from him and through him. By making our own the words of the Angel Gabriel and Saint Elizabeth contained in the *Hail Mary*, we find ourselves constantly drawn to seek out afresh in Mary, in her arms and in her heart, the "blessed fruit of her womb" (cf. Lk 1:42).

MYSTERY OF CHRIST, MYSTERY OF MAN

25.   In my testimony of 1978 mentioned above, where I described the Rosary as my favorite prayer, I used an idea to which I would like to return. I said then that "the simple prayer of the Rosary marks the rhythm of human life."[31]

In the light of what has been said so far on the mysteries of Christ, it is not difficult to go deeper into this *anthropological significance* of the Rosary, which is far deeper than may appear at first sight. Anyone who contemplates Christ through the various stages of his life cannot fail to perceive in him *the truth about man*. This is the great affirmation of the Second Vatican Council which I have so often discussed in my own teaching since the Encyclical Letter *Redemptor hominis*: "it is only in the mystery of the Word made flesh that the

---

30. No. 515.

31. Angelus Message of 29 October 1978 : *Insegnamenti*, I (1978), 76.

mystery of man is seen in its true light."[32] The Rosary helps to open up the way to this light. Following in the path of Christ, in whom man's path is "recapitulated,"[33] revealed and redeemed, believers come face to face with the image of the true man. Contemplating Christ's birth, they learn of the sanctity of life; seeing the household of Nazareth, they learn the original truth of the family according to God's plan; listening to the Master in the mysteries of his public ministry, they find the light which leads them to enter the Kingdom of God; and following him on the way to Calvary, they learn the meaning of salvific suffering. Finally, contemplating Christ and his Blessed Mother in glory, they see the goal towards which each of us is called, if we allow ourselves to be healed and transformed by the Holy Spirit. It could be said that each mystery of the Rosary, carefully meditated, sheds light on the mystery of man.

At the same time, it becomes natural to bring to this encounter with the sacred humanity of the Redeemer all the problems, anxieties, labors and endeavors which go to make up our lives. "Cast your burden on the Lord and he will sustain you" (Ps 55:23). To pray the Rosary is to hand over our burdens to the merciful hearts of Christ and his Mother. Twenty-five years later, thinking back over the difficulties which have also been part of my exercise of the Petrine ministry, I feel the need to say once more, as a warm invitation to everyone to experience it personally: the Rosary does indeed "mark the rhythm of human life," bringing it into harmony with the "rhythm" of God's own life, in the joyful communion of the Holy Trinity, our life's destiny and deepest longing.

CHAPTER III
"FOR ME, TO LIVE IS CHRIST"

THE ROSARY, A WAY OF ASSIMILATING THE MYSTERY

26.   Meditation on the mysteries of Christ is proposed in the Rosary by means of a method designed to assist in their assimilation. It is a method *based on repetition*. This applies above all to the *Hail Mary*, repeated ten times in each mystery. If this repetition is considered superficially, there could be a temptation to see the Rosary as a dry and boring exercise. It is quite another thing, however, when the Rosary is thought of as an outpouring of that love which tirelessly returns to the person loved with expressions similar in their content but ever fresh in terms of the feeling pervading them.

In Christ, God has truly assumed a "heart of flesh." Not only does God have a divine heart, rich in mercy and in forgiveness, but also a human heart, capable of all the stirrings of affection. If we needed evidence for this from the Gospel, we could easily find it in the touching dialogue between Christ and Peter after the Resurrection: "Simon, son of John, do you love me?" Three times this question is put to Peter, and three times he gives the reply: "Lord, you know that I love you" (cf. Jn 21:15–17). Over and above the specific meaning of this passage,

---

32. Second Vatican Ecumenical Council, Pastoral Constitution on the Church in the Modern World *Gaudium et spes*, 22.

33. Cf. Saint Irenaeus of Lyons, *Adversus haereses*, III, 18, 1: PG 7, 932.

so important for Peter's mission, none can fail to recognize the beauty of this triple repetition, in which the insistent request and the corresponding reply are expressed in terms familiar from the universal experience of human love. To understand the Rosary, one has to enter into the psychological dynamic proper to love.

One thing is clear: although the repeated *Hail Mary* is addressed directly to Mary, it is to Jesus that the act of love is ultimately directed, with her and through her. The repetition is nourished by the desire to be conformed ever more completely to Christ, the true program of the Christian life. Saint Paul expressed this project with words of fire: "For me to live is Christ and to die is gain" (Phil 1:21). And again: "It is no longer I that live, but Christ lives in me" (Gal 2:20). The Rosary helps us to be conformed ever more closely to Christ until we attain true holiness.

A VALID METHOD . . .

27.   We should not be surprised that our relationship with Christ makes use of a method. God communicates himself to us respecting our human nature and its vital rhythms. Hence, while Christian spirituality is familiar with the most sublime forms of mystical silence in which images, words and gestures are all, so to speak, superseded by an intense and ineffable union with God, it normally engages the whole person in all his complex psychological, physical and relational reality.

This becomes apparent *in the Liturgy*. Sacraments and sacramentals are structured as a series of rites which bring into play all the dimensions of the person. The same applies to non-liturgical prayer. This is confirmed by the fact that, in the East, the most characteristic prayer of Christological meditation, centered on the words "Lord Jesus Christ, Son of God, have mercy on me, a sinner"[34] is traditionally linked to the rhythm of breathing; while this practice favors perseverance in the prayer, it also in some way embodies the desire for Christ to become the breath, the soul and the "all" of one's life.

. . . WHICH CAN NEVERTHELESS BE IMPROVED

28.   I mentioned in my Apostolic Letter *Novo millennio ineunte* that the West is now experiencing *a renewed demand for meditation*, which at times leads to a keen interest in aspects of other religions.[35] Some Christians, limited in their knowledge of the Christian contemplative tradition, are attracted by those forms of prayer. While the latter contain many elements which are positive and at times compatible with Christian experience, they are often based on ultimately unacceptable premises. Much in vogue among these approaches are methods aimed at attaining a high level of spiritual concentration by using techniques of a psychophysical, repetitive and symbolic nature. The Rosary is situated within this broad gamut of religious phenomena, but it is distinguished by characteristics of its own which correspond to specifically Christian requirements.

---

34. *Catechism of the Catholic Church*, 2616.
35. Cf. no. 33: AAS 93 (2001), 289.

In effect, the Rosary is simply *a method of contemplation*. As a method, it serves as a means to an end and cannot become an end in itself. All the same, as the fruit of centuries of experience, this method should not be undervalued. In its favor one could cite the experience of countless Saints. This is not to say, however, that the method cannot be improved. Such is the intent of the addition of the new series of *mysteria lucis* to the overall cycle of mysteries and of the few suggestions which I am proposing in this Letter regarding its manner of recitation. These suggestions, while respecting the well-established structure of this prayer, are intended to help the faithful to understand it in the richness of its symbolism and in harmony with the demands of daily life. Otherwise there is a risk that the Rosary would not only fail to produce the intended spiritual effects, but even that the beads, with which it is usually said, could come to be regarded as some kind of amulet or magic object, thereby radically distorting their meaning and function.

ANNOUNCING EACH MYSTERY

29.   Announcing each mystery, and perhaps even using a suitable icon to portray it, is as it were *to open up a scenario* on which to focus our attention. The words direct the imagination and the mind towards a particular episode or moment in the life of Christ. In the Church's traditional spirituality, the veneration of icons and the many devotions appealing to the senses, as well as the method of prayer proposed by Saint Ignatius of Loyola in the Spiritual Exercises, make use of visual and imaginative elements (the *compositio loci*), judged to be of great help in concentrating the mind on the particular mystery. This is a methodology, moreover, which *corresponds to the inner logic of the Incarnation*: in Jesus, God wanted to take on human features. It is through his bodily reality that we are led into contact with the mystery of his divinity.

This need for concreteness finds further expression in the announcement of the various mysteries of the Rosary. Obviously these mysteries neither replace the Gospel nor exhaust its content. The Rosary, therefore, is no substitute for *lectio divina*; on the contrary, it presupposes and promotes it. Yet, even though the mysteries contemplated in the Rosary, even with the addition of the *mysteria lucis*, do no more than outline the fundamental elements of the life of Christ, they easily draw the mind to a more expansive reflection on the rest of the Gospel, especially when the Rosary is prayed in a setting of prolonged recollection.

LISTENING TO THE WORD OF GOD

30.   In order to supply a Biblical foundation and greater depth to our meditation, it is helpful to follow the announcement of the mystery with *the proclamation of a related Biblical passage*, long or short, depending on the circumstances. No other words can ever match the efficacy of the inspired word. As we listen, we are certain that this is the word of God, spoken for today and spoken "for me."

If received in this way, the word of God can become part of the Rosary's methodology of repetition without giving rise to the ennui derived from the simple recollection of something already well known. It is not a matter of recalling information but of *allowing God to speak*. In certain solemn communal celebrations, this word can be appropriately illustrated by a brief commentary.

SILENCE

31. *Listening and meditation are nourished by silence.* After the announcement of the mystery and the proclamation of the word, it is fitting to pause and focus one's attention for a suitable period of time on the mystery concerned, before moving into vocal prayer. A discovery of the importance of silence is one of the secrets of practicing contemplation and meditation. One drawback of a society dominated by technology and the mass media is the fact that silence becomes increasingly difficult to achieve. Just as moments of silence are recommended in the Liturgy, so too in the recitation of the Rosary it is fitting to pause briefly after listening to the word of God, while the mind focuses on the content of a particular mystery.

THE "OUR FATHER"

32. After listening to the word and focusing on the mystery, it is natural for *the mind to be lifted up towards the Father*. In each of his mysteries, Jesus always leads us to the Father, for as he rests in the Father's bosom (cf. Jn 1:18) he is continually turned towards him. He wants us to share in his intimacy with the Father, so that we can say with him: "Abba, Father" (Rom 8:15; Gal 4:6). By virtue of his relationship to the Father he makes us brothers and sisters of himself and of one another, communicating to us the Spirit which is both his and the Father's. Acting as a kind of foundation for the Christological and Marian meditation which unfolds in the repetition of the *Hail Mary*, the *Our Father* makes meditation upon the mystery, even when carried out in solitude, an ecclesial experience.

THE TEN "HAIL MARYS"

33. This is the most substantial element in the Rosary and also the one which makes it a Marian prayer *par excellence*. Yet when the *Hail Mary* is properly understood, we come to see clearly that its Marian character is not opposed to its Christological character, but that it actually emphasizes and increases it. The first part of the *Hail Mary*, drawn from the words spoken to Mary by the Angel Gabriel and by Saint Elizabeth, is a contemplation in adoration of the mystery accomplished in the Virgin of Nazareth. These words express, so to speak, the wonder of heaven and earth; they could be said to give us a glimpse of God's own wonderment as he contemplates his "masterpiece"—the Incarnation of the Son in the womb of the Virgin Mary. If we recall how, in the Book of Genesis, God "saw all that he had made" (Gen 1:31), we can find here an echo of that "pathos with which God, at the dawn of creation, looked upon the work of his hands."[36] The repetition of the *Hail Mary* in the Rosary gives us a share in God's own wonder and pleasure: in jubilant amazement we acknowledge the greatest miracle of history. Mary's prophecy here finds its fulfillment: "Henceforth all generations will call me blessed" (Lk 1:48).

---

36. John Paul II, *Letter to Artists* (April 4, 1999), 1: AAS 91 (1999), 1155.

The center of gravity in the *Hail Mary*, the hinge as it were which joins its two parts, is *the name of Jesus*. Sometimes, in hurried recitation, this center of gravity can be overlooked, and with it the connection to the mystery of Christ being contemplated. Yet it is precisely the emphasis given to the name of Jesus and to his mystery that is the sign of a meaningful and fruitful recitation of the Rosary. Pope Paul VI drew attention, in his Apostolic Exhortation *Marialis cultus*, to the custom in certain regions of highlighting the name of Christ by the addition of a clause referring to the mystery being contemplated.[37] This is a praiseworthy custom, especially during public recitation. It gives forceful expression to our faith in Christ, directed to the different moments of the Redeemer's life. It is at once *a profession of faith* and an aid in concentrating our meditation, since it facilitates the process of assimilation to the mystery of Christ inherent in the repetition of the *Hail Mary*. When we repeat the name of Jesus—the only name given to us by which we may hope for salvation (cf. Acts 4:12)—in close association with the name of his Blessed Mother, almost as if it were done at her suggestion, we set out on a path of assimilation meant to help us enter more deeply into the life of Christ.

From Mary's uniquely privileged relationship with Christ, which makes her the Mother of God, *Theotókos*, derives the forcefulness of the appeal we make to her in the second half of the prayer, as we entrust to her maternal intercession our lives and the hour of our death.

THE "GLORIA"

34.   Trinitarian doxology is the goal of all Christian contemplation. For Christ is the way that leads us to the Father in the Spirit. If we travel this way to the end, we repeatedly encounter the mystery of the three divine Persons, to whom all praise, worship and thanksgiving are due. It is important that the *Gloria, the high point of contemplation*, be given due prominence in the Rosary. In public recitation it could be sung, as a way of giving proper emphasis to the essentially Trinitarian structure of all Christian prayer.

To the extent that meditation on the mystery is attentive and profound, and to the extent that it is enlivened—from one *Hail Mary* to another—by love for Christ and for Mary, the glorification of the Trinity at the end of each decade, far from being a perfunctory conclusion, takes on its proper contemplative tone, raising the mind as it were to the heights of heaven and enabling us in some way to relive the experience of Tabor, a foretaste of the contemplation yet to come: "It is good for us to be here!" (Lk 9:33).

THE CONCLUDING SHORT PRAYER

35.   In current practice, the Trinitarian doxology is followed by a brief concluding prayer which varies according to local custom. Without in any way diminishing the value of such invocations, it is worthwhile to note that the contemplation

---

37. Cf. no. 46: AAS 66 (1974), 155. This custom has also been recently praised by the Congregation for Divine Worship and for the Discipline of the Sacraments in its *Direttorio su pietà popolare e liturgia. Principi e orientamenti* (December 17, 2001), 201, Vatican City, 2002, 165.

of the mysteries could better express their full spiritual fruitfulness if an effort were made to conclude each mystery with *a prayer for the fruits specific to that particular mystery*. In this way the Rosary would better express its connection with the Christian life. One fine liturgical prayer suggests as much, inviting us to pray that, by meditation on the mysteries of the Rosary, we may come to "imitate what they contain and obtain what they promise."[38]

Such a final prayer could take on a legitimate variety of forms, as indeed it already does. In this way the Rosary can be better adapted to different spiritual traditions and different Christian communities. It is to be hoped, then, that appropriate formulas will be widely circulated, after due pastoral discernment and possibly after experimental use in centers and shrines particularly devoted to the Rosary, so that the People of God may benefit from an abundance of authentic spiritual riches and find nourishment for their personal contemplation.

THE ROSARY BEADS

36.   The traditional aid used for the recitation of the Rosary is the set of beads. At the most superficial level, the beads often become a simple counting mechanism to mark the succession of *Hail Marys*. Yet they can also take on a symbolism which can give added depth to contemplation.

Here the first thing to note is the way *the beads converge upon the Crucifix*, which both opens and closes the unfolding sequence of prayer. The life and prayer of believers is centered upon Christ. Everything begins from him, everything leads towards him, everything, through him, in the Holy Spirit, attains to the Father.

As a counting mechanism, marking the progress of the prayer, the beads evoke the unending path of contemplation and of Christian perfection. Blessed Bartolo Longo saw them also as a "chain" which links us to God. A chain, yes, but a sweet chain; for sweet indeed is the bond to God who is also our Father. A "filial" chain which puts us in tune with Mary, the "handmaid of the Lord" (Lk 1:38) and, most of all, with Christ himself, who, though he was in the form of God, made himself a "servant" out of love for us (Phil 2:7).

A fine way to expand the symbolism of the beads is to let them remind us of our many relationships, of the bond of communion and fraternity which unites us all in Christ.

THE OPENING AND CLOSING

37.   At present, in different parts of the Church, there are many ways to introduce the Rosary. In some places, it is customary to begin with the opening words of Psalm 70: "O God, come to my aid; O Lord, make haste to help me," as if to nourish in those who are praying a humble awareness of their own insufficiency. In other places, the Rosary begins with the recitation of the Creed, as if to make

---

38. ". . . *concede, quaesumus, ut haec mysteria sacratissimo beatae Mariae Virginis Rosario recolentes, et imitemur quod continent, et quod promittunt assequamur.*" *Missale Romanum* 1960, in festo B. M. Virginis a Rosario.

the profession of faith the basis of the contemplative journey about to be undertaken. These and similar customs, to the extent that they prepare the mind for contemplation, are all equally legitimate. The Rosary is then ended with a prayer for the intentions of the Pope, as if to expand the vision of the one praying to embrace all the needs of the Church. It is precisely in order to encourage this ecclesial dimension of the Rosary that the Church has seen fit to grant indulgences to those who recite it with the required dispositions.

If prayed in this way, the Rosary truly becomes a spiritual itinerary in which Mary acts as Mother, Teacher and Guide, sustaining the faithful by her powerful intercession. Is it any wonder, then, that the soul feels the need, after saying this prayer and experiencing so profoundly the motherhood of Mary, to burst forth in praise of the Blessed Virgin, either in that splendid prayer the *Salve Regina* or in the *Litany of Loreto*? This is the crowning moment of an inner journey which has brought the faithful into living contact with the mystery of Christ and his Blessed Mother.

DISTRIBUTION OVER TIME

38.   The Rosary can be recited in full every day, and there are those who most laudably do so. In this way it fills with prayer the days of many a contemplative, or keeps company with the sick and the elderly who have abundant time at their disposal. Yet it is clear—and this applies all the more if the new series of *mysteria lucis* is included—that many people will not be able to recite more than a part of the Rosary, according to a certain weekly pattern. This weekly distribution has the effect of giving the different days of the week a certain spiritual "color," by analogy with the way in which the Liturgy colors the different seasons of the liturgical year.

According to current practice, Monday and Thursday are dedicated to the "joyful mysteries," Tuesday and Friday to the "sorrowful mysteries," and Wednesday, Saturday and Sunday to the "glorious mysteries." Where might the "mysteries of light" be inserted? If we consider that the "glorious mysteries" are said on both Saturday and Sunday, and that Saturday has always had a special Marian flavor, the second weekly meditation on the "joyful mysteries," mysteries in which Mary's presence is especially pronounced, could be moved to Saturday. Thursday would then be free for meditating on the "mysteries of light."

This indication is not intended to limit a rightful freedom in personal and community prayer, where account needs to be taken of spiritual and pastoral needs and of the occurrence of particular liturgical celebrations which might call for suitable adaptations. What is really important is that the Rosary should always be seen and experienced as a path of contemplation. In the Rosary, in a way similar to what takes place in the Liturgy, the Christian week, centered on Sunday, the day of Resurrection, becomes a journey through the mysteries of the life of Christ, and he is revealed in the lives of his disciples as the Lord of time and of history.

CONCLUSION

39.   What has been said so far makes abundantly clear the richness of this traditional prayer, which has the simplicity of a popular devotion but also the theological depth of a prayer suited to those who feel the need for deeper contemplation.

The Church has always attributed particular efficacy to this prayer, entrusting to the Rosary, to its choral recitation and to its constant practice, the most difficult problems. At times when Christianity itself seemed under threat, its deliverance was attributed to the power of this prayer, and Our Lady of the Rosary was acclaimed as the one whose intercession brought salvation.

Today I willingly entrust to the power of this prayer—as I mentioned at the beginning—the cause of peace in the world and the cause of the family.

PEACE

40.   The grave challenges confronting the world at the start of this new Millennium lead us to think that only an intervention from on high, capable of guiding the hearts of those living in situations of conflict and those governing the destinies of nations, can give reason to hope for a brighter future.

The Rosary is by its nature a prayer for peace, since it consists in the contemplation of Christ, the Prince of Peace, the one who is "our peace" (Eph 2:14). Anyone who assimilates the mystery of Christ—and this is clearly the goal of the Rosary—learns the secret of peace and makes it his life's project. Moreover, by virtue of its meditative character, with the tranquil succession of *Hail Marys*, the Rosary has a peaceful effect on those who pray it, disposing them to receive and experience in their innermost depths, and to spread around them, that true peace which is the special gift of the Risen Lord (cf. Jn 14:27; 20:21).

The Rosary is also a prayer for peace because of the fruits of charity which it produces. When prayed well in a truly meditative way, the Rosary leads to an encounter with Christ in his mysteries and so cannot fail to draw attention to the face of Christ in others, especially in the most afflicted. How could one possibly contemplate the mystery of the Child of Bethlehem, in the joyful mysteries, without experiencing the desire to welcome, defend and promote life, and to shoulder the burdens of suffering children all over the world? How could one possibly follow in the footsteps of Christ the Revealer, in the mysteries of light, without resolving to bear witness to his "Beatitudes" in daily life? And how could one contemplate Christ carrying the Cross and Christ Crucified, without feeling the need to act as a "Simon of Cyrene" for our brothers and sisters weighed down by grief or crushed by despair? Finally, how could one possibly gaze upon the glory of the Risen Christ or of Mary Queen of Heaven, without yearning to make this world more beautiful, more just, more closely conformed to God's plan?

In a word, by focusing our eyes on Christ, the Rosary also makes us peacemakers in the world. By its nature as an insistent choral petition in harmony with Christ's invitation to "pray ceaselessly" (Lk 18:1), the Rosary allows us to hope that, even today, the difficult "battle" for peace can be won. Far from offering an escape from the problems of the world, the Rosary obliges us to see them with responsible and generous eyes, and obtains for us the strength to face them with the certainty of God's help and the firm intention of bearing witness in every situation to "love, which binds everything together in perfect harmony" (Col 3:14).

THE FAMILY: PARENTS . . .

41.   As a prayer for peace, the Rosary is also, and always has been, *a prayer of and for the family*. At one time this prayer was particularly dear to Christian families, and it certainly brought them closer together. It is important not to lose this precious inheritance. We need to return to the practice of family prayer and prayer for families, continuing to use the Rosary.

In my Apostolic Letter *Novo millennio ineunte* I encouraged the celebration of the *Liturgy of the Hours* by the lay faithful in the ordinary life of parish communities and Christian groups;[39] I now wish to do the same for the Rosary. These two paths of Christian contemplation are not mutually exclusive; they complement one another. I would therefore ask those who devote themselves to the pastoral care of families to recommend heartily the recitation of the Rosary.

The family that prays together stays together. The Holy Rosary, by age-old tradition, has shown itself particularly effective as a prayer which brings the family together. Individual family members, in turning their eyes towards Jesus, also regain the ability to look one another in the eye, to communicate, to show solidarity, to forgive one another and to see their covenant of love renewed in the Spirit of God.

Many of the problems facing contemporary families, especially in economically developed societies, result from their increasing difficulty in communicating. Families seldom manage to come together, and the rare occasions when they do are often taken up with watching television. To return to the recitation of the family Rosary means filling daily life with very different images, images of the mystery of salvation: the image of the Redeemer, the image of his most Blessed Mother. The family that recites the Rosary together reproduces something of the atmosphere of the household of Nazareth: its members place Jesus at the center, they share his joys and sorrows, they place their needs and their plans in his hands, they draw from him the hope and the strength to go on.

. . . AND CHILDREN

42.   It is also beautiful and fruitful to entrust to this prayer *the growth and development of children*. Does the Rosary not follow the life of Christ, from his conception to his death, and then to his Resurrection and his glory? Parents are finding it ever more difficult to follow the lives of their children as they grow

---

39. Cf. no. 34: AAS 93 (2001), 290.

to maturity. In a society of advanced technology, of mass communications and globalization, everything has become hurried, and the cultural distance between generations is growing ever greater. The most diverse messages and the most unpredictable experiences rapidly make their way into the lives of children and adolescents, and parents can become quite anxious about the dangers their children face. At times parents suffer acute disappointment at the failure of their children to resist the seductions of the drug culture, the lure of an unbridled hedonism, the temptation to violence, and the manifold expressions of meaninglessness and despair.

To pray the Rosary *for children*, and even more, *with children*, training them from their earliest years to experience this daily "pause for prayer" with the family, is admittedly not the solution to every problem, but it is a spiritual aid which should not be underestimated. It could be objected that the Rosary seems hardly suited to the taste of children and young people of today. But perhaps the objection is directed to an impoverished method of praying it. Furthermore, without prejudice to the Rosary's basic structure, there is nothing to stop children and young people from praying it—either within the family or in groups— with appropriate symbolic and practical aids to understanding and appreciation. Why not try it? With God's help, a pastoral approach to youth which is positive, impassioned and creative—as shown by the World Youth Days!—is capable of achieving quite remarkable results. If the Rosary is well presented, I am sure that young people will once more surprise adults by the way they make this prayer their own and recite it with the enthusiasm typical of their age group.

THE ROSARY, A TREASURE TO BE REDISCOVERED

43.   Dear brothers and sisters! A prayer so easy and yet so rich truly deserves to be rediscovered by the Christian community. Let us do so, especially this year, as a means of confirming the direction outlined in my Apostolic Letter *Novo millennio ineunte*, from which the pastoral plans of so many particular Churches have drawn inspiration as they look to the immediate future.

I turn particularly to you, my dear Brother Bishops, priests and deacons, and to you, pastoral agents in your different ministries: through your own personal experience of the beauty of the Rosary, may you come to promote it with conviction.

I also place my trust in you, theologians: by your sage and rigorous reflection, rooted in the word of God and sensitive to the lived experience of the Christian people, may you help them to discover the Biblical foundations, the spiritual riches and the pastoral value of this traditional prayer.

I count on you, consecrated men and women, called in a particular way to contemplate the face of Christ at the school of Mary.

I look to all of you, brothers and sisters of every state of life, to you, Christian families, to you, the sick and elderly, and to you, young people: *confidently take up the Rosary once again.* Rediscover the Rosary in the light of Scripture, in harmony with the Liturgy, and in the context of your daily lives.

May this appeal of mine not go unheard! At the start of the twenty-fifth year of my Pontificate, I entrust this Apostolic Letter to the loving hands of the Virgin Mary, *prostrating myself in spirit before her image in the splendid Shrine built for her by Blessed Bartolo Longo*, the apostle of the Rosary. I willingly make my own the touching words with which he concluded his well-known *Supplication to the Queen of the Holy Rosary*: "O Blessed Rosary of Mary, sweet chain which unites us to God, bond of love which unites us to the angels, tower of salvation against the assaults of Hell, safe port in our universal shipwreck, we will never abandon you. You will be our comfort in the hour of death: yours our final kiss as life ebbs away. And the last word from our lips will be your sweet name, O Queen of the Rosary of Pompei, O dearest Mother, O Refuge of Sinners, O Sovereign Consoler of the Afflicted. May you be everywhere blessed, today and always, on earth and in heaven."

From the Vatican, on the 16th day of October in the year 2002, the beginning of the twenty-fifth year of my Pontificate.

IOANNES PAULUS PP. II

LETTER OF HIS HOLINESS POPE JOHN PAUL II TO ARTISTS

PASTORAL EXHORTATION
APRIL 4, 1999

AN OVERVIEW OF THE *LETTER OF HIS HOLINESS POPE JOHN PAUL II TO ARTISTS*

Rev. J. Philip Horrigan

The *Letter to Artists* is one of the literary gems from the prolific writing endeavors of John Paul II during the years of his pontificate, 1978–2005. Published on Easter Sunday 1999, the *Letter to Artists* is in the form of a pastoral exhortation to a particular constituent of the Church, namely artists. It is not an encyclical nor does it contain any legislative prescriptions. It has a certain "personal" overtone, as one artist (the pope was an accomplished) to his colleagues in ministry. The pope writes more in his role as a pastor to those whom he regards not only as fellow sojourners in the pursuit of great art, but also as friends who share a deep spiritual desire to inspire that "beauty will save the world."[1]

The primary purpose of the *Letter to Artists* is twofold: to encourage all artists to regard their vocation as a sharing in the creative Spirit of God, the original artist; and to assure those men and women who create art that they enjoy a special partnership with the Church, which is the source of mutual spiritual enrichment. In the words of the pope, "In writing this letter, I intend to follow the path of the fruitful dialogue between the Church and artists, which has gone on unbroken through two thousand years of history, and which still, at the threshold of the Third Millennium, offers rich promise for the future."[2]

THE ARTIST, IMAGE OF GOD THE CREATOR

The task of the artist is to craft from the existing material elements of creation that reflect the creative activity of God. The artist expresses his or her genius in their particular craft and in so doing mirrors the image of God as Creator. The artist takes up something that already exists and gives it both form and meaning so that it continues the work of creation and becomes a hymn of praise to God.

THE VOCATION OF THE ARTIST

The vocation of the artist is first a reflection of the artist's spiritual insight and growth. Although the artist speaks through his or her art to others who contemplate their work, artists see in their work a part of their own being and express a spirituality that interprets the world in a particular way. The gift of the artist is that he or she reveals the beauty that is hidden in the created work of the Divine Artist. This beauty is the visible form of the good that God bestowed on all that was made. In a very particular way the artistic talent of the artist is the gift of beauty that God as Creator bestows on the artist and it is this "divine

---

1. *Letter to Artists* (LetArt), 16; quoting from F. Dostoyevsky, *The Idiot*, Part III, chap. 5.
2. LetArt, 1.

spark"[3] that finds expression through the hand of the artist. Thus, does the artist perform a great service to the whole of humanity in its search for goodness and beauty.

In his letter the pope turns to the Scriptures as the source for both the inspiration and the subject matter for artists.

He quotes the great master Marc Chagall who referred to Sacred Scripture as an "iconographic atlas"[4] from which both Christian culture and art have drawn inspiration and vision.

Throughout history, artists have reflected upon the mystery of the divine presence in the world and thereby informed generations. Through their art, creative men and women have sought to reveal the spiritual depths hidden in the stories, people, events, and images of the Scriptures.

Art continues to be a distinct form of catechesis for people of faith, assisting others who seek to access and understand the rich treasures of Scripture. The vocation that artists enjoy is intimately tied to the mission of the Church, which is to open up the revealed Word of God to all who seek a friendship with the Lord.

Just as the Scriptures unfold and reveal the hidden mystery of the Spirit in salvation history, artists plumb the depths of that same mystery through their art. This alliance between art and the revealed Word of God, especially in Christ, the Word made flesh, is a singular conversation between the spiritual seeker of faith and the material expression of the artist through their craft.

This dialogue between the inner, invisible reality of mystery and the outer, visible expression of material is a form of epiphany to be cherished and celebrated.

ART IN HISTORY

There is historical evidence that the early Christian community used depictions of Christian symbols in the ornamentation of the places where they gathered for worship. The widespread growth of Christian architecture after the fourth century provided opportunities for architects and other artists to offer their imagination and craft to the faithful as vehicles of both identity and inspiration. Although art had its share of contention, giving way to the iconoclastic controversies in the early centuries of the Christian tradition—a conflict that was repeated in the years following the Protestant Reformation—nonetheless, art in the Christian Church continued to be regarded as a worthy expression of the God-given talent of artists and a source of inspiration and beauty.

The artistic expression of the icon flourished in the Eastern Church while the Western Church developed various architectural styles that came from the imagination of the architect and reflected the genius of artists and the cultures of the people. In painting, sculpture, and music, artists continued the exploration of the alluring importance and mystery of God in the human experience throughout the centuries.

---

3. Ibid., 3.
4. Ibid., 5.

The "extraordinary artistic flowering"[5] that marked the Renaissance may well have been the apex of sacred art in its variety, a wealth of subject matter and diversity of form and expression. The patronage of the Church as "a universally hospitable community"[6] for artists and a source of enrichment and inspiration for all manner of art, continued to encourage artists to search for the divine in and through their particular genius.

A RENEWED DIALOGUE

Calling to mind the long-standing tradition of the Church as a patron of the arts and supporter of artists, the pope invites artists of contemporary times to once again enter a dialogue between faith and art. He notes that in the modern world and its cultures there has often been a separation of faith and art and he seeks to renew the gift of art as a bridge to religious experience. He expresses the hope that there will be a new alliance in our own time between the Church and artists so that artists will once again give voice to "the universal desire for redemption."[7]

In the spirit of the documents of the Second Vatican Council (1963–1965), the pope reminds artists of their "noble ministry,"[8] which, when placed in service of the faith community "knowledge of God can be better revealed and the preaching of the Gospel can become clearer to the mind."[9] In light of this invitation to a new dialogue, the pope states clearly that the Church needs art and that artists need the Church. The mission of the Church to bring all people to Christ is supported and enriched by the diverse artistic expressions of artists—including architects, musicians, visual artists, sculptors, and painters. The breadth and depth of the mystery of God is never captured or contained in one form or symbol, so the great font of artistic expression can contribute to the thirst of the faithful for new avenues to the Divine Presence.

At the same time, art needs the Church as the source of rich inspiration and in some instances, as the arbiter of what constitutes sacred art that is worthy of the Christian tradition. As the Church continues to explore the truths of the Gospel she offers to artists new opportunities to engage in a partnership of "mutual spiritual enrichment."[10]

AN APPEAL TO ARTISTS

In the closing paragraphs of the *Letter to Artists*, the pope invites artists to "rediscover the depth of the spiritual and religious dimension that has been typical of art in its noblest forms in every age."[11] He appeals to artists in every field, the traditional areas that have marked the Christian tradition, those who are in the more contemporary fields of plastic arts, and those engaged in more recent endeavors of communication and technologies. All Christian artists share in a

---

5. Ibid., 9.
6. Ibid.
7. Ibid., 10.
8. Ibid., 11.
9. Ibid., 11; quoting *Gaudium et spes*, 62.
10. LetArt, 13.
11. Ibid., 14.

close alliance between the Gospel and art so they are invited in a particular way to use their creative gifts to enter into the "heart of the mystery of the Incarnate God and at the same time into the mystery of humanity."[12]

This invitation to artists appeals to their own impulses that can inspire their talents and lift their souls to recognize the great gift they have that "contains some tremor"[13] of the very breath of the Creator Spirit. The singular vocation and gift of the artist echoes the creative act of God and in turn brings a new illumination to the work of creation and genuine inspiration to people of faith. These "moments of grace"[14] bring the artist and all those who contemplate their art to a genuine experience of beauty and truth.

The pope concludes his letter in the form of a prayer, and with these words of hope and affection for artists:

> May the beauty that you pass on to generations still to come be such that it will stir them to wonder!

> May your many different paths all lead to that infinite ocean of beauty where wonder becomes awe, exhilaration, unspeakable joy.

> May you be guided and inspired by the mystery of the Risen Christ, whom the Church in these days contemplates with joy.

> May your art help to affirm that true beauty which, as a glimmer of the Spirit of God, will transfigure matter, opening the human soul to the sense of the eternal.[15]

A LITURGICAL CONTRIBUTION

Despite its brevity, the *Letter to Artists* contains a number of insights that should appeal to those concerned with the liturgical life of the Church.

First, every artist has a ministry that can serve the liturgy of the Church and the liturgical celebrations of the faithful. The pope makes it clear that the artist is imbued with the creative spirit of God whose act of creation was an act of love. The artist offers his or her gift of genius in artistic creations with that same gesture of love that speaks of beauty and of goodness. This is the heart of any ministry in the Church, and the artist whose work is intended both to adorn and to inspire expresses his or her ministry in a particularly visible and public fashion.

Second, the artist is, in a sense, an example for other ministers in the life of the Church. As the artist draws on an inner spirituality that is made visible with a particular artistic form, so other ministers must be conscious of their own inner spirituality so that their own ministry—in proclaimed Word or song, in greeting or serving, in presiding or preaching, in attending to others in any number of ways will be a visible expression of the Spirit of the Lord.

Third, the vocation of the artist is a mirror of the vocation of every disciple. Every follower of Christ is called to be in the world—yet, not of the world. As

---

12. Ibid.
13. Ibid., 15.
14. Ibid.
15. Ibid., 16.

the artist takes up the elements of the created world and shapes them to be vehicles of the mystery of God so every disciple finds his or her place in the world as a moment of grace—an opportunity to bring the Word of God to bear on the times and events that he or she encounters in life. As the pope noted, the artist engages in that dialogue, which brings together the human search for the ineffable and the divine assurance of hope, love, and joy for every creature. The faithful disciple is the artist of the ordinary unfolding of life, but with the extraordinary vocation to be a vessel of the promise of Christ, "will also do the works that I do and, in fact, will do greater works than these."[16]

Fourth, the *Letter to Artists* offers a unique insight into the nature of liturgy itself. For those who prepare, preside, minister, and study the liturgy, the *Letter to Artists* is a worthy resource for reflection. The liturgy in its fullness is a work of art. Many bring their gifts to each liturgical gathering and celebration; each gift is unique, yet all are needed for the "full, conscious, and active participation"[17] of the community. The liturgical palette is composed of the offerings of those who assemble, and when all contribute to the one common purpose of the liturgy it is as though a new tapestry, a new work of art is created. Yet each liturgy is an unfinished masterpiece. As Pope John Paul II remarked in his apostolic letter *Dies Domini*, the liturgy is not finished at the church doors. There remains the work of discipleship; the imperative of liturgy is a liturgy of neighbor—the work of the Gospel in the world. The liturgy, in the words of John Paul II is thus the school of discipleship; it is where we learn who we are, who we are to become, and what we are to do in the service of the Gospel. In this understanding, liturgy, like art, is catechetical and can bring all who engage in it closer to the mystery that is celebrated. It could be said that art is a form of liturgical expression, just as liturgy is a form of art.

Fifth, the *Letter to Artists* should reawaken an awareness among all who are involved in the design and ornamentation of churches of the importance of giving artists and their respective art a recognized voice in the design of new places of worship or in the renovation of existing ones. The pope makes it very clear how important good art is for the spiritual enrichment of believers. This should encourage artists to offer their work, with just compensation, to communities of faith. At the same time, members of diocesan commissions, pastoral leaders, liturgy committees, and community members should seek out the genius of such artists who can inspire faith and contribute to the beauty and spiritual goodness that is within the heart of every person and was truly in the creative act of God, the first artist.

The *Letter to Artists* is a call to all the faithful to remember and celebrate their own being as one in the image of God. We are indeed God's work of art. The Divine Artist passed on to us the Spirit of life and instilled in every soul a desire for beauty and goodness. Those who consider themselves artists and those who contemplate their work are joined in a profound spiritual communion that is rooted in the mystery of God that "engulfs and inhabits the world."[18]

---

16. John 14:12.

17. *Constitution on the Sacred Liturgy* (CSL), 14.

18. LetArt, 5.

LETTER OF HIS HOLINESS
POPE JOHN PAUL II
TO ARTISTS
1999

To all who are passionately dedicated
to the search for new "epiphanies" of beauty
so that through their creative work as artists
they may offer these as gifts to the world.

"God saw all that he had made, and it was very good." (Genesis 1:31)

THE ARTIST, IMAGE OF GOD THE CREATOR

1.　　None can sense more deeply than you artists, ingenious creators of beauty that you are, something of the pathos with which God, at the dawn of creation, looked upon the work of divine hands. A glimmer of that feeling has shone so often in your eyes when—like the artists of every age, captivated by the hidden power of sounds and words, colors and shapes—you have admired the work of your inspiration, sensing in it some echo of the mystery of creation with which God, the sole creator of all things, has wished in some way to associate you.

That is why it seems to me that there are no better words than the text of Genesis with which to begin my letter to you, to whom I feel closely linked by experiences reaching far back in time and which have indelibly marked my life. In writing this letter, I intend to follow the path of the fruitful dialogue between the Church and artists, which has gone on unbroken through two thousand years of history and which still, at the threshold of the Third Millennium, offers rich promise for the future.

In fact, this dialogue is not dictated merely by historical accident or practical need, but is rooted in the very essence of both religious experience and artistic creativity. The opening page of the Bible presents God as a kind of exemplar of everyone who produces a work: The human who crafts something mirrors the image of God as Creator. This relationship is particularly clear in the Polish language because of the lexical link between the words *stwórca* (creator) and *twórca* (craftsperson).

What is the difference between "creator" and "craftsperson"? The one who creates bestows being itself, bringing something out of nothing—*ex nihilo sui et subiecti*, as the Latin puts it—and this, in the strict sense, is a mode of operation which belongs to the Almighty alone. The craftsperson, by contrast, uses something that already exists, giving it form and meaning. This is the mode of operation peculiar to human beings as made in the image of God. In fact, after saying that God created man and woman "in his image" (cf. Genesis 1:27), the Bible adds that he entrusted to them the task of dominating the earth (cf. Genesis 1:28). This was the last day of creation (cf. Genesis 1:28–31). On the previous days, marking as it were the rhythm of the birth of the cosmos, God had created the universe. Finally he created the human being, the noblest fruit of divine design, to whom he made the visible world subject, as a vast field in which human inventiveness might assert itself.

God, therefore, called man and woman into existence, committing to them the task of craft. Through "artistic creativity" human beings appear more than ever "in the image of God," and accomplish this task above all in shaping the wondrous "material" of their own humanity and then exercising creative dominion over the universe that surrounds them. With loving regard, the divine Artist passes on to the human artist a spark of surpassing wisdom, calling him or her to share in divine creative power. Obviously, this is a sharing that leaves intact the infinite distance between the Creator and the creature, as Cardinal Nicholas of Cusa made clear: "Creative art, which it is the soul's good fortune to entertain, is not to be identified with that essential art, which is God himself, but is only a communication of it and a share in it."[1]

That is why artists, the more conscious they are of their "gift," are led all the more to see themselves and the whole of creation with eyes able to contemplate and give thanks, and to raise to God a hymn of praise. This is the only way for them to come to a full understanding of themselves, their vocation and their mission.

THE SPECIAL VOCATION OF THE ARTIST

2.   Not all are called to be artists in the specific sense of the term. Yet, as Genesis has it, all men and women are entrusted with the task of crafting their own life: In a certain sense, they are to make of it a work of art, a masterpiece.

It is important to recognize the distinction, but also the connection, between these two aspects of human activity. The distinction is clear: It is one thing for human beings to be the authors of their own acts, with responsibility for their moral value; it is another to be an artist, able, that is, to respond to the demands of art and faithfully to accept art's specific dictates.[2] This is what makes artists capable of producing objects, but it says nothing as yet of their moral character. We are speaking not of molding oneself, of forming one's own personality, but simply of actualizing one's productive capacities, giving aesthetic form to ideas conceived in the mind.

The distinction between the moral and artistic aspects is fundamental, but no less important is the connection between them. Each conditions the other in a profound way. In producing a work, artists express themselves to the point where their work becomes a unique disclosure of their own being, of what they are and of how they are what they are. And there are endless examples of this in human history. In shaping a masterpiece, the artist not only summons a work into being, but also in some way reveals his or her own personality by means of

---

1. *Dialogus de Ludo Globi*, lib. II: Philosophisch-Theologische Schriften, Vienna 1967, III, p. 332.

2. The moral virtues, and among them prudence in particular, allow the subject to act in harmony with the criterion of moral good and evil: according to *recta ratio agibilium* (the right criterion of action). Art, however, is defined by philosophy as *recta ratio factibilium* (the right criterion of production).

it. For the artist, art offers both a new dimension and an exceptional mode of expression for his or her spiritual growth. Through their works, artists speak to others and communicate with them. The history of art, therefore, is not only a story of works produced but also a story of men and women. Works of art speak of their authors; they enable us to know their inner life, and they reveal the original contribution that artists offer to the history of culture.

THE ARTISTIC VOCATION IN THE SERVICE OF BEAUTY

3.   A noted Polish poet, Cyprian Norwid, wrote that "beauty is to enthuse us for work, and work is to raise us up."[3] The theme of beauty is decisive for a discourse on art. It was already present when I stressed God's delighted gaze upon creation. In perceiving that all he had created was good, God saw that it was beautiful as well.[4] The link between good and beautiful stirs fruitful reflection. In a certain sense, beauty is the visible form of the good, just as the good is the metaphysical condition of beauty. This was well understood by the Greeks who, by fusing the two concepts, coined a term which embraces both: *kalokagathía*, or beauty-goodness. On this point Plato writes: "The power of the Good has taken refuge in the nature of the Beautiful."[5]

It is in living and acting that a person establishes a relationship with being, with the truth and with the good. The artist has a special relationship to beauty. In a very true sense it can be said that beauty is the vocation bestowed on the artist by the Creator in the gift of "artistic talent." And, certainly, this too is a talent that ought to be brought to fruition, in keeping with the sense of the Gospel parable of the talents (cf. Matthew 25:14–30).

Here we touch on an essential point. Those who perceive in themselves this kind of divine spark, which is the artistic vocation—as poet, writer, sculptor, architect, musician, actor and so on—feel the obligation not to waste this talent, but to develop it in order to put it at the service of their neighbor and humanity as a whole.

THE ARTIST AND THE COMMON GOOD

4.   Society needs artists, just as it needs scientists, technicians, workers, professional people, witnesses of the faith, teachers, fathers and mothers, who ensure the growth of the individual and the development of the community by means of that supreme art form which is "the art of education." Within the vast cultural panorama of each nation, artists have their unique place. Obedient to their inspiration in creating works both worthwhile and beautiful, they not only enrich the cultural heritage of each nation and of all humanity, but they also render an exceptional social service in favor of the common good.

The particular vocation of individual artists decides the arena in which they serve and points, as well, to the tasks they must assume, the hard work

---

3. *Promethidion, Bogumil*, vv. 185–86: Pisma wybrane, Warsaw 1968, vol. 2, p. 216.

4. The Greek translation of the *Septuagint* expresses this well in rendering the Hebrew term *t(o-)b* (good) as *kalón* (beautiful).

5. *Philebus*, 65 A.

they must endure and the responsibility they must accept. Artists who are conscious of all this know too that they must labor without allowing themselves to be driven by the search for empty glory or the craving for cheap popularity, and still less by the calculation of some possible profit for themselves. There is therefore an ethic, even a "spirituality" of artistic service, which contributes in its way to the life and renewal of a people. It is precisely this to which Cyprian Norwid seems to allude in declaring that "beauty is to enthuse us for work, and work is to raise us up."

ART AND THE MYSTERY OF THE WORD MADE FLESH

5.   The Law of the Old Testament explicitly forbids representation of the invisible and ineffable God by means of "graven or molten image" (Deuteronomy 27:15), because God transcends every material representation: "I am who I am" (Exodus 3:14). Yet in the mystery of the Incarnation, the Son of God becomes visible in person: "When the fullness of time had come, God sent forth his Son born of woman" (Galatians 4:4). God became human in Jesus Christ, who thus becomes "the central point of reference for an understanding of the enigma of human existence, the created world and God himself."[6]

This prime epiphany of "God who is Mystery" is both an encouragement and a challenge to Christians, especially at the level of artistic creativity. From it has come a flowering of beauty that has drawn its sap precisely from the mystery of the Incarnation. In becoming human, the Son of God has introduced into human history all the evangelical wealth of the true and the good. With this he has also unveiled a new dimension of beauty, of which the Gospel message is filled to the brim.

Sacred Scripture has thus become a sort of "immense vocabulary" (Paul Claudel) and "iconographic atlas" (Marc Chagall), from which both Christian culture and art have drawn. The Old Testament, read in the light of the New, has provided endless streams of inspiration. From the stories of the creation and sin, the flood, the cycle of the patriarchs, the events of the Exodus to so many other episodes and characters in the history of salvation, the biblical text has fired the imagination of painters, poets, musicians, playwrights and film-makers. A figure like Job, to take but one example, with his searing and ever-relevant question of suffering, still arouses an interest that is not just philosophical but literary and artistic as well. And what should we say of the New Testament? From the Nativity to Golgotha, from the Transfiguration to the Resurrection, from the miracles to the teachings of Christ, and on to the events recounted in the Acts of the Apostles or foreseen by the Book of Revelation in an eschatological key, on countless occasions the biblical word has become image, music and poetry, evoking the mystery of "the Word made flesh" in the language of art.

In the history of human culture, all of this is a rich chapter of faith and beauty. Believers above all have benefited from it in their experience of prayer and Christian living. Indeed for many of them, in times when few could read or

---

6. John Paul II, Encyclical Letter *Fides et ratio* (September 14, 1998), 80: AAS 91 (1999), 67.

write, representations of the Bible were a concrete mode of catechesis.[7] But for everyone, believers or not, the works of art inspired by scripture remain a reflection of the unfathomable mystery that engulfs and inhabits the world.

6.   Every genuine artistic intuition goes beyond what the senses perceive and, reaching beneath reality's surface, strives to interpret its hidden mystery. The intuition itself springs from the depths of the human soul, where the desire to give meaning to one's own life is joined by the fleeting vision of beauty and the mysterious unity of things. All artists experience the unbridgeable gap that lies between the work of their hands, however successful it may be, and the dazzling perfection of the beauty glimpsed in the ardor of the creative moment: What they manage to express in their painting, their sculpting, their creating is no more than a glimmer of the splendor which flared for a moment before the eyes of their spirit.

Believers find nothing strange in this: They know that they have had a momentary glimpse of the vastness of light that has its original wellspring in God. Is it in any way surprising that this leaves the spirit overwhelmed as it were, so that it can only stammer in reply? True artists above all are ready to acknowledge their limits and to claim as their own the words of the Apostle Paul, who says, "God does not dwell in shrines made by human hands," therefore, "we ought not to think that the deity is like an image fashioned from gold or silver or stone by human art and imagination" (Acts 17:24, 29). If the intimate reality of things is always "beyond" the powers of human perception, how much more so is God in the depths of unfathomable mystery!

The knowledge conferred by faith is of a different kind: It presupposes a personal encounter with God in Jesus Christ. Yet this knowledge too can be enriched by artistic intuition. An eloquent example of aesthetic contemplation sublimated in faith is, for example, the works of Fra Angelico. No less notable in this regard is the ecstatic *lauda,* which Saint Francis of Assisi twice repeats in the *chartula,* which he composed after receiving the stigmata of Christ on the mountain of La Verna: "You are beauty. . . . You are beauty!"[8] Saint Bonaventure comments: "In things of beauty, he contemplated the One who is supremely beautiful, and, led by the footprints he found in creatures, he followed the Beloved everywhere."[9]

A corresponding approach is found in Eastern spirituality, where Christ is described as "the supremely Beautiful, possessed of a beauty above all the children of earth."[10] Macarius the Great speaks of the transfiguring and liberating beauty of the Risen Lord in these terms: "The soul that has been fully illumined

---

7. This pedagogical principle was given authoritative formulation by Saint Gregory the Great in a letter of 599 to Serenus, Bishop of Marseilles: "Painting is employed in churches so that those who cannot read or write may at least read on the walls what they cannot decipher on the page." *Epistulae,* IX, 209: CCL 140A, 1714.

8. *Lodi di Dio Altissimo,* vv. 7 and 10: *Fonti Francescane,* No. 261, Padua 1982, p. 177.

9. *Legenda Maior,* IX, 1: *Fonti Francesane,* No. 1162, loc. cit., p. 911.

10. *Enkomia* of the Orthós of the Holy and Great Saturday.

by the unspeakable beauty of glory shining on the countenance of Christ over-flows with the Holy Spirit . . . it is all eye, all light, all countenance."[11]

Every genuine art form, in its own way, is a path to the inmost reality of the human being and the world. It is therefore a wholly valid approach to the realm of faith, which gives human experience its ultimate meaning. That is why the Gospel fullness of truth was bound from the beginning to stir the interest of artists, who by their very nature are alert to every "epiphany" of the inner beauty of things.

THE ORIGINS

7.   The art Christianity encountered in its early days was the ripe fruit of the classical world, articulating its aesthetic canons and embodying its values. Not only in their way of living and thinking, but also in the field of art, faith obliged Christians to a discernment which did not allow an uncritical acceptance of this heritage. Art of Christian inspiration began, therefore, in a minor key, strictly tied to the need for believers to contrive scripture-based signs to express both the mysteries of faith and a "symbolic code" by which they could distinguish and identify themselves, especially in the difficult times of persecution. Who does not recall the symbols that marked the first appearance of an art both pictorial and plastic? The fish, the loaves, the shepherd: In evoking the mystery, they became almost imperceptibly the first traces of a new art.

When the Edict of Constantine allowed Christians to declare themselves in full freedom, art became a privileged means for the expression of faith. Majestic basilicas began to appear, and in them the architectural canons of the pagan world were reproduced and at the same time modified to meet the demands of the new form of worship. How can we fail to recall at least the old Saint Peter's Basilica and the Basilica of Saint John Lateran, both funded by Constantine himself? Or Constantinople's Hagia Sophia built by Justinian, with its splendors of Byzantine art?

While architecture designed the space for worship, gradually the need to contemplate the mystery and to present it explicitly to the simple people led to the early forms of painting and sculpture. There appeared as well the first elements of art in word and sound. Among the many themes treated by Augustine we find *De Musica*; and Hilary of Poitiers, Ambrose, Prudentius, Ephrem the Syrian, Gregory of Nazianzus and Paulinus of Nola, to mention but a few, promoted a Christian poetry which was often of high quality not just as theology but also as literature. Their poetic work valued forms inherited from the classical authors, but was nourished by the pure sap of the Gospel, as Paulinus of Nola put it succinctly: "Our only art is faith and our music Christ."[12] A little later, Gregory the Great compiled the *Antiphonarium* and thus laid the ground for the organic development of that most original sacred music which takes its name from him. Gregorian chant, with its inspired modulations, was to become down the centuries the music of the Church's faith in the liturgical celebration of the

---

11. Homily I, 2: PG 34, 451.

12. *"At nobis ars una fides et musica Christus"*: Carmen 20, 31: CCL 203, 144.

sacred mysteries. The "beautiful" was thus wedded to the "true," so that through art too souls might be lifted up from the world of the senses to the eternal.

Along this path there were troubled moments. Precisely on the issue of depicting the Christian mystery, there arose in the early centuries a bitter controversy known to history as "the iconoclast crisis." Sacred images, which were already widely used in Christian devotion, became the object of violent contention. The council held at Nicaea in 787, which decreed the legitimacy of images and their veneration, was a historic event not just for the faith but for culture itself. The decisive argument to which the bishops appealed in order to settle the controversy was the mystery of the Incarnation: If the Son of God had come into the world of visible realities—his humanity building a bridge between the visible and the invisible—then, by analogy, a representation of the mystery could be used, within the logic of signs, as a sensory evocation of the mystery. The icon is venerated not for its own sake, but points beyond to the subject it represents.[13]

THE MIDDLE AGES

8.   The succeeding centuries saw a great development of Christian art. In the East, the art of the icon continued to flourish, obeying theological and aesthetic norms charged with meaning and sustained by the conviction that, in a sense, the icon is a sacrament. By analogy with what occurs in the sacraments, the icon makes present the mystery of the Incarnation in one or other of its aspects. That is why the beauty of the icon can be best appreciated in a church where, in the shadows, burning lamps stir infinite flickerings of light. As Pavel Florensky has written: "By the flat light of day, gold is crude, heavy, useless, but by the tremulous light of a lamp or candle, it springs to life and glitters in sparks beyond counting—now here, now there, evoking the sense of other lights, not of this earth, which fill the space of heaven."[14]

In the West, artists start from the most varied viewpoints, depending also on the underlying convictions of the cultural world of their time. The artistic heritage built up over the centuries includes a vast array of sacred works of great inspiration, which still today leave the observer full of admiration. In the first place, there are the great buildings for worship, in which the functional is always wedded to the creative impulse inspired by a sense of the beautiful and an intuition of the mystery. From here came the various styles well known in the history of art. The strength and simplicity of the Romanesque, expressed in cathedrals and abbeys, slowly evolved into the soaring splendors of the Gothic. These forms portray not only the genius of an artist, but the soul of a people. In the play of light and shadow, in forms at times massive, at times delicate, structural considerations certainly come into play, but so too do the tensions peculiar to the experience of God, the mystery both "awesome" and "alluring." How is one to summarize with a few brief references to each of the many different art forms, the creative power of the centuries of the Christian Middle Ages? An entire culture, albeit with the inescapable limits of all that is human, had become

---

13. Cf. John Paul II, Apostolic Letter *Duodecimum saeculum* (December 4, 1987), 8–9: AAS 80 (1988), pp. 247–249.

14. "La prospettiva rovesciata ed altri scritti," Rome 1984, p. 63.

imbued with the Gospel; and where theology produced the *Summa* of Saint Thomas, church art molded matter in a way which led to adoration of the mystery, and a wonderful poet like Dante Alighieri could compose "the sacred poem, to which both heaven and earth have turned their hand,"[15] as he himself described the Divine Comedy.

HUMANISM AND THE RENAISSANCE

9.   The favorable cultural climate that produced the extraordinary artistic flowering of humanism and the Renaissance also had a significant impact on the way in which the artists of the period approached the religious theme. Naturally their inspiration, like their style, varied greatly, at least among the best of them. But I do not intend to repeat things which you, as artists, know well. Writing from this Apostolic Palace, which is a mine of masterpieces perhaps unique in the world, I would rather give voice to the supreme artists who, in this place, lavished the wealth of their genius, often charged with great spiritual depth. From here can be heard the voice of Michelangelo, who, in the Sistine Chapel, has presented the drama and mystery of the world from the Creation to the Last Judgment, giving a face to God the Father, to Christ the Judge, and to human beings on this arduous journey from the dawn to the consummation of history. Here speaks the delicate and profound genius of Raphael, highlighting in the array of his paintings, and especially in the "Dispute" in the Room of the Signatura, the mystery of the revelation of the Triune God, who in the Eucharist befriends humanity and sheds light on the questions and expectations of human intelligence. From this place, from the majestic Basilica dedicated to the Prince of the Apostles, from the Colonnade which spreads out from it like two arms open to welcome the whole human family, we still hear Bramante, Bernini, Borromini, Maderno, to name only the more important artists, all rendering visible the perception of the mystery that makes of the Church a universally hospitable community, mother and traveling companion to all men and women in their search for God.

This extraordinary complex is a remarkably powerful expression of sacred art, rising to heights of imperishable aesthetic and religious excellence. What has characterized sacred art more and more, under the impulse of humanism and the Renaissance, and then of successive cultural and scientific trends, is a growing interest in everything human, in the world, and in the reality of history. In itself, such a concern is not at all a danger for Christian faith, centered on the mystery of the Incarnation and, therefore, on God's valuing the human being. The great artists mentioned above are a demonstration of this. One needs only to think of the way in which Michelangelo represents the beauty of the human body in his painting and sculpture.[16]

Even in the changed climate of more recent centuries, when a part of society seems to have become indifferent to faith, religious art has continued on its

---

15. *Paradiso* XXV, 1–2.

16. Cf. John Paul II, Homily at the Mass for the Conclusion of the Restoration of Michelangelo's Frescoes in the Sistine Chapel, 8 April 1994: *Insegnamenti*, XVII, 1 (1994), 899–904.

way. This can be more widely appreciated if we look beyond the figurative arts to the great development of sacred music through this same period, either composed for the liturgy or simply treating religious themes. Apart from the many artists who made sacred music their chief concern—how can we forget Pier Luigi da Palestrina, Orlando di Lasso, Tomás Luis de Victoria?—it is also true that many of the great composers—from Handel to Bach, from Mozart to Schubert, from Beethoven to Berlioz, from Liszt to Verdi—have given us works of the highest inspiration in this field.

TOWARD A RENEWED DIALOGUE

10.   It is true nevertheless that, in the modern era, alongside this Christian humanism that has continued to produce important works of culture and art, another kind of humanism, marked by the absence of God and often by opposition to God, has gradually asserted itself. Such an atmosphere has sometimes led to a separation of the world of art and the world of faith, at least in the sense that many artists have a diminished interest in religious themes.

You know, however, that the Church has not ceased to nurture great appreciation for the value of art as such. Even beyond its typically religious expressions, true art has a close affinity with the world of faith, so that, even in situations where culture and the Church are far apart, art remains a kind of bridge to religious experience. Insofar as it seeks the beautiful, as the fruit of an imagination which rises above the everyday, art is by its nature a kind of appeal to the mystery. Even when they explore the darkest depths of the soul or the most unsettling aspects of evil, artists give voice, in a way, to the universal desire for redemption.

It is clear, then, why the Church is especially concerned for the dialogue with art and desires that in our own time there be a new alliance with artists, as called for by my revered predecessor Paul VI in his vibrant speech to artists during a special meeting he had with them in the Sistine Chapel on 7 May 1964.[17] From such cooperation the Church hopes for a renewed "epiphany" of beauty in our time and apt responses to the particular needs of the Christian community.

IN THE SPIRIT OF THE SECOND VATICAN COUNCIL

11.   The Second Vatican Council laid the foundation for a renewed relationship between the Church and culture, with immediate implications for the world of art. This is a relationship offered in friendship, openness and dialogue. In the *Pastoral Constitution on the Modern World (Gaudium et Spes)*, the fathers of the Council stressed "the great importance" of literature and the arts in human life: "They seek to probe the true nature of humanity, its problems and experiences, as men and women strive to know and perfect themselves and the world, to discover their place in history and the universe, to portray their miseries and joys, their needs and strengths, with a view to a better future."[18] On this basis,

---

17. Cf. AAS 56 (1964), 438–44.
18. No. 62.

at the end of the Council the fathers addressed a greeting and an appeal to artists: "This world," they said, "in which we live needs beauty in order not to sink into despair. Beauty, like truth, brings joy to the human heart and is that precious fruit which resists the erosion of time, which unites generations and enables them to be one in admiration!"[19] In this spirit of profound respect for beauty, the *Constitution on the Sacred Liturgy (Sacrosanctum Concilium)* recalled the historic friendliness of the Church toward art and, referring more specifically to sacred art, the "summit" of religious art, did not hesitate to consider artists as having "a noble ministry" when their works reflect in some way the infinite beauty of God and raise people's minds to him.[20] Thanks also to the help of artists, "the knowledge of God can be better revealed and the preaching of the Gospel can become clearer to the human mind."[21] In this light, it comes as no surprise when Father Marie Dominique Chenu claims that the work of the historian of theology would be incomplete if it failed to give due attention to works of art, both literary and figurative, which are in their own way "not only aesthetic representations, but genuine 'sources' of theology."[22]

THE CHURCH NEEDS ART

12.   In order to communicate the message entrusted to us by Christ, the Church needs art. Art must make perceptible, and as far as possible attractive, the world of the spirit, of the invisible, of God. It must therefore translate into meaningful terms that which is in itself ineffable. Art has a unique capacity to take one or another facet of the message and translate it into colors, shapes and sounds that nourish the intuition of those who look or listen. It does so without emptying the message itself of its transcendent value and its aura of mystery.

The Church has need especially of those who can do this on the literary and figurative level, using the endless possibilities of images and their symbolic force. Christ himself made extensive use of images in his preaching, fully in keeping with his willingness to become, in the Incarnation, the icon of the unseen God.

The Church also needs musicians. How many sacred works have been composed through the centuries by people deeply imbued with the sense of the mystery! The faith of countless believers has been nourished by melodies flowing from the hearts of other believers, either introduced into the liturgy or used as an aid to dignified worship. In song, faith is experienced as vibrant joy, love, and confident expectation of the saving intervention of God. The Church needs architects, because we need spaces to bring the Christian people together and celebrate the mysteries of salvation. After the terrible destruction of the last World War and the growth of great cities, a new generation of architects showed themselves to be adept at responding to the exigencies of Christian worship, confirming that the religious theme can still inspire architectural design in our

---

19. "Message to Artists," December 8, 1965: AAS 58 (1966), 13.
20. Cf. No. 122.
21. Second Vatican Ecumenical Council, Pastoral Constitution *Gaudium et spes*, 62.
22. *La teologia nel XII secolo*, Milan 1992, p. 9.

own day. Not infrequently these architects have constructed churches that are both places of prayer and true works of art.

DOES ART NEED THE CHURCH?

13. The Church therefore needs art. But can it also be said that art needs the Church? The question may seem like a provocation. Yet, rightly understood, it is both legitimate and profound. Artists are constantly in search of the hidden meaning of things, and their torment is to succeed in expressing the world of the ineffable. How then can we fail to see what a great source of inspiration is offered by that kind of homeland of the soul that is religion? Is it not perhaps within the realm of religion that the most vital personal questions are posed, and answers both concrete and definitive are sought?

In fact, the religious theme has been among those most frequently treated by artists in every age. The Church has always appealed to their creative powers in interpreting the Gospel message and discerning its precise application in the life of the Christian community. This partnership has been a source of mutual spiritual enrichment. Ultimately, it has been a great boon for an understanding of humanity, of the authentic image and truth of the person. The special bond between art and Christian revelation has also become evident. This does not mean that human genius has not found inspiration in other religious contexts. It is enough to recall the art of the ancient world, especially Greek and Roman art, or the art that still flourishes in the very ancient civilizations of the East. It remains true, however, that because of its central doctrine of the Incarnation of the Word of God, Christianity offers artists a horizon especially rich in inspiration. What an impoverishment it would be for art to abandon the inexhaustible mine of the Gospel!

AN APPEAL TO ARTISTS

14. With this letter, I turn to you, the artists of the world, to assure you of my esteem and to help consolidate a more constructive partnership between art and the Church. Mine is an invitation to rediscover the depth of the spiritual and religious dimension that has been typical of art in its noblest forms in every age. It is with this in mind that I appeal to you, artists of the written and spoken word, of the theater and music, of the plastic arts and the most recent technologies in the field of communication. I appeal especially to you, Christian artists: I wish to remind each of you that, beyond functional considerations, the close alliance that has always existed between the Gospel and art means that you are invited to use your creative intuition to enter into the heart of the mystery of the Incarnate God and at the same time into the mystery of humanity.

Human beings, in a certain sense, are unknown to themselves. Jesus Christ not only reveals God, but "fully reveals humanity to humanity."[23] In Christ, God has reconciled the world to himself. All believers are called to bear witness to this; but it is up to you, men and women who have given your lives to art, to

---

23. Second Vatican Ecumenical Council, *Pastoral Constitution on the Church in the Modern World (Gaudium et spes)*, 22.

declare with all the wealth of your ingenuity that in Christ the world is redeemed: The human person is redeemed, the human body is redeemed, and the whole creation which, according to Saint Paul, "awaits impatiently the revelation of the children of God" (Romans 8:19), is redeemed. The creation awaits the revelation of the children of God also through art and in art. This is your task. Humanity in every age, and even today, looks to works of art to shed light upon its path and its destiny.

THE CREATOR SPIRIT AND ARTISTIC INSPIRATION

15.   Often in the Church there resounds the invocation to the Holy Spirit: *Veni, Creator Spiritus* . . . "Come, O Creator Spirit, visit our minds, fill with your grace the hearts you have created."[24]

The Holy Spirit, "the Breath" (in Hebrew, *ruah*), is the One referred to already in the Book of Genesis: "The earth was without form and void, and darkness was on the face of the deep; and the Spirit of God was moving over the face of the waters" (1:2). What affinity between the words "breath–breathing" and "inspiration"! The Spirit is the mysterious Artist of the universe. Looking to the Third Millennium, I would hope that all artists might receive in abundance the gift of that creative inspiration which is the starting-point of every true work of art.

Dear artists, you know well that there are many impulses that, either from within or from without, can inspire your talent. Every genuine inspiration, however, contains some tremor of that "breath" with which the Creator Spirit suffused the work of creation from the very beginning. Overseeing the mysterious laws governing the universe, the divine breath of the Creator Spirit reaches out to human genius and stirs its creative power. The Spirit touches it with a kind of inner illumination, which brings together the sense of the good and the beautiful, and he awakens energies of mind and heart that enable it to conceive an idea and give it form in a work of art. It is right then to speak, even if only analogically, of "moments of grace," because the human being is able to experience in some way the Absolute who is utterly beyond.

THE BEAUTY THAT SAVES

16.   On the threshold of the Third Millennium, my hope for all of you who are artists is that you will have an especially intense experience of creative inspiration. May the beauty that you pass on to generations still to come be such that it will stir them to wonder! Faced with the sacredness of life and the human person, and before the marvels of the universe, wonder is the only appropriate attitude.

From this wonder can come the enthusiasm of which Norwid spoke in the poem to which I referred earlier. People of today and tomorrow need this enthusiasm if they are to meet and master the crucial challenges that stand before us. Thanks to this enthusiasm, humanity, every time it loses its way, will be able

---

24. Hymn at vespers on Pentecost.

to lift itself up and set out again on the right path. In this sense it has been said with profound insight that "beauty will save the world."[25]

Beauty is a key to mystery and a call to transcendence. It is an invitation to savor life and to dream of the future. That is why the beauty of created things can never fully satisfy. It stirs that hidden nostalgia for God which a lover of beauty like Saint Augustine could express in incomparable terms: "Late have I loved you, beauty so old and so new: late have I loved you!"[26]

Artists of the world, may your many different paths all lead to that infinite ocean of beauty where wonder becomes awe, exhilaration, unspeakable joy.

May you be guided and inspired by the mystery of the Risen Christ, whom the Church in these days contemplates with joy. May the Blessed Virgin Mary be with you always: She is the *tota pulchra* portrayed by countless artists, she whom Dante contemplates among the splendors of Paradise as "beauty that was joy in the eyes of all the other saints."[27]

"From chaos there rises the world of the spirit." These words of Adam Mickiewicz, written at a time of great hardship for his Polish homeland,[28] prompt my hope for you: May your art help to affirm that true beauty which, as a glimmer of the Spirit of God, will transfigure matter, opening the human soul to the sense of the eternal.

WITH MY HEARTFELT GOOD WISHES!
JOHN PAUL II, POPE
FROM THE VATICAN,
APRIL 4, 1999,
EASTER SUNDAY

---

25. F. Dostoyevsky, *The Idiot*, Part III, chap. 5.

26. *"Sero te amavi! Pulchritudo tam antiqua et tam nova, sero te amavi!" Confessions*, 10, 27: CCL 27, 251.

27. *Paradiso* XXXI, 134–35.

28. *"Oda do mlodosci,"* v. 69: *Wybór poezji*, Wroclaw 1986, vol. 1, p. 63.

NATIONAL DIRECTORY
FOR CATECHESIS
LITURGICAL EXCERPTS,
CHAPTERS 3 AND 5

DIRECTORY

DEVELOPED BY THE UNITED STATES CONFERENCE
OF CATHOLIC BISHOPS, COMMITTEE ON EDUCATION
APPROVED BY THE UNITED STATES CONFERENCE
OF CATHOLIC BISHOPS
JUNE, 2003

RECOGNITIO GRANTED BY THE CONGREGATION
FOR THE CLERGY
DECEMBER 16, 2004

AN OVERVIEW OF THE *NATIONAL DIRECTORY FOR CATECHESIS*
(CHAPTERS 3 AND 5)
Jo-Ann Metzdorff

It is the responsibility of all the baptized to be agents of evangelization follow-ing Jesus's command to "Go therefore and make disciples of all nations."[1] How we do this is determined by our state in life, our particular gifts and talents, and in many ways by the culture in which we live. Evangelization is carried out through Word and sacrament, through the example of Christian living, through service to those in need, and through the ministry of catechesis. While particu-lar people in the Church are called to be catechists, teachers of the faith, "cat-echesis always has been and always will be a work for which the whole Church must feel responsible and must wish to be responsible."[2] This is the vision of the *National Directory for Catechesis* (NDC).

The NDC, published in 2005 by the United States Conference of Catholic Bishops, is the result of years of work and study to present the vision of the Second Vatican Council with regard to catechesis of the faithful to Catholics in the United States. It takes the place of *Sharing the Light of Faith: National Catechetical Directory for Catholics of the United States*, the 1979 document written following the promulgation of the *General Catechetical Directory* (GCD) in 1971 by the Congregation for the Clergy. The GCD was written to guide the world in the renewal of catechesis and evangelization after the Second Vatican Council. In the years since both those documents were published much has changed in the area of catechesis. Increasing numbers of lay people are now involved in full-time catechetical ministry and the *Rite of Christian Initiation of Adults* has become a model for catechesis of both adults and children. The call for renewed efforts at evangelization and catechesis aimed at adults as seen in the publication of the *Catechism of the Catholic Church* and other docu-ments such as Pope Paul VI's 1975 apostolic exhortation, *Evangelii nuntiandi*, and Pope John Paul II's 1979 apostolic exhortation, *Catechesi tradendae*, pre-cipitated a revision of the GDC in 1997 under the title *General Directory for Catechesis* (GDC).

The promulgation of the GDC and the publication of the United States Conference of Catholic Bishops' 1999 document on adult faith formation, *Our Hearts Were Burning Within Us*, contributed to the need to update *Sharing the Light of Faith*. There were also many new challenges that bishops, pastors, and catechetical leaders needed to address in the years since *Sharing the Light of Faith* was published. The world is rapidly changing, especially in the area of technology, and the way we catechize needs to keep up with these changes and developments. The shifting demographics of long established parishes, an influx

---

1. Matthew 28:19.
2. *Catechesi tradendae* (CT), 16.

of people with different cultural backgrounds, catechizing people with disabilities, and opening and continuing a dialogue with or catechizing people from different faith communities all called for a revision of the text to meet these changes. Shifting parish structures, changing family life, a diminishing of Catholic identity even among those who attend Mass regularly, increased secularism, moral uncertainties and issues relating to religious freedom, and changing worldviews all contribute to the need to constantly evaluate how the faithful are catechized and to offer further assistance to those who engage in this essential ministry. The NDC strives to address these developing needs and challenges and devotes several chapters to these important issues.

The NDC provides the framework for catechesis aimed at both children and adults in parishes and Catholic schools throughout the United States. In tandem with the *Catechism of the Catholic Church* (CCC) it also assists in the formulation and publication of programs and materials for catechesis to make sure they conform to Church teaching. In addition, it aids bishops, priests, and catechetical leaders on both the diocesan and parish levels in the implementation and evaluation of their catechetical programs.

There is always a question as to the level of authority an official Church document or publication carries. Some documents carry more weight than others. Using the *General Directory for Catechesis* as the norm for the entire Church; episcopal conferences were called to develop their own directories to assist in the endeavor of catechizing the faithful in their particular countries and regions. As an official document of the United States Conference of Catholic Bishops, the NDC fulfills this request. The NDC has been reviewed and approved by the Congregation of the Clergy.[3] The NDC is used along with the CCC to ensure that texts and programs are in conformity with both magisterial teaching and pastoral directives and as such it carries a significant level of authority. However, not everything in the NDC carries the same level of authority. Pastoral directives included in the text, although far from simply being suggestions, do not carry as much authority and are presented as "prudential judgments, applications, or guidelines that may continue to evolve."[4] These pastoral directives are exceedingly helpful in assisting catechetical leaders and publishers to understand the needs and diversity of those they catechize, and to adequately meet those needs.

The rationale for including chapters from the NDC in this volume of *The Liturgy Documents* is because, as we read in John Paul II's apostolic exhortation, *Catechesi tradendae*, "catechesis is intrinsically linked with the whole of liturgical and sacramental activity, for it is in the sacraments, especially in the Eucharist, that Christ Jesus works in fullness for the transformation of human beings."[5] The NDC contains a chapter specifically on liturgy and catechesis. Chapter 5, "Catechesis in a Worshiping Community," contains concise but comprehensive sections on catechizing and formation of children and adults for the reception of the sacraments. It also contains sections on prayer, both liturgical and personal, as well as on the liturgical year, art, architecture, music,

---

3. See *National Directory for Catechesis* (NDC), 7.

4. Ibid.

5. CT, 23.

popular piety, and devotions. Adequate catechesis in these areas is essential in order to "promote an active, conscious, genuine participation in the liturgy of the Church."[6] Liturgical catechesis and formation not only serves to assure the faithful are knowledgeable about the liturgical life of the Church, but more important, it "aims to initiate people into the mystery of Christ."[7]

The NDC is not only essential for those involved in catechetical ministry but also serves as a valuable resource and guide for those engaged in liturgical ministry. Catechetical leaders have a great responsibility to form children and adults to prepare for and better participate in the Church's sacraments and liturgies, and the NDC greatly aids them in that task, however, they cannot do this alone. Formation for worship involves the entire parish community, especially those involved in liturgical ministry. Individuals in liturgical leadership roles, such as diocesan and parish directors of liturgy, parish liturgy committees, directors of music ministry, coordinators of the Rite of Christian Initiation of Adults, and those responsible for art and environment, will find the NDC compliments and enhances other liturgical and theological resources they might use. In the same way that it is important for those in catechetical ministry to be acquainted with liturgical documents, becoming familiar with catechetical documents assists liturgical ministers in expanding their knowledge, getting a sense of challenges facing the formation of the faithful, and gaining insight as to how to carry out their own ministry in union with other diocesan and parish ministries.

The *Catechism of the Catholic Church* states that the liturgy is the "privileged place for catechizing the People of God."[8] It is in the Church's liturgy that people encounter Christ in a unique way as we enter into his Paschal Mystery. All liturgy is catechetical in that it is through our prayer and worship that we come to know God. It is through the proclamation of the Scriptures and the breaking open the Word in the homily that we encounter Christ and are called to go forth to spread the Good News and to fulfill our baptismal responsibilities. Through the study of the NDC, especially chapter 5, liturgical leaders are drawn into an understanding of important aspects of sacramental preparation and catechesis for liturgy in order that they too can best form their own ministers and volunteers and be better able to catechize the faithful through their particular ministry.

Chapter 3 has also been included in this volume. It is a brief but concise exploration of how the faithful are called to hand on the Catholic faith to others focusing on the "Authentic presentation of the Christian message" through Scripture, Tradition, and the *Catechism of the Catholic Church.*[9] Section 25, found in this chapter, especially offers liturgical ministers a brief yet ample exploration of how presentation of the Christian message takes place and offers several criteria for this presentation. This section stands out in that it not only presents the criteria but also affords the catechist or liturgical minister an opportunity to reflect on their own understanding of the basic teachings of the Church

---

6. *General Catechetical Directory* (GCD), 25.

7. *Catechism of the Catholic Church* (CCC), 1075.

8. Ibid., 1074.

9. NDC, 25.

and evaluate their efforts in evangelizing and handing on the faith to others. It offers the catechist and liturgical minister a common language and understanding of "the deposit of faith that was first entrusted to the apostles by Christ himself."[10]

Adequate comprehensive catechesis is needed today more than ever in order that future generations will be strong in their knowledge of the faith, and in their convictions to live out their lives as disciples of Christ through prayer, worship, and service. The NDC can guide us in our efforts to achieve this as both catechists and liturgical ministers as we live out our ministry of evangelization.

---

10. NDC, 26.

NATIONAL DIRECTORY FOR CATECHESIS

DIRECTORY
UNITED STATES CONFERENCE OF CATHOLIC BISHOPS
MAY 2005

CHAPTER 3
THIS IS OUR FAITH; THIS IS THE FAITH OF THE CHURCH

For I handed on to you as of first importance what I also received: that Christ died for our sins in accordance with the scriptures; that he was buried; that he was raised on the third day in accordance with the scriptures; that he appeared to Cephas, then to the Twelve. (1 Cor 15:3–5)

23. INTRODUCTION

In expressing and handing on the faith that Jesus entrusted to them before he ascended to his Father, the apostles made use of brief summaries by which all could come to know the fundamental content of Christian belief and preaching. These initial creedal statements synthesized the Christian faith and became the original catechetical reference points for the apostolic Church. They were the first professions of faith; they were intended especially for candidates for Baptism; and they have preserved the substance of the Christian message for people of all the nations for more than two thousand years.

Since the *Catechism of the Catholic Church* is a catechesis of the Creed, this chapter presents a brief introduction to it in order to facilitate its better understanding and use in the catechetical ministry. This chapter also provides the criteria for the authentic presentation of the Christian message in the United States at this time in history.

24. THE SYMPHONY OF THE FAITH

A. Normative Instruments of Catechesis

Sacred Scripture, the *Catechism of the Catholic Church*, the *General Directory for Catechesis*, and this *National Directory for Catechesis* are distinct yet complementary instruments that serve the Church's catechetical activity. The *General Directory for Catechesis* provides "the basic principles of pastoral theology taken from the Magisterium of the Church, and in a special way from the Second

Vatican Council, by which pastoral action in the ministry of the word can be more fittingly directed and governed."[1] This *National Directory for Catechesis* contains the general guidelines for catechesis in the United States and has been prepared by the United States Conference of Catholic Bishops. *Our Hearts Were Burning Within Us* gives a plan and strategies for development of an effective ministry of adult faith formation in parish life.

B. Sacred Scripture

Sacred Scripture, the word of God written under the inspiration of the Holy Spirit, has the preeminent position in the life of the Catholic Church and especially in the ministry of evangelization and catechesis. The earliest forms of Christian catechesis made regular use of the Old Testament and the personal witness of the apostles and disciples that would become the New Testament. Much of the catechesis of the patristic period took the form of commentary on the word of God contained in Sacred Scripture. Through all the ages of the Church, the study of Sacred Scripture has been the cornerstone of catechesis. The Second Vatican Council advised that catechesis, as one form of the ministry of the word, should be nurtured and should thrive in holiness through the word of the Scripture.[2] Catechesis should take Sacred Scripture as its inspiration, its fundamental curriculum, and its end because it strengthens faith, nourishes the soul, and nurtures the spiritual life. "Scripture provides the starting point, foundation, and norm of catechetical teaching."[3] Catechesis should assume the thought and perspective of Sacred Scripture and make frequent direct use of the biblical texts themselves. "The presentation of the Gospels should be done in such a way as to elicit an encounter with Christ, who provides the key to the whole biblical revelation and communicates the call of God that summons each one to respond."[4]

C. The Catechism of the Catholic Church

The Catechism of the Catholic Church is an act of the Magisterium promulgated by Pope John Paul II by virtue of his apostolic authority.[5] It is "a statement of the Church's faith and of catholic doctrine, attested to or illumined by Sacred Scripture, the Apostolic Tradition, and the Church's Magisterium."[6] It "aims at presenting an organic synthesis of the essential and fundamental contents of Catholic doctrine, as regards both faith and morals, in the light of the Second Vatican Council and the whole of the Church's Tradition."[7] The *Catechism of the Catholic Church* is a valid and legitimate instrument for ecclesial communion; it is a sure norm for teaching the faith and an authentic reference text for

---

1. GDC, no. 120.

2. Cf. DV, no. 12.

3. Pontifical Biblical Commission, *The Interpretation of the Bible in the Church* (Washington, DC: USCCB, 1994), 39.

4. *The Interpretation of the Bible in the Church*, 39.

5. Cf. John Paul II, *On the Publication of the "Catechism of the Catholic Church"* (*Fidei Depositum*) (FD), no. 3. In CCC.

6. FD, no. 3.

7. CCC, no. 11.

teaching Catholic doctrine and particularly for preparing local catechisms. However, the Catechism is not just an authentic reference text; it is a beautiful collection of the truths of the Catholic faith, following in the footsteps of the early Church. The foundation of the *Catechism* is Sacred Scripture, and it includes writings of the Fathers, doctors, and saints of the Church. It is not intended to replace local catechisms, but rather to encourage the preparation of new local catechisms that take into account particular cultures and preserve the unity of faith and fidelity to Catholic doctrine.[8]

This *National Directory for Catechesis*, as far as the content of the Christian message is concerned, presumes and refers to the *Catechism of the Catholic Church*. The following exposition of the Catechism of the Catholic Church seeks not to summarize its content but instead to facilitate its better understanding and use in the catechetical ministry in the United States.

Pope John Paul II has called the *Catechism of the Catholic Church* "the 'symphony' of the faith"[9] because it is the result of the collaboration of the whole Episcopate of the Catholic Church throughout the world and because it expresses the harmony of their confession of the faith.

The *Catechism of the Catholic Church* is structured around four fundamental dimensions of the Christian life: (1) the profession of faith, (2) the celebration of the Liturgy, (3) Christian moral life, and (4) prayer. These four parts correspond to the essential aspects of the Christian mystery: (1) belief in the Triune God and his saving plan in Jesus Christ, (2) celebration of Christ's saving actions in the sacramental life, (3) living life in Christ, and (4) expression of the Christian faith in prayer. This structure in turn derives from the profound unity of the Christian life.

> The Church professes this mystery [of the faith] in the Apostles' Creed (*Part One*) and celebrates it in the sacramental liturgy (*Part Two*), so that the life of the faithful may be conformed to Christ in the Holy Spirit to the glory of God the Father (*Part Three*). This mystery, then, requires that the faithful believe in it, that they celebrate it, and that they live from it in a vital and personal relationship with the living and true God. This relationship is prayer (*Part Four*).[10]

The *Catechism of the Catholic Church* is the doctrinal point of reference for education in the basic tasks of catechesis.[11] However, it does not impose a predetermined format for the presentation of doctrine.

The inspiration of the *Catechism of the Catholic Church* derives from the person of Jesus Christ as he reveals the mystery of the Holy Trinity and the mystery of the human person. Through Jesus Christ, we come to know God and his divine plan for our salvation, we come to know ourselves and our destiny, and we come to know how to live. These are the four golden threads of the *Catechism*:

---

8. Cf. FD, no. 3.

9. FD, no. 1.

10. CCC, no. 2558.

11. See Chapter 2 of this *Directory*.

the Blessed Trinity; Jesus as God and Man; the Paschal Mystery of Jesus' passion, death, Resurrection, and Ascension into heaven attaining our salvation; the dignity of the human person.

As the central mystery of the Catholic faith, the mystery of the Triune God animates and orders the presentation of the Christian message in the *Catechism of the Catholic Church*. The profession of faith is precisely a confession of faith in the Holy Trinity. It is divided into the fundamental doctrinal formulations that state Christian belief in the Father, the Son, and the Holy Spirit. It presents the sacraments and the Liturgy as the "work of the Holy Trinity."[12] It presents the Christian life as directed by the Trinity: "Everyone who follows Christ does so because the Father draws him and the Spirit moves him."[13] The profession of faith presents the prayer of the believer as "a communion with the Holy Trinity."[14]

The mystery of the human person is woven throughout the *Catechism of the Catholic Church* as well. Every human person longs to know God. "'Believing' is a human act, conscious and free, corresponding to the dignity of the human person."[15] The celebration of the Christian mystery in the Church's Liturgy and sacraments expresses the faith in words and signs that make sense to the human person. "It is with and through their own human culture, assumed and transfigured by Christ, that the multitude of God's children has access to the Father, in order to glorify him in the one Spirit."[16] In seeking to conform their lives to Christ, Christians are called to lead a life "worthy of the gospel of Christ."[17] "The vocation of humanity is to show forth the image of God and to be transformed into the image of the Father's only Son."[18] By deliberate actions, the human person "does, or does not, conform to the good promised by God and attested by moral conscience."[19] Christian prayer is "the life of the new heart. It ought to animate us at every moment."[20]

The *Catechism of the Catholic Church* is a catechism for the universal Church. As a catechism, it is *an organic presentation* of the Catholic faith in its entirety."[21] It is universal in scope because it presents the "events and fundamental salvific truths which express the faith common to the People of God and which constitute the indispensable basic reference for catechesis."[22] It seeks "to link the wondrous unity of the Christian mystery with the varied needs and conditions of those to whom this message is addressed."[23] However,

---

12. CCC, no. 1077.

13. CCC, no. 259.

14. CCC, no. 2655.

15. CCC, no. 180.

16. CCC, no. 1204.

17. Phil 1:27.

18. CCC, no. 1877.

19. CCC, no. 1700.

20. CCC, no. 2697.

21. CCC, no. 18.

22. GDC, no. 124.

23. John Paul II, *Apostolic Letter in Which the Latin Typical Edition of the "Catechism of the Catholic Church" Is Approved and Promulgated (Laetamur Magnopere)* (LM) (1997), xv. In CCC.

by design, this *Catechism* does not set out to provide the adaptation of doctrinal presentations and catechetical methods required by the differences of culture, age, spiritual maturity, and social and ecclesial condition among all those to whom it is addressed. Such indispensable adaptations are the responsibility of particular catechisms and, even more, of those who instruct the faithful.[24]

The *Catechism of the Catholic Church* presents and preserves the deposit of faith. The deposit of faith is the heritage of faith contained in Sacred Scripture and Tradition and handed on in the Church from the time of the apostles—a heritage from which the Magisterium draws all that it proposes for belief as being divinely revealed. "Catechesis will find in this genuine, systematic presentation of the faith and of Catholic doctrine a totally reliable way to present, with renewed fervor, each and every part of the Christian message to the people of our time. This text will provide every catechist with sound help for communicating the one, perennial deposit of faith within the local Church."[25]

Sacred Scripture has a preeminent position in catechesis because Sacred Scripture "present[s] God's own Word in unalterable form" and "make[s] the voice of the holy Spirit resound again and again in the words of the prophets and apostles."[26] The *Catechism of the Catholic Church* is intended to complement Sacred Scripture. Together with Sacred Tradition, Sacred Scripture constitutes the supreme rule of faith.

In practice, this means that catechesis must be permeated with biblical and evangelical thought, spirit, and attitudes through constant use of and reference to the word of God. The *Catechism of the Catholic Church* is not superior to the word of God but is, rather, at its service. Each nourishes the ministry of catechesis: "Both Sacred Scripture and the *Catechism of the Catholic Church* must inform biblical as well as doctrinal catechesis so that they become true vehicles of the content of God's word."[27]

In addition, the *Catechism of the Catholic Church* retrieves several important aspects of the catechetical tradition of the Church Fathers, who placed a high priority on the baptismal catechumenate in the life of the local churches. They emphasized the gradual and progressive movement of Christian initiation and formation through a series of stages and rituals. This was acknowledged when the Fathers of the Second Vatican Council called for the restoration of the adult catechumenate largely as it was celebrated and preserved in the patristic tradition.[28]

---

24. CCC, no. 24.
25. LM, p. xv.
26. DV, no. 21.
27. GDC, no. 128.
28. Cf. SC, no. 64.

25. CRITERIA FOR THE AUTHENTIC PRESENTATION OF THE CHRISTIAN MESSAGE

The word of God contained in Sacred Scripture and Sacred Tradition is the single source of the fundamental criteria for the presentation of the Christian message. The presentation of the Christian message

- Centers on Jesus Christ
- Introduces the Trinitarian dimension of the Gospel message
- Proclaims the Good News of salvation and liberation
- Comes from and leads to the Church
- Has a historical character
- Seeks inculturation and preserves the integrity and purity of the message
- Offers the comprehensive message of the Gospel and respects its inherent hierarchy of truths
- Communicates the profound dignity of the human person
- Fosters a common language of the faith

A. The Christian Message, Centered on Christ

The Christian message concentrates on the person of Jesus Christ. Above all, catechesis must transmit this centrality of Christ in the Gospel message. Catechesis that is centered on Christ presents Christ first and presents everything else with reference to him,[29] for he is the center of the Gospel message. "At the heart of catechesis we find, in essence, a Person, the Person of Jesus of Nazareth, 'the only Son from the Father . . . full of grace and truth.'"[30]

Catechesis that is centered on Christ presents Christ as "the center of the history of salvation."[31] He came "in the fullness of time."[32] As the definitive Revelation of God, he is the point in salvation history toward which the created order proceeds from the beginning of time and the final event toward which it converges. "Jesus Christ is the same yesterday, today, and forever."[33] He is "the key, the center and the purpose of the whole of man's history."[34]

Christ-centered catechesis presents the Gospel message as the word of God written down by human authors under the inspiration of the Holy Spirit.[35]

---

29. Cf. CT, no. 6.
30. CT, no. 5.
31. *General Catechetical Directory*, no. 41.
32. Eph 1:10.
33. Heb 13:8.
34. Second Vatican Council, *Pastoral Constitution on the Church in the Modern World* (*Gaudium et Spes*) (GS), no. 10.
35. CCC, nos. 105–106.

It transmits "the teaching of Jesus Christ, the Truth that he communicates or, to put it more precisely, the Truth that he is."[36]

Because the Gospels narrate the life of Jesus and the mystery of our redemption after Christ and the Reign of God that he proclaimed, catechesis will also be centered on Christ if the Gospels occupy a pivotal place within it. They "are our principal source for the life and teaching of the Incarnate Word, our Savior."[37] They transmit the life, message, and saving actions of Jesus Christ and express the teaching that was proposed to the first Christian communities. Catechesis must be centered in the Gospels, because "Jesus Christ is their center."[38]

In presenting catechesis that is centered on Christ, dioceses and parishes should

- Explicitly and consistently proclaim the name, teaching, promises, and mystery of Jesus Christ, as well as his announcement of the coming of the Reign of God

- Develop, through effective preaching, teaching, adult faith formation, and catechist formation programs, the personal relationship that Christ has initiated with each of his disciples

- Promote conversion to Jesus Christ and communion with him through the sacraments, especially the Holy Eucharist

- Teach, in a way that can be understood by specific cultures, that Christ is the ultimate meaning and purpose of history; and provide programs that help all who catechize to present the teachings of Christ "about God, man, happiness, the moral life, death, etc. without in any way changing his thought"[39]

- Help all who catechize to understand that, like Jesus, their teaching is not their own but, rather, comes from God[40]

B. The Trinitarian Character of the Christian Message

The Christian message is inherently Trinitarian because its source is the incarnate Word of the Father, Jesus Christ, who speaks to the world through his Holy Spirit.[41] Anointed by the Holy Spirit, Jesus' life is constantly oriented to the Father. He teaches in communion with the Father and the Holy Spirit. He leads us to the mystery of God in himself: Father, Son, and Holy Spirit. The Christian life and the Christian message are radically Trinitarian.

---

36. CT, no. 6.
37. DV, no. 18.
38. CCC, no. 139.
39. GDC, no. 98.
40. Cf. Jn 7:16.
41. The witness of the Eastern Catholic Churches to the explicitly Trinitarian character of Christian theology, liturgy, and spirituality has been a fruitful source of inspiration for the whole Church.

In presenting catechesis that is Trinitarian in nature, dioceses and parishes should help all who catechize to

- Understand that their presentation of the Gospel message must always proceed "through Christ, to the Father, in the Holy Spirit"[42] and "lead to [a] confession of faith in God, Father, Son and Holy Spirit"[43]

- Present God's plan of loving kindness, which was conceived by the Father, was fulfilled in the Son, and is directed by the Holy Spirit in the life of the Church

- Understand that the primary subject of catechesis is the mystery of the Holy Trinity, "the central mystery of Christian faith and life"[44]

- Present the fact that the innermost being of God, in whose image all are made, is a communion of love with vital implications for Christian living

- Draw out the moral implications for Christians who are called to be a people gathered in the unity of the Father, Son, and Holy Spirit

C. The Christian Message That Proclaims the Good News of Salvation and Liberation from Sin

The Christian message proclaims the gift of salvation in Jesus Christ. Jesus' announcement of the Kingdom of God marks a new and definitive intervention by God "with a transforming power equal and even superior to his creation of the world."[45] Christ's proclamation of salvation is the "center of his Good News."[46]

The Good News of the Kingdom of God, which proclaims salvation, includes a message of liberation for all, but especially for the poor. Jesus addressed his announcement of the kingdom principally to the frail, the vulnerable, the disabled, and the poor—not only the economically poor, but the culturally and religiously poor as well.[47] The Beatitudes proclaim the liberation that the kingdom brings. It is not merely a liberation from all the forms of injustice that oppress people; it is especially a liberation from sin.

Liberation from sin is the fundamental form of freedom from which all liberation emerges. Christ's message of liberation brought "glad tidings to the poor." He was sent "to proclaim liberty to captives / and recovery of sight to the blind, / to let the oppressed go free, / and to proclaim a year acceptable to the Lord,"[48] precisely so that the oppressed might be open to the action of the Holy Spirit in their lives.

---

42. *General Catechetical Directory*, no. 41.

43. GDC, no. 99.

44. CCC, no. 234.

45. GDC, no. 101.

46. EN, no. 9.

47. Cf. John Paul II, *On the Hundredth Anniversary of Rerum Novarum* (*Centesimus Annus*) (CA) (Washington, DC: USCCB, 1991), no. 57.

48. Lk 4:18–19.

In presenting catechesis that proclaims the Good News of salvation, dioceses and parishes should transmit the fundamental message of the Kingdom of God by emphasizing several basic points that Jesus made throughout his preaching:

1. God is a loving Father who abides with his people.

2. With the coming of the kingdom, God offers us salvation, free us from sin, brings us into communion with him and all humanity, and promises eternal salvation.

3. The Kingdom of God is one of justice, love, and peace, in the light of which we shall be judged.

4. The Kingdom of God is inaugurated in the person of Jesus Christ;[49] it is in mystery present now on the earth and will be perfected when the Lord returns.

5. The Church, the community of disciples, "is, on earth, the seed and the beginning of that kingdom"[50] and "is effectively and concretely at the service of the Kingdom."[51]

6. The Church offers a foretaste of the world to come, and human life is a journey back to God.

Catechesis helps the Christian faithful to integrate Christ's message of liberation in several important ways. It first situates his message of liberation within the "specifically religious objective of evangelization."[52] Therefore, dioceses and parishes should help the Christian faithful to integrate Christ's message of liberation by

- Situating his message of liberation within the "specifically religious finality of evangelization"[53]

- Ensuring that the message of liberation "cannot be contained in the simple and restricted dimension of economics, politics, social or cultural life"[54]

- Presenting Christian social morality as a demand of the Gospel's message of liberation and a consequence of the great commandment of love

- Arousing "a love of preference for the poor"[55] in those being catechized

- Emphasizing that "what is already due in justice is not to be offered as a gift of charity"[56]

---

49. Cf. LG, no. 3.
50. LG, no. 5.
51. RM, no. 20.
52. EN, no. 32.
53. EN, no. 32.
54. EN, no. 33.
55. John Paul II, *On Social Concern (Sollicitudo Rei Socialis)* (SRS) (Washington, DC: USCCB, 1988), no. 42.
56. Second Vatican Council, *Decree on the Apostolate of the Lay People (Apostolicam Actuositatem)* (AA), no. 8.

D. The Ecclesial Character of the Christian Message

Catechesis has a distinctly ecclesial character because the Christian community transmits the Gospel essentially as it has received it, understands it, celebrates it, lives it and communicates it.[57] Apostles received the Gospel message directly from Christ under the action of the Holy Spirit and preached it to the first Christian communities. Martyrs bore witness to it by their blood. Saints have lived it deeply. Fathers and Doctors of the Church have taught it wisely. Bishops have carefully preserved it with zeal and love and interpreted it authentically. Missionaries have proclaimed it courageously. Theologians have helped others understand it.[58] The People of God have applied it more fully in their daily lives. All continue these efforts today.

Although the community of the disciples of Jesus Christ is spread throughout the world, the Gospel message that binds them together is one; it is the same faith that is transmitted in many different languages and through many cultures. The Church has constantly and consistently confessed this: "one Lord, one faith, one baptism; one God and Father of all, who is over all and through all and in all."[59]

"Catechesis originates in the Church's confession of faith and leads to the profession of faith of the catechumen and those to be catechized."[60] In presenting catechesis, dioceses and parishes should ensure that catechesis

- Transmits the one faith to all peoples

- Introduces catechumens and those to be catechized to the unity of the profession of faith

- Nourishes the unity of the Body of Christ

E. The Historical Character of the Christian Message

The Gospel message of salvation in Jesus Christ has a distinctly historical character. Jesus Christ is a historical figure who preached the Good News of the coming of the Kingdom of God in time. The Incarnation, passion, death, and Resurrection of Christ are real historical events. Jesus Christ poured out his Holy Spirit and established the Church on Pentecost, hereby ushering in a new era of salvation history: the age of the Church. During this era, Christ is revealing the work of salvation in the life of the Church "until he comes" again.[61]

While the Church transcends history, she is also part of it. For her part, the Church remembers the saving events of the past and makes them known in every age. These events constitute the "constant 'memory'" of the Church.[62] Christ lives now and acts now in and with his Church. His gift to the Church,

---

57. Cf. CCC, no. 2558.

58. Cf. GDC, no. 105.

59. Eph 4:5–6.

60. GDC, no. 105.

61. 1 Cor 11:26.

62. GDC, no. 107.

the Holy Spirit, continues to "renew the face of the earth"[63] as the Church awaits the return of her Lord and Savior.

In presenting the historical character of the Christian message, dioceses and parishes should ensure that catechesis

- Proclaims the words and deeds of God throughout history

- Presents salvation history as it is set forth in Sacred Scripture through

  1. The various stages of Revelation in the Old Testament

  2. The fulfillment of Revelation in the life and teaching of Jesus

  3. The history of the Church whose responsibility it is to transmit Revelation to future generations

- Helps to interpret the meaning of the events of salvation history for the present age in light of Revelation

- Situates the sacraments within the history of salvation and helps those being catechized to "re-read and re-live the great events of salvation history in the 'today' of [the Church's] liturgy"[64]

- Helps those being catechized to understand the mystery at work in the historical events of salvation: the mystery of the Son of God at work in his humanity, the mystery of salvation at work in the history of the Church, and the evidence of God's presence at work in the signs of the times[65]

- Contributes to a healing of memories, to the reevaluation of past animosities and stereotypes among Christians, and to the interpretation of the past in a new way in the light of ecumenical developments

F. The Inculturation of the Christian Message

The inculturation of the Gospel is also a key criterion for the pastoral presentation of the Christian message because the Good News of Jesus Christ is intended for people of all cultures. It is not a superficial adaptation designed to make the Gospel more pleasing to its hearers. It is, rather, a process that brings the transforming power of the Gospel to touch persons in their hearts and cultures at their deepest levels.

In presenting catechesis that is both an inculturation of the Christian message and a careful preservation of the authenticity of that message, dioceses and parishes are encouraged to

- Present the same Gospel message that was given by Jesus Christ in its integrity and purity, avoiding any division, subtraction, or distortion of it

---

63. Ps 104:30.
64. CCC, no. 1095.
65. Cf. GDC, no. 108.

- Look to the Church as the principal agent of inculturation and involve persons of various cultures in planning the catechetical mission

- Gather information on the diverse cultural makeup of the community

- Develop and use culturally appropriate catechetical methods, tools, texts, and resources

- Cultivate catechetical leadership that reflects the cultural diversity of the locality

- Prepare catechists in their native language and cultural situations

- Rely on catechists who not only have "a profound religious sense [but] also possess a living social conscience and [are] well rooted in [their] cultural environment"[66]

- Ensure that catechesis is grounded in the cultural environment in which it is presented

- Respond to the various requirements of diverse cultures

- Ensure that catechesis employs popular devotions and the distinctive symbols of faith common to various cultural groups

- Ensure that catechetical initiatives work toward making the catechumenate and catechetical formation programs into centers of inculturation that employ, with proper discernment, the language, symbols, and values of the catechumens and those being catechized

- Enable those being catechized to become more able to explain the faith to others in the culture in which they live and to be able to give "reason for [their] hope"[67]

G. The Comprehensive Hierarchical Character of the Christian Message

The "organic hierarchical character"[68] of the Christian message is another vital criterion for the presentation of the Gospel. The harmony and coherence of the Christian message require that the different truths of the faith be organized around a center, the mystery of the Most Holy Trinity: "the source of all the other mysteries of faith, the light that enlightens them."[69]

"In Catholic doctrine there exists an order or 'hierarchy' of truths, since they vary in their relation to the foundation of the Christian faith."[70] The existence of a hierarchy of truths does not provide the grounds for ignoring or eliminating some truths of the faith. Neither should such a hierarchy be confused with the assignment of degrees of certainty to the individual truths of the faith: "This

---

66. GDC, no. 110.

67. 1 Pt 3:15.

68. CT, no. 31.

69. CCC, no. 234.

70. Second Vatican Council, *Decree on Ecumenism* (*Unitatis Redintegratio*) (UR), no. 11.

hierarchy does not mean that some truths pertain to faith itself less than others, but rather that some truths are based on others as of a higher priority, and are illumined by them."[71]

All levels of catechesis should carefully consider the hierarchy of truths in the presentation of the Christian message. All aspects and dimensions of the Christian message are related to these principle truths. In presenting the comprehensive hierarchical character of the Christian message, dioceses and parishes should ensure that catechesis presents

- The Christian message, organized around its central truths: "the mystery of God the Father, the Son, and the Holy Spirit, Creator of all things; the mystery of Christ the incarnate Word, who was born of the Virgin Mary, and who suffered, died, and rose for our salvation; the mystery of the Holy Spirit, who is present in the Church, sanctifying it and guiding it until the glorious coming of Christ, our Savior and Judge; and the mystery of the Church which is Christ's Mystical Body, in which the Virgin Mary holds the preeminent place"[72]

- Baptism as the foundational sacrament of Christian life, which celebrates the saving action of Christ's life, death, and Resurrection; which grafts us onto the vine that is Christ; and which gives us a share in his mission to realize the Reign of God

- The history of salvation, organized in reference to Jesus Christ, the "center of the history of salvation"[73]

- The Apostles' Creed as "a synthesis of and a key to reading all of the Church's doctrine, which is hierarchically ordered around it"[74]

- The sacraments as "an organic whole in which each particular sacrament has its own vital place"[75]

- The Eucharist as the "Sacrament of sacraments," to which all the other sacraments are ordered as to their end[76]

- The double commandment of love of God and neighbor as the centerpiece of Jesus' moral teaching, summing up the Decalogue and lived in the spirit of the Beatitudes—"the whole law and the prophets depend on these two commandments"[77]

- The Our Father as the synthesis of prayer contained in Sacred Scripture and in the life of the Church[78]

---

71. *General Catechetical Directory,* no. 43.
72. *General Catechetical Directory,* no. 43.
73. *General Catechetical Directory,* no. 41.
74. GDC, no. 115.
75. CCC, no. 1211.
76. Cf. CCC, no.1211.
77. Mt 22:40.
78. Cf. GDC, no. 115.

H. The Communication of Profound Meaning for the Human Person

Another criterion for the presentation of the Christian message is that it must convey a profoundly meaningful message for the human person. Jesus Christ is "the image of the invisible God, / the firstborn of all creation."[79] In the mystery of his incarnation, Christ has united himself to every human being. He is the perfect man who reveals to all human beings their own true nature and their eternal destiny in communion with God. If we seek to know ourselves and the meaning of our lives, we should look to Christ, for "he worked with human hands, he thought with a human mind. He acted with a human will, and with a human heart he loved."[80]

In presenting catechesis that communicates profound meaning for the human person, dioceses and parishes should ensure

- That catechesis not only reveals God's identity but, in doing so, reveals the deepest truths about human beings: that we are made in God's image, that we are religious beings by nature, that the desire for God is written on our hearts, that God never ceases to draw us to himself, and that we are made to live in communion with him

- That catechesis is concerned with the ultimate meaning of life and its deepest questions

- That catechesis examines the more significant experiences of life in light of the Gospel

- That the initial proclamation of the Gospel is done with an awareness of human nature and shows how the Gospel fully satisfies the aspirations of the human heart[81]

- That biblical catechesis helps to interpret human experiences in the light of the experiences of the people of Israel and of Jesus Christ and his Church

- That doctrinal catechesis, based on the Creed, shows how the great themes of the faith are sources of life and enlightenment for human beings

- That moral catechesis is a *"catechesis of the beatitudes*, for the way of Christ is summed up in the beatitudes, the only path that leads to the eternal beatitude for which the human heart longs"[82]

- That liturgical catechesis explains the signs and symbols of the sacred rites corresponding to human experiences[83]

---

79. Col 1:15.
80. GS, no. 22.
81. Cf. AG, no. 8.
82. CCC, no. 1697.
83. Cf. GDC, no. 117.

- That ecumenical catechesis helps all the faithful who are called upon to make a personal commitment toward promoting increasing communion with other Christians[84]

- That catechesis seeks to dispose people "to hope in the future life that is the consummation of the whole history of salvation"[85]

I. The Promotion of a Common Language of Faith in Transmitting the Christian Message

The final criterion for the presentation of the Christian message is that it should foster a common language of the faith so that it may be proclaimed, celebrated, lived, and prayed in words familiar to all the faithful. "We do not believe in formulas, but in those realities they express, which faith allows us to touch."[86] But as Catholics we do rely on the formulations of the faith to express and probe the meanings of the mysteries that the formulas attempt to describe. We also need familiar formulations of the faith in order to hand it on to future generations of believers. The Church has guarded the words of the Lord since he spoke them and since apostolic times has preserved the formulations of the faith.

In presenting catechesis that fosters a common language of the faith, dioceses and parishes should ensure that catechesis

- Respects and values "the language proper to the message, especially biblical language, as well as the historical-traditional language of the Church (*creed, liturgy*) and doctrinal language (*dogmatic formulations*)"[87]

- Uses the technical language of the faith while also demonstrating the contemporary relevance of the traditional formulas for communicating the faith

- Enters into dialogue with the particular people to whom the Christian message is being presented

- Avoids terminology that would alter the substance of faith

- Employs language suited to today's children, young people, and adults in general, as well as to many other categories of people: for example, students, intellectuals and scientists, those who are illiterate, and persons with disabilities[88]

26. CONCLUSION

The sacred duty and the joy of each succeeding generation of Christian believers has been to hand on the deposit of faith that was first entrusted to the apostles by Christ himself. We have received this gift, the deposit of faith—we have

---

84. Cf. UUS, no. 8.
85. Col 1:23.
86. CCC, no. 170.
87. Cf. GDC, no. 208.
88. Cf. CT, no. 59.

not conceived it. It is the heritage of the whole Church. It is our privilege and our responsibility to preserve the memory of Christ's words and the words themselves and to teach future generations of believers to carry out all that Christ commanded his apostles.

Sound catechesis, however, involves more than the presentation of the content of Christ's message according to the criteria outlined above. The effective presentation of the content of the Christian faith also depends on the methodology employed in the transmission of the Good News. That methodology is the subject of the next chapter.

CHAPTER 5
CATECHESIS IN A WORSHIPING COMMUNITY

> They devoted themselves to the teaching of the apostles and to the communal life, to the breaking of the bread and to the prayers.
> (Acts 2:42)

32. INTRODUCTION

The Jerusalem community of disciples concentrated on adherence to the teachings of the Twelve, the Eucharistic Liturgy, living the way of Christ, and prayer. These fundamental elements of ecclesial life have remained constant for more than two thousand years. Faith and worship are as closely related to one another as they were in the early Church: faith gathers the community for worship, and worship renews the faith of the community.

The Holy Spirit draws together the community of the faithful as the Church, the Body of Christ, and leads the Church in giving praise and thanks to the Father. The Church, then, is a worshiping community of believers in the Lordship of Jesus Christ—believers who, through the outpouring of the Holy Spirit, acknowledge their absolute dependence on God, the Father. The Liturgy is the official worship of the Church. In her Liturgy, the Church celebrates what she professes and lives, above all the Paschal Mystery, by which Christ accomplished the work of our salvation.

The rites of the Church are now—more than before the Second Vatican Council—clearly identified with the Paschal Mystery of Christ, adequately integrated with the Eucharist as the principal celebration of that mystery, and directly related to the experiences of individual Christians and communities of faith. The retrieval of Sacred Scripture in the Lectionary and the restoration of the liturgy of the word are an integral component in all sacramental celebrations and other liturgical rites. This restoration is a significant achievement in the renewal of the Liturgy. Liturgical renewal has also brought the Christian ecclesial communities closer to one another in their faith and forms of worship and has emphasized the common riches that they share on the road to full communion.

This chapter describes the relationship between catechesis and Liturgy. It also treats liturgical and personal prayer, catechesis for the sacramental life, sacred time and space, and sacramentals, popular piety, and popular devotions.

33. THE RELATIONSHIP BETWEEN CATECHESIS AND LITURGY

In the Church's mission of evangelization, catechesis and Liturgy are intimately connected. "Catechesis is intrinsically linked with the whole of liturgical and sacramental activity."[89] Catechesis and Liturgy originate in the faith of the Church; they proclaim the Gospel; they call its hearers to conversion to Christ; they initiate believers into the life of Christ and his Church; and they look for the coming of the kingdom in its fullness when "God may be all in all."[90] "The liturgy is the summit toward which the activity of the Church is directed; it is also the fount from which all her power flows."[91] The history of salvation, from the creation of the world to its redemption and eschatological fulfillment in Jesus Christ, is celebrated in the sacraments, especially in the Eucharist. That is why the Liturgy is "the privileged place for catechizing the People of God."[92]

Catechesis both precedes the Liturgy and springs from it. It prepares people for a full, conscious, and active participation in the Liturgy by helping them understand its nature, rites, and symbols. It stems from the Liturgy insofar as it helps people to worship God and to reflect on their experience of the words, signs, rituals, and symbols expressed in the Liturgy; to discern the implications of their participation in the Liturgy; and to respond to its missionary summons to bear witness and offer service. And Liturgy itself is inherently catechetical. As the Scriptures are proclaimed and reflected upon and as the Creed is articulated, the truths of the faith shape more and more profoundly the faith of the People of God. Through the Eucharist, the People of God come to know the Paschal Mystery ever more intimately and experientially. They come not simply to the knowledge of God—they come to know the living God.

"Liturgical catechesis aims to initiate people into the mystery of Christ . . . by proceeding from the visible to the invisible, from the sign to the thing signified, from the 'sacraments' to the 'mysteries.'"[93] It promotes a more informed knowledge and a more vital experience of the Liturgy. Liturgical catechesis fosters a deeper sense of the meaning of the Liturgy and the sacraments. "In other words, sacramental life is impoverished and very soon turns into hollow ritualism if it is not based on serious knowledge of the meaning of the sacraments, and catechesis becomes intellectualized if it fails to come alive in sacramental practice."[94]

---

89. CT, no. 23.
90. 1 Cor 15:28.
91. SC, no. 10; cf. CCC, no. 1069.
92. CCC, no. 1074.
93. CCC, no. 1075.
94. CT, no. 23.

34. LITURGICAL AND PERSONAL PRAYER

God draws every human being toward himself, and every human being desires communion with God. Prayer is the basis and expression of the vital and personal relationship of a human person with the living and true God: "God tirelessly calls each person to that mysterious encounter known as prayer."[95] His initiative comes first; the human response to his initiative is itself prompted by the grace of the Holy Spirit. That human response is the free self-surrender to the incomprehensible mystery of God. In prayer, the Holy Spirit not only reveals the identity of the Triune God to human persons, but also reveals the identity of human persons to themselves. It has been expressed throughout the history of salvation in the words and actions of prayer.

Liturgical prayer is the participation of the People of God in Christ's work. "Every liturgical celebration, because it is an action of Christ the Priest and of his Body, which is the Church, is a sacred action surpassing all others. No other action of the Church can equal its efficacy by the same title and to the same degree."[96] The sacraments, especially the Eucharist, are the Church's preeminent experiences of liturgical prayer.

"In the liturgy, all Christian prayer finds its source and goal."[97] The rhythms of prayer within the life of the Church are both liturgical and personal. Liturgical prayer is the public prayer of the Church. It is the work of Christ, and as such it is the work of the Church. Personal prayer is an essential aspect of the human person's relationship with God, which can find expression in and be nourished by various devotional prayers, such as the Holy Rosary, Stations of the Cross, and novenas.

Since the time of the apostles, the Church has abided by the exhortation "to pray constantly" (1 Thes 5:17) The Liturgy of the Hours, or the Divine Office, is the daily public prayer of the Church; in it "the whole course of the day and night is made holy by the praise of God."[98] Catechists especially would benefit greatly from participating in the Liturgy of the Hours. "Pastors of souls should see to it that the principal hours, especially Vespers, are celebrated in common in church on Sundays and on the more solemn feasts. The laity, too, are encouraged to recite the divine office, either with the priests, or among themselves, or even individually."[99]

The living Tradition of the Church, however, contains more than the great treasury of liturgical prayer. Personal prayer is God's gift to the "humble and contrite heart."[100] It expresses the covenant relationship that binds God to the person and the person to God. The connection is Christ, the Son of God made flesh. He is the new and eternal covenant whose blood "will be shed on behalf

---

95. CCC, no. 2567.
96. SC, no. 7.
97. CCC, no. 1073.
98. SC, no. 84.
99. SC, no. 100.
100. Ps 51:19.

of many for the forgiveness of sins"[101] so that humanity may be redeemed and restored to communion with God. Personal prayer expresses communion with the life of the Blessed Trinity. The Holy Spirit inspires hearts to pray, removes obstacles to living life in Christ, and leads humanity into communion with the Father and the Son. Personal prayer permeates the daily life of the Christian and disposes him or her toward liturgical, communal, or public prayer.

Because catechesis seeks to lead persons and communities to deeper faith, it is oriented to prayer and worship. Catechesis for prayer emphasizes the major purposes for prayer—adoration, thanksgiving, petition, and contrition—and includes various prayer forms: communal prayer, private prayer, traditional prayer, spontaneous prayer, gesture, song, meditation, and contemplation. Catechesis for prayer accompanies a person's continual growth in faith. It is most effective when the catechist is a prayerful person who is comfortable leading others to prayer and to participation in liturgical worship. "When catechesis is permeated by a climate of prayer, the assimilation of the entire Christian life reaches it summit."[102]

Catechesis for prayer begins when children see and hear others praying and when they pray with others, especially in the family. Young children seem to have a special sense of wonder, a recognition of God's presence in their lives, and a capacity for prayer. They should be encouraged by parents and catechists to call upon the Father, the Son, and the Holy Spirit as well as the Mother of God, the angels, and the saints. From infancy they should be inculturated into the daily prayer life of the family, thereby learning the prayers and prayer forms of the Catholic tradition and becoming accustomed to praying daily: e.g., morning and evening prayer, prayer before and after meals, and prayer at special moments in the life of the family.

35. CATECHESIS FOR THE SACRAMENTS IN GENERAL

A. Sacraments as Mysteries

The liturgical life of the Church revolves around the sacraments, with the Eucharist at the center. "The sacraments are efficacious signs of grace, instituted by Christ and entrusted to the Church," by which divine life is given to us and celebrated.[103] The Church celebrates seven sacraments: Baptism, Confirmation or Chrismation, Eucharist, Penance, Anointing of the Sick, Holy Orders, and Matrimony.[104]

---

101. Mt 26:28
102. GDC, no. 85.
103. CCC, no. 1131.
104. Many Eastern Traditions call this sacrament of Matrimony the mystery of "Holy Crowning." Cf. below in this *Directory*, no. 36 ("Catechesis for the Particular Sacraments"), section C ("The Sacraments at the Service of Communion"), subsection 2 ("Catechesis for the Sacrament of Matrimony").

B. General Principles for Sacramental Catechesis

Some fundamental principles apply to catechesis for each of the sacraments. Dioceses and parishes should present sacramental catechesis that

- Is a comprehensive and systematic formation in the faith, one that integrates knowledge of the faith with living the faith

- Is fundamentally Trinitarian and centers on initiation into the life of the Triune God

- Presents Christian life as a lifelong journey to the Father in the Son and through the Holy Spirit

- Is appropriate to the age level, maturity, and circumstances of those being catechized

- Is intended for all members of the Christian community, takes place within the community, and involves the whole community of faith

- Involves parents in the preparation of their children for the sacraments

- Is integrated into a comprehensive catechetical program

- Focuses primarily on the symbols, rituals, and prayers contained in the rite for each sacrament

- Enables the believer to reflect on the meaning of the sacrament received by implementing a thorough experience of *mystagogia* following the celebration

C. Catechetical Guidelines for Celebration of the Sacraments

The Church provides official catechetical norms and guidelines for the celebration of the sacraments. These are essential tools for sacramental catechesis. The *General Instruction of the Roman Missal*[105] provides the general guidelines for the celebration of the Eucharist. The introductions to each rite contain catechetical norms and guidelines appropriate to each sacrament. The *Rite of Christian Initiation of Adults* sets forth the directives to be followed throughout the process of the initiation of adults and children of catechetical age into the life of the Church. Our 1995 statement entitled *Guidelines for the Celebration of the Sacraments with Persons with Disabilities*[106] stresses the need to include persons with disabilities in the celebration of all the sacraments and provides general catechetical guidelines for celebrating the sacraments with persons with a variety of disabilities. The *Directory for Masses with Children*[107] contains the norms for Eucharistic liturgies with children. The *Directory for the Application of Principles and Norms on Ecumenism* outlines Catholic principles and

---

105. Cf *General Instruction of the Roman Missal* (GIRM) (2001) (Washington, DC: USCCB, 2003).

106. Cf. USCCB, *Guidelines for the Celebration of the Sacraments with Persons with Disabilities* (Washington, DC: USCCB, 1995).

107. Cf. Sacred Congregation for Divine Worship, *Directory for Masses with Children* (1973).

practice in sacramental sharing with other Christians.[108] The *Directory on Popular Piety and the Liturgy*[109] addresses the need for multicultural parishes to make special efforts to celebrate culture and traditions and employ the language, music, and art of each culture represented. In addition to the documents listed above, the prayers that are the form of the sacraments are also essential tools for sacramental catechesis.

D. Baptismal Catechumenate: Inspiration for All Catechesis

The baptismal catechumenate is the source of inspiration for all catechesis. This process of formation includes four stages, as well as rituals that mark those stages. The first stage, the pre-catechumenate, coincides with the first evangelization, in which the primary proclamation of the Gospel and the initial call to conversion to Christ takes place. The handing on of the Gospels accompanies the second stage, the catechumenate, and begins the period in which a more integral and systematic catechesis is presented to the catechumens and candidates. The third stage, purification and enlightenment, is characterized by the celebration of the scrutinies, by more intense prayer, and by the study and conferral of the Creed and the Lord's Prayer. This time is characterized by a more intense preparation for the sacraments of initiation. Fourth, the mystagogy, or post-baptismal catechesis, marks the time in which the neophyte experiences the sacraments and enters fully into the life of the community.[110] "These stages, which reflect the wisdom of the great catechumenal tradition, also inspire the gradual nature of catechesis."[111]

While a distinction is made between catechumens and those already baptized who are being catechized,[112] some elements of the baptismal catechumenate are instructive for post-baptismal catechesis. In that sense, the baptismal catechumenate inspires a continuing catechesis. It reminds the Church that her catechesis accompanies a continual conversion to Christ and an ongoing initiation into the celebration of the sacraments and the life of the Church. Just as the baptismal catechumenate is the responsibility of the entire Christian community, so too does the whole Church bear the obligation to provide an ongoing catechesis for the faithful. The baptismal catechumenate accompanies the catechumen's passage with Christ from the initial proclamation of his name, through "burial together with him in the death of baptism,"[113] and then to the newness of life. All catechesis should provide those being catechized with the opportunity to journey with Christ through the stages of his Paschal Mystery. The baptismal catechumenate is where the Gospel message deliberately engages the

---

108. Cf. Pontifical Council for Promoting Christian Unity, *Directory for the Application of Principles and Norms on Ecumenism* (Washington, DC: USCCB, 1993), Chapter 4.

109. Cf. Congregation for Divine Worship and the Discipline of the Sacraments, *Directory on Popular Piety and the Liturgy: Principles and Guidelines* (2002), http://www.vatican.va/roman _curia/congregations/ccdds/documents/rc_con_ccdds_doc_20020513_vers-direttorio_en.html (accessed on August 29, 2003).

110. Cf. RCIA, nos. 9–40.

111. GDC, no. 89.

112. Cf. *Directory for the Application of Principles and Norms on Ecumenism*, nos. 92–100.

113. Congregation for Divine Worship, *Rite of Baptism* (1969), no. 91.

culture of the catechumens. All catechesis must "take flesh" in the various cultures and environments in which the Gospel message is proclaimed.

The baptismal catechumenate is both "a process of formation and a true school of the faith."[114] It is a fruitful blend of instruction and formation in the faith; it progresses through gradual stages; it unfolds the Church's rites, symbols, and biblical and liturgical signs; and it incorporates the catechumens into the Christian community of faith and worship. While mystagogical, or post-baptismal, catechesis should not slavishly imitate the structure of the baptismal catechumenate, it should recognize that the baptismal catechumenate provides an admirable model for the whole of the Church's catechetical efforts and especially emphasizes the necessity for lifelong catechesis.[115]

More specifically, the time that follows the celebration of the sacraments of initiation—i.e., the period of post-baptismal catechesis or, mystagogy—"is a time for the community and the neophytes together to grow in deepening their grasp of the paschal mystery and in making it part of their lives through meditation on the Gospel, sharing in the Eucharist, and doing the works of charity."[116] It is the phase of liturgical catechesis that aims to incorporate the neophytes more deeply into the mystery of Christ through reflection on the Gospel message and the experience of the sacraments they have received. It gives them the opportunity to relive the great events of salvation history and helps them to open themselves to the spiritual understanding of the economy of salvation. Mystagogical, or post-baptismal, catechesis also helps the newly baptized to internalize the sacraments of initiation to deepen and nourish their life of faith and to enter more deeply into the community.

Through the period of post-baptismal catechesis, the neophytes "should experience a full and joyful welcome into the community and enter into closer ties with the other faithful. The faithful, in turn, should derive from it a renewal of inspiration and of outlook."[117] Sunday Masses during the Easter season following the neophytes' reception of the sacraments of initiation provide particularly favorable opportunities for them to gather with the community of faith, to hear readings from the Word of God specifically chosen for the period of post-baptismal catechesis, and to partake fully in the Eucharist. "Out of this experience, which belongs to Christians and increases as it is lived, [the neophytes] derive a new perception of the faith, of the Church, and of the world."[118]

In the broader sense, mystagogy represents the Christian's lifelong education and formation in the faith. By analogy it signifies the continuous character of catechesis in the life of the Christian. Conversion to Christ is a lifelong process that should be accompanied at every stage by a vital catechesis that leads Christians on their journey towards holiness. Lifelong catechesis should take many forms and use a variety of means: participation in the Sunday Eucharist and study of

---

114. GDC, no. 91.
115. Cf. Synod of Bishops, *Message to the People of God* (October 28, 1977), no. 8.
116. RCIA, no. 244.
117. RCIA, no. 246.
118. RCIA, no. 245.

the Liturgy, the study and exploration of Sacred Scripture and the social teachings of the Church, reflection on the important events of life in the light of Christian faith, opportunities for prayer, spiritual exercises, acts of charity that involve self-sacrifice, especially toward those in need, and more formal theological and catechetical instruction. Among these forms of continuing catechesis, the homily occupies a privileged position since it "takes up again the journey of faith put forward by catechesis, and brings it to its natural fulfillment."[119]

36. CATECHESIS FOR THE PARTICULAR SACRAMENTS

A. Sacraments of Initiation

Christian initiation is celebrated in Baptism, Confirmation or Chrismation, and Eucharist. These sacraments are efficacious signs of God's love and stages of a person's journey toward communion with the Trinity. Through these sacraments, a person is incorporated into the Church, is strengthened for participation in the Church's mission, and is welcomed to partake of the Body and Blood of Jesus Christ. As indicated above, the Rite of Christian Initiation of Adults provides the norm for catechetical as well as liturgical practice for the sacraments of initiation. In the Eastern Churches, Baptism, Chrismation, and Eucharist are celebrated together in infancy, and their intimate relationship is apparent. While the Latin Church has separated the celebration of Baptism from Confirmation and Eucharist, she also recognizes their essential interconnection.

Dioceses and parishes should present catechesis for Christian initiation that

- Summons the catechumen to profess faith in the person of Jesus Christ from the heart, to follow him faithfully, and to become his disciple

- Recognizes that Christian initiation is an apprenticeship of the entire Christian life and so should include more than instruction[120]

- Presents a comprehensive and systematic formation in the faith so that the catechumen or candidate can enter deeply into the mystery of Christ

- Incorporates the catechumen into the life of the Christian community, which confesses, celebrates, and bears courageous witness to the faith of Jesus Christ

- Includes instruction on the rites of Christian initiation, their basic symbols and forms, and the offices and ministries at work in them

For the purpose of Christian initiation, children who have reached the age of reason, generally understood as seven years of age, are considered adults in a limited sense.[121] As much as possible, their formation in the faith should follow the general pattern of the ordinary catechumenate, making use of the appropriate adaptations permitted in the rite. "They should receive the sacraments

---

119. CT, no. 48.
120. GDC, no. 67.
121. Cf. Canon Law Society of America (CLSA), *Code of Canon Law, Latin-English Edition, New English Translation* (CIC) (Washington, DC: CLSA, 1999), c. 852 §1.

of baptism, confirmation, and eucharist at the Easter Vigil, together with the older catechumens."[122]

The initiation of children who have not been baptized as infants, but who have attained the use of reason and have reached catechetical age, is ordinarily sought by their parents or guardians or, with parental permission, by the children themselves. These children are capable of receiving and nurturing a personal faith. They are also capable of a conversion appropriate to their age. They can receive a catechesis that is suited to their circumstances. The process of their initiation must be adapted to their ability to grow in faith and their capacity to understand the faith. Their initiation should proceed through the same steps that the initiation of adults does. While the process may take several years before they receive the sacraments, "their condition and status as catechumens . . . should not be compromised or confused, nor should they receive the sacraments of initiation in any sequence other than that determined in the ritual of Christian initiation."[123]

Children's catechetical formation should lead up to and follow the steps of the initiation process. Ordinarily the children to be initiated are part of a group of children of similar age and circumstances, some of whom have already been baptized and are preparing for Confirmation and Eucharist. In general, catechesis for such children should incorporate appropriate elements of the same thorough and systematic catechetical instruction of baptized children before reception of the Sacraments of Confirmation and the Eucharist.

The family is the child's first experience of a faith community and, as such, deserves careful attention in all catechetical endeavors. Throughout the period of initiation of children of catechetical age, the parents of the children should be encouraged to be involved. If the children are determined to be ready to receive the sacraments, the final period of preparation should proceed, if possible, during the season of Lent; the final step, the celebration of the sacraments of initiation, should normally take place at the Easter Vigil.[124] "Celebration at this time must also be consistent with the program of catechetical instruction they are receiving, since the candidates should, if possible, come to the sacraments of initiation at the time that their baptized companions are to receive confirmation or eucharist."[125]

I. CATECHESIS FOR BAPTISM

Catechesis for Baptism is directed primarily to adults: that is, catechumens— including children who have reached the age of reason—as well as the parents and godparents of infants who are to be baptized. Catechumens and candidates should be led through the stages of Christian initiation set forth in the *Rite of Christian Initiation of Adults*. This process provides helpful guidelines for the catechesis of parents and godparents who are preparing for the Baptism of an infant or child. All those preparing for Baptism, including parents and godparents,

---

122. RCIA, Appendix III, no. 18.
123. RCIA, Appendix III, no. 19.
124. Cf. RCIA, Part II, no. 256.
125. RCIA, Part II, no. 256.

need the prayerful support and apostolic witness of the people of the local community of faith—the parish. This preparation is an especially important opportunity for the Church to encourage the parents and godparents of infants to reexamine the meaning of the Christian message in their own lives. It is also the proper time to remind the parents and godparents that "an infant should be baptized within the first weeks after birth. If the child is in danger of death, it is to be baptized without delay."[126] For pastoral reasons, Baptism may be deferred if there is no assurance that the child's faith will be nurtured. The parish should give attention to the families of these children through pastoral outreach and evangelization.

Dioceses and parishes should present baptismal catechesis that

- Teaches that Baptism (1) is the foundation of the Christian life because it is the journey into Christ's death and Resurrection, which is the foundation of our hope; (2) gives sanctifying grace, that is, God's life; (3) gives them a new birth in which they become children of God, members of Christ, and temples of the Holy Spirit; (4) cleanses people from original sin and from all personal sins; (5) incorporates them into the life, practices, and mission of the Church; and (6) imprints on their souls an indelible character that consecrates them for Christian worship and is necessary for salvation in the case of all those who have heard the Gospel and have been able to ask for this sacrament[127]

- Teaches that through Baptism we receive a share in the mission of Christ as king, priest, and prophet

- Teaches that Baptism "symbolizes the catechumen's burial into Christ's death, from which he rises up by resurrection with him, as 'a new creature'"[128]

- Teaches that Baptism is "the basis of the whole Christian life, the gateway to life in the Spirit . . . and the door which gives access to the other sacraments"[129]

- Teaches that through Baptism the faithful "share in the priesthood of Christ, in his prophetic and royal mission"[130]

- Teaches that "the Most Holy Trinity gives the baptized sanctifying grace, the grace of *justification*" (thus "the whole organism of the Christian's supernatural life has its root in baptism")

  —"enabling them to believe in God, to hope in him, and to love him through the theological virtues"

---

126. Congregation for Divine Worship, *Rite of Baptism of Children*, no. 8, in *The Rites of the Catholic Church* (New York: Pueblo Publishing, 1983).

127. Cf. CCC, no. 1257.

128. CCC, no. 1214.

129. CCC, no. 1213.

130. CCC, no. 1268.

—"giving them the power to live and act under the prompting of the Holy Spirit through the gifts of the Holy Spirit"

—"allowing them to grow in goodness through the virtues"[131]

- Teaches that "having become a member of the Church, the person baptized belongs no longer to himself, but to him who died and rose for us. From now on he is called to be subject to others, to serve them in the communion of the Church, and to 'obey and to submit' to the Church's leaders, holding them in respect and affection"[132]

- Includes a thorough explanation of the Rite of Baptism together with the fundamental signs and symbols that it employs: immersion in or the pouring of water, the words of the Trinitarian formula, and the anointing with oil

- Teaches that the ordinary minister for the Sacrament of Baptism is a priest or deacon (in the Eastern Catholic Churches the priest is the only ordinary minister of Baptism, since Chrismation follows immediately) but that, in the case of necessity, any person who intends to do what the Church does can baptize by pouring water on the candidate's head and saying the Trinitarian formula

2. CATECHESIS FOR CONFIRMATION/CHRISMATION

The revised *Rite of Confirmation*[133] indicates that episcopal conferences may designate the appropriate age for Confirmation. In the United States the age of Confirmation in the Latin Church for children and young people varies widely from diocese to diocese; it can be designated between the age of discretion through around sixteen years. Since the sacramental practice for Confirmation in the United States is so diverse, a single catechesis cannot be prescribed for Confirmation. However, some general guidelines can be articulated.

Catechesis for adults preparing for Confirmation follows the pattern recommended in the *Rite of Christian Initiation of Adults*. Dioceses and parishes should present catechesis for the Sacrament of Confirmation that

- Teaches that Confirmation increases and deepens the grace of Baptism, imprinting an indelible character on the soul

- Teaches that Confirmation strengthens the baptismal conferral of the Holy Spirit on those confirmed in order to incorporate them more firmly in Christ, strengthen their bond with the Church, associate them more closely with the Church's mission, increase in them the gifts of the Holy Spirit,[134] and help them bear witness to the Christian faith in words and deeds

- Teaches about the role of the Holy Spirit, his gifts, and his fruits

131. CCC, no. 1266.
132. CCC, no. 1269.
133. Cf. Sacred Congregation for Divine Worship, *Rite of Confirmation* (1971).
134. Cf. CCC, no. 1303.

- Is developmentally appropriate and includes retreat experiences

- Includes instruction on the Rite of Confirmation and its basic symbols: the imposition of hands, the anointing with Sacred Chrism, and the words of the sacramental formula

- Ensures that parents and sponsors are involved in the catechetical preparation of the children for Confirmation

- Teaches that the bishop is the ordinary minister of the Sacrament of Confirmation (in the Eastern Catholic Churches, however, the priest is the ordinary minister of Chrismation)

3. CATECHESIS FOR EUCHARIST[135]

The Sacrament of the Eucharist is one of the sacraments of Christian initiation. "Those who have been raised to the dignity of the royal priesthood by Baptism and configured more deeply to Christ by Confirmation participate with the whole community in the Lord's own sacrifice by means of the Eucharist."[136]

The Eucharist is the ritual, sacramental action of giving thanks and praise to the Father. It is the sacrificial memorial of Christ and his body, the Church, and is the continuing presence of Christ in his Word and in his Spirit.

In the Mass, or "the Divine Liturgy" as it is termed in the Eastern Catholic Churches, the Eucharist constitutes the principal liturgical celebration of the Paschal Mystery of Christ and the ritual memorial of our communion in that mystery. Acting through the ministry of the priests, the bread and wine become— through Transubstantiation—Christ himself. Christ offers the Eucharistic sacrifice and is really present under the species of bread and wine.

Since the Eucharist is the "source and summit of the Christian life,"[137] catechesis for the Eucharist recognizes it as the heart of Christian life for the whole Church, for the dioceses and parishes, and for each individual Christian. Dioceses and parishes should present lifelong catechesis for the Eucharist that

- Helps people understand that the Eucharist is the mystery in which Christ's sacrifice on the cross is perpetuated; that it is a memorial of Christ's passion, death, and Resurrection; and that it is a sacred banquet in which the People of God share the benefits of the Paschal Mystery, renew the covenant that God has made through the blood of Christ, and anticipate the heavenly banquet

---

135. Cf. Congregation for Rites, *Instruction on Eucharistic Worship* (1967). In this document is a seven-part article (article 3) that deals specifically with "The Principal Points of Doctrine" and eleven articles (articles 5–15) that deal specifically with "Some General Principles of Particular Importance in the Catechesis of the People on the Mystery of the Eucharist." Cf. also John Paul II, *On the Eucharist* (*Ecclesia de Eucharistia*) (EE) (Washington, DC: USCCB, 2003).
136. CCC, no. 1322.
137. LG, no. 11.

- Helps people understand that the work of salvation accomplished by these events is made present by the liturgical action that Christ himself offers in every celebration of the Eucharist

- Teaches that through the priest—the other Christ—the bread and wine are transformed, through the Eucharistic Prayer, into the Body and Blood of Christ

- Includes instruction that the Eucharist is the Body and Blood of Christ, his real presence under the appearances of bread and wine, and that the Eucharist nourishes the Body of Christ the Church, and each individual communicant

- Teaches that Christ is present whole and entire, God and man, substantially and permanently, and in a unique way under the species of bread and wine[138]

- Teaches that Christ is also present in his word, in the body of the faithful gathered in his name, and in the person of the priest who acts in the person of Christ, the Head of his Body, the Church

- Includes the effects of the sacrament: unity in the Body of Christ and provision of spiritual food for the Christian's journey through life

- Teaches that the reception of the Body and Blood of Christ signifies and effects communion with the most Holy Trinity, forgives venial sins, and, through the grace of the Holy Spirit, helps the communicant to avoid mortal sin

- Helps the People of God to understand that, through the power of the Holy Spirit, the Eucharist forms the Church

- Helps the faithful to understand that, in the Eucharist, "Christ associates his Church and all her members with his sacrifice of praise and thanksgiving offered once for all on the cross to his Father"[139]

- Gives instruction about the meaning of the ritual, symbols, and parts of the Mass

- Presents the Jewish roots of the Last Supper as the renewal of God's covenant with his people in the blood of his beloved Son

- Teaches that essential signs of the Eucharistic sacrament are bread and wine, on which the power of the Holy Spirit is invoked and over which the priest pronounces the words of consecration spoken first by Jesus during the Last Supper

- Teaches that the "bread and wine are changed, a change traditionally and appropriately expressed by the word 'Transubstantiation,' so that,

---

138. Cf. USCCB, *The Real Presence of Jesus Christ in the Sacrament of the Eucharist: Basic Questions and Answers* (Washington, DC: USCCB, 2001), 1–2.
139. CCC, no. 1407.

while the appearances of bread and wine remain, the reality is the Body and Blood of Christ"[140]

- Teaches that the Eucharist commits those who receive it to serve the poor[141]

- Reminds the faithful that the Sacrament of the Eucharist is the preeminent sign of the unity of the Church

- Teaches that the Eucharist is an effective sign of the unity of all Christians and that one day—that is, the Parousia—by the grace of the Holy Spirit, the divisions that separate Christians will be healed

- Presents the guidelines for Eucharistic sharing that have been set forth by the United States Catholic bishops[142]

- Considers the mystery of the Eucharist in all its fullness and consequently teaches that the celebration of the Eucharist in the sacrifice of the Mass is the origin and consummation of the worship shown the Blessed Sacrament outside of Mass[143]

- Encourages visits to the Blessed Sacrament and other Eucharistic devotions, and teaches appropriate devotional gestures, postures, and proper conduct in church

- Includes instruction on the implications of the Eucharist for the Church's mission in the world and for social justice

- Clarifies the roles and ministries within the sacred action so that all may experience full, active, and conscious participation in the celebration of the Mass

- Includes an explanation of the theology and practice of celebrating the Eucharist in the Eastern Churches

- Makes people aware of their obligation to be free of mortal sin before receiving Holy Communion

- Teaches that Catholics must receive Holy Communion at least once a year during the Easter season

- Recommends that the faithful receive Holy Communion when they participate in the celebration of the Eucharist

- Instructs the faithful concerning the Eucharistic fast and the conditions under which Holy Communion may be received a second time on the same day

---

140. *National Catechetical Directory*, no. 121.
141. Cf. CCC, no. 1397.
142. Cf. USCCB, *Guidelines for the Reception of Communion* (November 14, 1996).
143. Cf. Sacred Congregation for Divine Worship, *Holy Communion and Worship of the Eucharist Outside of Mass* (1973).

- Instructs the faithful that we are called to realize that we become what we receive—which has great implications for how we live and act

3A. CATECHESIS FOR CHILDREN'S FIRST RECEPTION OF THE EUCHARIST

Children's preparation for first reception of the Eucharist begins in the home. The family has the most important role in communicating the Christian and human values that form the foundation for a child's understanding of the Eucharist. Children who participate with their family in the Mass experience the Eucharistic mystery in an initial way and gradually learn to join with the liturgical assembly in prayer.

Parents and the parish catechetical leader or catechist, together with the pastor, are responsible for determining when children have attained the age of reason and are ready to receive First Communion.[144] Because reception of the Eucharist, especially for the first time, is integral to the child's full incorporation into the ecclesial community, the pastor has a responsibility in determining every child's readiness to receive First Communion. Parents also have the right and the duty to be involved in preparing their children for First Communion. The catechesis offered should help parents grow in their own understanding and appreciation of the Eucharist and enable them to catechize their children more effectively.

The *Directory for Masses with Children* "sets the framework for catechizing children for eucharistic celebration."[145] Catechesis on the Mass provided in systematic parish catechetical programs is an indispensable part of the preparation of children for their first reception of the Eucharist. Suited to the children's age and abilities, catechesis should help children participate actively and consciously in the Mass. During planning, it is essential to remember that children around the age of reason ordinarily think concretely. Dioceses and parishes should present catechesis in preparation for the first reception of the Eucharist that

- Teaches that the Eucharist is the living memorial of Christ's sacrifice for the salvation of all and the commemoration of his last meal with his disciples

- Teaches not only "the truths of faith regarding the Eucharist but also how from First Communion on . . . they can as full members of Christ's Body take part actively with the People of God in the Eucharist, sharing in the Lord's table and the community of their brothers and sisters"[146]

- Ensures that the baptized have been prepared, according to their capacity, for the Sacrament of Penance prior to their First Communion

- Develops in children an understanding of the Father's love, of their participation in the sacrifice of Christ, and of the gift of the Holy Spirit

---

144. Cf. CIC, cc. 914, 777 2°; cf. *Code of Canons of the Eastern Churches* (CCEO), c. 619.
145. *National Directory for Catechesis*, no. 135.
146. *Directory for Masses with Children*, no. 12.

- Teaches that "the Holy Eucharist is the real body and blood of Christ" and that "what appear to be bread and wine are actually His living body"[147]

- Teaches the difference between the Eucharist and ordinary bread

- Teaches the meaning of reception of the Holy Eucharist under both species of bread and wine

- Helps them to participate actively and consciously in the Mass

- Helps children to receive Christ's Body and Blood in an informed and reverent manner

Traditional practice in some Eastern Churches in the United States calls for the newly baptized and chrismated infant or adult to receive the Holy Eucharist. The infant's first reception of the Eucharist, therefore, occurs in conjunction with the sacraments or mysteries of Baptism and Chrismation, because the culmination of initiation into the community of faith is sharing in the communal meal. In these situations, Eucharistic catechesis ordinarily follows reception of the sacrament and supports the young Christian's growth into the mystery of the Eucharist and the life of the Church.

3B. THE EUCHARISTIC LITURGY FOR SPECIAL GROUPS

The parish Sunday Mass, or Divine Liturgy, is the normative celebration of the Eucharistic Liturgy. It is the whole parish community's central act of worship, through which Christ unites the faithful to himself and to one another in his perfect sacrifice of praise. While every parish is made up of different groups, associations, and smaller religious communities, through the Sunday Eucharist Christ provides the opportunity for everyone to move beyond their particular circles to celebrate in common the sacrament of unity. "This is why on Sunday, the day of gathering, small group Masses are not to be encouraged: it is not only a question of ensuring that parish assemblies are not without the necessary ministry of priests, but also of ensuring that the life and unity of the Church community are fully safe, guarded and promoted."[148] Occasionally, however, Mass may be celebrated with groups whose members share special ties or a particular need. Such celebrations should help the members to grow in their faith and unite them more deeply to one another, to the parish community, and to the whole Church.

The *General Instruction of the Roman Missal* is the normative point of reference for the celebration of the Mass. Only the Holy See can change the liturgical books of the Roman Rite. Only the United States Conference of Catholic Bishops can propose adaptations of those rites to the Holy See, for the regulation of the Liturgy is strictly assigned to bishops alone. "'No other person, not even if he is a priest, may on his own initiative add, remove, or change anything in

---

147. *National Catechetical Directory*, no. 122.

148. John Paul II, *On Keeping the Lord's Day Holy (Dies Domini)* (DD) (Vatican City, 1998), no. 36, http://www.vatican.va/holy_father/john_paul_ii/apost_letters/documents/hf_jp-ii _apl_05071998_dies-domini_en.html (accessed on August 29, 2003).

the liturgy.' Inculturation is not left to the personal initiative of celebrants or to the collective initiative of an assembly."[149] Only in those instances clearly indicated in the *Roman Missal* may the celebrant choose from the options provided or add his own words to those prescribed. Catechists are often called upon to assist in planning these Masses and in preparing the groups to participate in them. The catechists should themselves have adequate liturgical preparation and should always work closely with these special groups, their pastors, and others trained in Liturgy.

3B-L. CHILDREN

Young children sometimes are not able to participate fully in Masses that are prepared primarily for adults since they may have difficulty understanding the words, symbols, and actions of the Eucharist. The *Directory for Masses with Children* is the normative reference for the preparation and celebration of Masses with children. It is "concerned with children who have not yet entered the period of pre-adolescence."[150] Such Eucharistic celebrations "must lead children toward the celebration of Mass with adults, especially the Masses at which the Christian community must come together on Sundays."[151] The authorization for the adaptation of the Liturgy given by the *Directory for Masses with Children* does not apply to Masses with adolescents or other special groups. While particular sensitivity to the cultural and age-specific needs of every group is a pre-condition for every celebration of the Eucharist, the requirements of the *Roman Missal* must always determine the parameters of such adaptation.

3B-2. RACIAL, CULTURAL, AND ETHNIC GROUPS

The celebration of the Liturgy should reflect the particular gifts and cultures of the different peoples; however, only those cultural adaptations approved by the Holy See for use in the United States or in the country of origin of a particular group are suited for use in the Liturgy. People express their worship of God most fruitfully through their particular culture as it has been assumed and transformed by Christ. In these celebrations, "homogenous cultural, racial, or ethnic communities have the right to use their own language and cultural expressions of faith in ritual, music, and art."[152]

Such liturgical diversity can be a source of enrichment to the whole Church, but it must not diminish the unity of the Church. Any adaptation must avoid all distortion of the celebration of the Liturgy as it is prescribed in the universal liturgical laws of the Church. No matter which particular group is celebrating the liturgy, it must express the one faith of the Church, always respecting "the

---

149. Congregation for Divine Worship and Discipline of the Sacraments, *Inculturation and the Roman Liturgy (Varietates Legitimae)*, no. 37 (quoting SC, no. 22), Appendix B in *Liturgiam Authenticam: Fifth Instruction on Vernacular Translation of the Roman Liturgy* (Washington, DC: USCCB, 2001).

150. *Directory for Masses with Children*, no. 6.

151. *Directory for Masses with Children*, no. 21.

152. *National Catechetical Directory*, no. 137.

substantial unity of the Roman Rite as expressed in the liturgical books."[153] "The liturgical assembly derives its unity from the 'communion of the Holy Spirit' who gathers the children of God into the one Body of Christ. This assembly transcends racial, cultural, social—indeed, all human affinities."[154]

3B-3. PERSONS WITH DISABILITIES[155]

Catholics with disabilities have the right to participate in the sacraments as full functioning members of the local ecclesial community. All forms of the liturgy should be completely accessible to persons with disabilities, since these forms are the essence of the spiritual tie that binds the Christian community together. As much as possible they should also be invited to play a more active role in the liturgy and should be provided with proper training and aids to do so. In some situations, special liturgies for persons with disabilities may be appropriate.

It is the responsibility of the pastor and lay leaders to make sure that the door to participation in the life of the Church is always open for persons with disabilities. To that end, the physical design of parish buildings must include easy accessibility for persons with disabilities.

Guidelines for the Celebration of the Sacraments with Persons with Disabilities provides general catechetical guidelines for the celebration of the sacraments, including the Eucharist, with persons with a variety of disabilities. Special liturgies for persons with disabilities, however, should never replace their inclusion in the larger worshiping community. Rather, these liturgies should always orient the participants back to the parish celebration of the Eucharist where the fundamental encounter between Christ and his people unfolds. Parishes should provide the means for inclusion of persons with disabilities, for example, sign language interpreters, hearing devices, Braille texts, etc. The Church "must recognize and appreciate the contributions that persons with disabilities can make to the Church's spiritual life and encourage them to do the Lord's work in the world according to their God-given talents and capacity."[156]

B. Sacraments of Healing

Through the sacraments of initiation, believers are drawn into the communion of the Holy Trinity. They become partakers in God's own life, are incorporated into the Body of Christ, and are strengthened for discipleship by the Holy Spirit. Ever present in the sacraments of initiation, however, is the sacrifice of Christ, which has reconciled the believers to the Father through the action of the Holy

---

153. John Paul II, *On the Twenty-Fifth Anniversary of the Constitution on the Sacred Liturgy* (*Vicesimus Quintus Annus*) (VQA) (Vatican City, 1988), no. 16, http://www.vatican.va/holy _father/john_paul_ii/apost_letters/documents/hf_jp-ii_apl_04121988_vicesimus-quintus -annus_en.html (accessed on August 29, 2003).

154. CCC, no. 1097.

155. For a fuller presentation of the participation of persons with disabilities in the Church's sacramental life see *Guidelines for the Celebration of the Sacraments with Persons with Disabilities* (1995) and *Pastoral Statement of U.S. Catholic Bishops on Persons with Disabilities* (Washington, DC: USCCB, 1978).

156. *Welcome and Justice for Persons with Disabilities*, no. 7.

Spirit. This constant awareness of the redemptive sacrifice of Christ in the sacraments of initiation reminds the faithful of their need for conversion, penance, and forgiveness, because they "hold this treasure in earthen vessels."[157] This treasure of new life in Christ can be gradually squandered or lost entirely by sin.

But the Father's design for his creation intends that all people be saved by Christ's self-sacrificial love. Toward that end, Christ founded his Church to continue his work of healing and salvation through the power of the Holy Spirit. Immediately after he called his first disciples, Christ cured many who were sick with various diseases,[158] exorcized demons, cleansed lepers, and forgave the sins of a paralytic, restoring him to physical and spiritual health. Christ's healing and reconciling ministry is carried on in the Church principally through the two sacraments of healing: the Sacrament of Penance and Reconciliation and the Sacrament of the Anointing of the Sick.

I. CATECHESIS FOR THE SACRAMENT OF PENANCE AND RECONCILIATION[159]

On the evening of his Resurrection, Jesus sent his apostles out to reconcile sinners to his Father and commissioned them to forgive sins in his name: "'Peace be with you. As the Father has sent me, so I send you.' And when he had said this, he breathed on them and said to them, 'Receive the holy Spirit. Whose sins you forgive are forgiven them, and whose sins you retain are retained.'"[160]

Catechesis for the Sacrament of Penance and Reconciliation first depends on the person's acknowledgment of God's faithful love, of the existence of sin, of the capacity to commit sin, and of God's power to forgive sin and reconcile the sinner with himself and with the Church. "If we say, 'We are without sin,' we deceive ourselves, and the truth is not in us."[161] The normative point of reference for catechesis for the Sacrament of Penance and Reconciliation is the *Rite of Penance*.[162]

Dioceses and parishes should present catechesis for the Sacrament of Penance and Reconciliation that

- Emphasizes God's plan for the salvation of all, his desire for every person to be reconciled with him and live in communion with him, and his gift of the grace of conversion

- Reveals a merciful and loving father who runs to greet the repentant sinner, throws his arms around him, and welcomes him home with a banquet[163]

---

157. 2 Cor 4:7
158. Cf. Mk 1:21–2:12.
159. In addition to using the term "sacrament of Penance and Reconciliation" for this sacrament, the *Catechism of the Catholic Church* also uses "sacrament of Conversion," "sacrament of Confession," and "sacrament of Forgiveness." Cf. nos. 1423–1424.
160. Jn 20:21–23.
161. 1 Jn 1:8.
162. Cf. Sacred Congregation for Divine Worship, *Rite of Penance* (1973).
163. Cf. Lk 15:11–32.

- Reveals the love of Christ, the Redeemer who, through the action of the Holy Spirit, pours himself out with a "love more powerful than death, more powerful than sin"[164]

- Teaches that Christ is at work giving actual graces in the sacrament, thereby effecting what the sacrament signifies, namely "reconciliation with God by which the penitent recovers grace; reconciliation with the Church; remission of the eternal punishment incurred by mortal sins; remission, at least in part, of temporal punishments resulting from sin; peace and serenity of conscience, and spiritual consolation; and an increase of spiritual strength for the Christian battle"[165]

- Teaches that "individual, integral confession and absolution remain the only ordinary way for the faithful to reconcile themselves with God and the Church, unless physical or moral impossibility excuses from this kind of confession";[166] the faithful are "obliged to confess in kind and in number all serious sins committed after baptism and not yet directly remitted through the keys of the Church nor acknowledged in individual confession, of which [they are] conscious after diligent examination of conscience"[167]

- Teaches that the Sacrament of Penance and Reconciliation consists of repentance, confession, reparation on the part of the penitent, and the priest's absolution

- Teaches that "mortal sin is sin whose object is grave matter and which is also committed with full knowledge and deliberate consent"[168]

- Teaches that one who desires to obtain sacramental Reconciliation with God and the Church must confess to a priest all unconfessed mortal sins; calls attention to the obligation to celebrate the sacrament whenever one has committed mortal sin, at least once a year[169]

- Teaches that "only priests who have received the faculty of absolving from the authority of the Church can forgive sins in the name of Christ"[170]

- Informs the faithful that priests are bound by the seal of confession, under the most severe penalties,[171] to keep absolute secrecy regarding the sins that penitents have confessed to them

164. John Paul II, *Rich in Mercy* (*Dives in Misericordia*) (Vatican City, 1980), no. 8, http://www.vatican.va/edocs/eng0215/_index.htm (accessed on August 29, 2003).

165. CCC, no. 1496.

166. Introduction, *Rite of Penance*, no. 31.

167. CIC, c. 988 § 1.

168. John Paul II, *Reconciliation and Penance* (*Reconciliatio et Paenitentia*) (RP) (Washington, DC: USCCB, 1984), no. 17.

169. Cf. CIC, c. 989.

170. CCC, no. 1495.

171. Cf. CIC, c. 1388 §1; cf. CCEO, c. 728 1°.

- Instructs those being catechized about the forms and options for celebrating the sacrament, the words and gestures of the rite, how to examine one's conscience, and how to make a good confession

- Reminds the faithful that the Penitential Rite in the Eucharistic Liturgy is a means of repentance for venial sin and that the confession of venial sins—"sin that merits merely temporal punishment"[172]—is strongly recommended by the Church

- Prepares the community to celebrate in ritual the realities of repentance, conversion, and reconciliation

- Challenges the individual and the community to recognize the presence of evil in the social order, to evaluate that evil in light of the Gospel values as articulated in the Church, to accept appropriate individual and corporate responsibility, and to seek forgiveness for participation in social evil, or the evil of society

- Reminds even those who have "put on Christ"[173] in the sacraments of initiation that they are all sinners and that, in the Sacrament of Penance and Reconciliation, they have an opportunity to acknowledge their sinfulness, their estrangement from God and his Church, and their need for conversion and forgiveness

- Encourages Christians to grow in their awareness of their solidarity with other human beings, to seek forgiveness from them, and to offer forgiveness to them when necessary

2. CATECHESIS FOR CHILDREN'S FIRST RECEPTION OF THE SACRAMENT OF PENANCE AND RECONCILIATION

Like preparation for Confirmation and First Communion, parents and the parish catechetical leader, together with the pastor, are responsible for determining when children are ready to receive First Penance and Reconciliation. Readiness for reception of this sacrament includes knowledge of the person of Jesus and the Gospel message of forgiveness, knowledge of sin and its effect, and understanding and experience of sorrow, forgiveness, and conversion.

In the Latin Church, children must receive the Sacrament of Penance and Reconciliation for the first time prior to their first reception of the Eucharist.[174] Since the celebration of First Confession precedes First Communion,

> catechesis for the Sacrament of Reconciliation is to precede First Communion and must be kept distinct by a clear and unhurried separation. This is to be done so that the specific identity of each sacrament is apparent and so that, before receiving First Communion, the child will be familiar with

---

172. CIC, c. 988 §2.
173. Cf. Gal 3:27.
174. Cf. *General Catechetical Directory*, Addendum, no. 5.

the revised Rite of Reconciliation and will be at ease with the reception of the sacrament.[175]

Catechesis for children prior to their first reception of the Sacrament of Penance and Reconciliation must always respect their natural disposition, ability, age, and circumstances. Since the family is intimately involved with the formation of a child's moral conscience and ordinarily integrates the child into the wider ecclesial communities, parents should be involved in the preparation of their children for this sacrament so that they can affirm and reinforce frequent participation in the sacraments. They orient the child toward God and encourage continual growth in the understanding of God's mercy and love.

Dioceses and parishes should present catechesis for the first reception of the Sacrament of Penance and Reconciliation that helps children to

- Acknowledge God's unconditional love for us

- Turn to Christ and the Church for sacramental forgiveness and reconciliation

- Recognize the presence of good and evil in the world and their personal capacity for both

- Recognize their need for forgiveness, not only from parents and others close to them, but from God

- Explore the meaning of the symbols, gestures, prayers, and scriptures of the Rite of Reconciliation

- Understand how to celebrate the Rite of Reconciliation

- Understand that "sacramental Confession is a means offered children of the Church to obtain pardon for sin, and furthermore that it is even necessary *per se* if one has fallen into serious sin"[176]

Since conversion is a lifelong process, catechesis for the Sacrament of Penance and Reconciliation is ongoing. Children have a right to a fuller catechesis each year.[177]

3. CATECHESIS FOR THE SACRAMENT OF THE ANOINTING OF THE SICK

The Gospels are filled with signs of Jesus' compassion for the sick, both in spirit and in body. Jesus charged his disciples and with them the whole Church to "cure the sick."[178] His love for the sick continues in the Church today. His healing power is a definitive sign that the Kingdom of God is close at hand and is a clear announcement of his victory over sin, suffering, and death. His Spirit draws all Christians to care for those who suffer in body and soul. Jesus, the divine physician of our souls and bodies, is at work in the Sacrament of the Anointing

---

175. *National Catechetical Directory*, no. 126.

176. *General Catechetical Directory*, Addendum, no. 3.

177. Cf. *National Catechetical Directory*, no. 126.

178. Mt 10:8.

of the Sick: touching our wounds in order to heal us and restoring us to communion with his Father in the Holy Spirit. Christ's personal solicitude for the sick is expressed in the words of James: "Is anyone among you sick? He should summon the presbyters of the church, and they should pray over him and anoint [him] with oil in the name of the Lord, and the prayer of faith will save the sick person, and the Lord will raise him up. If he has committed any sins, he will be forgiven."[179] In the Latin Church, the normative reference point for catechesis for the Anointing of the Sick is the *Rite of Anointing and Pastoral Care of the Sick*.[180]

Dioceses and parishes should present a catechesis for the Sacrament of the Anointing of the Sick that

- Examines the meaning of human suffering, sickness, aging, healing, and death in the light of the Christian faith

- Emphasizes the solidarity with the suffering Christ that Christians experience through their own illness—Christ was no stranger to the world of human suffering, for he took human suffering upon himself, voluntarily and innocently

- Includes instruction on the basic symbols of the sacrament: the laying-on of hands, the anointing of the head and hands with blessed oil, and the words of the sacramental formula[181]

- Teaches that "like all the sacraments the Anointing of the Sick is a liturgical and communal celebration, whether it takes place in the family home, a hospital or church, for a single sick person or a whole group of sick persons"[182]

- Clarifies that the Sacrament of the Anointing of the Sick "is not a sacrament intended only for those who are at the point of death,"[183] but that any baptized person who is seriously or chronically ill or in danger of death from advancing age may receive this sacrament

- Makes clear, equally, that the Anointing of the Sick is also a preparation for death, to be received by those at the point of death; integral to the last rites with which the Church fortifies her faithful in their last hours and which Catholics value so highly, Anointing of the Sick, with the Sacrament of Penance and the Eucharist as Viaticum, form the sacraments of departure[184]

- Explains the effects of the sacrament: "the uniting of the sick person to the passion of Christ, for his own good and that of the whole Church; the strengthening, peace, and courage to endure in a Christian manner

---

179. Jas 5:14–15.
180. Cf. Sacred Congregation for Divine Worship, Rite of Anointing and Pastoral Care of the Sick (1972).
181. Cf. CCC, no. 1519.
182. CCC, no. 1517.
183. SC, no. 73.
184. Cf. CCC, nos. 1523, 1525.

the sufferings of illness or old age; the forgiveness of sins, if the sick person was not able to attain it through the Sacrament of Penance and Reconciliation; the restoration of health, if it is conducive to the salvation of his soul; and the preparation for passing over to eternal life"[185]

- Teaches that a person who has previously received the Sacrament of the Anointing of the Sick may receive it again if the condition worsens still or if the condition initially improves and then worsens again

- Explains that those preparing for serious surgery, the elderly whose infirmity declines further, and seriously ill children should ask for sacramental anointing

- Encourages the members of the parish to visit and care for the sick and express concern and love for them

- Teaches that only bishops and priests are ministers of the Sacrament of the Anointing of the Sick

In some of the Eastern Churches, the Sacrament of the Anointing of the Sick is available to all the baptized on the Wednesday or Thursday before Easter and on certain other occasions, such as in the context of a pilgrimage. In these Churches, different parts of the body are anointed, according to the particular Eastern tradition.

Faithful to Christ's command to "heal the sick," the Church offers to those who are about to leave earthly life the Eucharist as *viaticum*, the Body and Blood of Christ, that goes "on the way with" or accompanies the dying person as he or she passes from this life to the next. In these circumstances, the Eucharist is the seed of eternal life that completes the pilgrim's earthly journey from birth through death to life. Catechesis on *viaticum* should include careful instruction so that the faithful can arrange for *viaticum* to be brought while the dying person is able to receive it.

C. The Sacraments at the Service of Communion

Jesus Christ, the only Son of God, leads all people to the Father through the Holy Spirit into communion with the Holy Trinity. This is the end toward which the Father's eternal plan for the salvation of humanity advances. To achieve this end, Christ pours out the Holy Spirit in the Church through the sacraments at the service of communion so that the baptized may bear witness to him and join themselves to his sacrificial offering of praise to the Father. Holy Orders and Matrimony are the sacraments at the service of communion because they "confer a particular mission in the Church and serve to build up the People of God."[186] The Eastern Catholic Churches call these the "Mysteries of Vocation."

---

185. CCC, no. 1532.
186. CCC, no. 1534.

Catechesis for the Sacrament of Holy Orders should be given to all members of the Christian community. Catechesis should teach that the whole Church is a priestly people and that through Baptism all the faithful share in the priesthood of Christ, the common priesthood of the faithful. Those who have been consecrated by the Sacraments of Baptism, Confirmation or Chrismation, and Eucharist share the vocation to holiness and to the mission of proclaiming the Gospel to all nations.[187] That call, issued by Jesus Christ, establishes the common priesthood of the faithful.

Within this common priesthood of the faithful, some are consecrated through the Sacrament of Holy Orders as members of the ministerial priesthood "to nourish the Church with the word and grace of God."[188] Catechesis should, therefore, teach that "based on this common priesthood and ordered to its service, there exists another participation in the mission of Christ: the ministry conferred by the Sacrament of Holy Orders, where the task is to serve in the name and in the person of Christ the Head in the midst of the community."[189] Catechesis should teach that "the ministerial priesthood differs in essence from the common priesthood of the faithful because it confers a sacred power for the service of the faithful."[190] It should teach that there are three degrees of the ordained ministry: that of bishops, that of priests, and that of deacons.

The ministerial priesthood and the common priesthood of the faithful participate "each in its own proper way, in the one priesthood of Christ."[191] Though they are ordered to each other, they differ essentially.[192] The ministerial priesthood is at the service of the common priesthood of the faithful. It is essential that all the faithful understand that the Sacrament of Holy Orders "is the sacrament through which the mission entrusted by Christ to his apostles continues to be exercised in the Church until the end of time."[193]

Catechesis concerning the Sacrament of Holy Orders should be provided for all the faithful so that they may have a clear understanding that bishops, priests, and deacons are called by Christ and, through sacramental ordination, are empowered to minister in his name and in the name of the Church. Such catechesis clarifies the specific roles and tasks of those in Holy Orders. It emphasizes the intimate connection between the ministerial priesthood and the common priesthood of the faithful. It encourages support for bishops, priests, and deacons so that they may remain faithful to their call and be effective in their ministry. It includes prayer for those in Holy Orders and for new vocations to the ordained ministry. Finally, such catechesis provides opportunities for young men to consider the call to the ministerial priesthood.

---

187. Cf. CIC, c. 1008.
188. LG, no. 11.
189. CCC, no. 1591.
190. CCC, no. 1592.
191. CCC, no.1547.
192. Cf. LG, no 10.
193. CCC, no. 1536.

Dioceses and parishes should present catechesis for the Sacrament of Holy Orders that

- Explains that the whole Church is a priestly people and that, through Baptism, all the faithful share in the priesthood of Christ, the common priesthood of the faithful

- Teaches that "the ministerial priesthood differs in essence from the common priesthood of the faithful because it confers a sacred power for the service of the faithful"[194]

- Sets forth the effects of the sacrament: that it configures a man to Christ either in the priesthood or diaconal service by a special grace of the Holy Spirit and imprints an indelible sacramental character that marks him permanently

- Teaches that "Church authority alone has the responsibility and right to call someone to receive the Sacrament of Holy Orders"[195]

- Teaches that the Church, in the person of the bishops, confers the Sacrament of Holy Orders only on baptized men: "priestly ordination, which hands on the office entrusted by Christ to his Apostles of teaching, sanctifying, and governing the faithful, has in the Catholic Church from the beginning always been reserved to men alone"[196]

- Teaches the symbols, gestures, prayers, and scriptures of the Rite of Ordination,[197] including the laying-on of hands and the bishop's prayer of consecration

- Describes the three degrees of the ordained ministry: that of bishops, that of priests, and that of deacons

- Explains that the grace of the Holy Spirit empowers bishops, priests, and deacons—each in ways particular to their order—to share in the saving action of Jesus Christ's ministry of teaching, sanctifying, and building up the Church

- Makes clear that the Latin Church calls ordained ministers, with the exception of permanent deacons, to consecrate themselves with undivided heart to the Lord by committing themselves to celibacy as a sign of the new life of service to which they are consecrated; ordinarily, the Sacrament of Holy Orders is conferred only on men who freely promise to embrace celibacy for the length of their lives[198]

- Teaches that, in the Eastern Churches, priests and deacons are ordinarily permitted to marry before their ordination

---

194. CCC, no. 1592.
195. CCC, no. 1598.
196. John Paul II, *Reserving Priestly Ordination to Men Alone* (*Ordinatio Sacerdotalis*) (OS) (Washington, DC: USCCB, 1994), no. 1.
197. Cf. CCC, no. 1573.
198. Cf. CCC, no. 1579.

- Teaches that permanent deacons may be men who are already married but that, after ordination to the deaconate, they cannot enter into another marriage

Catechesis on the value and importance of religious life should also be provided for the faithful. It should teach that religious life "derives from the mystery of the Church"[199] and is "distinguished from other forms of consecrated life by its liturgical character, public profession of the evangelical counsels" of poverty, chastity, and obedience; of "fraternal life led in common"; and of "witness given to the union of Christ with the Church."[200] It should also include instruction on secular institutes, societies of apostolic life, and other forms of consecrated life recognized by the Church.[201]

2. CATECHESIS FOR THE SACRAMENT OF MATRIMONY

Christian marriage is the union of a baptized man and woman who freely enter into a loving covenant with each other in Christ. "The matrimonial covenant, by which a man and a woman establish between themselves a partnership of the whole of life and which is ordered by its nature to the good of the spouses and the procreation and education of offspring, has been raised by Christ the Lord to the dignity of a sacrament between the baptized."[202]

This self-giving love of husband and wife represents the mutual love of Christ for his bride, the Church, and the love of the Church for her bridegroom, Christ. "Thus, the *marriage bond* has been established by God himself in such a way that a marriage concluded and consummated between baptized persons can never be dissolved."[203] It gives permanent witness to the fidelity of love. "This bond, which results from the free human act of the spouses and their consummation of the marriage, is a reality, henceforth irrevocable, and gives rise to a covenant guaranteed by God's fidelity. The Church does not have the power to contravene this disposition of divine wisdom."[204]

Catechesis for the Sacrament of Matrimony is addressed to the whole parish community. It is addressed directly to couples intending to marry in the parish and often takes the form of a diocesan or parish preparation program. Catechesis specifically for adults should be offered through all the stages of married life and should be the model for all other forms of catechesis on Christian marriage. Catechesis on Christian marriage and distinctively Christian family values should be given to adolescents and teenagers during their high school years. Children begin learning the meaning of married love at a very early age from their parents, both through the example of their lives and through their more formal instruction. The family is the most effective school for catechesis on Christian marriage and family life.

---

199. CCC, no. 926.
200. CCC, no. 925.
201. Cf. CCC, nos. 914–933.
202. CIC, c. 1055 §1; cf. CCEO, c. 776 §§1–2.
203. CCC, no. 1640.
204. CCC, no. 1640.

Dioceses and parishes should present catechesis on the Sacrament of Matrimony that

- Encourages the care and concern of the whole Christian community for married couples by public recognition of couples planning marriage, modeling by couples in successful marriages, and support of couples in challenged marriages

- Stresses marriage as a distinct and dignified vocation in the Church

- Explains the effects of the Sacrament of Matrimony: the establishment of a perpetual and exclusive bond between the spouses that is sealed by God himself,[205] the perfection of the mutually exclusive and permanent love of the couple, the strengthening of their indissoluble unity, and the experience of a foretaste of the Kingdom of God

- Encourages marriages within the Catholic faith and explains why this is desirable (the Church requires marriage within the Catholic faith; permission or a dispensation from the bishop is necessary for a Catholic to marry a non-Catholic or an unbaptized person, respectively)

- Teaches that marriage is a covenant of love in which God participates as an active member

- Acknowledges that it is in the love and struggles of marriage that a couple attains the holiness of their vocation

- Teaches that in Christian marriage the unity of the couple is a unity founded in an equal personal dignity and expressed in an unreserved mutuality of self-giving

- Teaches that the family is the first and essential center of faithful living, the domestic Church

- Teaches that the home is the first school of Christian life and human enrichment

- Teaches that a couple's marriage in Christ is a sacred relationship that is supported for the length of their lives by the grace to love each other with the love Christ has for the Church

- Teaches that fidelity, indissolubility, and openness to children are essential to Christian marriage

- Teaches that Christian marriage is for the mutual support of the spouses, their growth in love, and the procreation and education of their children

- Includes a clear presentation of the Church's teaching on the morally acceptable methods of regulating birth and the immorality of artificial birth control, of sterilization for that purpose, and of abortion

- Emphasizes their personal responsibility to protect the human life that they co-create with God from the moment of conception to natural death

---

205. Cf. Mk 10:9.

- Includes a clear presentation of the Church's teaching on mixed and interreligious marriages

- Includes instruction on the rite of the sacrament

- Teaches that the couple themselves are the ministers of the sacrament and that their consent should be publicly exchanged in their vows before a priest or deacon (or a witness authorized by the Church) and two other witnesses, ideally in the presence of an assembly of the faithful[206]

- Assists the couple in deepening their understanding of the nature of Christian marriage as a covenant between a man and a woman whereby the spouses establish between themselves a partnership of their whole life that is ordered to the well-being of the spouses and to the procreation and upbringing of children

Catechesis for those preparing for ecumenical or interreligious marriages should encourage them to discuss openly and honestly the challenges and opportunities that the respective faith traditions present for their relationship, the education and formation of their children, and the harmony of the family. It should also recognize the sacramental nature of a marriage between a baptized Catholic and a spouse baptized in another Christian tradition. Catechesis is also needed for non-sacramental baptized Catholic and an unbaptized person. It should clarify that for marriages between a Catholic and another Christian, the Catholic spouse must request a canonical dispensation from the diocesan bishop; likewise, the Catholic spouse must request a canonical dispensation in order to marry a member of a non-Christian religion or of no religion.

Dioceses and parishes should also present catechesis to the whole Catholic community that

- Encourages the care and concern of the whole Christian community for those who have suffered the trauma of divorce

- Encourages the Christian community to welcome divorced persons and their children into the parish as truly integral members

- Makes clear that, while the fact of divorce itself does not prevent reception of the sacraments, Catholics who are divorced and remarried without having obtained a declaration of nullity cannot participate in the sacramental life of the Church

- Explains that a Church annulment or "declaration of nullity" is an official decision by the Church that a marriage was invalid from the beginning, but that it does not affect the legitimacy of children resulting from the union

- Encourages those Catholics who are divorced and remarried outside the Church to seek to regularize their marriage if possible, "to listen to the word of God, to attend the sacrifice of the Mass, to persevere in prayer,

---

206. In Byzantine Catholic Churches, the priest is the minister of the sacrament. In addition, the vows are optional because the statement of the intention is made in a different manner.

to contribute to works of charity and to community efforts in favor of justice, to bring up their children in the Christian faith, to cultivate the spirit and practice of penance and thus implore, day by day, God's grace"[207]

37. THE SACRED: TIME (LITURGICAL YEAR) AND SPACE (ART)

A. Sacred Time: The Liturgical Year

"In Christianity time has a fundamental importance."[208] Christ inaugurates "the last days"[209] and the time of the Church that extends to the definitive coming of the Kingdom of God in Jesus Christ. *"In Jesus Christ, the Word made flesh, time becomes a dimension of God,* who is himself eternal."[210] Because of God's presence in time in the person of Jesus Christ, time is sacred. Christians mark time itself in relation to Christ.

The Latin Church lives and celebrates the mystery of Christ in the span of a calendar year that re-presents the mystery of the incarnation and redemption beginning with the First Sunday of Advent and concluding on the Solemnity of Christ the King. The Eastern Catholic Churches begin and end the liturgical year in accord with their particular traditions and follow the pattern of the Church year by means of their own particular lectionaries.

The economy or history of salvation unfolds throughout the liturgical year. Each day of the liturgical year is sanctified primarily by Christ's presence in it, but also by the prayer and the liturgical celebrations of the People of God, especially by the Mass and the Divine Office. The liturgical year exerts "a special sacramental power and influence which strengthens Christian life."[211]

From the time of the apostles, beginning with the actual day of Christ's Resurrection, the Church has celebrated the Paschal Mystery every first day, Sunday, the Lord's Day. "The intimate bond between Sunday and the Resurrection of the Lord is strongly emphasized by all the Churches of the East and West."[212] Sunday is the weekly Easter. The day of Christ's Resurrection is both the first day of the week in the new creation and the "eighth day" of the week, the image of eternity, which anticipates the glorious return of Christ and the fulfillment of God's reign. In the Byzantine Liturgy, Sunday is called "the day that knows no evening."

"The weekdays extend and develop the Sunday celebration."[213] As the Church celebrates the mystery of Christ throughout the liturgical year, she honors especially Mary, the Mother of God, and Mother of the Church, who is "inseparably linked with her son's saving work. In her the Church admires and exalts the most excellent fruit of redemption, and joyfully contemplates, as in a faultless

---

207. FC, no. 84.
208. TMA, no. 10.
209. TMA, no. 10, citing Heb 1:2.
210. TMA, no. 10.
211. Sacred Congregation of Rites, *Maxima Redemptionis Nostrae Mysteriis* (1955).
212. DD, no. 19.
213. *National Catechetical Directory*, no. 144.

image, that which she herself desires and hopes wholly to be."[214] The Church also commemorates the lives of the apostles, martyrs, and other saints, for they have been glorified with Christ. They are heroic examples of Christian life and intercede for the faithful on earth.

The liturgical year is divided into seasons that correspond to the major events in the history of salvation in Christ. The Christmas season celebrates the birth of the Savior in the mystery of the incarnation. In the Eastern Churches, after the close of the Christmas cycle, the Baptism of the Lord, called the "Theophany," is celebrated with great solemnity. Christ's baptism is seen as the paradigm or model for our own baptism.

For all the baptized, Lent is likewise the time to deepen and renew our own baptismal commitment. It is the primary penitential season in the Church's liturgical year, during which the faithful embrace the traditional practices of fasting, prayer, and almsgiving in preparation to renew their baptismal promises on Easter. These expressions of penance and self-denial manifest the Christian's continual need for conversion. Lent reflects the forty days that Jesus spent in the desert in fasting and prayer. It is also the time when the Church journeys with her catechumens and draws them toward the celebration of the Paschal Mystery in the final stages of their Christian initiation.

The Easter Triduum celebrates the Lord's passion, death, and Resurrection and is the culmination of the entire liturgical year. The Easter Vigil marks the sacramental initiation of the catechumens into God's own life and the life of the Church. The Easter season extends for fifty days to the celebration of Pentecost, which commemorates the mission of the Holy Spirit from the Father and the Son to the Church.

In the Latin Church, Ordinary Time, which spans the periods from Christmas to Lent and from Pentecost to the Feast of Christ the King, celebrates different aspects of the fullness of the mystery of Christ from week to week. The Eastern Catholic Churches do not designate a season of Ordinary Time, but some dedicate a season to the power of the cross, beginning with the Feast of the Holy Cross, in which the cross is celebrated with great solemnity as the standard for Christian living as the believers await the second coming of Christ.

Catechesis for recognizing God's presence in time, for keeping time holy, and for the interiorization of the liturgical year is directed to every Christian. The *Commentary on the Revised Liturgical Year* and the *General Norms for the Liturgical Year and the Calendar*[215] provide many examples for the development of catechesis for the liturgical year. The religious customs and traditions of the diverse cultural and ethnic heritages of the many peoples who make up the Catholic Church in the United States also offer countless opportunities to mark the more significant moments throughout the liturgical year. The celebration of these religious customs and traditions provide genuine opportunities to evangelize the culture and cultures of the United States.

---

214. SC, no. 103.
215. Cf. USCCB, *Roman Calendar, Text and Commentary* (1976).

B. Sacred Art, Architecture, and Music

I. SACRED ART

In sacred art human hands express the infinite beauty of God and prompt praise and thanks. "*Sacred art* is true and beautiful when its form corresponds to its particular vocation: evoking and glorifying, in faith and adoration, the transcendent mystery of God—the surpassing invisible beauty of truth and love visible in Christ."[216] While the particular expressions of sacred art vary from culture to culture, authentic sacred art turns human minds, hearts, and souls toward God. "Art is meant to bring the divine to the human world, to the level of the senses, then, from the spiritual insight gained from the senses and the stirring of the emotions, to raise the human world to God, to his inexpressible kingdom of mystery, beauty and life."[217] Sacred art "should be worthy, becoming, and beautiful, signs and symbols of things supernatural."[218]

Sacred art also has both a liturgical and catechetical purpose. Sacred art expresses the reverence and honor that are due the sacred. It conveys faith and fosters the expression of faith in the Liturgy. Sacramental celebrations depend on signs, symbols, and gestures to effect the grace they signify. Sacred art forms an essential part of the sacred Liturgy; it is "integral to the Church at prayer because these objects and actions are [sacred] 'signs and symbols of the supernatural world' and expressions of the divine presence."[219] Whether traditional or contemporary, sacred art is suitable for religious worship as long as it expresses divine in the midst of the human and leads to prayer.

Especially in the Eastern Churches, the liturgical icon portrays sacred images of Christ, the Mother of God, the saints, or the angels. These icons represent various aspects of the mystery of the incarnation of the Son of God. "Christian iconography expresses in images the same Gospel message that Scripture communicates by words. Image and word illuminate each other."[220] In Eastern spirituality, iconography depicts redeemed creation as a manifestation of the Divine Creator. Sacred images of the Mother of God, the angels, and the saints signify Christ, who is glorified in them. These sacred images lead the faithful to contemplate the mystery they depict, to meditate on the Word of God, and to enter more deeply into communion with God.

Dioceses and parishes should present catechesis on sacred art that

- Includes an introduction to the religious art of the past and the present in both the Eastern and Latin Churches

- Revives the tradition of using great works of art, such as music, stained glass windows, paintings, mosaics, and sculpture to instruct the faithful on the fundamental truths of the faith

---

216. CCC, no. 2502.
217. Paul VI, Address to the Pontifical Commission for Sacred Art in Italy (December 17, 1969).
218. SC, no. 122.
219. USCCB, *Built of Living Stones: Art, Architecture, and Worship* (Washington, DC: USCCB, 2000), no. 146.
220. CCC, no. 1160.

- Employs contemporary examples of sacred art of different cultures to imprint the mystery of Christ on the memories and experiences of those being catechized

- Encourages the placement of religious art in the home, such as the crucifix, statuary, sculpture, painting, mosaics, and other sacred images of Christ, the Virgin Mary, and the saints

2. SACRED ARCHITECTURE

In sacred architecture, the Church "demonstrates God's reign over all space by dedicating buildings to house the Church and its worship."[221] Christians build churches to worship God, but churches are not simply gathering spaces for the Christian assembly. Rather, "the church building is a sign and reminder of the immanence and transcendence of God—who chose to dwell among us and whose presence cannot be contained or limited to any single place."[222] A church is the house of God, his dwelling with those who have been reconciled to him by Christ and united to him by the Holy Spirit. A church building signifies the Church, the Body of Christ, alive in a particular place and among a particular people. It is the building in which the Christian community gathers to hear the word of God, to celebrate the Eucharist, to receive the sacraments, and to pray. It must have a place of great honor for God to dwell and for the faithful to pray. It should be a place appropriate for the reservation of the Eucharist and befitting the adoration of the Blessed Sacrament. It should be a form of worship itself, lifting the hearts and minds of the people to give praise and thanks to God. A church also signifies the Father's house, toward which his people journey and for which his people long. It should be easily accessible to all. The church building, in short, is a "sign of the pilgrim Church on earth and reflects the Church dwelling in heaven."[223]

3. SACRED MUSIC

Because sacred music gives glory and praise to God, it has been an integral part of the life of the Church from the very beginning. Jesus sang hymns with his apostles at the Last Supper,[224] and the first Christian writers attested to the customary inclusion of sacred music even in the earliest forms of Eucharistic Liturgy. Sacred music can be sung or performed on instruments. It can take a variety of forms, such as chant or polyphony, and can be ancient, medieval, modern, or contemporary. "Among the many signs and symbols used by the Church to celebrate its faith, music is of preeminent importance."[225]

---

221. *Built of Living Stones*, no. 20.

222. *Built of Living Stones*, no. 50.

223. Congregation for the Sacraments and Divine Worship, *Rite of Dedication of a Church and an Altar* (1978), ch. 1, no. 2.

224. Cf. Mk 14:26.

225. USCCB Bishops' Committee on the Liturgy, *Music in Catholic Worship*, rev. ed. (Washington, DC: USCCB, 1983), no. 23.

Thus, sacred music forms an integral part of the Church's Liturgy. More than just hymns, sacred music especially includes the Mass parts, so as to enrich the people's active participation in the Liturgy. It exhibits a "certain holy sincerity of form"[226] and performs a ministerial role in the celebration of divine worship. It serves—but does not dominate. "Liturgical worship is given a more noble form when divine offices are celebrated solemnly in song with the assistance of sacred ministers and the active participation of the people."[227]

In the Roman Liturgy, "Gregorian chant holds pride of place."[228] Along with it, polyphony in particular is allowed, and other forms of sacred music as well, "provided that they correspond to the spirit of liturgical action and that they foster the participation of all the faithful."[229] It is also desirable that everywhere the faithful "know how to sing together at least some parts of the Ordinary of the Mass in Latin, especially the Creed and the Lord's Prayer, set to the simpler melodies."[230]

Consequently, sacred music also has a distinct catechetical purpose. Sacred music invites the faithful to give glory to God; it enhances their prayer, fosters the unity of their minds and hearts, and aims to draw them closer to Christ. Sacred music "should assist the assembled believers to express and share the gift of faith that is written within them and to nourish and strengthen their interior commitment of faith."[231] Within the scope of sacred music, special attention should be given "to the *songs used by the assembly*, since singing is a particularly apt way to express a joyful heart, accentuating the solemnity of the celebration and fostering the sense of a common faith and a shared love."[232] Parishes should provide opportunities for their people to learn sacred hymns in order that they may fully participate in the liturgical life of the Church.

38. SACRAMENTALS AND POPULAR DEVOTIONS[233]

A. Sacramentals

Sacramentals "are sacred signs which bear a resemblance to the sacraments. They signify effects, particularly of a spiritual nature, which are obtained through the Church's intercession."[234] They prepare the faithful to receive and cooperate with grace and so are catechetical by nature. They are liturgical actions in which the faithful are invited to participate. In general, sacramentals sanctify the lives of the faithful by linking them to Christ's Paschal sacrifice.

---

226. Congregation for Divine Worship and Discipline of the Sacraments, *Instruction on Music in the Liturgy (Musicam Sacram)* (MusSacr), no. 4, in Flannery.

227. SC, no. 113.

228. GIRM, no. 41.

229. GIRM, no. 41.

230. GIRM, no. 41.

231. *Music in Catholic Worship*, no. 23.

232. DD, no. 50.

233. Cf. *Directory on Popular Piety and the Liturgy: Principles and Guidelines.*

234. SC, no. 60.

Sacramentals are instituted by the Church in order to sanctify certain ministries, certain states of life, and certain objects Christians use in their daily lives. Sacramentals are often concrete examples of the inculturation of the faith since they express the faith in the particular language, customs, and traditions of a specific culture. "They always include a prayer, often accompanied by a specific sign, such as the laying on of hands, the sign of the cross, or the sprinkling of holy water (which recalls Baptism)."[235]

Blessings of persons, meals, occasions, objects, and places are the most important kinds of sacramentals.[236] Certain blessings consecrate persons to God, such as the abbot or abbess of a monastery, virgins or widows, and the members of vowed communities. Other blessings designate persons for ministry in the Church, such as catechists, lectors, acolytes, and so forth. Still other blessings consecrate objects for liturgical use. Thus, the church building, the altar, the baptistry, oils to be used in celebrating the sacraments, sacred vessels, vestments, holy water, crosses and crucifixes, rosaries, palms, ashes, candles, medals, and various types of religious art and artifacts are all sacramentals. Some cultures have emphasized some sacramentals; the faith has been inculturated through them.

Catechesis on sacramentals should describe their relationship to faith in Jesus Christ and their function in the Church and in the lives of individual Christians. It should especially seek out examples of sacramentals that are common to all cultures in order to reveal their relationships to the Christian message.

B. Popular Piety and Popular Devotion

Especially in light of the cultural, ethnic, and religious diversity of the United States, popular piety is a vital element in Catholic life that is expressed in a wide variety of popular devotions, such as various forms of prayers for the souls in purgatory, the use of sacramentals, and pilgrimages to shrines of Christ, the Blessed Virgin Mary, and the saints.[237] In the United States, popular piety is a mode of the inculturation of the faith that is deeply rooted in the many cultures represented in its population. All racial, ethnic, and cultural groups have devotional practices that spring from their particular expressions of the one faith. Popular piety and the popular devotion it inspires provide many opportunities to encounter Christ in the particular circumstances of ethnic, cultural, and religious customs. If popular piety "is well oriented, above all by a pedagogy of evangelization, it is rich in values. It manifests a thirst for God which only the simple and poor can know. It makes people capable of generosity and sacrifice even to the point of heroism, when it is a question of manifesting belief."[238]

The large and growing number of immigrants in the United States requires careful attention to the role of popular piety in many people's lives.[239] This is true, for example, in the lives of Catholics whose roots are in Africa. The Church

---

235. CCC, no. 1668.
236. Cf. *Book of Blessings* (New York: Catholic Book Publishing Co., 1989).
237. Cf. EA, no. 16.
238. EN, no. 48.
239. Cf. USCCB, *Together a New People: Pastoral Statement on Migrants and Refugees* (Washington, DC: USCCB, 1986), no. 31.

"recognizes that it must approach these Americans from within their own culture, taking seriously the spiritual and human riches of that culture which appear in the way they worship, their sense of joy and solidarity, their language and their traditions."[240] As another example, Hispanics/Latinos "tend to view all of life as sacred and have generally developed a profound sense of the divine in daily living. This is evident in their popular religiosity. . . . In small communities, [they] find support to retrieve this sense of popular piety and to reaffirm the values contained in these celebrations."[241]

Asian and Pacific Catholic Americans and immigrants sustain their faith through devotional prayers and practices. They "migrated with the experience and sensibilities of the great religions and spiritual traditions of the world . . . together with Christianity. Their experience of the great religions and spiritual traditions teaches them to live with profound presence of the sacred, a holistic approach to life and salvation, and spirituality adapted to their needs and a life-giving vitality."[242] They "bring popular devotions from their homelands and share them with fellow parishioners."[243]

In the Latin Church in the United States, the Blessed Sacrament, the Sacred Heart, the Blessed Virgin Mary, and many saints are very important in popular devotion. "Hispanic/Latino spirituality," for example, "places strong emphasis on the humanity of Jesus, especially when he appears weak and suffering, as in the crib and in his passion and death. . . . The Blessed Virgin Mary, especially under the titles of Our Lady of Guadalupe (Mexico), Our Lady of Providence (Puerto Rico), and Our Lady of Charity (Cuba), occupies a privileged place in Hispanic/Latino popular piety."[244]

African Americans likewise weave the message of evangelization into the cultural environment of their distinctive spirituality. The roots of African American spirituality are found in the family and issue from their history and lived experience. Their art, music, language, dance, and drama—as well as those of other Black cultures—should be incorporated into liturgical celebrations that are always "authentically black . . . truly Catholic . . . well-prepared and well-executed."[245] The Kingship of Jesus Christ, the pouring of libations, and an emphasis on Mary as the "Great Mother" are a few examples of popular devotion that express the profound biblical themes of freedom and hope that are so integral to African American culture and spirituality.

240. EA, no. 16.
241. USCCB Committee on Hispanic Affairs, *Communion and Mission: A Guide for Bishops and Pastoral Leaders on Small Church Communities* (Washington, DC: USCCB, 1995), no. 5.
242. USCCB, *Asian and Pacific Presence: Harmony in Faith* (Washington, DC: USCCB, 2001), 15.
243. *Asian and Pacific Presence*, 16.
244. USCCB, *The Hispanic Presence: Challenge and Commitment* (1983), no. 12, in *Hispanic Ministry: Three Major Documents* (Washington, DC: USCCB, 1995).
245. *What We Have Seen and Heard*, 31.

In Eastern Catholic communities, *Akathistos, Paraklesis, Molebens,*[246] devotion to the Blessed Virgin Mary, reverence for icons, and offices to the saints are important forms of popular devotion.

C. Marian Devotion

Devotion to the Blessed Virgin Mary deserves special attention because it is such an important part of worship in the United States. The United States of America is under the patronage of the Immaculate Conception. The various forms of devotion to the Blessed Virgin Mary reflect many different cultures, religious convictions, and popular sensibilities that make up the Church in the United States. Catholic people of all cultures have a deep love for the Mother of God. They employ many different expressions of that love to show the one faith that characterizes their particular prayer life and spirituality.

In this country, as well as throughout the world, the Rosary holds a place of honor as the most popular prayer devotion to the Blessed Virgin Mary. In October 2002, Pope John Paul II called for a renewed focus on the Rosary in his apostolic letter *On the Most Holy Rosary (Rosarium Virginis Mariae).*[247] In that letter, the Holy Father also suggested five new Mysteries, which he called the "Luminous Mysteries." These Mysteries focus on events in the public life of Jesus.

Dioceses and parishes should present catechesis on piety that

- Promotes the exercise of sound pastoral judgment in order to ensure that popular devotions and the religious sensibility that underlies them lead the faithful to a deeper knowledge of the mystery of Jesus Christ and a true encounter with him

- Promotes Marian devotion that clearly expresses "intrinsic Trinitarian, Christological and ecclesiological aspects of Mariology"[248]

- Discovers the authentic spiritual values present in popular piety and enriches it with genuine Catholic doctrine so that it might lead to a sincere conversion and a practical exercise of charity[249]

- Recognizes the cultural and religious diversity of the United States and promotes awareness of how important popular piety and popular devotion are in the lives of many of the Christian faithful

Provides opportunities for a more complete inculturation of the Gospel so that the seeds of the Word found in the culture may come to their fulfillment in Christ

---

246. *Akathistos, Paraklesis,* and *Molebens* are various types of prayer services. *Akathistos,* literally "standing prayer," is the oldest version and involves prayers of devotion to Mary, to Jesus, or to the Sacred Hearts of Jesus or Mary. *Paraklesis* is a prayer service of intercession to a saint. *Molebens* is a somewhat shorter version of a Paraklesis.

247. Cf. John Paul II, *On the Most Holy Rosary (Rosarium Virginis Mariae)* (Washington, DC: USCCB, 2002).

248. GDC, no. 196.

249. Cf. EA, no. 16.

- Ensures that the various forms of popular devotion radiate from the Church's sacramental life but do not replace it

- Leads the faithful to a deeper sense of their membership in the Church, which increases the fervor of their love for the Church and offers an effective response to the challenges of today's secularization[250]

- Distinguishes between appropriate popular devotion and the requirements of the Christian faith

- Relies on valid elements of popular piety to be effective instruments in the new evangelization

39. CONCLUSION

Gathered to worship the Father in Christ and through the Holy Spirit, the whole Church is one and is profoundly aware of her mission to the world. In the Liturgy, the Church at once expresses her faith and by God's grace deepens that faith. In the Eucharist, Christ leads the community of the baptized to continual conversion in him, to deeper communion with the Father, and to life in the Holy Spirit. The Liturgy both enables and inspires the faithful to live the Christian faith: dedication to the teaching of the apostles, the communal life, the breaking of the bread, and prayer. The participation in the liturgical life of the Church presupposes support of and engagement in all forms of catechetical life in the parish and in the home. The liturgical life of the Church is integrated with her moral life. The next chapter describes how catechesis prepares and strengthens the believer for life in Christ: a life of faith, hope, charity, justice, and peace.

---

250. Cf. EA, no. 16.

SUMMORUM PONTIFICUM
ON THE USE OF THE ROMAN LITURGY
PRIOR TO 1970

APOSTOLIC LETTER ISSUED *MOTU PROPRIO*
POPE BENEDICT XVI
JULY 7, 2007

LETTER OF HIS HOLINESS BENEDICT XVI TO THE BISHOPS ON THE
OCCASION OF THE PUBLICATION OF THE APOSTOLIC LETTER
"MOTU PROPORIO DATA"

SUMMORUM PONTIFICUM

ON THE USE OF THE ROMAN LITURGY PRIOR
TO THE REFORM OF 1970
JULY 7, 2007

UNIVERSAE ECCLESIA

INSTRUCTION ON THE APOSTOLIC LETTER SUMMORUM
PONTIFICUM OF HIS HOLINESS BENEDICT XVI GIVEN
MOTU PROPRIO
PONTIFICIAL COMMISSION *ECCLESIA DEI*
APRIL 30, 2011

AN OVERVIEW OF *SUMMORUM PONTIFICUM* AND ITS ACCOMPANYING DOCUMENTS

Deacon Francis L. Agnoli

On July 7, 2007, Pope Benedict XVI promulgated his apostolic letter *motu proprio, Summorum pontificum* (SP). It took effect on September 14 of that year, the Feast of the Exaltation of the Holy Cross. The publication of the *motu proprio* was accompanied by a letter (*epistula*) from the pontiff to his "Brother Bishops" further explaining his decision to allow for wider use of the liturgical books in effect prior to the Second Vatican Council, what he referred to as the "extraordinary form" of the liturgy. On April 30, 2011, the Pontifical Commission *Ecclesia Dei*, which has competence in the area of the extraordinary form, published an instruction on the application of SP entitled *Universae Ecclesiae* (UE).

BACKGROUND OF THE DOCUMENT

The immediate background to the *motu proprio* is given in the introductory paragraphs of SP. Pope Benedict XVI recalled there that in some parts of the world "no small number"[1] of Catholics continued to adhere to the pre-Vatican II liturgical forms even after the Council. In response, Pope John Paul II issued the indult *Quattuor abhinc annos* and the *motu proprio Ecclesia Dei*. By these efforts, those faithful who were so inclined were granted access to the Mass celebrated according to the Missal of 1962.[2] However, as Pope Benedict mentions in his *epistula* to the bishops, application of those norms was uneven, due in part—according to the pontiff—to unfounded fears that such usage would call the Second Vatican Council into question.

PURPOSE OF THE DOCUMENT

It was against this backdrop that SP was issued. In the document itself, the Holy Father simply states that the purpose of the document is to respond to the expressed pastoral needs of those who adhere to the pre-Conciliar liturgy[3] and

---

1. *Summorum pontificum* (SP), introduction.

2. The conditions for taking advantage of the indult were: (1) the legitimacy and doctrinal exactitude of the post-Conciliar Missal had to be accepted; (2) the rites had to be celebrated in a church designated by the bishop; and (3) the rites had to be celebrated according to the 1962 Missal without adding anything from the post-Conciliar liturgy. See "Forty Questions on the Apostolic Letter *Summorum Pontificum*," 24, developed by the USCCB's Secretariat for Liturgy in April 2007. While sent to bishops and not published, it is available online at www.cdop.org /pdfs/40QuestionsonSummorumPontificum.pdf.

3. It is interesting to see how the numbers of those who adhere to the extraordinary form are referred to in these various documents. *Summorum pontificum* (SP) uses "no small number." The *epistula* refers to "a good number." *Universae Ecclesiae* (UE), 5 states that "many" of the faithful expressed a desire to keep celebrating according to the old form.

ensure more ready access to it. Pope Benedict XVI goes further in his accompanying *epistula*.

To begin with, the *motu proprio* was issued in order to give clearer juridical norms and to "free bishops from constantly having to evaluate anew how they are to respond to various situations,"[4] that is, in responding not only to those who have remained attached to the pre-Conciliar liturgy because that was their experience growing up, but also to a new generation of Catholics who have found that the extraordinary form responds to their spiritual needs. In addition, he makes the claim that some remain attached to the extraordinary form of the liturgy because in the aftermath of the Council there were "deformations of the liturgy which were hard to bear" and "caused deep pain to individuals totally rooted in the faith of the church."[5] Finally, he explicitly mentions that he sees his initiative as an important aspect of promoting "interior reconciliation in the heart of the church"—especially with the schismatic Society of St. Piux X. While the instruction from *Ecclesia Dei* echoes both SP[6] and its accompanying *epistula*,[7] *Ecclesia Dei* also uses language that seems to be more expansive, stating that the pope's desire was to offer *all* the faithful access to the extraordinary form (called a "precious treasure to be preserved").[8]

AUTHORITY OF THE DOCUMENT

A papal *motu proprio* is true legislation (*lex*). Therefore, it has binding power as universal law for the Church. As the document itself states, the Pontifical Commission *Ecclesia Dei* is charged with "supervising the observance and application"[9] of this new law. The *epistula* accompanying SP is not law, but it does reveal the mind of the legislator and thus can aid in the proper interpretation of the *motu proprio*.[10] The closing paragraph of the document contains the typical formula for revoking all contrary previous laws: "whatever there may be to the contrary."

Normally, the dicasteries of the Roman Curia exercise executive rather than legislative power, including the power[11] if so granted to issue instructions. Instructions are intended to "clarify the prescripts of laws and elaborate on and determine the methods to be observed in fulfilling them."[12] They are executive (administrative) in nature, and therefore have lesser juridic weight than

---

4. *Epistula* accompanying SP.

5. *Epistula* accompanying SP. But, as Nathan Mitchell notes after listing numerous examples: "The postconciliar liturgy, therefore, hardly has a monopoly on 'hard to bear,' 'arbitrary,' liturgical 'deformations.' There were plenty to go around during the four hundred years between" the Missals of 1570 and 1970 . As quoted in *"Summorum pontificum," Worship* 81, no. 6 [November 2007]: 559.

6. UE, 8b.

7. Ibid., 8c.

8. Ibid., 8a. It is interesting that SP itself makes no mention of this "universal" aim; rather, it is very specific that it was directed at those who adhered to the older form of the liturgy.

9. SP, 11–12.

10. *Code of Canon Law* (CIC) c. 17.

11. See UE, 12. In this article, the Pontifical Commission *Ecclesia Dei* specifically mentions that it has this faculty and that the instruction is being issued in accord with canon 34.

12. CIC c. 34§1.

legislative documents. Only if issued *in forma specifica* are they legislative. *Universae Ecclesiae* was issued *in forma communi* and thus it is not a legislative document.[13] It is law in the broad sense (*ius*) but not in the more narrow sense of legislation (*lex*). However, it does flow from the particular competence of the commission and thus needs to be considered a legitimate instrument for the implementation of applicable law: *Summorum pontificum, Ecclesiae unitatem*,[14] and the *Code of Canon Law* (1983).[15]

In UE, the Pontifical Commission *Ecclesia Dei* specifically states that SP is to be "interpreted in a sense favorable to the faithful."[16] As John Foster points out, this is an important distinction. Favors in the law are to be amplified; a broad rather than restrictive reading of the *motu proprio* is intended.[17]

What of the authority of a bishop in his own diocese? According to the *epistula*—citing the *Constitution on the Sacred Liturgy*, 22—SP in no way lessens the authority or responsibility of the bishop as the "moderator of the liturgy in his own diocese."[18] While UE reiterates SP in that regard,[19] it also states that bishops are to ensure that the extraordinary form is respected[20] and mentions that the Pontifical Commission *Ecclesia Dei* will intervene if any bishop takes an action "which appears to be contrary to" SP.[21]

EXTRAORDINARY FORM

Summorum pontificum refers to the celebration of the liturgy according to the books in force prior to the reforms of the Second Vatican Council as the extraordinary form of the liturgy, while liturgical celebrations according to the revised (post-Conciliar) books are termed the "ordinary form."[22] John Huels has pointed out that the term "extraordinary" has various shades of meaning in the law.[23] For example, a minister who under specific exceptional circumstances may replace an ordinary minister is called "extraordinary"—such as laypersons serving as extraordinary ministers of Holy Communion.[24] The third rite of

---

13. It does not create new law; therefore, it is important to keep in mind c. 34§2: "The ordinances of instructions do not derogate from laws. If these ordinances cannot be reconciled with the prescripts of laws, they lack all force."

14. Benedict XVI's *motu proprio* linking the Pontifical Commission *Ecclesia Dei* with the Congregation for the Doctrine of the Faith in order to facilitate reconciliation with the Society of St. Pius X (SSPX), issued on July 2, 2009. Available at: www.vatican.va/holy_father/benedict _xvi/apost_letters/documents/hf_ben-xvi_apl_20090702_ecclesiae-unitatem_en.html.

15. John J. M. Foster, "Reflexiones canónicas acerca de *Universae Ecclesiae*, Instrucción sobre la Aplicación de *Summorum Pontificum* (Spanish)," *Ius Canonicum*, 52, no. 103 (January 2012): pp. 193–4. The English translation of this work was kindly supplied by the author and will be published in *The Jurist*.

16. UE, 8b.

17. c. 36 §1; Foster, 196–197.

18. *Epistula* accompanying SP; see also SP, 5 §1, 7, and 8.

19. UE, 13.

20. Ibid., 14.

21. Ibid, 10.

22. SP, 1.

23. John M. Huels, "Reconciling the Old with the New: Canonical Questions on *Summorum Pontificum*," *The Jurist* 68 (January 2008): pp. 93–4.

24. CIC, c. 910 §2.

penance is termed "extraordinary" because of the significant restrictions placed on its use.

Neither definition fits this situation. Rather, the term here—according to Huels—is more analogous to the way the term is used in reference to the Synod of Bishops. "An extraordinary synod, convoked outside the cycle of ordinary synods, is an additional form of synod subordinate to the ordinary form."[25] So, in that sense, the "extraordinary" form of the liturgy is not the usual form; its use is still exceptional to some degree and subject to some conditions, as spelled out in SP. It should also be noted that the extraordinary form includes more than celebrating the Eucharist according to the Missal of John XXIII. *Summorum pontificum* specifically mentions that "baptism, marriage, penance and the anointing of the sick"[26] and Confirmation[27] may be celebrated according to liturgical books in force in 1962. Likewise, clerics are given permission to use the Breviary of 1962.[28]

GENERAL THEMES OF *SUMMORUM PONTIFICUM*

As explicitly stated in his *epistula* to the bishops, Pope Benedict XVI's "primary motivation for the *motu proprio* is to achieve the reconciliation of Catholics who felt alienated by the liturgical reforms."[29] Pope Benedict stresses that the fear that his *motu proprio* in some way undoes the work of the Second Vatican Council is "unfounded," as is the concern that its implementation "would lead to disarray or even divisions within parish communities."[30] By stating that the liturgical formation and language skills needed to celebrate the extraordinary form of the liturgy appropriately are not common,[31] the Holy Father maintained that the ordinary form would remain not only juridically but practically the most common form of the liturgy celebrated in parishes. In those parishes where a group of the faithful requests to celebrate the extraordinary form of the Mass, such a request must be "harmonize[d] with the ordinary care of the parish . . . avoiding discord and favoring the unity of the whole church."[32] The requirements for celebrating the Mass in the extraordinary form will be discussed below.

The Holy Father's primary aim is pastoral—he is not thereby setting aside liturgical concerns. First, he sees the extraordinary form, in and of itself, as a

---

25. Huels, "Reconciling the Old with the New," 94. See c. 345.

26. SP, 9 §1. See UE, 35, which mentions the *Pontificale Romanum and Ceremoniale Episcoporum* in addition to the *Rituale Romanum*. The edition of the *Collectio Rituum* in force in 1962 should be used. However, the 1961 edition of the *Collectio Rituum* for the United States, which was in force in 1962, is no longer in print. Therefore, the 1964 edition (which contains some minor adaptations added between 1960 and 1962) may be used if the 1961 edition is not available.

27. SP, 9 §2. See also UE, 29–31, which adds Holy Orders to the list—but only for Institutes of Consecrated Life and Societies of Apostolic Life that fall under the Pontifical Commission *Ecclesia Dei*.

28. SP, 9 §3; see also UE, 32. The Breviary is to be prayed entirely and in Latin.

29. Huels, "Reconciling the Old with the New," 112.

30. *Epistula* accompanying SP.

31. Ibid.

32. SP, 5 §1.

"treasure" that should not be discarded. He argues that while liturgy changes, it cannot be ripped from its historical roots. The pope adds. "What earlier generations held as sacred, remains sacred and great for us too, and it cannot be all of a sudden entirely forbidden or even considered harmful."[33]

Second, he argues that the two "forms" or "usages" of the liturgy can be "mutually enriching."[34] In particular, Pope Benedict XVI suggests that certain liturgical texts and saints found in the ordinary form could also find a place in the extraordinary, and that the "sacrality which attracts many people to the former usage" might also color the way that the ordinary form is celebrated.[35] The two forms, however, are not to be mixed in any way.[36] An often-cited example of a community that has been successful in celebrating both forms harmoniously is the parish of St. John Cantius in Chicago.[37]

Related to Pope Benedict XVI's assertion that what was held sacred for generations cannot be all of a sudden forbidden is his claim that the Missal of John XXIII was never abrogated.[38] Whatever the Holy Father had in mind by using this term, canonists agree that it cannot mean abrogation in the technical, juridical sense.[39] Rather, he seems to be using the term idiosyncratically—most likely referring to the fact that its *use* was not completely forbidden after the Council, but allowed (initially) only by rare exception.[40] However, as Chad J. Glendinning points out, "prohibition" and "abrogation" are not synonymous; one may abrogate a liturgical rite yet still permit its use under specific circumstances.[41]

Underlying the themes above is the particular theological perspective proposed by Pope Benedict XVI. In article 1 of his apostolic letter, Pope Benedict XVI

---

33. *Epistula* accompanying SP; repeated in UE, 7.

34. *Epistula* accompanying SP; see also USCCB, "40 Questions," 38.

35. Ibid.

36. USCCB, "40 Questions," 25, 27; see also UE, 24. Readers might refer to the website of St. John Cantius Parish, www.cantius.org.

37. Steven A. Kiczek, "Pope Benedict XVI's *Summorum Pontificum*: Reconciling Conflicting Values," *Journal of Religious and Theological Information* 8, no. 1/2 (January 2009): pp. 59–60. The article also mentions that the implementation of SP has been divisive in other places (see pp. 58–9).

38. SP, 1.

39. Chad J. Glendinning, "Was the 1962 *Missale Romanum* Abrogated? A Canonical Analysis in Light of *Summorum Pontificum*," *Worship* 85, no. 1 (January 2011): pp. 15–37. See also John F. Baldovin, "Reflections on *Summorum Pontificum*," *Worship* 83, no. 2 (March 2009): 104–5; Huels, "Reconciling the Old with the New," pp. 94–5; and Nathan Mitchell, "*Summorum pontificum*," *Worship* 81, no. 6 (November 2007): pp. 557–58. Glendinning mentions that Archbishop Marcel Lefebvre, founder of the SSPX, held the position that the 1962 Missal was never abrogated (in the technical sense) because the pope had no authority to do so because it had been canonized by Pius V.

40. Initially, permission was given for elderly or infirm priests who would have difficulty moving to the post-Conciliar liturgy to retain the use of the 1962 liturgical books on celebrations without the people (Sacred Congregation for Divine Worship, Notification *Instrucione de Constitutione*, June 14, 1971; published in AAS (63): pp. 712–15; available at: www.vatican.va/archive/aas/documents/AAS%2063%20[1971]%20-%20ocr.pdf). Later, Pope John Paul II broadened this use for public liturgy in *Quattuor Abhinc Annos* (October 3, 1984) and *Ecclesia Dei* (July 2, 1998).

41. Glendinning, "Abrogated," p. 29. He also points out that neither is "abrogation" synonymous with "condemnation" or "reprobation" (see pp. 30–1).

states that while in the Catholic Church's Latin Rite there are two expressions of the *lex orandi* (law of prayer)—the ordinary and extraordinary—both express the Church's one *lex credendi* (law of belief).[42] For that reason, he speaks of two "uses"[43] and not two "rites."

The above considerations reveal Pope Benedict XVI's vision of the relationship between the two forms, or expressions, of the liturgy. For Benedict, the key to liturgical development is continuity as opposed to rupture, with continuity seeming to imply a linear relationship: one might build on the past, one does not replace it. He holds both the post-Conciliar liturgy as well as the provisions of SP as consonant with that continuity.[44]

REQUIREMENTS: WHEN AND HOW MAY THE EXTRAORDINARY FORM BE CELEBRATED?

Summorum pontificum replaces the norms found in *Quattuor abhinc annos* and *Ecclesia Dei* and provides new laws governing the use of the pre-Conciliar liturgy. These norms touch on the community that may celebrate this form of the liturgy as well as the priest who may preside at these rites. While SP addressed some practical concerns, it raised many others. For that reason, the Pontifical Commission *Ecclesia Dei* published its instruction, UE. As will be seen below, implementation of the *motu proprio* raises numerous issues.

THE PRIEST

In Masses without the people, any Latin Rite Catholic priest may use the 1962 Missal; no special permission is required, even if some of the faithful are in attendance.[45] "Priests who use the Missal of John XXIII must be qualified (*idonei*) to do so and not juridically impeded."[46] What does "qualified" entail? As Pope Benedict notes in his *epistula*, "The use if the old missal presupposes a certain degree of liturgical formation and some knowledge of the Latin language; neither of these is found very often."[47] Therefore, at a minimum, a qualified priest (*sacerdos idoneus*) should know enough Latin to "pronounce the words correctly and understand their meaning."[48] Regarding the ability to enact the rubrics properly, UE simply states that "priests are presumed to be qualified" to celebrate the extraordinary form if they present themselves to do so and have done so in the past.[49] Other than those minimal requirements, a priest is considered "qualified" as long as he is not impeded by law.[50]

---

42. SP, 1.

43. For a critique of this language, see Baldovin, pp. 103–4.

44. SP, 1. For further discussion, refer to the articles by Baldovin, Mitchell, and Kiczek.

45. SP, 2. Except during the Triduum, when private Masses—using either Missal—are not permitted. See also UE, 16, 23.

46. SP, 5 §4.

47. *Epistula* accompanying SP.

48. UE, 20b; Huels, "Reconciling the Old with the New," p. 99.

49. UE, 20c.

50. UE, 20a; see also CIC, cc. 290, 292, 901–11, 1044, 1331–33, 1336, and 1338 and Foster, pp. 212–52.

The first requirement for celebrating the extraordinary form in parishes is that the request to do so would come from a "stable (*'stabiliter'*) group of the faithful (*'coetus fidelium'*) who adhere to the earlier liturgical tradition;"[51] it cannot be imposed on the community by the pastor or another priest. When SP was promulgated, the question of what constituted a "stable group of the faithful" was raised. How long should the group have been in existence and how large must it be before it meets the requirements of SP? The instruction UE clarified the definition by stating that a "stable group of the faithful" is simply one that is made up of a group of people from a parish, or from more than one parish or diocese, who join together in a specific church, oratory, or chapel because of their veneration of the pre-Conciliar liturgy and request its celebration.[52] The size of the group, or how long it might have been in existence, is not relevant. As Huels notes, this excludes those who want to celebrate the extraordinary form out of curiosity or a sense of novelty.[53]

John Huels reminds us that the norm of active participation of all in the liturgy applies to the extraordinary form as well. Therefore, he suggests that—in addition to having properly trained celebrants, servers, and choir—a community wishing to celebrate the pre-Conciliar liturgy ought to be able to "read their parts in Latin . . . and to sing the chants for the Kyrie, Sanctus, Pater noster, Agnus Dei, and if not sung by the choir, to sing or recite the Gloria and Credo."[54]

Finally, while not mentioned specifically in SP or in the accompanying *epistula*, it is presumed there that the "stable group of the faithful" does not deny the legitimacy of the ordinary form of the liturgy.[55] This requirement is made explicit in UE 19: "The faithful who ask for the celebration of the *forma extraordinaria* must not in any way support or belong to groups which show themselves to be against the validity or legitimacy of the Holy Mass or the Sacraments celebrated in the *forma ordinaria* or against the Roman Pontiff as Supreme Pastor of the Universal Church."[56]

The second requirement is that the use of the extraordinary form "harmonizes with the ordinary pastoral care of the parish."[57] For example, the Holy Father specifically states that the ordinary form cannot be abandoned for the extraordinary form.[58] Canon 905 is not set aside: A priest cannot celebrate more than two Masses on a weekday or three on Sunday.[59] The extraordinary form may only be celebrated once per day, unless the community had permission prior to SP to celebrate Mass using the 1962 Missal.[60]

---

51. SP, 5 §1; Huels, "Reconciling the Old with the New," p. 98.

52. UE, 15.

53. Huels, "Reconciling the Old with the New," p. 99.

54. Ibid.

55. USCCB, "40 Questions," #25.

56. UE, 19.

57. SP, 5 §1.

58. *Epistula* accompanying *Summorum Pontificum*. See USCCB, "40 Questions," 23.

59. Huels, "Reconciling the Old with the New," p. 99.

60. SP, 5 §2; Huels, "Reconciling the Old with the New," p. 98.

Regarding the Triduum,[61] the general rule is that only a single celebration of the Mass of the Lord's Supper, the Good Friday liturgy, and the Easter Vigil is permitted in any one place. The Mass of the Lord's Supper and, in the United States, the Good Friday liturgy may be celebrated a second time in one place, but only with the permission of the local ordinary (Holy Thursday) or diocesan bishop (Good Friday).[62] Yet, UE states that the community of the faithful that celebrates the extraordinary form has a *right* to celebrate the Triduum according to that form.[63] How does one balance this right versus the directive to harmonize the celebration of the extraordinary form of the liturgy with ordinary pastoral care of the parish? The instruction presumes that the celebration of the Triduum in the extraordinary form will take place in a church or oratory separate from the usual parish church, so as to avoid the duplication of the Triduum in one place. However, if no other arrangements can be made, the celebration of the Triduum in both the ordinary and extraordinary forms in the same place is not excluded.[64] The timing of the Triduum liturgies is the same, regardless of the form followed.[65] Of particular note, on Good Friday the Prayer for the Jewish People as revised by Pope Benedict, rather than the version of the prayer found in the 1962 Missal, must be used.[66]

As the example of the Triduum shows, one of the underlying values being stressed in both SP and UE is the extension of a "liturgical hospitality" on the part of bishops and pastors to those who adhere to the pre-Conciliar liturgy. Pastors are to allow the celebration of the Mass and the other sacraments in the extraordinary form for those priests and faithful who request so on occasion, for example, as part of a pilgrimage or if they have no other place to meet.[67] Likewise, if necessary, the ordinary may erect a personal parish to ensure access to the extraordinary form.[68] In choosing a site for the celebration of the extraordinary form, the rubrical requirements regarding liturgical space should be kept in mind.[69] Of course, all of this presumes the presence of a qualified priest.

Finally, SP provides norms for religious communities wishing to celebrate the extraordinary form of the Mass. The major superiors of such communities, in accord with their proper statutes, may elect to celebrate conventual Masses using the 1962 Missal.[70] Such Masses may "be attended by faithful who of their

---

61. Foster, pp. 225–28.

62. Third edition of *The Roman Missal*; see the rubrics for Holy Thursday (3) and Good Friday 4).

63. UE, 33. Foster (p. 225) states that the official English translation is mistaken; the Latin is stronger than "can also celebrate" and should be translated as "enjoys the right . . . of celebrating" the Triduum in the extraordinary form.

64. UE, 33.

65. Foster, pp. 227–28; Huels, "Reconciling the Old with the New," p. 109.

66. Secretariat of State of the Holy See, "Note from the Secretary of State Concerning the New Dispositions by the Holy Father Benedict XVI for the Liturgical Celebrations of Good Friday," (February 4, 2008). Available at: www.vatican.va/roman_curia/secretariat_state/2008 /documents/rc_seg-st_20080204_nota-missale-romanum_en.html.

67. SP, 5 §2 and 9 §1; UE, 16–18.

68. SP, 10; see also UE, 22. If the bishop cannot supply what is needed, he should refer the matter to the Pontifical Commission. *Ecclesia Dei* (SP, 7–8).

69. USCCB, "40 Questions," 9.

70. SP, 3.

own free will ask to be admitted."[71] *Universae Ecclesiae* clarified that the liturgical books proper to religious orders that were in force in 1962 may also be used.[72] Only for Institutes of Consecrated Life and Societies of Apostolic Life that are under the Pontifical Commission *Ecclesia Dei* may the Roman Pontifical of 1962 be used for the conferral of minor and major orders; the clerical state, however, is entered only with ordination to the diaconate as specified in canon 266 §2.[73]

PRACTICAL QUESTIONS AND CONCERNS

As might be expected, the promulgation of SP raised numerous practical questions. For example, could the extraordinary form still be celebrated if certain items—such as maniples—were no longer available? After all, the 1962 Missal listed numerous "defects" in celebrating the Mass. What readings and liturgical calendar are to be used? Are contemporary liturgical practices—such as women proclaiming the readings or serving at the altar; or the reception of Holy Communion—standing, in the hand, and under both species—permitted? How long should one fast before receiving Holy Communion? Is concelebration allowed?

Summorum pontificum does not answer these questions. Even the manner in which the question of the readings is answered raises more questions.[74] Huels maintains that "recognized" in article 6 refers specifically to those liturgical books granted the *recognitio* of the Holy See; in other words, approved Lectionaries. That would seem to imply that the editions of the 1962 Missal, which included vernacular translations of the readings, are indicated.[75] Huels, however, concludes that the use of the Lectionary of 1970 is allowed.[76]

The question of which readings to use was taken up by UE. First, it lays out the general principle that "[t]he liturgical books of the *forma extraordinaria* are to be used as they are."[77] In addressing the question raised by SP 6, UE specifies how the readings may be proclaimed: (1) in Latin only, (2) in Latin followed by the vernacular, or (3) at Low Masses in the vernacular only.[78] Unfortunately, UE still does not specify the sources for those readings. In his analysis of UE, Foster agrees with Huels's reading, but also notes that in 1991 the Pontifical Commission *Ecclesia Dei* cautioned that the use of the 1970 Lectionary should not be imposed and in a 2010 private response stated that the calendar, readings,

---

71. Ibid., 4.

72. UE, 34.

73. UE, 30–31.

74. SP, 6: "In Masses celebrated in the presence of the people in accordance with the missal of Blessed John XXIII, the readings may be given in the vernacular, using editions recognized by the Apostolic See."

75. See site.adw.org/pdfs/Norms_14_Extraordinary.pdf, footnote 1531. What if the edition of the liturgical book from 1962 does not contain a vernacular translation? It would seem then that one could read the same pericope from the 1970 Lectionary (Second edition in 1998–2000), but one could not simply read from a Bible.

76. Huels, "Reconciling the Old with the New," pp. 100–1.

77. UE, 24. See CIC, c. 846 §1.

78. UE, 26.

or Prefaces of the 1970 Missal may not replace those of the 1962 Missal.[79] Interestingly, in article 25, UE states that the Pontifical Commission *Ecclesia Dei* is studying the addition of some of the saints and prefaces found in the ordinary form to the extraordinary.

Regarding to the other questions that have been raised, UE provides the following guidance. As Foster states, these two paragraphs must be read together—the first providing the general principle and the second the exception:[80]

> With regard to the disciplinary norms connected to celebration, the ecclesiastical discipline contained in the *Code of Canon Law* of 1983 applies.[81]

> Furthermore, by virtue of its character of special law, within its own area, the *motu proprio Summorum pontificum* derogates from those provisions of law, connected with the sacred rites, promulgated from 1962 onward and incompatible with the rubrics of the liturgical books in effect in 1962.[82]

Foster holds that paragraph 28 is mistranslated; the derogation is more properly from "all liturgical laws, connected with the sacred rites."[83] So, while the rubrics of the 1962 liturgical books are binding (liturgical law), so too are the disciplinary laws of the 1983 *Code of Canon Law* and related documents. As Foster asks. "where does one draw the line between disciplinary norms connected with the liturgy and liturgical laws (which are certainly part of ecclesiastical discipline) on the other?"[84] Even before UE was promulgated, John Huels made a similar argument: "while the rubrical laws of the 1962 Missal are to be observed for the proper performance of the rite, the disciplinary laws in force today must be the basis for determining the outcome of any disputed question or practice related to liturgical and sacramental discipline."[85]

Based on these careful distinctions, what can be said about such practices as women serving in liturgical ministries, contemporary practices regarding the distribution of Holy Communion, and concelebration? Based on the canonical analyses by John Huels,[86] John Foster,[87] and Chad J. Glendinning,[88] it may be concluded that because these are disciplinary and not rubrical issues, it is indeed permissible in the extraordinary form for women to proclaim the Scriptures and serve at the altar,[89] to distribute Holy Communion under both species, to receive Holy Communion in the hand and/or standing, to fast for

---

79. Foster, pp. 215–17. In footnote 64, he mentions that while private responses are not binding, they do illustrate the *praxis curiae* (CIC, c. 19).

80. Foster, p. 217.

81. UE, 27.

82. Ibid., 28.

83. Foster, p. 218.

84. Ibid., p. 219.

85. Huels, "Reconciling the Old with the New," pp. 105–6.

86. Ibid., pp. 105–8.

87. Foster, pp. 219–22.

88. Chad J. Glendinning, "CIC, c. 230: Use of Female Altar Servers in Liturgical Celebrations using the Extraordinary Form," in *2008 Roman Replies & CLSA Advisory Opinions*, ed. Ronny E. Jenkins, et al., Washington, DC: Canon Law Society of America (2008): pp. 77–9.

89. A private (and therefore non-binding) communication from the secretary of the Pontifical Commission *Ecclesia Dei* states otherwise. See 2.bp.blogspot.com/-7WMG0TN-m4Y/

only one hour before receiving Holy Communion (instead of three, or from midnight), to have laypersons serve as extraordinary ministers of Holy Communion, and to concelebrate the Mass. Regarding concelebration and the distribution of Holy Communion under both species, since the 1962 Missal is rubrically silent, the rubrics for doing so are to be found in the 1965 *Rite of Concelebration* and *Rite of Communion Under Both Kinds*.[90] However, as some have asked, if these practices are allowed, will the extraordinary form remain that form to which people adhere, or will it have become something different and perhaps not recognizable?[91] In the end, individuals and communities may choose to follow the older discipline if so desired—such as observing a longer Eucharistic fast or not calling women to liturgical ministries—while respecting the rights of others (for example, to stand for Holy Communion or to receive Holy Communion under the form of wine if unable to receive under the form of bread).

Of what were once considered "defects" in celebrating Mass? In general, what were once listed as "defects" refers to disciplinary matters. As such, newer practices are allowed. For example, the maniple has been suppressed—so while it *may* be used, its use is not required.[92] Is there a role for "permanent" deacons in the extraordinary form? Yes. Any deacon may exercise his liturgical ministry under the 1962 Missal provided that, like the priest, he is competent in the rubrics and language. However, there is no provision for a deacon at a low or high (sung) Mass in the 1962 Missal; it is not permitted to fabricate a role for the deacon at these rites. While there is a role for a deacon at a solemn high Mass, a priest may serve in this role, but vested as a deacon. Likewise, a priest or deacon, vested as a subdeacon, could serve in the ministry of subdeacon at a solemn high Mass; an instituted acolyte may also serve in this capacity—but does not wear the maniple or biretta and does not wipe out the chalice after the ablution.[93]

Which liturgical calendar should be followed by communities celebrating the extraordinary form? As noted above, communities adhering to the extraordinary form follow the calendar in force in 1962. In addition to possibly creating conflicts in parishes that celebrate both forms,[94] the issue of solemnities of precept is raised, since in many of the ecclesiastical provinces of the United States some of these Holydays of Obligation (such as Epiphany, Ascension, and *Corpus Christi*) have been transferred to Sunday. In those cases, the feast *may* still be celebrated in the extraordinary form on the assigned day (for example, January 6 for Epiphany, Thursday for Ascension) but the obligation is dispensed. In addition,

Te7Mm4vCWpI/AAAAAAAAE2A/MxCpAdH5Odw/s1600/extraordinary-form-latin-mass-altar-girls-whatdoestheprayerreallysay-zuhlsdorf-PCED-letter.jpg.

90. *Ritus servandus in concelebratione Missae et Ritus Communionis sub utraque species* (March 7, 1965); Huels, "Reconciling the Old with the New," p. 106.

91. Kiczek, pp. 60–1.

92. Huels, "Reconciling the Old with the New," p. 110. Huels discusses many other issues, for example: altar linens and candles, previously required blessings, servers, and the material used for sacred vessels.

93. See www.sanctamissa.org/en/faq/concelebration.html#R1 and www.ewtn.com/library/liturgy/zlitur236.htm.

94. For example, the Ordinary Form community is still in Ordinary Time while the Extraordinary Form community is observing the Sundays before Lent (Septagesima, Sexagesima, Quinquagesima).

the "external solemnity" (the celebration of a feast, without an office, for the good of the faithful; akin to a votive Mass) can be moved to the Sunday, and such observance can even be mandated by the bishop.

In the end, as SP is being implemented, it may be necessary in order to offer clear guidance and direction to those communities which celebrate the extraordinary form, for individual bishops to promulgate particular law, or at least policies, in their dioceses.[95] Such laws may be modified as directives from the Pontifical Commission *Ecclesia Dei* or national Conferences of Bishops become available and specific issues are clarified. It seems that we are in a time of liturgical development, and higher authorities are still not ready to legislate every detail relative to enacting SP and UE.

A BRIEF NOTE ON CONFIRMATION

Summorum pontificum gave permission for *ordinaries*[96] to use the extraordinary form (Roman Pontifical in force in 1962) in celebrating the Sacrament of Confirmation "if the good of souls would seem to require it."[97] By doing so, an immediate question was raised: Since the earlier sacramental form of the sacrament had been abrogated by the apostolic constitution promulgating the revised *Rite of Confirmation*, and replaced with the new formula, "Be sealed with the gift of the Holy Spirit,"[98] must the new form be used, or may the old form be utilized? On the one hand, Huels argues that an apostolic constitution is of greater weight than an apostolic letter, and so the new formula would seem to be required. On the other, he mentions that Pope Benedict XVI may have intended to derogate from his predecessor's legislation and so allow the use of the older form without restriction—as suggested by the general revoking formula at the end of the *motu proprio*. Regardless, there is at the very least a doubt of law—so Huels concludes that either formula is permissible.[99]

The matter was taken up in UE, which states: "Permission to use the older formula for the rite of confirmation was confirmed by the *motu proprio Summorum pontificum* (cf. art. 9 § 2). Therefore, in the *forma extraordinaria* it is not necessary to use the newer formula of Pope Paul VI as found in the *Ordo Confirmationis*."[100] As Foster reads this provision, UE is simply acknowledging that a doubt in the law exists and therefore reiterates that it is not required to use the older form. It should be noted that the use of the older sacramental form ("*Signo te signo crucis et confirmo te chrismate salutis, in nomine Patris et Filii et Spiritus Sanctus. Amen*") is not mandated.[101]

---

95. For example, as we have done in the Diocese of Davenport. Our policy is available at www.davenportdiocese.org/lit/liturgylibrary/Policies/litImplementationSummorumPontificum-101512.pdf

96. Huels, "Reconciling the Old with the New," 109. He notes, therefore, that priests (whether presbyters or bishops) who are not ordinaries may not celebrate confirmation in the extraordinary form without an indult from the Holy See. Neither can a bishop who is an ordinary delegate this faculty to another.

97. SP, 9 §2.

98. Huels, "Reconciling the Old with the New," p. 103.

99. Ibid., 104–5.

100. UE, 29.

101. Foster, pp. 222–23.

RESOURCES FOR CELEBRATING THE EXTRAORDINARY FORM

- The website for the Pontifical Commission *Ecclesia Dei* may be found at: www.vatican.va/roman_curia/pontifical_commissions/ecclsdei.

- The Canons Regular of St. John Cantius host an extensive website (www .sanctamissa.org) with links to numerous resources (www.sanctamissa .org/en/resources/) and tutorials, including scheduled workshops (www .sanctamissa.org/workshops).

- Print resources (store.fraternitypublications.com/) and workshops for learning the extraordinary form of the liturgy (www.fssptraining.org) are also offered by the Priestly Fraternity of Saint Peter.

- The standard guide for celebrating the Mass according to the 1962 Missal is *The Ceremonies of the Roman Rite Described*, by Adrian Fortescue, J.B. O'Connell, and Alcuin Reid, OSB (15th rev. ed., 2009). Another helpful source is *The Celebration of Mass: A Study of the Rubrics of the Roman Missal* by John Berthram O'Connell, Bruce Publishing Co., 1964 (2007 reprint by Loreto Publishing).

CONCLUSION

While liturgical and theological considerations informed Pope Benedict XVI's decision to promulgate SP, his overarching concern was pastoral: to care for those who adhere to the preconciliar liturgical forms and to offer to the schismatic Society of St. Pius X an avenue for returning to communion with the Church. Implementation of SP has raised numerous practical and pastoral questions. Will SP be instrumental in healing the schism of the Society of St. Pius X? Will the ordinary and extraordinary forms of the liturgy mutually inform and enrich one another? These were the hopes of Pope Benedict XVI. The degree to which these hopes are realized waits to be seen as the Church lives with the novel situation of having two "uses" of the one Roman Rite.

LETTER OF HIS HOLINESS BENEDICT XVI TO THE BISHOPS ON THE OCCASION OF THE PUBLICATION OF THE APOSTOLIC LETTER "MOTU PROPRIO DATA"

SUMMORUM PONTIFICUM

ON THE USE OF THE ROMAN LITURGY PRIOR TO THE REFORM OF 1970

My dear Brother Bishops,

With great trust and hope, I am consigning to you as Pastors the text of a new Apostolic Letter "Motu Proprio data" on the use of the Roman liturgy prior to the reform of 1970. The document is the fruit of much reflection, numerous consultations and prayer.

News reports and judgments made without sufficient information have created no little confusion. There have been very divergent reactions ranging from joyful acceptance to harsh opposition, about a plan whose contents were in reality unknown.

This document was most directly opposed on account of two fears, which I would like to address somewhat more closely in this letter.

In the first place, there is the fear that the document detracts from the authority of the Second Vatican Council, one of whose essential decisions—the liturgical reform—is being called into question.

This fear is unfounded. In this regard, it must first be said that the Missal published by Paul VI and then republished in two subsequent editions by John Paul II obviously is and continues to be the normal Form—the *Forma ordinaria*—of the Eucharistic Liturgy. The last version of the *Missale Romanum* prior to the Council, which was published with the authority of Pope John XXIII in 1962 and used during the Council, will now be able to be used as a *Forma extraordinaria* of the liturgical celebration. It is not appropriate to speak of these two versions of the Roman Missal as if they were "two Rites." Rather, it is a matter of a twofold use of one and the same rite.

As for the use of the 1962 Missal as a *Forma extraordinaria* of the liturgy of the Mass, I would like to draw attention to the fact that this Missal was never juridically abrogated and, consequently, in principle, was always permitted. At the time of the introduction of the new Missal, it did not seem necessary to issue specific norms for the possible use of the earlier Missal. Probably it was thought that it would be a matter of a few individual cases which would be resolved, case by case, on the local level. Afterwards, however, it soon became apparent that a good number of people remained strongly attached to this usage of the Roman Rite, which had been familiar to them from childhood. This was especially the case in countries where the liturgical movement had provided many people with a notable liturgical formation and a deep, personal familiarity with the earlier Form of the liturgical celebration. We all know that, in the movement led by Archbishop Lefebvre, fidelity to the old Missal became an external mark of identity; the reasons for the break which arose over this, however, were at a deeper level. Many people who clearly accepted the binding character of the Second Vatican Council, and were faithful to the Pope and the Bishops, nonetheless also desired to recover the form of the sacred liturgy that was dear to them. This occurred above all because in many places celebrations were not faithful to the prescriptions of the new Missal, but the latter actually was understood as authorizing or even requiring creativity, which frequently led to deformations of the liturgy which were hard to bear. I am speaking from experience, since I too lived through that period with all its hopes and its confusion. And I have seen how arbitrary deformations of the liturgy caused deep pain to individuals totally rooted in the faith of the Church.

Pope John Paul II thus felt obliged to provide, in his Motu Proprio *Ecclesia Dei* (July 2, 1988), guidelines for the use of the 1962 Missal; that document, however, did not contain detailed prescriptions but appealed in a general way to the generous response of Bishops towards the "legitimate aspirations" of those members of the faithful who requested this usage of the Roman Rite. At the time, the Pope primarily wanted to assist the Society of Saint Pius X to recover full unity with the Successor of Peter and sought to heal a wound experienced ever more painfully. Unfortunately this reconciliation has not yet come about. Nonetheless, a number of communities have gratefully made use of the possibilities provided by the Motu Proprio. On the other hand, difficulties remain concerning the use of the 1962 Missal outside of these groups, because of the lack of precise juridical norms, particularly because Bishops, in such cases, frequently feared that the authority of the Council would be called into question. Immediately after the Second Vatican Council it was presumed that requests for the use of the 1962 Missal would be limited to the older generation which had grown up with it, but in the meantime it has clearly been demonstrated that young persons too have discovered this liturgical form, felt its attraction, and found in it a form of encounter with the Mystery of the Most Holy Eucharist particularly suited to them. Thus the need has arisen for a clearer juridical regulation which had not been foreseen at the time of the 1988 Motu Proprio. The present norms are also meant to free Bishops from constantly having to evaluate anew how they are to respond to various situations.

In the second place, the fear was expressed in discussions about the awaited Motu Proprio, that the possibility of a wider use of the 1962 Missal would lead to disarray or even divisions within parish communities. This fear also strikes me as quite unfounded. The use of the old Missal presupposes a certain degree of liturgical formation and some knowledge of the Latin language; neither of these is found very often. Already from these concrete presuppositions, it is clearly seen that the new Missal will certainly remain the ordinary Form of the Roman Rite, not only on account of the juridical norms, but also because of the actual situation of the communities of the faithful.

It is true that there have been exaggerations and at times social aspects unduly linked to the attitude of the faithful attached to the ancient Latin liturgical tradition. Your charity and pastoral prudence will be an incentive and guide for improving these. For that matter, the two Forms of the usage of the Roman Rite can be mutually enriching: new Saints and some of the new Prefaces can and should be inserted in the old Missal. The *"Ecclesia Dei"* Commission, in contact with various bodies devoted to the *usus antiquior*, will study the practical possibilities in this regard. The celebration of the Mass according to the Missal of Paul VI will be able to demonstrate, more powerfully than has been the case hitherto, the sacrality which attracts many people to the former usage. The most sure guarantee that the Missal of Paul VI can unite parish communities and be loved by them consists in its being celebrated with great reverence in harmony with the liturgical directives. This will bring out the spiritual richness and the theological depth of this Missal.

I now come to the positive reason which motivated my decision to issue this Motu Proprio updating that of 1988. It is a matter of coming to an interior reconciliation in the heart of the Church. Looking back over the past, to the divisions which in the course of the centuries have rent the Body of Christ, one continually has the impression that, at critical moments when divisions were coming about, not enough was done by the Church's leaders to maintain or regain reconciliation and unity. One has the impression that omissions on the part of the Church have had their share of blame for the fact that these divisions were able to harden. This glance at the past imposes an obligation on us today: to make every effort to enable for all those who truly desire unity to remain in that unity or to attain it anew. I think of a sentence in the Second Letter to the Corinthians, where Paul writes: "Our mouth is open to you, Corinthians; our heart is wide. You are not restricted by us, but you are restricted in your own affections. In return . . . widen your hearts also!" (2 Cor 6:11–13). Paul was certainly speaking in another context, but his exhortation can and must touch us too, precisely on this subject. Let us generously open our hearts and make room for everything that the faith itself allows.

There is no contradiction between the two editions of the Roman Missal. In the history of the liturgy there is growth and progress, but no rupture. What earlier generations held as sacred, remains sacred and great for us too, and it cannot be all of a sudden entirely forbidden or even considered harmful. It behooves all of us to preserve the riches which have developed in the Church's faith and prayer, and to give them their proper place. Needless to say, in order to experience full communion, the priests of the communities adhering to the former usage cannot, as a matter of principle, exclude celebrating according to the new books.

The total exclusion of the new rite would not in fact be consistent with the recognition of its value and holiness.

In conclusion, dear Brothers, I very much wish to stress that these new norms do not in any way lessen your own authority and responsibility, either for the liturgy or for the pastoral care of your faithful. Each Bishop, in fact, is the moderator of the liturgy in his own Diocese (cf. *Sacrosanctum Concilium*, 22: "Sacrae Liturgiae moderatio ab Ecclesiae auctoritate unice pendet quae quidem est apud Apostolicam Sedem et, ad normam iuris, apud Episcopum").

Nothing is taken away, then, from the authority of the Bishop, whose role remains that of being watchful that all is done in peace and serenity. Should some problem arise which the parish priest cannot resolve, the local Ordinary will always be able to intervene, in full harmony, however, with all that has been laid down by the new norms of the Motu Proprio.

Furthermore, I invite you, dear Brothers, to send to the Holy See an account of your experiences, three years after this Motu Proprio has taken effect. If truly serious difficulties come to light, ways to remedy them can be sought.

Dear Brothers, with gratitude and trust, I entrust to your hearts as Pastors these pages and the norms of the Motu Proprio. Let us always be mindful of the words of the Apostle Paul addressed to the presbyters of Ephesus: "Take heed to yourselves and to all the flock, in which the Holy Spirit has made you overseers, to care for the Church of God which he obtained with the blood of his own Son" (Acts 20:28).

I entrust these norms to the powerful intercession of Mary, Mother of the Church, and I cordially impart my Apostolic Blessing to you, dear Brothers, to the parish priests of your dioceses, and to all the priests, your co-workers, as well as to all your faithful.

Given at Saint Peter's, July 7, 2007.

BENEDICTUS PP. XVI

SUMMORUM PONTIFICUM

APOSTOLIC LETTER ISSUED MOTU PROPRIO

POPE BENEDICT XVI

Up to our own times, it has been the constant concern of supreme pontiffs to ensure that the Church of Christ offers a worthy ritual to the Divine Majesty, "to the praise and glory of His name," and "to the benefit of all His Holy Church."

Since time immemorial it has been necessary—as it is also for the future—to maintain the principle according to which "each particular Church must concur with the universal Church, not only as regards the doctrine of the faith and the sacramental signs, but also as regards the usages universally accepted by uninterrupted apostolic tradition, which must be observed not only to avoid errors but also to transmit the integrity of the faith, because the Church's law of prayer corresponds to her law of faith."[1]

Among the pontiffs who showed that requisite concern, particularly outstanding is the name of St. Gregory the Great, who made every effort to ensure that the new peoples of Europe received both the Catholic faith and the treasures of worship and culture that had been accumulated by the Romans in preceding centuries. He commanded that the form of the sacred liturgy as celebrated in Rome (concerning both the Sacrifice of Mass and the Divine Office) be conserved. He took great concern to ensure the dissemination of monks and nuns who, following the Rule of St. Benedict, together with the announcement of the Gospel illustrated with their lives the wise provision of their Rule that "nothing should be placed before the work of God." In this way the sacred liturgy, celebrated according to the Roman use, enriched not only the faith and piety but also the culture of many peoples. It is known, in fact, that the Latin liturgy of the Church in its various forms, in each century of the Christian era, has been a spur to the spiritual life of many saints, has reinforced many peoples in the virtue of religion and fecundated their piety.

Many other Roman pontiffs, in the course of the centuries, showed particular solicitude in ensuring that the sacred liturgy accomplished this task more effectively. Outstanding among them is St. Pius V who, sustained by great pastoral zeal and following the exhortations of the Council of Trent, renewed the entire liturgy of the Church, oversaw the publication of liturgical books amended and

---

1. *General Instruction of the Roman Missal*, 3rd ed., 2002, no. 397.

"renewed in accordance with the norms of the Fathers," and provided them for the use of the Latin Church.

One of the liturgical books of the Roman rite is the Roman Missal, which developed in the city of Rome and, with the passing of the centuries, little by little took forms very similar to that it has had in recent times.

"It was towards this same goal that succeeding Roman Pontiffs directed their energies during the subsequent centuries in order to ensure that the rites and liturgical books were brought up to date and when necessary clarified. From the beginning of this century they undertook a more general reform."[2] Thus our predecessors Clement VIII, Urban VIII, St. Pius X,[3] Benedict XV, Pius XII and Blessed John XXIII all played a part.

In more recent times, Vatican Council II expressed a desire that the respectful reverence due to divine worship should be renewed and adapted to the needs of our time. Moved by this desire, our predecessor, the Supreme Pontiff Paul VI, approved, in 1970, reformed, and partly renewed liturgical books for the Latin Church. These, translated into the various languages of the world, were willingly accepted by bishops, priests, and faithful. John Paul II amended the third typical edition of the Roman Missal. Thus Roman pontiffs have operated to ensure that "this kind of liturgical edifice . . . should again appear resplendent for its dignity and harmony."[4]

But in some regions, no small numbers of faithful adhered and continue to adhere with great love and affection to the earlier liturgical forms. These had so deeply marked their culture and their spirit that in 1984 the Supreme Pontiff John Paul II, moved by a concern for the pastoral care of these faithful, with the special indult *Quattuor abhinc annos*, issued by the Congregation for Divine Worship, granted permission to use the Roman Missal published by Blessed John XXIII in the year 1962. Later, in the year 1988, John Paul II with the Apostolic Letter given as Motu Proprio, *Ecclesia Dei*, exhorted bishops to make generous use of this power in favor of all the faithful who so desired.

Following the insistent prayers of these faithful, long deliberated upon by our predecessor John Paul II, and after having listened to the views of the Cardinal Fathers of the Consistory of March 22, 2006, having reflected deeply upon all aspects of the question, invoked the Holy Spirit, and trusting in the help of God, with these Apostolic Letters we establish the following:

Art 1. The Roman Missal promulgated by Paul VI is the ordinary expression of the *Lex orandi* (Law of prayer) of the Catholic Church of the Latin rite. Nonetheless, the Roman Missal promulgated by St. Pius V and reissued by Bl. John XXIII is to be considered as an extraordinary expression of that same *Lex orandi*, and must be given due honor for its venerable and ancient usage. These two expres-

---

2. John Paul II, Apostolic Letter *Vicesimus quintus annus*, December 4, 1988, 3: AAS 81 (1989), 899.

3. Ibid.

4. St. Pius X, Apostolic Letter Motu propio data, *Abhinc duos annos*, October 23, 1913: AAS 5 (1913), 449–450; cf John Paul II, Apostolic Letter *Vicesimus quintus annus*, no. 3: AAS 81 (1989), 899.

sions of the Church's *Lex orandi* will in no any way lead to a division in the Church's *Lex credendi* (Law of belief). They are, in fact, two usages of the one Roman rite.

It is, therefore, permissible to celebrate the Sacrifice of the Mass following the typical edition of the Roman Missal promulgated by Bl. John XXIII in 1962 and never abrogated, as an extraordinary form of the Liturgy of the Church. The conditions for the use of this Missal as laid down by earlier documents *Quattuor abhinc annos* and *Ecclesia Dei*, are substituted as follows:

Art. 2. In Masses celebrated without the people, each Catholic priest of the Latin rite, whether secular or regular, may use the Roman Missal published by Bl. Pope John XXIII in 1962, or the Roman Missal promulgated by Pope Paul VI in 1970, and may do so on any day with the exception of the Easter Triduum. For such celebrations, with either one Missal or the other, the priest has no need for permission from the Apostolic See or from his Ordinary.

Art. 3. Communities of Institutes of consecrated life and of Societies of apostolic life, of either pontifical or diocesan right, wishing to celebrate Mass in accordance with the edition of the Roman Missal promulgated in 1962, for conventual or "community" celebration in their oratories, may do so. If an individual community or an entire Institute or Society wishes to undertake such celebrations often, habitually, or permanently, the decision must be taken by the Superiors Major, in accordance with the law and following their own specific decrees and statues.

Art. 4. Celebrations of Mass as mentioned above in art. 2 may—observing all the norms of law—also be attended by faithful who, of their own free will, ask to be admitted.

Art. 5. § 1. In parishes, where there is a stable group of faithful who adhere to the earlier liturgical tradition, the pastor should willingly accept their requests to celebrate the Mass according to the rite of the Roman Missal published in 1962 and ensure that the welfare of these faithful harmonizes with the ordinary pastoral care of the parish, under the guidance of the bishop in accordance with canon 392, avoiding discord and favoring the unity of the whole Church.

§ 2. Celebration in accordance with the Missal of Bl. John XXIII may take place on working days; while on Sundays and feast days one such celebration may also be held.

§ 3. For faithful and priests who request it, the pastor should also allow celebrations in this extraordinary form for special circumstances such as marriages, funerals or occasional celebrations, e.g. pilgrimages.

§ 4. Priests who use the Missal of Bl. John XXIII must be qualified to do so and not juridically impeded.

§ 5. In churches that are not parish or conventual churches, it is the duty of the Rector of the church to grant the above permission.

Art. 6. In Masses celebrated in the presence of the people in accordance with the Missal of Bl. John XXIII, the readings may be given in the vernacular, using editions recognized by the Apostolic See.

Art. 7. If a group of lay faithful, as mentioned in art. 5 § 1, has not obtained satisfaction to their requests from the pastor, they should inform the diocesan bishop. The bishop is strongly requested to satisfy their wishes. If he cannot arrange for such celebration to take place, the matter should be referred to the Pontifical Commission *Ecclesia Dei*.

Art. 8. A bishop who, desirous of satisfying such requests, but who for various reasons is unable to do so, may refer the problem to the Commission *Ecclesia Dei* to obtain counsel and assistance.

Art. 9. § 1. The pastor, having attentively examined all aspects, may also grant permission to use the earlier ritual for the administration of the Sacraments of Baptism, Marriage, Penance, and the Anointing of the Sick, if the good of souls would seem to require it.

§ 2. Ordinaries are given the right to celebrate the Sacrament of Confirmation using the earlier Roman Pontifical, if the good of souls would seem to require it.

§ 3. Clerics ordained *in sacris constitutis* may use the Roman Breviary promulgated by Bl. John XXIII in 1962.

Art. 10. The ordinary of a particular place, if he feels it appropriate, may erect a personal parish in accordance with can. 518 for celebrations following the ancient form of the Roman rite, or appoint a chaplain, while observing all the norms of law.

Art. 11. The Pontifical Commission *Ecclesia Dei*, erected by John Paul II in 1988,[5] continues to exercise its function. Said Commission will have the form, duties and norms that the Roman Pontiff wishes to assign it.

Art. 12. This Commission, apart from the powers it enjoys, will exercise the authority of the Holy See, supervising the observance and application of these dispositions.

We order that everything We have established with these Apostolic Letters issued as Motu Proprio be considered as "established and decreed," and to be observed from 14 September of this year, Feast of the Exaltation of the Cross, whatever there may be to the contrary.

From Rome, at St. Peter's, July 7, 2007, third year of Our Pontificate.

BENEDICTUS PP. XVI

---

5. Cf. John Paul II, Apostolic Letter Motu proprio data *Ecclesia Dei*, July 2, 1988, 6: AAS 80 (1988), 1498.

OUTLINE

The following outline applies to the Instruction, Universae Ecclesiae, *found on page 654. Outlines are not provided for the other two documents because they do not include article numbers.*

UNIVERSAE ECCLESIAE

PONTIFICAL COMMISSION ECCLESIA DEI

INSTRUCTION ON THE APPLICATION OF THE APOSTOLIC LETTER
SUMMORUM PONTIFICUM OF HIS HOLINESS BENEDICT XVI GIVEN
MOTU PROPRIO

I. INTRODUCTION

1.   The Apostolic Letter *Summorum Pontificum* of the Sovereign Pontiff
Benedict XVI given *Motu Proprio* on July 7, 2007, which came into effect on
September 14, 2007, has made the richness of the Roman Liturgy more acces-
sible to the Universal Church.

2.   With this Motu Proprio, the Holy Father Pope Benedict XVI promulgated
a universal law for the Church, intended to establish new regulations for the
use of the Roman Liturgy in effect in 1962.

3.   The Holy Father, having recalled the concern of the Sovereign Pontiffs in
caring for the Sacred Liturgy and in their recognition of liturgical books, reaffirms the traditional principle, recognized from time immemorial and necessary
to be maintained into the future, that *"each particular Church must be in accord
with the universal Church not only regarding the doctrine of the faith and sacramental signs, but also as to the usages universally handed down by apostolic
and unbroken tradition. These are to be maintained not only so that errors
may be avoided, but also so that the faith may be passed on in its integrity,
since the Church's rule of prayer* (lex orandi) *corresponds to her rule of belief*
(lex credendi)."[1]

4.   The Holy Father recalls also those Roman Pontiffs who, in a particular
way, were notable in this task, specifically Saint Gregory the Great and Saint
Pius V. The Holy Father stresses moreover that, among the sacred liturgical
books, the *Missale Romanum* has enjoyed a particular prominence in history,
and was kept up to date throughout the centuries until the time of Blessed Pope
John XXIII. Subsequently in 1970, following the liturgical reform after the Second
Vatican Council, Pope Paul VI approved for the Church of the Latin rite a new
Missal, which was then translated into various languages. In the year 2000,
Pope John Paul II promulgated the third edition of this Missal.

5.   Many of the faithful, formed in the spirit of the liturgical forms prior to
the Second Vatican Council, expressed a lively desire to maintain the ancient
tradition. For this reason, Pope John Paul II with a special Indult *Quattuor abhinc
annos* issued in 1984 by the Congregation for Divine Worship, granted the faculty under certain conditions to restore the use of the Missal promulgated by

---

1. Benedict XVI, *Litterae Apostolicae Summorum Pontificum motu proprio datae*, I: AAS 99
(2007), 777; cf. *Institutio Generalis Missalis Romani*, tertia editio, 2002, n. 397.

Blessed Pope John XXIII. Subsequently, Pope John Paul II, with the Motu Proprio *Ecclesia Dei* of 1988, exhorted the Bishops to be generous in granting such a faculty for all the faithful who requested it. Pope Benedict continues this policy with the Motu Proprio *Summorum Pontificum* regarding certain essential criteria for the *Usus Antiquior* of the Roman Rite, which are recalled here.

6.   The Roman Missal promulgated by Pope Paul VI and the last edition prepared under Pope John XXIII, are two forms of the Roman Liturgy, defined respectively as *ordinaria* and *extraordinaria*: they are two usages of the one Roman Rite, one alongside the other. Both are the expression of the same *lex orandi* of the Church. On account of its venerable and ancient use, the *forma extraordinaria* is to be maintained with appropriate honor.

7.   The Motu Proprio *Summorum Pontificum* was accompanied by a letter from the Holy Father to Bishops, with the same date as the Motu Proprio (July 7, 2007). This letter gave further explanations regarding the appropriateness and the need for the Motu Proprio; it was a matter of overcoming a lacuna by providing new norms for the use of the Roman Liturgy of 1962. Such norms were needed particularly on account of the fact that, when the new Missal had been introduced under Pope Paul VI, it had not seemed necessary to issue guidelines regulating the use of the 1962 Liturgy. By reason of the increase in the number of those asking to be able to use the *forma extraordinaria*, it has become necessary to provide certain norms in this area.

Among the statements of the Holy Father was the following: *"There is no contradiction between the two editions of the Roman Missal. In the history of the Liturgy growth and progress are found, but not a rupture. What was sacred for prior generations, remains sacred and great for us as well, and cannot be suddenly prohibited altogether or even judged harmful."*[2]

8.   The Motu Proprio *Summorum Pontificum* constitutes an important expression of the Magisterium of the Roman Pontiff and of his *munus* of regulating and ordering the Church's Sacred Liturgy.[3] The Motu Proprio manifests his solicitude as Vicar of Christ and Supreme Pastor of the Universal Church,[4] and has the aim of:

a) offering to all the faithful the Roman Liturgy in the *Usus Antiquior*, considered as a precious treasure to be preserved;

b) effectively guaranteeing and ensuring the use of the *forma extraordinaria* for all who ask for it, given that the use of the 1962 Roman Liturgy is a faculty generously granted for the good of the faithful and therefore is to be interpreted in a sense favorable to the faithful who are its principal addressees;

c) promoting reconciliation at the heart of the Church.

---

2. Benedict XVI, *Epistola ad Episcopos ad producendas Litteras Apostolicas motu proprio datas, de Usu Liturgiae Romanae Instaurationi anni 1970 praecedentis*, *AAS* 99 (2007) 798.

3. Cf. *Code of Canon Law*, Canon 838 §1 and §2.

4. Cf. *Code of Canon Law*, Canon 331.

II. THE RESPONSIBILITIES OF THE PONTIFICAL COMMISSION ECCLESIA DEI

9.   The Sovereign Pontiff has conferred upon the Pontifical Commission *Ecclesia Dei* ordinary vicarious power for the matters within its competence, in a particular way for monitoring the observance and application of the provisions of the Motu Proprio *Summorum Pontificum* (cf. art. 12).

10.   § 1. The Pontifical Commission exercises this power, beyond the faculties previously granted by Pope John Paul II and confirmed by Pope Benedict XVI (cf. Motu Proprio *Summorum Pontificum*, art. 11–12), also by means of the power to decide upon recourses legitimately sent to it, as hierarchical Superior, against any possible singular administrative provision of an Ordinary which appears to be contrary to the Motu Proprio.

§ 2. The decrees by which the Pontifical Commission decides recourses may be challenged *ad normam iuris* before the Supreme Tribunal of the Apostolic Signatura.

11.   After having received the approval from the Congregation for Divine Worship and the Discipline of the Sacraments, the Pontifical Commission *Ecclesia Dei* will have the task of looking after future editions of liturgical texts pertaining to the *forma extraordinaria* of the Roman Rite.

III. SPECIFIC NORMS

12.   Following upon the inquiry made among the Bishops of the world, and with the desire to guarantee the proper interpretation and the correct application of the Motu Proprio *Summorum Pontificum*, this Pontifical Commission, by virtue of the authority granted to it and the faculties which it enjoys, issues this Instruction according to can. 34 of the *Code of Canon Law*.

The Competence of Diocesan Bishops

13.   Diocesan Bishops, according to Canon Law, are to monitor liturgical matters in order to guarantee the common good and to ensure that everything is proceeding in peace and serenity in their Dioceses,[5] always in agreement with the *mens* of the Holy Father clearly expressed by the Motu Proprio *Summorum Pontificum*.[6] In cases of controversy or well-founded doubt about the celebration in the *forma extraordinaria*, the Pontifical Commission *Ecclesia Dei* will adjudicate.

14.   It is the task of the Diocesan Bishop to undertake all necessary measures to ensure respect for the *forma extraordinaria* of the Roman Rite, according to the Motu Proprio *Summorum Pontificum*.

---

5. Cf. *Code of Canon Law*, Canons 223 § 2 or 838 §1 and §4.

6. Benedict XVI, *Epistola ad Episcopos ad producendas Litteras Apostolicas motu proprio datas, de Usu Liturgiae Romanae Instaurationi anni 1970 praecedentis*: AAS 99 (2007), 799.

15.   A *coetus fidelium* ("group of the faithful") can be said to be *stabiliter existens* ("existing in a stable manner"), according to the sense of art. 5 § 1 of the Motu Proprio *Summorum Pontificum*, when it is constituted by some people of an individual parish who, even after the publication of the Motu Proprio, come together by reason of their veneration for the Liturgy in the *Usus Antiquior*, and who ask that it might be celebrated in the parish church or in an oratory or chapel; such a *coetus* ("group") can also be composed of persons coming from different parishes or dioceses, who gather together in a specific parish church or in an oratory or chapel for this purpose.

16.   In the case of a priest who presents himself occasionally in a parish church or an oratory with some faithful, and wishes to celebrate in the *forma extraordinaria*, as foreseen by articles 2 and 4 of the Motu Proprio *Summorum Pontificum*, the pastor or rector of the church, or the priest responsible, is to permit such a celebration, while respecting the schedule of liturgical celebrations in that same church.

17.   § 1. In deciding individual cases, the pastor or the rector, or the priest responsible for a church, is to be guided by his own prudence, motivated by pastoral zeal and a spirit of generous welcome.

   § 2. In cases of groups which are quite small, they may approach the Ordinary of the place to identify a church in which these faithful may be able to come together for such celebrations, in order to ensure easier participation and a more worthy celebration of the Holy Mass.

18.   Even in sanctuaries and places of pilgrimage the possibility to celebrate in the *forma extraordinaria* is to be offered to groups of pilgrims who request it (cf. Motu Proprio *Summorum Pontificum*, art. 5 § 3), if there is a qualified priest.

19.   The faithful who ask for the celebration of the *forma extraordinaria* must not in any way support or belong to groups which show themselves to be against the validity or legitimacy of the Holy Mass or the Sacraments celebrated in the *forma ordinaria* or against the Roman Pontiff as Supreme Pastor of the Universal Church.

Sacerdos idoneus *("Qualified Priest")*
(cf. Motu Proprio Summorum Pontificum, *art 5 § 4)*

20.   With respect to the question of the necessary requirements for a priest to be held *idoneus* ("qualified") to celebrate in the *forma extraordinaria*, the following is hereby stated:

   a)   Every Catholic priest who is not impeded by Canon Law[7] is to be considered *idoneus* ("qualified") for the celebration of the Holy Mass in the *forma extraordinaria*.

---

7. Cf. *Code of Canon Law*, Canon 900 § 2.

b) Regarding the use of the Latin language, a basic knowledge is necessary, allowing the priest to pronounce the words correctly and understand their meaning.

c) Regarding knowledge of the execution of the Rite, priests are presumed to be qualified who present themselves spontaneously to celebrate the *forma extraordinaria*, and have celebrated it previously.

21.   Ordinaries are asked to offer their clergy the possibility of acquiring adequate preparation for celebrations in the *forma extraordinaria*. This applies also to Seminaries, where future priests should be given proper formation, including study of Latin[8] and, where pastoral needs suggest it, the opportunity to learn the *forma extraordinaria* of the Roman Rite.

22.   In Dioceses without qualified priests, Diocesan Bishops can request assistance from priests of the Institutes erected by the Pontifical Commission *Ecclesia Dei*, either to the celebrate the *forma extraordinaria* or to teach others how to celebrate it.

23.   The faculty to celebrate *sine populo* (or with the participation of only one minister) in the *forma extraordinaria* of the Roman Rite is given by the Motu Proprio to all priests, whether secular or religious (cf. Motu Proprio *Summorum Pontificum*, art. 2). For such celebrations therefore, priests, by provision of the Motu Proprio *Summorum Pontificum*, do not require any special permission from their Ordinaries or superiors.

Liturgical and Ecclesiastical Discipline

24.   The liturgical books of the *forma extraordinaria* are to be used as they are. All those who wish to celebrate according to the *forma extraordinaria* of the Roman Rite must know the pertinent rubrics and are obliged to follow them correctly.

25.   New saints and certain of the new prefaces can and ought to be inserted into the 1962 Missal,[9] according to provisions which will be indicated subsequently.

26.   As foreseen by article 6 of the Motu Proprio *Summorum Pontificum*, the readings of the Holy Mass of the Missal of 1962 can be proclaimed either solely in the Latin language, or in Latin followed by the vernacular or, in Low Masses, solely in the vernacular.

27.   With regard to the disciplinary norms connected to celebration, the ecclesiastical discipline contained in the Code of Canon Law of 1983 applies.

---

8. Cf. *Code of Canon Law*, Canon 249; Second Vatican Ecumenical Council, Constitution *Sacrosanctum Concilium*, 36; Declaration *Optatum totius*, 13.

9. Benedict XVI, *Epistola ad Episcopos ad producendas Litteras Apostolicas motu proprio datas, de Usu Liturgiae Romanae Instaurationi anni 1970 praecedentis*: AAS 99 (2007), 797.

28. Furthermore, by virtue of its character of special law, within its own area, the Motu Proprio *Summorum Pontificum* derogates from those provisions of law, connected with the sacred Rites, promulgated from 1962 onwards and incompatible with the rubrics of the liturgical books in effect in 1962.

Confirmation and Holy Orders

29. Permission to use the older formula for the rite of Confirmation was confirmed by the Motu Proprio *Summorum Pontificum* (cf. art. 9 § 2). Therefore, in the *forma extraordinaria*, it is not necessary to use the newer formula of Pope Paul VI as found in the *Ordo Confirmationis*.

30. As regards tonsure, minor orders and the subdiaconate, the Motu Proprio *Summorum Pontificum* does not introduce any change in the discipline of the *Code of Canon Law* of 1983; consequently, in Institutes of Consecrated Life and Societies of Apostolic Life which are under the Pontifical Commission *Ecclesia Dei*, one who has made solemn profession or who has been definitively incorporated into a clerical institute of apostolic life, becomes incardinated as a cleric in the institute or society upon ordination to the diaconate, in accordance with canon 266 § 2 of the *Code of Canon Law*.

31. Only in Institutes of Consecrated Life and Societies of Apostolic Life which are under the Pontifical Commission *Ecclesia Dei*, and in those which use the liturgical books of the *forma extraordinaria*, is the use of the *Pontificale Romanum* of 1962 for the conferral of minor and major orders permitted.

Breviarium Romanum

32. Art. 9 § 3 of the Motu Proprio *Summorum Pontificum* gives clerics the faculty to use the *Breviarium Romanum* in effect in 1962, which is to be prayed entirely and in the Latin language.

The Sacred Triduum

33. If there is a qualified priest, a *coetus fidelium* ("group of faithful"), which follows the older liturgical tradition, can also celebrate the Sacred Triduum in the *forma extraordinaria*. When there is no church or oratory designated exclusively for such celebrations, the parish priest or Ordinary, in agreement with the qualified priest, should find some arrangement favorable to the good of souls, not excluding the possibility of a repetition of the celebration of the Sacred Triduum in the same church.

The Rites of Religious Orders

34. The use of the liturgical books proper to the Religious Orders which were in effect in 1962 is permitted.

35.   The use of the *Pontificale Romanum*, the *Rituale Romanum*, as well as the *Caeremoniale Episcoporum* in effect in 1962, is permitted, in keeping with n. 28 of this Instruction, and always respecting n. 31 of the same Instruction.

The Holy Father Pope Benedict XVI, in an audience granted to the undersigned Cardinal President of the Pontifical Commission Ecclesia Dei on April 8, 2011, approved this present Instruction and ordered its publication.

Given at Rome, at the Offices of the Pontifical Commission Ecclesia Dei, April 30, 2011, on the memorial of Pope Saint Pius V.

WILLIAM CARDINAL LEVADA
PRESIDENT

MONS. GUIDO POZZO
SECRETARY

GLOSSARY
Rev. Msgr. Patrick R. Lagges

Apostolic Constitution: A document issued by the Roman Pontiff that "constitutes" something (establishing a diocese, instituting laws, defining doctrine, etc.). It is one of the most solemn declarations of the Church.

Apostolic Exhortation: A document issued by the Roman Pontiff that is "exhortative" in nature. It is not primarily legislative. Apostolic exhortations are often issued after a synod of bishops has addressed an issue of pastoral importance for the Church. An apostolic exhortation can be issued to the whole Church or to a portion of the Church.

Apostolic Letter issued *motu proprio*: A document issued by the Roman Pontiff "on his own initiative (*motu proprio*)." This type of document is primarily legislative, and sets forth norms for the entire Church.

Apostolic See: The Roman Pontiff, along with the various offices that assist him in the leadership of the Church.

Authentic Interpretations: A document containing an authoritative interpretation of a law whose meaning was previously unclear, or extending a law to cover a situation that was not explicit in the law. Because it is a legislative document, it can only be issued by someone with legislative power. Authentic interpretations are given by the Pontifical Council for Legislative Texts. In the past, they were given by the Pontifical Commission for the Interpretation of the Second Vatican Council or by the Consilium for Liturgy.

Circular Letter: A document, issued by an office of the Roman Curia, which usually explains certain procedural matters in the Church. It is not legislative because the offices of the Curia do not possess legislative authority. Circular letters are more along the lines of guidelines that ought to be followed when carrying out certain aspects of Church life. The use of circular letters has increased in recent years.

Commission: An office of the Roman Curia, usually designated a "Pontifical Commission." At the present time, there are Pontifical Commissions for the Cultural Heritage of the Church, for Sacred Archaeology, for Latin America, and for the Vatican City State, as well as the Pontifical Biblical Commission and the International Theological Commission.

Committee: An office of the Roman Curia, usually designated a "Pontifical Committee." At the present time, there are Pontifical Committees for the International Eucharistic Congresses and for the Historical Sciences.

Conference of Bishops: A grouping of bishops of a nation or a certain territory, established by the Holy See, which jointly exercises certain pastoral functions within its territory. The Conference of Bishops possesses teaching authority under certain conditions, legislative authority as specified in the *Code of Canon Law* (CIC), and some executive authority. The conference is not an intermediary institution between the Holy See and the individual diocesan bishops, and cannot interfere in the diocesan bishop's power of governance in his diocese. The norms issued by the conference of bishops are binding throughout the territory. Norms binding in the United States can be found on the website of the United States Conference of Catholic Bishops at www.usccb.org.

Congregations: An office of the Holy See that assists the Roman Pontiff in day-to-day Church operations. They are part of the Roman Curia. Congregations are not primarily legislative, but can be given legislative authority by the Roman Pontiff in specific instances. They are governed by their own special law, at present the apostolic constitution, *Pastor Bonus*. Currently, there are Congregations for the Doctrine of the Faith; for the Oriental Churches; for Divine Worship and the Discipline of the Sacraments; for the Causes of Saints; for Bishops; for the Evangelization of Peoples; for the New Evangelization; for the Clergy; for Institutes of Consecrated Life and Societies of Apostolic Life; and for Catholic Education.

Council: A gathering of particular Churches. Councils can be ecumenical (for all the bishops of the Church); plenary (consisting of all the particular Churches within the territory of a conference of bishops); or provincial (consisting of all the particular Churches of the same ecclesiastical province). Plenary and provincial councils are legislative in nature and can establish norms for their particular territory.

Curia: The administrative offices of the universal or particular Church. They assist the Roman Pontiff or the diocesan bishop in the day-to-day governance of the Christian faithful who have been entrusted to his care. They are not legislative in nature.

Customary Law: A law introduced into a community by a custom that is not contrary to divine law or forbidden by law, and which has been observed for thirty continuous and complete years.[10] Canon 27 refers to custom as "the best interpreter of laws."

Declaration: A statement from one with executive authority concerning the proper way to carry out a law—in which case it would be akin to a general executory decree, an instruction, a precept, or other singular administrative decree—or a statement from one with legislative authority concerning an authentic interpretation or modification of the law. It could also be a statement from an ecclesiastical authority that an automatic penalty has been incurred. Declarations were not specified in the 1983 CIC.

Decretal Letter: A solemn pronouncement of the Roman Pontiff, usually concerned with the beatification or canonization of saints. They are not generally legislative in nature.

Dicastery: Another name for one of the Roman Curial offices. In practical terms, *dicastery* is most often used as a synonym for the Roman Congregations rather than Commissions, Committees, or Tribunals.

---

10. See *Code of Canon Law* (CIC), § 23–28.

Diocesan Bishop: A bishop who has been entrusted with a portion of the people of God as their proper pastor. The diocesan bishop possesses all of the legislative, executive, and juridical authority needed to carry out his office, although he does so with the assistance of other members of the faithful, who are sometimes referred to as the diocesan curia. When the law specifies that the diocesan bishop can do something, it refers only to him, and not to others who may have delegated authority (vicar general, judicial vicar, episcopal vicars, vicars forane, deans, etc.). Ecclesiastical territories that are not dioceses are pastored by territorial prelates, territorial abbots, apostolic vicars, or apostolic prefects who are equivalent to diocesan bishops. A diocese that is vacant may also be pastored by an apostolic administrator.

Diocesan Synod: A gathering within a diocese of the bishops, diocesan priests, members of religious institutes, and the faithful. The synod assists the diocesan bishop with the pastoral care of the diocese. The synod usually results in particular law, although it is the bishop alone who is the legislator.

Directory: A form of general executory decree that determines how a law ought to be applied or that urges the observance of a law. There are directories, for example, on ecumenism and on the pastoral ministry of bishops. A directory is not a law in itself, but it explains how to carry out the law.

Disciplinary Decree: A document that indicates how something is to be done in the Church. As such, it indicates the "discipline" that is to be followed in carrying out Church functions. It is distinguished from a "penal decree," which imposes a penalty on someone for an offense.

Dispensation: A relaxation of a merely ecclesiastical law in a particular case for a spiritual purpose. Laws stating how something or some action is constituted are not subject to dispensation. While the diocesan bishop can generally dispense from disciplinary laws in the Church, he cannot dispense from laws that establish a penalty or that describe a procedure. In addition, the dispensation from some laws is reserved to the Holy See.

Ecclesiastical Authority: The person who has responsibility for governance in a particular case or in all cases. It is always necessary to determine who has the authority to act in a particular situation.

General Decree: A provision made by one with legislative authority for a community that is capable of receiving laws. For example, a diocesan bishop would establish particular law (policies, procedures, or protocols) for his diocese by means of a general decree.

General Executory Decree: A provision made by one with executive authority that more precisely determines the way laws are to be observed or that urges their observance. A directory is a type of general executory decree.

Holy See: Another name for the Apostolic See; namely, the Roman Pontiff and the offices that assist him in the leadership of the Church.

Indult: A singular administrative act that grants an individual or group something beyond what is stated in a law. Indults are sometimes granted to individual countries or regions to celebrate liturgical ceremonies in a certain way.

Instruction: A document issued by one with executive authority that clarifies what is contained in the law and determines the methods to be used in observing the law. The *General Instruction of the Roman Missal* is a good example of an instruction.

Liturgical Law: Generally refers to a body of law that is contained in the rites themselves or various directories, instructions, or particular law. For the most part, the CIC does not define the rites themselves. The individual ritual editions, particularly their *praenotandae*, ought to be consulted.

Local Ordinary: A term used for one who has executive authority over a certain territory. In addition to the Roman Pontiff and the diocesan bishop, local ordinaries include vicars general and episcopal vicars. The vicar general has authority over the whole territory, while the episcopal vicar has authority over either the whole territory or a part of the territory, depending on the decree appointing him. Religious superiors have authority over certain groups of persons and would not be considered "local ordinaries."

Norms: A document issued by one with executive authority that more precisely determines how laws are to be carried out in the Church. Norms must always be reconciled to the actual laws that they seek to explain or clarify. When their meaning is unclear, the laws on which they are based ought to be consulted.

Notification: A document issued by one with executive authority, which usually serves as a reminder of something contained in the law, or explains more clearly the meaning of a law.

Ordinary: A term used for one who has executive authority over a certain territory or a certain group of people. In addition to the Roman Pontiff and the diocesan bishop, ordinaries include the vicar general, the episcopal vicars, and the major superiors of clerical religious institutes and societies of apostolic life or pontifical right.

Papal Address: A talk given by the Roman Pontiff about an element of Church teaching, practice, or legislation. Papal addresses are not considered legislative in nature, but they indicate the thinking of the Roman Pontiff on various matters of importance to the Church.

Papal Allocution: A particular form of papal address that is usually more formal than a simple talk and is usually directed toward one of the dicasteries of the Holy See.

Papal Nuncio: The representative of the Roman Pontiff for the Church in a particular country, whose task is to strengthen the bond of unity between the Holy See and the Churches of that country. If there are no diplomatic relations between the Holy See and the civil state in a country, the papal representative is called the "apostolic delegate."

Particular Law: Laws established for a particular group of people, such as a diocese. They are sometimes referred to as "policies," "guidelines," "procedures," or "protocols," although these terms can sometimes be misleading.

Plenary Council: A gathering of all the churches of an individual conference of bishops. The council provides for the pastoral needs of the people of God within the territory of the conference, particularly those concerning "the increase of faith, the organization of common pastoral action, and the regulation of morals and of the common ecclesiastical discipline which is to be observed, promoted, and protected."[11] A plenary council is legislative in nature, with the bishops having deliberative vote and the clergy and laity having consultative vote. The Councils of Baltimore in the United States were plenary councils.

Praenotanda: The introductory section to a ritual established for the Church. It provides essential information about the nature of the ritual and how to carry it out.

Privilege: A favor given to an individual or group of individuals. It could be in the form of an indult or other type of singular administrative act, or it could be a centenary or immemorial privilege that has always existed for the individual or group.

Promulgation: The act of making a law public and assigning a date when it will become effective. If no date is assigned for a law to take effect, and the law is issued by the Holy See, the effective date is three months after it has been promulgated; if the law is issued by another entity, the effective date is one month after it has been promulgated. Laws issued by the Holy See are generally promulgated in the *Acta Apostolicae Sedis*, but could be promulgated in another forum.

Province: A grouping of dioceses or ecclesiastical territories for pastoral purposes. The province is headed by an archbishop, who is also called the *metropolitan*. He does not have any governing authority over the other bishops of the province, but exercises vigilance over the faith and ecclesiastical discipline within the province; he reports to the Roman Pontiff if there are any difficulties in these areas.

Provincial Council: A gathering of all the churches within an ecclesiastical province that is concerned with the pastoral care of the faithful within a certain territory. It is legislative in nature, with the bishops having deliberative vote and the clergy and laity having consultative vote.

Recognitio: The required approval given by the Holy See to legislative acts of the conference of bishops. The *recognitio* guarantees that the legislation does not harm the unity of the Church. It is an act of executive authority, with the legislative authority coming from the conference of bishops.

Recourse: The process used when there is disagreement over an action. The person who disagrees with the action has ten days to ask that the decision be changed. Church law recommends that such disputes be settled through conciliation,

---

11. Canon 445.

mediation, or arbitration, but also provides for recourse to the person's hierarchical superior should attempts at conciliation fail.

Region: A grouping of provinces, requested by the conference of bishops and established by the Holy See, to promote the pastoral good of a larger portion of the faithful within a certain territory.

Regulation: Similar to a norm, a regulation specifies how a law is to be carried out. Regulations are issued by those who possess executive authority, and must be harmonized with existing legislation.

Rescript: A singular administrative act, giving a decision or making provision for a particular case. Dispensations, privileges, and other favors are examples of rescripts.

Responses: A document that provides an answer to a specific question that has been posed to one of the dicasteries of the Holy See. Recent responses concerned the invalidity of Baptism in the Church of Jesus Christ of Latter Day Saints and the inability of deacons to celebrate the Sacrament of the Anointing of the Sick.

Rubric: A form of liturgical law that indicates how a rite is to be performed. It gets its name from the fact that these instructions were usually written in red within the ritual, giving rise to the phrase, "Read the black; do the red."

Singular Decree: A singular administrative act that contains a decision or makes provision in a particular case, not necessarily in response to a request. Like all decrees, it should be made in writing, and only after the person with executive authority issuing the decree has gathered the necessary information and heard those whose rights could be injured.[12]

Singular Precept: A singular administrative act that directly and legitimately orders an individual or a group of individuals to do something or to refrain from or avoid doing something. It should be issued in writing, and only after the person with executive authority issuing the precept has gathered the necessary information and heard those whose rights could be injured.[13]

Special Law: A law given for specific situations. For example, the laws concerning canonizations and concerning the dissolution of marriages could be considered special law. It differs from particular law, in that a special law is not given to a particular group of people, but generally covers special processes in the Church.

Synod of Bishops: A gathering of bishops from different regions of the world that meets periodically to foster greater unity between the Roman Pontiff and the bishops; to assist the Roman Pontiff with their counsel regarding faith, morals, and ecclesiastical discipline; and to consider questions pertaining to the activity of the Church in the world. The synod of bishops is not a legislative body. After listening to the counsel of the bishops, the Roman Pontiff usually issues an apostolic exhortation on the topic of the synod, which represents the counsel of the bishops throughout the world.

---

12. See Canon 50.
13. Ibid.

Universal Law: Law that is given for the entire Church. It could be contained in the CIC or in the rites of the Church. It binds all the members of the Church, and must be made known to them through publication in some form.

Vatican II Documents: The sixteen official documents of the Second Vatican Council. They are divided into three categories:

Constitutions, which are called either dogmatic (on the Church and on Divine Revelation) or pastoral (on the Church in the Modern World) or simply a Constitution (on the Sacred Liturgy), without any particular explanation for the differing titles;

Decrees on the Instruments of Social Communication, on Ecumenism (two documents), on the Eastern Catholic Churches, on the Bishop's Pastoral Office, on Priestly Formation, on the Renewal of Religious Life, on the Apostolate of the Laity, on the Ministry and Life of Priests, and on the Church's Missionary Activity;

Declarations on the Relationship of the Church to Non-Christian Religions and on Religious Freedom.

INDEX

References are to article numbers of individual documents that are included in The *Liturgy Documents, Volume Four.* For a list of abbreviations of document names, see pages ix–x. Because of space constraints, citations are limited. See also the detailed outlines which precede each document.

ADAPTATION(S)
SacCar 54; VD 114; VL 52–69; PGR 13, 17–20, 24–28, 30, 33, 41, 68; DPPL 24, 92, 223; RVM 38; NDC 24C, 25F, 36A.3B

ADORATION
SacCar 4, 29, 66–69, 81, 93; VD 86; MND 18; OU 2; VL 42; PGR 89; DPPL 32, 127, 141, 164–65, 177–78, 218, 245, 286; MarCult 5, 50; RVM 10, 33; LetArt 8; NDC 34, 37A.1, 37A.2

ADVENT
VD 65; GMEF 9, 11, 13–14, 30; PGR 22; DPPL 96–105, 191, 221; MarCult 3–4; NDC 37A

AFRICAN AMERICAN:
See *Plenty Good Room*

ALTAR
SacCar 2, 6, 9, 13, 23, 36, 41, 47, 53, 55, 68–70, 75, 93, 96; VD 56, 68; MND 30–31; GCE 11, 14, 21–22, 24–25, 34, 44, 48–50, 53; VL 24, 43, 54; PGR 17, 119, 120; DPPL 141, 160–61, 164, 215, 235, 237, 244; NDC 38A

AMBO
SacCar 41; VD 68

ANOINTING OF THE SICK:
SacCar 22, 56; VD 61; VL 26; DAPNE 123, 125, 129, 131; DPPL 42, 269, 270; NDC 35A, 36B

ANTHROPOLOGY/ ANTHROPOLOGICAL
SacCar 28; VD 110; VL 30; DPPL 12, 75, 178, 180, 186–87, 232–233, 247, 257, 286; MarCult 29, 34, 36–37; RVM 25

ARS CELEBRANDI
SacCar 38–43, 64

ASSEMBLY (LITURGICAL)
SacCar 23, 41, 57, 66–67, 73, 79, 96; VD 57, 59; MND 17; OU 2, 6, App. 3, 7, 14, 16–17; GCE 14–15, 51; VL 14, 22, 37, 41, 53; GMEF 2–3, 16, 22, 26; PGR 3, 9, 16, 19, 21, 60, 89, 94, 96, 98, 101–102, 104, 107, 109, 112–14, 117, 119, 177; NDC 36A.3, 36C.2, 37B.2, 37B.3

BAPTISM
SacCar 17, 19, 20, 27, 76, 79, 92; VD 77, 84, 94; OU 9, App. 3, 4; VL 22, 43, 53, 56; PGR 15, 17–18, 59, 109; DPPL 77, 79, 119, 121, 124, 153, 156, 175, 191, 204–5, 223–25, 235, 245, 250, 257; MarCult 14, 19; RVM 15, 19, 21; See *Directory for the Application of Ecumenism* and *National Directory for Catechesis.*

BAPTIZED
SacCar 58, 83, 94, 96; OU App. 3; PGR 16, 52; DPPL 125, 157, 224–25, 245, 270; MarCult 32; RVM 24; See *Directory for the Application of Ecumenism* and *National Directory for Catechesis.*

BEAUTY
SacCar 24, 35–36, 41, 53, 66–67, 82, 94, 96–97; VD 2, 70, 93, 108, 112; MND 30; GCE 16; VL 43; PGR 8, 69, 115; DPPL 18, 26, 40, 79, 202–3, 243, 263, 271, 276, 286; MarCult 57; RVM 1, 9, 26, 43; LetArt 1, 3–6, 8–11, 16; NDC 37B.1

BIBLE
SacCar 56; VL 9, 23, 28, 41, 53; GMEF 6, 15, 31, 51–52, 54, 61–62; PGR 116; DAPNE 183, 185–86; DPPL 42, 87, 280; MarCult 30, 51; RVM 13; LetArt 1, 5; See *Verbum Domini*

BLACK CHURCH
See *Plenty Good Room*

BLESSED VIRGIN MARY
SacCar 12, 15, 33, 94, 96–97; VD 7, 15, 19, 27–28, 48–49, 66, 79, 83, 87–89, 94, 124; MND 9–10, 18, 31; VL 44; PGR 10, 65; DPPL 6, 8, 41, 48, 56–57, 62, 68–69, 79, 84, 95, 97, 99, 101–2, 107–9, 112, 115, 122, 136–37, 145, 147, 149, 155, 157, 170–71, 174, 180–81, 183, 185, 187–89, 191, 193–97, 201, 203–7, 214, 218–21, 225, 229, 234, 261, 263, 275; LetArt 16; NDC 25G, 37, 38; See *Marialis Cultus* and *Rosarium Virginis Mariae*

BOOK OF BLESSINGS
VD 63

CANON LAW
SacCar 29; OU 13; DPNE 120, 130, 150–51, 183; DPPL 266

CATECHIST(S)
VD 75; GMEF 21; See *National Directory for Catechesis*

CATECHESIS
SacCar 20–21, 44, 64–65, 67, 86; VD 5, 41, 74, 81, 85; MND 17; GMEF 20; PGR 10, 27, 29, 113; DPPL 33, 37, 42, 59, 95, 191, 194, 212–13, 240, 255; LetArt 5; See *National Directory for Catechesis*

CELEBRANT
SacCar 13, 39, 41, 69; MND 13; OU 7–8, 14; VL 37; DAPNE 97, 157; DPPL 251, 269; NDC 36A.3B; See *Guidelines for Concelebration of the Eucharist*

CELIBACY
SacCar 24, 81; DPPL 220; NDC 36C.1

CHARITY
SacCar 1, 5, 27, 29, 73, 82, 88, 90–91; VD 46, 48, 87, 103, 107, 123; MND 28; DAPNE 104–5, 109, 149; DPPL 6, 23, 41, 61, 66, 113, 121, 156, 164, 166, 206, 212, 234, 242, 251, 263, 268, 275–76, 286; MarCult 16, 20, 26, 35, 37, 56–57; RVM 40; NDC 36C.2, 38B, 38C, 39

CHILDREN
SacCar 17–19, 25, 27, 29, 67, 73, 77, 79, 82–83, 90; VD 50–51, 84–85, 91; VL 11, 22; GMEF 24–25; PGR 52, 56, 72, 86; DAPNE 144, 150–52; DPPL 81, 104, 109, 112–13, 118–19, 152, 204, 211, 224, 269, 275; MarCult 14, 18–19, 23, 39, 56–57; RVM 15, 40, 42; LetArt 6, 14; See *National Directory for Catechesis*.

CHRISTOLOGY
VD 11–13

CHRISTIAN INITIATION
SacCar 17–19, 26, 48, 56; PGR 9; DAPNE 99–100; DPPL 85, 124, 150, 191, 270; NDC 24C, 36A, 37A

CHRISTIAN WITNESS
VD 97; DPPL 231

CHRISTMAS TIME
VD 65; PGR 17; DPPL 25, 27, 98, 101–120, 177, 200, 221; MarCult 3, 5, 19; NDC 37A

CLERGY SHORTAGE
SacCar 25

COMMON GOOD
SacCar 74, 83; VD 100, 118; VL 64; PGR 24; DPPL 100; LetArt 4

CONFERENCE(S) OF BISHOPS
SacCar 18, 54, 75; VD 45, 118; VL 3, 27, 30–32, 36–37, 49, 51, 54–68, 70; DAPNE 94, 99, 130, 139, 143, 146, 150, 154; DPPL 2, 92, 245, 264; MarCult 24, 40; NDC 36A.2

CONFIRMATION
SacCar 17, 19, 79; OU 8–9; VL 56; DAPNE 99, 101; DPPL 79, 156, 191, 204; NDC 35A, 36A, 36B.2, 36C.1

CULTURE(S)
SacCar 12, 20, 28, 54, 65, 77–78; VD 4, 29, 32, 92–93, 96, 109–117; MND 25–26; PGR 13–28, 30, 32, 37–42, 48, 68, 78, 85, 105, 107, 109, 123–124; DPPL 1, 9, 23, 29, 36, 42–43, 45, 52–53, 61, 63, 75, 82, 91, 95, 153, 156, 160, 242–243, 276; MarCult 36; RVM 5, 42; LetArt 2, 5, 7–8, 10–11; NDC 24C, 25A, 25D, 25F, 35C–D, 36A.3B-2, 37A–B.1, 38; See *Varietates legitimae*

DANGER OF DEATH
DAPNE 130; DPPL 269; NDC 36A.1, 36B.3

DEVOTION(S)
SacCar 24, 26, 41, 66–68, 77, 81, 94; MND 5, 11, 18; OU 3, 16; VL 45; PGR 15, 18, 20–21, 27; DAPNE 112, 152; LetArt 7; NDC 25F, 32, 34, 36A.3, 38B–C; See *Directory on Popular Piety and the Liturgy, Marialis Cultus,* and *Rosarium Virginis Mariae*

ABOUT THE AUTHORS

Authors are listed in the order in which their articles appear in this publication.

Rev. Michael S. Driscoll, PHD, STD, is a presbyter of the Diocese of Helena and an associate professor of sacramental theology and liturgy at the University of Notre Dame. Besides having a theoretical appreciation of the liturgy, he is actively involved in pastoral practice: he has worked as choir director of the Cathedral of St. Helena and as a liturgical consultant across the country. He is the founding director of the graduate program in sacred music and the undergraduate minor in liturgical music ministry at the University of Notre Dame. He is the current president of the Catholic Academy of Liturgy and is past president of the North American Academy of Liturgy.

Rev. Mark E. Wedig, OP, is a Dominican friar of the Province of St. Martin de Porres, the associate dean for graduate studies, professor, and chair of the Department of Theology and Philosophy, College of Arts and Sciences, Barry University in Miami Shores, Florida. He holds a doctorate in liturgical studies from the Catholic University of America. His scholarly interests lie at the intersection of liturgy, the hermeneutics of visual Christianity, and culture studies. He is an active member of the North American Academy of Liturgy, the Catholic Academy of Liturgy, the American Academy of Religion, and the Catholic Theological Society of America. Wedig contributed to *A Commentary on the Order of Mass of The Roman Missal* (Liturgical Press, 2011) and *A Commentary on the General Instruction of the Roman Missal 2002* (Liturgical Press, 2007).

S. Joyce Ann Zimmerman, CPPS, PHD, STD, is the director of the Institute for Liturgical Ministry in Dayton, Ohio; adjunct professor of liturgy at the Athenaeum of Ohio; a liturgical consultant; frequent speaker and facilitator of workshops on liturgy, spirituality, and other related topics; and an award-winning author of numerous books and articles on liturgy and spirituality. She is the recipient of the Notre Dame Center for Liturgy 2008 Michael Mathis Award and the 2010 Georgetown Center for Liturgy National Award for Outstanding Contributions to the Liturgical Life of the American Church. She is a theological consultant to the United States Conference of Catholic Bishops' Committee on Divine Worship.

Corinna Laughlin, PHD, is the director of liturgy for St. James Cathedral in Seattle. She also serves on the Liturgical Commission for the Archdiocese of Seattle. She co-authored *The Liturgical Ministry Series: Guide for Sacristans* and *The Liturgical Ministry Series: Guide for Servers* (both LTP), and is a frequent contributor to *Sourcebook for Sundays, Seasons, and Weekdays: The Almanac for Parish Liturgy*. Corinna has also written articles for *Pastoral Liturgy, Today's Liturgy, Ministry & Liturgy,* and *AIM*. She holds a doctorate in English from the University of Washington and a bachelor's degree in English from Mount Holyoke College.

Paul F. Ford, PHD, studied for the priesthood for the then Diocese of Monterey-Fresno, 1961-1973, but was never ordained. He was a Benedictine monk at St. Andrew's Abbey, Valyermo, from 1973-1978. Dr. Ford was the first Roman Catholic in the doctoral program at Fuller Theological Seminary in Pasadena. His primary areas of competence are ecclesiology, spirituality, and music and liturgy; his secondary areas are Mariology and chant. He is an internationally recognized authority on the life and writings of C.S. Lewis. His award-winning book, *Companion to Narnia* (HarperCollins) is now in its fourth edition. Cardinal Roger Mahony honored him with the Laudatus Award in 1995 "for excellence in the promotion of the liturgical life of parishes and the people of the Archdiocese of Los Angeles." Dr. Ford's latest publications are eleven entries in *C.S. Lewis: A Reader's Encyclopedia* (Zondervan, 1998) and *By Flowing Waters: Chant for the Liturgy* (Liturgical Press, 1999).

Rev. Msgr. Joseph DeGrocco, pastor of Our Lady of Perpetual Help Church, Lindenhurst, New York and former professor of liturgy and director of liturgical formation at the Seminary of the Immaculate Conception in Huntington, New York, holds a master's in theology (liturgical studies) from the University of Notre Dame and a doctor of ministry from the Seminary of the Immaculate Conception. He is the author of *A Pastoral Commentary on the General Instruction of the Roman Missal,* the *Dictionary of Liturgical Terms, The Church at Worship: Theology, Spirituality and Practice of Parish Liturgy,* the "Q & A" column in *Pastoral Liturgy* (all from LTP), and is a member of his diocese's liturgical commission.

Rev. Ricky Manalo, CSP, PHD, is a Paulist priest who teaches at Santa Clara University and the Jesuit School of Theology in Berkeley, California. He studied music composition and piano at the Manhattan School of Music, theology at the Washington Theological Union, and liturgy, culture, and sociology at the Graduate Theological Union. His music is published by OCP and GIA Publications. He is a member of the American Academy of Religion, the North American Academy of Liturgy, the Catholic Theological Society of America, *Societas Liturgica,* and the National Association of Pastoral Musicians (Board Member, 2008-12). He also directs the Cultural Orientation Program for International Ministers/Priests (COPIM) of Loyola Marymount University, and serves as an advisor to the United States Conference of Catholic Bishops' Committee on Cultural Diversity in the Church and the Secretariat on Divine Worship. Currently, he resides at Old St. Mary's Cathedral in Chinatown, San Francisco, California.

Rev. John T. Pawlikowski, OSM, has extensively studied the Nazi Holocaust, which has enabled him to appreciate the ethical challenges facing the human community as it struggles with greatly enhanced power and extended responsibility for the future of all creation. His scholarly interests include the theological and ethical aspects of the Christian-Jewish relationship and public ethics.

A leading figure in the Christian-Jewish dialogue, he was the two-term president and chair of the theology committee of the International Council of Christians and Jews (ICCJ). He remains on ICCJ's board as immediate past president. Pawlikowski is a member of the Catholic Theological Society, the

American Academy of Religion, the Society of Christian Ethics (past board member), the Ethics Working Group of the World Conservation Union, and the Association of University Leaders for a Sustainable Future. He also served as the principal theological consultant for the United States Conference of Catholic Bishops' Statement on Energy.

Pawlikowski is the author/editor of more than fifteen books including *The Challenge of the Holocaust for Christian Theology*; *Christ in the Light of the Christian-Jewish Dialogue*; *Jesus and the Theology of Israel*; *Biblical and Theological Reflections on The Challenge of Peace*; *Justice in the Marketplace: CTU's Pastoral Commentary on the Bishops' letter on the Economy*; *The Ecological Challenge: Ethical, Liturgical, and Spiritual Responses*; *Reinterpreting Revelation and Tradition: Jews and Christians in Conversation*; *Good and Evil after Auschwitz*; and *Ethics in the Shadow of the Holocaust*. He also is a contributor to many journals and has served on the editorial boards of numerous publications including: *Journal of Ecumenical Studies*, *Journal of Holocaust and Genocide Studies*, *Explorations*, *Shofar: An Interdisciplinary Journal of Jewish Studies*, and *Bridges: An Interdisciplinary Journal*. Pawlikowski also served as editor of *New Theology Review* for seven years.

Archbishop Wilton Gregory was ordained a priest for the Archdiocese of Chicago on May 9, 1973. Three years after his ordination he began graduate studies at the Pontifical Liturgical Institute (Sant'Anselmo) in Rome. There he earned his doctorate in sacred liturgy in 1980.

After having served as an associate pastor of Our Lady of Perpetual Help Parish in Glenview, Illinois, as a member of the faculty of St. Mary of the Lake Seminary in Mundelein and as a master of ceremonies to Cardinals John Cody and Joseph Bernardin, he was ordained an auxiliary bishop of Chicago on December 13, 1983. On February 10, 1994, he was installed as the seventh bishop of the Diocese of Belleville, Illinois, where he served for the next eleven years.

On December 9, 2004, Pope John Paul II appointed Bishop Gregory as the sixth archbishop of the Archdiocese of Atlanta. He was installed on January 17, 2005. Archbishop Gregory has also contributed a leading role in the U.S. Church. In November 2001, he was elected president of the United States Conference of Catholic Bishops following three years as vice president under Bishop Joseph Fiorenza of the Diocese of Galveston-Houston. During his tenure in office, the crisis of sex abuse by Catholic clergy escalated, and under his leadership, the bishops implemented the "Charter for the Protection of Children and Young People."

Rev. Paul Turner is pastor of St. Anthony Parish in Kansas City, Missouri. A priest of the Diocese of Kansas City-St. Joseph, he holds a doctorate in sacred theology from Sant'Anselmo in Rome. His publications include *At the Supper of the Lamb* (LTP, 2011); *Glory in the Cross* (Liturgical Press, 2011); *ML Bulletin Inserts* (Resource Publications, 2012); and *Celebrating Initiation: A Guide for Priests* (World Library Publications, 2008). He is a former president of the North American Academy of Liturgy and a team member for the North American Forum on the Catechumenate. He is a member of *Societas Liturgica* and the Catholic Academy of Liturgy. He serves as a facilitator for the International Commission on English in the Liturgy.

Rev. Mark Francis, CSV, has lived and ministered in both Latin America and Europe. After earning his doctorate in liturgy at the Pontifical Liturgical Institute of Sant' Anselmo, he taught liturgy at Catholic Theological Union in Chicago for thirteen years. He has written numerous articles on liturgical topics and is especially interested in the relationship between liturgy and culture. With John Page and Keith Pecklers he edited Archbishop Piero Marini's recent book: A Challenging Reform. Francis serves as superior general of his religious community, the Viatorians, lives in Rome, and teaches the course on liturgical inculturation at Pontifical Liturgical Institute of Sant'Anselmo.

Michael R. Prendergast, MTS, MA, is a seasoned pastoral musician and liturgist with experience at the parish, cathedral, and diocesan levels. He is a frequent speaker and clinician for conferences, dioceses, and parishes. He has edited and authored numerous books and articles, including *The Liturgical Ministry Series: Guide for Liturgy Committees* (LTP), co-authored with Paul Turner. Prendergast holds advanced degrees in theological studies and liturgy. Prendergast is coordinator of liturgy at St. Andrew Church in Portland, Oregon; an instructor in the lay ministry formation program for the Archdiocese of Portland; and an instructor in the theology department at the University of Portland. Prendergast is founder and executive director of Sacred Liturgy Ministries, a liturgical consulting firm; find out more at www.sacredliturgyministries.org.

Rev. Thomas P. Looney, CSC, a priest of the Congregation of Holy Cross, presently serves as the college chaplain and director of campus ministry at King's College in Wilkes-Barre, Pennsylvania. He holds a bachelor's in psychology from Stonehill College, an a master's of divinity from the University of St. Michael's College and a doctorate from the Catholic University of America. A tenured member and former chair of the Department of Theology at King's College, he has also served as the vice president of Catholic Identity and Mission at Stonehill College and as the provincial superior of the former Eastern Province of the Congregation of Holy Cross. In addition to serving on the board of directors of Renew International, Stonehill College and the Father Peyton Centre in Ireland, he has preached numerous retreats and parish missions.

Rev. J. Philip Horrigan, STB, MED, MTH, DMIN, is a presbyter of the Archdiocese of Kingston, Ontario, Canada. As a pastor he was responsible for starting a new parish and leading a parish through a new church building project. He served as the director of the Department of Art and Architecture, Office for Divine Worship, Archdiocese of Chicago (1997– 2009). He acted as a resource/consultant for those parishes involved in building or renovation projects. He is an independent liturgical design consultant on several projects in Canada and the United States. He is a frequent speaker at conferences and workshops on topics related to the building and renovation of liturgical spaces; the liturgical environment; and the history, documents, and components of liturgical design. His particular interest is understanding and exploring the relationship between ritual space and ritual event.

Jo-Ann Metzdorff DMIN, director of religious education and RCIA at the parish of St. Agnes Cathedral in Rockville Centre, New York, holds a bachelor's in art education from St. John's University, New York, a master's in Elementary

Education from Adelphi Univerity and a master's in theology from the Seminary of the Immaculate Conception, New York and the University of Notre Dame. Her doctor of ministry degree is from the Seminary of the Immaculate Conception. Jo-Ann serves on the diocesan Liturgy Commission and the RCIA committee. She is an instructor for the Pastoral Formation Institute of the Diocese of Rockville Centre and is also involved in formation of liturgical ministers on both parish and diocesan levels, adult faith formation programs, retreat and presentations on spirituality, liturgy, and stewardship. She has written for a number of publications in the area of liturgy, liturgies with children, catechesis, and RCIA.

Deacon Francis L. Agnoli, DMin, was ordained for the Diocese of Lexington, Kentucky, in 2002, and serves as the director of liturgy and director of deacon formation for the Diocese of Davenport, Iowa. Agnoli is married to Marianne, and they have two children. He worked as a family physician in rural Kentucky for a number of years before returning to school to earn his master of divinity and master of arts in theology degrees at St. John's University School of Theology and Seminary. He and his family then returned to Kentucky where he served for five years as the primary pastoral caregiver for two parishes that did not have a resident priest. He earned a doctorate of ministry in preaching from the Aquinas Institute of Theology in 2009 and is currently completing a certificate program in homiletic supervision at the St. Meinrad School of Theology and Seminary. In addition to his diocesan responsibilities, he has taught in the deacon formation programs sponsored by Brescia University and by St. Meinrad's.

Rev. Msgr. Patrick R. Lagges, JCD, PhD, is a presbyter of the Archdiocese of Chicago. He is chaplain and director of Calvert House, the Catholic center at the University of Chicago, and director of the Hesburgh Sabbatical Program at Catholic Theological Union. His articles have been published in *Studia canonica*, *The Jurist*, *Proceedings of the Canon Law Society of America*, *Fidelium iuris*, *CLSA Advisory Opinions*, *The Liguorian*, *Catechumenate*, and *Marriage and Family*. Canon law studies were done at St. Paul University, Ottawa, Ontario, Canada, where he received a doctorate in canon law.